Management Science

A Spreadsheet Approach

Management Science

A Spreadsheet Approach

Donald R. Plane
Crummer Graduate School
Rollins College

▲ *The Scientific Press Series*
boyd & fraser publishing company

Dedication

*This book is dedicated to the glory of God.
It is my way of saying "Thanks, God, for the gift of so many blessings."*

MANAGEMENT SCIENCE: A SPREADSHEET APPROACH
by Donald R. Plane

 The Scientific Press Series

Senior Acquisitions Editor: DeVilla Williams
Developmental Editor: Gene Smith
Copy Editor: Dave Rich
Text Design and Compositor: Gene Smith
Cover Design: John Craig
Cover Photo: Stan Osolinski

 © 1994 by boyd & fraser publishing company
A Divison of South-Western Publishing Co.
One Corporate Place • Ferncroft Village
Danvers, Massachusetts 01923

I(T)P International Thomson Publishing
boyd & fraser publishing company is an ITP company.
The ITP trademark is used under license.

Manufactured in the United States of America

ISBN 0-89426-225-4

1 2 3 4 5 6 7 8 9 10 D 7 6 5 4 3   Stock Number: SP 2254

 This book is printed on recycled, acid-free paper that meets Environmental Protection Agency standards.

CONTENTS

Preface xi
Foreword to Instructors xiii

Chapter **1** Managerial Models for Decisions 1

Why Construct a Model? 1
Modeling for *Ad Hoc* Decisions or Repeated Decisions 2
Two Approaches to End-User Spreadsheet Modeling 2
Vacation Budget: An Example of an Influence Chart and Top-Down Modeling 3
Some Guidelines for Constructing an Influence Chart 5
Using the Influence Chart to Construct a Model 6
What Use Is a Model? 8
Roll Out the Barrel: Another Scenario and Influence Chart for Top-Down Modeling . . 8
Continuing with the Influence Chart 10
Constructing a Model from the Influence Chart 11
Why Use Influence Charts? 12
Worksheets with Many Columns 14
Documentation of Worksheets with Many Columns 16
Exercises 17
Case Study: Rangely Lakes Company 21
Case Study: Sunsoak Products 22

Chapter **2** The Details of Constructing an Influence Chart & a Model 25

Constructing an Influence Chart for Rangely Lakes 25
Constructing the Model from the Influence Chart 28

Chapter **3** Optimization of a Managerial Spreadsheet Model 43

The Rangely Lakes Company Case 43
Components of an Optimization Problem 46
Solving Optimization Problems with the What's *Best!* Solver 49

The Optimized Spreadsheet 54
What Is an Optimization Problem? 56
Modeling for Optimization: Some Comparisons and Comments 57
Questions for Thought and Discussion 58
Exercises 60

Chapter 4 Linear Programming 65

What Is Linear Programming? 65
What Is Linearity? 66
What Might Cause Nonlinearity? 68
Spreadsheet Nonlinearities for Reporting 69
A Mathematical View of Linear Programming 71
Questions 81
Exercises 82

Chapter 5 Managerial Information from Linear Programming 87

Marginal (or Dual) Value Associated with a Constraint 89
Validity Range for Marginal Values 92
What Does It Cost to Do Something Optimization Doesn't Recommend? 94
Finding the Cost of Admission (Dual Value for a Decision Variable) 96
The What'sBest! Solution Report 96
Exercises 97

Chapter 6 Examples of Optimization Models 99

Example 1: Developing a New Product 99
Some Tips About Using What'sBest! 104
Example 2: Production Quantities 105
Example 3: Process Selection 109
Example 4: Process Selection in Transportation 112
Exercises 114
Case Study: Agribusiness 116
Case Study: Tucker Development Corporation 118

Chapter 7 More Modeling Examples:
Transportation & Assignment Problems 125

Example 1: A Transportation Problem 125
Example 2: Expanding the Transportation Problem 128
Example 3: An Assignment Problem: Xaja Construction Company 129
Dealing with Too Many Crews or Projects 132

A Variation on the Assignment Problem 134
Solving Transportation and Assignment Problems 134
Exercises 134
Case Study: Delta Company 137
Case Study: Delta Company (B) 138
Case Study: Delta Company (C) 138

Chapter **8** Optimization of Network Models 139

Project Scheduling 139
Case Scenario: Soft Ideas, Inc. 140
Using Optimization to Determine Project Completion Time 143
Tradeoffs in Scheduling: Cost and Time 147
Flows in Networks 151
Fast Pack Delivery Company 151
Finding the Shortest Path Through a Network 158
Exercises 160

Chapter **9** Optimization Models Involving Time 165

Example: Purchasing in a Fluctuating Market 165
A Cash Planning Scenario 169
Case Study: Novana Company 172
Exercises 184
Case Study: Sawgrass Canning Company 186

Chapter **10** Improving Modeling Skills:
How to Maintain Linearity in Some Models 189

Nonlinearities in Optimization 191
Illustration: A Problem in Blending 193
Case Study: Sparkling Clean 199
Case Study: Rangely Lakes Company (B) 201
Another Example of Piecewise Linearity: Production Planning 205
Case Study: Production Planning 206
Exercises 210
Case Study: Hanley Electronics 212

Chapter **11** Optimization with Integer Variables 219

A Knapsack Problem: Do I Pack It? 221
Extending the Knapsack Problem 224

The Capital Budgeting Problem 225
Location Problems: Where to Put Recycling Centers 225
The Fixed Charge Problem: Using Binary Variables 228
Optimizing Chris's Spreadsheet with Fixed Charges 230
Exercises 232
Case Study: Long Plains Fire Services 234

Chapter 12   Inventory Analysis: An Example of Nonlinear Optimization . . 239

Inventory Management: An Example of Nonlinear Optimization 240
Specialty Products Incorporated 240
Economic Order Quantity 245
A Comparison: Modeling and Formulas 249
An Inventory System with Multiple Items 250
Optimizing the Multi-Item Inventory System 252
Managerial Information from Nonlinear Optimization 253
Quantity Discounts and Nonlinear Optimization 253
Exercises 257
Modeling Case: Economic Production Quantity 258
Case Study: Golden Ear Audio Distributor (A) 260
Case Study: Golden Ear Audio Distributor (B) 262
Case Illustration: An Efficient Portfolio 263
Case Illustration: Stratified Sampling and Sample Allocation 267

Chapter 13   Decision Analysis: Dealing with Uncertainty 271

Narrowing the Scope of the Analysis: A First Step in Decision Analysis 271
Four Components of a Decision Analysis 275
Payoff Table: Combining the Events, Acts, Payoffs, and Probabilities 276
Expected Value: Combining Payoffs and Probabilities 227
Comment: Payoff Tables and Their Uses 279
An Illustration of Decision Analysis: Choosing a Production Process 279
Using a Spreadsheet for J.D.'s Problem 281
Additional Information 282
Perfect Information for J.D.'s Problem 283
Decision Trees: Decision Problems with a Sequence of Decisions 284
Computing Terminal Values for a Decision Tree 286
Exercises 287
Cases in Spreadsheet Modeling and Decision Analysis: J.D.'s Decision (B) . 291
A Case Using a Decision Tree and a Spreadsheet: YumYum Corporation . . 296

Chapter 14 The Monte Carlo Method:
Incorporating Uncertainty into a Spreadsheet 303

Generating Random Numbers on a Spreadsheet 303
Using Data Tables (What-If) to Keep Track of Monte Carlo Replications . . . 304
Applying Monte Carlo Simulation to J.D.'s Problem 305
Expanding J.D.'s Scenario 307
Using the Results of J.D.'s Simulation: The Cumulative Frequency Distribution . . 309
More Uncertainty for J.D. 311
Generating Other Probability Distributions for Monte Carlo Analysis 315
Converting Managerial Descriptions of Uncertainty into Spreadsheet Formulas . . 318
Exercises 321
Case Analysis: Using Monte Carlo to Support Novana's Decisions 323
Case Study: Soft Ideas (B) 330
Supplement: Random Number Generation with What's*Best!* Functions 335

Chapter 15 Uncertainty in Inventory Management: Analysis & Simulation . 339

Monte Carlo Simulation in Inventory Management 340
Inventory Simulation: Golden Ear Audio (C) 340
Simulating a Hundred Days: Historical Demand, Next-Day Replenishment . . . 341
A Longer Simulation: Generating Random Demand Data 344
Inventory Analysis: When Should I Reorder? 348
Demand During a Lead Time: A Historical Approach 349
Demand During a Lead Time: A Statistical Approach 351
Simulation of Golden Ear Audio with Three-Day Replenishment Lead Time . . . 352
Exercises 356
Supplement: The Central Limit Theorem & The Runs Test 360
Case Study: Golden Ear Audio (D) 364

Chapter 16 Simulation & Analysis of Waiting Lines 371

Case Example: Quick-Serve Software Help 371
Analysis of Waiting Lines with Poisson Arrivals and Exponential Service Times . . 373
Spreadsheet Simulation of a Single-Server Waiting Line 376
Case Study: Lines at the Copier, North-South Insurance Company 380
Exercises 394

Appendix A Installing What's*Best!* 399

System Requirements 399
Quick Installation 399

Installation Details 401
Installation Related Problems 402

Appendix **B** What's*Best!* Commands & Error Messages 405

The What's*Best!* Commands 405
Advanced Commands 409
Messages for Errors and Troubleshooting 418

Appendix **C** Using the Solvers in Excel 4.0
& Quattro Pro for Windows 1.0 427

Using the Solver in Excel Release 4.0 427
Using the Optimizer in Quattro Pro for Windows Version 1.0 428
Using the Quattro Pro Release 4.0 Optimizer 429
Optimizers in Quattro Pro 2.0 and 3.0 429

Index 431

PREFACE

Spreadsheets are widely used in making business decisions. This quantitative language, which managers use more widely than they use algebraic notation, is a very effective language for telling students and managers about management science modeling and solutions. This text assumes that readers have some familiarity with spreadsheets, and have a beginner's ability to use a spreadsheet for managerial purposes. Experience has shown that this spreadsheet approach to teaching management science accomplishes two purposes:

- Students learn management science in a spreadsheet language they will continue to use throughout their careers, and
- Students improve their proficiency with spreadsheets.

The idea of a model is at the heart of management science analysis. The author's experience is that optimization modeling using spreadsheets is an excellent way to practice and improve modeling skills. This modeling method is also useful in many management science techniques, from optimization to decision analysis, risk analysis, inventory models, and waiting line simulation. Each of these topics is included in this text.

This text uses DOS-based spreadsheets, Lotus 1-2-3 Release 2.x and Quattro Pro Version 4, which are widely used by business students. The optimization modeling in Chapters 2 through 12 uses the What's*Best!* solver software that accompanies this text. What's*Best!* uses spreadsheet models to find optimal solutions to linear, nonlinear, and mixed integer programming problems. The models are documented in a way that lets the reader understand and implement the *logic* on any spreadsheet, including spreadsheets with built-in solvers. Appendix C discusses the use of the solvers that are a part of Quattro Pro for DOS or Windows and Excel for windows. The final four chapters of the text deal with uncertainty. The Monte Carlo techniques used in these chapters use the data table (what-if) capabilities found in almost all spreadsheets.

Acknowledgments

There are many people I thank for giving me the impetus and support to develop these ideas and write this text. The first is Professor Martin Schatz, Dean Emeritus of the Crummer Graduate School at Rollins College. Marty provided the impetus and years of support as these ideas unfolded. Many others have had an impact, including Professor David Monarchi ("I know, Don, formulas look nicer to you, but will the manager agree with you?") of the University of Colorado at Boulder, and Professors Asim Roy of Arizona State University and David Eldredge of Murray State University, who classrooom-tested this material. Valuable contributions have been made by reviewers, including: Stephen Powell, Dartmouth College; Stephan Bloomfield and Dale McFarlane, Oregon State University; Jack Yurkiewicz, Pace University; Rick Hesse, Mercer University; Larry Weatherford, University of Wyoming; Yiannis Glegles, Suffolk University; Dinesh Dave, Appalachian State University; and Paul Gray, Claremont Graduate School.

Special thanks go to four classes of Executive MBA students at the Crummer Graduate school, who have used most of this text in earlier versions. In addition, more than three hundred other MBA students at the Crummer School have had an opportunity to make the text better by pointing out rough spots.

Without a family who so generously shares the love we have all been freely given, this text would never have been completed. May you be rewarded as you become involved in teaching or learning management science using spreadsheets!

Winter Park, Florida
December, 1993

FOREWORD

TO INSTRUCTORS

By tradition, we teach management science topics using algebraic notation and expect managers and students to become proficient in symbolic algebraic manipulation before they learn management science. The author's experience is that we discourage too many people by this process. Yet the traditional course expects the user (the student) to bend to fit the teaching methods of the instructor. The approach in this text is to use a management language, spreadsheets, instead of algebraic notation. The anticipated result: managers and students who learn spreadsheet modeling continue to use these tools in other courses and in their jobs. How often does this happen among students who learn management science using algebraic notation? In summary, the carry-over skills of both spreadsheets and management science are improved by using the methods of this text. It requires a different way of thinking, but the rewards make it worth the effort involved in changing the teaching methods.

Teaching a course that relies heavily upon spreadsheets presents many challenges to the instructor. A major challenge is documenting the logic of a spreadsheet model. Nearly all of the models shown in the text have English-like documentation, which is a useful way to encourage students to replicate these models for themselves. The following additional material is available from boyd & fraser publishing company:

- Virtually every model shown in the text on a diskette for instructors as a *.WK1 file;
- What's *Best!* software on a 5¼" diskette;
- A linear-only version of What's *Best!* for students with 640K hard-disk computers.

This range of material provides the models that best fit individual classroom demands and the software that satisfies individual student requirements.

A key idea used in developing this text is that it is primarily for "the course in management science" and not "the first course in management science." By teaching as if there is no follow-on course, the text provides managerial usefulness instead of foundations that most students don't build upon.

An important technique in this text is *influence charts* to aid in constructing models. This new term describes a device that has some characteristics of influence diagrams (from decision analysis) and flow charts (from computer programming). Students may be very good at building a spreadsheet model for a system they understand (such as an income statement), because the spreadsheet is a faster way of doing the familiar. But the essence of analysis is addressing new problems, never before seen by the analyst. A student may know that a spreadsheet would help in the analysis, but really doesn't have the experience to construct a useful spreadsheet for a new problem. An influence chart is a structured approach to aid in designing and constructing a spreadsheet model. How often have you known of a situation where hours (days) are spent on a spreadsheet, only to be stopped by the questions "Now what do I have here?" and "Now where do I go?" Influence charting starts with the desired outputs, the most important part of a model, before worrying about "what to multiply and divide, add and subtract."

Flexibility is provided for classes with different backgrounds and ability. For students without much spreadsheet experience, many "spreadsheet tips" appear throughout the text, to stretch students' abilities to use spreadsheets for decision support.

For mature students, several challenging cases are provided. These are often at the end of a chapter, so they can be omitted without losing continuity. While a junior-level undergraduate class would perhaps spend class time dealing with the models in the first part of chapter six, a graduate class might be assigned the Tucker Development Company case at the end of the chapter. In the graduate class, time would be spent discussing models and analysis for Tucker. Another example of this flexibility is the organization of Chapter 9, Optimization Models Involving Time. A beginning course might cover only two models (Hesse Corporation and Highint Company) showing decisions over a finite time horizon. A graduate course might spend only a limited amount of time on these simple illustrations, but spend a great deal of class time looking at models for the Novana Company. This sets the stage for a major case study, Sawgrass Canning Company, which integrates many functions across a business: production planning, purchasing, financing, terms of sale, working capital, and human resources management. A course of some depth can be developed by using these cases:

Chapter 6	Tucker
Chapter 7	Delta
Chapter 9	Novana, Sawgrass
Chapter 10	Hanley Electronics
Chapter 11	Long Plains Fire Services

Chapter 12   Economic Production Quantity, Golden Ear Audio, Efficient Portfolio, Stratified Sample Allocation

Chapter 13   J.D.'s Decision, YumYum Corporation

Chapter 14   Novana revisited, Soft Ideas revisited

Chapter 15   Golden Ear Audio revisited

Note that several cases are repeated. This emphasizes the importance of models, not techniques; the same scenario and very similar spreadsheet models can be used with several different tools of management science. It helps drive home the point that modeling is the unifying concept of management science.

The diskette provided with this text includes the What's *Best!* software (student version) and several other files that are required for various parts of the text. Two of these files, for Golden Ear Audio and North-South Insurance Company, provide large datasets not shown completely in the text. (Why should we show 200 observations in the text, and expect students to key them?) Waiting line formulas are not shown in the text, because there is little learning that takes place by pushing calculator buttons. Instead, the formulas are on two spreadsheets (provided on the diskette) which are discussed in the waiting line chapter (Chapter 16). Finally, students are provided with completed optimization spreadsheets for Rangely Lakes, RANGELY.WK1 and RANGELY.WQ1, which contain the optimization instructions. This scenario is discussed extensively in the text; the file is provided as a concrete example showing all the details that may have been overlooked, misunderstood (or explained poorly?) in developing the first optimization illustration. All of these files may be optionally installed on the student's computer during installation of What's *Best!* by following the on-screen installation instructions.

So let's roll up our sleeves and get on with it!

1

Management Models
for Decisions

Management science is the use of quantitative methods to support managerial decisions. Fundamental to management science is a model, which is a representation of reality. A youngster enjoys a model airplane or a model railroad. An engineer uses a model of an airfoil in a wind tunnel. An architect uses a set of blueprints as a model to show what is to be built. NASA uses computer models of a spacecraft to determine the impact of a new condition that arises during a space flight, so that a new flight plan can be developed.

A manager's model may be as simple as "back of an envelope" calculations leading to a price quotation, or as complex as a large model representing a financial consolidation with a proposed merger partner. A manager uses a model to evaluate alternative courses of action. Within the last decade, managers have become much more directly involved in using a computer in the modeling process. Although computer-based managerial modeling has been around for decades, use of models that were created by the manager, rather than by some other part of the organization (such as data processing, analysis, operations research, or planning), has become widespread in only the last ten years. This relatively new concept of end-user modeling has been fostered by computer software oriented around a spreadsheet.

Why Construct a Model?

Most models are constructed so that the user can see what happens if something changes. Generally, it is more efficient to try out a change on a model than it is to test it in the reality represented by the model. It is easier to test an airfoil in a wind tunnel than on an aircraft flying at 30,000 feet; or to "put the bathroom at this end of the hall" on an architect's drawing to physically build it to see how it

1

affects other parts of the floor plan. During a space flight, it is better to experiment with a new flight plan on a computer simulation model than with the real spacecraft.

A manager uses a model in these same ways. The manager may wish to look at alternative inventory control methods with a model, rather than implementing the methods only to find out that the stockout level has reached unacceptable levels. It is better to experiment with conditions of a new financing plan on a worksheet than in the financial markets, or to determine the staffing requirements with a planning model than by finding out that the company needed a third shift "yesterday."

Modeling for *Ad Hoc* Decisions or Repeated Decisions?

A useful classification of models is by whether the situation being modeled is a "one-time" affair or a repeated situation. A decision to build a new plant using new technology would require an *ad hoc* model, while the monthly budget variance report is repeated monthly. The focus of this chapter is on managerial development of *ad hoc* models. By contrast, computer models that are used repeatedly may be more likely to benefit from an information systems professional who is skilled at tasks such as dressing up the reports and making the software more friendly to a new user.

Two Approaches to End-User Spreadsheet Modeling

How does an end-user (such as a manager) go about constructing a spreadsheet model for a scenario that has never been encountered before, and that may never be encountered again? There are two extreme approaches:

Do it the way I would do it by hand. If a manager's job requires evaluating a proposal, chances are that the manager will eventually be able to figure out how to go about "developing the numbers" that are useful in evaluating a proposal. A model can be constructed that mimics this "traditional" approach, which uually involves starting with detail and following a procedure or set of calculations that eventually (we hope) leads to the "answer" being sought by the modeler.

Build the model "top down" with an influence chart.* This method of modeling requires starting the process with the "bottom line" or the

---

*Influence charts, as used in this book, have evolved from *influence diagrams* used in the literature of Decision Analysis. The influence charts used here are somewhat similar to the influence diagrams used by Samuel E. Bodily, *Modern Decision Making: A Guide to Modeling with Decision Support Systems* (New York: Mc-Graw-Hill Book Company, 1984). For a description of influence diagrams as used in the literature of decision analysis, see Peter McNamee, *Supertree* (South San Francisco: The Scientific Press, 1992), revised edition. The term *influence chart* has been selected for this book to distinguish the modeling uses of influence charts and the focus on uncertainty in influence diagrams. The word *chart* relates to a *flow chart*, which has long been used as a schematic device developed prior to a computer program. However, influence charts show relationships among variables, while flow charts show flow of control in a computer program. For those with an information systems inclination, it may be useful to view influence charts as a non-procedural equivalent of a flow chart.

numbers that are the desired output of the model. (Unfortunately, there is a conflict of terms: The accountant's *bottom* line is the *top* of the hierarchy in the language of information systems.) From this end result, the modeler works lower and lower, with increasing detail, until the model is complete. This process is called *top-down modeling*, because it starts with the desired output from the model, and then works downward to the details necessary to calculate this output. This process is guided by the construction of an *influence chart* to show how many variables are related in the model.

Vacation Budget: An Example of an Influence Chart and Top-Down Modeling

Our first example of using an influence chart and top-down modeling is a vacation budget. While this example is simple enough that its model could be constructed "the way I'd do it with pencil and paper," it is a good illustration of top-down modeling and an influence chart.

The vacationer, DP, wants to project the total expenses for a trip to New York. DP breaks expenses into two categories: "living expenses" for food and lodging, and "vacation expenses" for travel and entertainment. For planning purposes, DP plans to spend $90 per day for food and $170 per day for lodging. Travel will cost $375, including airline tickets and transportation to and from both airports. Entertainment costs are estimated to be $50 per day, plus $140 for two "big evenings" on Broadway. DP will decide on the number of days for the trip after looking at the output of the model; tentatively, a five-day trip is planned.

The information that is desired from the model is total expenses, which becomes the first entry on the influence chart. The next entries for the chart are living expenses and vacation expenses: if DP knew these two items, total expenses could be calculated by finding their sum. At this point, the influence chart looks like Figure 1.1. An important aspect of this influence chart is what is not shown, as well as what is shown. It is true that TOTAL EXPENSES are influenced by LIVING EXPENSES, but there are many other items or variables that also influence TOTAL EXPENSES. These other variables, however, have an indirect influence, through LIVING EXPENSES and VACATION EXPENSES. At this point, the influence chart is showing the variables that directly influence TOTAL EXPENSES, rather than the variables which influence TOTAL EXPENSES indirectly, or through other variables. Another example: the food cost per day clearly influences total expenses. But the food cost per day directly influences food expenses, which directly affects living expenses. These influencing variables will be shown later in the chart.

The next step is to decompose each of these variables, by asking "What variables do I need to know to calculate living expenses" and "What variables do I need to know to calculate vacation expenses?" Again, we want the variables

---
Figure 1.1

Influence Chart for Vacation Budget: Step 1

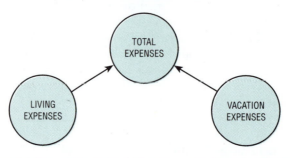

Figure 1.2

Influence Chart for Vacation Budget: Step 2

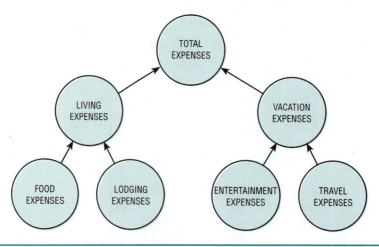

---

that directly influence living expenses and vacation expenses, to make the logic of the influence chart as clear and simple as possible. Living expenses are directly influenced by food expenses and lodging expenses; knowing these two variables, we could calculate living expenses. Vacation expenses are directly influenced by entertainment expenses and travel expenses; knowing these two variables, we could calculate vacation expenses. This gives us Figure 1.2, showing the second step in the influence chart. Note that with each step we are "peeling the onion" one more layer.

We continue the process of decomposing each variable into its direct influences. We can list these influences as follows:

Food expenses are directly influenced by *food cost per day*, and by the *number of days*.

Figure 1.3

Influence Chart for Vacation Budget: Step 3

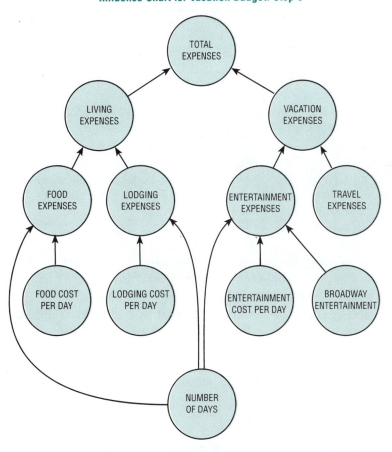

Lodging expenses are directly influenced by *lodging cost per day,* and by the *number of days.*

Entertainment expenses are directly influenced by *entertainment cost per day,* the *number of days,* and by *Broadway entertainment.*

Note that travel expenses is already decomposed as far as it can go: the scenario simply states a lump sum figure of $375 for travel expenses. Figure 1.3 shows the final step in the influence chart for the vacation budget. Even though NUMBER OF DAYS influences three variables, it appears only once in the chart. Multiple arrows from NUMBER OF DAYS show the multiple influences.

Some Guidelines for Constructing an Influence Chart

The influence chart is constructed so the modeler can understand the logic of the model before attempting to enter it into a spreadsheet. The chart separates the tasks of model logic and spreadsheet formulas. Because the chart is a tool for the user, the issue is not to define the correct way to construct a chart; the issue is how charts can be a useful step that a manager would use in constructing a spreadsheet model. In that spirit, we suggest these guidelines:

> Start by asking which spreadsheet cells or variables the decision maker will look at to evaluate the plan described by the spreadsheet model. These are the "bottom line" cells or variables that let the decision maker evaluate the plan of the model. The values for these cells or variables are what we want the spreadsheet to calculate; we start the influence chart with these cells and then develop logic to calculate these cell values.

> After you have started the chart, pick a variable and ask what influencing variables you need to calculate this variable. Don't worry yet about how to calculate these influencing variables; that comes later. Add new variables, as they are suggested in this step. Show the influences with arrows.

> A variable should have as few influences as possible. To implement this, ask yourself, "What two (or three, or four . . .) variables do I need to calculate this?" Notice that the question starts with the variable on the chart, and asks what influences this variable. This guideline helps make models simple to construct and easy to understand.

> A variable is shown only once on a chart. If that variable influences several other variables (such as NUMBER OF DAYS influences three variables), show it with several arrows from one variable on the chart.

> Don't fall into the trap of asking "What does this variable influence?" This question reverses the logic of influence chart construction and leads to useless charts. For example, if you ask whether the number of days influences total expenses, the answer is yes. But there is no arrow from NUMBER OF DAYS to TOTAL EXPENSES, because it is an indirect influence operating through many other variables.

When an influence chart is complete, any variable which does not have an arrow pointing into it is considered to be data. (Starting with Chapter 3 we'll use the term *decision variables* for some of these variables with no influencing variables. These will be the variables that are controlled in the decision process. For now, however, we'll include these variables as data.) These data values must be known from outside the system being modeled. It is often convenient to write these values beside the circle on the chart.

Using the Influence Chart to Construct a Model

It is rather straightforward to construct the spreadsheet model (shown in the top portion of Figure 1.4) from the influence chart, because the logic of the model has been understood in the process of constructing the chart. The author's favorite way to accomplish this is to start by listing the variable names in column A (which has been widened to 30 spaces); the formulas can be placed in column B, next to

---------------------- **Figure 1.4** ----------------------

Vacation Budget Spreadsheet

	A	B	C
1	Vacation Budget		
2			
3	Total Expenses	$2,065	
4	Living Expenses	1,300	
5	Vacation Expenses	765	
6	Food Expenses	450	
7	Lodging Expenses	850	
8	Entertainment Expenses	390	
9	Travel Expenses	375	
10	Food Cost per Day	90	
11	Lodging Cost per Day	170	
12	Entertainment Cost per Day	50	
13	Broadway Entertainment	140	
14	Number of Days	5	
15			
16			

	A	B
1	Vacation Budget	
2		
3	Total Expenses	+B4+B5
4	Living Expenses	+B6+B7
5	Vacation Expenses	+B8+B9
6	Food Expenses	+B10*B14
7	Lodging Expenses	+B11*B14
8	Entertainment Expenses	+B12*B14+B13
9	Travel Expenses	375
10	Food Cost per Day	90
11	Lodging Cost per Day	170
12	Entertainment Cost per Day	50
13	Broadway Entertainment	140
14	Number of Days	5
15		
16		

the text labels in column A. The influence chart indicates which cells are to be involved in each formula. For example, the formula for TOTAL EXPENSES in cell B3 is logically and symbolically:

TOTAL EXPENSES = LIVING EXPENSES + VACATION EXPENSES

Cell B3 contains the formula +B4+B5

This formula is easily entered either by pointing or by keying the formula directly.* (Experience has shown that there are fewer errors if one points to cells rather than keying cell addresses. As spreadsheet models become larger, pointing

---

*Chapter 2 contains a complete description of the keystrokes involved in creating a spreadsheet model. It focuses on the Rangely Lakes Company case, at the end of this chapter. It is designed for the reader with limited experience in creating spreadsheet models. If you have limited spreadsheet experience, you should spend several hours studying Chapter 2 and Rangely Lakes before you complete your study of Chapter 1.

Figure 1.5

Verbal Documentation of Vacation Budget Model

```
Total Expenses = Living Expenses + Vacation Expenses
Living Expenses = Food Expenses + Lodging Expenses
Vacation Expenses = Entertainment Expenses + Travel Expenses
Food Expenses = Food Cost per Day * Number of Days
Lodging Expenses = Lodging Cost per Day * Number of Days
Entertainment Expenses = Entertainment Cost per Day * Number of Days + Broadway Entertainment
Travel Expenses = 375
Food Cost per Day = 90
Lodging Cost per Day = 170
Entertainment Cost per Day = 50
Broadway Entertainment = 140
Number of Days = 5
```

---

becomes the only attractive option for building formulas.) The spreadsheet is shown in Figure 1.4, with the numerical values in the first part and the formulas in the second part. The formulas can be displayed by changing the **Format** in column B cells to **Text**.

We have represented a model by an influence chart, and by a spreadsheet model. A third way of representing the model is with a verbal documentation of the relationships. This style of verbal documentation* will be used throughout the text, to communicate the formulas in a model clearly. This documentation is shown in Figure 1.5.

What Use Is a Model?

When studying the values computed by the model with five days vacation, DP was disappointed with the results. DP had hoped that the expenses for the vacation would be less than $2,000; could something be changed? This introduces one of the powerful uses of management science models: responding to "What If" questions. What if DP reduces lodging costs to $135 a day by staying at lesser hotels? What if the number of days is reduced? What if we cut the daily entertainment cost, but increase the Broadway entertainment? Any of these questions can be pursued by using the model. In this introductory example, the relationships are so simple that mental calculations could answer many of the queries; this is not always the case!

Roll Out the Barrel: Another Scenario and Influence Chart for Top-Down Modeling

As another illustration of top-down modeling with an influence chart, we use a scenario which is less familiar; there is no "obvious" way to construct the model, which makes the use of an influence chart more important.

---

*This documentation is very similar to modeling statements used in the IFPS descriptive modeling language (Execucom Systems Corporation, Austin, Texas). It is also very similar to the spreadsheet documentation output produced by the CellMate software (Clarity Software Corp., Austin, Texas).

A beer wholesaler, LB, wants to find out the average price per gallon for beer sold by the distributorship. The average price is the total revenue from kegs and six-packs divided by the number of gallons sold in kegs and six-packs. Last year, LB sold 400,000 gallons of beer; of that, 100,000 gallons was sold in kegs and 300,000 gallons was sold in cans and bottles.

LB sells a six-pack for $1.45. Bottles and cases (cans or bottles) sell for about the same price (per ounce or per gallon) as a six-pack. Beer sold by the keg sells at about 45% of the six-pack price per ounce (or per gallon); there are 1.778 six-packs in a gallon.

As we work through the modeling process, we are really separating it into two steps:

What variables are involved in the model, and what variables influence each variable? This is shown in an influence chart.

What is the exact form of the relationship, showing how each variable is influenced by other variables? This is shown in the model constructed with the aid of the influence chart.

The modeling process starts with the influence chart. First, the modeler determines the desired output from the model, or the "bottom line" or the "end result" of using the model. For LB, this desired output is the AVERAGE PRICE PER GALLON. As before, the process is like peeling an onion, one layer at a time. We peel the next layer by asking what we need to calculate AVERAGE PRICE PER GALLON; we want to answer this question with a short list. In this situation, we know the TOTAL REVENUE and the GALLONS SOLD; these two variables directly influence the AVERAGE PRICE PER GALLON. Each of these, in turn, is subjected to "peeling a layer." TOTAL REVENUE is influenced by KEG REVENUE and CAN REVENUE (where CAN refers to bottles, cans, six-packs, and cases). GALLONS SOLD is influenced by GALLONS IN KEGS and GALLONS IN CANS.

This gets difficult to follow in text format. At this point, the paragraph above can be shown as the influence chart of Figure 1.6. The information in the influence chart shows visually that:

AVERAGE PRICE PER GALLON *is influenced by* TOTAL REVENUE *and by* GALLONS SOLD

TOTAL REVENUE *is influenced by* KEG REVENUE *and by* CAN REVENUE

GALLONS SOLD *is influenced by* GALLONS IN KEGS *and by* GALLONS IN CANS

From an understanding of the situation, the modeler knows the nature of the relationships:

$$\text{AVERAGE PRICE PER GALLON} = \text{TOTAL REVENUE} \, / \, \text{GALLONS SOLD}$$

$$\text{TOTAL REVENUE} = \text{KEG REVENUE} + \text{CAN REVENUE}$$

$$\text{GALLONS SOLD} = \text{GALLONS IN KEGS} + \text{GALLONS IN CANS}$$

Now it's time to peel the onion again. What influences gallons in kegs and gallons in cans? What influences keg revenue and can revenue? We get different types of answers for these two questions:

Figure 1.6

The Beginnings of an Influence Chart

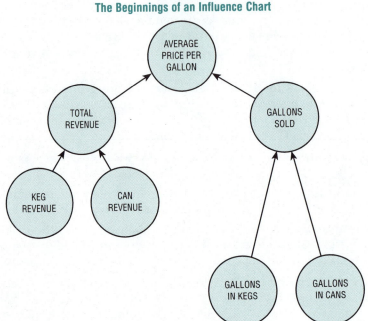

From the scenario, we know the values for gallons in kegs and gallons in cans. These values are data, not influenced by other variables in the model under construction. In the influence chart, there will be no arrows pointing into these circles, because they aren't influenced by (or calculated by) any other variables.

The variables, keg revenue and can revenue, are influenced by the price and quantity for each product. Specifically, the modeler knows that keg revenue is the product of gallons in kegs and keg price per gallon; and that can revenue is the product of gallons in cans and can price per gallon.

The expanded influence chart is shown in Figure 1.7. Note that both GALLONS IN KEGS and GALLONS IN CANS influence two variables, which is indicated by two arrows leading from GALLONS IN KEGS and GALLONS IN CANS. *Reminder:* A variable is shown only once on an influence chart, even though that variable may influence many variables.

Continuing with the Influence Chart

Back to peeling the onion. What influences the can price per gallon? This is influenced by the price of six pack and the number of six packs per gallon. Since both of these new variables are data known from the situation, we won't need to peel any more here.

Figure 1.7

Continuing with the Influence Chart

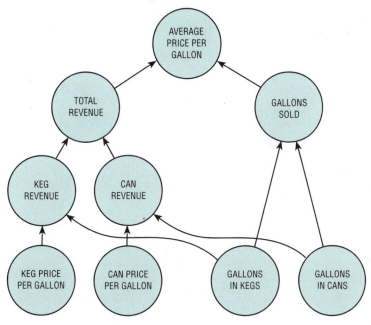

The final variable to be considered is the keg price per gallon. From understanding the situation, we know that keg price per gallon is 45% of the can price per gallon. If we call this value (45%) the KEG PRICE RATIO, we are finished. The final influence chart is shown in Figure 1.8.

Constructing a Model from the Influence Chart

The influence chart guides the modeler in constructing the model. In a spreadsheet, a straightforward approach to constructing the model is to list the variable names in column A on the worksheet. For the beer price scenario, the list of variables (with obvious abbreviations) might be placed in column A. The next step is to enter the formulas in column B, typically using the pointing capabilities of the spreadsheet to place cell addresses in formulas. The completed spreadsheet and numerical values are shown in Figure 1.9. For convenience, the cell formulas have been placed beside the values in Figure 1.9, although they do not appear in the worksheet as a separate column. Below the worksheet, the verbal documentation of the model is also shown.*

---

*The "range (block) name" capability of spreadsheets can also be used to provide internal documentation for a spreadsheet. By naming the cells in column B from the labels in column A, the cell formulas in column B will be displayed in the control panel with range names instead of cell addresses. If the format of the formula cells in column B is changed to Text format, the spreadsheet itself will display the formulas using range names (if the column width is sufficient).

Figure 1.8

The Completed Influence Chart

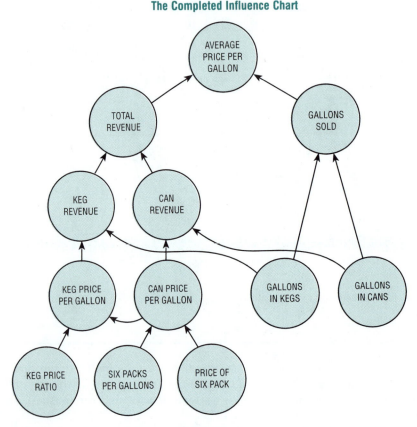

Why Use Influence Charts?

When we calculate something with a calculator or by hand, we are forced to start with what we know, and from that calculate a value. We start with the data and proceed to calculate additional intermediate values until we end up with what we want. A potential problem with this approach is that the intermediate values we keep calculating may not lead us to what we want. Many times we seem to end up pursuing blind alleys, having calculated intermediate value after intermediate value without ever reaching something that is useful.

Compare this with the influence chart approach: we start the chart with where we want to be, and decide what we need to know to get there. This approach has several advantages:

There are fewer blind alleys to be pursued, because each intermediate value leads along the pathway to a desired end result.

The process clearly identifies the data that need to be gathered before the model can be completed.

--- **Figure 1.9** ---

Worksheet for Roll Out the Barrel

	A	B	
1	Avg Price per Gal	$2.224	+B3/B7
2			
3	Total Revenue	$889,445	+B4+B5
4	Keg Revenue	$116,015	+B8*B11
5	Can Revenue	$773,430	+B9*B12
6			
7	Gallons Sold	400,000	+B8+B9
8	Gallons in Kegs	100,000	
9	Gallons in Cans	300,000	
10			
11	Keg Price per Gal	$1.160	+B12*B16
12	Can Price per Gal	$2.578	+B14*B15
13			
14	Price of Six Pak	$1.45	
15	Six Paks per Gal	1.778	
16	Keg Price Ratio	0.45	
17			

```
Avg Price per Gal = Total Revenue / Gallons Sold
Total Revenue = Keg Revenue + Can Revenue
Keg Revenue = Gallons in Kegs * Keg Price per Gal
Can Revenue = Gallons in Cans * Can Price per Gal
Gallons Sold = Gallons in Kegs + Gallons in Cans
Gallons in Kegs = 100000
Gallons in Cans = 300000
Keg Price per Gal = Can Price per Gal * Keg Price Ratio
Can Price per Gal = Price of Six Pak * Six Paks per Gal
Price of Six Pak = 1.45
Six Paks per Gal = 1.778
Keg Price Ratio = 0.45
```

The influence chart is a very useful way to communicate to a colleague the assumptions that are made in a model.

There are disadvantages to an influence chart. For a small problem, some modelers feel it is not worth the time to construct an influence chart. As a counterpoint to this possible disadvantage, the reality is that a modeler's influence charts are seldom as neat as those in a printed document! A freehand influence chart helps the modeler think about a problem; it becomes a living scratchpad, with changes frequently being made as the modeler understands the problem.

Another possible disadvantage is that an influence chart may not be very useful in constructing a model to replicate something a modeler does frequently. You don't need an influence chart to tell you that your cash balance is equal to your previous balance plus your receipts less your expenditures, if you have gone through that process a number of times. But if a model is for a new problem, an influence chart is a very useful tool for constructing a model.

Many modelers do not use influence charts; experience of the author, however, has shown that complex *ad hoc* problems are modeled more quickly and more correctly with the use of influence charts. The mental structuring of the problem that is enforced by the top down logic tends to produce models that are better because they are easier for the modeler to understand, and easier for others to understand as they use and modify the model.

Worksheets with Many Columns

The model and influence chart for "Roll Out the Barrel" were one-column; all of the numbers referred to the same item (beer) and the same point in time (last year). Although the worksheet used two columns (column A for the variable names, and column B for the variable definitions) the model itself referred to only one entity, beer last year. For example, Total Revenue referred to the total amount of revenue for beer last year.

Many models use columns to represent several time periods. Total Revenue, for example, refers to the total amount of revenue for beer last year. But it could also have referred to the total amount of revenue for beer the year before, or for other years. A modeler will frequently have columns headed with January, February, . . . , or with 1994, 1995, 1996, and so on.

Another way that multiple columns are used in worksheets is to represent different entities. For example, the beer distributor might have three products: beer, light beer, and ale. A separate column—each with the logic copied from column B with the original logic—would calculate the Avg Price per Gallon for each of the different entities.

When additional columns in a model are used to represent different periods of time, or different entities, the influence chart for one time period (or for one entity) is often suitable for each time period or entity. This is the case when we add more entities (light beer, ale) to the scenario. For example, Keg Revenue for each entity (product column) is calculated using identical logic. A spreadsheet showing the Avg Price per Gal for Beer, Light, and Ale is shown in Figure 1.10. Notice that each product has its own gallons and price. The physical constant, Six Paks per Gal, is the same across all columns. According to the numbers in the spreadsheet, the pricing factor between keg price and can price is also the same for each product.

A typical reaction from a manager looking at the spreadsheet of Figure 1.10 might be "How did we do for the entire product line?" What is the average price per gallon for all items? This suggests a second common use for additional columns: some form of aggregation, such as a sum or an average. The influence chart could be expanded to show this added information, but there are tradeoffs to consider. While incorporating this information would complete the influence chart, it would also clutter the chart. A judgment call: The additional clutter is not worth a modest increase in clarity.

The additional information is primarily a horizontal summation of various columns. For the entire product line, each revenue term (Total Revenue, Keg Revenue, Can Revenue) and each gallon term (Gallons Sold, Gallons in Kegs, Gallons in Cans) is calculated by summing the three terms in parentheses. We have elected not to diagram the information for the Product Line column, but a warning must be included. The average price per gallon should be calculated by

---

Figure 1.10

A Model with Three Products

	A	B	C	D
1		Beer	Light	Ale
2				
3	Avg Price per Gal	$2.224	$1.706	$2.720
4				
5	Total Revenue	$889,445	$554,292	$108,814
6	Keg Revenue	$116,015	$232,029	$0
7	Can Revenue	$773,430	$322,263	$108,814
8				
9	Gallons Sold	400,000	325,000	40,000
10	Gallons in Kegs	100,000	200,000	0
11	Gallons in Cans	300,000	125,000	40,000
12				
13	Keg Price per Gal	$1.160	$1.160	$1.224
14	Can Price per Gal	$2.578	$2.578	$2.720
15				
16	Price of Six Pak	$1.45	$1.45	$1.53
17	Six Paks per Gal	1.778	1.778	1.778
18	Keg Price Ratio	0.45	0.45	0.45

---

using the revenue and gallons information from the entire product line. It would be incorrect to average just the three prices, because different amounts of each product are sold. (If you bought nine drinks at $2 and one drink at $1, is your average price $1.50, an unweighted average, or $1.90, obtained by adding the amount spent and dividing by the number of drinks?) A model with the column for the Product Line is shown in Figure 1.11.

Figure 1.11

A Model with a Total Column for the Product Line

	A	B	C	D	E
1		Beer	Light	Ale	Product Line
2					
3	Avg Price per Gal	$2.224	$1.706	$2.720	$2.029
4					
5	Total Revenue	$889,445	$554,292	$108,814	$1,552,550
6	Keg Revenue	$116,015	$232,029	$0	$348,044
7	Can Revenue	$773,430	$322,263	$108,814	$1,204,506
8					
9	Gallons Sold	400,000	325,000	40,000	765,000
10	Gallons in Kegs	100,000	200,000	0	300,000
11	Gallons in Cans	300,000	125,000	40,000	465,000
12					
13	Keg Price per Gal	$1.160	$1.160	$1.224	
14	Can Price per Gal	$2.578	$2.578	$2.720	
15					
16	Price of Six Pak	$1.45	$1.45	$1.53	
17	Six Paks per Gal	1.778	1.778	1.778	
18	Keg Price Ratio	0.45	0.45	0.45	

───────────────────────────── **Figure 1.12** ─────────────────────────────

Verbal Documentation of a Four-Column Model

```
Avg Price per Gal[Beer THRU Product Line] = Total Revenue / Gallons Sold

Total Revenue[Beer THRU Ale] = Keg Revenue + Can Revenue
Total Revenue[Product Line] = SUM (Total Revenue[Beer] THRU Total Revenue[Ale])

Keg Revenue[Beer THRU Ale] = Gallons in Kegs * Keg Price per Gal
Keg Revenue[Product Line] = SUM (Keg Revenue[Beer] THRU Keg Revenue[Ale])

Can Revenue[Beer THRU Ale] = Gallons in Cans * Can Price per Gal
Can Revenue[Product Line] = SUM (Can Revenue[Beer] THRU Can Revenue[Ale])

Gallons Sold[Beer THRU Ale] = Gallons in Kegs + Gallons in Cans
Gallons Sold[Product Line] = SUM (Gallons Sold[Beer] THRU Gallons Sold[Ale])

Gallons in Kegs[Beer] = 100000
Gallons in Kegs[Light] = 200000
Gallons in Kegs[Ale] = 0
Gallons in Kegs[Product Line] = SUM (Gallons in Kegs[Beer] THRU Gallons in Kegs[Ale])

Gallons in Cans[Beer] = 300000
Gallons in Cans[Light] = 125000
Gallons in Cans[Ale] = 40000
Gallons in Cans[Product Line] = SUM (Gallons in Cans[Beer] THRU Gallons in Cans[Ale])

Keg Price per Gal[Beer THRU Ale] = Can Price per Gal * Keg Price Ratio

Can Price per Gal[Beer THRU Ale] = Price of Six Pak * Six Paks per Gal

Price of Six Pak[Beer THRU Light] = 1.45
Price of Six Pak[Ale] = 1.53

Six Paks per Gal[Beer THRU Ale] = 1.778

Keg Price Ratio[Beer THRU Ale] = 0.45
```

Documentation of Worksheets with Many Columns

Both cell formulas and verbal documentation were used to document the single-column models described earlier in this chapter. Cell formula documentation on the spreadsheet model screens or printouts becomes almost useless as a model expands. As a remedy, we will usually present verbal documentation of a model after the model is shown. The general scheme of the spreadsheet models is to use a column of labels as variable names (often column A). In verbal documentation, these variable names will be presented first.

Looking again at the model, the entity or time period names are given as labels in a header row (often Row 1). In the documentation, these column labels will be shown in square brackets, e.g., [Light]. In the model, the cell referenced by Total Revenue and Light is obvious from the appearance of the spreadsheet as the intersection of the row with the Total Revenue label and the column with the Light label. In the documentation, the intersection is shown as Total Revenue[Light]. Figure 1.12 illustrates verbal documentation for the multi-column model shown in Figure 1.11.

An important part of verbal documentation is the use of the word THRU to designate columns that were computed using identical logic. For example, the documentation of Keg Revenue illustrates that one definition is used for columns

[Beer THRU Ale], while another definition is used for column [Product Line]. Note also that some column labels have been omitted. The first line of the documentation is:

```
Avg Price per Gal[Beer THRU Product Line] + Total Revenue / Gallons Sold
```

This line of documentation could have been written more completely, but less clearly, as

```
Avg Price per Gal[Beer THRU Product Line] + Total Revenue[Beer THRU
     Product Line] / Gallons Sold[Beer THRU Product Line]
```

This elaborates the obvious: Avg Price per Gal for Beer is calculated using Total Revenue and Gallons Sold from column Beer; each column is calculated using its own column of values.

Exercises

1. The amount of your paycheck is determined by your wages and your travel reimbursement. Wages are determined by the number of hours and the hourly wage rate. Travel reimbursement is determined by the distance driven and the mileage reimbursement rate. Construct an influence chart to determine the amount of your paycheck. Use the influence chart to construct a spreadsheet model to calculate the amount of your paycheck. Assume reasonable data values.

2. A rectangular area is to be enclosed by a fence; the land owner wants as large an enclosed area as possible. The land owner has purchased some fencing, and has constructed this spreadsheet model to calculate the enclosed area and the perimeter (amount of fence) for a rectangle of any length and width:

	A	B
1	Fence Exercise	
2		
3	Length	50
4	Width	100
5		
6	Area	5000
7	Perimeter	300

Construct an influence chart to show influences among Length, Width, Area, and Perimeter. Construct the spreadsheet model and verify its correctness by changing the length to 20 feet and the width to 10 feet; the area should be 200, and the perimeter should be 60.

3. Jan Hixler, a second-year college student, is interested in calculating the grade point average earned through the first three semesters. This average is defined as the total "points" earned divided by the total number of hours attempted. Semester grade reports show the total number of hours attempted and the total points for each semester. Construct an influence chart showing the desired output, the intermediate variables, and the data required.

4. Your school budget is met from savings and earnings. Of critical importance to you is the amount required from savings, which is the difference between total

expenses and earnings. When you are working, your living expenses are $740 per month and your earnings are $1200 per month. When you are in school, your living expenses are $530 a month and your school expenses are $2100 per course. When you are neither in school nor working, your expenses are $290 per month (thanks to your parents). Construct an influence chart to calculate the impact of various proposals you might have for spending your time during the next twelve months. From the influence chart, construct a spreadsheet model to assist in your planning.

5. There are three activities you enjoy on vacation: biking, sailing, and sunning. You are very concerned about the time and money required for various proposed vacations. Each hundred miles of biking requires two days, and you spend $41 for hostel expenses and food; each day of sailing costs $75; and each day of sunning costs $35. Construct an influence chart to assist you in your planning. From the chart, construct a spreadsheet model.

6. You want to build a spreadsheet to calculate various costs for making a metal can (a "tin can") for a food product. A can is completely described by its diameter and its height. There are two cost elements: metal cost and labor cost. The metal cost is incurred for the metal in the can wall and the ends. The amount of metal used in the wall is

   HEIGHT × DIAMETER × π where π is 3.14159 . . . , or @PI on a spreadsheet.

   The amount of metal used in each of two ends (or the top and the bottom) is

   DIAMETER × DIAMETER

   which assumes the round ends are cut from a square. Metal costs 0.02 cents ($0.0002) per square inch. At this point, these variables have been introduced:

METAL COST	END METAL USED
METAL COST PER SQUARE INCH	HEIGHT
TOTAL METAL USED	DIAMETER
WALL METAL USED	

   Construct an influence chart to calculate METAL COST, for a can of any HEIGHT and DIAMETER. (Looking ahead at the next part of this problem, use only half of your sheet of paper for this influence chart.)

   The labor cost is incurred for "seaming" for the side wall and for the joint between the ends and the side wall. The side wall seaming costs 0.1 cents per inch; the seam between an end and a side wall costs 0.15 cents per inch. The amount of side wall seaming is equal to the height of the can. The amount of side wall to end seaming for one end is

   DIAMETER × π where π is 3.14159 . . . , or @PI on a spreadsheet.

   These additional variables have been introduced:

TOTAL SEAM COST	UNIT COST FOR WALL SEAM
WALL SEAM COST	LENGTH OF END SEAMS
END SEAM COST	UNIT COST FOR END SEAMS
LENGTH OF WALL SEAM	

Construct an influence chart to calculate TOTAL SEAM COST, for a can of any HEIGHT and DIAMETER. *Note carefully* that any variables (such as HEIGHT and DIAMETER) that have already been entered into the influence chart should not be entered again. (Since you looked ahead, you may now use the other half of the paper you used for the previous influence chart.)

The total cost of the can is the sum of TOTAL METAL COST and TOTAL SEAM COST. On the paper you have used for the influence charts, show the influence arrows between the two charts already drawn and the TOTAL CAN COST.

7. Using the variables listed in Exercise 6, build a spreadsheet model to calculate the cost of a can that is six inches high and three inches in diameter. A good model should be constructed so that any number may be changed without changing any cell formulas. To assist in verifying your work, the cost for the proposed can is 4.918 cents.

8. A manufacturer of hammers has two models, standard and deluxe. Each standard hammer contributes $4 to profit; each deluxe hammer contributes $7 to profit. Both hammers require metal and labor, in different quantities. A standard hammer requires 21 ounces of metal and 0.8 hours of labor. A deluxe hammer requires 18 ounces of metal and 1.1 hours of labor. For the planning period, no more than 20,000 ounces of metal or 950 hours of labor can be used. A plan will include the number of standard hammers and the number of deluxe hammers to produce.

   a. Build an influence chart that shows the influences among these variables for a standard hammer:

PROFIT	UNIT PROFIT CONTRIBUTION
METAL USED	METAL PER HAMMER
LABOR USED	HOURS PER HAMMER
QUANTITY MADE	

   b. Construct a spreadsheet model, assuming that 700 standard hammers and 100 deluxe hammers will be produced. Compare this plan with the resource limitations. *Note:* a good model would be constructed so that any number could be changed without changing any formulas. The model should show a total for profit, as well as totals for metal used and labor used. Check the accuracy of your spreadsheet with mental arithmetic or a calculator. (For verification purposes, the profit from this plan is $3500.)

   c. Change the plan so that 500 standard hammers and 600 deluxe hammers will be produced. Which do you prefer, this plan or the plan for 700 standard and 100 deluxe hammers?

9. Another manufacturer is making pliers. Each economy plier sells for $3 and requires 3 ounces of metal and 10 minutes of labor. Each standard plier sells for $4 and requires 7 ounces of metal and 12 minutes of labor. Each deluxe plier sells for $5 and requires 6 ounces of metal and 15 minutes of labor. There is a

limit, unknown at this moment, for the number of ounces of metal and the number of minutes of labor can be used during the planning period. Each ounce of metal costs $0.04; each minute of labor costs $0.20. The manufacturer wants to maximize profit, which is the total revenue (price × quantity) less the cost of resources.

a. Build an influence chart that shows the influences among these variables, for an economy plier:

PROFIT	MINUTES PER UNIT
METAL USED	COST OF RESOURCES USED
LABOR USED	COST OF METAL USED
REVENUE	COST OF LABOR USED
UNIT SELLING PRICE	COST PER OUNCE
QUANTITY MADE	COST PER MINUTE
METAL PER UNIT	

b. Construct a spreadsheet model, assuming that 10 economy pliers, 100 standard pliers, and 1000 deluxe pliers will be produced and sold. Check the correctness of your spreadsheet model with a mental arithmetic or a calculator. Note that with the suggested quantities, mental arithmetic can be used for many of the computations, as a check on the correctness of spreadsheet construction.

10. You are concerned about the number of calories you consume from ice cream and cookies, but you also want to get a lot of "total satisfaction" measured in "yums"; you are also concerned about protein intake. Each serving of ice cream provides 40 yums and 25 grams of protein. Each cookie provides 50 yums and 15 grams of protein. Unfortunately, a serving of ice cream has 300 calories, and a cookie has 350 calories. You have no difficulty in eating a partial serving of ice cream, or a partial cookie. Plan your ice cream and cookie consumption for this situation, using these steps:

a. Build an influence chart that shows the influences among these variables, for your consumption of ice cream:

CALORIES CONSUMED	CALORIES PER SERVING
YUMS OBTAINED	YUMS PER SERVING
PROTEIN CONSUMED	PROTEIN PER SERVING
QUANTITY EATEN	

b. Construct a spreadsheet model, assuming that you eat 1.4 servings of ice cream and 0.8 cookies. Note: a good model would be constructed so that any number could be changed without changing any formulas. The model should show a total for calories, as well as totals for yums obtained and protein consumed. Check the accuracy of your spreadsheet model with mental arithmetic or a calculator.

Rangely Lakes Company

In early August, 1988, J. L. Duckworth began thinking about the winter activities of Rangely Lakes Company. J.L. was particularly concerned about the cash budgets for the winter, when revenue was quite limited. The other major concern J.L. was addressing was the need to keep the golf course maintenance staff busy during the winter.

The Rangely Lakes Company operates a summer-only golf course in northern Maine. To keep the maintenance employees on the workforce during the winter, they have developed two "Maine Woods Souvenirs" made out of forest products from the Rangely Lakes area. For our purposes, they have two products: Mallard decoys and Mallard wall hangings. Both of these products are hand-made; they have developed procedures so that skilled (but unartistic) maintenance workers can produce the two items. These souvenirs are marketed through numerous gift shops in New England. Rangely Lakes has priced the items attractively, so that they have never had any problems selling all of the souvenirs they can produce. From a budgeting standpoint, J. L. Duckworth needed to know how much profit would be generated from the souvenirs made during the winter. For planning purposes, J.L. calculated profit as revenue (price × quantity) less the cost of the wood used and the cost of the labor in the products.

Most gift shops sell the Mallard decoy for $26.95 and the Mallard wall hanging for $34.95. Rangely Lakes sells to the gift shops at $12 and $15 each. The average labor content is 1.1 hours for a decoy, and 0.5 hours for a wall hanging. Each labor hour costs Rangely Lakes $7.15, including fringe benefits. Although Rangely has some flexibility in the amount of labor it uses, it monitors labor use very closely to be certain that enough production is planned to keep the workforce employed, and that the production plan doesn't require more labor than the amount that can be available.

The souvenirs are made from native lumber, carefully selected during the summer as forest operations are performed. Each decoy requires 2.9 board feet of this special lumber; each wall hanging requires 4.8 board feet. (A board foot is 144 cubic inches of lumber.) More than 25,000 board feet were available for last winter's production season; this number may be somewhat higher or lower, depending upon lumbering activities during the next month. The anticipated market price for the wood is about $1.30 per board foot.

For J. L. Duckworth's "first cut" at the budget for the winter months, the plan was to make the same number of decoys and wall hangings as last year. A search of the records showed that 3500 decoys and 2500 wall hangings had been made. How would this plan affect J.L.'s concerns?

Note: Chapter 2 goes through a detailed explanation of the steps for constructing Rangely's influence chart and spreadsheet model. Chapter 2 may be skipped by students thoroughly familiar with using spreadsheets, since there is essentially no new material on developing influence charts. In any case, the following questions are designed to be used without reference to Chapter 2, it only for later verification and clues.

Case Questions

1. What information does J. L. Duckworth want as output of the model? These output variables will become the starting point for the influence chart.

2. The influence chart for J. L. Duckworth may be thought of as applying only to Decoys. Would the chart for hangings be identical (except for data values)? Construct the influence chart for J. L. Duckworth.

3. The model constructed for J. L. Duckworth should have variable names shown as labels in column A. Column B should contain formulas and values for decoys; column C should contain formulas and values for hangings. What should be shown in column D? Will every variable have an entry in column D? Construct the model for J. L. Duckworth. Use the model to address the question raised in the last paragraph of the case scenario.

CASE STUDY:

Sunsoak Products

Sunsoak Products is a relatively new contender in the skin care market. Its primary focus is on products for protection against potential dangers of exposure to sun. Its general advertising theme has been successful; a substantial number of people "Don't soak the sun without Sunsoak." The success of the product line has caused capacity problems in its manufacturing operations. Although raising prices is often one approach to rationing scarce capacity, retail commitments make it inappropriate for Sunsoak to change its prices. Sunsoak must decide how to use its scarce manufacturing capacity and imported oil in a fashion that is as profitable as possible.

The production operations for Sunsoak are relatively simple; an imported oil is the primary ingredient of each product. For the near term, oil is arriving from the supplier at the rate of 300 liters per day. Although Sunsoak has made inquiries, there seems to be no way to change this rate in time to affect the current planning period. Each retail container of the product labeled *Screen* requires 140 milliliters (ml) of oil. As there are 1000 ml of oil in a liter, slightly more than seven containers of *Screen* can be made from each liter of oil. The other two products do not use as much oil. The *Block* product requires 85 ml per container; and *Soak* requires 130 ml. Although there are other ingredients in each of the products, their availability is essentially unlimited; the cost of these ingredients is inconsequential to Sunsoak's planning.

The manufacturing operations for the three products, *Screen*, *Block*, and *Soak* are described in this report from the product manager:

The first product, *Screen*, requires time in our mixing machine. When we are mixing *Screen*, we turn out enough mixture for six containers each minute, or 360 each hour. That means each container requires ten seconds. The mixture goes to the filling machine, where it is placed into containers. This product has the largest containers, and its viscosity makes it a slower job to get into the containers. We can do only four containers a minute, or 240 each hour. Another way of stating this is that each container requires fifteen seconds for filling. The packaging for *Screen*, like all products in this line, is a plastic container mounted on cardboard, which is then placed in a "blister pack" so it can be hung on display racks that are on countertops in stores. The container is large, but the profile is simple; the operation that turns out the "blister pack" is pretty good for this product. We can do four a minute, or 240 each hour; this is equivalent to fifteen seconds per container. The operations are quite smooth when we are working on *Screen*, because the mixing and blistering are so nicely balanced.

The second product in the line, *Block*, goes through the same three processes: mixing, filling, and blister-packaging. A variety of ingredients is used in *Block*, so it takes longer to mix this product. A recent study of the mixing operation indicated that a typical mixing operation for *Block* is sufficient for fifty containers; this mixing required fifteen minutes. On the average, we mix enough for one container every eighteen seconds. The filling operation requires only eight seconds per container. The odd shape of the product makes the blister-packaging time consuming; on the average, twenty-two seconds are required to package one container.

The third product, *Soak*, can be mixed at an average time of nine seconds per container. Filling a container requires twelve seconds. It can be blister-packaged in eighteen seconds.

A quick phone call provided information about the cost and availability of the machines necessary for each of the three operations. The plant had recently switched to a new work schedule, with each person working four shifts each week; each shift is ten hours long. The mixing and filling operations can be run only one shift each day for these products, because it is used for other products during the other hours of the day. The blister-packaging can be run two shifts each day, because no other parts of the company utilize this equipment. The cost to operating the mixing operation is $45 per hour, which includes operators, supervision, and estimated maintenance. The filling operation costs $50 per hour; the blister-packaging operation costs $55 per hour.

The marketing campaign for these products is based upon Sunsoak selling at fixed (but perhaps high) prices. The company receives $8.00 for each container of *Screen*, $10.00 for each container of *Block*, and $12.00 for each container of *Soak*.

Case Assignment

1. Develop an influence chart for Sunsoak Products. This influence chart is to show the logic to calculate (for one product) the information that management wants in order to evaluate a production plan. This information includes:

What is the daily profit for the product?

How many hours of mixing are required each day?

How many hours of filling are required each day?

How many hours of blister-packaging are required each day?

Although the influence chart is for only one product, its logic is identical for all products. In the model, determine appropriate methods of aggregation for the individual products to the product line.

2. Construct a spreadsheet model from the influence chart. Use the model to evaluate the proposed production plan to produce 800 containers of *Screen*, 1000 containers of *Block*, and 1200 containers of *Soak* each day.

3. Discuss the proposed production plan in terms of resources available and in terms of profit. Compare the proposed production plan with each of these alternative plans:

> Plan A: 500 containers of each product
> Plan B: 1000 containers of each product
> Plan C: 1500 containers of each product

4. Can you find a production plan that is better than any of those proposed? In what ways do you use the model in searching for a better plan?

2

The Details of Constructing
an Influence Chart & a Model

Learning takes place through repetition; there are rather large doses of repetition in this chapter! The chapter goes through the steps in creating an influence chart for the Rangely Lakes case, and then uses that influence chart to construct a spreadsheet model. For those readers who are relatively inexperienced in model construction, the detailed steps to create the model are described using both the Lotus 1-2-3 commands and the commands for Quattro Pro for DOS. For classes with students thoroughly familiar with spreadsheet modeling, this chapter may be skipped.

Constructing an Influence Chart for Rangely Lakes

For convenience, the scenario for Rangely Lakes from the case study at the end of Chapter 1 is repeated here.

> In early August, 1988, J. L. Duckworth began thinking about the winter activities of Rangely Lakes Company. J.L. was particularly concerned about the cash budgets for the winter, when revenue was quite limited. The other major concern J.L. was addressing was the need to keep the golf course maintenance staff busy during the winter.
>
> The Rangely Lakes Company operates a summer-only golf course in northern Maine. To keep the maintenance employees on the workforce during the winter, they have developed two "Maine Woods Souvenirs" made out of forest products from the Rangely Lakes area. For our purposes, they have two products: Mallard decoys and Mallard wall hangings. Both of these products are hand-made; they have developed procedures so that skilled (but unartistic) maintenance workers can produce the two items. These souvenirs are marketed through numerous gift shops in New England. Rangely Lakes has priced the

items attractively, so that they have never had any problems selling all of the souvenirs they can produce. From a budgeting standpoint, J. L. Duckworth needed to know how much profit would be generated from the souvenirs made during the winter. For planning purposes, J.L. calculated profit as revenue (price $\times$ quantity) less the cost of the wood used and the cost of the labor in the products.

Most gift shops sell the Mallard decoy for $26.95, and the Mallard wall hanging for $34.95. Rangely Lakes sells to the gift shops at $12 and $15 each. The average labor content is 1.1 hours for a decoy, and 0.5 hours for a wall hanging. Each labor hour costs Rangely Lakes $7.15, including fringe benefits. Although Rangely has some flexibility in the amount of labor it uses, it monitors labor use very closely to be certain that enough production is planned to keep the workforce employed, and that the production plan doesn't require more labor than the amount that can be available.

The souvenirs are made from native lumber, carefully selected during the summer as forest operations are performed. Each decoy requires 2.9 board feet of this special lumber; each wall hanging requires 4.8 board feet. (A board foot is 144 cubic inches of lumber.) More than 25,000 board feet were available for last winter's production season; this number may be somewhat higher or lower, depending upon lumbering activities during the next month. The anticipated market price for the wood is about $1.30 per board foot.

For J. L. Duckworth's "first cut" at the budget for the winter months, the plan was to make the same number of decoys and wall hangings as last year. A search of the records showed that 3,500 decoys and 2,500 wall hangings had been made. How would this plan affect J.L.'s concerns?

As a prelude to constructing the influence chart, we recognize that the influence chart for decoys is identical to the chart for hangings; we will construct the chart as if it is only for decoys. When we build the spreadsheet model, we'll use a column for decoys, and two additional columns: one for hangings and one for a total.

What is the output from the model? J. L. Duckworth is contemplating a production plan of 3500 decoys and 2500 wall hangings; if this plan is carried out, J.L. will want to know these things:

      a. How much profit will be made?

      b. How many hours of labor will be used?

      c. How many board feet of lumber will be used?

The influence chart has these three output or "bottom line" variables, which are shown as three circles which cannot yet be connected. Find these three circles in

Figure 2.1

Influence Chart for Rangely Lakes

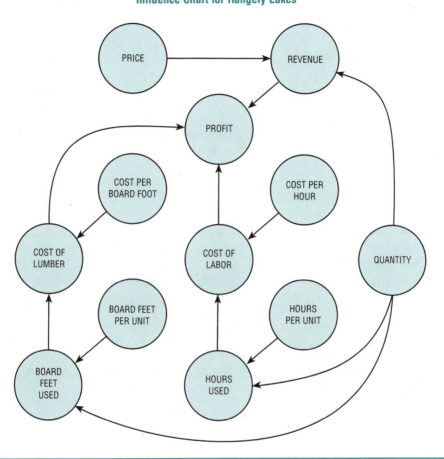

the influence chart of Figure 2.1, and mark them so you know they are where the chart started.

Step 2: The influence chart for decoys is identical to the chart for hangings; therefore, we will construct the chart as if it were only for decoys. We look for the variables that immediately influence each of the three items already identified. Much of this information is detailed in the case scenario.

Profit is revenue less cost of labor, less cost of lumber. Hence, PROFIT is influenced by:

REVENUE
COST OF LABOR
COST OF LUMBER

Hours used is the quantity of decoys (or hangings), multiplied by the hours required per unit. Hence, HOURS USED is influenced by:

QUANTITY OF DECOYS (or HANGINGS)

HOURS PER UNIT

Board feet used is the quantity of decoys (or hangings), multiplied by the board feet required per unit. Hence, BOARD FEET USED is influenced by:

QUANTITY OF DECOYS (or HANGINGS)

BOARD FEET PER UNIT

Find each of the six variables that influence the three output variables, and mark them on Figure 2.1 so you know they are the next "layer" in constructing the influence chart.

Step 3: Identify the immediate influencing variables for each of the new variables from Step 2.

Revenue is price multiplied by quantity. Hence, REVENUE is influenced by:

PRICE

QUANTITY

Cost of labor is the cost per hour multiplied by the number of hours used. Hence, COST OF LABOR is influenced by:

COST PER HOUR

HOURS USED

Cost of lumber is cost per board foot multiplied by the number of board feet used. Hence, COST OF LUMBER is influenced by:

COST PER BOARD FOOT

BOARD FEET USED

Several items in this list have already appeared on the influence chart. The only new items are cost per hour and cost per board food. The influence chart (Figure 2.1) can now be completed; all influences have been described. The variables without arrows into them are not influenced by other variables in the chart; these are often data values for the model.

Constructing the Model from the Influence Chart

Constructing an influence chart is an art; constructing the model is also an art. Just as no two artists would interpret a scene with identical paintings, we anticipate that a variety of analysts would create a variety of influence charts from the same scenario. We also anticipate a variety of models stemming from the same influence chart. What follows is not "the correct model," but it is one of many useful models that depict the relationships from the influence chart.

In this text, a common spreadsheet layout is to show variable names in the rows of column A, with values for the variables in column B, column C, column

Figure 2.2

Rangely Lakes Spreadsheet Layout

	A	B	C	D
1		Decoy	Hanging	Total
2	Quantity			
3	Price			
4	Revenue			
5				
6	Board Feet Used			
7	Cost of Lumber			
8				
9	Hours Used			
10	Cost of Labor			
11				
12	Profit			
13				
14	Board Feet per Item			
15	Hours per Item			
16				
17				
18	Price per Board Foot			
19	Price per Hour			

D, and so on. For Rangely Lakes, we'll use column A for variable names, column B for decoys, column C for hangings, and column D for totals. In many other problems, the columns will represent various time periods, or perhaps various locations, various people, and so on. Other modelers may prefer other layout styles; no layout is right or wrong! The criterion is its usefulness.

The next decision is the order in which variables are to be listed in column A. Each variable has already been named from the influence chart; any order of listing them in column A is acceptable. A common way to list variables is to approximate the way a business income statement might appear. Another order for listing variables might be the order in which they were entered into the influence chart. Another might be alphabetically! Each has its advantages: the income statement enhances communication between people familiar with its format; the influence chart order reinforces the logic that went into the influence chart; alphabetical listing makes it easier to find a particular variable in a long model. The key point of this paragraph is to emphasize that the first step in actual construction of the model is to list all of the variables in column A, usually starting in cell A2 and working down. This leaves row 1 for entering column titles, such as Decoy, Hanging, and Total. Figure 2.2 shows this portion of the model, using a layout which approximates a business income statement.

The spreadsheet keystrokes to enter this portion of the model are listed below, in some detail. The term *arrow keys* refers to the four directional arrows: up [↑], down [↓], right [→], and left [←]. These four keys are typically located near each other on the keyboard, often as a part of a separate keypad with numbers. Don't confuse the arrow keys with the "backspace" and "tab" keys, whose functions are different from the arrow keys.

1. Use the arrow keys to position the cell pointer in cell A2. Enter the keystrokes:

    Quantity[←⎟Enter]

    where the key enclosed by square brackets, [ ], is a named key. The [←⎟Enter] key may be called a [Return] key on some keyboards, or it may be identified by a hooked left arrow symbol, ←⎟, without a text label.

2. Next use the arrow keys to move the cell pointer to A3. Enter the keystrokes:

    Price[←⎟Enter]

3. Then use the arrow keys to move the cell pointer to A4. Enter the keystrokes:

    Revenue[←⎟Enter]

4. Move the cell pointer to A6. (A5 is left blank.) Enter the keystrokes:

    Board Feet Used[←⎟Enter]

5. At this point, the width of column A may be too small to show all of the characters, although they are temporarily spilling into column B because the adjacent cell (B6) is not yet used. To widen column A to 20 characters, these keystrokes are used for Lotus 1-2-3 spreadsheets:

/	to invoke the commands in Lotus 1-2-3
W	to select **Worksheet**; or highlight **Worksheet**, then [←⎟Enter]
C	to select **Columns**; or highlight **Columns**, then [←⎟Enter]
S	to select **Set Width**; or highlight **Set Width**, then [←⎟Enter]
20[←⎟Enter]	to specify a width of 20 characters

    In Quattro Pro, the keystrokes are:

/	to invoke the commands
S	to select **Style**; or highlight **Style**, then [←⎟Enter]
C	to select **Column Width**; or highlight **Column Width**, then [←⎟Enter]
20[←⎟Enter]	to specify a width of 20 characters

6. Using the arrow keys to move from one cell to the next, enter the remaining information to complete the worksheet as shown in Figure 2.2:

A7 :	Cost of Lumber [←⎟Enter]
A8 :	(*intentionally left blank, for clarity*)
A9 :	Hours Used[←⎟Enter]
A10:	Cost of Labor[←⎟Enter]
A11:	(*intentionally left blank, for clarity*)
A12:	Profit[←⎟Enter]
A13:	(*intentionally left blank, for clarity*)
A14:	Board Feet per Item[←⎟Enter]
A15:	Hours per Item[←⎟Enter]
A16:	(*intentionally left blank, for clarity*)
A17:	(*intentionally left blank, for use later—stay tuned*)
A18:	Price per Board Foot[←⎟Enter]
A19:	Price per Hour[←⎟Enter]

    Tip: After the keystrokes for A7, Cost of Lumber, have been concluded, the [↓] key may be depressed without using the [←⎟Enter] key. After using the alphanumeric keys to enter the information for a spreadsheet cell, an arrow key serves a dual purpose: it enters the information, and it also moves the cell pointer in the direction of the arrow key.

7. To enter the column titles, these keystrokes are used:

[Home]	to move the cell pointer to cell A1
[→]	to move the cell pointer to B1
Decoy	to enter the label *Decoy*
[→]	to finish the entry and move the cell pointer to C1
Hanging	to enter the label *Hanging*
[→]	to finish the entry and move the cell pointer to D1
Total	to enter the label *Total*
[←Enter]	to conclude the labels shown in Figure 2.2.

Entering Values and Formulas into the Model: Column B

The next step is to enter the information for decoys into column B. We start with the cell pointer in B2, which will contain the information for the Quantity[Decoy]. On the influence chart, there are no arrows pointing to this cell; this cell contains data, or values specified outside the model. The appropriate keystrokes for this cell are:

B2:	3500[↓]	to enter the value and move the pointer

Next is cell B3, which shows Price[Decoy]. This is also a data value, which can be entered in this way:

B3:	12[↓]	to enter the value and move the pointer

Because this is a dollar value, it is tempting to use the dollar sign to indicate the format. In many spreadsheets, this won't work. To make the dollar sign appear, the format of the cell must be changed with these keystrokes, with the cell pointer positioned in B3. For Lotus 1-2-3:

/	to invoke the commands
R	to select **Range**; or highlight **Range**, [←Enter]
F	to select **Format**; or highlight **Format**, then [←Enter]
C	to select **Currency**; or highlight **Currency**, then [←Enter]
0	to indicate no decimals displayed, then [←Enter]
[←Enter]	to accept the displayed range, B3..B3

For Quattro Pro, the keystrokes are:

/	to invoke the commands
S	to select **Style**; or highlight **Style**, then [←Enter]
N	to select **Numeric** format; or highlight **Numeric** format, then [←Enter]
C	to select **Currency**; or highlight **Currency**, then [←Enter]
0	to indicate no decimals displayed, then [←Enter]
[←Enter]	to accept the displayed range, B3..B3

Tip: Using the **Currency** format with 0 decimals makes the worksheet look "neat and tidy" but it may be dangerous: If a price such as $12.75 is entered, the decimals won't be displayed, although they are correctly entered into the spreadsheet. For display purposes, the spreadsheet would show $13; for computational purposes, $12.75 would be used. Use formats with 0 decimals with care . . . the unwary user may be led astray with no effort at all!

The next step is to enter the formula to calculate Revenue[Decoy], in cell B4. From the logic used in constructing the influence chart, we know that REVENUE is calculated as PRICE × QUANTITY. One way to do this (which isn't recommended) is to enter these keystrokes in this cell:

B4:   +B3*B2[←┘Enter]

The "+" sign indicates that the following information is to be treated as a formula, rather than as a label. Keystrokes beginning with a letter are understood by most spreadsheets to be labels; keystrokes beginning with a number or a symbol used in formulas, such as [+], [−], or [(], are understood to be formulas.

The keystroke method of entering formulas is not recommended, because errors are easy to make in determining rows and columns in the lower right portion of the screen, and because it is very difficult to find these addresses when the spreadsheet is larger than one screen.

The recommended way to enter the information is to place the cell pointer in cell B4, and then enter the plus symbol keystroke to begin a formula. When the plus symbol is entered, the status indicator in the upper (or lower) right corner switches from **Ready** to **Value**, indicating that a **Value** or a formula is being placed in this cell. Instead of keying cell addresses directly, the cell pointer may be used to point to a cell. After the plus symbol, use the arrow keys to move the cell pointer to cell B3. Note that the status indicator changes from **Value** to **Point**. With the cell pointer on B3, press the [*] key. With this keystroke, the upper left corner of the spreadsheet indicates that the formula being constructed is currently +B3*. The formula is completed by using the arrow keys to move the cell pointer to B2, and pressing [←┘Enter] to complete entering the information for the cell.

Continuing down the column, cell B6 or Board Feet Used[Decoy] is next. From the influence chart, this is influenced by QUANTITY and BOARD FEET PER ITEM; the scenario and logic tell us that BOARD FEET USED is QUANTITY multiplied by BOARD FEET PER ITEM. To use the cell pointer to enter cells in formulas, these steps are followed:

Start with the cell pointer in Board Feet Used[Decoy] (B6).

Begin the formula with the + symbol.

Use the arrow keys to move the cell pointer to Quantity[Decoy] (B2), then press [*] to indicate multiplication. Note that the cell pointer returns to the beginning cell, B6, when [*] is pressed.

Use the arrow keys to move the cell pointer to Board Feet per Item [Decoy] (B14), which is currently blank.

Complete the formula by pressing [←┘Enter]. The value in B6 will temporarily be 0, because the blank cell (B14) is understood by the spreadsheet to have a value of 0.

Tip: Beginning users sometimes confuse the cell containing a label with the cell containing the value indicated by the label. When you are instructed to move the cell pointer to Board Feet per Item[Decoy], move the cell pointer to the cell next to the label Board Feet per Item, and in the column marked Decoy. Although a label (such as cell A14) may be used in a formula, such a use is almost always an error. The spreadsheet treats a formula by arbitrarily giving it a value of zero.

The next cell is B7, Cost of Lumber[Decoy], which is calculated as the product of Board Feet Used[Decoy] and Price per Board Foot. Start with the cell pointer in B7, and begin the formula with [+]. Move the cell pointer to Board Feet Used [Decoy] (B6), then press [*]. Move the cell pointer to Price per Board Foot (B18), and complete the formula by pressing [←Enter]. Again, a blank cell (Price per Board Foot) has been understood as 0 by the spreadsheet, so the value in B7 is temporarily 0.

The next cell is B9, Hours Used[Decoy], which is calculated as the product of Quantity[Decoy] and Hours per Item[Decoy]. Start with the cell pointer in B7, and begin the formula with [+]. Move the cell pointer to Quantity[Decoy] (B2), then press [*]. Move the cell pointer to Hours per Item[Decoy] (B15), and complete the formula by pressing [←Enter]. Again, a blank cell has caused this value to be 0 (temporarily).

The next cell is B10, Cost of Labor[Decoy], which is calculated as the product of Hours Used[Decoy] and Price per Hour. Start with [+], move the cell pointer to Hours Used[Decoy] (B9), press [*], move the cell pointer to Price per Hour (B19), then press [←Enter].

The next cell is B12, Profit[Decoy], which is calculated as the Revenue[Decoy] less Cost of Lumber[Decoy], less Cost of Labor[Decoy]. Starting with the cell pointer in B12, begin the formula with [+], move the cell pointer to Revenue[Decoy] (B4), press [–], move the cell pointer to Cost of Lumber[Decoy] (B7), press [–], move the cell pointer to Cost of Labor[Decoy] (B10), then complete the formula by pressing [←Enter].

Data values need to be entered for Board Feet per Item, Hours per Item, Price per Board Foot, and Price per Hour. These values, from the scenario, are entered by placing the cell pointer in the appropriate cell, and keying the numbers, followed by [←Enter]. The values are:

B14	Board Feet per Item[Decoy]	2.9
B15	Hours per Item[Decoy]	1.1
B18	Price per Board Foot	1.30
B19	Price per Hour	7.15

The current model is shown in Figure 2.3.

Some of the values in Figure 2.3 are shown without the dollar sign, even though they are actually currency values. To dress up the spreadsheet, we need to change Revenue[Decoy], Cost of Lumber[Decoy], and Profit[Decoy] to **Currency** format with 0 decimals; we also need to change Price per Board Foot and Price per Hour to **Currency** format, but with two decimals. These appearance

---

Figure 2.3

Partial Spreadsheet Model for Rangely Lakes

	A	B	C	D
1		Decoy	Hanging	Total
2	Quantity	3500		
3	Price	$12		
4	Revenue	42000		
5				
6	Board Feet Used	10150		
7	Cost of Lumber	13195		
8				
9	Hours Used	3850		
10	Cost of Labor	27528		
11				
12	Profit	1277		
13				
14	Board Feet per Item	2.9		
15	Hours per Item	1.1		
16				
17				
18	Price per Board Foot	1.30		
19	Price per Hour	7.15		

---

items are incorporated into the spreadsheet with these commands starting at cells B4, B7, and again at B10. For Lotus 1-2-3:

/	to invoke the commands
R	to select **Range**; or highlight **Range**, then [←Enter]
F	to select **Format**; or highlight **Format**, then [←Enter]
C	to select **Currency**; or highlight **Currency**, then [←Enter]
0	to indicate no decimals displayed, then [←Enter]
[←Enter]	to accept the displayed range

For Quattro Pro, the keystrokes are:

/	to invoke the commands
S	to select **Style**; or highlight **Style**, then [←Enter]
N	to select **Numeric** format; or highlight **Numeric** format, then [←Enter]
C	to select **Currency**; or highlight **Currency**, then [←Enter]
0	to indicate no decimals displayed, then [←Enter]
[←Enter]	to accept the displayed range

Cells B18 and B19 can be formatted with one command, because they are in adjacent cells. Start with the cell pointer in B18. For Lotus 1-2-3:

/	to invoke the commands
R	to select **Range**; or highlight **Range**, then [←Enter]
F	to select **Format**; or highlight **Format**, then [←Enter]
C	to select **Currency**; or highlight **Currency**, then [←Enter]
2	to indicate two decimals displayed, then [←Enter]
[↓]	to expand the displayed range to B18..B19, then [←Enter]
[←Enter]	to accept the displayed range, B18..B19

For Quattro Pro, the keystrokes are:

/	to invoke the commands
S	to select **Style**; or highlight **Style**, then [←Enter]
N	to select **Numeric** format; or highlight **Numeric** format, then [←Enter]
C	to select **Currency**; or highlight **Currency**, then [←Enter]
2	to indicate two decimals displayed, then [←Enter]
[↓]	to expand the displayed block to B18..B19
[←Enter]	to accept the displayed block, B18..B19

Entering Values and Formulas into the Model: Column C

The next step in constructing the model for Rangely Lakes is to enter the information for column C, which is already labeled for Hangings. For the most part, this will be replicating the information shown for Decoys in column B. However, there are three different types of information in column B. Each type of information requires a different treatment. Data values that change from one column to the next will be entered with keystrokes. Formulas that apply to both columns will be copied, using the spreadsheet commands. Data values that are the same from one product to the next will use *absolute addresses*, which will be discussed later in this section.

The cells for Quantity, Price, Board Feet per Item, and Hours per Item (cells B2, B14, and B15) contain data that is unique for Decoys, and will change for Hangings in column C. This information should be keyed directly in these cells:

Cell	Name of Variable	Key In
C2	Quantity[Hanging]	2500
C3	Price[Hanging]	15
C14	Board Feet per Item[Hanging]	4.8
C15	Hours per Item[Hanging]	0.5

Change the format of C3 to **Currency** with 0 decimals, as explained earlier.

The formulas in B4..B12 can apply (with some modifications to be handled just a bit later) to column C for Hanging, just as they apply to column B for Decoys. Our next step is to copy these formulas from column B to column C with the keystrokes shown below. For purposes of understanding a bit more about spreadsheets, this step will be performed imperfectly now, and then done again after we have observed some things about the way **Copy** operates. Starting with the cursor in B4, we enter these commands for Lotus 1-2-3:

/	to invoke the commands
C	to select **Copy**; or highlight **Copy**, then [←Enter]

Respond to the prompt Copy From (or Copy What?): B4..B4 range by repeatedly pressing [↓], until the desired range B4..B12 is highlighted and displayed. Press [←Enter] to accept this range. We are now copying a range which is a column of nine cells.

Respond to the prompt Copy To (or To where?): B4 range by pressing [→] one time, so the Copy To: C4 range is highlighted and displayed.

Figure 2.4

Rangely Lakes Model After an Imperfect Copy Operation

	A	B	C	D
1		Decoy	Hanging	Total
2	Quantity	3500	2500	
3	Price	$12	$15	
4	Revenue	$42,000	$37,500	
5				
6	Board Feet Used	10150	12000	
7	Cost of Lumber	$13,195	$0	
8				
9	Hours Used	3850	1250	
10	Cost of Labor	$27,528	$0	
11				
12	Profit	$1,277	$37,500	
13				
14	Board Feet per Item	2.9	4.8	
15	Hours per Item	1.1	0.5	
16				
17				
18	Price per Board Foot	$1.30		
19	Price per Hour	$7.15		

This shows the starting point of the range we are copying. Press [←Enter] to accept this range.

For Quattro Pro, the keystrokes are:

/	to invoke the commands
E	to select **Edit**; or highlight **Edit**, then [←Enter]
C	to select **Copy**; or highlight **Copy**, then [←Enter]

Respond to the prompt for the Source block: B4..B4 range by repeatedly pressing [↓], until the desired block B4..B12 is highlighted and displayed. Press [←Enter] to accept this block. We are now copying a block which is a column of nine cells.

Respond to the prompt for the Destination block: B4 by pressing [→] one time, so the Destination block: C4 block is highlighted and displayed. This shows the starting point of the block we are copying. Press [←Enter] to accept this block.

The spreadsheet now appears as shown in Figure 2.4, which has some problems we'll handle soon!

Tip: In the copy command, two different types of range are displayed as spreadsheet prompts. For the initial Copy From: B4..B4 prompt, an *anchored* range is shown by the spreadsheet, as indicated by the appearance of the two-address range, separated by the "." symbols. This Copy From range was expanded by using the arrow keys and pointing to change the second address in the range. For the initial Copy To: B4 prompt, an *unanchored* range is shown by the spreadsheet, as indicated by the appearance of the one-address range without the "." symbols.

This range was moved by the arrow keys, to the new destination C4. Pressing [←Enter] copied the entire source range (B4..B12) into the destination indicated by the starting range C4.

Another Tip: An *anchored* range may be changed to an *unanchored* range to pressing [Backspace] or [Esc]. An *unanchored* range may be changed to an *anchored* range by pressing the "period" key [.].

Copying Spreadsheet Formulas: Relative and Absolute Cell Addresses

It is always a good idea to look at the results of a new operation and see what happened. When we look at the revenue for hangings, it is logically correct: 2500 units at $15, for a revenue of $37,500. But the cost of lumber is incorrect; it isn't $0 as the spreadsheet indicates. To see what went wrong, we need to examine the **Copy** command a lot closer. While displaying a spreadsheet with the appearance of Figure 2.4, place the cell pointer on cell B4. The upper left corner shows the formula: +B2*B3, calculating revenue for decoys as the product of quantity and price for decoys. This formula says that the current cell (B4) is the product of the cell two above (B2) and the cell one above (B3). Now move the cell pointer to cell C4, whose formula was copied from B4. The formula here is +C2*C3. This formula, resulting from the copy operation, is still the product of the cell two above (now C2) and the cell one above (now C3). This illustrates what is called *relative addresses* for cell locations. The key item is that when a cell formula is copied, it is the logic of the cell formula, rather than the specific addresses, that is copied. This means that the logic, expressed in cell location relative to the current cell, could be stated as:

> This cell (B4), is the product of the cell two above (B2) and the cell one above (B3). When it is copied to C4, that relative logic stays the same (the cell two above multiplied by the cell one above), but it is now expressed as +C2*C3.

This relative address copy works correctly for Revenue, Board Feet Used, Hours Used, and Profit. But Profit has an incorrect value for Hangings, because the relative copy was not correct for two of its influencing variables, Cost of Lumber and Cost of Labor. Pause for a moment and reflect on why this copy worked for some variables, and not for others.

The problem arises because we have some data that is the same for both Decoy and Hanging. Neither the Price per Board Foot nor the Price per Hour depends upon whether we are talking about Decoy or Hanging. It would be poor practice to enter these values ($1.30 and $7.15) into each column, because a change in one of the prices would require multiple changes in the spreadsheet. Spreadsheets allow for this situation by using *absolute addresses* as well as the relative addresses we have been describing. An absolute address copies to its destination cell exactly as it appears in the source (or Copy From:) cell. An absolute address is indicated by a dollar sign before the column letter and another dollar sign before the row number. In a formula, the cell address $B$18 will copy as cell $B$18, while the relative address B18 will copy according to its position relative to the cell containing the formula using B18. We need to go back to the cells that used `Price per Board Foot` and `Price per Hour`, and change the cell addresses to absolute addresses, so the copy command will be correct when it is performed again.

`Price per Board Foot` is used in calculating the `Cost of Lumber` (as shown in the influence chart). On the spreadsheet, place the cell pointer in B7, `Cost of Lumber[Decoy]`. The formula displayed is +B6*B18. There are several ways one could enter the formula with absolute cell reference; one way (not recommended) is to key in the new formula directly:

+B6*$B$18

Another way is to use the editing capabilities of the spreadsheet. With the cell pointer in B7, press [F2] (the [EDIT] key). This brings the formula to be edited into the control panel in the upper left corner, with the edit cursor placed at the end of the formula, closest to the B18 portion of the formula. Pressing [F4] (the [ABS] or ABSolute key) automatically inserts the dollar signs in the address at the edit cursor. The formula is now

+B6*$B$18

which is accepted by pressing [←Enter].

A similar change is made in cell B10, which calculates `Cost of Labor[Decoy]`. With the cell pointer in B10, press [F2] ([EDIT]); the edit cursor is at the end of the formula, or closest to the B19 portion of the formula. Pressing [F4] ([ABS]), the dollar signs appear, making the formula

+B9*$B$19

indicating the absolute address has been entered for B19, but not for B9. To emphasize the fact that cells B18 and B19 apply to several columns, it is helpful to put in a label such as `Data` in cell B17.

Tip: Other cell addresses in a formula may be made absolute by moving the edit cursor to the appropriate cell address, and pressing [F4] ([ABS]). When using the cell pointer to construct a formula "from scratch," [F4] may be used with the cell pointer on the appropriate cell. [F4] makes an address absolute both in *edit* mode and in *point* mode. There is more to the [F4] key than we have described here. Knowing this much is useful, and not dangerous. But we haven't told the whole story.

To illustrate the **Copy** command with absolute addresses, we'll start out by erasing the previously copied cells. (This erase isn't really necessary, but it gives a reason to illustrate a few more commands in the spreadsheet language.) To erase the results of the previous imperfect copy, start with the cell pointer in C4. Use these keystrokes in Lotus 1-2-3:

/	to invoke the commands
R	to select **Range**; or highlight **Range**, then [←Enter]
E	to select **Erase**; or highlight **Erase**, then [←Enter]

Respond to the prompt for Enter Range to Erase: C4..C4 by repeatedly pressing [↓], until the desired range (C4..C12) is highlighted and displayed. Press [←Enter] to accept this range.

The keystrokes for Quattro Pro are:

/	to invoke the commands
E	to select **Edit**; or highlight **Edit**, then [←Enter]
E	to select **Erase**; or highlight **Erase**, then [←Enter]

Respond to the prompt for Block to be modified: C4..C4 by repeatedly pressing [↓], until the desired block (C4..C12) is highlighted and displayed. Press [←Enter] to accept this block.

Tip: A common mistake made by beginners is to "erase" a spreadsheet cell by putting a space into that cell. This is dangerous. Don't do it! A blank cell (all cells when a new spreadsheet is started) contains nothing. A cell with a space in it appears to be blank, but it isn't. In the wonderful world of computers, a space (such as the space between words in a sentence) is something, even though it appears to be nothing. To get something out of a cell and make that cell blank again, use the **Erase** command. Any other approach may lead to incorrect answers later on, because a cell with a space isn't empty . . . and sometimes we want to count non-empty cells!

Another Tip: In Lotus 1-2-3 release 2.3 and higher, and in Quattro Pro, a cell may be erased with the [Delete] key.

The next step is to perform the copy once again, with the absolute addresses in place. Move the cell pointer to B4. Perform the copy, using these keystrokes in Lotus 1-2-3:

/	to invoke the commands
C	to select **Copy**; or highlight **Copy**, then [←Enter]

Respond to the prompt for the Copy From (Copy What?): B4..B4 range by repeatedly pressing [↓], until the desired range (B4..B12) is highlighted and displayed. Press [←Enter] to accept this range. We are now copying a range which is a column of nine cells.

Respond to the prompt for the Copy To (To where?): B4 range by pressing [→] one time, so the Copy To: C4 range is highlighted and displayed. This shows the starting point of the range we are copying. Press [←Enter] to accept this range.

For Quattro Pro, the keystrokes are:

/	to invoke the commands
E	to select **Edit**; or highlight **Edit**, then [←Enter]
C	to select **Copy**; or highlight **Copy**, then [←Enter]

Respond to the prompt for the Source block: B4..B4 range by repeatedly pressing [↓], until the desired block (B4..B12) is highlighted and displayed. Press [←Enter] to accept this block. We are now copying a block which is a column of nine cells.

Respond to the prompt for the Destination: B4 range by pressing [→] one time, so the Destination: C4 is highlighted and displayed. This shows the starting point of the destination block. Press [←Enter] to accept this destination.

If everything has been completed correctly, the value for Profit[Hanging] should be $12,963.

The values for Price per Board Foot and Price per Hour apply to both columns, although they appear in the column labeled Decoy. For clarity, we previously entered the label Data in cell B17, to make it clear that these values apply to more than just the Decoy product.

Entering Values and Formulas into the Model: Column D

The next step is to provide the totals for appropriate rows. Three totals are required by the scenario:

> Board Feet Used[Total]
> Hours Used[Total]
> Profit[Total]

Several other totals may be useful information, although they have not explicitly been discussed in the scenario:

Quantity[Total]   shows the total number of items available for the plan.
Revenue[Total]   is commonly shown in business income statements.
Cost of Lumber[Total]   may be useful for materials budgeting.
Cost of Labor[Total]   may be useful for human resource budgeting.

There are several items which would be meaningless to total; the total of Price, Board Feet per Item, and Hours per Item would be meaningless if they were shown on the spreadsheet model.

One formula can be entered, and then copied to appropriate cells for the total for the firm. Since each total is the value two cells to the left, plus the value one cell to the left, relative cell addresses (without the dollar signs) are correctly used. The first of the Total cells can be entered by placing the cell pointer at cell D2. Begin the formula with the + symbol, then point "two cells to the left" to B2, enter [+], then point "one cell to the left" to C2, and finish by pressing [←Enter].

Using the copy command, this formula can be copied to the other six cells in the Total column. These copy operations, with keystrokes similar to those used above, are:

> Copy From: D2   Copy To: D4
> Copy From: D2   Copy To: D6..D7
> Copy From: D2   Copy To: D9..D10
> Copy From: D2   Copy To: D12

For appearance, change the format of cells D4, D7, D10, and D12 to **Currency** with 0 decimals. The complete worksheet shown in Figure 2.5. The verbal documentation for the worksheet is shown in Figure 2.6.

─────────────── **Figure 2.5** ───────────────

Spreadsheet for Rangely Lakes Production Plan

	A	B	C	D
1		Decoy	Hanging	Total
2	Quantity	3500	2500	6000
3	Price	$12	$15	
4	Revenue	$42,000	$37,500	$79,500
5				
6	Board Feet Used	10150	12000	22150
7	Cost of Lumber	$13,195	$15,600	$28,795
8				
9	Hours Used	3850	1250	5100
10	Cost of Labor	$27,528	$8,938	$36,465
11				
12	Profit	$1,277	$12,963	$14,240
13				
14	Board Feet per Item	2.9	4.8	
15	Hours per Item	1.1	0.5	
16				
17		Data		
18	Price per Board Foot	$1.30		
19	Price per Hour	$7.15		

─────────────── **Figure 2.6** ───────────────

Verbal Documentation for Rangely Lakes Spreadsheet

```
Quantity[Decoy] = 3500
Quantity[Hanging] = 2500
Quantity[Total] = Quantity[Decoy] + Quantity[Hanging]

Price[Decoy] = 12
Price[Hanging] = 15

Revenue[Decoy THRU Hanging] = Quantity * Price
Revenue[Total] = Revenue[Decoy] + Revenue[Hanging]

Board Feet Used[Decoy THRU Hanging] = Quantity * Board Feet per Item
Board Feet Used[Total] = Board Feet Used[Decoy] + Board Feet Used[Hanging]

Cost of Lumber[Decoy THRU Hanging] = Board Feet Used * Price per Board Foot[Data]
Cost of Lumber[Total] = Cost of Lumber[Decoy] + Cost of Lumber[Hanging]

Hours Used[Decoy THRU Hanging] = Quantity * Hours per Item
Hours Used[Total] = Hours Used[Decoy] + Hours Used[Hanging]

Cost of Labor[Decoy THRU Hanging] = Hours Used * Price per Hour[Data]
Cost of Labor[Total] = Cost of Labor[Decoy] + Cost of Labor[Hanging]

Profit[Decoy THRU Hanging] = Revenue − Cost of Lumber − Cost of Labor
Profit[Total] = Profit[Decoy] + Profit[Hanging]

Board Feet per Item[Decoy] = 2.9
Board Feet per Item[Hanging] = 4.8

Hours per Item[Decoy] = 1.1
Hours per Item[Hanging] = 0.5

Price per Board Foot[Data] = 1.3

Price per Hour[Data] = 7.15
```

Saving the Spreadsheet and Exiting the Spreadsheet

This spreadsheet should be saved to the appropriate disk, using the **File Save** commands. To save the file to a disk in the A: drive, with a file named RANGELY, the commands would be:

/	to invoke the commands
F	to select **File**; or highlight **File**, then [←┘Enter]
S	to select **Save**; or highlight **Save**, then [←┘Enter]

Respond as shown to the prompt Enter Name of File to Save: A:RANGELY

The file, named RANGELY.WK?, is now on the disk. (The "?" character depends upon the software being used.)

Note for Lotus 1-2-3 and Quattro Pro: Depending upon the way your software is installed on the computer you are using, you may need to press [Esc] once (or several times) to be able to enter the filename for saving as A:RANGELY.

Note for Quattro Pro: The menu choice **File Save** will save the file with the name which was used to retrieve the file. To save a file with a new name, use the **Save As** command.

After saving the file, the user may be ready to leave the spreadsheet software. To exit the spreadsheet, these keystrokes may be used:

/	to invoke the commands in Lotus 1-2-3
Q	to select **Quit**; or highlight **Quit**, then [←┘Enter]

Respond to any prompts that may appear on the screen.

For Quattro Pro, the keystrokes are:

/	to invoke the commands
F	to select **File**; or highlight **File**, then [←┘Enter]
X	to select **eXit**; or highlight **eXit**, then [←┘Enter]

Respond to any prompts that may appear on the screen.

3

Optimization of a Managerial Spreadsheet Model

The Rangely Lakes case and the Sunsoak case (from Chapter 1) provide opportunities to construct models for managerial use. This chapter uses the Rangely Lakes case to demonstrate an important managerial use of a model, optimization of a spreadsheet model, in order to provide management with useful support for a decision. Chapter 2 presented a complete description of the influence chart for Rangely Lakes, along with a keystroke commentary to construct the spreadsheet model. We start this chapter by repeating the case scenario, followed by a dialogue extending that scenario. The case and the accompanying model provide illustrations of managerial uses of optimization of a spreadsheet model. After we have described optimization of a managerial spreadsheet model, the chapter is concluded with a discussion of situations in which optimization is helpful, and when it is not useful in supporting a managerial decision.

The Rangely Lakes Company Case

In early August, 1988, J. L. Duckworth began thinking about the winter activities of Rangely Lakes Company. J.L. was particularly concerned about the cash budgets for the winter, when revenue was quite limited. The other major concern J.L. was addressing was the need to keep the golf course maintenance staff busy during the winter.

The Rangely Lakes Company operates a summer-only golf course in northern Maine. To keep the maintenance employees on the workforce during the winter, they have developed two "Maine Woods Souvenirs" made out of forest products from the Rangely Lakes area. For our purposes, they have two products: Mallard decoys and Mallard wall hangings. Both of these products are hand-made; they have developed procedures so that skilled (but unartistic) maintenance workers can produce the two items. These souvenirs are marketed through numerous gift shops in New England. Rangely Lakes has priced the items attractively, so that they have never had any problems selling all of the souvenirs they can produce. From a budgeting standpoint, J. L. Duckworth needed to know how much profit would be generated from the souvenirs made during the winter. For planning purposes, J.L. calculated profit as revenue (price × quantity) less the cost of the wood used and the cost of the labor in the products.

Most gift shops sell the Mallard decoy for $26.95 and the Mallard wall hanging for $34.95. Rangely Lakes sells to the gift shops at $12 and $15 each. The average labor content is 1.1 hours for a decoy, and 0.5 hours for a wall hanging. Each labor hour costs Rangely Lakes $7.15, including fringe benefits. Although Rangely has some flexibility in the amount of labor it uses, it monitors labor use very closely to be certain that enough production is planned to keep the work-force employed, and that the production plan doesn't require more labor than the amount that can be available.

The souvenirs are made from native lumber, carefully selected during the summer as forest operations are performed. Each decoy requires 2.9 board feet of this special lumber; each wall hanging requires 4.8 board feet. (A board foot is 144 cubic inches of lumber.) More than 25,000 board feet were available for last winter's production season; this number may be somewhat higher or lower, depending upon lumbering activities during the next month. The anticipated market price for the wood is about $1.30 per board foot.

For J. L. Duckworth's "first cut" at the budget for the winter months, the plan was to make the same number of decoys and wall hangings as last year. A search of the records show that 3500 decoys and 2500 wall hangings had been made. How would this plan affect J.L.'s concerns?

The model (constructed in Chapter 2) showing J.L.'s proposed production plan is shown in Figure 3.1. If the proposed plan of 3500 Mallard decoys and 2500 Mallard wall hangings is implemented, the profit for Rangely Lakes Company would be $14,240. This plan requires 22,150 board feet of lumber and 5100 hours. To understand the managerial uses J. L. Duckworth might have for this infor-mation, eavesdrop on this dialogue between J.L. Duckworth and an assistant:

J.L.: Oh, that profit—more than fourteen grand—really looks nice. If we had done that well last year, we would have shown nearly twice the profit that we did for the whole year, since we had that rainy weather last year that kept people off the golf course so much of July. Let's go ahead and make this our working plan for the winter. What do you think? Can we squeeze any more profit out of this souvenir business during the winter?

Assistant: Well, that profit contribution ought to look nice. There's no way we can get 22,150 board feet of lumber. Without the lumber, we can't make that fourteen grand.

J.L.: Why not? We got offers last year of twice that much lumber.

Assistant: I know, but the excessive rains last year reduced the number of trees the mills had to process. So the mills spent more time carefully

---

Figure 3.1

Spreadsheet for Rangely Lakes Production Plan

	A	B	C	D
1		Decoy	Hanging	Total
2	Quantity	3500	2500	6000
3	Price	$12	$15	
4	Revenue	$42,000	$37,500	$79,500
5				
6	Board Feet Used	10150	12000	22150
7	Cost of Lumber	$13,195	$15,600	$28,795
8				
9	Hours Used	3850	1250	5100
10	Cost of Labor	$27,528	$8,938	$36,465
11				
12	Profit	$1,277	$12,963	$14,240
13				
14	Board Feet per Item	2.9	4.8	
15	Hours per Item	1.1	0.5	
16				
17		Data		
18	Price per Board Foot	$1.30		
19	Price per Hour	$7.15		

---

preserving the scrap from each tree. But this year they have so many trees they aren't spending much time working the scrap that we need to make our souvenirs.

J.L.: I know that's right. I talked with our four suppliers just last week. They are able to guarantee us a total of about 17,000 board feet. That may change a little, but it looks pretty firm right now. Our anticipated price of $1.30 per board foot looks good.

Assistant: Have you done any analysis to see how many hours we need to plan to use during the winter?

J.L.: I checked back to last year. We used something like 6000 hours during the winter last year, if these records are any good. But Jo and Ev have already told me that they don't want to work at all in December and January. I'm not sure I know why; I'd go crazy in these woods without anything to do. Do you think they are going to Florida for those two months?

Assistant: Oh, they both stopped by early today and told me that their trip to Florida is "iffy" at best. If there isn't any work for them, that's OK. On the other hand, they're both willing to work a regular schedule, as long as we let them know in the next two months before they buy their super-saver tickets.

J.L.: It sounds to me, then, that we should plan to use someplace between 4000 and 6000 hours this winter. No one seems to complain too much if we cut back to about a thirty-hour week. When we look at the holiday schedule, and the number of people we want to keep busy, that range looks about right to me now.

From this dialogue, it seems rather obvious that the plan shown on the spreadsheet won't work. What parts of the spreadsheet could J.L. manipulate to improve the situation? (Please take a minute to answer this question before you continue reading.)

In order to get "better" answers to the amount of lumber used, the number of hours used, and profit, J.L. is able to manipulate the quantity of decoys and hangings. From the influence chart, one can follow arrows from QUANTITY to BOARD FEET USED, HOURS USED, and PROFIT. This means that changing the quantity of the products planned does influence the things that are important to J.L.: board feet used, hours used, and profit. Thus, J.L. is in a position to play "What If" games with the spreadsheet; changes can be made in Quantity to see the changes in the variables being watched. (Take some time now to make What If changes in Quantity on your spreadsheet, and observe how these changes affect the variables being watched: Board Feet Used, Hours Used, and Profit, all in the Total column.)

Components of an Optimization Problem

The problem J.L. is addressing can be viewed as an optimization problem. An optimization problem has three components: *decision variables*, *constraint variables*, and *objective cell*. In a nutshell,

> Optimization is a process of adjusting *decision variables* to make the *objective* as large (or small) as possible, without exceeding limits specified by the *constraints*.

The three components of an optimization problem are listed more fully below.

Part 1: *Decision Variables.* Decision variables are variables that are under the control of the decision maker. These are the worksheet cells that the manager would change in performing What If analyses on the spreadsheet. Using a colloquial phrase, these are the values that the manager can "diddle with" to improve the situation. Decision cells are often called *adjustable cells* because they are adjusted by the optimization software. The term *what-if cell* is sometimes used to describe decision variables. This describes managerial behavior of trying many possible values to see *what* happens *if* various values are used.

> For Rangely Lakes, the decision variables (adjustable cells) are the quantity of decoys and the quantity of wall hangings. Using brackets to indicate columns, the decision variables are Quantity[Decoy] and Quantity[Hanging].

Part 2: *Constraint Cells.* The constraint cells are the cells that the manager watches to make sure that known limits aren't violated. Some general examples are:

> Some things must always be positive or zero (example: a bank balance).

> Other things can't exceed specified limits (example: an upper limit or

ceiling on office supply expenditures). When there is an upper limit, something must be less than or equal to this upper limit.

Other things can't go below specified limits (example: the contract requires that we deliver at least 5000 items this month). When there is a lower limit, something must be greater than or equal to this lower limit.

Some things must stay within a range (example: our inventory level must be between a lower limit of $25,000 to meet customer needs, and an upper limit of $50,000 to avoid financial problems). A constraint variable which must stay within a range is a combination of a constraint specifying an upper limit, and a constraint specifying a lower limit.

Some things must be exactly equal to a target value (example: the inventory at a warehouse must be exactly 400 units at the end of the year; there is no room to store any more, and fewer units would result in poor customer service).

Each of these items illustrates a possible constraint in a managerial setting. The bank doesn't complain as long as the bank balance is positive. The controller doesn't complain as long as office supply expenditures are within budget. The buyer doesn't complain as long as we meet the 5000 minimum delivery this month. We don't get complaints from either customers or the controller as long as the inventory level stays between $25,000 and $50,000. The warehouse manager has performed the job correctly if the year-end inventory is the target value of 400 units.

For Rangely Lakes, the constraints are Board Feet Used[Total] (which must be less than or equal to 17,000 board feet) and Hours Used[Total] (which must be greater than or equal to 4000 hours, and less than or equal to 6000 hours).

Objective Cell. The objective cell is the cell on the spreadsheet that the decision maker wants to make either "as big as I can" (like profit maximization) or "as small as I can" (like cost minimization). We will be studying optimization problems with only one objective cell. The objective cell is sometimes called the *best* cell.

For Rangely Lakes, the objective cell is the total profit. Using brackets to indicate the column, the objective cell is Profit[Total]. This objective is to be maximized.

A linkage between the model and the influence chart can be developed by using specific shapes to designate optimization components. We will use these shapes throughout this book:

A decision variable will be shown as a square on an influence chart.

The objective cell will be shown as a rectangle with rounded corners on an influence chart.

Constraint cells will be shown as triangles on an influence chart.

Figure 3.2

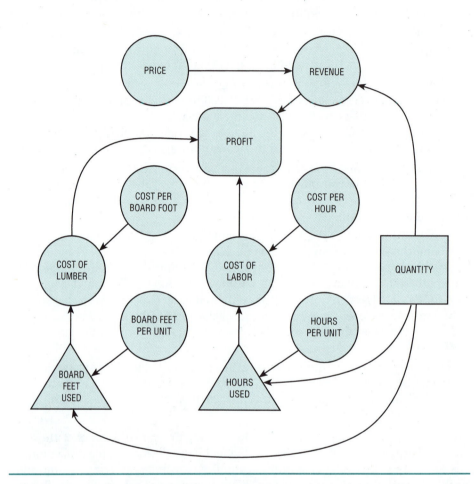

The influence chart with these shapes is shown as Figure 3.2. There is substantial "artistic license" taken with this influence chart. The chart is constructed as if it were for only one product, because the logic for the second product is copied from one spreadsheet column to the next. Then obvious horizontal summations are made to get a total for the product line. The objective and constraint designations apply only to the total, while the decision variable designations apply only to the two individual product values for QUANTITY. While the influence chart could be modified to show these distinctions, the additional clutter tends to detract more than it adds to understanding. Because an influence chart is a modeler's tool to understand the scenario before turning to the spreadsheet, these tradeoffs between usefulness and ambiguity will often be encountered in developing influence charts. Our attempt will be to let usefulness win out over other choices!

Each of these optimization components has important characteristics that show up on an influence chart. The decision variables have no arrows leading into them; they must logically be constants (not formulas) in the spreadsheet model. If a cell is influenced by other cells and is also declared to be a decision variable, there is a logical inconsistency: the variable cannot be under management control (a decision variable) and still be defined in terms of other variables. There may be constraints which limit management control, but these limitations must be described as constraints rather than influences on the chart and in the model. In a way, decision variables are much like data values because they have no arrows leading into them. They are conceptually different because data values are "givens" in a scenario, while decision variables are controlled by management, using the guidance of optimization.

Each constraint cell must have arrows pointing to it; there may be arrows leading from the constraint cells. Each constraint cell must be directly or indirectly influenced by at least one decision variable, or there would be nothing that management can do that affects the feasibility of a proposed plan. The constraint cells must be formulas (not constants) in a spreadsheet model. (There is an exception to observation that a constraint must apply to a formula cell: sometimes a decision variable has limits associated with it. These decision cells with limits contain constants, which are adjusted by the optimization process. These cells have no arrows leading into them.)

The objective cell must have arrows pointing to it; there may be arrows leading from it. The objective cell must be directly or indirectly influenced by at least one decision variable. Otherwise, management decisions would have no impact on the desirability of the outcome, which would mean that it doesn't matter what management does! The objective cell must be a formula (not a constant) in the spreadsheet model. There is an exception to the rule that the objective must be a formula cell: Sometimes a decision variable is the objective. This decision cell will be adjusted by the optimization process, to find the largest (or smallest) value consistent with the constraints. This objective cell will have no arrows leading into it.

Solving Optimization Problems with the What's*Best!* Solver

The optimization software What's*Best!* (bundled with this text) optimizes a spreadsheet model, such as the one we have created for Rangely Lakes. A special spreadsheet menu structure is used to define the optimization instructions for a solver or optimizer by specifying the *adjustable* or *decision* cells, the *best* or *objective* cell, and the *constraint* cells.

Before starting the optimization, it is good practice to enter limiting values for the constraints into spreadsheet cells. We have three limits: no more than 17,000 board feet of lumber, at least 4000 hours of labor, and no more than 6000 hours. To prepare the spreadsheet (Figure 3.1) for optimization, enter these numerical values in the cells shown:

Cell F6:	17000	(board feet must be less than or equal to 17,000)
Cell F9:	4000	(hours used must be greater than or equal to 4000)
Cell H9:	6000	(hours used must be less than or equal to 6000)

Here's an overview of the way the What's*Best!* solver works with your spreadsheet software. What's*Best!* is "add on" software for the spreadsheets. It is invoked by the user, through the appropriate operating system command. The spreadsheet, in turn, is invoked by the solver software. Next, the optimization problem is described using the solver's menu. During the optimization process, spreadsheet files will be saved, optimization software will be invoked, and then the spreadsheet software will once again be run. All of this is performed by What's*Best!* without user intervention.

> *Note:* Before using the What's*Best!* solver, it must be installed according to the instructions in Appendix A at the end of this text. Appendix B at the end of this text is reference material that supplements the description of What's*Best!* in this chapter. Appendix C discusses other spreadsheet solvers that may be used with many of the examples in this text.

The two sections that follow are parallel for Lotus 1-2-3 (Release 2.2, 2.3, or 2.4) and Quattro Pro (Release 4.0). What's*Best!* will operate with Quattro Pro Release 2.0 and 3.0, but its appearance on the screen will be different from that shown in this text. You may skip the section for the spreadsheet that you won't be using.

Using What's*Best!*: Lotus 1-2-3, Release 2.2 and 2.3
(This section should be omitted by readers not using Lotus 1-2-3)

The first step in using the solver is to invoke What's*Best!* from the subdirectory containing the spreadsheet software and What's*Best!* files. For example, if the 1-2-3 spreadsheet software is in subdirectory C:\123R23, that directory should be made the default directory with a change directory command such as:

```
CD C:\123R23
```

Then invoke the solver with the command WB, which will cause the normal spreadsheet logo and screen to appear.

After the solver and spreadsheet are started, retrieve the file containing the Rangely model into the spreadsheet. The next step is to describe the Rangely optimization problem to What's*Best!*, making menu choices to describe the decision variables (called the **Adjustable** cells on the menu), the constraints, and the objective cell (called the **Best** cell on the menu). At any point, What's*Best!* help is available with the [F1] key. In detail:

Step 1: *Decision (Adjustable) Cells:* We first identify the adjustable cells for Rangely Lakes, as modeled in Figure 3.1. Move the cell pointer to cell B2, then invoke the What's*Best!* menu ([Alt]+[F7], depending upon the key selected during installation). Next, move the menu pointer to **Adjustable** and press [←Enter], or press the [A] key. From this menu, choose **Adjust**. (The other choices are more advanced than we need to discuss right now.) Following the instructions on the menus, select the adjustable cells in the same manner you select any spreadsheet range. When you have moved the cell pointer to the beginning of the adjustable cells, anchor the range with the anchor key (a "period" [.]). When the desired decision cells B2..C2 are selected, press [←Enter] to finish your selection. Note that adjustable cells appear in a different color or intensity on the spreadsheet screen.

For a spreadsheet with more than one range of adjustable cells, repeat the process. Choose **Adjustable**, then **Adjust**, and then move the cell pointer to select the next range of adjustable cells. For Rangely, there is only one range of decision cells.

Step 2: ***Constraint Cell:*** Constrain D6, Board Feet Used[Total] to be less than or equal to 17,000 board feet. From the What's *Best!* menu, choose **Constrain**. The next prompt is to "Enter range of cells to be constrained:" which instructs you to use typical spreadsheet range selection techniques to select the cell or range of cells to be constrained. With the cell pointer at D6, Board Feet Used[Total], the constraint cell is selected by pressing the [←Enter] key.

The next menu choice is **Less than** (which is shorthand for the wordy "less than or equal to"). Choosing **Less than** calls the next menu, which requests a selection of either:

Range   (constraining limits are located in a range of cells),

Cell   (a single constraining limit, which may apply to many constraint cells, is located in a cell), or

Value   (a single constraining limit, which may apply to many constraint cells, is to be entered from the keyboard).

Because we have the constraining limit of 17,000 in spreadsheet cell F6, we choose **Cell**, and respond to the prompt "Enter limits as Cell or Range of Cells" with typical spreadsheet cell selection techniques ("pointing" or keying the cell location, F6).

The final prompt for this constraint is "Enter range to store constraints:". The constraint must be stored in a spreadsheet cell. We could select any blank cell; for clarity, move the pointer to E6, which is adjacent to the cell being constrained. After pressing [←Enter] with the cell pointer on E6, the symbol "Not <=" appears in the spreadsheet cell, indicating this cell contains a "<=" constraint which is not satisfied. A special function named @WB is used to generate this display.

Step 3: ***Other Constraints:*** The concepts of Step 2 must be followed for each constraint. Cell D9, Hours Used[Total], must be greater than or equal to 4000 hours (a constant contained in cell F9), and less than or equal to 6000 hours (a constant contained in H9). Store these constraints in cells E9 and G9 with these steps:

From the What's *Best!* menu, choose **Constrain**. Select D9 as the range to be constrained. Choose **Greater than**; choose **Cell**; select cell F9 as the constraint limit; store the constraint in cell E9. This will be displayed by the @WB function as ">=" indicating that a constraint of this type is stored in E9; the constraint is satisfied, because 5100 (the value of the expression in D9) is greater than 4000 (the value stored in F9).

From the What's *Best!* menu, choose **Constrain**; select D9 as the range to be constrained. Choose **Less than**; choose **Cell**; select cell H9 as the constraint limit; store the constraint in cell G9. This will be displayed by the

@WB function as "<=" indicating that a constraint of this type is stored in F9; the constraint is satisfied because 5100 (the value of the expression in D9) is less than 6000 (the value stored in H9).

Step 4: ***Objective Cell:*** This step identifies total profit as the objective cell to be maximized. From the What's*Best!* menu, choose **Best**. Then choose **Profit/Maximize**; move the cell pointer to D12 (Profit[Total]) and select this cell. The optimization problem will then be completely defined for What's*Best!*.

Step 5: ***Solve the Optimization Problem.*** From the What's*Best!* menu, choose **Solve**. What's*Best!* will set up the problem, optimize the values of the decision variable, and return to the spreadsheet with the optimized values placed in the adjustable decision cells.

Tip: What's*Best!* is designed to be friendly to your files. The original spreadsheet file before optimization is left unchanged, with the name WBTO.WK1. The spreadsheet with the optimized values will have the name WBFR.WK1. The WBTO file is what went *to* optimization; the WBFR file is what came *from* optimization.

Using What's*Best!*: Quattro Pro, Release 4.0
(This section should be omitted by readers not using Quattro Pro)

The first step in using the solver is to invoke What's*Best!* from the subdirectory containing the spreadsheet software and What's*Best!* files. For example, if the Quattro Pro spreadsheet software is in subdirectory QPR04, that directory should be made the default directory with a change directory command such as:

```
CD C:\QPR04
```

Then invoke the solver with the command **WBQ**, which will cause the normal spreadsheet logo and screen to appear.

After the solver and spreadsheet are started, retrieve the file containing the Rangely model into the spreadsheet. The next step is to describe the Rangely optimization problem to What's*Best!*, making menu choices to describe the decision variables (called the **Adjustable** cells on the menu), the constraints, and the objective cell (called the **Best** cell on the menu). In detail:

Step 1: ***Decision (Adjustable) Cells:*** We first identify the adjustable cells for Rangely Lakes, as modeled in Figure 3.1. Move the cell pointer to cell B2, then choose **WB!** from the main Quattro Pro menu. (The single-letter choice B is equivalent to highlighting **WB!**.) Then press [←Enter]. Next, move the menu pointer to **Adjustable** and press [←Enter], or press the [A] key. From this menu, choose **Adjust**. (The other choices are more advanced than we need to discuss right now.) Following the instructions on the menus, select the adjustable cells in the same manner you select any spreadsheet range. When you have moved the cell pointer to the beginning of the adjustable cells, anchor the range with the anchor key (a "period" or "dot". When the desired decision cells B2..C2 are selected, press [←Enter] to finish your selection. Note that adjustable cells appear in a different color or intensity on the spreadsheet screen.

For a spreadsheet with more than one block of adjustable cells, repeat the process. Choose **Adjustable** and **Adjust**, then move the cell pointer to select the next block of adjustable cells. For Rangely, there is only one range of decision cells.

Step 2: *Constraint Cell:* Constrain D6 (Board Feet Used[Total]) to be less than or equal to 17,000 board feet. From the What's*Best!* menu, choose **Constraints**. From the next menu option, choose **Less than** (which is shorthand for the wordy "less than or equal to"). The constraint must be stored in a spreadsheet cell. The next prompt for this constraint is to place the cursor on the cell where you want the constraint put, and then press [←Enter]. We could select any blank cell; for clarity, move the pointer to E6, which is adjacent to the cell being constrained.

The final prompt is to enter the cell to be constrained and the constraining limit. Following the prompts and instruction on the screen, move the cell pointer to D6 (the cell to be constrained) and press [←Enter]; move the cell pointer to F6 (the constraining limit) and press [←Enter] again. (If preferred, a limiting value could have been entered from the keyboard instead of pointing to the cell containing the constraining limit.)

Tip: In this sequence of steps, screen messages will be cleared by any keystroke. Close attention to the screen will clarify whether a keystroke was taken as an entry, or was simply interpreted as instructions to clear a message from the screen. The message will be cleared immediately, so read the entire message carefully before you strike another key.

After completing this constraint,, the symbol "Not <=" appears in the spreadsheet cell, indicating that this cell contains a "<=" constraint that is not satisfied. A special function named @WB.CON is used to generate this display.

Step 3: *Other Constraints:* Step 2 must be followed for each constraint. Cell D9 (Hours Used[Total]) must be greater than or equal to 4000 hours (contained in cell F9) and less than or equal to 6000 hours (contained in H9). Store these constraints in cells E9 and G9 with these steps:

From the What's*Best!* menu, choose **Constraints**. Choose **Greater than** from the menu. Then select E9 as the cell in which to put the constraint function. Next select D9 as the cell to be constrained and cell F9 as the constraining limit. This will be displayed in cell E9 by the @WB.CON function as ">=" indicating that a constraint of this type is stored in E9; the constraint is satisfied, because 5100 (the value of the expression in D9) is greater than 4000 (the value stored in F9).

From the What's*Best!* menu, choose **Constraints**; Choosse **Less than** from the menu. Then select G9 as the cell in which to put the constraint function. Next select D9 as the cell to be constrained and cell H9 as the constraining limit. This will be displayed in cell G9 by the @WB.CON function as "<=" indicating that a constraint of this type is stored in G9; the constraint is satisfied because 5100 (the value of the expression in D9) is less than 6000 (the value stored in H9).

Step 4: *Objective Cell:* This step identifies total profit as the objective cell to be maximized. From the What's*Best!* menu, choose **Best**. Then choose **Profit/Maximize**; move the cell pointer to D12 (Profit[Total]) and select this cell. The optimization problem will then be completely defined for What's*Best!*.

Step 5: *Solve the Optimization Problem.* From the What's*Best!* menu, choose **Solve**. What's*Best!* will set up the problem, optimize the values of the decision variable, and return to the spreadsheet with the optimized values placed in the adjustable decision cells.

> *Tip:* What's*Best!* is designed to be friendly to your files. The original spreadsheet file before optimization is left unchanged, with the name WBTO.WQ1. The spreadsheet with the optimized values will have the name WBFR.WQ1. The WBTO file is what went *to* optimization; the WBFR file is what came *from* optimization.

Tip for Advanced Spreadsheet Users

Here's some insight into the way the What's*Best!* software places optimization instructions in the spreadsheet. The decision (adjustable) cells are identified by *unprotecting* those cells. The constraint cells are stored in the spreadsheet, with one cell for each constraint. In Lotus 1-2-3 Release 2.x, and in Quattro Pro Release 4.0, a special add-in function, @WB or @WB.CON, describes the constraints. The objective cell is identified by the single-cell range (block) named WBMAX or WBMIN, for profit/maximize or cost/minimize. In earlier versions of Quattro Pro, a strange looking @IF function describes the constraint information. The What's*Best!* menu also provides an option to generate the @IF function in Lotus. The @IF form and the translation feature are described in Appendix B at the end of this text.

Throughout this text, we assume that the @WB function is used to describe the constraints.

The Optimized Spreadsheet

Figure 3.3 shows the Rangely Lakes spreadsheet as it has been returned from optimization (named WBFR.W??). The production plan from optimization maximizes profit while keeping labor use and lumber use within the required limits. The optimal decision values are about 2794 decoys and 1854 wall hangings. This will yield a profit of about $10,630, use up all of the available lumber, and keep labor at its lower limit of 4000 hours. Your optimized spreadsheet may be slightly different from what is shown here; the amount of lumber used may be very close to the limiting value, such as 16,999.99, which is effectively 17,000 for managerial purposes. Optimization software will often leave values "almost but not quite" specified values, because of tolerances incorporated within the software. Optimization mathematics requires a large number of arithmetic operations, causing the roundoff error to be larger than we typically encounter in spreadsheet operations. Occasionally, this roundoff may cause a display such as

---
Figure 3.3

Rangely Lakes After Optimization

	A	B	C	D	E	F	G	H
1		Decoy	Hanging	Total				
2	Quantity	2793.733	1853.785	4647.51				
3	Price	$12	$15					
4	Revenue	$33,525	$27,807	$61,332				
5								
6	Board Feet Used	8101.827	8898.171	16999.9	=<=	17000		
7	Cost of Lumber	$10,532	$11,568	$22,100				
8								
9	Hours Used	3073.107	926.8928	3999.99	=>=	4000	<=	6000
10	Cost of Labor	$21,973	$6,627	$28,600				
11								
12	Profit		$1,020	$9,612	$10,632			
13								
14	Board Feet per Item	2.9	4.8					
15	Hours per Item	1.1	0.5					
16								
17			Data					
18	Price per Board Foot	$1.30						
19	Price per Hour	$7.15						

Note: The contents of the constraint cells inserted in a Lotus spreadsheet by What'sBest! are:

```
E6:   @WB(D6,"<=",F6)
E9:   @WB(D9,"<=",F9)
G9:   @WB(D9,">=",H9)
```

The contents of the constraint cells inserted in a Quattro Pro spreadsheet by What'sBest! are:

```
E6:   @WB.CON(D6,"<=",F6)
E9:   @WB.CON(D9,"<=",F9)
G9:   @WB.CON(D9,">=",H9)
```

"Not >=" when the constraint is satisfied, according to the mathematical instructions used in the optimization solver.

What'sBest! displays constraints in eight different ways, to indicate both the type of constraint (<=, >=, or =) and whether it is satisfied. A constraint which is not satisfied is shown with the word Not preceding the symbols. A constraint which is exactly satisfied is displayed with the "=" sign preceding the symbol. More specifically, the constraint displays are listed here:

<=   A "less than or equal to" constraint that is "loose" at the current solution. This means that the constraint cell is less than (and not equal to) the constraint limit.

=<=   A "less than or equal to" constraint that is "tight" at the current solution. This means that the constraint cell is equal to (and not less than) the constraint limit.

Not <= A "less than or equal to" constraint that is violated (or not satisfied) at the current solution. The means that the constraint cell is not less than or equal to the constraint limit.

>=   A "greater than or equal to" constraint that is "loose" at
            the current solution. This means that the constraint cell is
            greater than (and not equal to) the constraint limit.

=>=   A "greater than or equal to" constraint that is "tight" at the
            current solution. This means that the constraint cell is equal
            to (and not greater than) the constraint limit.

Not >=   A "greater than or equal to" constraint that is violated (or
            not satisfied) at the current solution. This means that the
            constraint cell is not greater than or equal to the constraint
            limit.

=   An "equal to" constraint that is satisfied at the current solu-
            tion. This means that the constraint cell is equal to the con-
            straint limit.

Not =   An "equal to" constraint that is not satisfied at the current
            solution. This means that the constraint cell is not equal to
            the constraint limit.

All of these constraint displays will be left justified within a cell. Because numbers are usually right justified within a cell, use care in determining the column
for a constraint specification.

It is often desirable to review the optimization settings that generated an
optimized spreadsheet. All of the specifications of the optimization problem are
stored as a part of the spreadsheet model, so they can be found using What's *Best!*
commands. From the main solver menu, choose **Report**, then **Locate**, then either
Adjustable, **Best**, or **Constrain**. Following the prompts will lead to each of the components of the optimization problem. Another way to look at the complete problem formulation is the *Solutions Report*, which is described in Appendix B (from
the What's *Best!* menu, select **Report**, **Solution**, **Enable**, and follow the prompts).
This report also contains additional information that is discussed in a later chapter of this text.

What Is an Optimization Problem?

The Rangely Lakes case demonstrates that optimization may be viewed simply
as asking "What's Best?" on a spreadsheet. But there are many attributes to
various kinds of What's Best? questions; not all of these questions look like the
Rangely Lakes scenario. In this section, we discuss various characteristics of
What's Best? questions that may arise with spreadsheet models.

Some managerial models are built to answer "yes or no" questions. Do
I build the plant or don't I? Do I make the merger proposal or don't I?
Do I accept the offer or refuse it? Spreadsheet models are often constructed to support decisions like these. The spreadsheet is designed to
help the manager decide which is better. Although these questions are
optimization questions, they might be viewed as informal optimization.
Spreadsheets are used to "chase out the consequences" of pursuing an
alternative, which will be either accepted or rejected.

Some spreadsheet models address "multiple choice" questions to find the best of the several choices. Do I build the plant in Denver, Orlando, Dallas, or Evansville? Each of these alternative locations may have substantially different logic brought about by differences in factors such as terrain, culture, tax environment, labor availability, and legal environment. Thus, the What's Best? question is addressed by comparing the information generated from four models, one model for each proposed location. Although this is a What's Best? question, this use of spreadsheet models might again be viewed as informal optimization.

Both of the examples of informal optimization have very limited numbers of alternatives. A "yes or no" question has the two obvious alternatives. A "multiple choice" informal optimization problem has so few alternatives that a separate model can be used to evaluate each alternative. The formal optimization methods available to work in conjunction with spreadsheet software are of no real benefit for problems having only a few alternatives to evaluate. Problems of this type may be optimized without special software, by trying all possible choices.

The Rangely Lakes analysis clearly benefitted from the use of optimization software. A manager could have played "What If" games for a long time, without finding a production plan with as much profit as the solution generated by the optimization software, and without violating the constraints about lumber used and hours used. A key difference between Rangely Lakes and the "informal optimization" situations is that the Rangely Lakes case posed a "How Much?" or "How Many?" question for the manager. In contrast, the informal optimization models look at "Should I?" or "Which One?" questions. Although more advanced optimization and modeling addresses the "Which?" questions when there are many alternatives, for now we limit the discussion of optimization to questions involving "How Much?" or "How Many?"

Modeling for Optimization: Some Comparisons and Comments

A reader who has studied optimization in its traditional format has not found much familiar material in this chapter. A traditional view of optimization involves algebraic notation, using the language of the mathematician. This chapter has presented a manager's view of optimization using a spreadsheet, a manager's language. Chapter 3 presents a traditional view of linear programming, a very important type of optimization.

Another useful comparison can be made between the modeling presented in this chapter and the modeling that would be more natural if we simply asked "How many decoys should we make?" But there are two distinct modeling approaches that should be compared:

The Optimization Modeling Approach: We constructed the model so that it could be used to evaluate any plan (any number of decoys and hangings). The influence chart and model were intended to be constructed at the conclusion of Chapter 1, before we made any mention of optimization! The motivation for the model was "What happens if I . . ." Optimization software was then applied to this model.

The "What Should I Do" Approach: Suppose this book had started with the Rangely Lakes scenario and asked readers unfamiliar with either spreadsheets or optimization, "How many decoys, and how many hangings should we make?" There would be nearly as many ways to develop an answer as there are readers; we conjecture that many readers would use rules of thumb, and develop an answer based on calculations such as the number of decoys we could make if we made only decoys, to use up all the lumber, and so on. These clues would be used informally to develop a plan.

It is important to understand these differences, because beginning users of spreadsheet optimization tend to drift into the "what should I do" computations instead of the "what happens if I . . . " modeling. Although optimization provides answers to the "what should I do" questions, the model is always constructed to evaluate proposals. Then the optimization software finds the best possible proposal, consistent with all of the constraints.

Questions for Thought and Discussion

The following situations briefly describe managerial situations in which spreadsheets might be used to support a decision. Discuss whether each situation is a candidate for formal optimization. Recall that problems with limited alternatives, characterized as "Which?" problems, are typically not candidates for formal optimization, while problems with many alternatives, often characterized as "How Many?" or "How Much?" problems, may be candidates for formal optimization.

a. *I've got to place an order for computer paper. When I order a lot at one time, we hear from the controller complaining that we have too much money tied up in inventories. When I order in smaller quantities, I get complaints from the purchasing department that they spend all their time processing our purchase orders.*

    Discussion: The issue is "How Much?" should I order. Formal optimization may be useful in this situation.

b. *I've got to place an order for computer paper. When I go to the Office Supply Warehouse, I need to buy four cases to meet their purchase minimums. Gosh, that's a lot. When I buy from the Computer Store, they deliver it a box at a time because they have a small truck. Sometimes I get it from a catalog, ordering the minimum quantity, which is plenty for us.*

    Discussion: This is a question with a limited number (three) of alternatives. Since the "How Much?" question has already been decided for each alternative, the analysis would involve comparing the costs and benefits for each of the three alternatives. Formal optimization would not likely be useful in this situation.

c. *In preparing mixed cattle feed, our problem is to get the desired nutrient level for the mixture, but still make as much profit as we can. What should the percentage of oat grain be in the mixture?*

Discussion: The question is "How Much?" oat grain should be in the mixture. This is a candidate for formal optimization.

d. *In preparing mixed cattle feed, our problem is to get the desired nutrient level for the mixture, but still make as much profit as we can. Should we use sunflower seeds in the mixture?*

Discussion: At first it appears that the question involves a simple comparison of the alternatives "Use sunflower seeds" and "Don't use sunflower seeds." But each of those alternatives has an optimization problem hidden behind it. If I use sunflower seeds, how much should I use? How much will that mix cost? If I don't use sunflower seeds, what mix should I use, and how much will that mix cost? This is a candidate for a pair of formal optimization problems.

e. *Should we make cattle feed or pet food?*

Discussion: Much like the sunflower seed question above, this problem would benefit from formal optimization before the two product lines are compared.

f. *Should we invest in the apartment complex or the warehouse building?*

Discussion: This problem is the comparison of two alternatives. It is unlikely that formal optimization would enhance the analysis of the decision.

g. *In order to minimize the shipping costs from warehouses to stores, should we build our new warehouse in Huntington, Bloomington, Evansville, or Louisville?*

Discussion: This is the comparison of four alternatives. However, the underlying question of "How Many?" to ship from each warehouse to each store needs to be answered with each prospective warehouse in place. This analysis would benefit from formal optimization. After this formal optimization, the four alternatives can be compared.

h. *In order to meet our peak winter customer demand for snow blowers, should we use overtime, add workforce just before the peak season, or use level production and build up inventory levels during the slow months?*

Discussion: The question is really how many to hire each month, how many to dismiss each month, and how much overtime to use each month. Formal optimization is a good candidate for aiding the analysis of this problem. However, it may be that labor contracts and other considerations limit the alternatives so severely that the consequences of a small number of alternatives can be evaluated effectively without the use of formal optimization.

i. *I've got lots of crop land and a limited irrigation water allocation for the growing season. Should I irrigate the wheat field?*

Discussion: There is not enough information to determine whether the question is "Which crop should I irrigate?" or "How much water should I use on each crop?" The first question is a multiple choice question; it is unlikely that formal optimization would effectively support this decision. However, if all crops can be irrigated in various amounts, the determination of the amount of water for each crop is a candidate for formal optimization.

j. *How should I divide my investment funds between Certificates of Deposit, bonds, and notes? I want to get as much interest as I can, but I have a series of payments to make from the money returned from the investments. Each investment has a specified maturity. If I use long term investments, I get a good return; if I use short term investments, the yield isn't as good. But if I use too much long term investment, the money isn't available when I need to make the payments.*

> *Discussion:* This is a "How Much?" question: "How much should I invest in each security each month?" Constraints need to be established so that there is enough money each period to meet the payments due.

Exercises

1. Use the spreadsheet model for Rangely Lakes as described in Chapter 2 and as shown in Figure 3.1 of this chapter. Using the keystrokes as outlined in this chapter, enter the optimization specifications and solve, obtaining the optimal solution shown in Figure 3.3.

2. (This scenario is from Chapter 1, Exercise 2.) A rectangular area is to be enclosed by a fence; the land owner wants as large an enclosed area as possible. The land owner has purchased 500 feet of fence and has constructed this spreadsheet model to calculate the enclosed area and the perimeter (amount of fence) for a rectangle of any length and width:

	A	B
1	Fence Exercise	
2		
3	Length	50
4	Width	100
5		
6	Area	5000
7	Perimeter	300

a. Construct a spreadsheet model to duplicate the calculations shown in the spreadsheet model above. Verify the correctness of your model by showing that changing the length to 10 feet changes the area to 1000 and the perimeter to 220.

b. What are the two decision variables?

c. What is the one constraint?

d. What is the objective? Is the objective maximization or minimization?

e. Enter the optimization specifications into the spreadsheet to prepare for solution by What's*Best!*.

f. Solve the optimization problem. You may receive a message that there are nonlinearities in the model; these will be discussed later in the text.

For now, ignore the message, following the instructions at the top of the error report to return to the optimized spreadsheet.

g. What is the recommendation for the size of the enclosed area? (Some readers may already know that a square encloses more area than any rectangle of the same perimeter. This optimization result should verify that fact. This exercise is designed to provide practice for entering optimization information into the spreadsheet.)

3. (This is the scenario from Exercise 6, Chapter 1.) You want to build a spreadsheet to calculate the cost for making a metal can (a "tin can") for a food product. A can is completely described by its diameter and its height. There are two cost elements: metal cost and labor cost. The metal cost is incurred for the metal in the can wall and the ends. The amount of metal used in the wall is

HEIGHT × DIAMETER × π where π is 3.14159 . . . , or @PI on a spreadsheet.

The amount of metal used in each of two ends (or the top and the bottom) is

DIAMETER × DIAMETER

which assumes the round ends are cut from a square. Metal costs 0.02 cents ($0.0002) per square inch.

The labor cost is incurred for the "seaming" for the side wall and for the joint between the ends and the side wall. The side wall seaming costs 0.1 cents per inch; the seam between and end and a side wall costs 0.15 cents per inch. The amount of side wall seaming is equal to the height of the can. The amount of side wall to end seaming for one end is

DIAMETER × π where π is 3.14159 . . . , or @PI on a spreadsheet.

The total cost of the can is the sum of total metal cost and total seam cost. A spreadsheet model to calculate the cost of a can is shown here:

	A	B
1	Can Exercise	
2		
3	Metal Cost	1.490973
4	Metal Cost per Sq In	0.02
5	Total Metal Used	74.54866
6	Wall Metal Used	56.54866
7	End Metal Used	18
8		
9	Height	6
10	Diameter	3
11		
12	Total Seam Cost	3.427433
13	Wall Seam Cost	0.6
14	End Seam Cost	2.827433
15	Length of Wall Seam	6
16	Unit Cost for Wall Seam	0.1
17	Length of End Seams	18.84955
18	Unit Cost for End Seams	0.15
19		
20	Total Can Cost	4.918406

The volume of a can is the height multiplied by the area of one end of the can. The area of one end is the square of the radius, multiplied by @PI (3.14159 . . .). The radius of the can is half of the diameter.

   a. Include the volume of the can in the influence chart (from Chapter 1 Exercise 6) and in the spreadsheet model.

   b. The volume of the can to be produced must be at least 40 cubic inches. The can may not be more than eight inches high; its diameter must be between 2.5 and 4 inches. Within these limitations, a can that costs less is preferred to one that costs more. Identify the decision variables, the constraints, and the objective.

   c. Specify the optimization settings in the spreadsheet for What's*Best!*. Solve the optimization problem, and recommend dimensions for the can. For verification purposes, the cost of the optimal can is 4.701 cents. You may receive a message that there are nonlinearities in the model; these will be discussed later in the text. For now, ignore the message, following the instructions at the top of the report to return to the optimized spreadsheet.

4. (This scenario is from Chapter 1, Exercise 8.) A manufacturer of hammers has two models, standard and deluxe. Each standard hammer contributes $4 to profit; each deluxe hammer contributes $7 to profit. Both hammers require metal and labor, in different quantities. A standard hammer requires 21 ounces of metal and 0.8 hours of labor. A deluxe hammer requires 18 ounces of metal and 1.1 hours of labor. For the planning period, no more than 20,000 ounces of metal or 950 hours of labor can be used. Obviously, more profit is preferred to less profit.

   a. Identify the decision variables for the hammer company. Use a square to identify the decision variable on the influence chart from Chapter 1, Exercise 8.

   b. Identify the constraints for the hammer company. Use a triangle to identify the constraints on the influence chart.

   c. Identify the objective for the hammer company. Use an oval to identify the objective on the influence chart.

   d. Using What's*Best!* enter the optimization information into the spreadsheet.

   e. Find the optimal solution, using the model and What's*Best!*. For verification, the optimal value of profit is about $6045.5 if one could construct and sell a fractional hammer).

   f. If the profit contribution of a standard hammer increases to $6, would you recommend a change in the production plan? To answer this question, change the profit contribution in the spreadsheet, and optimize again.

5. (This scenario is from Chapter 1, Exercise 9.) Another manufacturer is making pliers. Each economy plier sells for $3 and requires 3 ounces of metal and 10

minutes of labor. Each standard plier sells for $4 and requires 7 ounces of metal and 12 minutes of labor. Each deluxe plier sells for $5 and requires 6 ounces of metal and 15 minutes of labor. No more than 1400 ounces of metal and 4000 minutes of labor can be used during the planning period. Each ounce of metal costs $0.04; each minute of labor costs $0.20. The manufacturer wants to maximize profit, which is the total revenue (price × quantity) less the cost of resources.

    a. Identify the decision variables for the plier company. Use a square to identify the decision variable on the influence chart.

    b. Identify the constraints for the plier company. Use a triangle to identify the constraints on the influence chart.

    c. Identify the objective for the plier company. Use an oval to identify the objective on the influence chart.

    d. Using What's*Best!*, enter the optimization information into the spreadsheet.

    e. Find the optimal solution, using the model and What's*Best!*. For verification purposes, the optimal profit is slightly more than $410 if one could make a fractional plier.

    f. If the selling price for a deluxe plier changes to $8, would you recommend a change in the production plan? To answer this question, change the selling price in the spreadsheet, and optimize again.

6. (This scenario is similar to Chapter 1, Exercise 10.) You want to minimize the number of calories you consume from ice cream and cookies, but have "total satisfaction" of at least 100 "yums" and protein intake of at least 50 grams. Each serving of ice cream provides 40 yums and 25 grams of protein. Each cookie provides 50 yums and 15 grams of protein. Unfortunately, a serving of ice cream has 300 calories, and a cookie has 350 calories. You have no difficulty in eating a partial serving of ice cream or a partial cookie. Plan your ice cream and cookie consumption for this situation, using these steps:

    a. Identify the decision variables for the nutrition plan. Use a square to identify the decision variable on the influence chart.

    b. Identify the constraints for the nutrition plan. Use a triangle to identify the constraints on the influence chart.

    c. Identify the objective for the nutrition plan. Use an oval to indicate the objective on the influence chart.

    d. Using What's*Best!* and the spreadsheet model you constructed in Chapter 1, Exercise 10, enter the optimization information into the spreadsheet.

    e. Find the optimal solution, using the model and What's*Best!* For verification, you can find a nutrition plan that provides 730.8 calories.

7. (This exercise continues from Exercise 1 of this chapter.) J. L. Duckworth has been toying with changing the prices. A member of the sales force had men-

tioned that an interesting marketing strategy would be to charge the same price for each product. J.L. believed that the only price that would work is $13.50, splitting the difference between the two existing prices. Evaluate this strategy, based on the assumption that you can still sell all you can make with this new pricing policy. To evaluate this policy, it is necessary to change the data values for the two prices, optimize once again, and compare the results of optimizing with each set of prices.

8. (This exercise continues from Exercise 1 of this chapter. The price changes from Exercise 7 are not used in this exercise.) By paying $1.50 per board foot for all the lumber used, J.L. believes it may be possible to obtain as much as 27,000 board feet. Is this worth pursuing?

9. After studying the optimal solution based on the Exercise 1 scenario (2794 decoys, 1854 hangings), J.L. was concerned. The sales forces keeps talking about "excess ducks" as being hard to sell; customers seem to want as many hangings as decoys, yet the proposed optimal solutions has 940 excess ducks (the difference between 2794 and 1854). J.L. wants to modify the influence chart and model to keep track of the number of excess ducks.

   a. Make the appropriate additions to the influence chart to show excess ducks.

   b. Make the appropriate additions to the model to calculate excess ducks.

   c. The number of excess ducks is limited to 500. Use What's *Best!* to determine the mix of products that will make as much profit as possible under the original pricing policy and lumber availability of 17,000 board feet.

10. Identify the components of an optimization problem in the Sunsoak case (from Chapter 1). Indicate the components on the influence chart using a square for a decision variable, a triangle for a constraint, and a rectangle with rounded corners for the objective. Using the What's *Best!* software, optimize the spreadsheet model. Describe the optimized spreadsheet to management, in terms of a recommended course of action.

4

Linear Programming

What Is Linear Programming?

The purpose of this chapter is to build a bridge between the spreadsheet view of optimization and more traditional concepts of optimization, such as linear programming. You may encounter optimization in a format that is very different from the spreadsheet view; this chapter shows other more traditional ways of looking at some optimization problems. If you are interested only in the spreadsheet view of optimization, you could safely omit most of this chapter without a loss of continuity. But then it would be difficult to relate this book to others that treat the same topics in a very different manner.

Linear programming is one of the most important topics of management science. It is used in many different situations, as the variety of applications in the next several chapters will demonstrate. The Rangely Lakes optimization problem in Chapter 3 is an example of a linear programming problem, which is a specific type of optimization problem. A linear programming problem is an optimization problem in which there are linear relationships between the decision variables and the constraints, and between the decision variables and the objective.

The What's *Best!* software can determine whether an optimization problem is linear. After the **Solve** menu choice has been selected, you will be notified if there is a nonlinear constraint or objective in the optimization problem. (This can be changed by selecting different options from the What's *Best!* menu.) To understand this report, we need to understand linearity.

Our first task is to describe some characteristics of linearity. Then we consider the mathematical definition of linearity, followed by a graphical method for solving simple linear programming problems. At first, the description that follows may seem lengthy. That shouldn't alarm you, however, because optimization software includes the intelligence to determine whether a model is linear. Even though the software makes this determination, a managerial understanding of linearity is important to be able to construct linear models, if possible, because they are solved more quickly than nonlinear models by the computer software.

What Is Linearity?

The relationship between two variables is said to be linear if a "unit change" in the first variable is always accompanied by a constant amount of change in the second variable. A "unit change" is an increase of one unit, such as from zero to one, from ten to eleven, from 213 to 214, from 4326.4 to 4327.4, or from −874 to −873. For a linear relationship, the change in the second variable caused by any of these unit changes would be identical. On a graph, a linear relationship between two variables is a straight line.

An example of a linear relationship in Rangely Lakes is the one between Quantity[Decoy] and Revenue[Decoy]. Each unit change in Quantity[Decoy] is accompanied by a $12 change in Revenue[Decoy]. This is true because the revenue from each decoy is $12. Is there a linear relationship between Quantity[Decoy] and Profit[Total]? Between Quantity[Hanging] and Hours Used[Total]?

If an optimization problem is linear, the following relationships must all be linear in the spreadsheet model:

The relationship between the first decision variable and the objective.

The relationship between the second decision variable and the objective.

. . . and so on for each decision variable.

The relationship between the first decision variable and the first constraint variable.

The relationship between the first decision variable and the second constraint variable.

. . . and so on for the first decision variable and each constraint variable.

. . . and so on for each decision variable and each constraint variable.

Linearity in an optimization model is easy to demonstrate graphically with a spreadsheet, as shown in Figure 4.1. (There is some additional information, shown in row 3 of the spreadsheet, that should be ignored for now. It will be discussed later.) The upper portion of the spreadsheet in Figure 4.1 is the Rangely Lakes model used in the two previous chapters (with Quantity[Hanging] set at 100 to keep the numbers manageable). The lower half of the spreadsheet shows values of Profit[Total], Lumber Used[Total], and Hours Used[Total] for various values of Quantity[Decoy]. For example, look at spreadsheet row 25: if 100 is used as the value for Quantity[Decoy], Profit will be $555.00; 770 board feet of lumber will be used; 160 hours will be used.

Spreadsheet Tip: Data Tables (What-If Tables). To create a data table, the user enters a column of potential values for the decision variable, Quantity [Decoys], in A25..A35. The text labels (Profit, Lumber Used, Hours Used) shown in A22..D23 are for the reader's use only; they aren't part of the

Figure 4.1

Model and Data Table to Illustrate Linearity

	A	B	C	D	E
1		Decoy	Hanging	Total	
2	Quantity	3500	100	3600	
3	Qty as pct of Total	97.2%	2.8%		
4	Price	$12	$15		
5	Revenue	$42,000	$1,500	$43,500	
6					
7	Board Feet Used	10150	480	10630	
8	Cost of Lumber	$13,195	$624	$13,819	
9					
10	Hours Used	3850	50	3900	
11	Cost of Labor	$27,528	$358	$27,885	
12					
13	Profit	$1,277	$519	$1,796	
14					
15	Board Feet per Item	2.9	4.8		
16	Hours per Item	1.1	0.5		
17					
18		Data			
19	Price per Board Foot	$1.30			
20	Price per Hour	$7.15			
21					
22		Quantity	Profit	Lumber	Hours	Decoys
23		[Decoys]		Used	Used	as pct
24			1796.0	10630	3900	97.2%
25		0	518.5	480	50	0.0%
26		100	555.0	770	160	50.0%
27		200	591.5	1060	270	66.7%
28		300	628.0	1350	380	75.0%
29		400	664.5	1640	490	80.0%
30		500	701.0	1930	600	83.3%
31		600	737.5	2220	710	85.7%
32		700	774.0	2510	820	87.5%
33		800	810.5	2800	930	88.9%
34		900	847.0	3090	1040	90.0%
35		1000	883.5	3380	1150	90.9%

data table. The user provides the data table heading row, B24..E24. These headings contain the formulas that show the values to be placed in the table for the values of Quantity[Decoys] shown in column A. Cell B24 contains the formula +D13; since the profit is calculated in D13, the table heading in B22 also shows profit. Similarly, cell C24 contains the formula +D7; D24 contains the formula +D10. (For use later, cell E24 contains the formula +B3.) After the user enters the command for a one-way data table (/DT1 for **Data Table 1-way** in Lotus 1-2-3, or /TW1 for **Tools What-if 1-variable** in Quattro Pro), the software prompt requests the location of the table, A24..E35. The software prompt also requests the location of the spreadsheet cell into which the values from A25..A35 are to be placed. The user responds with "B2", the cell address for Quantity[Decoys]. The software then substitutes the data from column A into cell B2 during the data table operation, and places the results in B25..E35.

───────────────── **Figure 4.2** ─────────────────

Graph Showing Linearity Between Objective, Constraints, and Decision

Rangely Lakes Company—Linearity
Objective and Constraints vs. Decision

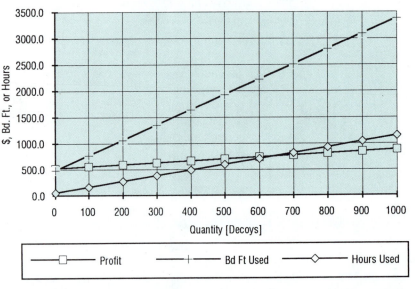

You are encouraged to replicate this data table on a spreadsheet. The graph is an XY graph, with Quantity[Decoy] in the X range, and the remaining three columns plotted in ranges A, B, and C (Lotus 1-2-3) or 1st Series, 2nd Series, 3rd Series (Quattro Pro). Straight lines result from this exercise, as shown in Figure 4.2. A similar data table and graph could be constructed for Quantity[Hanging]; straight lines would result from this exercise as well.

What Might Cause Nonlinearity?

Linearity for Rangely Lakes could be disturbed in a number of ways. The following items are examples of scenario changes that would affect the linearity of the Rangely Lakes optimization model.

A lumber supplier provides quantity discounts for the lumber used in making souvenirs. This would cause the profit to "jump down" when the price break point is reached if the discount applies to all lumber purchased. It would cause a "kink" when the price break point is reached if the discount applies only to lumber purchased after the discount applies. Neither the "jump" nor the "kink" is linear (although they may be made up of straight lines).

There is a reduction in the shipping cost per board foot of lumber if more than 15,000 board feet is purchased during the season. This would cause the same "jump" or "kink" as the price break.

There is learning involved in making the souvenirs, so that souvenirs made later in the season use less labor than those made earlier in the season. The profit curve would start to bend up slightly as the workers become experienced, and production becomes less expensive.

Boredom sets in, so that souvenirs made later in the season use more labor than those made earlier in the season. The profit curve would start to bend down slightly as boredom sets in, and production becomes more expensive.

The percentage rate on a payroll tax, such as social security contribution (FICA) by the employer, changes during the season. This might happen if an employee was paid so much overtime during the summer that December pay was exempt from social security payroll tax, but the January pay was not exempt. Exercise: describe the shape of the profit curve.

Quantity discounts are granted to a customer. This means that the first souvenirs sold to this customer bring more revenue than the last souvenirs sold to this customer. Exercise: describe the shape of the profit curve.

Overtime pay is required for labor in excess of 5000 hours. Exercise: describe the shape of the profit curve.

Each item in this list causes a change in the relationship between a decision variable and the objective and/or a constraint. As an example of a change that makes the model nonlinear, a learning curve means that the first souvenir uses more hours than the last souvenir, and that the first souvenir has a smaller profit than the last souvenir. This means that making one more souvenir (a unit change in a decision variable) does not have the same impact on profit (the objective) for all values of that decision variable. Similarly, making one more souvenir has a different impact on hours used (a constraint) depending upon whether the change in the number of souvenirs is from 0 to 1, from 10 to 11, or from 1000 to 1001.

There is another characteristic of linearity that we mention for completeness. For the original Rangely Lakes scenario, each decoy used 2.9 board feet. The property of linearity that we have discussed above is that a unit change in Quantity[Decoy] is accompanied by a 2.9 change in Board Feet Used[Total], regardless of the number of decoys made. The additional characteristic of linearity is that this value, 2.9, is the same regardless of the value of the other decision variable(s), Quantity[Hanging] in this case. Optimization software that we will use in this text makes this check as well, so we need not be intimately involved in this property of linearity. The mathematical definition of linearity, discussed later, is the best way to thoroughly understand this property of linearity.

Spreadsheet Nonlinearities for Reporting

There may be parts of a spreadsheet that have nonlinear relationships that do not affect the linearity of the optimization model. For example, J. L. Duckworth

─────────────────────────── **Figure 4.3** ───────────────────────────

Nonlinearity for Reporting Only

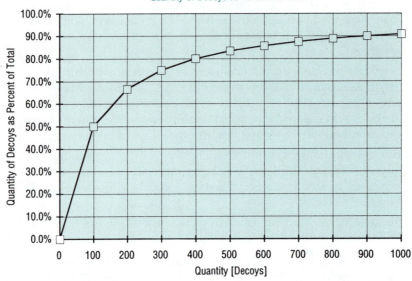

Rangely: Nonlinearity for Reporting
Quantity of Decoys as Percent of Total

might be interested in the number of decoys and hangings, expressed as a percent of total units produced. These values have been shown in row 3 of the spreadsheet in Figure 4.1. The relationships are:

```
Qty as pct of Total[Decoy]   = Quantity[Decoy]   / Quantity[Total]
Qty as pct of Total[Hanging] = Quantity[Hanging] / Quantity[Total]
```

In these relationships, the numerator (top of the fraction) of the right-hand side is a decision variable; the denominator (bottom of the fraction) of the right-hand side is calculated from the decision variables. This ratio of two terms, both depending upon decision variables, is a nonlinear relationship.

Figure 4.3 shows this relationship in graphical form, plotting the quantity of decoys as a percent of total against quantity of decoys. Clearly, this is a non-linear relationship. The What's*Best!* solver will detect the nonlinear relationship, but determines that these cells are for reporting purposes only.

The key issue, however, is that the optimization model itself is a linear model, although there are nonlinear relationships in the spreadsheet. Linear algorithms will be used by What's*Best!* to solve the problem. If there are many cells used for reporting only, solution time may be improved by using the option to specify a WBOMIT range, instructing the solver to omit the reporting cells in solving the optimization problem. The reporting cells are B3..C3; these are omitted from optimization with these instructions:

From the What's *Best!* menu, choose **Options**, then **Omit**.

The suggested range (block) name WBOMIT may be used, or additional characters may be added after the six characters, "WBOMIT". (Names such as WBOMIT1, WBOMIT2 are convenient.) Then the cells to be omitted, B3..C3, are selected in the usual manner.

If the spreadsheet contains cells which are calculated from the omitted cells, these cells must also be contained in a WBOMIT range. For example, cell E24 in Figure 4.1 contains a simple formula, +B3. But B3 is included in a WBOMIT range that requires cell E24 to be included in another WBOMIT range, which might be named WBOMIT1.

An influence chart is useful to reinforce the concept of "reporting only" variables. Figure 4.4 is the Rangely influence chart from Chapter 3 with these two additional variables, which were used in defining cells B3..C3:

Quantity[Total]

Qty as pct of Total

None of the "output variables" for optimization (constraints, objective) is calculated from Qty as pct of Total. Even though Qty as pct of Total is calculated using a nonlinear relationship, the optimization is still linear because nothing that enters into the optimization problem needs to know the value of Qty as pct of Total.

A Mathematical View of Linear Programming

This section presents a mathematical view of linear programming, to serve as a bridge to understanding traditional optimization literature. Subscript notation is used throughout optimization literature. Traditionally, the decision variables are identified as values of X; the first decision variable is called X_1, the second is called X_2, and so on. (Sometimes these are called X[1], X[2], and so on, for typographical convenience.) In generic terms, the letter j is used to indicate the decision variable in position j in the list. Because the decision variables are traditionally viewed as a row of variables, the value of j indicates the column location of a particular decision variables.

The traditional literature views linear programming constraints as rows. Each row is given a subscript notation. The limiting value for the first constraint is called b_1; the limiting value for the second constraint is called b_2; the limiting value for constraint i is called b_i. As we get further into this mathematical view of linear programming, we'll be using coefficients at the intersection of each row and column. These coefficients are named with subscripts as well. The coefficient in row 1, column 2, is called a_{12}; the coeffieicnt in row i column j is called a_{ij}.

Management scientists use this notation to examine a problem to determine whether it is linear. An optimization problem is a linear optimization problem, or a linear programming problem, if it can be stated in this way:

Figure 4.4

Influence Chart with Nonlinear Relationships for Reporting Only

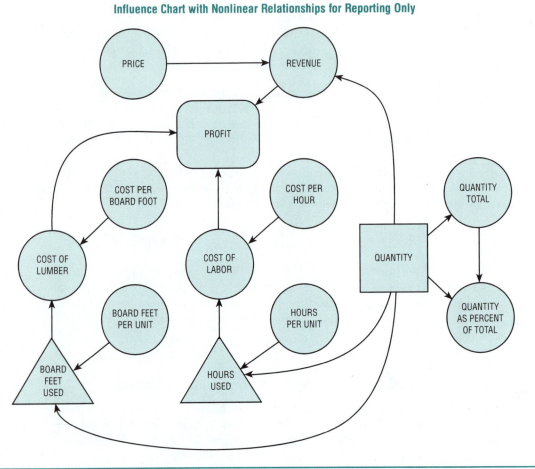

Objective: Maximize or Minimize $c_1 X_1 + c_2 X_2 + \cdots$

where $c_1, c_2, \ldots$ are constants

Subject to these constraints:

$$a_{11} X_1 + a_{12} X_2 + \cdots \text{ [relation] } b_1, \quad \text{and}$$
$$a_{21} X_2 + a_{22} X_2 + \cdots \text{ [relation] } b_2, \quad \text{and}$$
$$a_{31} X_3 + a_{32} X_2 + \cdots \text{ [relation] } b_3, \quad \text{and}$$
$$\cdot$$
$$\cdot$$
$$\cdot$$

where each [relation] can be $\leq$, $\geq$, or $=$; each value of a_{ij} is a constant; and b_i is a limiting value. The values of b are sometimes called the "right-hand side" values because they are on the right-hand side of the constraints.

To determine whether Rangely Lakes fits this definition of a linear optimization problem, we need to see if there is a set of constants (a, b, and c) that can be used to state the problem in this form.

For the objective, each value of c_j is the amount of change in the objective that accompanies a unit change in decision variable j. More specifically, c_1 is the profit change that accompanies a unit change in the value of Quantity[Decoy]; c_2 is the profit change that accompanies a unit change in the value of Quantity [Hanging]. These profit changes can be calculated as:

Decoys: $12 selling price, less 2.9 board feet at $1.30 per board foot, less 1.1 hours at $7.15 per hour. The unit profit for decoys is $0.365, which is the value of c_1.

Hangings: $15 selling price, less 4.8 board feet at $1.30 per board foot, less 0.5 hours at $7.15 per hour. The unit profit for decoys is $5.185, which is the value of c_2.

The objective for Rangely Lakes can be stated as:

$$\text{Maximize} \quad \text{Profit[Total]}, \quad \text{or}$$
$$\text{Maximize} \quad 0.365\,X_1 + 5.185\,X_2$$

which is the format for a linear relationship, as shown earlier in this chapter. These coefficients, $c_1 = 0.365$ and $c_2 = 5.185$, are called *objective coefficients*.

The first constraint is the number of board feet used, or the lumber constraint. Each value of a_{1j} is the amount of board feet that accompanies a unit change in decision variable j. The value of a_{11} is 2.9, which is the number of board feet (constraint 1) used by a decoy (decision variable 1). The value of a_{12} is 4.8, which is the number of board feet (constraint 1) used by a wall hanging (decision variable 2). The first constraint can be written as:

$$\text{Board Feet Used[Total]} \quad \text{<=} \quad 17000, \quad \text{or}$$
$$2.9X_1 + 4.8X_2 \quad \leq \quad 17{,}000$$

which is in the form of a linear relationship.

The second constraint is the number of hours used. Each value of a_{2j} is the number of hours that accompanies a unit change in decision variable j. The value of a_{21} is 1.1, which is the number of hours (constraint 2) used by a decoy (decision variable 1). The value of a_{22} is 0.5, which is the number of hours (constraint 2) used by a wall hanging (decision variable 2). The second constraint can be written as:

$$\text{Hours Used[Total]} \quad \text{>=} \quad 4000, \quad \text{or}$$
$$1.1X_1 + 0.5X_2 \quad \geq \quad 4000$$

The third constraint sets 6000 hours as the upper limit on the number of hours that can be used. This constraint is:

$$\text{Hours Used[Total]} \quad \text{<=} \quad 6000, \quad \text{or}$$
$$1.1X_1 + 0.5X_2 \quad \leq \quad 6000$$

both of which are in linear relationship form. There are many software packages that can be utilized to optimize the problem once it is formulated in this manner. Many of them, such as LINDO,* accept input information in a format similar to that used above. Other software requires the information to be provided in the form of a *coefficient matrix*, with each column representing a variable (such as X_1), and each row representing a constraint (such as the lumber constraint). This coefficient matrix in a spreadsheet may be augmented by a column showing the form of the relationship (<=, =, or >=) and the constraining values or *right hand side* values. This format requires specifying the *objective coefficients*, one for each decision variable, along with the sense of the optimization (maximize or minimize). This is shown here as the top row of the coefficient (although it may be in other locations, depending upon specific software being used). The coefficient matrix, relations, and right hand side for this problem have this appearance:

X_1	X_2		
0.365	5.185	MAX	
2.9	4.8	<=	17000
1.1	0.5	<=	6000
1.1	0.5	>=	4000

A key factor in applying spreadsheet optimization software, such as What's-Best!, is that the user does not need to construct the optimization problem in this mathematical format. The constants c_1 and c_2, used in the expression showing the amount of profit generated, never appear in the spreadsheet. Yet the software determines the values of these coefficients, and others as necessary, from the spreadsheet model. The software then determines whether the form of the optimization problem is linear, freeing the user of that task. Although this mathematical view of linear programming is widespread, the manager using spreadsheet optimization may not need this view of optimization to use it effectively in supporting decisions. Instead of performing an analysis thinking of a mathematical form, the the user is free to use whatever spreadsheet structure meets the users' needs.

Linear Programming: A Graphical Solution

While the mathematics involved in solving large linear programming problems is more interesting to mathematicians than to managers, some managerial insight may be gained by looking at a graphical solution to a simple linear programming problem. This graphical solution method is presented for these insights, not for its usefulness in solving linear programming problems. Only problems with two decision variables can be viewed with a two-dimensional graph. We continue with Rangely Lakes and its graphical solution.

---

*Linus Schrage, *LINDO: An Optimization Modeling System*. South San Francisco, CA: The Scientific Press, 1991, 4th edition.

In a graphical linear programming solution, each decision variable is shown on one of the graph's axes. (This is different from the graphs we used to demonstrate linearity, in which one decision variable was on the horizontal axis, and the objective or a constraint was on the vertical axis.) We'll plot X_1, the quantity of decoys, on the horizontal axis, and X_2, the quantity of hangings, on the vertical axis. (On the graphs, the notation X[1] and X[2] is used for typographical convience.) The first step in the graphical solution is to determine the *feasible region*, which is the region on the graph that shows values of the two quantities that meet all of the constraints. Our approach is to consider each constraint one at a time, starting with the lumber constraint:

Constraint 1:   Board Feet Used[Total]   <=   17000,   or

$$2.9X_1 + 4.8X_2 \quad \leq \quad 17{,}000$$

Suppose we made no hangings; then $X_2 = 0$. How many decoys could be made, considering only the lumber constraint? With 17,000 board feet available, and each decoy requiring 2.9 board feet, we could make up to:

17,000/2.9 = 5862 decoys, if we made no hangings.

Similarly, if we made no decoys, we could make up to:

17,000/4.8 = 3541 hangings.

These two extremes represent alternatives that would use up all of the lumber; in terms of the graph, these two alternatives are the *intercepts* on the two axes. Any point on the line connecting these two intercepts is also an alternative that would use up all of the lumber. This line is shown in Figure 4.5. The constraint, however, is that the board feet used must be less than or equal to 17,000, not exactly equal to 17,000. The line represents using up all of this resource; points below and to the left of the line use less than 17,000 board feet; points above and to the right of the line use more than 17,000 board feet. The line serves as the boundary between the production quantities that satisfy the lumber constraint, and those that do not satisfy the lumber constraint.

We next consider the requirement that we must use at least 4000 hours to satisfy the needs of the members of the work force:

Constraint 2:   Hours Used Used[Total]   >=   4000,   or

$$1.1X_1 + 0.5X_2 \quad \geq \quad 4000$$

Using the procedures outlined for the first constraint, we find the intercepts. One alternative is to make all decoys, and no hangings. Considering only the requirement specified by constraint 2, the number of decoys we could make is

4000/1.1 = 3636 decoys, if we made no hangings.

Similarly, considering only this constraint, the number of hangings we could make is:

4000/0.5 = 8000 hangings, if we made no decoys.

—————————————————— **Figure 4.5** ——————————————————

Lumber Constraint

Graphical Solution
First Constraint

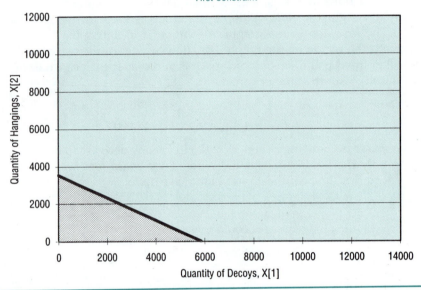

These two intercepts represent extreme product mix plans that would use exactly 4000 hours. The line connecting the intercepts shows all plans using exactly 4000 hours. Any product mix below or to the left of the line uses less than 4000 hours; any product mix above or to the right of the line uses more than 4000 hours. This line is shown in Figure 4.6, along with the line from the lumber constraint. The small shaded triangle shows the *feasible region* of all feasible product mix plans, considering the lumber constraint, and the lower limit of 4000 hours.

We next consider the requirement that we use no more than 6000 hours:

Constraint 3:   Hours Used Used[Total]   <=   6000,   or
$$1.1X_1 + 0.5X_2 \qquad \leq \quad 6000$$

As before, we find the intercepts. Considering only this constraint, if we made only decoys the quantity made would be:

$$6000/1.1 = 5454.$$

If we made only hangings, the quantity made would be:

$$6000/0.5 = 12,000.$$

Placing these two intercepts on the graph and connecting them, we have the set of product mix plans that would use exactly 6000 hours. Any point below or to the left of the line uses fewer than 6000 hours, and is feasible. Any point above

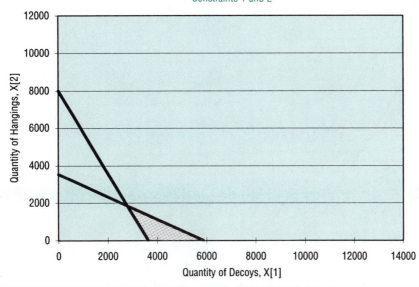

Figure 4.6

Two Constraints

Graphical Solution
Constraints 1 and 2

and to right of the line uses more than 6000 hours, and does not satisfy this constraint. This line is shown in the graph, Figure 4.7. Note that the feasible region (considering all three constraints) is smaller, with the extreme right corner cut off when we introduce this third constraint.

The constraints on the graph show the feasible region; which point in the feasible region is optimal because it has the highest profit? To see how to answer that question, we first pick an arbitrary profit target of $5000, and determine all the ways we could make $5000. Recall that the objective function is:

$$\text{Maximize} \quad \text{Profit[Total]}, \quad \text{or}$$
$$\text{Maximize} \quad 0.365\,X_1 + 5.185\,X_2$$

If we made no hangings, we could obtain a profit of $5000 by making this quantity of decoys:

$$5000/0.365 = 13{,}699 \text{ decoys.}$$

Similarly, if we made no decoys, a profit of $5000 could be obtained by producing this quantity of hangings:

$$5000/5.185 = 964 \text{ hangings.}$$

The line connecting these two intercepts shows all of the ways we can make a profit of $5000.

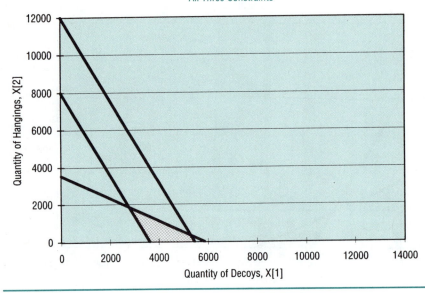

———————————————— **Figure 4.7** ————————————————

All Three Constraints

Graphical Solution
All Three Constraints

Next we consider all of the ways to make $2000 profit (again, $2000 is an arbitrary number). This can be accomplished by making:

2000/0.365 = 5479 decoys, if we made no hangings, or
2000/5.185 = 386 hangings, if we made no decoys.

The line connecting these two intercepts shows all of the ways we can make a profit of $2000. These two lines are shown in Figure 4.8. The line further away from the origin is the $5000 line; the line closer to the origin is the $2000 line. Note that the two lines are parallel to each other. From this we observe what mathematicians can prove:

As profit increases, the profit lines are further from the origin; and

All lines of equal profit are parallel to each other.

The next step is to place a profit line on the same graph as the feasible region. Combining the $5000 profit line from Figure 4.8 and the feasible region from Figure 4.7, we obtain Figure 4.9. Note that the profit line cuts through the feasible region. In Figure 4.8 we compared two profit lines. The higher profit line was further from the origin. If we found another profit line in Figure 4.9, profit lines further from the origin have higher profit. What profit line is furthest from the origin, yet still touches the feasible region? Because all lines of equal profit are parallel to each other, imagine moving the profit line (parallel to itself) further from the origin, until it just barely touches the feasible region. Visually, one can

Figure 4.8

Two Profit Lines: $5,000 and $2,000

Graphical Solution
Two Levels of Profit

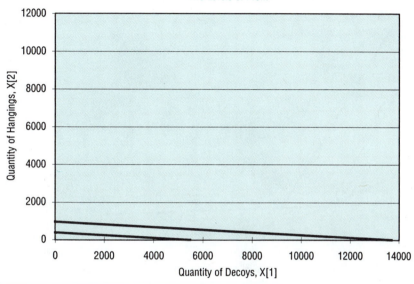

Figure 4.9

Feasible Region with $5,000 Profit Line

Graphical Solution
All Constraints and a Profit Line

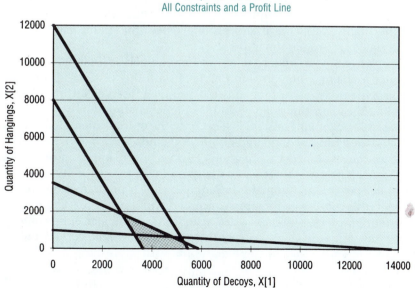

Figure 4.10

Optimal Solution

Graphical Solution
All Constraints and Best Profit Line

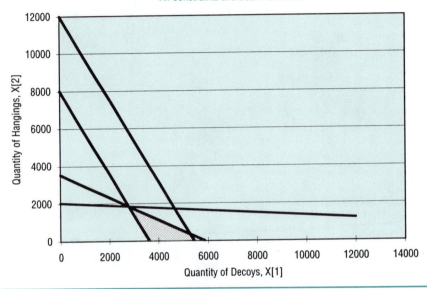

see that the upper left corner of the feasible region is the last point on the feasible region touched by the line of equal profit as we imagine sliding it further from the origin. This is shown in Figure 4.10. The optimal solution is at the point where the 4000 hour constraint and the lumber constraint intersect. Moving to a profit line further from the origin would not be feasible; moving to a profit line closer to the origin would have less profit. Hence, this point is the optimal solution to the linear programming problem.

The *simplex method* is widely used to obtain algebraic solutions to linear programming problems; the software provided with this text uses the simplex method to solve optimization problems that are diagnosed as linear. Although understanding the algorithmic details of the simplex method has no managerial importance, its logic provides useful insights into the optimization process. In an oversimplified description, the simplex method finds a corner of the feasible region. It then moves from corner to corner, always improving the profit, until it finds that every adjacent corner has a lower profit. Mathematicians can prove that this corner point is an optimal solution to the linear programming problem.

Although this chapter is primarily concerned with linear programming, this graphical solution process also provides insight into nonlinear optimization. If there are nonlinearities in the objective, the profit lines will be curved and may not be parallel to each other. If there are nonlinearities in the constraints, the constraints will appear as curved lines. Either of these changes may cause an optimal solution to be something other than a corner point. In linear programming, the search process can be limited to corner points on the boundary of the feasible region. In nonlinear programming, the search must consider the entire feasible region, not just the corner points and not just the boundaries. When nonlinearities are caused by discontinuous functions (such as @MAX, @ABS, @MIN, @VLOOKUP, @IF, and so on), the profit line and the feasible region may have sharp features that inhibit the search process. For these reasons, a future chapter (Chapter 10) discusses ways that some nonlinear problems can become linear.

Questions

The following questions give you an opportunity to think about whether there is a linear relationship between a decision variable and an objective or constraint variable. Discuss the linearity or nonlinearity of each of the relationships suggested by the situation.

a. *I sell each box of candy for $5.* **Decision:** *Number of Boxes of Candy.* **Objective:** *Revenue.*

> *Discussion:* Each unit change in Number of Boxes of Candy is accompanied by a $5 change in revenue. The relationship is linear.

b. *I sell each box of candy for $5, up to ten boxes; after that, I sell each box for $4.50.* **Decision:** *Number of Boxes of Candy.* **Objective:** *Revenue.*

> *Discussion:* The revenue change accompanying a unit change in the number of boxes of candy depends upon whether the number of boxes of candy is above or below ten. The relationship is nonlinear. Technically, it is called a "piecewise linear" relationship, because two straight line pieces describe the graph of revenue vs. boxes.

c. *Although I try to sell candy for $5 a box, I need to reduce the price just a little bit to sell each additional box. An economist once told me this means I have a "downward sloping demand curve."* **Decision:** *Number of Boxes of Candy.* **Objective:** *Revenue.*

> *Discussion:* Each box of candy that is sold brings in slightly less revenue than its predecessor, because of the slight price reduction. This is a nonlinear relationship.

d. *I'm deciding how many boxes of candy to order from my wholesaler. Each box is 100 cubic inches. I need to be able to fit all the candy I order in my closet, which has six cubic feet available.* **Decision:** *Order Quantity.* **Constraint:** *Closet Space Available.*

> *Discussion:* If we neglect the issue of the "fit" of the boxes in the closet (i.e., forget about problems arising when we try to fit a box 10" by 10" into a space 5" by 20"), a unit change in the number of boxes of candy is accompanied by a 100 cubic inch change in the amount of closet space used. The relationship is linear.

e. **Decision:** *Amount of Income to make next year.* **Constraint:** *Amount of Federal Income Tax I am willing to pay next year.*

> *Discussion:* The marginal tax rate increases with the amount of taxable income. The first dollar is tax free; later dollars are taxed at rates over 30

percent. This is a nonlinear relationship; more specifically, the amount of income tax paid is piecewise linear.

f. *Decision:* *Amount of Revenue to achieve for my retail store next year.* **Objective:** *Amount of State Sales Tax for my retail store next year.*

> *Discussion:* Typically, the sales tax rate is the same for sales of all levels. For example, the first dollar incurs a six cent tax liability; the millionth dollar also incurs a six cent tax liability. This is a linear relationship.

g. *A packaging consultant is designing a cylindrical package for bath salts.* **Decision:** *Diameter of the cylinder.* **Constraint:** *Amount of Material Used for the circular cylinder ends (the walls are made of a different material).*

> *Discussion:* You might recall from geometry class that the area of a circle is πr^2, "pi r squared." Increasing the radius from 1 to 2 changes the area of the circle from π to 4π, or an increase of 3π. Increasing the radius from 2 to 3 changes the area of the circle from 4π to 9π, or an increase of 5π. The amount of change in area accompanying a unit change in the decision variable depends upon the value of the decision variable; hence, the relationship is nonlinear.

h. *Decision:* *Amount of Funds to Invest in 8% bonds.* **Objective:** *Net Return from the 8% bonds.*

> *Discussion:* The relationship is linear because adding another bond to the portfolio makes the same change in return regardless of the number of bonds already in the portfolio.

i. *Decision:* *Amount of Funds to invest in 8% bonds.* **Objective:** *Net Return from the 8% bonds. Note: The bond broker uses a "sliding scale" for commissions: The rate of commission goes down as the purchase goes up.*

> *Discussion:* The introduction of the sliding scale for commission means that the return (net of commission) from the purchase of a small lot may be different from the net return from the purchase of a large lot. The large lot will have a lower commission rate per bond, so the relationship is nonlinear.

j. *Decision:* *Speed to drive.* **Constraint:** *Distance Required to Stop the car.*

> *Discussion:* From driving experience or from the tables you memorized when you took your last test for your driver's license, you know that doubling the speed more than doubles the stopping distance. This is a nonlinear relationship.

Exercises

Note: These problems provide practice in finding the mathematical formulation of an optimization problem, and investigating linearity from a mathematical and numerical standpoint. They are designed to reinforce the student's understanding of the traditional view of linear programming as a complement to the student's understanding of the spreadsheet view of optimization. The remainder of this text does not depend upon your ability to state an optimization problem in its traditional or mathematical form; rather, the expertise built into What's*Best!* is available for your use.

1. The DRP company makes two products, Standard and Deluxe. The Standard contributes $2 per unit to profit; the Deluxe contributes $3 per unit. There are two scarce resources: time and materials. Each Standard uses 2 hours of time and 3 pounds of material; each Deluxe uses 4 hours of time and 4 pounds of material. There are 500 hours available, and 600 pounds of material.

   a. Using X_1 and X_2 to represent the quantity of each product, state the expression that represents the DRP company's objective.

   b. State the relationship that must be satisfied if the proposed manufacturing quantities are feasible, as far as time is concerned.

   c. State the relationship that must be satisfied if the proposed manufacturing quantities are feasible, as far as materials are concerned.

   d. Are the relationships you have stated linear in form?

   e. Construct a graph with X_1 and X_2 as the axes. Plot the line that uses up all of the time. Plot a second line that uses up all of the materials. Identify the feasible region on your graph.

   f. On the graph you just constructed, plot a line that represents all of the ways DRP company can make a profit contribution of $150.

   g. Find the point on the graph that represents the optimal solution for DRP Company.

2. Construct an influence chart and a spreadsheet model for the DRP Company. This model should show the value of the objective and each constraint for any production plan that DRP may suggest.

   a. Use the model to construct a data table, showing the value of the objective and each constraint for 100 Standard and these values of quantity for Deluxe: 0, 10, 20, 30, 40, 50, 60, 70, 80, 90, and 100.

   b. Construct graphs showing the value of the objective and each constraint for the values of the quantity for Deluxe shown in (a) above. If your model and data table are correct, these lines should be straight.

   c. Use the spreadsheet model and optimization software to find the optimal solution to DRP's problem.

3. (This scenario is from the fence problem, Chapter 1 Exercise 2, and Chapter 3 Exercise 2.) A rectangular area is to be enclosed by a fence; the land owner wants as large an enclosed area as possible. The land owner has purchased 500 feet of fence and has constructed a spreadsheet model (shown in Chapter 3) to calculate the enclosed area and the perimeter (amount of fence) for a rectangle of any length and width. Now the landowner wants to view the problem mathematically, using the symbols L for Length and W for Width; L and W are the decision variables (instead of X_1 and X_2).

a. State the constraint (perimeter must not be more than 500 feet) in mathematical form. Is this a linear relationship?

b. State the objective (maximize area) in mathematical form. Is this a linear relationship?

c. Is this a linear programming problem? Compare your diagnosis with the diagnosis from What's Best!, using the optimization instructions you used for Exercise 2 Chapter 3.

4. (This scenario is from Chapter 1 Exercise 8, and Chapter 3 Exercise 4.) A manufacturer of hammers has two products, standard and deluxe. Each standard hammer contributes $4 to profit; each deluxe hammer contributes $7 to profit. Both hammers require metal and labor, in different quantities. A standard hammer requires 21 ounces of metal and 0.8 hours of labor. A deluxe hammer requires 18 ounces of metal and 1.1 hours of labor. For the planning period, no more than 20,000 ounces of metal or 950 hours of labor can be used. Obviously, more profit is preferred to less profit.

a. Using the symbols X_1 and X_2 for the decision variables, the quantity of standard hammers and the quantity of deluxe hammers, state the optimization problem in mathematical form.

b. If you want experience in graphical solution of linear programming problems, solve this problem graphically and compare it with the solution you obtained using What's Best!.

5. (This scenario is from Chapter 1 Exercise 9, and Chapter 3 Exercise 5.) Another manufacturer is making pliers. Each economy plier sells for $3 and requires 3 ounces of metal and 10 minutes of labor. Each standard plier sells for $4 and requires 7 ounces of metal and 12 minutes of labor. Each deluxe plier sells for $5 and requires 6 ounces of metal and 15 minutes of labor. No more than 1400 ounces of metal and 4000 minutes of labor can be used during the planning period. Each ounce of metal costs $0.04; each minute of labor costs $0.20. The manufacturer wants to maximize profit, which is the total revenue (price × quantity) less the cost of resources.

a. Find the objective coefficient for each economy plier. For this scenario, the objective coefficient is the contribution to profit, which is calculated as the revenue per unit, less the cost of the resources that each unit uses.

b. Find the objective coefficient for each standard plier and for each deluxe plier.

c. State the objective in mathematical form.

d. State the metal constraint in mathematical form.

e. State the labor constraint in mathematical form.

f. State the problem in "coefficient matrix" format, as shown in the text.

g. Is this a linear programming problem? Does your result agree with the diagnosis you obtained using What's Best! in solving Exercise 5 Chapter 3?

6. (This scenario is similar to Chapter 1 Exercise 10, and Exercise 6 Chapter 3.) You want to minimize the number of calories you consume from ice cream and cookies, but have "total satisfaction" of at least 100 "yums" and protein intake of at least 50 grams. Each serving of ice cream provides 40 yums and 25 grams of protein. Each cookie provides 50 yums and 15 grams of protein. Unfortunately, a serving of ice cream has 300 calories, and a cookie has 350 calories. You have no difficulty in eating a partial serving of ice cream or a partial cookie.

   a. State in mathematical form the optimization problem to plan your ice cream and cookie consumption for this situation. Use the symbols X_1 for the number of servings of ice cream, and X_2 for the number of cookies.

   b. If you want experience in graphical solution of linear programming problems, solve this problem graphically and compare it with the solution you obtained using What's *Best!*.

5

Managerial Information from Linear Programming

Optimizing the values of the decision variables on a spreadsheet provides obvious information for management; these optimized values of the decision variables make the objective as large (or small) as possible, without violating any of the constraints. In addition to the optimized decision variable values, the optimized spreadsheet shows the optimized value of each constraint cell, so that manager can see how close that optimized value is to the limit specified in the optimization instructions.

Managerial uses of optimization are seldom as exact as the optimized spreadsheet makes it appear. The model includes many assumptions; the manager is often interested in whether changes in these assumptions have a big impact on the decision suggested by optimization. Sometimes it is appropriate for management to introduce changes: obtain more resources, change a performance requirement, or change a price. What is the impact of these changes? Traditionally, management scientists have developed sophisticated methods to evaluate changes without solving the optimization problem once again. Because this information is available as a result of finding an optimal solution, the material described in this chapter is often called *postoptimality analysis*. Another common term is *duality*, from some mathematical history we won't explore here. Other common terms are *sensitivity analysis* and *ranging*. This chapter explores these ideas, and shows how What's *Best!* provides this information.

One of the advantages of managerial analysis with a spreadsheet is that it is easy to make a change, and immediately see the impact. This advantage carries over to optimization with a spreadsheet model. If there is a change, simply change the cell(s) involved and optimize again. Even though postoptimality analysis is designed for the traditional mathematical formulation of optimization problems, the information it provides can be very useful in guiding the analyst to try new ideas suggested by the results of optimization. The What's *Best!* menu, beginning with the **Dual** menu choice, provides extensive capabilities for post-optimality analysis.

Throughout this chapter we continue an assumption that has been made in our previous discussions: The decision variables are not limited to integer values; rather, fractional values are quite legitimate. In many decision situations, that assumption is perfectly correct. We can indeed refine any quantity of oil we want to; we aren't limited to refining whole numbers of barrels. Similarly, we can make any quantity of lotion we want.

There are other situations where the assumption that fractional values are acceptable isn't strictly true, but it is so close to reality that it doesn't matter. If we have decided that we will sell lotion in 5-oz. jars, we can't very well produce 1253.35 jars. However, the assumptions that went into the model that generated such a precise number aren't perfect. Our plans might very well be to make 1250 jars; whether we end up making 1250 or 1200 or 1300 jars will depend upon things like the number of machine breakdowns we have, the number of sick days employees have, and other factors that are not in our current planning project. In these situations there is no point in debating whether we really can make a fractional jar of lotion; we have no ability or desire to plan that closely anyway!

Our explanation of the managerial information that is available from optimization will be based upon the scenario of the Rangely Lakes Company, originally presented in Chapter 1. The complete scenario, as we will be discussing it, follows.

In early August, 1988, J. L. Duckworth began thinking about the winter activities of Rangely Lakes Company. J.L. was particularly concerned about the cash budgets for the winter, when revenue was quite limited. The other major concern J.L. was addressing was the need to keep the golf course maintenance staff busy during the winter. It appeared that there would be a need to have at least 4000 hours of work available during the winter; after discussing the winter plans with more employees, J.L. had concluded that no more than 6000 hours of employee time would be available during the winter season.

The Rangely Lakes Company operates a summer-only golf course in northern Maine. To keep the maintenance employees on the work-force during the winter, they have developed two "Maine Woods Souvenirs" made out of forest products from the Rangely Lakes area. For our purposes, they make two products: Mallard decoys and Mallard wall hangings. Both of these products are handmade; they have developed procedures so that skilled (but unartistic) maintenance workers can produce the two items. These souvenirs are marketed through numerous gift shops in New England. Rangely Lakes has priced the items attractively, so that they can sell all of the souvenirs they produce. From a budgeting standpoint, J. L. Duckworth needs to know how much profit would be generated from the souvenirs made during the winter. For planning purposes, J.L. calculated profit as revenue (price × quantity) less the cost of the wood used and the cost of the labor in the products.

Figure 5.1

Optimization Components for Rangely Lakes

Decision (Adjustable) Cells:	B2	Quantity[Decoy]
	C2	Quantity[Hanging]
Objective:	D12	*Maximize* Profit[Total]
Constraints	E6	Board Feet Used[Total] <= 17000
	E9	Hours Used[Total] >= 4000
	G9	Hours Used[Total] <= 6000

Most gift shops sell the Mallard decoy for $26.95 and the Mallard wall hanging for $34.95. Rangely Lakes sells to the gift shops at $12 and $15 respectively. The average labor content is 1.1 hours for a decoy and 0.5 hours for a wall hanging. Each labor hour costs Rangely Lakes $7.15, including fringe benefits. Although Rangely has some flexibility in the amount of labor it uses, it monitors labor usage very closely to be certain that enough production is planned to keep the workforce employed, without planning for more labor than reasonable expectations of availability.

The souvenirs are made from native lumber, carefully selected during the summer as forest operations are performed. Each decoy requires 2.9 board feet of this special lumber; each wall hanging requires 4.8 board feet. (A board foot is 144 cubic inches of lumber.) About 17,000 board feet will be available for the winter production season. The anticipated market price for the wood is about $1.30 per board foot.

Figure 5.1 shows the optimization components for Rangely Lakes. The optimized spreadsheet is shown in Figure 5.2. If the model completely represents the situation faced by J. L. Duckworth, the optimal plan is to produce about 2793 decoys and about 1853 Hangings. This will use up all of the lumber available, and will use exactly the 4000 hours of labor that Duckworth set as the minimum amount. The mathematics of linear optimization provides answers to several What If questions about changes in the optimization problem and its solution; although the answers to these hypothetical questions assume the optimization has been performed again, the power of the mathematics provides answers without actually solving the optimization again.

Marginal (or Dual) Value Associated with a Constraint

The optimization problem in Figures 5.1 and 5.2 has three constraints: We can't use more than 17,000 board feet of lumber; we must use at least 4000 hours of labor; we can't use more than 6000 hours of labor. We see from Figure 5.2 that two of these constraints are "binding" or have values at their limits; all of the lumber is being used, and the minimum number of hours is being used. The third constraint is not binding; we are not using as many labor hours as we have available. What happens if we make (small) changes in the limiting values of the constraint cells?

Figure 5.2

Optimized Spreadsheet for Rangely Lakes

	A	B	C	D	E	F	G	H
1		Decoy	Hanging	Total				
2	Quantity	2793.733	1853.785	4647.51				
3	Price	$12	$15					
4	Revenue	$33,525	$27,807	$61,332				
5								
6	Board Feet Used	8101.827	8898.171	16999.9	=<=	17000		
7	Cost of Lumber	$10,532	$11,568	$22,100				
8								
9	Hours Used	3073.107	926.8928	3999.99	=>=	4000	<=	6000
10	Cost of Labor	$21,973	$6,627	$28,600				
11								
12	Profit		$1,020	$9,612	$10,632			
13								
14	Board Feet per Item	2.9	4.8					
15	Hours per Item	1.1	0.5					
16								
17		Data						
18	Price per Board Foot	$1.30						
19	Price per Hour	$7.15						

Note: The contents of the constraint cells inserted by What'sBest! are:

E6:	@WB(D6,"<=",F6)	or	@WB.CON(D6,"<=",F6)
E9:	@WB(D9,"<=",F9)	or	@WB.CON(D9,"<=",F9)
G9:	@WB(D9,"<=",H9)	or	@WB.CON(D9,">=",H9)

It is easy to explain the impact of changing the limit on the maximum amount of labor available. If J. L. Duckworth explained that the upper limit on labor availability had changed from 6000 hours to (say) 6100 hours, you might require only a few seconds to respond, "so what?" That limit was "loose" in the optimal solution; we had unused or slack labor hours available. So if J.L. makes more labor available, we wouldn't change a thing. You won't make any more profit as a result of being able to use more labor, because you've already seen that you don't want to use all that you have. We can generalize this idea:

> If a constraint is not tight, changing the limiting value of that constraint (by a small amount) will not have any impact upon the optimal value of the objective.

If the constraint represents a resource (such as labor), we say that the marginal value of that resource is zero.

Things aren't so simple for limits of tight constraints. We specified that we had only 17,000 board feet of lumber available; the optimal solution uses all 17,000 board feet. So if J. L. Duckworth explained that the upper limit on lumber usage might go up a bit, you might become interested: There is economic value because lumber is a scarce resource. The optimization mathematics makes available to us a value called the *marginal value** associated with a constraint limit.

---

*In the technical literature, *marginal value* is given a variety of names. Among them are shadow price, dual value, and sea-jay minus zee-jay ($c_j - z_j$).

From What's*Best!* we will learn that the marginal value for the lumber constraint is $1.442. (Details about obtaining this value from What's*Best!* follow shortly.) This means that the next board foot of lumber, in excess of 17,000, has an economic value of $1.442. We can generalize the concept of a marginal value or dual value for a "less than or equal to" or a "greater than or equal to" constraint:

> The *marginal value* associated with a constraint is the amount the objective value would change (after optimization) if the constraint limit is increased by one unit, and all other resource limits stay the same. A positive marginal value indicates that increasing a constraint limit will increase the optimal value of the objective; a negative marginal value indicates that increasing a constraint limit will decrease the optimal value of the objective.

If the constraint represents a resource (such as lumber), the marginal value from the optimization process is the economic value of expanding the availability of a scarce resource. A resource that is not being fully utilized (that is, a resource whose constraint is not binding) is not really a scarce resource; hence, such a resource has no marginal value.

There is also a nonzero marginal value for the constraint stating that the number of hours used must be greater than or equal to 4000; that marginal value is −$3.469. This means that if the limit on this constraint is increased from 4000 units, profit (the objective) will change by −3.469 for each increase of one hour. As the minimum hour requirement goes up, profit goes down. In other words, we could make more money from the souvenir business if we didn't require the usage of 4000 hours, but that would be contrary to the reason for being in this business in the first place.

The concept of a marginal value is sometimes a puzzling one because we can't do anything with just 1 board foot of lumber or 1 hour of labor. But that ignores the fact that marginal values are calculated as if optimization has been performed again. It is as if we added a board foot of lumber, and *then we perform the optimization again*. Hence, the marginal value is based on the premise that everything will change as necessary to find the optimal value of the objective, when we change the limit of a constraint.

Obtaining Marginal (Dual) Values for Constraints

The What's*Best!* menu allows you to place the marginal values on the spreadsheet. The traditional term "dual value" is used on the menu. For Lotus 1-2-3, the steps to follow are:

1. Activate the What's*Best!* menu.
2. Choose **Dual**, then **Value** from the menu.
3. Follow the prompt "Enter range that you want the dual value of:" by highlighting the range as requested. Each cell in this range must be a constraint cell placed by What's*Best!* *Hint:* Recall that a constraint has several parts: the formula that is being constrained, which is the cell in the left-hand side of the constraint; the limiting value (or formula),

which is the right-hand side of the constraint; and the cell in which the @WB function is stored. This prompt refers to the cell in which the @WB function is stored.

4. Follow the prompt "Enter the range where you want the dual values put:" by highlighting the range to receive the dual values. Each cell in this range should be blank, because it will be erased when the dual values are placed in these cells. When the dual value is first requested, its value is zero until the optimization is solved once again.

For Quattro Pro 4, the steps to follow are:

1. Activate the What's*Best!* menu from the main menu.

2. From the What's*Best!* menu, choose **Dual**, then **Value**.

3. The constraint must be stored in a spreadsheet cell. The next prompt for this dual value is to place the cursor on the cell where you want the dual value information put, and then press [←Enter]. A special function, @WB.DUAL, will be stored in the cell you identify.

4. The final prompt is to enter the cell that you want the dual information on. Following the prompts and instruction on the screen, move the cell pointer to the cell containing the @WB.CON constraint function whose dual value you want, and press [←Enter] again. In this sequence of steps, screen messages will be cleared by any keystroke. Close attention to the screen will clarify whether a keystroke was taken as an entry or was simply interpreted as an instruction to clear a message from the screen. The message will be cleared as soon as another key is used, so read the entire message carefully before you strike aanother key.

Tip for Experienced Lotus 1-2-3 and Quatro Pro Users: The spreadsheet copy commands can be used to copy the cells containing the special @ functions which report the dual information. Suppose you want to put the dual value beneath a number of constraint cells (that is, just below the indicator, such as Not = or =<=). Use the solver commands to establish the first dual value reported by @WBDUAL or @WB.DUAL), then use spreadsheet copy commands to copy that cell to any cell just below a constraint cell.

Validity Range for Marginal Values

The marginal values as we have been describing them are based upon "small" changes in resource availability. Unfortunately, "small" has a definition that changes with each situation. Although the marginal value always shows the *rate* of change in the objective as the constraint limit is changed, that rate may be valid for a change of any amount between a trivial change (zero, for all practical purposes) and a very large change (increasing a resource manyfold). If the mathematical form of the problem is nonlinear, we can't determine the validity range for the marginal value without changing numbers on the spreadsheet and optimizing again. But when the problem is a linear optimization problem, the optimization software provides the validity range for the marginal values. The validity ranges are based on "upper range limit" and "lower range limit" values obtained from the optimization software. The upper range limit sets a limit on the amount the constraint can be increased without changing the marginal (dual) value. The lower range limit sets a limit on the amount the constraint can be decreased without changing the marginal (dual) value. These range limits have the following economic interpretations:

> The marginal value for Board Feet Used[Total] is $1.442. The upper range limit is 21,400. This means that the marginal value is unchanged as long as the constraint limit (17,000 board feet) is increased by as much as 21,400 board feet, to 17,000 + 21,400 = 38,400 board feet, *while all other constraint limits remain unchanged.*
>
> The lower range limit for Board Feet Used[Total] is 6454.5 board feet. The marginal value ($1.442) remains unchanged as long as the constraint limit (currently 17,000 board feet) is reduced by as much as 6455 board feet, to 17,000 − 6,455 = 10,545 board feet, *while all other constraint limits remain unchanged.*
>
> For the constraint setting a 4000 hour lower limit on Labor Hours[Total], the upper range limit for Labor Hours[Total] is 2000 hours. The marginal value is −$3.469. This marginal value remains unchanged as long as the constraint limit (4000 hours) is increased by no more than 2000 hours to 4000 + 2000 = 6000 hours. The lower range limit for this constraint is 2229 hours. If the constraint is decreased by no more than 2229 hours to 4000 − 2229 = 1771 hours, the marginal value is unchanged.
>
> The marginal value is $0 for the constraint requiring a 6,000 hour upper limit on Labor Hours[Total]. This marginal value remains unchanged as long as the constraint limit (6000 hours) is increased by any amount (shown as a very large number, such as 1.0E+20 on the spreadsheet). This marginal value also remains at a value of 0 if the constraint is decreased by as much as the lower range limit of 2000 hours, to 6000 − 2000 = 4000 hours, *while all other constraint limits remain unchanged.*

Obtaining Validity Ranges for Marginal (Dual) Values

The What's *Best!* keystrokes to find the validity range start with the What's *Best!* menu. The steps to find the upper range are listed below; the steps for the lower range are obviously similar. For Lotus 1-2-3:

1. Activate the What's *Best!* menu (typically, [Alt]+[F7]).
2. Choose **Dual**, then **Upper** from the menu.
3. Follow the prompt "Enter range that you want the Upper Ranges of:" by highlighting the range as requested. Each cell in this range should be a constraint cell placed by What's *Best!*
4. Follow the prompt "Enter the range where you want the Upper Ranges put:" by highlighting the range to receive the upper range values. Each

cell in this range should be blank, because it will be erased when the dual values are placed in these cells.

For Quattro Pro 4, the steps to follow are:

1. Activate the What's*Best!* menu from the main menu.

2. From the What's*Best!* menu, choose **Dual**, then **Upper** from the menu.

3. The upper range must be stored in a spreadsheet cell. The next prompt for this dual value is to place the cursor on the cell where you want the upper range information put, and then press [←Enter]. A special function, @WB.UPPER, will be stored in the cell you identify.

4. The final prompt is to enter the cell that you want the range information on. Following the prompts and instruction on the screen, move the cell pointer to the cell containing the @WB.CON constraint function whose range you want, and press [←Enter] again. In this sequence of steps, screen messages will be cleared by any keystroke. Close attention to the screen will clarify whether a keystroke was taken as an entry or was simply interpreted as an instruction to clear a message from the screen. The message will be cleared immediately by another keystroke, so read the entire message carefully before you strike another key.

What Does It Cost to Do Something Optimization Doesn't Recommend?

The Rangely Lakes optimization (Figure 5.2) recommended producing all (both) of the products; in more general terms, we could say that all activities should be undertaken, or that all decision variables have nonzero values. It is often managerially interesting to find out the consequences of producing a product that is not recommended by optimization. More generally, this is equivalent to undertaking an activity that is not in the optimal solution, or implementing a plan with a decision variable at a nonzero value when optimization has recommended it be at a zero value.

Obviously, the example needs to be changed to illustrate this point, because we don't have any nonzero decision values in the optimal solution shown in Figure 5.2. The validity range for the marginal value of lumber indicated that a new marginal value would appear at or above 38,400 board feet. If we change the lumber availability to 39,000 board feet, we find that it is no longer "optimal" to produce decoys. The optimal solution, with 39,000 board feet available, is shown in Figure 5.3.

The zero value for Quantity[Decoy] may cause problems for J. L. Duckworth. The product line is now incomplete; will the assumptions on which the model was constructed still be valid? How expensive (in terms of foregone profit, as measured by the model) would it be if we produced some decoys? Obviously, one way to address this issue is to constrain the value of Quantity[Decoy] to some lower bound. Optimizing the spreadsheet with this new requirement would answer the question.

Figure 5.3

Rnagely Lakes Optimal Solution with 39,000 Board Feet

	A	B	C	D	E	F	G	H
1		Decoy	Hanging	Total				
2	Quantity	0	8125	8125				
3	Price	$12	$15					
4	Revenue	$0	$121,875	$121,875				
5								
6	Board Feet Used	0	39000	39000	=<=	39000		
7	Cost of Lumber	$0	$50,700	$50,700				
8								
9	Hours Used	0	4062.5	4062.5	>=	4000	<=	6000
10	Cost of Labor	$0	$29,047	$29,047				
11								
12	Profit		$0	$42,128	$42,128			
13								
14	Board Feet per Item	2.9	4.8					
15	Hours per Item	1.1	0.5					
16								
17		Data						
18	Price per Board Foot	$1.30						
19	Price per Hour	$7.15						

Another approach is to use the dual value for the decision variable, Quantity [Decoy]. The dual value for Quantity[Decoy] shows what it would "cost" to "admit" decoys into the plan. The dual value for Quantity[Decoy] is $2.7676; this means that "admitting" decoys into the plan would reduce profit at the rate of $2.7676 for each decoy we choose to manufacture.

We need to generalize the concept of the cost of admission. Because there is no widely-used nontechnical term for this concept, we will continue to use the term *cost of admission** with this definition:

> For a decision variable whose optimized value is zero, the *cost of admission* is the rate at which the value of the objective will deteriorate if the decision variable is admitted into the solution. For a profit maximization problem, the cost of admission shows the profit *reduction* that will accompany a change in the value of the decision variable from 0 to 1. For a cost minimization problem, the cost of admission shows the cost *increase* that will accompany a change in the value of the decision variable from 0 to 1. (This assumes that one unit of the decision variable is within the validity range for the cost of admission.)

The cost of admission is one way a manager can utilize a model that is known to be somewhat different from reality. Although it is well known that product synergy often makes a product line more profitable than unrelated individual products would be, it is difficult to state these relationships in a model. In the unusual situation in which the relationships are understood well enough to include in the model, a nonlinear model would almost certainly be the result. If the manager builds the model as if there were no product synergy, the "optimal"

---

*Technical terms for the *cost of admission* include *reduced cost* and *dual value*.

Figure 5.4

Solution Report for Rangely Lakes with 17,000 Board Feet (From Figure 5.2)

OBJECTIVE CELL:

CELL ADDRESS	VALUE	INITIAL VALUE	TYPE
D12	10631.59	14240	MAX

ADJUSTABLE CELLS:

CELL ADDRESS	VALUE	INITIAL VALUE	TYPE	DUAL VALUE
B2	2793.734	3500	>	0
C2	1853.786	2500	>	0

CONSTRAINT CELLS:

CELL ADDRESS	VALUE	TYPE	DUAL VALUE	UPPER RANGE	LOWER RANGE	FORMULA
E6	0	<	1.441514	21400	6454.545	D6,<=,F6
E9	0	>	-3.468538	2000	2229.167	D9,>=,F9
G9	2000	<	0	+Inf	2000	D9,<=,H9

---

solution to that model is known to be nonoptimal because synergy has been ignored. However, it can be subjectively included into the manager's decision by using the concept of cost of admission to decide whether it appears the benefits of including the product are worth the cost of admission.

Finding the Cost of Admission
(Dual Value for a Decision Variable)

The dual value for a decision (adjustable) variable is the cost of admission, if that decision variable has an optimal value of zero. Its value is found by using the What's *Best!* menu choice **Dual Value**, and responding to the prompts to identify the the decision variable whose dual value is desired, and where this value is to be stored on the spreadsheet.

The What's*Best!* Solution Report

What's *Best!* can produce a solution report, which shows the components of the optimization problem (decision variables, constraints, and objective), all marginal values and their validity ranges, and the values for the cost of admission. To obtain this report, these What's *Best!* menu selections are chosen: **Report, Solution, Enable**. Then respond to the prompts to give the report file a name (by default, WBSOLN.PRN) and a cell to store the file name. After the optimization problem is solved (and after enabling the report), a text file is created with the name assigned for the report. This text file may be:

Figure 5.5

Solution Report for Rangely Lakes with 39,000 Board Feet (From Figure 5.3)

OBJECTIVE CELL:

CELL ADDRESS	VALUE	INITIAL VALUE	TYPE
D12	42128.13	10631.59	MAX

ADJUSTABLE CELLS:

CELL ADDRESS	VALUE	INITIAL VALUE	TYPE	DUAL VALUE
B2	0	2793.734	>	2.767604
C2	8125	1853.786	>	0

CONSTRAINT CELLS:

CELL ADDRESS	VALUE	TYPE	DUAL VALUE	UPPER RANGE	LOWER RANGE	FORMULA
E6	0	<	1.080208	18600	600	D6, <=, F6
E9	62.5	>	0	62.5	+Inf	D9, >=, F9
G9	1937.5	<	0	+Inf	1937.5	D9, <=, H9

---

printed using DOS commands or a word processor,

imported into a spreadsheet using spreadsheet commands, or

retrieved onto the spreadsheet with the menu options, **Report**, **Solution**, **Retrieve**.

If you retrieve the report into the spreadsheet, follow the instructions at the top of the report to return to the model. (*Tip for advanced spreadsheet users:* This text file is placed in the same directory as your spreadsheet software, unless you specify a path name along with the file name.)

The solution reports are shown in Figure 5.4 for the optimized spreadsheets shown in Figure 5.2 and in Figure 5.5 for Figure 5.3 The information labeled Value for a constraint is the amount of slack in that constraint. (Although the solution report may give range information for dual values for adjustable cells, this information is not particularly useful.)

Exercises

1. Exercises 1(a) through 1(f) ask you to make changes in the constraint limit values specified in the optimization problem. After you make each change, perform the optimization again. Then you are to verify that changes in the objective value are in accordance with the predictions of the marginal values and the validity range for the marginal values.

   a. Using optimization with your spreadsheet model for Rangely Lakes, show that increasing the lumber available from 17,000 board feet to

17,001 board feet increases the profit by $1.442. *Note:* It may be necessary to change the display format of the worksheet objective cell in order to verify all of the decimals in the change.

b. Using optimization with your spreadsheet model for Rangely Lakes, show that increasing the lumber available from 17,000 board feet to 18,000 board feet increases the profit by 1000 × $1.442, or $1442.

c. Using optimization with your spreadsheet model for Rangely Lakes, show that increasing the lumber available from 17,000 board feet to 117,000 board feet does *not* increase the profit by 100,000 × $1.442. Explain how this could have been predicted by using the validity range for the marginal value.

d. Using optimization with your spreadsheet model for Rangely Lakes, show that increasing the minimum requirement on labor usage from 4000 hours to 4001 hours decreases the profit by $3.469.

e. Using optimization with your spreadsheet model for Rangely Lakes, verify the validity range for the marginal value for reducing the 4000 hour minimum labor usage constraint. Note that the upper range for the dual value is 2000 hours to a new value of 6000 hours available. The lower range for the dual value is 2229 hours to a new value of 1771 hours available. Perform this verification by making a change in the minimum labor usage limit to 1900 hours and showing that the marginal value (−3.468) multiplied by the amount of change in the limit (−2100) is equal to the change in the objective. Then make a change in the minimum labor usage to 1500 hours and show that the marginal value multiplied by the amount of change in the limit is *not* equal to the change in the objective. You may need to use data precise to several decimals for your calculations.

f. Using optimization with your spreadsheet model for Rangely Lakes, verify that there is no marginal value associated with changing the labor availability (from 6000 hours) to various values between 4000 hours and (say) 1,000,000 hours.

2. Change the optimization specifications for the Rangely Lakes problem so that 39,000 board feet of lumber are available; optimize the spreadsheet. Then introduce a constraint requiring a lower bound of 1 on the quantity of decoys. Show that the change in profit is consistent with the cost of admission identified in the solution report in Figure 5.5.

3. Change the availability of lumber to 60,000 board feet. Interpret the meaning of all values of cost of admission and marginal values that are obtained from the solution report.

4. Interpret the complete solution report for the Sunsoak case, described at the end of Chapter 1 and optimized in Exercise 10 Chapter 3.

5. Interpret the complete solution report for the diet problem described at the end of Chapter 1 and optimized in Exercise 6 Chapter 3.

6

Examples of
Optimization Models

Modeling is both an art and a science; it is improved through practice. Hence, the purpose of this chapter is to present several situations where modeling and optimization can support managerial decisions. The purpose of these illustrations is to show diverse uses of modeling for optimization, and to give the student an opportunity to practice modeling skills by constructing the models described in this chapter.

Example 1: Developing a New Product

Citrimagination is a small but growing food processor in central Florida. Their newest creation is an orange cheesecake to be sold to tourists at citrus stands, T-shirt stores, souvenir stores, and similar outlets. A particularly important part of the marketing appeal of the product is that it will be sold as a nutritionally sound product; the use of fresh fruit, Florida-grown sugar, and cottage cheese from Florida dairy herds are all part of the image the product will carry. An intriguing part of the product is a novel use of citrus by-products (pulp for texture and small amounts of rind for flavoring) and flour to create a new crust for the cheesecake. Avoidance of eggs and cream or condensed milk will substantially reduce the cholesterol count. In fact, some people who taste the product think it has a chance of becoming the "light choice" to join key lime pie as a famous Florida dessert.

There are some important restrictions in ingredient usage, in order to keep the product tasty and apparently nutritionally sound. The basic recipe to be developed is for a 1-kilogram cheesecake, which is called the standard cake; the same recipe will be used in smaller proportions for other sizes. In deciding how

─────────────────────────────── **Figure 6.1** ───────────────────────────────

Costs and Nutritional Values for Citrimagination

	Flour	Sugar	Cottage Cheese	Oranges	Citrus By-Products
Calories per 100 grams	365	385	105	35	—
Grams of protein per 100 grams	10	—	15	1	—
Grams of fat per 100 grams	1	—	5	—	—
Carbohydrate per 100 grams	70	100	3	10	—
Cost ($) per 100 grams	0.15	0.17	0.22	0.04	0.01

many hundred-grams of each ingredient to include in a standard cake, the following restrictions for a standard cake have been proposed:

No more than 1500 calories (150 calories for a 100-gm serving);

At least 80 grams of protein;

No more than 30 grams of fat;

No more than 300 grams of carbohydrate.

There must be between 50 and 200 grams of flour.

There must be between 150 and 400 grams of sugar.

There must be between 250 and 500 grams of cottage cheese.

There must be between 200 and 600 grams of oranges.

There must be between 20 and 30 grams of citrus byproducts, which are nutritionally insignificant.

The economic factors for each ingredient fluctuate from year to year, and from month to month within a year. However, the standard cake will be designed with the costs and nutritional values shown in Figure 6.1.

Although the manager of Citrimagination eventually wants to invent the recipe that will minimize the cost of making a standard cake, the first step is to build an influence chart that will show (for any recipe) the items of management concern:

To determine if the recipe is nutritionally sound, management must know:

the calorie count in a standard cake (CALORIES);
the amount of protein in a standard cake (PROTEIN);
the amount of fat in a standard cake (FAT); and
the amount of carbohydrates in a standard cake (CARBOHYDRATES).

To determine the economic desirability of the recipe, management must know:

the cost of a standard cake made with the recipe (COST).

Each ingredient must be kept within the range of consumer acceptance.

—————————————— **Figure 6.2** ——————————————

Partial Influence Chart for Calories for Citrimagination

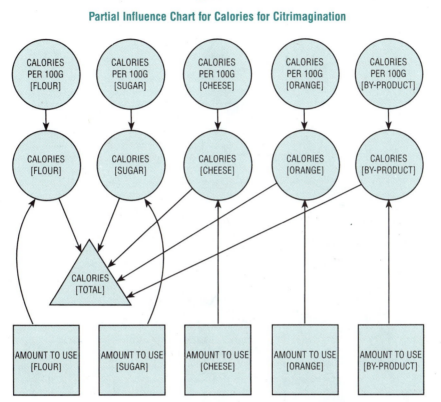

Before going any further, let's talk about units of measurement. It is common for nutritional information to be published in terms of 100 grams of the ingredient. Using this vocabulary makes it easier to communicate with people interested in the nutritional aspects of the product. When we talk about the amount of flour to use in a cake, we'll be measuring in 100-gram units; if we say that AMOUNT TO USE [FLOUR] = 2, we mean to use 2 of these 100-gram measures, or 200 grams of flour.

Let's first look at the CALORIES portion of the influence chart, shown in Figure 6.2. The CALORIES [TOTAL] value is of managerial interest, because there are limits on the total number of calories in a standard cake. This is a constraint placed on the design of the cake, so it is shown as a triangle on the influence chart. There are five values that influence CALORIES [TOTAL]: the calories from flour, CALORIES [FLOUR]; the calories from sugar, CALORIES [SUGAR], and so on for each of the five ingredients. Each of these calorie values is influenced by two values: the amount used of the ingredient, and the calories per 100 grams for the ingredient. Using flour as an example, this is shown on the influence chart: CALORIES [FLOUR] is influenced by AMOUNT TO USE [FLOUR] and by CALORIES PER 100G [FLOUR].

Figure 6.3

Influence Chart for Citrimagination

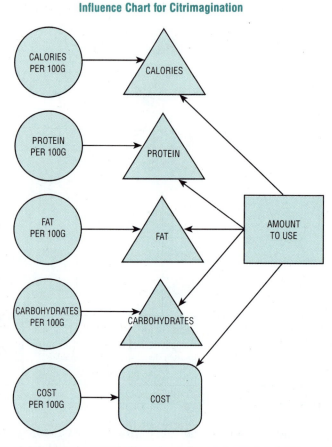

Although this detailed partial influence chart clearly shows the relationships in the model to be constructed, constructing a complete influence chart with this much detail would take a lot more effort than constructing the model. The diagram has five distinct columns, one for each ingredient. This is suggestive of the spreadsheet design: one worksheet column for each ingredient, and another column for the totals. If we simplify the influence chart, and allow the word CALORIES to represent the calories supplied by each ingredient as well as the total calories in a standard cake, the influence chart becomes useful and simple. This simplified influence chart is shown in Figure 6.3.

From this influence chart, the worksheet shown in Figure 6.4 can be constructed. As with all worksheets for optimization, we start with an arbitrary set of values for the decision variables, because optimization will be used to set their final values. However, starting with nonzero values gives us the ability to see the numbers that result from the logic of the spreadsheet.

Figure 6.4

Citrimagination Worksheet

	A	B	C	D	E	F	G	H	I
1		Flour	Sugar	Cheese	Orange	By-Prod	Total		Limit
2	Amt to Use	1	2	3	4	1	11	Not =	10
3									
4	WB Constraint	>=	>=	>=	>=	>=			
5	Lower Limit	0.5	1.5	2.5	2	0.2			
6									
7	WB Constraint	<=	<=	<=	<=	Not <=			
8	Upper Limit	2	4	5	6	0.3			
9									
10	Calories	365	770	315	140	0	1590	Not <=	1500
11	Protein	10	0	45	4	0	59	Not >=	80
12	Fat	1	0	15	0	0	16	<=	30
13	Carbos	70	200	9	40	0	319	Not <=	300
14	Cost	0.15	0.34	0.66	0.16	0.01	1.32		
15									
16	Calories per 100g	365	385	105	35	0			
17	Protein per 100g	10	0	15	1	0			
18	Fat per 100g	1	0	5	0	0			
19	Carbos per 100g	70	100	3	10	0			
20	Cost per 100g	0.15	0.17	0.22	0.04	0.01			

There are some additions to the worksheet that make this worksheet easier to use. We can add some rows underneath the Amt to Use section that show the managerially imposed upper and lower limits on the ingredients (rows 5 and 8). In the spreadsheet, there is space for the What's*Best!* constraints in rows 4 and 7 for the lower and upper limits. We also include column I showing the limit on each nutrient, and leave space for these constraints in column H. Of course, the constraints could be placed anywhere on the spreadsheet; it makes sense to put the constraints and limits near the cells being constrained. (On the other hand, if you were working with a spreadsheet that had been designed without What's*Best!* optimization in mind, you might choose to leave the spreadsheet unchanged, and place all constraints and limits in one section of the spreadsheet, such as below all other information.) The documentation for this model is shown in Figure 6.5. (The model shows the constraints stored by What's*Best!*, which will be discussed shortly. The documentation ignores these constraints.)

From the completed model, we can state the components of the optimization problem:

Decision Variables:

Amt to Use[Flour]
Amt to Use[Sugar]
Amt to Use[Cheese]
Amt to Use[Orange]
Amt to Use[By—Prod]

───────────── **Figure 6.5** ─────────────

Documentation of Worksheet for Citrimagination

```
Amt to Use[Flour THRU By-Prod] = 1, 2, 3, 4, 1
Amt to Use[Total] = SUM (Amt to Use[Flour] THRU Amt to Use[By-Prod])

Lower Limit[Flour THRU Total] = 0.5, 1.5, 2.5, 2, 0.2, 10
Upper Limit[Flour THRU Total] = 2, 4, 5, 6, 0.3, 10

Calories[Flour THRU By-Prod] = Amt to Use * Calories per 100g
Calories[Total] = SUM (Calories[Flour] THRU Calories[By-Prod])
Calories[Limit] = 1500

Protein[Flour THRU By-Prod] = Amt to Use * Protein per 100g
Protein[Total] = SUM (Protein[Flour] THRU Protein[By-Prod])
Protein[Limit] = 80

Fat[Flour THRU By-Prod] = Amt to Use * Fat per 100g
Fat[Total] = SUM (Fat[Flour] THRU Fat[By-Prod])
Fat[Limit] = 30

Carbos[Flour THRU By-Prod] = Amt to Use * Carbos per 100g
Carbos[Total] = SUM (Carbos[Flour] THRU Carbos[By-Prod])
Carbos[Limit] = 300

Cost[Flour THRU By-Prod] = Amt to Use * Cost per 100g
Cost[Total] = SUM (Cost[Flour] THRU Cost[By-Prod])
```

Constraints:

Amt to Use[Flour]	*between*	0.5 *and* 2
Amt to Use[Sugar]	*between*	1.5 *and* 4
Amt to Use[Cheese]	*between*	2.5 *and* 5
Amt to Use[Orange]	*between*	2 *and* 6
Amt to Use[By-Prod]	*between*	0.2 *and* 0.3
Amt to Use[Total]	=	10
Calories[Total]	<=	1500
Protein[Total]	>=	80
Fat[Total]	<=	30
Carbos[Total]	<=	300

Objective:

   Minimize Cost[Total]

Some Tips About Using What's*Best!*

The constraints on the usage of each ingredient are shown as "between" constraints. These require two sets of constraints: The Amt to Use for each of the five ingredients must be greater than or equal to the lower limit for that ingredient, and less than or equal to its upper limit.

Tip for Lotus 1-2-3 Users: The requirement that the AMT TO USE for each ingredient must be greater than or equal to the lower limit can be specified in one operation. Using the What's*Best!* menu **Constrain** selection, select cells B2..F2 as the cells to constrain. From the menu, select

Greater than. Then select the range B5..F5 as the constraining limits. Identify the storage cells as B4..F4 (or more simply as B4).

Tip for Quattro Pro Users: The requirement that the AMT TO USE for each ingredient must be greater than or equal to the lower limit can be specified one cell at a time, following the menu prompts, selecting **W B!**, then **Constraints**, then **Greater than**. The cell to put the constraint is identified, the constrained cell is identified, and the constraining limit is identified. For example, in cell B4 we place the constraint that B2 >= 5. The easiest way to identify the rest of the lower limit constraints is to exit the menu [Esc], then use the spreadsheet **Edit Copy** command to copy B4 to the block C4..F4.

Each spreadsheet cell storing a constraint displays the type of constraint.If the constraint is not satisfied, the indicator "Not" appears before the relation. If it is exactly satisfied (often called *tight*), an equality sign appears before the relation. In similar fashion, the upper limits may be identified.

It is left as an exercise to construct the model, fill in the optimization instructions for What's *Best!*, and find the values for the decision variables that yield a minimum ingredient cost per standard cake of $1.5036.

Example 2: Setting Production Quantities

Chris Hadley, a recent graduate of a leading business school, has developed several new paper products that are sold to souvenir stores throughout tourist areas. Each item requires cutting, printing, and folding on specialized equipment. Chris arranged with a large printing company to rent time during slack periods; unfortunately, there was not enough time available to meet all of the anticipated demand in Chris's plans. For the four items in the product line, Chris believed that there would be no difficulty in selling quantities within production capabilities at these prices:

Product A	$5
Product B	$7
Product C	$3.25
Product D	$3

Manufacturing each of the products required all three operations: cutting, printing, and folding. The printing company equipment had these hourly production capacities, shown in units per hour for each product in each piece of equipment:

	Cutting	Printing	Folding
Product A	1000	4000	500
Product B	2000	1000	350
Product C	4000	1000	750
Product D	3000	3000	600

Figure 6.6

Influence Chart for Chris's Printing Business

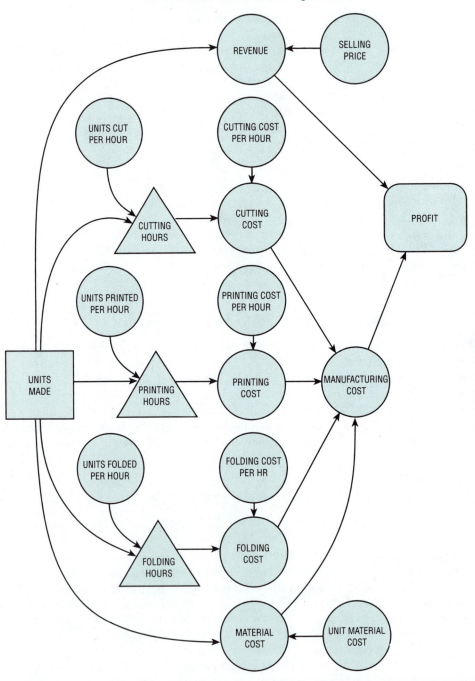

Figure 6.7

Worksheet Model for Chris Hadley (Arbitrary Decision Values)

	A	B	C	D	E	F	G	H
		Prod A	Prod B	Prod C	Prod D	Total	Constr	Limit
1								
2	Units Made	100	1000	2000	3000			
3	Low Lmt Constraint	Not >=	=>=	>=	>=			
4	Lower Limit	1000	1000	1000	1000			
5								
6	Selling Price	5	7	3.25	3			
7	Revenue	500	7000	6500	9000			
8								
9	Units Cut per Hr	1000	2000	4000	3000			
10	Cutting Hours	0.1	0.5	0.5	1	2.1	<=	12
11	Cutting Cost per Hr	100						
12	Cutting Cost	10	50	50	100			
13								
14	Units Printed per Hr	4000	1000	1000	3000			
15	Printing Hours	0.025	1	2	1	4.025	<=	20
16	Printing Cost per Hr	200						
17	Printing Cost	5	200	400	200			
18								
19	Units Folded per Hr	500	350	750	600			
20	Folding Hours	0.2	2.8571	2.6666	5	10.723	<=	30
21	folding Cost per Hr	300						
22	Folding Cost	60	857.14	800	1500			
23								
24	Unit Material Cost	0.3	0.3	0.3	0.3			
25	Material Cost	30	300	600	900			
26								
27	Manufacturing Cost	105	1407.1	1850	2700			
28								
29	Profit	395	5592.8	4650	6300	16937.		

The agreement with the printer required Chris to pay for time used, and also set limits on the number of hours available:

Cutting	$100 per hour	12 hours available
Printing	$200 per hour	20 hours available
Folding	$300 per hour	30 hours available

The raw materials for each product are $0.30 per unit, for any of the four products. In order to present a balanced product line, Chris believed that it was necessary to make at least a thousand units of each of the four products.

Chris knew that the only costs that depended upon the quantity made for each item were the manufacturing costs already considered: cutting cost, printing cost, folding cost, and material cost. Although there were substantial selling and administrative expenses, these overhead cost items were not influenced by the production quantity. Hence, what Chris wanted to do was find the quantity to produce for each product, to make the profit contribution (revenue less manufacturing cost) as large as possible. But it was important not to plan more machine usage than the printing company would be able to make available.

Figure 6.8

Documentation for Chris Hadley's Model (Shown in Figure 6.7)

Units Made[Prod A THRU Prod D] are decision variables
Low Lmt Constraint row is inserted using What'sBest!
Lower Limit[Prod A THRU PROD D] = 1000 (data values)
Selling Price[Prod A THRU Prod D] are data values

Revenue[Prod A THRU Prod D] = Units Made * Selling Price

Units Cut per Hr[Prod A THRU Prod D] are data values

Cutting Hours[Prod A THRU Prod D] = Units Made / Units Cut per Hr
Cutting Hours[Total] = SUM (Cutting Hours[Prod A] THRU Cutting Hours[Prod D])
Cutting Hours[Constraint] is inserted using What'sBest!
Cutting Hours[Limit] = 12 (a data value)

Cutting Cost per Hr[Prod A] = 100 (a data value applying to all products)

Cutting Cost[Prod A THRU Prod D] = Cutting Hours * Cutting Cost per Hr[Prod A]

Units Printed per Hr[Prod A THRU Prod D] are data values

Printing Hours[Prod A THRU Prod D] = Units Made / Units Printed per Hr
Printing Hours[Total] = SUM (Printing Hours[Prod A] THRU Printing Hours[Prod D])
Printing Hours[Constraint] is inserted using What'sBest!
Printing Hours[Limit] = 20 (a data value)

Printing Cost per Hr[Prod A] = 200 (a data value applying to all products)

Printing Cost[Prod A THRU Prod D] = Printing Hours * Printing Cost per Hr[Prod A]

Units Folded per Hr[Prod A THRU Prod D] are data values

Folding Hours[Prod A THRU Prod D] = Units Made / Units Folded per Hr
Folding Hours[Total] = SUM (Folding Hours[Prod A] THRU Folding Hours[Prod D])
Folding Hours[Constraint] is inserted using What'sBest!
Folding Hours[Limit] = 30 (a data value)

Folding Cost per Hr[Prod A] = 300 (a data value applying to all products)

Folding Cost[Prod A THRU Prod D] = Folding Hours * Folding Cost per Hr[Prod A]

Unit Material Cost[Prod A THRU Prod D] = 0.3 (data values)

Material Cost[Prod A THRU Prod D] = Units Made * Unit Material Cost

Manufacturing Cost[Prod A THRU Prod D] = Cutting Cost + Printing Cost + Folding Cost + Material Cost

Profit[Prod A THRU Prod D] = Revenue – Manufacturing Cost
Profit[Total] = SUM (Profit[Prod A] THRU Profit[Prod D])

To get started on an influence chart, Chris outlined the items that would be necessary to evaluate any production plan:

> The contribution to profit
> The number of cutting hours used
> The number of printing hours used
> The number of folding hours used

With values for these items, Chris could evaluate any proposed production plan. The influence chart for Chris might appear as shown in Figure 6.6. Again, this influence chart makes no distinction between the various columns; the term PRINTING HOURS refers to the values for Printing Hours[Prod A], Printing Hours [Prod B], Printing Hours[Prod C], Printing Hours[Prod D], and Printing Hours [Total]. Yet this imprecise influence chart is a very useful aid for constructing the model. The worksheet model, before optimization, is shown in Figure 6.7. This worksheet includes the symbols corresponding to the information added with What's*Best!*. The documentation is shown in Figure 6.8. The student is encouraged to construct the model, perform the necessary optimization, and find the values for Units Made that generate the optimal profit of $57,638.

Example 3: Process Selection

A manufacturer of amusement devices has a contract to produce 5000 electronic amusement devices. There are three ways these units can be manufactured:

Figure 6.9

Influence Chart for Amusement Devices Process Selection

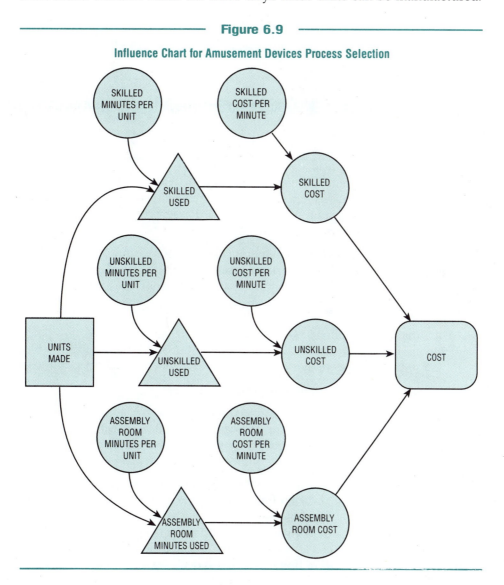

Figure 6.10

Worksheet Model for Amusement Devices Process Selection

	A	B	C	D	E	F	G
1	Amusement Devices						
2		Hand	Semi-Aut	Robotic	Total	Constr	Limit
3	Units Made	2000	4000	0	6000	Not =	5000
4							
5	Skilled Min per Unit	1	4	8			
6	Skilled Used	2000	16000	0	18000	<=	25000
7	Skilled Cost per Min	0.4					
8	Skilled Cost	800	6400	0			
9							
10	Unskilled Min per Unit	40	30	20			
11	Unskilled Used	80000	120000	0	200000	Not <=	140000
12	Unskilled Cost per Min	0.25					
13	Unskilled Cost	20000	30000	0			
14							
15	Asmby Room Min per Unit	3	2.5	4			
16	Asmby Room Min Used	6000	10000	0	16000	<=	20000
17	Asmby Room Cost per Min	4.25					
18	Asmby Room Cost	25500	42500	0			
19							
20	Cost	46300	78900	0	125200		

---

with hand assembly, semiautomated assembly, or with robotic assembly. Any of the assembly processes requires three types of resources: skilled labor, unskilled labor, and assembly room time. Hand assembly of one unit requires these resources:

- 1 minute of skilled labor, at a unit cost of $0.40 per minute
- 40 minutes of unskilled labor, at a unit cost of $0.25 per minute
- 3 minutes of assembly room time, at a unit cost of $4.25 per minute

Semiautomatic assembly of one unit requires these resources:

- 4 minutes of skilled labor, at a unit cost of $0.40 per minute
- 30 minutes of unskilled labor, at a unit cost of $0.25 per minute
- 2.5 minutes of assembly room time, at a unit cost of $4.25 per minute

Robotic assembly of one unit requires these resources:

- 8 minutes of skilled labor, at a unit cost of $0.40 per minute
- 20 minutes of unskilled labor, at a unit cost of $0.25 per minute
- 4 minutes of assembly room time, at a unit cost of $4.25 per minute

There are limits of 25,000 minutes of skilled labor available, 140,000 minutes of unskilled labor available, and 20,000 minutes of assembly room available. It has been proposed to make 2000 units with hand assembly and 4000 units with semiautomatic assembly, because these are the lowest-cost production methods. (Somebody really goofed here; this would produce too many units. Optimization will cure that problem, because cost minimization will be accomplished only when the required number of units are produced.)

Figure 6.11

Worksheet Documentation for Amusement Devices (Shown in Figure 6.10)

```
Units Made[Hand] = 2000
Units Made[Semi-Aut] = 4000
Units Made[Robotic] = 0
Units Made[Total] = SUM (Units Made[Hand] THRU Units Made[Robotic])
Units Made[Constraint] is inserted using What'sBest!
Units Made[Limit] = 5000

Skilled Min per Unit[Hand] = 1
Skilled Min per Unit[Semi-Aut] = 4
Skilled Min per Unit[Robotic] = 8

Skilled Used[Hand THRU Robotic] = Units Made * Skilled Min per Unit
Skilled Used[Total] = SUM (Skilled Used[Hand] THRU Skilled Used[Robotic])
Skilled Used[Constraint] is inserted using What'sBest!
Skilled Used[Limit] = 25000

Skilled Cost per Min[Hand] = 0.4 Note: Applies to all Processes

Skilled Cost[Hand THRU Robotic] = Skilled Used * Skilled Cost per Min[Hand]

Unskilled Min per Unit[Hand] = 40
Unskilled Min per Unit[Semi-Aut] = 30
Unskilled Min per Unit[Robotic] = 20

Unskilled Used[Hand THRU Robotic] = Units Made * Unskilled Min per Unit
Unskilled Used[Total] = SUM (Unskilled Used[Hand] THRU Unskilled Used[Robotic])
Unskilled Used[Constraint] is inserted using What'sBest!
Unskilled Used[Limit] = 140000

Unskilled Cost per Min[Hand] = 0.25 Note: Applies to all Processes

Unskilled Cost[Hand THRU Robotic] = Unskilled Used * Unskilled Cost per Min[Hand]

Asmby Room Min per Unit[Hand] = 3
Asmby Room Min per Unit[Semi-Aut] = 2.5
Asmby Room Min per Unit[Robotic] = 4

Asmby Room Min Used[Hand THRU Robotic] = Units Made * Asmby Room Min per Unit
Asmby Room Min Used[Total] = SUM (Asmby Room Min Used[Hand] THRU Asmby Room Min Used[Robotic])
Asmby Room Min Used[Constraint] is inserted using What'sBest!
Asmby Room Min Used[Limit] = 20000

Asmby Room Cost per Min[Hand] = 4.25 Note: Applies to all Processes

Asmby Room Cost[Hand THRU Robotic] = Asmby Room Min Used * Asmby Room Cost per Min[Hand]

Cost[Hand THRU Robotic] = Skilled Cost + Unskilled Cost + Asmby Room Cost
Cost[Total] = SUM (Cost[Hand] THRU Cost[Robotic])
```

To evaluate the proposed plan with a spreadsheet model, the manager needs to know the total units made, the cost of the plan, and whether there are sufficient amounts of skilled labor, unskilled labor, and assembly room time. An influence chart showing these values is shown in Figure 6.9. A worksheet model with the proposed plan is shown in Figure 6.10. Note that limiting values have been inserted in the model. What's*Best!* has also been used to insert the constraints, which appear on the spreadsheet as <=, >=, or =. If the symbol is preceded by Not, it is not satisfied (violated). If it is preceded by the equality sign, the constraint is exactly satisfied (tight). As decision variables are adjusted either by the user or by What's*Best!*, the information displayed by the constraint cell changes to reflect the current values of the decision variables. The model's documentation is shown in Figure 6.11. The reader is encouraged to construct the spreadsheet model, insert the optimizing information, and find the optimal solution. The optimal process selection has a cost of $104,100.

Example 4: Process Selection in Transportation

Heavy Haulers, Inc. has a contract to transport two types of machinery, presses and punches, from the factory to the port. This equipment is quite heavy, and requires modification of trucks so that the machinery is not damaged in transit. Special carrying racks, which are different for the two machine types, are installed in the trucks. Three different truck designs have been built by Heavy Haulers. Truck Design A has racks for three presses and one punch; Design B has racks for two presses and two punches; Design C has no press racks, but racks for four punches.

A delivery trip with a Design A truck costs $700; Design B, $500; Design C, $600. The contract requires delivery of 570 presses and 360 punches. The projected travel times for the three designs suggest that Design A can make no more than 100 trips; Design B, no more than 150 trips; and Design C, no more than 225 trips. Develop a schedule for Heavy Haulers, indicating the number of trips each design should make.

The influence chart, Figure 6.12, indicates that the spreadsheet model must calculate the COST, the number of PRESSES CARRIED, and the number of PUNCHES

Figure 6.12

Influence Chart for Heavy Haulers

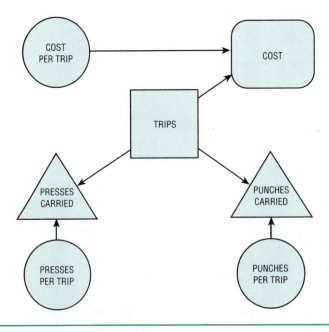

Figure 6.13

Worksheet Model for Heavy Haulers, Inc.

	A	B	C	D	E	F	G
1	Heavy Haulers, Inc.						
2							
3		Design A	Design B	Design C	Total	Constraint	Limit
4	Trips	10	20	30			
5	Trip Constraint	<=	<=	<=			
6	Trip Limit	100	150	225			
7							
8	Cost per Trip	700	500	600			
9	Cost	7000	10000	18000	35000		
10							
11	Presses per Trip	3	2	0			
12	Presses Carried	30	40	0	70	Not >=	570
13							
14	Punches per Trip	1	2	4			
15	Punches Carried	10	40	120	170	Not >=	360

Figure 6.14

Documentation for Heavy Haulers Worksheet

Trips[Design A] = 10
Trips[Design B] = 20
Trips[Design C] = 30

Trip Constraint[Design A THRU Design C] is is inserted using What'sBest!

Trip Limit[Design A] = 100
Trip Limit[Design B] = 150
Trip Limit[Design C] = 225

Cost per Trip[Design A] = 700
Cost per Trip[Design B] = 500
Cost per Trip[Design C] = 600

Cost[Design A THRU Design C] = Trips * Cost per Trip
Cost[Total] = SUM (Cost[Design A] THRU Cost[Design C])

Presses per Trip[Design A] = 3
Presses per Trip[Design B] = 2
Presses per Trip[Design C] = 0

Presses Carried[Design A THRU Design C] = Trips * Presses per Trip
Presses Carried[Total] = SUM (Presses Carried[Design A] THRU Presses Carried[Design C])
Presses Carried[Constraint] is inserted using What'sBest!
Presses Carried[Limit] = 570

Punches per Trip[Design A] = 1
Punches per Trip[Design B] = 2
Punches per Trip[Design C] = 4

Punches Carried[Design A THRU Design C] = Trips * Punches per Trip
Punches Carried[Total] = SUM (Punches Carried[Design A] THRU Punches Carried[Design C])
Punches Carried[Constraint] is inserted using What'sBest!
Punches Carried[Limit] = 360

CARRIED. The worksheet model (before optimization) is shown in Figure 6.13. The documentation for this worksheet is shown in Figure 6.14.

A special note is in order about the constraints used in optimization. The constraint on the number of presses (or punches) carried must be carefully stated; although we would not recommend carrying extra machines from the factory to the port, it may be desirable (or necessary) to run a truck with an empty machine rack. Thus, the number of machines carried must be greater than or equal to the limit specified. Requiring the number of machines carried to be exactly equal to the limit would cause problems (try it!). The reader is encouraged to construct the model, provide the optimization instructions, and verify an optimal cost of $137,500.

Exercises

1. Construct the spreadsheet model shown in Figure 6.4, and documented in Figure 6.5. Place all of the optimization instructions for What's *Best!* in the spreadsheet, using the What's *Best!* menu. Optimize to verify that the least-cost standard cake meeting all of Citrimagination's requirements is $1.5036.

2. Write a report to Citrimagination management describing the "best" course of action to follow, according to the optimization results of Exercise 1.

3. For Chris Hadley's printing business, classify each of these statements as applying directly to the objective, to the decision variables, to the limiting values, to data values, or to other spreadsheet formulas.

   a. The printing operation for Product A operates at 4000 units per hour.

   b. Chris desires to make the profit contribution as large as possible.

   c. The selling price of Product B is $7.

   d. The cost of the cutting operation is $100 per hour.

   e. The printing operation is limited to 20 hours during the planning period.

   f. Chris wants to find the quantity to produce for each product.

   g. The unit raw material cost is $0.30 for each unit of any product.

   h. Twelve hours of cutting operation are available.

   i. Chris believed that all feasible production could be sold at the stated prices.

   j. There is half again as much folding capacity (30 hours) as printing capacity (20 hours).

4. What are the optimization instructions to be applied to Chris Hadley's model, Figure 6.7?

5. Construct the spreadsheet model shown in Figure 6.7 and documented in Figure 6.8. Use What's *Best!* to find the optimal solution. You should obtain an optimal value of profit of $57,638.

6. Write a report to Chris Hadley describing the "best" course of action to follow, according to the optimization results of Exercise 5.

7. Find and interpret the marginal values associated with each of the constraints for Chris Hadley's problem.

8. For the process selection in amusement devices, classify each of these statements as applying to the objective, to the decision variables, to the limiting values, to data values, or to other spreadsheet formulas.

   a. The manufacturer has a contract to produce 5000 electronic amusement devices.

   b. How many devices should be produced using the hand assembly method?

   c. 25,000 minutes of skilled labor are available.

   d. Should any devices be produced using robotic assembly? If so, how many?

   e. The cost of skilled labor is $0.40 per minute.

   f. What is the cost of the resources necessary to implement a proposed production plan?

   g. Robotic assembly requires 4 minutes of assembly room time per device.

   h. How many devices should be produced using semiautomatic assembly?

   i. Unskilled labor is limited to a total usage of 140,000 minutes.

   j. Hand assembly uses less skilled labor than any other process.

   k. We can't use more than 20,000 minutes of assembly room floor time.

   l. Assembly room floor time costs more per minute than any other resource.

9. What are the What'sBest! optimization instructions to be applied to Amusement Devices' spreadsheet, Figure 6.10?

10. Construct the spreadsheet model shown in Figure 6.10, and documented in Figure 6.11. Use What'sBest! to find the "best" values for the decision variables. Interpret the results for management.

11. For the optimal solution to Exercise 10, interpret each marginal value (dual value) available from What'sBest!

12. What are the What'sBest! optimization instructions to be applied to Heavy Haulers' spreadsheet, Figure 6.13?

13. Construct the spreadsheet model shown in Figure 6.13, and documented in Figure 6.14. Use What'sBest! to perform optimization. Interpret the results for management.

CASE STUDY:

Agribusiness

An agribusiness manager is evaluating plans for the use of the acreage in Farm #39. Last year, this farm was completely planted in milo (400 acres) and wheat (600 acres). After studying market trends, the manager made a tentative decision to plant Farm #39 with 200 acres of milo, 500 acres of alfalfa, and the remaining 300 acres in wheat.

The market prices that are acceptable for planning purposes indicate that each acre in milo will yield a revenue of $600; alfalfa will yield $500; wheat will yield $450. Seed and fertilizer costs are $40 per acre for milo, and twice that for alfalfa and wheat. Labor costs $10 per hour, regardless of crop. However, each acre of milo requires 5 hours of labor; alfalfa requires 3.5 hours; wheat requires 4.5 hours.

Water is a scarce resource at Farm #39. Each acre of milo requires 0.6 acre-feet of water; alfalfa requires 0.3 acre-feet per acre; wheat requires 0.2 acre-feet per acre. Any plan under consideration must be evaluated for total water requirements, so that the feasibility of obtaining the required water supply can be investigated. For planning purposes, water costs $150 per acre-foot; the best estimate of the water availability is 450 acre-feet.

There is some unrest in the labor situation. Initially, there was reason to believe that at a total labor cost of $10 per hour, any quantity of labor could be obtained. However, recent changes in immigration law suggest that it is prudent to keep track of the amount of labor a plan will require before it is implemented. Currently, a plan is needed that will not count on more than 3800 hours of labor.

The management of the agribusiness is interested in getting as much cash flow as possible; for their purposes, this is considered to be the revenue from the crop, less the cost of seed, water, and labor.

Case Analysis Questions

1. What is the objective for Agribusiness?

2. What variables does management control in order to achieve the optimum value of the objective?

3. What limitations must Agribusiness observe as they attempt to optimize the value of the objective?

4. An influence chart, without shapes or arrows, is provided on the following page. Enclose each variable with the appropriate shape to indicate whether it is the objective, a decision variable, a constraining value, or an intermediate variable. Then complete the influence diagram.

5. Construct the model to describe the results of any plan Agribusiness might suggest.

6. Apply optimization to obtain the optimal plan for Agribusiness.

CASH FLOW

PRICE   REVENUE

WATER PRICE   COST OF   ACRES   COST OF
                   WATER   SEED

                         WATER
                         USED
                                                              SEED PRICE

                         WATER
                         PER ACRE

          COST   LABOR
          OF LABOR   USED

     LABOR PRICE   LABOR
                         PER ACRE

CASE STUDY:

Tucker Development Corporation

Note: Tucker Development Corporation case study is provided for additional practice in modeling and optimization. While it is a realistic situation, liberties have been taken in developing the case to provide experience in modeling. *Tucker Development Corporation is intended for students with some business coursework or experience.**

Sidney Tucker, President and Chief Executive Officer of Tucker Development Corporation (TUCKER), had just returned from vacation in October, 1984. Work was about to begin on the West Coast Center, a new strip shopping center just about ready to move from planning to site preparation and construction. Sidney was ready to evaluate a proposal about the types of business TUCKER should be inviting to occupy the West Coast Center. The West Coast Center was on a parcel of 100,000 square feet. As demolition was about to begin, it was time to decide about the kinds of business that would be desirable for the center.

The proposal Sidney Tucker was considering had come from an assistant, Jan Chingon. The proposal is contained in the memo shown as Exhibit 6.1.

Background

Sidney Tucker was one of a small group who had started developing commercial property in the early 1970s. At the time they started in the commercial development business, the opportunity to leave white-collar jobs and work for themselves had been an important motivator. A lot of hard work had let them take advantage of many talents possessed by the founding group. The group had founders whose individual specialties included real estate sales, both commercial and residential; financial planning, primarily for individuals; land use planning and architecture; and market research and planning. The West Coast Center was the seventh major project; some of the early projects had already been sold completely, which gave TUCKER a substantial financial base to use on current projects. Each of the six previous projects had been incorporated separately. This permitted investors to be found on a project-by-project basis, with TUCKER maintaining between 25% and 50% interest in each of the companies. Each individual project obtained its own financing, which insulated TUCKER from losses which might be felt by any individual project. Fortunately, there had been no financial problems with any of the projects undertaken to date. Some were more profitable than others, but none was considered to be a lemon.

Sidney Tucker had often thought about the various factors that had been important in the success of TUCKER. Perhaps the most important factor had been dealing with small businesses in a way that encouraged the success of each business in the center. Although TUCKER preferred to enter into leasing agreements with existing retail stores, the experience of any individual store owner

*This case is inspird by Rianhard Associates, Inc., copyright 1974 by the Board of Trustees of the Leland Stanford Junior University, reprinted in Christoph Haehling von Lanzenauer, *Cases in Operations Research.* San Francisco: Holden-Day, Inc., 1975.

───────────────────────   **Exhibit 6.1**   ───────────────────────

Memo to Sidney Tucker

Memo to: Sidney Tucker, President   October 14, 1984
From: Jan Chingon, Staff Assistant
Subject: Invitations for Occupants, West Coast Center

The market research for the West Coast Center, to be built in a suburban
 area which is growing even faster than the metropolitan area, is now
complete. There will be a substantial base of new housing near the
center, with suburban families eager to establish new shopping habits.
We believe we will offer our tenants a very profitable location.

As you well know, we need to begin the process of negotiating and signing
leases for a new shopping center some months before we begin construction.
Since we will be demolishing existing structures for the West Coast Center
sometime in November, I want to begin the process of planning our "invi-
tation list" of businesses to occupy the center. Is there any reason we
should deviate from the percentage allocations we used on our last project?

Our last project was the High Plains Shops, with a total store area of
40,000 square feet. Here is the way we started looking for tenants in
that center:

	Percent of Total Area
Hair Stylist	5
Grocery	20
Women's Clothing	19
Dry Goods and Fabric	7
Hardware	11
Drug	13
Ice Cream or Yogurt	10
Card and Gift	15

If we apply these percentages to the West Coast Center (with a rough
planning figure of 28,000 square feet), we would start inviting tenants
with approximately these square foot areas in mind:

	Square Feet
Hair Stylist	1400
Grocery	5600
Women's Clothing	5320
Dry Goods and Fabric	1960
Hardware	3080
Drug	3640
Ice Cream or Yogurt	2800
Card and Gift	4200

was not always as extensive as TUCKER would like. To compensate for this lack of retail background, TUCKER provided some consulting services to tenants. TUCKER also helped arrange joint neighborhood advertising campaigns for the occupants of each center. There was also a great deal of emphasis on the planning and design of each project that TUCKER started. All of these activities are very important to the success of a project, because the eventual market value of a property depends upon the revenue a center can generate. Although TUCKER always planned to be certain that each project was able to operate on the lease payments generated by the stores in the center, the big payoff comes from resale of the center; this resale value is where good revenue from tenant sales is very important.

The West Coast Center

In June, 1984, TUCKER had paid $20 per square foot for the 100,000 square foot site for the West Coast Center. The purchase was made with investor and company funds augmented by a ten-year non-amortizing loan of $612,000. The interest rate on the loan was 11.5%, with annual interest payments of $70,000. If everything continued on schedule, the site preparation would begin within the month, with construction scheduled to begin in early 1985. The architectural concept for the center, which was nearing completion, was based upon Miami Vice colors and bold angular lines in the retail structures. The architect and construction consultant had jointly estimated a cost of $16 per square foot for unfinished interior space, building structure, parking, site preparation, drainage, and other costs. The major cost element not included in this $16 estimate is interior finishing; the funds that would be used to finance the structure could not be used for this interior finishing without violating the terms of the loan. The main reason that TUCKER had obtained the $612,000 loan for the property purchase was so that there would be sufficient investor and company funds available for the building costs (based on a current estimate of 28,000 square feet at $16 per square foot).

In recent years the municipal zoning where West Coast Center was to be built had specified that no more than 30% of the land to be used for a shopping center could be used for retail space. The remaining 70% had to be used in the following way:

Parking	55%
Landscaping	10%
Surface Water Retention	5%

Sidney Tucker believed that changes in the IRS code indicated that 1985 would be a banner year for shopping center construction. There was concern that prices would begin to soften by the end of 1985; this made it even more important to get the center leased in the first half of 1985. Currently, the market had stabilized so that leases in the suburbs of the metropolitan area were nearly standard; the standard lease payment was a percentage of gross revenue, with a guaranteed minimum amount per month. Each type of store had slightly differ-

---
Exhibit 6.2

Research Report of Strip Center Profitability

Although there is no universal formula for determining the success of
a strip shopping center, our research has indicated the following profile
for centers that tend to be in the upper quartile of center profitability.
It is true that there are some centers which are very profitable with
very different profiles, and there are centers which meet this profile
very closely that have become lemons. However, we believe that our chance
of turning any Tucker Development Corporation project into a successful
venture is enhanced if we attempt to design a center with the characteristics of the successful strip center, described below.

The basic idea is to divide various types of stores into four groups.
We label these groups in this way:

Required:	Hair Stylist, Grocery
Soft Goods:	Women's Clothing, Dry Goods and Fabrics
Hard Goods:	Hardware, Variety, Drug
Niceties:	Ice Cream or Yogurt, Bakery, Card and Gift

The successful strip center (in our profile) has both a hair stylist and
a grocery store. There is at least one store from each of the other
groups. The successful center profile requires that a "meaningful" amount
of space be devoted to each group. Our research has indicated that the
following square foot minimum values are sufficient for a square footage
allocation to be meaningful:

Required Stores:	7000 square feet, total, minimum
Hair Stylist:	between 1000 and 1500 square feet
Grocery store:	at least 5500 square feet
Soft Goods:	5800 square feet, minimum
Hard goods:	5200 square feet, minimum
Niceties:	3700 square feet, minimum

ent provisions; the large "anchor" store would have a more attractive lease than
a small specialty store, because the anchor store brings in business to the center,
thereby assisting the small specialty stores. This means that TUCKER's experience
in real estate development would pay off, because competition would be based
on nonmonetary factors. TUCKER's experience in this area was certainly a plus for
the West Coast Center.

After Sidney Tucker had read the memo from Jan Chingon about allocation
of square footage to various types of stores, Tucker referred to Exhibit 6.2, a
recent report about the factors that affect the profitability of various strip shopping centers. In summary, this report had listed ten types of stores, two more
than recommended in Chingon's memo (Exhibit 6.1). There were various characteristics that successful centers possessed, as indicated in the exhibit.

Exhibit 6.3

Planning Data for West Coast Center

Type of Store	Factor 1 Initial Interior Cost Per Square Foot	Factor 2 Guaranteed Rent Per Square Foot	Factor 3 Present Value Per Square Foot
Hair Stylist	$40	$10.00	$238
Grocery	31	6.70	225
Women's Clothing	39	5.50	210
Dry Goods and Fabrics	35	5.80	200
Hardware	33	6.40	203
Variety	32	7.95	190
Drug	41	4.25	230
Ice Cream or Yogurt	46	8.20	250
Bakery	41	7.00	258
Card and Gift	31	4.20	235

The economics of the various stores include three factors, which are shown in Exhibit 6.3:

> Factor 1: Initial cost per square foot for interior finishing
> Factor 2: Annual guaranteed rent per square foot
> Factor 3: Present value per square foot

Each of these factors is important in its own way. Factor 1 (initial cost per square foot for interior finishing) is important because this must be financed with a new loan, yet to be negotiated. Sidney Tucker believed that it would be reasonable to obtain financing of $900,000 for the interior finishing, at an interest rate of 9%. Preliminary conversations with sources of financing indicated that there would be little difficulty in arranging an interest-only payment schedule for the first ten years of the loan. (Typically, TUCKER would have disposed of the center by that time, so ten years was an adequate horizon for this financing.) In addition to the anticipated $900,000 loan for interior finishing, up to $100,000 in investor and company funds could be used for interior finishing. However, these funds would not be used until the loan proceeds had been spent. The lender had indicated that if financing was to be provided for the interior finishing, the loan amount would be for $900,000. The lender was not interested in a smaller loan, and was unable to make a larger loan.

Factor 2 (annual guaranteed rent per square foot) is very important for all of TUCKER's planning. The key to obtaining good financing was to conclusively demonstrate that first-year guaranteed rentals would cover annual fixed charges (property management overhead, interest on debt from interior finishing, and interest on debt from land purchase). With this requirement, there were obvious advantages to obtaining solid tenants with high annual guarantees. Of course, guarantees that were unrealistically high would be inappropriate, because stores unable to meet unrealistic requirements would go out of business and provide little or no income to TUCKER. The initial research for West Coast Center had indicated that property management overhead would be between $40,000 and $60,000 annually.

Factor 3 (present value per square foot) had become TUCKER's primary "yardstick" for measuring the profitability of a strip shopping center. One of the founders of TUCKER had directed a research project to look at the pattern over time of various revenues and costs associated with typical strip shopping center projects. Initially, a project's revenues grew rather rapidly as consumer habits changed to include the new stores. Another factor providing for rapid initial growth was the managerial expertise of the individual store owners, who began to understand the wants and needs of the consumers in the market area. Overhead (including building maintenance) tended to stay steady for a number of years, which means that increasing revenues were not offset by increasing expenses. As the growth began to slow, however, newer projects became more attractive; new projects were more easily financed with the proceeds from the sale of older projects. By carefully considering all of these timing factors, TUCKER calculated Factor 3, which includes:

> Projected present value of the stream of income, after taxes, for each type of store. In calculating this factor, annual expenses such as property management overhead have already been considered. Although there is uncertainty in the first-year property management overhead (which is important for comparing first-year guaranteed rentals with first-year cash expenses), the first-year property management overhead has little if any impact on the value of Factor 3.

> Discounted value from the eventual sale of the center, for each type of store.

By multiplying Factor 3 by the square feet of each type of store, a gross measure of the attractiveness of that store is obtained. The gross measure of the attractiveness of the center is the total of these values for all stores in the center. As shown in Exhibit 6.3, the Present Value per Square Foot has not been reduced by the land costs, structure costs, or interior improvements. TUCKER believed that the ultimate factor to use for evaluating a center's design and tenant selection is the aggregate present value of the project, reduced by the land costs, structure cost, and the interior improvements. However, this factor is meaningless if the design and tenant selection make an unworkable project. Furthermore, TUCKER believes that this approach is valid only if the guidelines of Exhibit 6.2 are followed.

Case Analysis Questions

1. Classify each of these as an objective, a decision variable, or a constraint:

  How many square feet should be established for each store?

  The current plan is for 28,000 square feet of interior space.

  The hair stylist must be between 1000 and 1500 square feet.

  The grocery store must be at least 5500 square feet.

Required stores must have at least 7000 square feet.

Soft goods stores must have at least 5800 square feet.

Hard goods stores must have at least 5200 square feet.

Stores selling niceties must have at least 3700 square feet.

The difference between guaranteed annual rent and cash expenses (property management overhead, interest on purchase loan, and interest on interior finishing loan) cannot be negative.

The cost of interior finishing cannot exceed $1,000,000.

The evaluation of a center is based on the aggregate present value of the project, reduced by the land cost, structure cost, and the cost of interior improvements.

2. Construct an influence chart for TUCKER. The purpose of the model (to be constructed from the chart) is to evaluate the proposal in Exhibit 6.1, in terms of the objective and each constraint. There are a number of constraints relating the allocation of square feet to store types; it may not be useful to include each of these limits in a detailed influence chart.

3. Construct a spreadsheet model for TUCKER, based on the influence chart in the question above.

4. Optimize the spreadsheet model for TUCKER. Describe the results of the optimization to management.

5. Discuss the impact of the apparent disparity between a 28,000 square foot center (Exhibit 6.1) and the zoning laws permitting 30% of the 100,000 square foot site to be used for retail space.

7

More Modeling Examples: Transportation & Assignment Problems

This chapter shows more examples of managerial modeling for optimization, where optimization is useful to support a decision. All of the illustrations in this chapter are best modeled using a single variable name to identify a rectangular range of cells. (In traditional terms, these examples have a *matrix* layout.) In models we have been using before, a single variable name has represented a row of values, rather than a rectangular range.

Our first illustration is a "transportation problem," so named because it is often used to find the least-cost way to move items from one set of places (often factories) to another set of places (often warehouses). This is shown with an illustration of two factories and three warehouses. The purpose of this example is to illustrate the use of a rectangular range or matrix in a transportation problem.

Example 1: A Transportation Problem

A company has supplies at factories A, B, and C; they must be sent to the East and West warehouses. Factory A has 100 units; B has 200 units, and C has 300 units. East needs 350 units; West needs 250 units. The unit shipping costs are shown in Figure 7.1, in the rectangular range or matrix, B3..D4. The company wants to find the best way to ship units from the factories to the warehouses, shipping no more than the maximum number available from any factory, and shipping at least as many as required to each warehouse. An arbitrary shipping schedule (which doesn't even meet the requirements) is shown as a rectangular range or matrix in B8..D9. This arbitrary schedule, for example, suggests shipping 10 units from B to the East, and 200 units from B to the West, and so on. Note that we have used two matrices, Unit Cost and Shipping Schedule; each of

---

Figure 7.1

Transportation Example

	A	B	C	D	E	F	G
1	Unit Cost:						
2		From A	From B	From C			
3	Unit Cost East	8	7	4			
4	Unit Cost West	2	5	6			
5							
6	Shipping Schedule:						Minimum
7		From A	From B	From C	Total	Constraint	Required
8	Ship East	0	10	100	110	Not >=	350
9	Ship West	100	200	300	600	>=	250
10	Total Shipped	100	210	400	710		
11	Constraint	=<=	Not <=	Not <=			
12	Max Available	100	200	300			
13							
14	Shipping Cost:				3470		
15	(Using @SUMPRODUCT function)						
16							

---

these is a rectangular range of cells, with one label used to identify that range to the reader.

Most of the remaining parts of the model are logic. Cells E8..E9 are the row totals, showing the amount shipped to each warehouse. Cells B10..D10 are the column totals, showing the amount shipped from each factory. Next to each of these totals is the amount required (for warehouses) or the amount available (for factories). The constraints for the problem can be entered into the row and column with the constraint label. Specifically, these constraints are:

To each warehouse, you must ship at least as much as required, or

Total Shipped >= Minimum Required for Ship East and Ship West, or

    E8..E9   >=   G8..G9

From each factory, you can ship no more than the maximum available, or

Total Shipped <= Max Available From A, B, and C, or

  B10..D10   <=   B12..D12

There are several ways to construct the model to calculate the total shipping costs for the shipping schedule. It could be done with one long formula, like this:

```
Shipping Cost[Total] = +B3*B8 + C3*C8 + D3*D8 + B4*E9 + C4*C9 + D4*D9
                     =   8*0  + 7*10 + 4*100 + 2*100 + 5*200 + 6*300 = 3470
```

This would obviously become difficult if we added more factories or more warehouses! Another way would be to create a third matrix, showing the shipping cost for each factory/warehouse pair. This would be easy for a problem of any size, because one formula can be entered, then copied to the entire matrix in one operation.

A third way to calculate the total cost is to use the @SUMPRODUCT function (a function built into Quattro Pro, and automatically attached by installing

What's*Best!* for Lotus 1-2-3). This function uses two ranges of identical size; it multiplies the corresponding elements of each range, and then finds the sum of the products. The cell formula for this method is:

```
Cell E14:   @SUMPRODUCT(B3..D4,B8..D9)
```

Note that the first range, B3..D4, is the unit cost matrix; the second range, B8..D9, is the shipping schedule. The @SUMPRODUCT function calculates the total cost of the schedule as $3470.*

To find the best schedule, we can use What's*Best!* to find the shipping schedule that minimizes the grand total cost, in cell E14. The information to specify for the optimization software is:

Decisions
(adjustable cells): The shipping schedule matrix.

Constraints: The two sets of constraints were discussed above. We must deliver at least as many as required to each warehouse, and we must ship from each factory no more than the maximum available at that factory.

Objective: *Minimize* Shipping Cost[Total] *in cell* E14.

It is left as an exercise to use What's*Best!* to find the optimal shipping schedule, which has a total cost of $2500.

Several possible changes could be made in this example to illustrate situations that arise frequently in transportation problems. This started out as a "balanced" problem, with the supply exactly equal to the demand. We could have constrained the total shipped from each factory to be exactly equal to the supply at that factory; we could have constrained the total shipped to each warehouse to be exactly equal to the requirement at that warehouse. The result would have been identical, and could have been achieved by constraining the deliveries to each warehouse to be exactly equal to the requirements, and by constraining the quantity shipped from each factory to be exactly equal to the maximum available at that factory. If we had more units available than we required, we would incur additional shipping charges if we shipped more than needed to any warehouse. The original formulation of the problem would still find the best solution, because cost minimization would assure that we didn't ship more than we needed. But if we required more than we had available, no feasible solution could be found. One way this could be handled is to determine the penalty cost for failing to meet demand at each warehouse, and modifying the model to incorporate the incurred penalties into the total cost. A better way might be to look at the revenue and costs generated by a shipping schedule, and then instruct the software to maximize profit. This is the situation considered in the next section.

---

*The @SUMPRODUCT function can be used as an add-in for any Lotus 1-2-3 spreadsheet, release 2.x. However, it must be attached (by installing What's *Best!* or /Add-in Attach) before loading a file which uses @SUMPRODUCT. Files using Quattro's built-in @SUMPRODUCT function saved as *.WK1 files for a Lotus spreadsheet will not save the function in a form that permits its direct use with Lotus.

Example 2: Expanding the Transportation Problem

We introduce several modifications from the transportation problem illustrated above. First, the demand replaces the minimum required; if we don't meet the demand, we simply don't make any profit from that unfilled demand. The demand and the selling price for each warehouse is given as:

350 units at the East warehouse, where they will be sold at $145 each

300 units at the West warehouse, where they will be sold at $155 each (previously, only 250 units were available)

The quantities available at each factory are the same as above; however, the unit manufacturing cost information is now available:

$35 at factory A

$37 at factory B

$41 at factory C

It would be possible to calculate the unit profit for each factory/warehouse combination. But there are easier ways! The model we have already constructed handles the shipping cost, which is the only item that changes from factory to factory *and* from warehouse to warehouse. The selling price changes only from warehouse to warehouse, while the manufacturing cost changes only from factory to factory. We can calculate the revenue from the total shipped to each warehouse; we can calculate manufacturing cost from the total shipped from each factory. The logic from the first example calculates the shipping costs. All of this is shown in a model, with an arbitrary shipping schedule, in Figure 7.2.

There are some obvious and some subtle changes from Figure 7.1. The obvious changes are the addition of revenue, manufacturing cost, and shipping cost. Obvious data elements are shown in H8..H9 (price) and B13..D13 (unit manufacturing cost). To calculate the economic factors of the problem, these cell formulas are used:

Revenue	Cell E16	@SUMPRODUCT(H8..H9,E8..E9)
Mfg Cost	Cell E17	@SUMPRODUCT(B13..D13,B10..D10)
Shipping Cost	Cell E18	@SUMPRODUCT(B3..D4,B8..D9)
Profit	Cell E19	+E16−E17−E18

The reader is encouraged to verify that the ranges for each of these @SUMPRODUCT functions agrees with this verbal logic:

Revenue is calculated from the price at each warehouse and the quantity shipped to each warehouse.

Manufacturing cost is calculated from the unit manufacturing cost at each factory and the quantity shipped from each factory.

Shipping cost is calculated from the unit shipping cost and the shipping schedule for each factory/warehouse combination.

Profit is calculated as revenue less manufacturing cost less shipping cost.

Figure 7.2

Transportation Problem with Revenue and Manufacturing Cost

	A	B	C	D	E	F	G	H
1	Unit Cost:							
2		From A	From B	From C				
3	Unit Cost East	8	7	4				
4	Unit Cost West	2	5	6				
5								
6	Shipping Schedule:					Con-		
7		From A	From B	From C	Total	straint	Demand	Price
8	Ship East	0	10	100	110	<=	350	145
9	Ship West	100	200	300	600	Not <=	300	155
10	Total Shipped	100	210	400	710			
11	Constraint	=<=	Not <=	Not <=				
12	Max Available	100	200	300				
13	Unit Mfg Cost	35	37	41				
14								
15								
16	Revenue				108950			
17	Mfg Cost				27670			
18	Shipping Cost				3470			
19	Profit				77810			

An important change is required when we are maximizing profit, rather than minimizing cost. We need to permit unfilled demand for this unbalanced problem in which demand exceeds supply. We require that the total shipped to each warehouse must be less than or equal to the demand; we also require that the total shipped from each factory must be less than or equal to the maximum available at that factory. Because we are including the revenue for each item shipped, we will be certain to ship as many as we can (unless the price is too low). If we had used constraints like this for the problem to minimize shipping cost, we would have discovered that the least-cost shipping schedule is to ship nothing. It is left as an exercise to the reader to apply What's*Best!* to optimize the shipping schedule. The most profitable plan has a profit of $64,400.

Example 3: An Assignment Problem: Xaja Construction Company

The Xaja Construction Company has successfully captured five road maintenance projects for the next month. Each of the projects will require about a month to complete; overtime will be used if more than a month would normally be required. Xaja has grouped their workforce into five work crews, with different equipment assigned to each crew. Although any crew can theoretically complete any of the five projects, achieving the right match between projects and crews can reduce cost substantially. Crew 1, for example, has extra trucks for hauling materials to and from supply points; this crew is well-suited for work in urban areas, where supply points are located outside the urban area. Crew 2 has been given additional flagpeople, so that it can work effectively in areas with heavy

---
Figure 7.3

Xaja Construction Company Cost Table

	Crew 1	Crew 2	Crew 3	Crew 4	Crew 5
Project 1	352	503	398	418	99999
Project 2	93	115	132	99999	88
Project 3	83	109	141	145	112
Project 4	258	483	385	391	405
Project 5	412	390	405	405	395

traffic control needs. After considering all of these factors, the cost (in thousands of dollars) for assigning each crew to each project is shown in tabular form in Figure 7.3. Note that several entries in the table have very large costs (99999), to indicate that a crew is unsuited to a particular project.

From a clerical point of view, the problem can be viewed in this form: circle one entry in each row, and one entry in each column (i.e., five entries in all); add up the circled costs. The managerial task is to find the set of circles that makes the total cost of doing the five projects as small as possible. Instead of circling with a pencil, we'll indicate a crew assignment with a new table, using a 0 to indicate that cell is not circled, and a 1 to indicate a circled cell, as shown in Figure 7.4.

This set of assignments clearly has a problem: Project 1 has been assigned to two crews, while Project 3 has no crew assigned to it. This is indicated by the "Crews Assigned" heading, which is the sum of the entries in the row for each project. There are also problems with Crew 2 (too many projects) and Crew 3 (no project). These are indicated by the column sums in the row called "Projects Assigned."

At this point, let's reinforce one of the fundamental rules of modeling for optimization: let the optimization software take care of the problems dealing with feasibility. The assignment in Figure 7.4 is a "dumb" assignment of crews to projects, because it just won't work. But it is sufficient to get the optimization process started. We next need to address the issue of the cost of the assignment, so that the optimization process can find the cost of any assignment it evaluates.

Figure 7.4

Assignments for Xaja Construction Company

Assignments:	Crew 1	Crew 2	Crew 3	Crew 4	Crew 5	Crews Assigned
Project 1	1	1	0	0	0	2
Project 2	0	1	0	0	0	1
Project 3	0	0	0	0	0	0
Project 4	0	0	0	1	0	1
Project 5	0	0	0	0	1	1
Projects Assigned	1	2	0	1	1	

Figure 7.5

Incurred Costs for Xaja Construction Company

Incurred Costs:	Crew 1	Crew 2	Crew 3	Crew 4	Crew 5
Project 1	352	503	0	0	0
Project 2	0	115	0	0	0
Project 3	0	0	0	0	0
Project 4	0	0	0	391	0
Project 5	0	0	0	0	395

Total Cost: 1756

From a logical point of view, we want to create a new table with the project/crew cost carried down for each "1" in the assignment table, and a 0 entered for each "0" in the assignment table. This is done by multiplying the cost (shown in Figure 7.3) by the assignment, 0 or 1 (shown in Figure 7.4). This gives the result shown in Figure 7.5.

The spreadsheet model for optimization needs a few more parts. We need to assure that exactly one crew in each column is "circled" and exactly one project in each row is "circled." This is the same as requiring that the number of crews assigned to each project is exactly 1, and that the number of projects assigned to each crew is exactly 1. (This is a balanced problem, with five crews and five projects. We'll discuss unbalanced problems a bit later.) We accomplish this by using the **What'sBest!** option menu, selecting **Constraint**, to enter constraints into the worksheet.

The cell formulas for the model of Figure 7.6 are straightforward; for documentation, they are shown here:

Crews Assigned to Project 1	Cell G11	@SUM(B11..F11)	which copies to G12..G15
Projects Assigned to Crew 1	Cell B16	@SUM(B11..B15)	which copies to C16..F16
Incurred Cost, Project 1, Crew 1	Cell B21	+B4*B11	which copies to B21..B25
Total Cost	Cell B27	@SUM(B21..F25)	

The optimization instructions for finding the best assignment for Xaja Construction Company are quite straightforward:

The objective, to be minimized, is the value labeled Total Cost.

The decision variables are the Assignments (indicated by the 0s and 1s).

The constraints are shown in cells H11..H15, which require the number of crews assigned to each project to be exactly equal to 1. Constraints are also shown in cells B17..F17, which require that the number of projects assigned to each crew to be exactly equal to 1.

It is also logical that each decision variable must be limited so that its value is between 0 and 1; we can't have a crew assigned twice. But if any assignment is greater than 1, the row and column sums are violated, so we don't need to worry about it!

—————————————————— **Figure 7.6** ——————————————————

Spreadsheet Model for Xaja Assignment Problem

	A	B	C	D	E	F	G	H	I
1	Xaja Company – Cost for each crew to complete each project ($000)								
2									
3	Cost	Crew 1	Crew 2	Crew 3	Crew 4	Crew 5			
4	Project 1	352	503	398	418	99999			
5	Project 2	93	115	132	99999	88			
6	Project 3	83	109	141	145	112			
7	Project 4	258	483	385	391	405			
8	Project 5	412	390	405	405	395			
9							Crews		
10	Assignments	Crew 1	Crew 2	Crew 3	Crew 4	Crew 5	Assgnd	Constraint	
11	Project 1	1	1	0	0	0	2	Not =	
12	Project 2	0	1	0	0	0	1	=	
13	Project 3	0	0	0	0	0	0	Not =	
14	Project 4	0	0	0	1	0	1	=	
15	Project 5	0	0	0	0	1	1	=	
16	Proj Assgnd	1	2	0	1	1			
17	Constraint	=	Not =	Not =	=	=			
18									
19									
20	Incurred Cost	Crew 1	Crew 2	Crew 3	Crew 4	Crew 5			
21	Project 1	352	503	0	0	0			
22	Project 2	0	115	0	0	0			
23	Project 3	0	0	0	0	0			
24	Project 4	0	0	0	391	0			
25	Project 5	0	0	0	0	395			
26									
27	Total Cost:	1756							

The next question is a bit trickier: Do we need to worry about fractional assignments? From a logical standpoint, the answer is "maybe." If it makes sense to shift crews around in the middle of a month, and they don't conflict with each other (which is unlikely), and it doesn't increase costs to switch crews around (which is also unlikely), then we don't have to worry about fractional assignments. But the mathematics of this particular optimization problem are such that there is always a non-fractional assignment as the optimal solution, so this isn't a problem. Don't misunderstand: Most optimization problems tempt the optimizer to produce fractional solutions. But the mathematical form of this particular problem, which is called an assignment problem, guarantees that the optimizer will provide a solution of all 0s and 1s. (The mathematics of the proof is beyond the scope of this text.) Later in the text we'll demonstrate the use of What's*Best!* software for problems that specifically require variables to be either 0 or 1 when that doesn't automatically happen like it does here.

Dealing with Too Many Crews or Projects

The Xaja Construction Company assignment problem was nicely balanced; we have five crews and five projects. What happens if we had one more crew, or if we had one more project? This question really deserves a managerial answer:

What would happen if Xaja found itself in this situation? Without knowing the answer, we really can't proceed. Instead, we'll outline several managerial actions that might be forthcoming, and discuss the model construction that is appropriate for each of them.

Situation 1: An extra crew.

Managerial Action: Let the crew be unemployed.

Modeling Action: Put in a project called "unemployed" and extend the logic for this extra project; the tables are now square again (i.e., they are balanced). In the cost table for the "unemployed" project, enter whatever costs are incurred for each crew if it is unemployed. If equipment rental costs are included in the cost table, and if these costs go on even if the crew is not assigned to a real project, then the equipment rental costs for unemployed crews must be included in this "unemployed" project. Other costs might include added unemployment tax, supplemental unemployment benefits, and fringe benefits that continue through unemployment (if they have been included in the cost table for real projects). Obviously, if all of the costs in the cost table are discontinued when a crew is not assigned to a real project, and if there are no additional costs incurred from unemployment, then the cost table row for the unemployed project is all 0s.

Situation 2: An extra project.

Managerial Action: Use outside contractors.

Modeling Action: Put in a new crew called "outside contractor." Fill the cost table for that column with appropriate costs for the outside contractor.

Situation 3: An extra project.

Managerial Action: Let one of the projects slip to next month.

Modeling Action: Put in a crew called "delay a month." Fill the new column of the cost table with the costs or penalties that are associated with a delay. This may be trickier than it sounds, however, because it requires the manager to plan into the future and see if next month has the potential for being too busy as well.

Situation 4: An extra project.

Managerial Action: Forget about it.

Modeling Action: If "forget about it" really is a no-cost option, simply change the constraints from:

> the sum of the number of crews assigned to each project is *equal to* one,

to the constraints:

> the sum of the number of crews assigned to each project is *less than or equal to* one.

It turns out that this is the same thing as inserting a fictitious crew labeled "forget it" with all zero values in the cost table.

A Variation on the Assignment Problem

Although the Xaja Construction Company illustrates a cost minimization assignment problem, there can be profit maximization assignment problems as well. For example, how should the sales staff be assigned to clients? If the profit potential for each possible salesperson/client combination can be estimated, a straightforward assignment problem can be formulated. It is even possible to modify the formulation so that each salesperson can have no more than five clients, for example, if there are more clients than sales people (the usual situation, of course). Mathematicians assure us that this modification will still give us assignments without fractions. But be careful: Other optimization instructions (see Chapter 11) may be required if we add other constraints. Suppose that estimates of the time required for servicing a client are available. These can be included in the model, so that the sum of the hours required by an assignment does not exceed the number of hours available for a salesperson; this constraint, however, invites fractional assignments (which the sales manager may veto).

Solving Transportation and Assignment Problems

Historically, management science professionals have been very concerned about the mathematical structure of transportation and assignment problems. That interest has led to very fast solution methods for these problems. The spreadsheet optimization software we describe in this book does not utilize these faster solution techniques; rather, the general-purpose simplex algorithm is the basis for the software. If problems become so large that hardware or software limitations are reached, very large transportation and assignment problems can be solved by software that is based on the special mathematical formulation of these problems. It is even feasible (although totally unnecessary) to solve transportation and assignment problems with a dozen or so rows and columns without a computer.

Exercises _____

1. Using What's *Best!* and a model you construct, find the shipping schedule for the transportation example of Figure 7.1, which has the optimal cost of $2500.

2. Find the least-cost shipping schedule, where each supplier provides up to one hundred units and each customer demands fifty units. The shipping costs in dollars per unit, arranged from Customer #1 to Customer #6 are:

    From Supplier #1: $10, $11, $9, $8, $7, $12
    From Supplier #2: $15, $11, $19, $5, $12, $15
    From Supplier #3: $13 for all customers

3. Modify Exercise 2 above so that each customer demands only forty units. Any units available from suppliers but not shipped cost nothing.

4. Modify Exercise 2 above so that each customer demands sixty units. Any units demanded but not available incur a lost demand cost, which depends upon the customer. For each of the six customers, in order, the cost of a unit of lost demand is:

$$\$100, \$110, \$105, \$107, \$108, \$100$$

5. A company has four warehouses, each with a limited supply of seasonal candy. There are 25 cases at A, 40 cases at B, 35 cases at C, and 75 cases at D. Because of different market conditions at different stores, and different shipping costs from warehouse to store, there is a different profit at each store for each warehouse providing the candy. For a case of candy at each of the three stores, the unit profit per case is:

Warehouse A:	$15, $18, $14
Warehouse B:	$12, $12, $10
Warehouse C:	$17, $16, $19
Warehouse D:	$10, $20, $15

Each store has a minimum number of cases to permit company-wide advertising, and a maximum number of cases based upon the number of customers it serves. These limiting values are:

Store 1:	between 50 and 150 cases
Store 2:	between 25 and 200 cases
Store 3:	between 50 and 100 cases

Develop a plan for the company to use to send the candy to the stores.

6. A company has four warehouses, each with a limited supply of seasonal greeting cards. There are 85 cases at A, 70 cases at B, 35 cases at C, and 75 cases at D. Because of different market conditions at different stores, there is a different profit at each store for each warehouse providing the greeting cards. For a case of greeting cards at each of the three stores, the unit profit per case, before considering shipping costs, is:

Warehouse A:	$15, $18, $14
Warehouse B:	$12, $12, $10
Warehouse C:	$17, $16, $19
Warehouse D:	$10, $20, $15

The shipping cost, per case, from each warehouse to each of the three stores is:

Warehouse A:	$1, $2, $0
Warehouse B:	$1, $3, $1
Warehouse C:	$4, $3, $5
Warehouse D:	$1, $5, $2

Each store has a minimum number of cases to permit company-wide advertising, and a maximum number of cases based upon the number of customers it serves. These limiting values are:

Store 1:	between 50 and 150 cases
Store 2:	between 25 and 200 cases
Store 3:	between 50 and 100 cases

Develop a plan for the company to use to send the greeting cards to the stores.

7. A company has five employees, to be assigned to five tasks. The dollar cost of each assignment, arranged from Employee #1 to Employee #5, are:

Task #1:   4, 3, 7, 6, 8
Task #2:   3, 5, 4, 6, 3
Task #3:   100, 101, 102, 98, 103
Task #4:   0, 1, 4, 2, 3
Task #5:   46, 48, 47, 51, 55

Find the least-cost assignment.

8. Find the maximum-profit assignment from the data given in Exercise 7, assuming that the assignment costs are now profits resulting from an assignment.

9. There are four tasks to be completed: mow, edge, bag, and sweep. Jim can mow (2 hours) or edge (3 hours). Ev can mow (3 hours), edge (2 hours), bag (4 hours), or sweep (3 hours). Jan can mow (1 hour), edge (1 hour), bag (1 hour), or sweep (1 hour). Sam can edge (4 hours), bag (6 hours), or sweep (7 hours). Using a spreadsheet model and optimization software, find an assignment that will use as few hours as possible. Each person must do one task. *Tip:* to use a rectangular range for the decision cells, put in a very large number of hours (such as 999) for a task that a person is incapable of performing. This simplifies the spreadsheet model.

10. Four salespeople are to be assigned to territories. Each salesperson will be assigned to one territory. The best seller is Doni; it is estimated that Doni will generate sales (in hundreds of thousands) in each territory (North, South, East, West) as follows:

Estimated sales for Doni: $7, $9, $10, $6

For the other salespeople:

Estimated sales for Jami: $6, $5, $9, $7
Estimated sales for Sami: $1, $1, $2, $5
Estimated sales for Toni: $3, $5, $4, $1

Using a spreadsheet model and What's*Best!*, develop an assignment of employees to territories.

11. For the situation of Exercise 10, how much additional sales would be generated if any salesperson could handle two territories? (This would be accomplished by using private aircraft, teleconferencing, support staff, and incentives.)

12. For the situation of Exercise 10, how much additional sales would be generated if Sami's productivity could be increased (by training) so that Sami would sell $100,000 more in any territory? If this training could be offered to only one salesperson, with the same impact of a $100,000 increase, should it be given to Doni, Jami, Sami, or Toni?

CASE STUDY:
Delta Company

The Delta Company case presents a series of situations for you to address. For each situation you should construct a model and find the optimal solutions. This will introduce you to a variety of similar but intriguingly different situations where optimization is useful.

Jan Smythe is manager of transportation for the Delta Company. The Delta Company manufactures a modular building structure, used in apartment construction, at four different factories in the south. These factories were constructed several years ago, in cities where there was substantial apartment construction activity. Unfortunately, other cities had recently become "hot" with apartment construction, and Delta found itself with factories located in the wrong cities.

Jan had just come back from a meeting with Sid Johnes, who had just spent three weeks determining the markets that Delta would be concentrating on during the next quarter. Sid was convinced that the "hot" markets for the next quarter would be Orlando, St. Petersburg, Atlanta, and Charlotte. While visiting each of these cities, Sid paid some attention to the building activity and the competition in each market. Jan asked Sid about the number of modules that could be sold in each market; Sid's estimates were no more than 100 in Orlando, 200 at most in St. Petersburg, 250 as the ceiling in Atlanta, and 225 as the maximum in Charlotte.

At this point, Jan thought there was enough information available to decide which factories to use to supply each city. Jan already had collected information about the shipping cost ($2 per module per mile) and the mileage:

		Miles to Construction Site in:		
		Orlando	*St. Petersburg*	*Atlanta*	*Charlotte*
From:	Miami Factory	229	253	663	740
	Tampa Factory	82	22	452	584
	Atlanta Factory	426	474	7	240
	Jacksonville Factory	140	217	313	393

After studying this information, Jan concluded that Orlando should be supplied by Tampa, St. Petersburg should be supplied by Tampa, Atlanta should (obviously) be supplied by Atlanta, and Charlotte should be supplied by Atlanta. Each of these supply decisions is based upon the closest factory serving each market.

To confirm this decision, Jan met with the Vice-President for Operations, who didn't spend much time at all with Jan. The essence of the conversation was that this would certainly make shipping costs quite low, but it would use only two factories. Furthermore, there are limits on production at each factory. Jan felt a bit guilty for having ignored an earlier memo which contained this paragraph:

In planning the construction module business for the next quarter, the following plant capacities must be considered:

Miami	200 modules
Tampa	150 modules
Atlanta	150 modules
Jacksonville	175 modules

Some quick arithmetic indicated that some demand would not be met, even though Delta would send out all modules manufactured next quarter. A bit selfishly, Jan thought this was OK, because it would mean fewer units to be shipped, and the shipping budget would be less strained. Jan quickly dismissed these thoughts when they were pushed to their obvious conclusion: We can make shipping costs as low as possible if we don't ship anything.

CASE STUDY:

Delta Company (B)

Jan Smythe started to implement the shipping schedule that had been developed; this schedule had a total of 137,675 miles, or a total shipping cost of $275,350. When Jan presented the schedule to Sid Johnes, Sid was not at all happy: "You mean we're only going to send 125 modules to Charlotte? That's not very sensible. In Charlotte, we can get top dollar for a module." There's really quite a variation in the price in each market:

Orlando	$3700
St. Petersburg	3500
Atlanta	4000
Charlotte	4100

CASE STUDY:

Delta Company (C)

Maybe Murphy was right: if it can go wrong, it will. A memo just out of Operations describes a major change in capacity at the four plants. A major contract scheduled for the next quarter was postponed for six months. Not only does this affect the capacity available, it also affects the module cost at each factory. The postponed contract had been scheduled to use some new equipment with low labor cost, which would now be available to make construction modules. The new capacity limits, and the production cost per module at each factory, were shown in the memo:

Factory	Capacity	Cost per Module
Miami	250 modules	$700
Tampa	250 modules	900
Atlanta	200 modules	1300
Jacksonville	225 modules	1100

8

Optimization of Network Models

The word *network* brings many images to a manager: a computer network, a network of friends, a support network of professionals, or a telephone network. Each of these networks involves entities (PCs, friends, professionals, telephones) that are connected in some way to each other. By looking at the points, or *nodes*, and the connections, or *arcs*, between them, we have a network view of a system.

The purpose of this chapter is to provide the manager with tools that are useful for solving network problems that fit on a spreadsheet. Mathematicians have been very successful in developing special-purpose algorithms or procedures for solving many specialized network problems, such as the *transportation problem* and the *assignment problem* from Chapter 7. These special-purpose algorithms are very important for solving large problems with many thousands of nodes and arcs. Our purpose in using the general linear optimizer and the spreadsheet is to develop methods managers can use without probing into special methods or computer programs. We will show how end-users can solve real problems using the general-purpose linear optimizer. Like any optimization problem, a point may be reached where the spreadsheet formulation of the problem becomes too large for the software. When that happens, management science specialists, who know these special-purpose solution methods, need to become involved in the process, and will be successful in solving many very large network problems. The models in this chapter use more advanced spreadsheet concepts, including range names and cell addresses that are a mixture of absolute and relative addresses. These spreadsheet modeling and optimization skills have wide applicability; however, this chapter may be omitted without loss of continuity.

Project Scheduling

For many years, network scheduling models have been used to support management decisions in planning and monitoring large projects. These techniques are given a variety of names; the most common names are PERT (Program Evaluation and Review Technique) and CPM (Critical Path Method). Special-purpose computer programs, for both personal computers and larger computers, are readily available for managers who spend a lot of time managing and tracking projects that involve many activities. In this chapter, we'll show how optimization can be used to determine a completion date and to improve resource allocation in a project plan. As a case study to Chapter 14, we'll take a completely different spreadsheet view of the project planning network, and show how uncertainty can be addressed using that view.

Case Scenario: Soft Ideas, Inc.

Soft Ideas, Inc., is an established developer of software for personal computers. Its recent growth has caused the need for rapid expansion of office space. Over the past several months, its programmers and systems staff have been spread out over three different buildings in a four-block downtown area. A major problem arises because people who need to be able to communicate with each other haven't been close enough for effective working relationships to develop. The company has decided to plan and build a new building very quickly. Soft Idea's management team has decided to use some of the ideas of "fast track" construction: begin building the rough parts of the building without knowing the final details of the interior. This requires a great deal of coordination, so information about finishing details are available when irrevocable construction activities are performed.

There are a number of individual activities that must be performed. A report from the project coordinator identified the activities, with comments about each of them. The problem is to consider all activities and figure out how long it will take to complete the project.

> *Site Selection and Purchase:* If our new building is too far away from our present location, we'll lose some very talented people. We can get started on the site selection right away; I estimate it will take thirty days to select and purchase the site. Fortunately, we have a good idea about the space we need; we'll purchase the land with cash, which is already available. This will save us from any delays in arranging financing. Activity name: SITE.

> *Plans Preparation:* We have already retained an architect, who has assessed our needs and determined the requirements for the site. But the preparation of the plans can't begin until we have selected and purchased the site. Estimated time for plans preparation is forty-five days. Activity name: PLANS.

> *Revision of Plans:* Although we'll be working closely with the architect during the preparation of the plans, experience has shown that we should allow an additional thirty days to revise the plans after they have been prepared. This gives us time to consider unforeseen governmental

problems, or problems that come up when the plans receive wider distribution. Activity name: REVISE.

Arrange Financing: There's no way, of course, we want to pay for the construction with cash. In fact, we'll withdraw as much of the cash as we can from our site purchase, and arrange mortgage financing on the combined value of the land and building. So we'll start on this activity as soon as we have completed the site purchase. Estimated time to arrange financing is sixty days. Activity name: FINANCE.

Rough Construction: This phase of the construction involves site preparation, foundations, and structural elements. We'll begin on it as soon as the financing is complete and the plans are revised. Estimated time for rough construction is ninety days. Activity name: ROUGH.

Interior Design: When we can begin the rough construction, we can begin the detailed interior plans. The interior walls, plumbing, and electrical wiring don't need to be specified when we begin rough construction, so this design phase determines all of these details. This won't take too long; our estimate is twenty-five days. Activity name: INTERIOR DESIGN.

Purchase Furnishings: As soon as the interior design is completed, we need to order the furnishings (desks, tables, white boards, and similar items). This typically takes about 120 days, because we'll need some special items to fit our computing needs. Activity name: FURNISH.

Interior Construction: This is the final stage in the construction of the building. It can begin when two things have been finished: rough construction (above) and completion of the computer network design (discussed below). The current estimate for the time required for interior construction is seventy days. Activity name: INTERIOR CONSTRUCTION.

PC Selection: When we start looking for a site for the building, we'll also start selecting the PC equipment we'll use in the building. This process will take about 120 days, because everyone in the firm is a self-proclaimed expert in the field. Activity name: PC SELECT.

PC Purchase: After the PC equipment has been selected, we can begin the purchase process. We have enough clout with hardware vendors that we'll be able to get very good prices; since they think we're in a hurry, they won't budge for a while. So this step will require about ninety days to complete. Activity name: PC PURCHASE.

Network Design: All of our computing equipment will be interconnected with a network. Right now, it's not clear what type of cabling we'll use: it might be twisted pair (telephone wire), coaxial cable (much like TV antenna cable), optical fiber cabling, or we might even go with a wireless network. We can't begin the design until we have the PC equipment selected; the interior construction cannot begin until the network is designed, because cabling must be in place before interior walls are

---

Figure 8.1

Planning Network for Soft Ideas

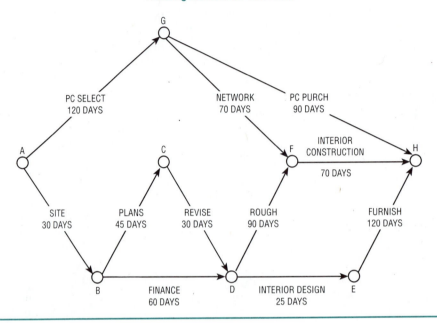

---

finished. This design process will take seventy days. Activity name: NETWORK.

To understand the way these activities fit together, a network is constructed. In general network terms, a network consists of arcs and nodes. In project planning terms, the network consists of activities and events.

An *activity* is a task that requires time to complete. Each activity is shown as an arc or arrow on the network. At each end of each activity is a node, which signifies an event. Associated with each activity is the time required to accomplish that activity. Each activity has a name associated with it, such as PC SELECT, NETWORK, and so on.

An *event* occurs when all of the activities pointing *to* that event have been completed; no activity which points *from* an event can begin until that event has occurred. We use letters to name events. In this scenario, we will have events A through H; the project is complete when event H occurs.

The network for Soft Ideas is shown in Figure 8.1. It begins at the left, when SITE and PC SELECT can begin; the project is complete when the rightmost events (PC PURCHASE, INTERIOR CONSTRUCTION, FURNISH) have all been finished. Each event has been given a letter name, A thru F. The activity times are also shown on the network.

Figure 8.2

Spreadsheet Model for Soft Ideas

	A	B	C	D	E	F	G
1		Scheduled					
2		Time of					
3	Event	Occurrence					
4	A	0					
5	B	25					
6	C	60					
7	D	120					
8	E	150					
9	F	200					
10	G	150					
11	H	250					
12							
13							
14							
15			Sched	Sched	Allowed		>= zero?
16	Activity	Duration	Start	Finish	by Sched	Slack	Constrnts
17	SITE	30	0	25	25	-5	Not >=
18	PLANS	45	25	60	35	-10	Not >=
19	REVISE	30	60	120	60	30	>=
20	FINANCE	60	25	120	95	35	>=
21	ROUGH	90	120	200	80	-10	Not >=
22	INT DES	25	120	150	30	5	>=
23	FURNISH	120	150	250	100	-20	Not >=
24	INT CONST	70	200	250	50	-20	Not >=
25	PC SELECT	120	0	150	150	30	>=
26	PC PURCH	90	150	250	100	10	>=
27	NETWORK	70	150	200	50	-20	Not >=

Using Optimization to Determine Project Completion Time

Finding the earliest time at which a project can be completed is an optimization problem.* For Soft Ideas, we want to find the earliest time at which event H can occur. Viewed in optimization terms, we want to minimize the time of occurrence for event H. To understand the spreadsheet model for optimizing the completion of the project, we start with an arbitrary schedule for each event. Then we check to see if that schedule will work. This is shown in the top part of Figure 8.2; event A is scheduled to start "now" or time 0; event B is scheduled to start at time 25, or 25 days from now.

The reader is encouraged to write these scheduled event times on Figure 8.1, and think about the proposed schedule. Will it work? How do you know? To answer that question, we look at the various activities, shown in the bottom part of the spreadsheet model of Figure 8.2. The first activity, SITE, requires 30 days. This activity is scheduled to start when event A occurs. On the spreadsheet,

---

*The calculation for determining the earliest time for which a project can be completed is not necessarily an optimization problem. An alternate view of the network will be used in a case following Chapter 14. This alternate view allows us to determine the earliest project completion using a completely different approach.

the value zero appears in cell C17, which agrees with the zero in the cell B4, showing the scheduled time for event A. The formula in cell C17 (row labeled SITE, in column labeled Sched Start) is +B4. This means that any change in the schedule for event A will be reflected in the Sched Start for SITE. Similarly, the Sched Finish for SITE is 25 (cell D17), in agreement with the time for event B in cell B5. Cell D17 (row SITE, column Sched Finish) contains the formula +B5, because the time for event B is shown in cell B5.

Tip: Keying this model can be simplified by using range (block) names. In the top part of the spreadsheet, the cell next to A is given the name A; the cell next to B is given the name B, and so on. These range names can easily be assigned by using the "Range Name Labels Right" command, /RNLR in Lotus 1-2-3 or /ENLR (Edit Name Labels Right) in Quattro Pro, and identifying the range (block) as A4..A11 (the cells that contain the event letters A thru H). When the information for each activity is keyed into the spreadsheet, the following process can be used, illustrated with the activity SITE in row 17:

A17: Enter the label for the activity, SITE.

B17: Enter the duration of the activity, 30.

C17: Enter the starting event, preceded by a "plus" sign: +A
(+A refers to the cell named A, which is cell B4.)

D17: Enter the ending event, preceded by a "plus" sign: +B
(+B refers to the cell named B, which is cell B5.)

This turns out to be considerably easier than using the cell pointer to point to cells for the formulas, because the information can be read directly from the picture of the network in Figure 8.1.

The next step is to create the information to determine if the schedule will work. The time allowed for each activity is computed by finding the difference between the Sched Finish time and the Sched Start time. If the time allowed is greater than the duration for an activity, there is *slack* on that activity. For each activity, the slack is calculated as the difference between the time allowed by the schedule and the duration of the activity. Positive slack means extra time has been allowed, while negative slack means that the schedule is infeasible. (When the What's*Best!* constraints are included in the worksheet, the symbols will indicate whether the amount of slack is greater than or equal to zero, as required by the constraint.)

Tip: The computations for the time Allowed by Sched and the slack can be keyed once into the spreadsheet, into cells E17..F17. Then these formulas can be copied for the rest of the activities, by copying from E17..F17 to D18..D27.

The optimization problem is now defined: we want to minimize the scheduled time for event H (the end of the project) by adjusting the scheduled times for each activity. To make sure the schedule is feasible, there can be no negative slack times. The complete optimization problem can now be stated as:

Figure 8.3

Influence Chart for Soft Ideas Model

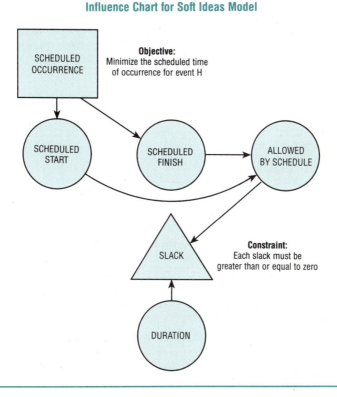

Decisions
(adjustable cells):   Scheduled times for each event B thru H. (The scheduled time for event A is set to zero.)

Constraints: The slack time for each activity must be greater than or equal to zero. These constraints are stored in G17..G27.

Objective: Minimize the scheduled time for event H.

Contrary to our usual habits, we have described the model by explaining the keystrokes involved in its construction. To solidify the reader's understanding of the logic of the model, the influence chart for the model is shown in Figure 8.3, with appropriate shapes for the optimization. In the influence chart, the schedule information (SCHEDULED OCCURRENCE) applies to the set of events; information about DURATION, SCHEDULED START, SCHEDULED FINISH, ALLOWED BY SCHEDULE, and SLACK applies to each activity. Verbal documentation is shown in Figure 8.4. Applying the optimization software yields Figure 8.5, which shows that the earliest the project can be completed is 265 days from now, the minimum completion time for event H.

The What's *Best!* software has been used to insert the marginal values (dual variables) in column H, adjacent to the constraints. Any constraint with a mar-

---

Figure 8.4

Verbal Documentation for Soft Ideas Model, Figure 8.2

In the documentation for this model, variable names are column labels on the worksheet; identifiers shown in square brackets, [ ], are taken from row labels. While this improves the readability of the documentation for this model, it is reversed from the customary practices of this book.

```
Scheduled Time of Occurrence[A] THRU[H] is shown in Figure 2, cells B4..B11

Duration[SITE] THRU[NETWORK] is shown in Figure 2, cells B17..B27

Sched Start[SITE] = Scheduled Time of Occurrence[A]
Sched Start[PLANS] = Scheduled Time of Occurrence[B]
Sched Start[REVISE] = Scheduled Time of Occurrence[C]
Sched Start[FINANCE] = Scheduled Time of Occurrence[B]
Sched Start[ROUGH THRU INT DES] = Scheduled Time of Occurrence[D]
Sched Start[FURNISH] = Scheduled Time of Occurrence[E]
Sched Start[INT CONST] = Scheduled Time of Occurrence[F]
Sched Start[PC SELECT] = Scheduled Time of Occurrence[A]
Sched Start[PC PURCH THRU NETWORK] = Scheduled Time of Occurrence[G]

Sched Finish[SITE] = Scheduled Time of Occurrence[B]
Sched Finish[PLANS] = Scheduled Time of Occurrence[C]
Sched Finish[REVISE] = Scheduled Time of Occurrence[D]
Sched Finish[FINANCE] = Scheduled Time of Occurrence[D]
Sched Finish[ROUGH] = Scheduled Time of Occurrence[F]
Sched Finish[INT DES] = Scheduled Time of Occurrence[E]
Sched Finish[FURNISH THRU INT CONST] = Scheduled Time of Occurrence[H]
Sched Finish[PC SELECT] = Scheduled Time of Occurrence[G]
Sched Finish[PC PURCH] = Scheduled Time of Occurrence[H]
Sched Finish[NETWORK] = Scheduled Time of Occurrence[F]

Allowed by Sched[SITE THRU NETWORK] = Sched Finish - Sched Start

Slack[SITE THRU NETWORK] = Allowed by Sched - Duration
```

---

ginal value of zero is not a tight constraint: Changing the constraint limit will not affect the objective (within the range of validity). Hence, none of the slack constraints with a zero marginal value is critical. On the other hand, all of the constraints with nonzero marginal values are *critical:* Changing the limiting value of the constraint will affect the objective or finish time. This is important because changing the slack from zero to one is conceptually identical to increasing the time required for an activity. Hence, the activities with nonzero marginal values are those which require the most managerial attention.

The path of activities with nonzero marginal values is called the *critical path* for a network. Any increase in time required for any of these activities will delay the project completion, on a day-for-day basis. From the marginal values, the activities SITE, PLANS, REVISE, ROUGH, and INT CONST make up the critical path. On the other hand, a slight slippage on the non-critical activities, FINANCE, INT DES, FURNISH, PC SELECT, PC PURCH, and NETWORK* will not affect the completion time.

---

*For those who like puzzles, contemplate the meaning of 0 slack *and* 0 marginal value for FURNISH and NETWORK. Together, these two values of 0 say that an activity has no slack, but it wouldn't delay the project if it had some. *Hint:* would it matter if event G had been scheduled for time 120 instead of 125? What would happen to the slack on PC SELECT? What would happen to the slack on NETWORK? What would happen to project completion?

Figure 8.5

Optimized Model for Soft Ideas

	A	B	C	D	E	F	G	H
1		Scheduled						
2		Time of						
3	Event	Occurrence						
4	A	0						
5	B	30						
6	C	75						
7	D	105						
8	E	130						
9	F	195						
10	G	125						
11	H	265						
12								
13								
14								
15			Sched	Sched	Allowed		>= zero?	Marginal
16	Activity	Duration	Start	Finish	by Sched	Slack	Constrnts	Value
17	SITE	30	0	30	30	0	=>=	1
18	PLANS	45	30	75	45	0	=>=	1
19	REVISE	30	75	105	30	0	=>=	1
20	FINANCE	60	30	105	75	15	>=	0
21	ROUGH	90	105	195	90	0	=>=	1
22	INT DES	25	105	130	25	0	=>=	0
23	FURNISH	120	130	265	135	15	>=	0
24	INT CONST	70	195	265	70	0	=>=	1
25	PC SELECT	120	0	125	125	5	>=	0
26	PC PURCH	90	125	265	140	50	>=	0
27	NETWORK	70	125	195	70	0	=>=	0

The sensitivity ranges can be used to tell how much each activity can be increased (by itself) without affecting project completion.

Tradeoffs in Scheduling: Cost and Time

In many situations, things can be done faster at a higher price. In a restaurant, this is called *tipping*. In the tax code, it might be called *facilitating payments*. In project scheduling, it is called *crashing* an activity. Crashing, or accomplishing an activity in less time than its original duration, can often be accomplished by overtime or by using additional resources. We now introduce this added information for Soft Ideas and the new building.

> We could accelerate the SITE selection process, but it means that we won't search or evaluate as thoroughly. These costs are difficult to assess, and we'll never really know what it cost to stop our search process three days early. As a planning figure, let's assume that we can cut off as much as five days for SITE selection, at a cost of $5000 per day.
>
> The architect informs us that we can pay the cost of overtime for the operators of the computer system that draws the plans. Each day of shortening the duration of PLANS costs $500, but we can only save two

days here. The rest of the activity is creative time, which is very difficult to accelerate.

We won't make any changes in the allowed time to REVISE the plans, because we might end up with a building that doesn't meet our needs.

Making the arrangements to FINANCE the project can be shortened substantially. We can put more people on the project, allowing us to cut this time to as little as forty-five days. Each day we shorten the time costs $100, when we consider the "learning time" of people we switch into this activity.

Preparing the INTerior DESign is another one of those creative activities. The clerical work involved is not very extensive, but with some additional staffing we can save up to five days at a cost of $50 per day.

We can obtain the FURNISHings quicker by using expedited shipping. This activity is already tightly scheduled, using leased trucks for delivery so we maintain control over the schedules. To get this done any faster, we would need to use air shipments. Each day we shorten this activity costs about $3000 in additional shipping costs. Even at that expense, we can't save more than ten days.

Both the ROUGH construction and the INTerior CONSTruction can be expedited. The contractor we have been talking with insists on a late construction penalty of no more than $5000 per day. Although we haven't talked explicitly about this, a bonus for early completion of $10,000 per day (for up to ten days on each activity) should be something we would negotiate. Of course, if we negotiate this into the contract, we want to be certain that it becomes *our* option, not the option of the contractor.

Each of the three PC related activities (PC SELECTion, PC PURCHase, and NETWORK selection) can be crashed up to ten days, at a cost we guess at $500 per day, by talking to fewer people in the selection phases and to fewer vendors in the purchase phase.

Soft Ideas would like to have the project completed in 250 days. Which activities should be crashed to reach this target? The influence chart of Figure 8.6 shows the introduction of a new decision variable, DAYS TO CRASH. Instead of finishing as quickly as possible, we now want to minimize the total cost of crashing. The cell Sched Finish (which has the same value as the scheduled time for event H) will be constrained by an upper limit of 250.

The spreadsheet model to perform this optimization is shown in Figure 8.7, which builds upon the optimized model shown in Figure 8.5. The column showing slack (before crashing) has been titled Slack W/Out Crash; other columns have been added: Days to Crash, Slack with Crash, Daily Crash Cost, and Crash Limit. Days to Crash is arbitrary at this point; optimization will adjust the values. The Slack with Crash is the previous definition of slack, plus the number of days we decide to crash. The Daily Crash Cost is from the scenario above. The Crash Limit is from the scenario. The Total Crash Cost is calculated using @SUMPRODUCT, with the Days to Crash and Daily Crash Cost ranges. As starting values, we have used

Figure 8.6

Influence Chart for Soft Ideas with Crashing

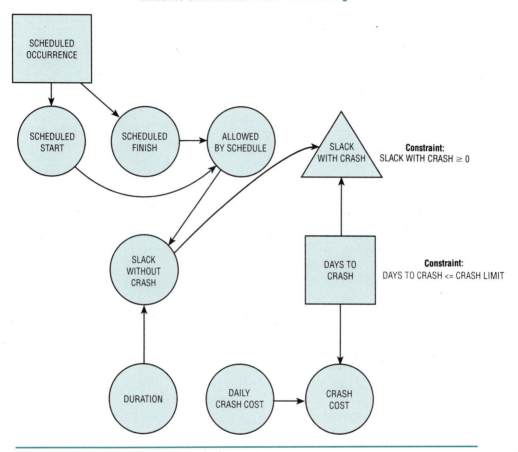

an arbitrary schedule and arbitrary crash times. This arbitrary schedule appears to get the project completed in time, because the scheduled time for event H is equal to the target of 250 days. But it isn't feasible; there are negative values for Slack with Crash.

The directions for the optimization problem are changed by the inclusion of crashing: We now want to find the least-cost way to complete the project in 250 days.

Decisions: Scheduled time for each event (as before).
Days to crash for each activity.

Constraints: The scheduled time for the occurrence of event H, the time at which the network is finished, must be less than or equal to 250 days, or the cell B11 must be equal to the target value shown in cell E11.

Figure 8.7

Soft Ideas' Spreadsheet Model with Crashing

	A	B	C	D	E	F	G	H	I	J	K	L
1		Scheduled										
2		Time of										
3	Event	Occurrence	Cnstrt	Target								
4	A	0										
5	B	25										
6	C	68										
7	D	98										
8	E	130										
9	F	188										
10	G	118										
11	H	250		=<=	250							

							Slack	Days			Slack	Daily
14			Sched	Sched	Allwd	W/Out	to Crash	Crash	With	Slack	Crash
15	Acvty	Durat	Start	Fnsh	bySch	Crash	Crash	Cnstr	Limit	Crash	Cnstr	Cost
17	SITE	30	0	25	25	-5	1	<=	5	- 4	Not >=	5000
18	PLANS	45	25	68	43	-2	2	=<=	2	0	=>=	500
19	REVISE	30	68	98	30	0	3	Not <=	0	3	>=	0
20	FINANC	60	25	98	73	13	0	<=	15	13	>=	100
21	ROUGH	90	98	188	90	0	0	<=	10	0	=>=	10000
22	INT DE	25	98	130	32	7	0	<=	5	7	>=	50
23	FURNIS	120	130	250	120	0	0	<=	10	0	=>=	3000
24	INT CO	70	188	250	62	-8	8	<=	10	0	=>=	10000
25	PC SEL	120	0	118	118	-2	1	<=	10	-1	Not >=	500
26	PC PUR	90	118	250	132	42	0	<=	10	42	>=	500
27	NETWOR	70	118	188	70	0	1	<=	10	1	>=	500

	A
30	Total Crash Cost
31	(using @SUMPRODUCT)
33	87000

There are crash constraints, stored in H17..H27. These constraints require that the Days to Crash must be less than or equal to the Crash Limit, for each activity.

There are slack constraints, stored in K17..K27. These constraints require that the Slack with Crash must be greater than or equal to zero, for each activity.

Objective: Minimize the Total Crash Cost (shown before optimization as $87,000 in Figure 8.7, using arbitrary values for Days to Crash). The value of the Total Crash Cost is calculated using the @SUMPRODUCT function, @SUMPRODUCT(G17..G27,I17..I27).

It is left as an exercise to demonstrate that the project can be completed in 250 days at a crash cost of $107,000.

Flows in Networks

A network of friends and associates focuses on the connections and relationships within the network. Our view of project planning focuses on the way the events are connected, or the way the activities relate to each other. But a pipeline network or a transportation network has additional dimensions: Things flow through the network, and each unit shipped through an arc of the network may have a cost of using that arc. The concepts of flows through networks are illustrated with the Fast Pack Delivery Company.

Fast Pack Delivery Company

Fast Pack is a small-package delivery company that has established a network of trucking lines with trucks that travel along arcs or routes between pairs of cities. There is an opportunity to go after extra business by accepting an order to ship a large number of packages from city 1 to city 7. The trucks have unused space on various arcs that connect cities near 1 and 7. How many packages can Fast Pack ship from 1 to 7 without adding any capacity to the network? The network between the cities is shown pictorially in Figure 8.8. All arcs have capacity limits, shown as a number of packages on each arc, with an arrow indicating the direction of travel. Arcs that permit traffic in both directions have two capacity values, with arrows indicating the capacity in each direction. This same information is shown as a table in Figure 8.9, with two-direction arcs shown as two separate lines on the table.

To construct an influence chart for Fast Pack, we start with what we want to find from the spreadsheet:

> The spreadsheet must calculate the number of packages entering each node. For the *sink* node or destination, this is the number of packages flowing through the network to the final destination.

Figure 8.8

Fast Pack's Network of Truck Routes

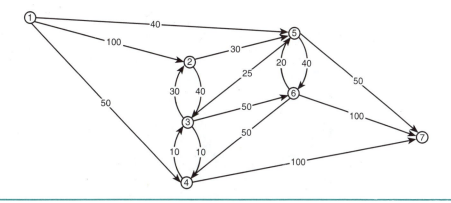

Figure 8.9

Network Capacity for Fast Pack's Extra Business

From	To	Capacity	From	To	Capacity
1	2	100	3	6	50
1	4	50	4	3	10
1	5	40	4	7	100
2	3	40	5	6	20
2	5	30	5	7	50
3	2	30	6	4	50
3	4	10	6	5	40
3	5	25	6	7	100

The spreadsheet must calculate the number of packages leaving each node. For the *source* node or the beginning of the network, this is the number of packages starting through the network. (Unless there are strange things happening, the number of packages entering the network will be the same as the number of packages arriving at the destination.)

The spreadsheet must show the flow along each arc of the network. These arc flows are used to calculate the flow to and from each of the nodes.

The influence chart (Figure 8.10) is quite simple: The flow to and from each node is influenced by the flow along the arcs. (As we will see, the spreadsheet logic to accomplish this is more interesting than the influence chart might indicate.)

The optimization instructions for this problem will be to maximize the number of packages shipped to the destination node. The flow along each arc will be adjusted to achieve this maximization, subject to constraints: No arc flow

---

Figure 8.10

Influence Chart for Fast Pack

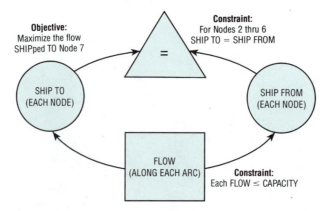

can exceed the capacity of the arc, and the number of packages shipped to each intermediate node must equal the number of packages shipped from that node.

Constructing a Spreadsheet Model for Fast Pack

The logic of the influence chart is quite simple, but the spreadsheet model we will develop to implement the logic is quite different from anything we have used before. To understand the spreadsheet logic, we walk through the spreadsheet rather slowly. The first step is to key into the spreadsheet the information shown in Figure 8.9. Allowing a few rows for headings, start with the first row (an arc from 1 to 2 with a capacity of 100 packages) in A3:

A3:	1	the beginning of the first arc
B3:	2	the ending of the first arc
C3:	100	the capacity of the first arc

This is repeated in the next row for the next arc, and so on for all sixteen arcs. The spreadsheet now has the appearance of the first three columns of Figure 8.11. Arbitrary Flow values have been assigned to represent flows in the network, shown in column D. These values may even be silly: flow occurs from 2 to 3, and then back from 3 to 2. Some arbitrary flows exceed the capacity of the arc. These arbitrary values, of course, will be adjusted in the optimization process.

Columns A thru D of the worksheet are straightforward; however, the constraints and objective have not yet been incorporated into the spreadsheet model. (Column E is reserved to store constraints.) Column F shows the various flows that come from node 1 (the source, or beginning of the network). If one were producing this column manually, it is a snap; we selectively transcribe either a flow or zero into this column:

──────────────── **Figure 8.11** ────────────────

Beginning Fast Pack's Spreadsheet Model

	A	B	C	D	E	F
1						From
2	From	To	Capacity	Flow		1
3	1	2	100	10		10
4	1	4	50	0		0
5	1	5	40	30		30
6	2	3	40	40		0
7	2	5	30	50		0
8	3	2	30	40		0
9	3	4	10	30		0
10	3	5	25	0		0
11	3	6	50	0		0
12	4	3	10	0		0
13	4	7	100	100		0
14	5	6	20	10		0
15	5	7	50	50		0
16	6	4	50	40		0
17	6	5	40	0		0
18	6	7	100	10		0

For each row: if there is a 1 in column A, transcribe the flow from column D into column F. If there is anything other than a 1 in column A, place a 0 in column F.

Accomplishing this selective transcription from column D to column F takes advantage of the spreadsheet's ability to use @IF logic to tell if there is a value of 1 in the first column. Consider this expression:

@IF(A3=1,1,0)　　　(the arc's beginning node is in cell A3)

This expression will have the value 1 if the arc starts at 1, and the value 0 if it does not. Now let's extend the expression, which will be entered in cell F3:

F3:　　@IF(A3=1,1,0)*D3　　　(the flow over the arc is in cell D3)

This expression in F3 will perform the selective transcription. If the node doesn't start at 1, the flow is multiplied by zero from the @IF function. Since anything multiplied by zero is zero, this will always insert a value of zero for arcs that don't start at 1. If the node starts at 1, the flow is transcribed because multiplying by 1 (from the IF clause) does not change anything.

The logic in the last paragraph is particularly important; if you are having trouble with it, get out the spreadsheet and experiment a bit! A reader unfamiliar with logic like this is encouraged to enter the spreadsheet model of Figure 8.11, and understand how it works. (It turns out that the documentation style we have been using in earlier models doesn't help much, because we are using things that aren't oriented into strict rows and columns.)

One could complete the spreadsheet with the logic we have just described. But constructing the spreadsheet is greatly simplified by using the spreadsheet capability of *absolute addresses*, as described in Figure 8.12. Our purpose in this section is to develop an expression that we can place in cell F3 (the "From 1" flow for arc 12) and copy into corresponding cells for all arcs and all originating nodes.

The "From 1" flow for arc 12 is in cell E3 of the spreadsheet, Figure 8.11. Instead of the expression we developed above, we use absolute addresses with this expression:

F3:　　@IF($A3=F$2,1,0)*$D3

which has this meaning:

If the beginning of the arc is equal to the node labeled at the top of this column, use the value 1 as the multiplier for the flow over this arc. Otherwise, use the value 0 as the multiplier for the flow over this arc.

The advantage of this expression is that it can be copied to a number of cells, into columns corresponding to the seven nodes and into rows corresponding to the sixteen arcs of the network, as shown in Figure 8.13. The expression in F3 has been copied to the rectangular range F3..L18. The value of each cell in this range F3..L18 shows the flow over the arc (row) that comes from the node shown by the column label.

—————————————— **Figure 8.12** ——————————————

A Summary of Absolute and Relative Addresses in Spreadsheets

A cell reference such as G4 has a clear meaning when it appears in a formula. But when that formula is copied into another cell, some things change. If the formula in cell F1 refers to cell G4, the reference to cell G4 really means the cell that is one column right (from F to G) and three rows down (from 1 to 4). If the contents of cell F1 are copied to cell F2, the cell reference will no longer be G4, but will be the cell G5, which is still one column right and three rows down. We illustrate these ideas with this simple spreadsheet, showing three people and amounts, the total, and the three amounts expressed as a percentage of the total.

	A	B	C
1	Jim	4	20%
2	Joe	6	30%
3	Jan	10	50%
4	Total	20	

The column total is in B4; cell C1 contains the formula to divide B1 by B4. However, copying the formula +B1/B4 would cause adjustments to be made in both B1 and B4; the problem is that we don't want the divisor (B4) to be adjusted when we copy from C1 to C2..C3. This is accomplished by referring not to cell B4, but to cell $B$4. The dollar signs keep the reference to the same cell, column B row 4. Next we look at the same spreadsheet, with the format of the formula cells changed to **Text** format, a format (which you may not have used) from the **Range** format section of the spreadsheet menu tree. The formula in C1 was entered from the keyboard; it was copied to C2..C3. The copy command automatically adjusts the numerator (upstairs) of the fraction, but makes no adjustments in the denominator (downstairs) of the fraction, because of the $ signs.

	A	B	C	
1	Jim	4	+B1/$B$4	<==This cell was entered from keyboard
2	Joe	6	+B2/$B$4	<==This cell was copied from C1
3	Jan	10	+B3/$B$4	<==This cell was copied from C1
4	Total	@SUM(B1..B3)		

If this isn't making sense, it's time to get out the spreadsheet and experiment with these concepts! It's getting a bit more complicated now, because we go to the concept of *mixed* addresses: those which are partially relative and partially absolute. In a mixed cell reference, only one dollar sign appears: a dollar sign before the column letter "fixes" the column; a dollar sign before the row number "fixes" the row. Suppose cell A1 has an expression which refers to cell B$4. When this expression is copied to another cell, it refers to the cell that is one column to the right (from column A to column B) and in row 4 (because the reference is to row $4). Copying cell A1 to B2 would change the cell reference (in A1) from B$4 to the cell reference (in B2) C$4, which is one column right, still in row 4. If cell A1 contains a reference to cell $B4 (always column B, three rows down), which is copied to cell B2, the cell reference $B4 (in A1) becomes $B5 (still column B, but three rows down).

The reader should have learned by now that this text advocates use of the cell pointer to enter cell addresses in formulas. But the discussion above talks about putting dollar signs into formulas as if they came from the keyboard. Using the dollar sign key gets the job done. But there is an alternative, which is usually better: Use the [F4] (absolute) key. After pointing to (say) cell B2 with the cell pointer, press [F4] one time and B2 becomes $B$2. Pressing [F4] again changes the cell reference to B$2. Next is $B2, followed by a return to B2.

This same process is used to find the flows that go to each node, shown in columns M thru S of the worksheet (Figure 8.13). This expression is entered in cell M3:

$$\text{M3:} \qquad \text{@IF(\$B3=M\$2,1,0)*\$D3}$$

Figure 8.13

Fast Pack's Model Showing Flows To and From Nodes

	A B	C	D	E	F	G	H	I	J	K	L	M	N	O	P	Q	R	S
1					From	—	—	—	—	—	—	To	—	—	—	—	—	—
2	FrTo	Capa	Flow	Cstr	1	2	3	4	5	6	7	1	2	3	4	5	6	7
3	1 2	100	10	<=	10	0	0	0	0	0	0	0	10	0	0	0	0	0
4	1 4	50	0	<=	0	0	0	0	0	0	0	0	0	0	0	0	0	0
5	1 5	40	30	<=	30	0	0	0	0	0	0	0	0	0	0	30	0	0
6	2 3	40	40	=<=	0	40	0	0	0	0	0	0	0	40	0	0	0	0
7	2 5	30	50	Not	0	50	0	0	0	0	0	0	0	0	0	50	0	0
8	3 2	30	40	Not	0	0	40	0	0	0	0	0	40	0	0	0	0	0
9	3 4	10	30	Not	0	0	30	0	0	0	0	0	0	0	30	0	0	0
10	3 5	25	0	<=	0	0	0	0	0	0	0	0	0	0	0	0	0	0
11	3 6	50	0	<=	0	0	0	0	0	0	0	0	0	0	0	0	0	0
12	4 3	10	0	<=	0	0	0	0	0	0	0	0	0	0	0	0	0	0
13	4 7	100	100	=<=	0	0	0	100	0	0	0	0	0	0	0	0	0	100
14	5 6	20	10	<=	0	0	0	0	10	0	0	0	0	0	0	0	10	0
15	5 7	50	50	=<=	0	0	0	0	50	0	0	0	0	0	0	0	0	50
16	6 4	50	40	<=	0	0	0	0	0	40	0	0	0	0	40	0	0	0
17	6 5	40	0	<=	0	0	0	0	0	0	0	0	0	0	0	0	0	0
18	6 7	100	10	<=	0	0	0	0	0	10	0	0	0	0	0	0	0	10
19	Totals				40	90	70	100	60	50	0	0	50	40	70	80	10	160
20	Constraints					Not	Not	Not	Not	Not	=							

This expression is copied to each cell in the rectangular range M3..S18. Each cell in this range now shows the flow over the arc (row) that goes to the node shown by the column label.

The next step in constructing the worksheet is to sum each of the flow columns. This is done using relative addresses (no dollar signs) in this way:

F19:   @SUM(F3..F18)   which is copied to the range G19..S19.

We are now ready to optimize. The instructions for the optimizer are quite straightforward:

Decisions: Adjust the flows in the various arcs, cells D3..D18.

Constraints: Each of the flows (D3..D18) must be less than or equal to the capacities, shown in cells C3..C18. These constraints are stored in E3..E18.

For each intermediate node (nodes 2 through 6) the *flow from* must be equal to the *flow to*. The flow from each node is calculated in G19..K19; these cells are constrained to be equal to the flow to these nodes, shown in N19..R19. These constraints are stored in G20..K20.

Objective: Maximize flow from node 1, which is calculated in cell F19 (or maximize the flow into node 7, which is calculated in cell S19).

The problem, formulated as we have described, is a linear optimization problem. The results of the optimization are shown in Figure 8.14. This shows

Figure 8.14

Optimized Spreadsheet for Fast Pack

					From							To						
Fr	To	Capa	Flow	Cstr	1	2	3	4	5	6	7	1	2	3	4	5	6	7
1	2	100	70	<=	70	0	0	0	0	0	0	0	70	0	0	0	0	0
1	4	50	50	=<=	50	0	0	0	0	0	0	0	0	0	50	0	0	0
1	5	40	40	=<=	40	0	0	0	0	0	0	0	0	0	0	40	0	0
2	3	40	40	=<=	0	40	0	0	0	0	0	0	0	40	0	0	0	0
2	5	30	30	=<=	0	30	0	0	0	0	0	0	0	0	0	30	0	0
3	2	30	0	<=	0	0	0	0	0	0	0	0	0	0	0	0	0	0
3	4	10	10	=<=	0	0	10	0	0	0	0	0	0	0	10	0	0	0
3	5	25	0	<=	0	0	0	0	0	0	0	0	0	0	0	0	0	0
3	6	50	30	<=	0	0	30	0	0	0	0	0	0	0	0	0	30	0
4	3	10	0	<=	0	0	0	0	0	0	0	0	0	0	0	0	0	0
4	7	100	60	<=	0	0	0	60	0	0	0	0	0	0	0	0	0	60
5	6	20	20	=<=	0	0	0	0	20	0	0	0	0	0	0	0	20	0
5	7	50	50	=<=	0	0	0	0	50	0	0	0	0	0	0	0	0	50
6	4	50	0	<=	0	0	0	0	0	0	0	0	0	0	0	0	0	0
6	5	40	0	<=	0	0	0	0	0	0	0	0	0	0	0	0	0	0
6	7	100	50	<=	0	0	0	0	0	50	0	0	0	0	0	0	0	50
Totals					160	70	40	60	70	50	0	0	70	40	60	70	50	160
Constraints					=	=	=	=	=									

that the network can handle 160 packages from the source node (1) to the destination node (7), without violating any arc capacities. This maximum flow, 160 packages, is the flow out of source node 1, as shown in cell F19 (and in cell S19, showing the flow into the sink node 7).

Combining Flows and Costs

After studying the results of the optimization, management of Fast Pack was concerned about the added costs that might result from accepting an additional 160 packages for shipping over the network. For many arcs, there is a shipping and handling cost associated with handling another package. What would it cost to handle more packages? The handling costs for each arc were determined, and the problem was restructured:

What is the minimum cost of accepting 100 packages?

What is the minimum cost of accepting 110 packages?

What is the minimum cost of accepting 120 packages?

and so on up to the maximum of 160 packages. The influence chart for costs is shown in Figure 8.15; the optimized spreadsheet (shipping 130 packages) is shown in Figure 8.16. The only modification is the addition of columns S and T: the unit cost of shipping on each arc, and the unit cost multiplied by the flow on that arc. The objective is to minimize the cost of the flow (cell T19). The former objective, flow from node 1, becomes a constraint: Cell F19 must be equal to 130. The results of optimization with flows from 100 packages to 160 packages are shown in Figure 8.17.

Figure 8.15

Influence Chart for Fast Pack with Costs

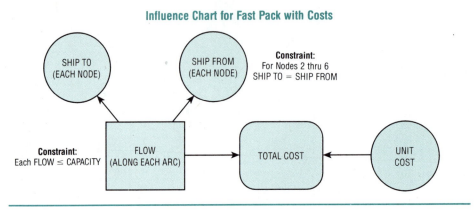

Figure 8.16

Optimized Network for Fast Pack with Costs for 130 Packages

	A	B	C	D	E	F	G	H	I	J	K	L	M	N	O	P	Q	R	S	T
1						From							To							Unit
2		Fr	To	Capa	Flow	Cstr 1	2	3	4	5	6	7	1	2	3	4	5	6	7	Cost
3	1	2	100	40	<=	40	0	0	0	0	0	0	0	40	0	0	0	0	0	2
4	1	4	50	50	=<=	50	0	0	0	0	0	0	0	0	0	50	0	0	0	3
5	1	5	40	40	=<=	40	0	0	0	0	0	0	0	0	0	0	40	0	0	0
6	2	3	40	30	<=	0	30	0	0	0	0	0	0	0	30	0	0	0	0	1
7	2	5	30	10	<=	0	10	0	0	0	0	0	0	0	0	0	10	0	0	4
8	3	2	30	0	<=	0	0	0	0	0	0	0	0	0	0	0	0	0	0	2
9	3	4	10	10	=<=	0	0	10	0	0	0	0	0	0	0	10	0	0	0	3
10	3	5	25	0	<=	0	0	0	0	0	0	0	0	0	0	0	0	0	0	4
11	3	6	50	20	<=	0	0	20	0	0	0	0	0	0	0	0	0	20	0	3
12	4	3	10	0	<=	0	0	0	0	0	0	0	0	0	0	0	0	0	0	5
13	4	7	100	80	<=	0	0	0	80	0	0	0	0	0	0	0	0	0	80	1
14	5	6	20	0	<=	0	0	0	0	0	0	0	0	0	0	0	0	0	0	2
15	5	7	50	50	=<=	0	0	0	0	50	0	0	0	0	0	0	0	0	50	2
16	6	4	50	20	<=	0	0	0	0	0	20	0	0	0	0	20	0	0	0	1
17	6	5	40	0	<=	0	0	0	0	0	0	0	0	0	0	0	0	0	0	0
18	6	7	100	0	<=	0	0	0	0	0	0	0	0	0	0	0	0	0	0	4
19	Totals					130	40	30	80	50	20	0	0	40	30	80	50	20	130	
20	Constraint				=>=	=	=	=	=	=		Total (using SUMPRODUCT)							590
21	Requirement				130															

These costs illustrate the economist's concept of increasing marginal cost. Moving from 100 to 140 packages increases the cost by $8 per package. But moving from 150 to 160 packages increases the cost by $12 per package. It becomes increasingly more expensive to ship additional packages as the network comes closer to its maximum capacity.

Finding the Shortest Path Through a Network

"What's the shortest way to get there?" That question seeks the shortest path through a network. One often wants to find the shortest (miles) or the quickest

---------- **Figure 8.17** ----------

Fast Pack's Network with Costs: Results of Multiple Optimizations

Number of Packages	Minimum Cost
100	$350
110	430
120	510
130	590
140	670
150	770
160	890

(minutes) or the cheapest (dollars) way to get from one place to another. All of these questions are "shortest path" problems. The technique we have used to find the minimum cost of achieving a specified flow through a network can be used to find the shortest path through a network. The cost along each arc is the measure of distance (miles, minutes, dollars) for each arc. We want to have a flow of one unit (the person or thing going from here to there), and we want to accomplish it at minimum miles, minutes, or dollars.

To illustrate a shortest path problem, we'll find the shortest path from Fast Pack's node 1 to node 7; we replace the unit cost column with a miles column. (We assume that one-way arcs indicate that travel is possible in only one direction on those arcs.) In the optimization, we want to have one entity (person or thing) flowing to node 7; this becomes a constraint. The capacity constraints are no

---------- **Figure 8.18** ----------

Shortest Path Through Fast Pack's Network: Optimal Solution

	A	B	C	D	E	F	G	H	I	J	K	L	M	N	O	P	Q	R	S	T
1						From								To						
2		FrToCapaFlowCstr				1	2	3	4	5	6	7	1	2	3	4	5	6	7	Mls
3	1	2	100	1	<=	1	0	0	0	0	0	0	0	1	0	0	0	0	0	10
4	1	4	50	0	<=	0	0	0	0	0	0	0	0	0	0	0	0	0	0	35
5	1	5	40	0	<=	0	0	0	0	0	0	0	0	0	0	0	0	0	0	50
6	2	3	40	1	<=	0	1	0	0	0	0	0	0	0	1	0	0	0	0	20
7	2	5	30	0	<=	0	0	0	0	0	0	0	0	0	0	0	0	0	0	40
8	3	2	30	0	<=	0	0	0	0	0	0	0	0	0	0	0	0	0	0	20
9	3	4	10	0	<=	0	0	0	0	0	0	0	0	0	0	0	0	0	0	10
10	3	5	25	1	<=	0	0	1	0	0	0	0	0	0	0	0	1	0	0	15
11	3	6	50	0	<=	0	0	0	0	0	0	0	0	0	0	0	0	0	0	25
12	4	3	10	0	<=	0	0	0	0	0	0	0	0	0	0	0	0	0	0	10
13	4	7	100	0	<=	0	0	0	0	0	0	0	0	0	0	0	0	0	0	65
14	5	6	20	0	<=	0	0	0	0	0	0	0	0	0	0	0	0	0	0	5
15	5	7	50	1	<=	0	0	0	0	1	0	0	0	0	0	0	0	0	1	25
16	6	4	50	0	<=	0	0	0	0	0	0	0	0	0	0	0	0	0	0	40
17	6	5	40	0	<=	0	0	0	0	0	0	0	0	0	0	0	0	0	0	5
18	6	7	100	0	<=	0	0	0	0	0	0	0	0	0	0	0	0	0	0	30
19	Totals					1	1	1	0	1	0	0	0	1	1	0	1	0	1	
20	Constraint			=>=	=	=	=	=	=			Total	(using	SUMPRODUCT)		70				
21	Requirement			1																

longer necessary (although they are shown in the model). The shortest path is shown in Figure 8.18; it is made up of the arcs with a flow of 1: from 1 to 2, 2 to 3, 3 to 5, and 5 to 7. The total distance traveled is 70 miles.

Exercises

1. A project has six tasks, whose duration and starting and ending nodes are shown in this table:

Activity 1	Starts at A	Terminates at B	Requires 2 hours
Activity 2	Starts at A	Terminates at C	Requires 4 hours
Activity 3	Starts at B	Terminates at E	Requires 8 hours
Activity 4	Starts at C	Terminates at E	Requires 5 hours
Activity 5	Starts at C	Terminates at D	Requires 1 hour
Activity 6	Starts at D	Terminates at E	Requires 6 hours

a. Construct the picture of the network. Start by placing the nodes (A through E) on paper, then connecting them with activities as shown above.

b. With some mental experimentation, verify by studying the picture that the shortest time to complete the project is 11 hours. You can use this as a check figure for the optimization model you will be building.

c. Construct a spreadsheet model similar to Figure 8.2, using scheduled times for A through E of 0, 2, 4, 6, and 8.

d. Using optimization, verify that 11 hours is the minimum time for project completion.

e. Using the marginal values from optimization, verify that the *critical path* is ACDE. Choose one of the three activities on the path, and lengthen its required time by one day. What is the impact on the minimum time for project completion? Is this consistent with the concept of marginal values and the critical path?

f. Choose an activity that is not on the critical path, and lengthen its require time by one day. What is the impact on the minimum time for project completion? Is this consistent with the concept of marginal values and the critical path?

2. There is an opportunity to crash some of the activities in the project of Exercise 1. No activity may be crashed by more than two hours; the minimum time (after crashing) cannot be less than one hour for any activity. The cost of crashing each activity is:

Activity 1 (AB):	$4 per hour
Activity 2 (AC):	$9 per hour
Activity 3 (BE):	$5 per hour
Activity 4 (CE):	$6 per hour
Activity 5 (CD):	$8 per hour
Activity 6 (DE):	$7 per hour

a. Construct a spreadsheet model similar to Figure 8.7 for this project. Find the minimum cost of completing the project in nine hours.

b. What is the minimum time in which the network can be completed with crashing?

c. What is the minimum cost of completing the project in the minimum time you identified in the previous question? (The minimum time just determined will be a constraint in this optimization problem.)

3. Construct a model for optimization to find the earliest project completion (starting at time 0) for this project planning network. Activities are given names such as ACT 1; events are given letter names.

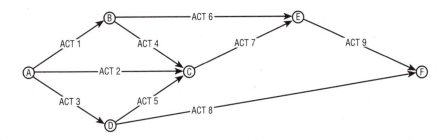

The number of days duration for each activity is shown in this table:

Activity 1	10 days
Activity 2	20 days
Activity 3	17 days
Activity 4	15 days
Activity 5	13 days
Activity 6	30 days
Activity 7	14 days
Activity 8	40 days
Activity 9	25 days

a. What is the shortest time in which the project can be completed?

b. Interpret the marginal values associated with the constraints on slack for each activity.

c. Identify the critical path.

d. Interpret the validity range for the marginal values associated with the constraints on slack for each activity.

4. The project in the exercise above must be completed in fifty days. Each activity can be crashed up to six days, at a cost of $100 per day for activities 1–4, and $150 per day for the remaining activities.

a. Modify the optimization model to include crashing and the associated costs.

b. What is the minimum cost for completing the project in fifty days?

c. Interpret the marginal values associated with the constraints on slack for each activity.

d. What is the shortest possible time to complete the project?

e. Using the shortest completion time (from the exercise above) as a constraint, what is the minimum cost of completing the project in this amount of time?

f. The company can spend only $900 in crash costs. What is the minimum time in which the project can be completed?

5. On the spreadsheet model for Soft Ideas, shown in Figure 8.2, change the duration of SITE to 35 days, PLANS to 30 days, and REVISE to 60 days. Apply optimization to find the minimum completion time for the project. Identify the activities that are on the critical path, using the marginal values for the slack constraints.

6. For Soft Ideas (using duration values shown in the chapter) verify that the optimal solution to the spreadsheet of Figure 8.7 results in a crash cost of $107,000.

7. Two new activities have been added to the Soft Ideas project. Activity AC is to TALK to contractors, to be in a better position to evaluate construction bids. This activity will require eighty days; it can be crashed by no more than 40 days, at a cost of $2000 per day. Activity CF is EVALUATE types of interior construction. This activity will require 100 days; it can be crashed up to 10 days at a cost of $3000 per day.

a. What is the minimum time for project completion?

b. What is the total cost of crashing, if the project must be completed in 250 days?

c. What is the shortest time to project completion, with a crash budget of $90,000?

d. What is the minimum crash cost for completing the project as quickly as possible?

8. A network has these arcs:

1 to 2	with a capacity of 100	and a unit cost of $2
1 to 4	with a capacity of 120	and a unit cost of $3
2 to 3	with a capacity of 40	and a unit cost of $4
3 to 2	with a capacity of 50	and a unit cost of $5
3 to 4	with a capacity of 60	and a unit cost of $6
2 to 5	with a capacity of 30	and a unit cost of $7
3 to 5	with a capacity of 50	and a unit cost of $8
4 to 5	with a capacity of 70	and a unit cost of $9

a. Construct the picture showing the network arcs. Start with the five nodes, 1, 2, 3, 4, and 5; add the arcs. *Hint:* place 1 on the left; 5 on the right, and 2, 3, and 4 arranged vertically between 1 and 5.

b. Construct a spreadsheet model similar to Figure 8.13. Use optimization to find the maximum flow from 1 to 5.

   c. Using a spreadsheet model similar to Figure 8.16, find the minimum cost of shipping 130 units from 1 to 5.

   d. What is the maximum number of units that can be shipped for a budget of $1200?

9. A pipeline network has capacity available along portions of its network. There is a need to ship as many units as possible from 1 to 7. The list of arcs, their beginning and ending nodes, and the capacity available on each arc is shown in this table, where the first number represents the origin of the arc, the second number represents the destination of the arc:

12	20	34	11
13	35	35	13
14	12	45	10
26	22	57	33
23	15	65	17
27	27	67	24

   a. Construct a diagram showing the network and the capacities.

   b. Using optimization, what is the maximum amount that can be sent from 1 to 7?

   c. The cost of shipping one unit along each arc is shown in this table:

12	2	34	1
13	3	35	4
14	1	45	1
26	2	57	3
23	1	65	1
27	2	67	2

     What is the minimum cost for sending forty units from 1 to 7?

10. Verify each of the cost figures shown in Figure 8.17 of the text.

11. The critical path for a project planning network (such as Soft Ideas) can be viewed as the longest path through the network. Using a spreadsheet similar in design to Figure 8.18, find the critical path (the longest path) for the Soft Ideas project, shown in Figure 8.1.

9

Optimization Models Involving Time

Spreadsheets are often ideal for depicting behavior over time; just as in many accounting statements, each column can be used to represent a different time period (or an aggregation of several time periods). This lets us build models for optimization to support decisions in which timing is important. We begin the chapter with an example illustrating purchasing in a fluctuating market.

Example: Purchasing in a Fluctuating Market

The Hesse Corporation purchases refrigerators for resale. It has found that prices fluctuate from month to month in a rather predictable manner. Hesse has the capacity to store up to 2500 refrigerators, but at a cost which also varies from month to month. For the next five months, Hesse is planning on these unit purchase costs and monthly storage costs:

January: $215 to purchase one refrigerator, $7 to store one
February: $225 to purchase one refrigerator, $2 to store one
March: $225 to purchase one refrigerator, $4 to store one
April: $228 to purchase one refrigerator, $3 to store one
May: $235 to purchase one refrigerator, $3 to store one

The storage costs are based on the number of refrigerators in stock at the end of each month. During the month, there is a flow of refrigerators into the warehouse (from purchases) and out of the warehouse (from sales); Hesse's experience has shown that using the ending inventory each month gives a good representation of the storage costs for the month.

Figure 9.1

Influence Chart for Hesse Corporation

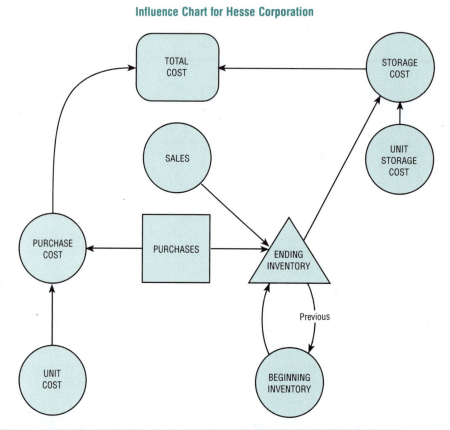

Hesse believes that 1400 refrigerators will be sold in each month, January through May. At the beginning of January, there is an inventory of 500 refrigerators; Hesse wants to plan to have 500 refrigerators in stock at the end of May as well. Hesse must develop a purchasing plan that will minimize the costs of purchase and storage for these five months, without ever running out of stock.

It would be possible for the Hesse Corporation to develop some effective rules for deciding how many refrigerators to purchase each month, based on the purchase cost and the storage cost. It is doubtful that a management science professional would consider using a traditional (non-spreadsheet) linear programming formulation. However, the spreadsheet model is straightforward, and illustrates concepts of time-based modeling. It may be much quicker to build the model on a spreadsheet and optimize it than it is to use other methods to solve the problem.

Hesse's spreadsheet model must calculate several values for each month. As an alternative to an influence chart, we'll list these items, starting with the objective for optimization, followed by indented influencing variables. (Variables shown in parentheses are repeat listings, and should not appear twice

---

Figure 9.2

Spreadsheet for Hesse Corporation

	A	B	C	D	E	F	G
1		Jan	Feb	Mar	Apr	May	Total
2	Beg Inventory	500	100	700	2300	900	
3	Purchases	1000	2000	3000	0	1000	
4	Sales	1400	1400	1400	1400	1400	
5	End Inventory	100	700	2300	900	500	
6	End Invty Cnstrnt<=		<=		<=	<=	
7	End Invty Limit	2500	2500	2500	2500		
8	Low Limit Cnstrnt>=		>=		>=	>=	
9	May Invty Cnstrnt					=	
10	May Invty Target					500	
11							
12	Purchase Cost	215000	450000	675000	0	235000	
13	Storage Cost	700	1400	9200	2700	1500	
14	Total Cost	215700	451400	684200	2700	236500	1590500
15							
16	Unit Cost	215	225	225	228	235	
17	Unit Storage Cost	7	2	4	3	3	

in the spreadsheet. They are shown to assist understanding the logic of the model.

> Total Cost
>> Purchase Cost
>>> Purchases
>>> Unit Cost
>> Storage Cost
>>> Unit Storage Cost
>>> Ending Inventory
>>>> Beginning Inventory
>>>>> (Last Month's Ending Inventory)
>>>> (Purchases)
>>> Sales

This same information is shown in the form of an influence chart in Figure 9.1. Note that the BEGINNING INVENTORY is influenced by last month's ENDING INVENTORY, with PREVIOUS marked on the arrow to indicate the time lag. As indicated on the influence chart by shapes, the decision variables are the PURCHASES. Constraints limit the ending inventory (January THRU April) to values between 0 and 2500. The May ending inventory is targeted to be 500.

The model and verbal documentation for Hesse are shown in Figures 9.2 and 9.3. Note that arbitrary values (1000, 2000, etc.) have been used for purchases, to make the logic of the model easier to follow.

You are encouraged to construct the model, and use What's Best! to optimize the purchase plan. For verification, the optimal value of Total Cost[Total] is $1,577,800. The optimization instructions are:

Figure 9.3

Verbal Documentation for Hesse Corporation Spreadsheet

```
Beg Inventory[Jan] = 500
Beg Inventory[Feb THRU May] = PREVIOUS End Inventory

Purchases[Jan] = 1000
Purchases[Feb] = 2000
Purchases[Mar] = 3000
Purchases[Apr] = 0
Purchases[May] = 1000

Sales[Jan THRU May] = 1400

End Inventory[Jan THRU May] = Beg Inventory + Purchases - Sales

May Invty Target[Total] = 500

Purchase Cost[Jan THRU May] = Purchases * Unit Cost

Storage Cost[Jan THRU May] = End Inventory * Unit Storage Cost

Total Cost[Jan THRU May] = Purchase Cost + Storage Cost
Total Cost[Total] = SUM (Total Cost[Jan] THRU Total Cost[May])

Unit Cost[Jan] = 215
Unit Cost[Feb THRU Mar] = 225
Unit Cost[Apr] = 228
Unit Cost[May] = 235

Unit Storage Cost[Jan] = 7
Unit Storage Cost[Feb] = 2
Unit Storage Cost[Mar] = 4
Unit Storage Cost[Apr THRU May] = 3
```

Decisions
(adjustable cells): Purchases[Jan THRU May]

Constraints: Ending Inventory[Jan THRU April] <= End Invty Limit
(*stored in row* 6)

Ending Inventory[Jan THRU April] >= 0
(*stored in row* 8)

Ending Inventory[May] = May Invty Target[May]
(*stored in cell* F9)

Objective: *Minimize* Total Cost[Total]

A basic concept in spreadsheet models involving time is the division of time into distinct and equal units. In the Hesse scenario, time is divided into months. Nothing is allowed to change during a month; all changes occur either at the beginning of the month or at the end of the month. It is important for the modeler to decide how things are to be viewed; there is no uniquely correct way of viewing time periods in a model, partially because the end of one month is the same point in time as the beginning of the next month. For Hesse, we treated purchases and sales within a month as being flexible, so that current purchases could be used for current sales. This assumption wouldn't make sense if we knew that all purchases arrived during the last ten days of the month, and all customers wanted refrigerators during the first ten days of the month. The timing assumptions may vary from one model to another, depending upon the scenario.

There are some elements of the Hesse model that are worth noting, because they will occur frequently in time-based models:

Initial conditions (such as Hesse's January beginning inventory) are known.

Closing conditions (such as Hesse's May ending inventory) are constrained.

Cost (or profit) is accumulated within one time period (purchase cost plus storage cost) and again over the planning horizon (total cost for the five months).

There are linkages from one period to the next (one period's beginning inventory is the previous period's ending inventory).

Many of these concepts are illustrated in the next example.

A Cash Planning Scenario

The Highint Company is planning investments and disbursements for the next five months. At the beginning of each of these monthly periods, a decision will be made about the amount of funds to be placed in one-month, two-month, and three-month investments. These investments are named A, B, and C. For the five-month planning period, Highint believes that each thousand dollars placed in one-month investments will return $1007.50 in principal and interest one month later. Two-month investments will return $1016.00 two months later. Three-month investments will return $1023.75 three months later. (Although these rates are quoted in return per thousand, there is no minimum required for any of the investments.)

Highint will begin the five months with $100,000. At the end of months two, three, and four, Highint will need to make disbursements of $20,000, for a total disbursement of $60,000. How should Highint schedule its investments so that it has as much money as possible at the end of five months, or the beginning of the sixth month?

In this scenario, time is again divided into months. Nothing is allowed to change during a month; all changes occur either at the beginning of the month or at the end of the month. It is important for the modeler to decide how things are to be viewed; for Highint, we make these assumptions about timing:

Securities are purchased at the beginning of the time period.

Withdrawals occur at the end of the time period.

Returns are credited at the beginning of the time period.

It is also important to understand terminology used in constructing a model. Although there is no universal standard, we'll use these terms for Highint's model:

Beginning balance is funds available at the beginning of a month, before any investment returns are considered.

Figure 9.4

Influence Chart for Highint Cash Planning

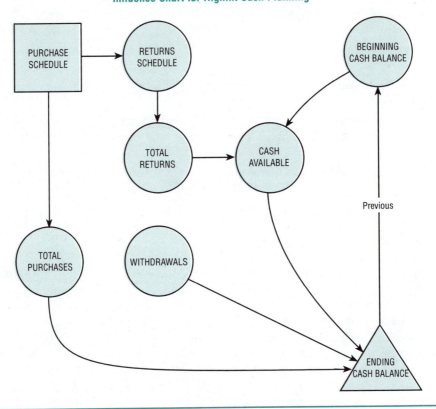

Cash available is funds available after investment returns are considered, but before any disbursements are made.

Ending balance is funds available at the completion of transactions during a month.

The influence chart of Figure 9.4 shows the logic of the model we will construct for Highint. We want the CASH AVAILABLE in Month 6 to be as large as possible. We decide on the PURCHASE SCHEDULE, a matrix showing securities purchased by type and by month. The PURCHASE SCHEDULE determines the RETURNS SCHEDULE, a matrix showing the dollar returns by type and by month. From these schedules, the TOTAL PURCHASES and TOTAL RETURNS can be determined for each month; these cash flows, along with required withdrawals, determine the changes in the cash balance each month.

A common characteristic of models involving time is the distinction between *flows* and *stocks*. A flow is analogous to water flowing from a faucet; a stock is analogous to the water in the bucket. A flow changes the related stock. Just as water flowing into a bucket changes the amount of water in the bucket, investment returns flowing into a cash balance increase the stock of cash, and with-

---

Figure 9.5

Spreadsheet Model for Highint Cash Planning

	A	B	C	D	E	F	G
1		Month 1	Month 2	Month 3	Month 4	Month 5	Month 6
2	Purchase Schedule:						
3	A's Purchased	40000	10000	0	0	0	
4	B's Purchased	20000	0	0	0	0	
5	C's Purchased	10000	0	10000	0	0	
6	Return Schedule:						
7	A Returns	0	40300	10075	0	0	0
8	B Returns	0	0	20320	0	0	0
9	C Returns	0	0	0	10237.5	0	10237.5
10							
11	Beginning Cash Balance	100000	30000	40300	40695	30932.5	30932.5
12	Total Returns	0	40300	30395	10237.5	0	10237.5
13	Cash Available	100000	70300	70695	50932.5	30932.5	41170
14	Total Purchases	70000	10000	10000	0	0	
15	Withdrawals	0	20000	20000	20000	0	
16	Ending Cash Balance	30000	40300	40695	30932.5	30932.5	
17	Cash Constraint	>=	>=	>=	>=	>=	
18	A Return per $	1.0075					
19	B Return per $	1.016					
20	C Return per $	1.02375					

---

drawals reduce the stock of cash. A common modeling statement calculates a stock by adding to its previous value all flows coming in, and subtracting all flows going out.

For Highint, we have these stocks:

> BEGINNING CASH BALANCE
> CASH AVAILABLE
> ENDING CASH BALLANCE

and these flows each month:

> TOTAL PURCHASES
> TOTAL RETURNS
> WITHDRAWALS

The spreadsheet model keeps track of these flows and stocks, as shown in Figure 9.5. The verbal documentation for this model is shown in Figure 9.6.

A manager studying the implications of the proposed (arbitrary) purchase schedule would immediately realize that there are unused cash balances which could be invested. However, the ending cash balance can never be negative, which would be a bank overdraft. This constraint, and the decisions contained in the investment schedule and the objective of maximizing cash available in Month 6, become the optimization instructions:

Decisions: A's Purchased[Month 1..Month 5]
             B's Purchased[Month 1..Month 5]
             C's Purchased[Month 1..Month 5]

Figure 9.6

Verbal Documentation for Highint Model, Figure 9.5

```
A's Purchased[Month 1] THRU C's Purchased[Month 5] is documented in cells B3..F5, Figure 5.

A Returns[Month 1] = 0
A Returns[Month 2 THRU Month 6] = PREVIOUS A's Purchased * A Return per $

B Returns[Month 1 THRU Month 2] = 0
B Returns[Month 3 THRU Month 6] = PREVIOUS 2 B's Purchased * B Return per $

C Returns[Month 1 THRU Month 3] = 0
C Returns[Month 4 THRU Month 6] = PREVIOUS 3 C's Purchased * C Return per $

Beginning Cash Balance[Month 1] = 100000
Beginning Cash Balance[Month 2 THRU Month 6] = PREVIOUS Ending Cash Balance

Total Returns[Month 1 THRU Month 6] = SUM (A Returns THRU C Returns)

Cash Available[Month 1 THRU Month 6] = Beginning Cash Balance + Total Returns

Total Purchases[Month 1 THRU Month 5] = SUM (A's Purchased THRU C's Purchased)

Withdrawals[Month 1] = 0
Withdrawals[Month 2 THRU Month 4] = 20000
Withdrawals[Month 5] = 0

Ending Cash Balance[Month 1 THRU Month 5] = Cash Available - Total Purchases - Withdrawals

A Return per $ = 1.0075
B Return per $ = 1.016
C Return per $ = 1.02375
```

Constraints: Ending Cash Balance[Month 1..Month 5] >= 0

Objective: *Maximize* Cash Available[Month 6]

It is left as an exercise to apply optimization and verify that the maximum value for available cash in Month 6 is $42,570.

Spreadsheet Tip: The format used to display the contents of a cell may cause your spreadsheet to have a different appearance from those shown here. This is particularly true for a spreadsheet showing the results of optimization. Optimization requires decisions for whether a value is truly zero. Sometimes a number such as −0.0000042 may be considered by the software to be zero; the spreadsheet will display it in various ways, depending upon format and column-width. It may appear to be 0, ($0), or −4E–6. For managerial purposes, any of these values is effectively zero!

CASE STUDY:

Novana Company

The Novana Company case study is an extensive application of modeling involving time. The case also illustrates another aspect of management science modeling: Models may expand and become more realistic as managers gain experience in using them. It is common for a model to be constructed and optimized, causing the modeler to exclaim "That's dumb!" because something was omitted from the model. Hence, the model evolves, coming closer to reality, and becoming more useful to managers. This evolution emphasizes the philosophy that management science is providing support for managerial decisions, rather than "making decisions with a computer."

Novana is a company founded in 1980 to market lightweight fitness equipment on Cable TV. It is planning its advertisements and product requirements for the first four months of next year for the SlimmerGymmer. S. T. Semoran, the controller, estimates that on January 1 next year Novana will have 1000 Slimmer-Gymmer units in stock, and a bank balance of $10,000. S.T. believes that this is the minimum cash balance that can be planned, to allow for some flexibility of payments and receipts within a month. Unfortunately, no bank credit is available to Novana. There is a limited amount of trade credit available; only one of the suppliers will sell to Novana "on credit."

There are two suppliers of the SlimmerGymmer, BenderMet and Flexo. BenderMet is the lower cost supplier, but orders must be placed by January 1 for delivery in the first four months of next year. Because BenderMet has had some difficulty in collecting from Novana in the past, their terms of sale are stringent: payment of $50 per unit in January, regardless of delivery date, and $10 per unit during the month of delivery. BenderMet will not deliver any units to Novana in January, to be certain that the funds paid for the order are properly deposited before any work is started on the order. The $50 January payment covers the manufacturing costs, while the $10 payment at delivery covers transportation costs.

The second supplier is Flexo, who has been a reliable supplier on two occasions in the past. Flexo does not have as much manufacturing experience as BenderMet, and charges more. Flexo charges $85 per unit, delivered. Payment is required during the month in which the unit is delivered.

Novana has enough experience in the Cable TV market to predict advertising effectiveness quite reliably. Novana views the calendar year as broken into three planning periods of four months each. The Winter season, which is now being planned, takes advantage of the holiday habits of overeating. The Summer season, May thru August, relies on bathing suit phobia as its primary appeal. The Fall season, September thru December, is the most difficult to classify. The planning for each of these three seasons has been based on fifty to one hundred ads each season. As the business has grown, it has been reaching this upper limit of one hundred. The experience of the past several Winter seasons has indicated that each ad generates sales of 25 units during the month the ad is run, 20 units the next month, and 10 units the third month. However, Novana has experienced a sharp drop-off in sales in the summer months; hence, Novana will not plan on any "residual effect" of Winter season ads in the Summer season months of May or June.

Novana receives $150 for each SlimmerGymmer it sells. Half of the orders are credit card sales, which are credited to their account the month of the sale. The other half are COD sales, for which they receive payment the following month. Novana's contract with the cable networks requires Novana to purchase

100 ads, at a cost of $1500 per ad, sometime during January, February, March, or April. Ads must be paid for during the month they are run; however, within each month the TV network permits Novana to pay within a few days of running each ad, so that credit card orders received as a result of running an ad can be deposited in the bank before the ad itself must be paid for.

S.T. had received a memo from an assistant recommending that all purchases be made from Flexo. The memo proposed a delivery schedule of 300 units in January, and 2000 in February and again in March. The memo commented that "BenderMet is just too stringent on their payment requests. We can't afford to do business with them, because we'd run out of cash." Furthermore, the recommendation was to run half the ads in January and half in February, to be able to take full advantage of the "residual effect" which would be lost by running ads in March or April.

Discussion: Novana Case

What information does Novana management need to support decisions being made? When S. T. Semoran was presented with the memo outlining the recommendations, the immediate reaction was:

What is the plan? This relates to the decisions:

Novana must decide how many ads to run in each month, and the number of SlimmerGymmers to purchase each month from each supplier. Once these planning values are set, all inventory levels and all financial values are determined by the assumptions in the scenario. The memo outlined the planned purchases and ad schedule for the season.

Can I implement this plan? This relates to the constraints:

There are two basic factors that affect the ability to implement a plan:

Is there enough product? (In other words, do we run out of Slimmer-Gymmers?)

Is there enough cash? (In other words, will the bank balance go too low?)

How profitable is this plan? This relates to the objective:

Money in the bank is a substitute for profit, in this situation. (We are assuming that the only income statement items that vary with our decision are those we have discussed: sales revenue, cost of goods sold, and the cost of advertising.) But "money in the bank" is ambiguous: money in the bank when? This answer is easy: whenever all transactions affected by decisions made during the first four months have been reflected in the bank balance.

To support the planning decisions, Novana needs a model to keep track of both the product and the cash. Figure 9.7 shows an influence chart showing the factors that influence cash. This influence chart shows stocks and flows that are common in time-based models. The logic used to keep track of cash is shown in the influence chart and with this explanation:

Figure 9.7

Influence Chart for Novana (Cash)

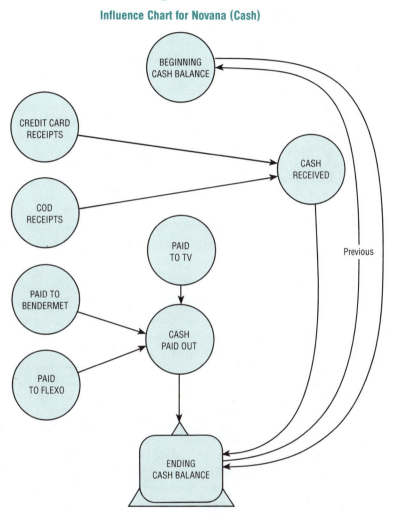

For any month, the cash at month-end is the cash at the beginning, plus the inflows (cash received), less the outflows (cash paid out).

The beginning cash balance for one month is the same as the ending cash balance for the previous month. We have shown this lagged relationship with an influence arrow from ENDING CASH BALANCE to BEGINNING CASH BALANCE; this arrow is noted "PREVIOUS" indicating that one month's beginning cash balance is influenced by the previous month's ending cash balance. (In this example, the influence is really an identity. February's beginning cash balance is January's ending cash balance.)

We need to construct a similar chart to show the stocks and flows for SlimmerGymmers for any month. This influence chart is shown in Figure 9.8.

Figure 9.8

Influence Chart for Novana (Inventory)

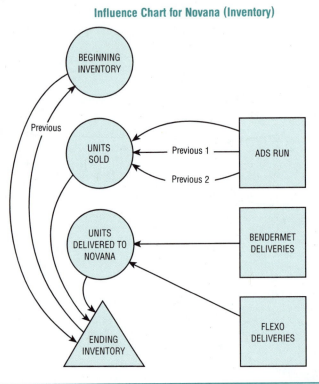

Many of the variables shown in the two previous influence charts need to be expanded to show additional influences. For example, in the first chart, the amounts paid to each of the suppliers are not explained in the chart. The variables needed to explain these "cash" variables are in the "inventory" influence chart. The receipts from credit card and COD sales are influenced by the number of units sold; again, these variables are in different influence charts. The complete influence chart for Novana is obtained by placing both charts side by side and showing the remaining influences, as shown in Figure 9.9.

This influence chart provides assistance in constructing a spreadsheet model. In this particular influence chart, we have settled for a somewhat simplified chart; no attempt has been made to show that various columns of a variable (i.e., various monthly values) are influenced by different things. For example, the January beginning cash balance is a data value; the February beginning cash balance is the ending January cash balance. Another slight difference between reality and the influence chart is that Units Sold[January] is influenced only by the current value of Ads Run. However, Units Sold[February] is influenced by the current value of Ads Run and by the previous value of Ads Run. Units Sold[March] is influenced by Ads Run[February], which is PREVIOUS 1, and by Ads Run[January], which is PREVIOUS 2. Although these matters could be described on the influence chart, such description might provide more clutter than under-

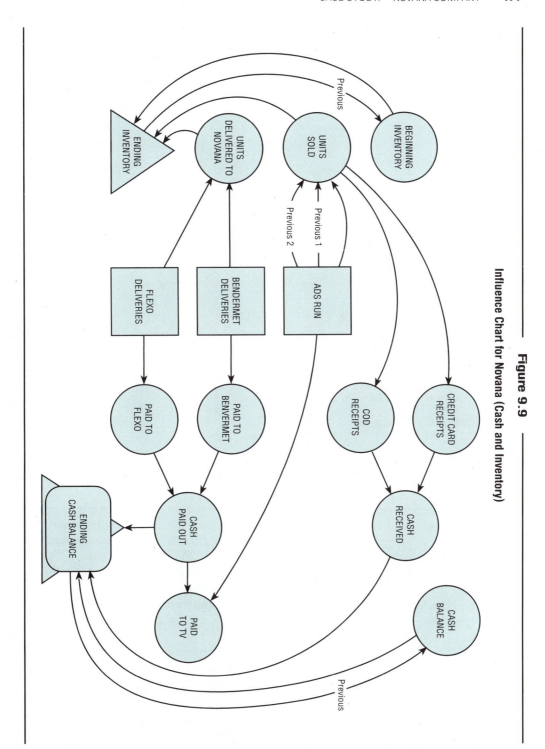

Figure 9.9

Influence Chart for Novana (Cash and Inventory)

---------- **Figure 9.10** ----------

Worksheet for Novana

	A	B	C	D	E	F	G
1		Jan	Feb	March	Apr	May	Total
2	Beginning Cash Balance	$10,000	$3,250	$20,750	$132,000	$282,000	
3	Cash Received	$93,750	$262,500	$281,250	$150,000	$37,500	
4	Credit Card Receipts	$93,750	$168,750	$112,500	$37,500		
5	COD Receipts	$0	$93,750	$168,750	$112,500	$37,500	
6	Cash Paid Out	$100,500	$245,000	$170,000	$0		
7	Paid to BenderMet	$0	$0	$0	$0		
8	Paid to Flexo	$25,500	$170,000	$170,000	$0		
9	Paid to TV	$75,000	$75,000	$0	$0		
10	Ending Cash Balance	$3,250	$20,750	$132,000	$282,000	$319,500	
11	Cash Constraint	Not >=	>=	>=	>=		
12	Minimum Cash Balance	$10,000	$10,000	$10,000	$10,000		
13							
14	Beginning Inventory	1,000	50	(200)	300		
15	Units Sold	1,250	2,250	1,500	500		
16	Units Delivered to Novana	300	2,000	2,000	0		
17	BenderMet Deliveries	0	0	0	0		0
18	Flexo Deliveries	300	2,000	2,000	0		
19	Ending Inventory	50	(200)	300	(200)		
20	Inventory Constraint	>=	Not >=	>=	Not >=		
21							
22	Ads Run	50	50	0	0		100
23	Ads Constraint						=
24	Target						100
25							
26	Selling Price		150				
27	BenderMet January Payment		50				
28	BenderMet Delivery Payment		10				
29	Flexo Delivery Payment		85				
30	Credit Card Percentage		0.5				
31	First Month Sales		25				
32	Second Month Sales		20				
33	Third Month Sales		10				
34	Ad Price		1500				

---

standing. There is an "artistic" aspect of influence charts; let the influence chart be your servant in helping understand the system, rather than your master in requiring a detailed set of arrows and shapes.

The spreadsheet model of Figure 9.10 is constructed from the influence chart, using the plan proposed in the Novana scenario. The reader should verify the numbers, to be able to see where each number originated. Notice that the construction of the worksheet is in four basic sections: cash, inventory, ads, and data values.

The influence chart only shows three sections: cash, inventory, and ads. The data values are not shown. Again, this illustrates the "artistic" nature of an influence chart. It clearly would be correct to show that cash Paid to TV is influenced by the Ad Price. The modeler needs to make a decision whether the clarity improvement from showing that price (and other data values) is worth expanding the number of circles on the chart by more than half. Indeed, such things as the Ad Price could be built into the formulas in the worksheet. That practice,

---

Figure 9.11

Documentation for Worksheet in Figure 9.10

Beginning Cash Balance[Jan] = 10000
Beginning Cash Balance[Feb THRU May] = PREVIOUS Ending Cash Balance

Cash Received[Jan THRU May] = Credit Card Receipts + COD Receipts

Credit Card Receipts[Jan THRU Apr] = Units Sold * Credit Card Percentage[Data] * Selling Price[Data]

COD Receipts[Jan] = 0
COD Receipts[Feb THRU May] = (1 − Credit Card Percentage[Data])
    * PREVIOUS Units Sold * Selling Price[Data]

Cash Paid Out[Jan THRU Apr] = Paid to BenderMet + Paid to Flexo + Paid to TV

Paid to BenderMet[Jan] = BenderMet Deliveries[Total] * BenderMet January Payment[Data]
    + BenderMet Deliveries[Jan] * BenderMet Delivery Payment[Data]
Paid to BenderMet[Feb THRU Apr] = BenderMet Deliveries * BenderMet Delivery Payment[Data]

Paid to Flexo[Jan THRU Apr] = Flexo Deliveries * Flexo Delivery Payment[Data]

Paid to TV[Jan THRU Apr] = Ads Run * Ad Price[Data]

Ending Cash Balance[Jan THRU May] = Beginning Cash Balance + Cash Received − Cash Paid Out

Minimum Cash Balance[Jan THRU Apr] = 10000

Beginning Inventory[Jan] = 1000
Beginning Inventory[Feb THRU Apr] = PREVIOUS Ending Inventory

Units Sold[Jan] = Ads Run[Jan] * First Month Sales[Data]
Units Sold[Feb] = Ads Run[Feb] * First Month Sales[Data] + Ads Run[Jan] * Second Month Sales[Data]
Units Sold[March THRU Apr] = Ads Run * First Month Sales[Data] +
    PREVIOUS Ads Run * Second Month Sales[Data] + PREVIOUS 2 Ads Run * Third Month Sales[Data]

Units Delivered to Novana[Jan THRU Apr] = BenderMet Deliveries + Flexo Deliveries

BenderMet Deliveries[Jan THRU Apr] = 0
BenderMet Deliveries[Total] = SUM (BenderMet Deliveries[Jan] THRU BenderMet Deliveries[Apr])

Flexo Deliveries[Jan] = 300
Flexo Deliveries[Feb THRU March] = 2000
Flexo Deliveries[Apr] = 0

Ending Inventory[Jan THRU Apr] = Beginning Inventory − Units Sold + Units Delivered to Novana

Ads Run[Jan THRU Feb] = 50
Ads Run[March THRU Apr] = 0
Ads Run[Total] = SUM (Ads Run[Jan] THRU Ads Run[Apr])

Target[Total] = 100

Selling Price[Data] = 150
BenderMet January Payment[Data] = 50
BenderMet Delivery Payment[Data] = 10
Flexo Delivery Payment[Data] = 85
Credit Card Percentage[Data] = 0.5
First Month Sales[Data] = 25
Second Month Sales[Data] = 20
Third Month Sales[Data] = 10
Ad Price[Data] = 1500

---

however, would illustrate poor modeling habits: Imbedding *true* constants (such as the number of inches in a foot) into formulas may be good modeling practice, but "constants" such as Ad Price and Credit Card Percentage are subject to change. It is much easier to change these values when they are separated as data values rather than embedded in formulas in the spreadsheet.

The verbal documentation for the spreadsheet is shown in Figure 9.11.

Clearly, the proposed plan is not feasible: We run out of product in February and April, and we run below the $10,000 cash balance in January. To find a better plan, we employ optimization with these instructions:

Decisions: Ads Run[Jan..Apr]
                    BenderMet Deliveries[Feb..Apr]
                    Flexo Deliveries[Jan..Apr]

Constraints: Ending Cash Balance[Jan..Apr] >= 10,000
                    (*stored in row* 11)

                    Ending Inventory[Jan..Apr] >= 0
                    (*stored in row* 20)

                    Ads Run[Total] = 100
                    (*stored in row* 23)

Objective: *Maximize* Ending Cash Balance[May]

It is left as an exercise to verify that applying optimization for Novana results in about $304,200 ending cash balance in May.

Marginal Values for Ads Run

S. T. Semoran studied the marginal values for the constraints, and observed that the marginal value associated with the Ads Run constraint was $1425. This value is calculated after considering the $1500 cost of an ad, which is built into the spreadsheet model. Would it be possible to run just a few more ads? The model was optimized, without constraining Ads Run[Total]. The result was a substantially improved cash position at the end of May: $428,200 at the end of May, achieved by running a total of 316 ads! This raised a serious question: Are the data valid for this substantial change in the scale of operations? Will each ad still be as productive? Will the suppliers be able to meet delivery times when production is increased to keep up with the ads? Will the $10,000 minimum cash balance be sufficient for this scale of operations? Before deciding whether to run more ads, S.T. decided to think about proposals to suppliers and to the banker for Novana.

Novana and the Friendly Banker

After studying the results of the analysis conducted to this point, S. T. Semoran realized that a lack of cash was possibly causing some problems. Just last week S.T. had approached both BenderMet and Flexo about changing the terms of sale. Both vendors were quite interested, until they discovered that S.T. was hoping for later payment, rather than earlier payment. S.T. was unable to persuade either supplier to provide more generous conditions for paying for SlimmerGymmer units.

The next attempt for S. T. Semoran was the bank. While Novana had reasonably good relations with the bank, the bank had viewed Novana more as a depositor than as a borrower. S.T. hoped that presenting the banker with projected cash flows for the next four months would be a good way to raise the question of a loan. In the past, S.T. hadn't known how much credit to request; the cash flow projections might help solve that problem. S.T. decided that any negotiations with the banker would keep the number of ads at or below one hundred; bankers aren't happy dealing with "What If" scenarios that are way outside the range of experience.

Some preliminary discussion with Scotia National Bank seemed somewhat encouraging. Scotia was talking about a $40,000 line of credit, which Novana could obtain for a payment in January of $1000 (whether the credit line was used or not). In addition, interest would be charged at the rate of 18% annually or 1.5% monthly. The bank explained the procedure that would be used for determining the month's interest:

> Each month, the "loan balance before interest" will be computed as the beginning loan balance, plus the amount borrowed that month, less the amount repaid that month. Then the loan interest will be determined using this balance and the interest rate. Finally, the ending loan balance will be determined by adding loan interest to the loan balance before interest. This ending loan balance becomes next month's beginning loan balance.

S.T. thought the additional cash from this line of credit would really enhance the profitability of the SlimmerGymmer operations. S.T. knew that the bank would require that enough of the loan balance and/or interest be paid each month so that the loan balance at the end of each month (after the interest has been added) never gets bigger than $40,000.

The discussions with the banker brought out another interesting possibility: The bank was willing to purchase the rights to the COD payments. The bank proposal worked this way: They would purchase the anticipated February COD receipts at ninety-five cents on the dollar, which the bank would deposit into Novana's account in January. This would require no "up front" charge comparable to the $1000 fee for the line of credit; however, the funds this would generate were limited to the amount of COD sales. In some situations, this would be less than the $40,000 available under the line of credit. The bank made it clear that any agreement about COD sales will apply to all COD orders Novana receives during this planning period.

Discussion: Novana and the Friendly Banker

What are the issues the analyst faces with this extension of the Novana case? One way to approach the case is to assert that S. T. Semoran's decision is a multiple choice decision:

> Accept neither the loan proposal nor the COD receipts proposal.
>
> Accept the COD receipts proposal.
>
> Accept the loan proposal.

The bank is unwilling to make the loan and also purchase the CODs. Although this is a multiple choice decision, optimization plays a very important role. We have already discussed optimization to evaluate the "status quo" of accepting

---

Figure 9.12

Influence Chart for Loan Account

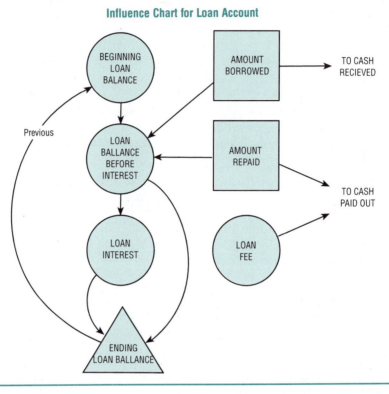

---

neither proposal: a May ending balance of $304,200. But the set of decisions that is best for the status quo is inappropriate for the other proposals; optimization is necessary to evaluate each of the other possible courses of action.

Of the remaining two choices, the COD receipts proposal is easier to evaluate. The only change in Novana's influence chart is that COD RECEIPTS are no longer influenced by the PREVIOUS value of UNITS SOLD; they are influenced by the UNITS SOLD in the current month. An additional influence is the COD discount factor, a data value of 95%. After making these changes in the model (about five minutes work, at most), the optimization operation can be performed again. It is left as an exercise to verify that the May ending balance for this scenario can be as high as $325,938.

The opportunity to establish a line of credit requires an addition to the model. In the current model, we are tracking two levels, or stocks: the stock of cash and the stock of inventory. If we include a loan, we have a third stock to track: the loan balance. There are also additional flows: Each month, S.T. must decide how much to borrow and how much to repay. After these decisions have been made each month, the values are used in conjunction with the beginning balance and the interest charged to determine the ending loan balance. This is shown in this influence chart of Figure 9.12. The only influence arrows connecting the previous influence chart and this one is that the loan fee, the AMOUNT BORROWED, and the

AMOUNT REPAID influence the ENDING CASH BALANCE. Performing these changes in the model is left as an exercise to demonstrate that the proposal for the loan results in a May ending balance of about $327,613. While this is an improvement of about $1700 over the COD receipts proposal, the difference may not be manageri- ally important in light of the accuracy of the data with which Novana is working.

Additional Comments About Novana

A number of things can be learned from the Novana case. The following para- graphs present some of the issues that apply to Novana, but more generally apply to time-based models and other models as well. Now that there is a "concrete example" to present these issues, it's time for their discussion.

Optimization can force you out of the range in which you have been think- ing. This is both good and bad. When new ways of doing things are uncovered through optimization, the result may be good. When doing things in new ways causes implicit or explicit assumptions to be incorrect, the relationships or num- bers in the "optimized" spreadsheet may be misleading or wrong. Notice what has happened in the Novana case:

> When we recognized through a marginal value that each additional ad increased profit by $1425, a model was presented that drove the number of ads above 300. But the case explicitly states that the response rate (units sold per ad) was based on running about a hundred ads in a four-month period. Can we justify extrapolating beyond the observed data? Clearly, that's a judgment issue with which management and the analyst (who may, of course, be one and the same) must wrestle.

> The initial formulation of the case indicated that a $10,000 cash balance would be enough to allow for matching receipts and payments within a month. But in some months for some situations we were dealing with monthly receipts and disbursements in excess of $300,000. It may be poor judgment to assume that this can be handled with a minimum balance of $10,000. This might be handled by raising the lower limit on the cash balance, or by constructing a weekly or even daily model instead of a monthly model.

Time-based models are always tricky in one sense: The assumption is made that all decisions and transactions occur at one point in the period. Although we haven't explicitly stated this, the Novana models in this chapter assume that all transactions occur at the beginning of the period. Note, for example, that loan interest is charged for a full month, based on the ending loan balance before interest; this full-month charge assumes that transactions take place at the begin- ning of the month. Similarly, we receive units from suppliers, ship them to customers, and receive credit card receipts from them all at one point in time. If this assumption seems unwarranted, it may be necessary to use smaller time periods until the assumption is reasonable.

Optimization is a support system, not a decision system. Answers from a model are seldom applied exactly as the report indicates. But optimization may cause thinking and planning to change directions, because assumptions about the structure of "good" solutions may be incorrect. Let these suggestions from optimization influence the analysis, but always be careful not to let optimization take you outside the range in which your data assumptions are valid.

Exercises

1. Construct the spreadsheet model for the Hesse Corporation, as shown in Figure 9.2. Using What's*Best!*, verify that the total cost can be no lower than $1,577,800.

2. The Hesse Corporation just received good news: demand is now projected to be 2000 refrigerators a month, instead of 1400. It was immediately suggested that more warehouse space should be rented, to take advantage of the lower unit cost in the early months. The proposal is to change the constraining value on ending inventory from 2500 refrigerators to 3500; this would cost $5000 for the planning period. The May target of 500 refrigerators is unchanged.
   a. Without the new warehouse space, what would be the total cost with the increased demand?
   b. If the new warehouse were available and free, what would be the total cost with the increased demand?
   c. Does it make economic sense to obtain the new warehouse space?

3. The Rick Corporation deals in refrigerators in a different market. They plan to sell 3000 refrigerators a month for the next twelve months. The unit cost of a refrigerator is $200 the first month, but it increases exactly 5% (not rounded) each month thereafter. Their storage costs will decline, however, as their warehouse employees gain additional experience. They project storage costs at $10 per month for the first month, declining 4% each month thereafter (again, this cost is not rounded). The Rick Corporation has a beginning balance of 2000 refrigerators; it is willing to end the year with only 1000 refrigerators on hand. Their storage limit (for any month-end) is 2000 refrigerators. Develop a spreadsheet model and optimization instructions for this situation. Find the optimal purchase plan for the Rick Corporation.

4. Build a spreadsheet model similar to Figure 9.5. Using What's*Best!*, find the purchase schedule for Highint that yields the optimal cash available in Month 6, $42,570.

5. The optimization instructions for Highint included these decisions:

```
A's Purchased[Month 1..Month 5]
B's Purchased[Month 1..Month 5]
C's Purchased[Month 1..Month 5]
```

This implies that Bs could be purchased in Month 5, even though they mature in Month 7, which is past the time horizon of this model. Similarly, it indicates that Cs could be purchased in Months 4 and 5, which also mature too late for this scenario.
   a. How could the instructions be changed to avoid this suggested difficulty?
   b. Is the difficulty described here real or imaginary? Why?

6. It has been suggested that diversification of the portfolio should be built into Highint's model. It is now required that no more than $25,000 should be invested in any one security at any one time. This is easy for security A; an upper limit of $25,000 purchased in any period will provide the required diversification for this security. However, security B is more difficult. New spreadsheet formulas will be needed so this constraint can be specified.

`Investment in B[Month 2] <= $25,000`

and so on for months 3 and 4. Note that the `Investment in B[Month 2]` is calculated by the spreadsheet formula:

```
Investment in B[Month 2] =
         B's Purchased[Month 1] + B's Purchased[Month 2]
```

For security C, three months of purchases must be summed to find the current Investment in C. Modify the model for Highint, and maximize the cash available in Month 6. How much does the diversification cost?

7. Continuing with the scenario for Highint as shown in Figure 9.5 (without the diversification requirement of Exercise 6), add a fourth security (D) which will return $1040 four months later. Using a spreadsheet model, find the maximum cash available for Month 6, and the optimal purchase schedule to obtain this cash.

8. After Novana's S. T. Semoran saw the results of the optimization of the model shown in Figure 9.10, there was a great deal of excitement. "You mean we can plan things so we can have over $304,200 in cash at the end of May? That's fantastic. What do we do to make that happen?"

   The analyst explained that Novana would order 300 SlimmerGymmers from BenderMet, to be delivered in February; the rest of the units would be supplied by Flexo. Contrary to intuition, Novana should run about 40 ads in January, 51 in February, and the remaining 9 in March. At first, there was a great deal of resentment about running those nine ads in March. A typical question asked of the analyst was, "You know we can't count on residual effect of March ads in May. Did you allow for that?" The analyst confirmed that losing the residual had been considered. Then the next question tended to be "That's silly. Why should we run ads in March when we get more benefit from running the ads in January or February? It seems to me that we're throwing away advertising money if we run ads in March that we could run in February. You know I just can't accept such a waste in any ad schedule that requires my signature."

   a. Using optimization software, verify the optimized value of ending cash balance ($304,200) and the purchase plan suggested in the preceding paragraph. Discuss the advisability of advertising in March.

   b. Discuss the objections raised to advertising late in the planning horizon, when there is less benefit obtained from the ads.

   c. In the course of further discussion about the plan for the next four months, someone said that the big problem was we weren't advertising enough. "Is it true that we can pay $1500 for an ad that increases our cash flow by $2925 before we pay for the ad, or $1425 after paying for the ad?" Determine whether $1425 is a correct value, first by changing the target number of ads to 101, and then by using the marginal values on an optimized spreadsheet.

d. Next the discussion focused upon whether they could get by with an ending cash balance of only $10,000. S. T. Semoran wanted to increase it to $15,000. To help evaluate this suggestion, find the changes in the "bottom line" costs that can come from changing this cash requirement. Use a spreadsheet model and optimization. Are there other considerations?

e. Using a spreadsheet model and What's*Best!*, find the advertising and purchasing schedules that maximize May's ending cash balance, when there is no limit on the number of ads that can be run.

9. Using a spreadsheet model and What's*Best!*, show that the proposal for Novana to sell the COD receivables for a 5% discount results in a May ending balance of $325,938.

10. Using a spreadsheet model and What's*Best!*, show that the proposal for Novana to engage in a line of credit, under the conditions described in the text, results in an ending cash balance of $327,613.

11. For each of these situations discussed for Novana, find the marginal value for increasing the number of ads:

> Discounting COD receipts
> Borrowing up to $40,000, with a $1000 loan fee

Why does the marginal value differ from one situation to the other?

12. Interpret the marginal value for the constraint on ending cash balance, month by month, for the basic Novana model (Figure 9.10).

CASE STUDY:

Sawgrass Canning Company*

The Sawgrass Canning Company is a small vegetable cannery processing vegetables grown near Florida's Gulf coast. Although it is technically operated as a cooperative, it makes its decisions using cash flow analysis. Sawgrass tries to use this rule: Consider the elements of cash flow that will be affected by the decision at hand; if a cash flow item will change depending upon a decision, then it is a relevant part of cash flow; on the other hand, omit those cash flow elements that don't change as a result of the decision being made. Applying this rule works in this way:

> The cost of cans for a new product is a relevant cash flow. Sawgrass will pay more for cans if more cans are used in processing. But the cost of the president's retirement pay isn't a relevant cash flow. The amount of

---

*This case is inspired by "Palmetto Canning Company," V. L. Andrews, C. W. Young, and P. Hunt, *Financial Management: Cases and Readings*, 3rd edition, Homewood, IL: Richard D. Irwin, Inc., 1982.

current expenditure for this item won't be affected by the amount of processing that is done for the new product.

The decision at hand is whether to accept two contracts for off-season use of the canning facilities. During the two growing seasons (spring and fall in Florida), the facilities are used intensively. But there is a twelve-week window when the facilities can be used to can soft drinks and concentrate-based fruit punch drinks.

The soft drink contract, which has not yet been signed by I. L. Kerf, the president of Sawgrass, is for 100,000 cans to be delivered any time during the twelve-week period. This contract is with a local soft drink bottler, who wants to build some inventory of a new generic soft drink that will be introduced shortly. The local bottler will provide all ingredients for this product; Sawgrass will provide the cans, labor, and equipment. The economics of this product are:

Revenue	$0.040 per can
Variable costs:	
Can material	0.017 per can
Labor	0.013 per can
Cash flow	0.010 per can

I. L. Kerf also has a contract awaiting signature for canning fruit punch for a large grocery chain. The chain requires delivery of at least 40,000 cans during the first six weeks, and a fixed quantity of 300,000 on any schedule during the last six weeks. The economics of this product are:

Revenue	$0.140 per can
Variable costs:	
Can material	0.017 per can
Ingredients	0.033 per can
Labor	0.020 per can
Cash flow	0.070 per can

Sawgrass is historically cash-starved. The only reason it is considering the soft drink contract when the punch is so much more profitable is that the payment terms are much better for the soft drinks. I. L. Kerf mentally went over these factors about the timing of receipts and expenditures for each possible new product, which Kerf mentally calls "Softy" and "Fruity" for simplicity.

Revenue: Softy pays on delivery. So soft drinks delivered in Week 2 are paid for in Week 2. Fruity pays three weeks after delivery, according to the contract. Cans of punch produced and delivered in Week 2 are paid for in Week 5. All cans are delivered to the customer in the week they are produced.

Can Material and Ingredients: These purchases are paid two weeks after they are used. Standard practice at Sawgrass is for the items to be ordered about two weeks before they are needed, on "net 30" terms. But the typical delay between the date of the invoice and the date the cans or ingredients are used is two weeks. That typically means that cans billed in Week 2 will be used in Week 4, and paid for in Week 6. Summing it up: Kerf plans for a two-week lag between usage and payment for can material and ingredients.

Labor: The workforce is accustomed to being paid each week, for the current week of work.

The rate of production is a maximum of 20,000 cans each day. All of the weeks have five work days, except Weeks 5 and 10, which have only three days because of holidays. There are no formal or informal commitments to produce the limit on any day, because the plant has typically been idle during this time period. Any new work will be welcomed by the workforce, which expects none.

There are several cash transactions yet to take place from other lines of business. These transactions affect cash available for the proposed new ventures. During each of the first four weeks, Sawgrass plans for $3000 cash inflow from existing receivables. Unfortunately, Sawgrass anticipates accounts payable of $3500 for each of the twelve weeks of the planning period. The major transaction worrying Kerf now is a note to a friend which comes due in the third week of the period. This will require a cash outlay of $12,000. Kerf has already asked the friend for an extension, and plans to pay the note on time after hearing the reply.

The current cash situation for Sawgrass is not particularly healthy. But Kerf is optimistic that the current cash balance of $17,000 will allow a nice profit to be made, without running out of cash any time during the period.

Case Exercises

1. Using a model with weekly time periods, develop a plan for Sawgrass. Study the results of optimization to determine whether Sawgrass really is cash starved.

2. Would profit be enhanced if Fruity could be persuaded to pay in two weeks instead of three weeks? Develop information to help Kerf decide whether to approach Fruity with this idea.

3. Would profit be enhanced if labor could be paid with a one-week delay, using checks instead of cash? Develop information to help Kerf decide whether to approach the workforce with this idea. (Keep Fruity on a three-week payment plan for this analysis.)

4. Would there be less profit if the beginning balance had been $13,000 instead of $17,000? What if the beginning balance had been $25,000? (Keep Fruity on a three-week payment plan, and the workforce paid in the week the work is performed for the analysis.)

5. Develop a plan to convince a banker that a loan of $10,000 would be very profitable.

10

Improving Modeling Skills: How to Maintain Linearity in Some Models

This chapter contains several modeling examples. First is a blending example, where a product (such as gasoline) is to be blended from a variety of possible ingredients. The second example returns to Rangely Lakes and its souvenirs, with a new twist: The same product may sell for two different prices, depending upon the quantity sold. The final illustration is determining the best way to use overtime, hiring, and firing in planning production to meet fluctuating demand.

What a diverse set of situations! They are held together by a common thread: There are "good" and "bad" formulations for each of these, and the natural formulation isn't the necessarily the best formulation. By "good" we mean a linear formulation. But if these problems are formulated in their natural way, they may end up as nonlinear problems. Although the What'sBest! software provided with this book is designed to determine whether a problem is linear or nonlinear, and solve either, we are concerned about the differences between linear and nonlinear optimization for these reasons:

1. Mathematicians have been able to develop very fast and effective ways to solve linear optimization problems; linear problems with thousands of decision variables are routinely solved in many businesses. Unfortunately, mathematical methods to solve nonlinear problems are neither as fast nor as effective as the methods for solving linear problems.

2. The term "solution" has a stronger meaning in a linear problem than in a nonlinear problem. When a linear problem is solved using a linear

189

————————————— **Figure 10.1** —————————————

An Example of a Smooth Nonlinearity

Objective (or Constraint) vs. Decision

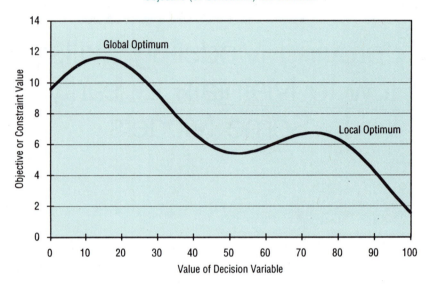

optimizer, mathematicians know that there is no better solution. Such a solution is called a *global optimum*. But a "solution" to a nonlinear optimization problem may terminate at a *local optimum*. This means that there is no better solution "close" to the one identified, but nonlinear optimizers are not able to guarantee that there is no better solution that is not "close" to the local optimum. Nonlinear optimizers operate much like a hiker along a mountain path in a dense fog. You know you are at the top of a hill when the trail descends regardless of the direction you walk. But the fog and the mountains don't permit you to see whether there is a higher hill at some other place on the trail.

3. Some nonlinear problems have *nonsmooth* nonlinearities; these problems don't solve well with nonlinear optimizers. Part of this chapter explores the differences between smooth and nonsmooth nonlinearities; nonlinear optimization methods are typically more effective at solving problems with smooth nonlinearities.

4. Most optimization software requires the user to understand the differences between linear programming and nonlinear programming. Although What's *Best!* contains expertise to determine whether a spreadsheet model is linear, this capability is the exception rather than the rule. Furthermore, there is an abundance of software for linear optimi-

—————————— **Figure 10.2** ——————————

An Example of a Nonsmooth Nonlinearity

Objective (or Constraint) vs. Decision

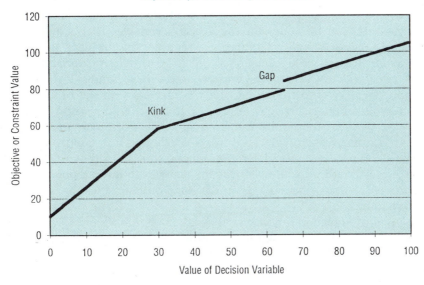

zation problems formulated in mathematical language, but nonlinear optimization software is harder to find.

Nonlinearities in Optimization

If there is a nonlinear relationship between a decision variable and either the objective or any constraint cell, the What's*Best!* software will detect that non-linearity and use a nonlinear algorithm for solving the problem. (Users of other software may need to perform that diagnosis using their own expertise, and then choose the software that matches the diagnosis.) The success of the nonlinear optimization depends upon the type of nonlinearity; different problems arise depending upon whether the nonlinearity is *smooth* or *nonsmooth*. Figure 10.1 shows an example of a smooth nonlinear relationship; Figure 10.2 shows a nonsmooth relationship, with a "kink" (or a point that is nondifferentiable, to the mathematician) and a "gap" (or a discontinuity, to a mathematician).

When there is a smooth nonlinearity, the difference between local and global optima may be important. Figure 10.1 shows two peaks; within the values shown for a decision on the horizontal axis, the higher peak is a global opti-mum for a maximization problem; the lower peak is a local optimum. The opti-mization process may locate either of these points. If the optimization search begins at the left edge of the values shown on the horizontal axis, the global optimum would be encountered, causing the search to terminate. On the other hand, starting at the right edge of the graph, the optimizer might stop at the local optimum. The optimizer has looked at the values "nearby" and found none that is better, in either case. Algorithms are not yet smart enough to know how to look long distances away. In more formal language, smooth nonlinearity leads to a set of values for the decision variables that is a local optimum but not necessarily a global optimum. To counter this problem, the analyst should attempt to start the optimization with a set of decision variable values that are "good" and let the software improve upon those values. If the analyst places "good" values into the spreadsheet before starting the optimization process, there is a better chance of finding a global optimum using optimization software. Better yet, optimize the model a number of times, starting each search with a different set of decision variable values. It is good practice to make these starting values quite different from one another. Although this won't guarantee a global optimum, it improves the chances of finding one. Unfortunately, one never knows whether a particular set of optimized values is a local or a global optimum.

Two kinds of nonsmooth nonlinearities are shown in Figure 10.2, marked "kink" and "gap." Either of these causes a problem. Kinks and gaps are caused by functions such as @IF, @ABS, @INT, and @MOD. A nonlinearity is present if any of these functions is in the computational path between a decision variable and either the objective variable or a constraint variable. (It is true that these functions do not necessarily generate nonsmooth nonlinearities, but they are used unnecessarily if they don't!) When many of these functions are used in a model (in the computation path between decisions and either objective or constraints) optimization may be useful to improve upon a good solution, but experience has shown that little more should be expected from the software. In effect, the search process is misled by the "kinks" and "gaps" that these functions introduce. Changing the starting point for the search, by changing the decision variable values in the spreadsheet, is occasionally helpful in finding a better solution; however, models with many nonsmooth functions have little hope of finding the global optimum.

In some situations, one can convert a nonsmooth nonlinear model into a linear model. Not every nonlinear problem can be converted to a linear model; in fact, most nonlinear problems have no linear formulation. However, the expertise of What's*Best!* can be used to find out just which formulas are nonlinear, to guide the modeler in investigating whether a linear formulation may be possible. To obtain this information, options must be selected from the What's*Best!* menu: **Options**, **Warning**, **Nonlinear**, and **Enable** (report any cells that contain nonlinear formulas).

This might be a good time to review the section in Chapter 3, "Spreadsheet Nonlinearities for Reporting." If a nonlinear relationship in the spreadsheet is not in the computational path between a decision variable and either a constraint or the objective, then the model is still linear. The software is smart enough to use the linear solver. In the blending problem which follows, however, the nonlinear cell is in the computational path between a decision variable and a

---

Figure 10.3

Influence Chart for Mixture

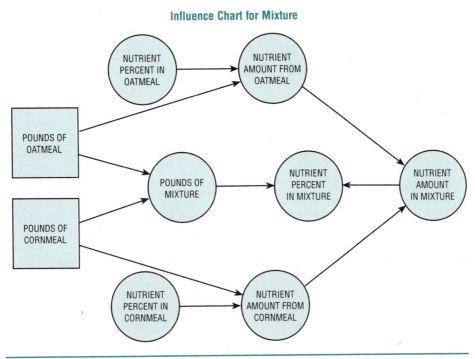

---

constraint. This blending problem illustrates how some nonlinear situations can be modeled in a different way to obtain linearity.

Illustration: A Problem in Blending

This illustration describes blending several ingredients into a final product. Although an optimal solution may be available by inspection, we'll spend several pages to show some useful concepts of mixtures.

Jan Chalk was contemplating various ways of mixing oatmeal and cornmeal to produce an animal food. Oatmeal is 10% nutrients; cornmeal is 15% nutrients. The mixture resulting from mixing cornmeal and oatmeal needs to be at least 12% nutrients. Jan has 100 pounds of oatmeal and 50 pounds of cornmeal, and wants to make as much animal food as possible. Jan started thinking about mixtures with this question:

> If 10 pounds of oatmeal is mixed with 40 pounds of cornmeal, what percent nutrient is in the mixture? On scratch paper, Jan wrote:
>
> $$[(10\% \times 10) + (15\% \times 40)] / (10 + 40) = (1 + 6) / (50) = 14\%$$
>
> to correctly calculate that the mixture is 14% nutrients.

Jan wanted to generalize, keeping the oatmeal content at 10 pounds and varying the amount of cornmeal. We'll use this illustration to investigate linearity and nonlinearity in blending.

─────────────────── **Figure 10.4** ───────────────────

Spreadsheet Model for Mixture

	A	B	C	D
1			Constrnt	Limit
2	Pounds of Oatmeal	10	<=	100
3	Pounds of Cornmeal	40	<=	50
4	Pounds of Mixture	50		
5				
6	Nutr percent in Oatmeal	10.00%		
7	Nutr percent in Cornmeal	15.00%		
8	Nutr Amount from Oatmeal	1		
9	Nutr Amount from Conrmeal	6		
10	Nutr Amount in Mixture	7		
11	Nutr percent in Mixture	14.00% >=		12.00%

In general, to find the percent nutrient in the mix, find the total amount of nutrient in the mixture and divide by the weight of the mixture. Ten pounds of oatmeal contains 1 pound of nutrient (10% × 10 pounds = 1 pound); 40 pounds of cornmeal contains 6 pounds of nutrient (15% × 40 pounds = 6 pounds). The mixture contains 7 pounds nutrients and 50 pounds of mixture; the nutrient percent of the mixture is 14% (7/50 = 14%). This logic is shown in the influence chart of Figure 10.3. A spreadsheet model for computing the nutrient percent in the mixture is shown in Figure 10.4; the documentation is shown in Figure 10.5. Is this a linear model? Jan used What's*Best!* with these optimization instructions:

Decisions:	Pounds of Oatmeal
	Pounds of Cornmeal
Constraints:	Nutr percent in Mixture >= Nutr percent in Mixture[Limit]
	Pounds of Oatmeal <= Pounds of Oatmeal[Limit]
	Pounds of Cornmeal <= Pounds of Cornmeal[Limit]
Objective:	*Maximize* Pounds of Mixture

With these instructions, What's*Best!* diagnoses the problem as nonlinear, with a nonlinear relationship in cell B11. To better understand the nonlinear nature in

─────────────────── **Figure 10.5** ───────────────────

Documentation for Mixture Worksheet

```
Pounds of Oatmeal = 10
Pounds of Oatmeal[Limit] = 100
Pounds of Cornmeal = 40
Pounds of Cornmeal[Limit] = 50
Pounds of Mixture = Pounds of Oatmeal + Pounds of Cornmeal
Nutr percent in Oatmeal = 0.1
Nutr percent in Cornmeal = 0.15
Nutr Amount from Oatmeal = Pounds of Oatmeal * Nutr percent in Oatmeal
Nutr Amount from Cornmeal = Pounds of Cornmeal * Nutr percent in Cornmeal
Nutr Amount in Mixture = Nutr Amount from Oatmeal + Nutr Amount from Cornmeal
Nutr percent in Mixture = Nutr Amount in Mixture / Pounds of Mixture
Nutr percent in Mixture[Limit] = 0.12
```

--- **Figure 10.6** ---

Data Table for Nutrient Percent in Mixture

Pounds of Cornmeal	Percent Nutrient	Pounds of Cornmeal	Percent Nutrient
0	10.00	13	12.83
1	10.45	14	12.92
2	10.83	15	13.00
3	11.15	16	13.08
4	11.43	17	13.15
5	11.67	18	13.21
6	11.87	19	13.28
7	12.06	20	13.33
8	12.22	.	.
9	12.37	.	.
10	12.50	.	.
11	12.62	40	14.00
12	12.73		

Note: Oatmeal is constant at ten pounds.

--- **Figure 10.7** ---

Graph of Data Shown in Figure 10.6

Nutrient Percent in Mixture
(Assuming Ten Pounds of Oatmeal)

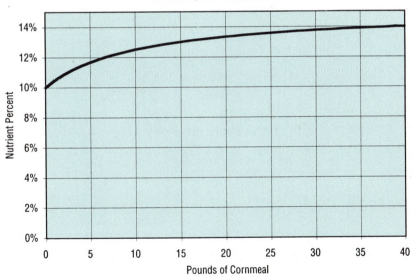

the mixture, the spreadsheet model was used to prepare a data table showing the nutrient percent in the mixture for various amounts of cornmeal in the mixture, keeping oatmeal constant at ten pounds. The data table is shown in Figure 10.6; the corresponding graph is shown in Figure 10.7. The graph clearly confirms the

―――――――――――――― **Figure 10.8** ――――――――――――――

Influence Chart for Mixture (Linear)

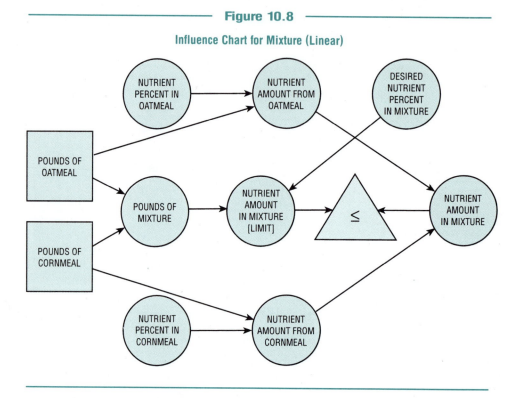

―――――――――――――― **Figure 10.9** ――――――――――――――

Spreadsheet Model for Mixture (Linear)

	A	B	C	D
1			Constrnt	Limit
2	Pounds of Oatmeal	10	<=	100
3	Pounds of Cornmeal	40	<=	50
4	Pounds of Mixture	50		
5				
6	Nutr percent in Oatmeal	10.00%		
7	Nutr percent in Cornmeal	15.00%		
8	Nutr Amount from Oatmeal	1		
9	Nutr Amount from Conrmeal	6		
10	Nutr Amount in Mixture	7	>=	6
11	Desired Nutr pct in Mixtur	12.00%		

diagnosis: there is a nonlinear relationship between the decision variables and the nutrient percent in the mixture.

The mixture problem, while quite simple, is nonlinear in this form. This model, however, can be converted to a linear relationship, although the new formulation is not quite as "natural" as the original model. *The key to the linear formulation is to calculate the amount of nutrient required, and see if ingredients in a proposed mixture have enough nutrients.*

—————————— **Figure 10.10** ——————————

Documentation for Mixture Worksheet (Linear)

```
Pounds of Oatmeal = 10
Pounds of Oatmeal[Limit] = 100

Pounds of Cornmeal = 40
Pounds of Cornmeal[Limit] = 50

Pounds of Mixture = Pounds of Oatmeal + Pounds of Cornmeal
Nutr percent in Oatmeal = 0.1
Nutr percent in Cornmeal = 0.15
Nutr Amount from Oatmeal = Pounds of Oatmeal * Nutr percent in Oatmeal
Nutr Amount from Cornmeal = Pounds of Cornmeal * Nutr percent in Cornmeal
Nutr Amount in Mixture = Nutr Amount from Oatmeal + Nutr Amount from Cornmeal
Nutr Amount in Mixture[Limit] = Pounds of Mixture * Desired Nutr pct in Mixture
Desired Nutr pct in Mixture = 0.12
```

Look again at the requirement that the mixture must have at least 12% nutrients. The original proposed mixture (10 pounds of oatmeal, 40 pounds of cornmeal) weighs 50 pounds, and has 7 pounds of nutrient. (All of this information was calculated in the previous worksheet.) A 12% mixture needs 6 pounds of nutrient for 50 pounds of mix ($12\% \times 50 = 6$). The nutrient constraint is satisfied, because the Nutr Amount in Mixture (7 pounds) is greater than the Nutr Amount in Mixture[Limit] (6 pounds). Figure 10.8 shows this logic in an influence chart. The computations are shown in the worksheet of Figure 10.9, which is documented in Figure 10.10.

The optimization instructions for this problem are:

Decisions: Pounds of Oatmeal
                   Pounds of Cornmeal

Constraints: Nutr Amount in Mixture >= Nutr Amt in Mixture[Limit]
                   Pounds of Oatmeal <= Pounds of Oatmeal[Limit]
                   Pounds of Cornmeal <= Pounds of Cornmeal[Limit]

Objective: *Maximize* Pounds of Mixture

Using What's *Best!*, the optimal mixture is to use 75 pounds of oatmeal, and 50 pounds of cornmeal, for a total of 125 pounds of mixture. This is the same optimal solution we reached using the nonlinear formulation earlier in the chapter.

The solver determines that the constraints and the objective are linear. The most important constraint is:

Nutr Amount in Mixture >= Nutr Amt in Mixture[Limit]

which compares two spreadsheet cells or variables; both of these variables change in value when the value of a decision variable is adjusted.

Our next task is to demonstrate linearity in a constraint; since this constraint contains two parts, the demonstration is simpler if we combine the two parts of the constraint into one part, by using this definition:

Excess Nutr Amount in Mixture = Nutr Amount in Mixture −
                                       Nutr Amount in Mixture[Limit]

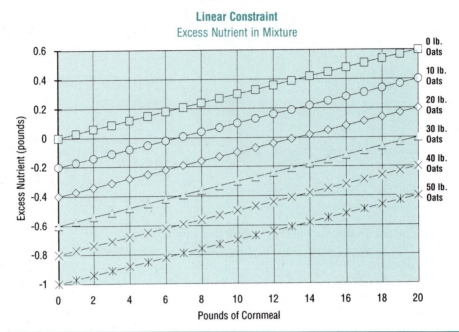

Figure 10.11

Linear Constraint
Excess Nutrient in Mixture

and this equivalent constraint:*

```
Excess Nutr Amount in Mixture >= 0
```

Figure 10.11 shows a graph of the amount of excess nutrient plotted against the number of pounds of cornmeal in the mixture. The excess nutrient is shown for various amounts of oatmeal in the mixture. Not only is there a linear relationship between the amount of cornmeal and the amount of excess nutrient, the slope of the line is the same for any amount of oatmeal. In summary, this illustration has shown that the straightforward method of calculating the percent nutrient in a mixture (the method Jan Chalk did on scratch paper at the beginning of the illustration) leads to a nonlinear relationship between the decision variable (pounds of cornmeal) and the percent nutrient in the mixture. This is nonlinear because the decision variable (pounds of cornmeal) affects both the numerator (upstairs) and denominator (downstairs) of a fraction. Looking at the same situation in a different way, we calculated the amount of nutrient contained in a mixture, and compared it with the amount of nutrient a mixture must have. This shows that the constraint

```
Nutr Amount in Mixture >= Nutr Amount in Mixture[Limit]
```

is a linear constraint. This method of modeling mixtures is applied in the Sparkling Clean case.

---

*If you are using the optimizer in Quattro Pro for Windows, this form of the constraint must be used for optimization. QPW is not designed to use constraints whose right-hand side varies with a decision variable.

CASE STUDY:
Sparkling Clean

The Sparkling Clean Company has five ingredients in its warehouse. They can be blended into an industrial strength cleaning solution which will be sold for $2.18 per gallon. This product will be offered only until the quantities of ingredient that are in stock are exhausted; these ingredients remain from a custom detergent blend which was shipped last week. Any ingredients not used in making this cleaning solution will be discarded. The ingredients available, according to a stock report from the warehouse, are as follows:

Super Clean	1700 gallons
All Round	1400 gallons
No Germ	800 gallons
Potency	1000 gallons
Bland	2000 gallons
Water	unlimited amount

The company believes that industrial cleaning solutions have three characteristics of concern to buyers:

The first characteristic, cleaning index, must be at least 75. The blending works in the straightforward way: 1 gallon of ingredient with a cleaning index of 60, mixed with 1 gallon of another ingredient with a cleaning index of 70, would result in a mixture with an index of 65. (The computation of the index for the mixture is exactly the same as the computation of the percent nutrient for the previous example.)

The second characteristic is the irritation index. The industrial strength cleaner to be blended must have an irritation index no larger than 60. If the irritation index is too high, the blend is too irritable to use. The irritation index of a blend behaves the same as the cleaning index.

The final characteristic is the disinfectant index. The company will not label the blend as industrial strength unless its disinfectant index is at least 45. The disinfectant index of a blend is computed in the same manner as the cleaning index.

The five ingredients plus water are used to blend industrial strength cleaner. The properties of water are obvious: Its cleaning index, irritation index, and disinfectant index are all zero. The properties of the remaining ingredients are:

Ingredient	Cleaning Index	Irritation Index	Disinfectant Index
Super Clean	80	35	60
All Round	70	50	50
No Germ	20	25	95
Potency	90	80	25
Bland	55	35	25
Limits:	at least 75	at most 60	at least 45

Figure 10.12

Spreadsheet Model for Sparkling Clean

	A	B	C	D	E	F	G
1		Gallons	Cnstr	Up Limit	Clng	Irritn	Disinf
2	Super Clean Index				80	35	60
3	All Round Index				70	50	50
4	No Germ Index				20	25	95
5	Potency Index				90	80	25
6	Bland Index				55	35	25
7	Water Index				0	0	0
8							
9	Super Clean Amount	2	<=	1700	160	70	120
10	All Round Amount	10	<=	1400	700	500	500
11	No Germ Amount	20	<=	800	400	500	1900
12	Potency Amount	100	<=	1000	9000	8000	2500
13	Bland Amount	200	<=	2000	11000	7000	5000
14	Water Amount	500			0	0	0
15	Total Amount	832			21260	16070	10020
16	Constraint				Not >=	<=	Not >=
17	Required Amount				62400	49920	37440
18	Required Index				75	60	45

Figure 10.13

Documentation for Sparkling Clean Worksheet

Super Clean Index[Cleaning]..Water Index[Disinfectant] is documented in cells C2..D7

Super Clean Amount[Gallons] = 2 (an arbitrary initial value)
Super Clean Amount[Up Limit] = 1700
Super Clean Amount[Cleaning THRU Disinfectant] = Super Clean Index * Super Clean Amount[Gallons]

All Round Amount[Gallons] = 10 (an arbitrary initial value)
All Round Amount[Up Limit] = 1400
All Round Amount[Cleaning THRU Disinfectant] = All Round Index * All Round Amount[Gallons]

No Germ Amount[Gallons] = 20 (an arbitrary initial value)
No Germ Amount[Up Limit] = 800
No Germ Amount[Cleaning THRU Disinfectant] = No Germ Index * No Germ Amount[Gallons]

Potency Amount[Gallons] = 100 (an arbitrary initial value)
Potency Amount[Up Limit] = 1000
Potency Amount[Cleaning THRU Disinfectant] = Potency Index * Potency Amount[Gallons]

Bland Amount[Gallons] = 200 (an arbitrary initial value)
Bland Amount[Up Limit] = 2000
Bland Amount[Cleaning THRU Disinfectant] = Bland Index * Bland Amount[Gallons]

Water Amount[Gallons] = 500 (an arbitrary initial value)
Water Amount[Cleaning THRU Disinfectant] = Water Index * Water Amount[Gallons]

Total Amount[Gallons] = SUM (Super Clean Amount THRU Water Amount[Gallons])

Total Amount[Cleaning THRU Disinfectant] = SUM (Super Clean Amount THRU Bland Amount)

Required Amount[Cleaning THRU Disinfectant] = Required Index * Total Amount[Gallons]
Required Index[Cleaning] = 75
Required Index[Irritation] = 60
Required Index[Disinfectant] = 45

Sparkling Clean: Discussion

In order to construct a model to support the decision in Sparkling Clean, management needs to know the number of gallons of a mixture that a particular "recipe" will produce, and whether the limits on cleaning, irritation, and disinfectant are met. Our typical approach has been to start with an influence chart, and then construct a model. The logic of the influence chart from Figure 10.8 applies to each of the three properties (Cleaning, Irritation, and Disinfectant) of the mixture. Because that logic is quite straightforward (once you have studied the mixture example above), we proceed directly to the spreadsheet model.

The spreadsheet to evaluate a proposed recipe is shown in Figure 10.12, and documented in Figure 10.13. The decisions are the values in the Gallons column for the six ingredients (Super Clean Amount[Gallons] THRU Water Amount [Gallons]). These values will be adjusted by the optimization software; their initial values have been selected to assist understanding the logic of the model by looking at the spreadsheet. Constraints arise from the requirements for Cleaning, Disinfectant, and Irritation. The objective is for Total Amount[Gallons].

It is left as an exercise to demonstrate that the company can make 4858.3 gallons of cleaner. The optimization instructions for Sparkling Clean are:

Decisions: Super Clean Amount[Gallons] THRU Water Amount[Gallons]

Constraints: Total Amount[Cleaning] >= Required Amount[Cleaning]
Ttotal Amount[Irritation] <= Required Amount[Irritation]
Total Amount[Disinfectant] >= Required Amount[Disinfectant]
Super Clean Amount[Gallons] <= 1700
All Round Amount[Gallons] <= 1400
No Germ Amount[Gallons] <= 800
Potency Amount[Gallons] <= 1000
Bland Amount[Gallons] <= 2000

Objective: *Maximize* Total Amount[Gallons]

CASE STUDY:

Rangely Lakes Company (B)

The Rangely Lakes Company was first presented in Chapter 1, and was extended in Chapter 3. We present the entire case, with an added final paragraph:

> In early August, 1988, J. L. Duckworth began thinking about the winter activities of Rangely Lakes Company. J.L. was particularly concerned about the cash budgets for the winter, when revenue was quite limited. The other major concern J.L. was addressing was the need to keep the golf course maintenance staff busy during the winter. It appeared that there would be a need to have at least 4000 hours of work available dur-

there would be a need to have at least 4000 hours of work available during the winter; after discussing the winter plans with more employees, J.L. had concluded that no more than 6000 hours of employee time would be available during the winter season.

The Rangely Lakes Company operates a summer-only golf course in northern Maine. To keep the maintenance employees on the workforce during the winter, they have developed two "Maine Woods Souvenirs" made out of forest products from the Rangely Lakes area. They produce only these two products: mallard decoys and mallard wall hangings. Both of these products are hand-made; they have developed procedures so that skilled (but unartistic) maintenance workers can produce the two items. These souvenirs are marketed through numerous gift shops in New England. Rangely Lakes has priced the items attractively, so that they can sell all of the souvenirs they can produce. From a budgeting standpoint, J. L. Duckworth needs to know how much profit would be generated from the souvenirs made during the winter. For planning purposes, J.L. calculated profit as revenue (price × quantity) less the cost of the wood used and the cost of the labor in the products.

Most gift shops sell the mallard decoy for $26.95, and the mallard wall hanging for $34.95. Rangely Lakes sells to the gift shops at $12 and $15 respectively. The average labor content is 1.1 hours for a decoy and 0.5 hours for a wall hanging. Each labor hour costs Rangely Lakes $7.15, including fringe benefits. Although Rangely has some flexibility in the amount of labor it uses, it monitors labor usage very closely to be certain that enough production is planned to keep the workforce employed, without planning for more labor than reasonable expectations of availability.

The souvenirs are made from native lumber, carefully selected during the summer as forest operations are performed. Each decoy requires 2.9 board feet of this special lumber; each wall hanging requires 4.8 board feet. (A board foot is 144 cubic inches of lumber.) About 17,000 board feet will be available for the winter production season. The anticipated market price for the wood is about $1.30 per board foot.

J. L. Duckworth made this statement, with new information: "I know I implied we could sell all the wall hangings we could make at $15 each. But I don't think so any more. I think we could sell about a thousand at $15 each. If we try to sell more than a thousand, we could still sell the first thousand at $15 each. After that, we'd need to cut the price to $11 each for those above a thousand."

How would this change affect the spreadsheet that was constructed for supporting the souvenir decision? In the last visit to Rangely, revenue for wall hangings was price multiplied by quantity. With the new information, that relationship is true only when the quantity of wall hangings is less than or equal

--- **Figure 10.14** ---

Nonlinear Objective for Rangely Lakes (B)
Rangely (B): Profit vs. Qty Hangings
(Assumes 1000 Decoys Made and Sold)

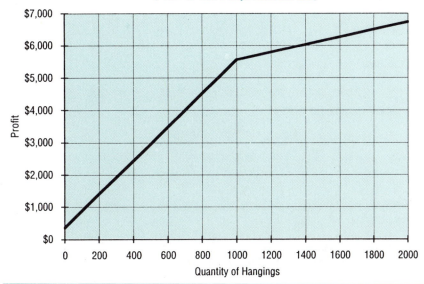

to 1000. Otherwise, the revenue is computed as 1000 wall hangings at $15 each, plus the remaining wall hangings at $11. In a spreadsheet formula, the revenue for wall hangings is:

```
@IF(Quantity<=1000,15*Quantity,15*1000+11*(Quantity-1000))
```

where `Quantity` refers to the cell containing the quantity of wall hangings. If it is true that the quantity is less than or equal to 1000, then the revenue is `15*Quantity`. But if the condition is false, then revenue is calculated as $15,000 plus the remainder at $11 each.

What is the impact of this change in the model? A bit of reflection reveals that the change in revenue, and hence the change in profit (the objective) depends upon whether the number of wall hangings is below or above 1000. Until a quantity of 1000 wall hangings is reached, a unit change in `Quantity` [Hangings] brought about a $15 change in revenue. After 1000 hangings have been produced, a unit change in `Quantity`[Hangings] brings about a change of $11 in revenue. This means that the optimization problem is nonlinear.

Figure 10.14 displays a graph of `Profit[Total]` vs. `Quantity[Hanging]`. The line will be straight, from no hangings up to 1000 hangings. Then the line has a kink, with another straight line segment joining the first one at 1000 hangings. There are two "straight line pieces" that show the relationship between the decision variable and the objective variable. Mathematicians call this a "piecewise linear relationship"; from the standpoint of optimization, it is nonlinear.

Figure 10.15

Rangely Lakes (B) Before Optimization

	A	B	C	D	E	F	G	H	I
1		Decoy	Hang I	Hang II	Total	Cnstr	Limit	Cnstr	Limit
2	Quantity	1000	400	100		<=	1000		
3	Price	$12	$15	$11					
4	Revenue	$12,000	$6,000	$1,100	$19,100				
5									
6	Board Feet Used	2900	1920	480	5300	<=	17000		
7	Cost of Lumber	$3,770	$2,496	$624	$6,890				
8									
9	Hours Used	1100	200	50	1350	Not >=	4000	<=	6000
10	Cost of Labor	$7,865	$1,430	$358	$9,653				
11									
12	Profit		$365	$2,074	$119	$2,558			
13									
14	Board Feet per Item	2.9	4.8	4.8					
15	Hours per Item	1.1	0.5	0.5					
16									
17		Data							
18	Price per Board Ft	$1.30							
19	Price per Hour	$7.15							

Note: The contents of the constraint cells inserted by What's*Best!* are:

    F2:   @WB(C2,"<=",G2)
    F6:   @WB(E6,"<=",G6)
    F9:   @WB(E9,">=",G9)
    H9:   @WB(E9,"<=",I9)

Rangely Lakes Company (B): Discussion

The kinky nonlinearity in Rangely Lakes (B) is caused by a reduction in the selling price from $15 to $11 for all wall hangings in excess of 1000. This non-linearity can be removed by imagining that there are really two different wall hangings: one that sells for $15, and another that sells for $11. It just so happens that they are alike in every way except the price tag! Let's call them Hang I (selling for $15) and Hang II (selling for $11). (If these hangings depicted surfers, additional kinks would bring us to Hang X.) Of course, Rangely would not want to make any Hang II items until 1000 Hang I items had been made. It would clearly be nonoptimal to make 500 of each product, because the resource use would be the same as making 1000 Hang I items, yet the revenue would be less when production is 500 of each. So all we need to do is limit the value of the decision variable Hang I so that it is between 0 and 1000; if it is profitable to make Hang II items after that, the optimization process will automatically recommend that in the solution. This approach is demonstrated in the spreadsheet (Figure 10.15) and documentation (Figure 10.16). The optimization instructions are:

          Decisions: Quantity[Decoy]
                        Quantity[Hang I]
                        Quantity[Hang II]

―――――――――――――――――― **Figure 10.16** ――――――――――――――――――

Rangely Lakes (B) Documentation

```
Quantity[Decoy]..Quantity[Hang II] are arbitrary initial values
Quantity[Limit] = 1000 (note:  an upper limit that applies to Hang I)
Price[Decoy] = 12
Price[Hang I] = 15
Price[Hang II] = 11
Revenue[Decoy THRU Hang II] = Quantity * Price
Revenue[Total] = SUM (Revenue[Decoy] THRU Revenue[Hang II])
Board Feet Used[Decoy THRU Hang II] = Quantity * Board Feet per Item
Board Feet Used[Total] = SUM (Board Feet Used[Decoy] THRU Board Feet Used[Hang II])
Board Feet Used[Limit] = 17000 (note:  an upper limit)
Cost of Lumber[Decoy THRU Hang II] = Board Feet Used * Price per Board Foot
Cost of Lumber[Total] = SUM (Cost of Lumber[Decoy] THRU Cost of Lumber[Hang II])
Hours Used[Decoy THRU Hang II] = Quantity * Hours per Item
Hours Used[Total] = SUM (Hours Used[Decoy] THRU Hours Used[Hang II])
Hours Used[Limit] = 4000 (note:  a lower limit)
Hours Used[Limit] = 6000 (note:  an upper limit)
Cost of Labor[Decoy THRU Hang II] = Hours Used * Price per Hour
Cost of Labor[Total] = SUM (Cost of Labor[Decoy] THRU Cost of Labor[Hang II])
Profit[Decoy THRU Hang II] = Revenue - Cost of Lumber - Cost of Labor
Profit[Total] = SUM (Profit[Decoy] THRU Profit[Hang II])
Board Feet per Item[Decoy] = 2.9
Board Feet per Item[Hang I THRU Hang II] = 4.8
Hours per Item[Decoy] = 1.1
Hours per Item[Hang I THRU Hang II] = 0.5
Price per Board Foot = 1.3
Price per Hour = 7.15
```

Constraints: Board Feet Used[Total] <= 17000
Hours Used[Total] >= 4000
Hours Used[Total] <= 6000
Quantity[Hang I] <= 1000

Objective: *Maximize* Profit[Total]

It is left as an exercise to demonstrate that the maximum profit in this situation is $7216.

Another Example of Piecewise Linearity: Production Planning

Production planning introduces another example of piecewise linearity. This application is somewhat like the treatment of loan transactions in the Novana case from the previous chapter. We broke the transactions into two parts: AMOUNT BORROWED and AMOUNT REPAID. In one sense, these are the same activity: changing the level of the loan balance. Because we usually think of these as different activities, they were modeled as two separate decision variables. This has an additional advantage: If there had been a transaction tax (which there wasn't), a different tax rate could have been applied to amounts borrowed and amounts repaid. Splitting an activity into its positive and negative components is also quite useful in production planning.

In planning production levels for a planning period, an important variable is the number of workers employed each month. From one month to the next, hiring and firing changes the number of workers employed each month. There are costs associated with hiring and with layoffs, but they generally are not the same. Some firms may find that it costs a lot more to increase the number of workers (hire) than it costs to reduce the number of workers (layoff); other firms may be in the opposite situation. There are at least three ways to set up this problem for optimization:

Method 1: Decide on the level of the workforce each period. From this, the number of workers hired and the number of workers placed on layoff can be determined. This requires logic (an @IF function) to determine whether we hired or fired this period. The IF function causes a piecewise linear relationship, which is nonlinear and troublesome to optimize.

Method 2: Decide on the change in the level of the workforce each period, allowing this change to be positive or negative (i.e., instruct What's*Best!* to allow the decision variable to be free, permitting negative values). This is straightforward: A positive change implies hiring, a negative change implies a layoff. Again, however, logic (an @IF function) will be required to apply the correct cost factor to the change in workforce level. The IF function causes a piecewise linear relationship, which is nonlinear and troublesome to optimize.

Method 3: Make two separate decisions: how many workers to hire, and how many workers to fire. Limit each of these decisions to nonnegative values. Then each may have its own cost applied to it, which becomes a linear relationship. The "kink" of IF logic does not exist, because the permitted values of the decision variables have a lower bound of zero. The kink in Method 2 arises when the variables go from positive to negative.

Any of these methods would work quite well in descriptive spreadsheet modeling. But in modeling for optimization, the third method is clearly superior to the other two, because the troublesome IF logic is avoided.

CASE STUDY:

Production Planning

This case is presented, along with a model and optimization instructions, to serve as an illustration of dealing with a piecewise linear situation in a time-based context.

A company is planning its production for the next four months. The company will have an inventory of 100 units at the end of the current month; the

---

Figure 10.17

Spreadsheet Model for Production Planning

	A	B	C	D	E	F	G
1		Mo. 1	Mo. 2	Mo. 3	Mo. 4	Mo. 5	Total
2							
3	Previous Workforce	30	35	35	25	25	
4	Workers Hired	5	0	0	0	0	
5	Workers Terminated	0	0	10	0	0	
6	Current Workforce	35	35	25	25	25	
7	Cnstrnt: WorkForce >=	>=	>=	>=	=		
8	Workforce Limit/Target	0	0	0	0	25	
9							
10	Beginning Inventory	100	200	225	400		
11	Regular Production	350	350	250	250		
12	Overtime Production	0	25	0	0		
13	Cnstrnt: Overtime Limit <=	=<=	<=	<=			
14	Overtime Limit	25	25	25	25		
15							
16	Units Available	450	575	475	650		
17	Shipments	250	350	75	450		
18	Ending Inventory	200	225	400	200		
20	Cnstrnt: Inventory >=	>=	>=	Not =			
19	End Invty Limit/Target	0	0	0	150		
21							
22	Hiring Cost	2500	0	0	0	0	
23	Termination Cost	0	0	4000	0	0	
24	Overtime Cost	0	1125	0	0		
25	Inventory Cost	10000	11250	20000	10000		
26	Monthly Cost	12500	12375	24000	10000	0	58875
27							
28	Units per Month	10					
29	Cost per Hire	500					
30	Cost per Termination	400					
31	Overtime Surcharge	45					
32	Monthly Inventory Charge	50					

---

current workforce is 30 workers. For the next four months, the projected shipments are 250 units, 350 units, 75 units, and 450 units. Each worker can produce
10 units per month. Hiring a worker costs $500; terminating a worker costs $400.
Carrying a unit from one month to the next costs $50. A surcharge of $45 is
incurred for every unit made on overtime. No more than 25 units can be made
on overtime each month. At the end of the fourth month (really, at the beginning
of the fifth month for modeling purposes) the company must have an inventory
of 150 units, and a workforce of 25 workers. Find the least-cost production plan
for the company.

The spreadsheet values for this problem, shown in Figure 10.17, are virtually
self-documenting. The student is encouraged to follow the logic for the cells in
the solution, first by following the numbers with a calculator, then by using the
documentation that follows. The values for the decision variables in this illustration are arbitrary. Another worthwhile activity for the student is to study this
spreadsheet solution, and mark the appropriate cells as *decision*, *constraint*, or
objective. The model is documented in Figure 10.18.

───────────────── **Figure 10.18** ─────────────────

Documentation for Spreadsheet in Figure 10.16

```
Previous Workforce[Mo. 1] = 30
Previous Workforce[Mo. 2 THRU Mo. 5] = PREVIOUS Current Workforce

Workers Hired[Mo. 1] = 5
Workers Hired[Mo. 2 THRU Mo. 5] = 0

Workers Terminated[Mo. 1 THRU Mo. 2] = 0
Workers Terminated[Mo. 3] = 10
Workers Terminated[Mo. 4 THRU Mo. 5] = 0

Current Workforce[Mo. 1 THRU Mo. 5] = Previous Workforce + Workers Hired - Workers Terminated
Workforce Limit/Target[Mo. 1 THRU Mo. 4] = 0
Workforce Limit/Target[Mo. 5] = 25

Beginning Inventory[Mo. 1] = 100
Beginning Inventory[Mo. 2 THRU Mo. 4] = PREVIOUS Ending Inventory

Regular Production[Mo. 1 THRU Mo. 4] = Current Workforce * Units per Month

Overtime Production[Mo. 1] = 0
Overtime Production[Mo. 2] = 25
Overtime Production[Mo. 3 THRU Mo. 4] = 0
Overtime Limit[Mo. 1 THRU Mo. 4] = 25

Units Available[Mo. 1 THRU Mo. 4] = Beginning Inventory + Regular Production + Overtime Production

Shipments[Mo. 1] = 250
Shipments[Mo. 2] = 350
Shipments[Mo. 3] = 75
Shipments[Mo. 4] = 450

Ending Inventory[Mo. 1 THRU Mo. 4] = Units Available - Shipments
End Invty Limit/Target[Mo. 1 THRU Mo. 3] = 0
End Invty Limit/Target[Mo. 4] = 150
Hiring Cost[Mo. 1 THRU Mo. 5] = Workers Hired * Cost per Hire

Termination Cost[Mo. 1 THRU Mo. 5] = Workers Terminated * Cost per Termination

Overtime Cost[Mo. 1 THRU Mo. 4] = Overtime Production * Overtime Surcharge

Inventory Cost[Mo. 1 THRU Mo. 4] = Ending Inventory * Monthly Inventory Charge

Monthly Cost[Mo. 1 THRU Mo. 5] = SUM (Hiring Cost THRU Inventory Cost)
Monthly Cost[Total] = SUM (Monthly Cost[Mo. 1] THRU Monthly Cost[Mo. 5])
Units per Month = 10
Cost per Hire = 500
Cost per Termination = 400
Overtime Surcharge = 45
Monthly Inventory Charge = 50
```

Note that this model uses five monthly columns, although there are only four months of activity. However, the problem requires the workforce level at the end of the fourth month to be 25 workers. The logic of the model permits the workforce decisions to be made at the beginning of each month; the workforce decisions for the fifth month must be included to allow the optimization software to return the workforce to the level of 25 workers. If the problem had been been modeled with decisions made at the end of each month, we would have needed a column at the beginning of the model for "now" so that decisions could be made to take effect at the beginning of the first month.

––––––––––––––––––––––––––––– **Figure 10.19** –––––––––––––––––––––––––––––

Optimized Spreadsheet for Production Planning

	A	B	C	D	E	F	G
1		Mo. 1	Mo. 2	Mo. 3	Mo. 4	Mo. 5	Total
2							
3	Previous Workforce	30	25	25	32.5	32.5	
4	Workers Hired	0	0	7.5	0	0	
5	Workers Terminated	5	0	0	0	7.5	
6	Current Workforce	25	25	32.5	32.5	25	
7	Cnstrnt: WorkForce	>=	>=	>=	>=	=	
8	Workforce Limit/Target	0	0	0	0	25	
9							
10	Beginning Inventory	100	100	0	250		
11	Regular Production	250	250	325	325		
12	Overtime Production	0	0	0	25		
13	Cnstrnt: Overtime Limit <=	<=	<=	=<=			
14	Overtime Limit	25	25	25	25		
15							
16	Units Available	350	350	325	600		
17	Shipments	250	350	75	450		
18	Ending Inventory	100	0	250	150		
19	Cnstrnt: Inventory	>=	=>=	>=	=		
20	End Invty Limit/Target	0	0	0	150		
21							
22	Hiring Cost	0	0	3750	0	0	
23	Termination Cost	2000	0	0	0	3000	
24	Overtime Cost	0	0	0	1125		
25	Inventory Cost	5000	0	12500	7500		
26	Monthly Cost	7000	0	16250	8625	3000	34875
27							
28	Units per Month	10					
29	Cost per Hire	500					
30	Cost per Termination	400					
31	Overtime Surcharge	45					
32	Monthly Inventory Charge	50					

Figure 10.19 shows the results of applying optimization to the spreadsheet. Notice that the "optimal" solution does some hiring, some termination, some overtime, and carries some inventory. One aspect of the "optimal" solution is that it implies hiring a fractional employee. Although it is often possible to have parttime workers, the training costs are not fractionally applied as they are in this model. A later chapter discusses the use of What's *Best!* to solve problems that must have integer answers. For now, one could argue that the data are not good enough to warrant a more sophisticated solution than shown here. We really don't believe that each worker will produce exactly 10 units each month; we really don't believe that all the dollar costs are just what they are stated to be. For this problem, then, managerial judgment could be applied to modify the "optimal" solution and find a workable solution. (There are other solutions that do not require fractional workers. For example, by hiring 7 workers in month 3, 1 in month 4, and terminating 8 in month 5, all constraints are met with a cost increase of only $200.)

Exercises

1. Whole milk is approximately 3.5% butterfat; skim milk is approximately 0.5% butterfat.

   a. If a mixture is blended of 200 quarts whole milk and 100 quarts skim milk, what is the butterfat percent of the blend?

   b. How much butterfat is contained in a blend of 200 quarts whole milk and 300 quarts skim milk?

   c. Does a proposed blend of 200 quarts whole milk and 300 quarts skim milk have excess butterfat or a deficiency of butterfat, for a 1% requirement? How much is the excess or deficit? Build a spreadsheet model to calculate the excess or deficit.

2. You have 1000 quarts of whole milk (3.5% butterfat), and 200 quarts of skim milk (0.5% butterfat). With the spreadsheet model you constructed in Exercise 1(c), use optimization to maximize the amount of 1% milk you can create from your resources.

3. Construct a model for Sparkling Clean case as shown in Figure 10.12, and use optimization to find the blend that yields the maximum output of 4858.3 gallons.

4. Sparkling Clean (from Exercise 3) has just discovered that it can sell its supplies of ingredients. The value of each ingredient is:

Super Clean	$3 per gallon
All Round	$1.40 per gallon
No Germ	$1.30 per gallon
Potency	$0.95 per gallon
Bland	$0.75 per gallon

   One of the employees of Sparkling Clean observed that the industrial strength cleaner (the subject of the blending model in Figure 10.12) sells for $2.18. This employee went on to argue that it wouldn't make any sense to blend the industrial strength cleaner, because the Super Clean can be sold for $3 per gallon, while the cleaner only brings $2.18. There is no cost associated with mixing. Recommend a course of action for Sparkling Clean. Check figure: A revenue of $12,783 can be attained.

5. This problem is an extension of Exercise 3 (before resale values were introduced). There was discussion about the desirability of designing a second product to use the surplus ingredients. A household cleaner was proposed; it would sell for $2.39 a gallon, while the industrial strength cleaner still sells for $2.18. The cleaning index of the household cleaner must be at least 70; however, its irritation index cannot exceed 35. It need not be a strong disinfectant; an index of 20 or larger is acceptable. How much (if any) of each product should be made, using what recipes? Check figure: A revenue of $11,850 can be obtained with these two products.

6. An agricultural feed is being blended from ingredients that change in price each month. It is important to have the capability to enter current prices, and determine the ingredients to use each month and how much feed to blend that

month. There are several nutrients, which must fall within prescribed bounds. The information is shown in this table:

	Nutrient 1	Nutrient 2	Nutrient 3	Nutrient 4	Available	Cost
Ingredient 1	23%	13%	2%	29%	1000	$2.50
Ingredient 2	27	11	20	28	2000	$3.50
Ingredient 3	23	5	25	5	1500	$1.50
Ingredient 4	4	21	25	1	1000	$2.00
Ingredient 5	17	20	27	14	3000	$2.75
Maximum	25%	15%	24%	25%		
Minimum	15%	5%	18%	15%		

This table shows that Ingredient 1 is 23% Nutrient 1, 13% Nutrient 2, and so on. This ingredient costs $2.50 per unit; no more than 1000 units are available for this month. The selling price of the blended feed is $3.25. The blended feed must be between 15% and 25% Nutrient 1, between 5% and 15% Nutrient 2, and so on. One of the managers suggested that "it would be dumb to use any of ingredient 2 because we buy it for $3.50 and sell it for $3.25." Recommend a course of action for the month. Check figure: Optimum value of profit is $5778.

7. In the discussion of production planning, three methods of making workforce decisions were described:

Method 1: Decide on the level of the workforce each period.

Method 2: Decide on the change in the level of the workforce each period.

Method 3: Decide on the number of workers to hire, and the number of workers to fire.

Each of these decisions eventually determines values for the cost of hiring and the cost of termination, and the level of the workforce. The variables involved in the influence chart are these:

PREVIOUS WORKFORCE	HIRING COST
WORKERS HIRED	COST PER HIRE
WORKERS TERMINATED	TERMINATION COST
CHANGE IN WORKFORCE LEVEL	COST PER TERMINATION
CURRENT WORKFORCE	

Construct an influence chart for each method, using a square shape to identify the decision variables. Point out each arrow or influence that is nonlinear in the first two methods.

8. Construct the model shown in Figure 10.17, documented in Figure 10.18. Use optimization to verify the optimal solution shown in Figure 10.19.

9. Using the model constructed in the previous exercise, change the surcharge for overtime production from $45 to $10. Find the optimal production plan with this change.

10. The Whipper company is planning its production of lawn mowers for the next four months, March through June. It has a current inventory of 1000 mowers; at

the end of four months, it wants to have only 200 mowers in inventory. The cost of carrying inventory is $1.50 per mower per month, based on the inventory at the end of each month. The shipping schedule requires shipment of 3000 mowers in March, 6000 in April, 7000 in May, and 4000 in June. The current workforce is 30 workers, each capable of producing 100 mowers in a month. The cost of hiring additional workers is $500 per worker; the cost of terminating is $750 per worker. At the beginning of July, the workfore must be at least 20 workers. Using a spreadsheet model and optimization, find a production plan that minimizes total cost of inventory, hiring, and firing.

11. The Whipper company (from the previous exercise) has determined that overtime production of 600 mowers a month is feasible. The additional cost of producing mowers on overtime is $4.50. Find a production plan that minimizes the total cost of inventory, hiring, firing, and overtime.

12. The Whipper company (from Exercise 10), which does not permit overtime, also produces chain saws using the same workers. Each worker can produce 200 chain saws in a month. The cost of chain saw inventory per month is $1 per saw per month, based on inventory at the end of each month. The shipping schedule requires shipment of 1000 saws in March, 1700 in May, 5000 in June, and 500 in July. The beginning saw inventory is 500; at the end of June the inventory is to be 100 saws. Overtime is not possible for this scenario. All personnel costs and mower costs and requirements are the same as previous exercises. Find a production plan that minimizes total cost of inventory, hiring, and firing.

CASE STUDY:

Hanley Electronics

In the fall of 1988, Chris Hanley, founder and President of Hanley Electronics, was ecstatic. Chris had just received a contract to supply a new electronics device, which would be used in light aircraft. Nearly a million dollars had gone into developing the device, which Hanley called the Whoami.

Hanley Electronics is located in Evansville, Indiana, a community of about 150,000. Evansville's economy is based on a mix that includes pharmaceuticals, manufacturing (primarily refrigerators and other home appliances), and agriculture. Although electronics is not a major factor in Evansville's economy, Hanley Electronics had been quite successful because of the educational base provided by two local universities, and the large number of people available for assembly work. The firm had been started several decades ago, around a nucleus of engineers from several prominent engineering schools who had met during their MBA coursework. Although the firm had been profitable for a number of years, Hanley had not yet grown to the size that it could take advantage of automated electronics assembly and other robotics.

The first deliveries of the Whoami are to be made in April, 1989, leaving about six months for planning the production of the item. Hanley's customer is a major electronics wholesaler, who sells to a number of "Fixed Base Operators" at airports through the country. The wholesaler also acts as a jobber, assisting Hanley in selling electronics items to manufacturers of light planes. New FAA rules, which just became effective, will eventually require all light planes to have this device, or one made by a competitor, in order to fly in designated air spaces around major airports. There are two markets for the device: the market for existing planes, and the market for new planes. As the effective date of the regulation gets closer, there will be a distinct peak in the rate at which Chris must supply the devices to Hanley's customer. The agreement with Hanley's customer specifies a schedule for the number of units to be delivered in each of the first six months. The schedule also shows the anticipated "steady state" delivery requirement of 2500 per month, after the regulations have been effective for a few months.

	April	May	June	July	August	September	Future Months
Delivery Schedule	500	1500	2500	3500	6400	3600	2500

Chris was contemplating two rather different plans for meeting the peak demand in the late summer of 1989. On the one hand, Chris wanted to continue the Hanley reputation of providing long-term employment for its production workers. With this type of delivery schedule, it would be possible but difficult to use periods of low demand to build inventory for the peak demand in August and September. This could require some overtime, but it would avoid large layoffs and help Hanley's reputation as a good place to work.

On the other hand, Chris knew that there were advantages to hiring to meet the July peak. Although there would be a reduction in the workforce when September was finished, both storage costs and overtime costs might be lower.

In making the proposal to the customer, these planning factors had been used. After some checking, Chris decided they were still appropriate.

Labor content: 5 hours per unit, at $14 per hour: $70 per unit

Material content: $230 per unit

Labor and Materials: $300 per unit

Selling Price, FOB Hanley's facilities: $580 per unit

When Chris began exploring the possibility of keeping the level of the workforce the same from April forward, the plans called for a "standard" month of 160 hours per worker per standard month. The average demand for April through September is 3000 units per month, which is 20% greater than the subsequent planning figure of 2500 units per month. Chris believed that 20% overtime was about the limit that could be sustained for any extended period of time, and wondered whether six months, including summer, was longer than reasonable for a 20% overtime rate. After all, Chris reasoned, 20% means a six day week every week; if a nine-hour working day is feasible, then Saturday work is not necessary every week. Regardless of the schedule, Chris knew that overtime premiums cost about $5.50 per hour. Although overtime is paid at a rate of 50% above base wages, fringe benefits such as vacations, holiday pay, and medical insurance do not cost any more just because overtime has been scheduled. Chris was firm about one thing regarding overtime: starting in October, Chris planned to have a workforce sized to produce 2500 Whoami units each month, in a standard month with 160 work hours.

There are also some difficulties associated with letting the workforce vary from month to month to follow the demand. Hanley was fortunate in being able to hire rather easily. Historically, Hanley hadn't hired very often because attrition was practically nil. Hanley believed in extensive screening and training, however, which resulted in a cost of about $800 for each worker hired for manufacturing the Whoami. Hanley had less experience in reducing the workforce, but knew that it would be a mistake to count on attrition to reduce the workforce after the peak demand. There were some tangible costs that were obvious. Among these costs Chris listed the following:

> Continuation of health insurance for 90 days, according to the labor contract Hanley had signed.

> Change in state unemployment tax rate, which is based on the number of unemployment claims filed by former Hanley employees.

> Termination physical exam, which Hanley routinely performed to avoid future disability claims from terminated employees.

But Chris was particularly concerned about the impact on the rest of the labor force and future hiring if Hanley developed a reputation for employment fluctuations. A particular concern was labor negotiations, which would begin in late 1989. Chris felt that these negotiations would be much more difficult if there is a recent history of terminations.

Considering all of these factors, Chris concluded that the total cost (tangible and intangible) of terminating an employee was somewhere between $1000 and $2000. Chris was "uncomfortably satisfied" with planning based on $1500 per termination.

The final factor that Chris worried about was the financial commitment required to use level production. Since only 500 Whoami units would be delivered in April, production of 3000 units in April would cause a substantial inventory of these units until late summer. Chris wasn't happy with these tentative calculations:

April production (tentative)	3000 Whoami Units
April deliveries (scheduled)	500 Whoami Units
April ending inventory	2500 Whoami Units

At a manufacturing cost of $300 for each Whoami, this amounted to an inventory at the end of April of about three-quarters of a million dollars. Chris realized this would get worse as the months got warmer. Chris believed that financing could be arranged to cover this investment, but it would be expensive. Furthermore, there would be storage costs. Because Hanley had not been involved in a product with demand peaking so sharply, they had typically delivered items rather quickly after their production. For the Whoami, Chris planned to rent warehouse space. The high value of the Whoami meant that security would need to be provided, which would increase the cost of the storage. After considering the cost of warehouse space and security, and the cost of borrowing money, Chris came to the startling realization that storing one Whoami for one month cost about $10.

Chris went through a quick calculation. The additional cost of producing a Whoami on overtime is about $27.50 (five hours at $5.50 per hour overtime surcharge). So overtime is cheaper than three months in storage, but more expensive than two months in storage. Chris wasn't sure just what to do with that tradeoff information, but it was interesting.

Chris thought about another tradeoff: hiring and firing as an alternative to overtime and/or inventory costs. Each worker hired and then terminated costs about $2300 ($800 hiring, $1500 termination). An employee who works for six months will produce about 192 Whoamis. (That result is based on a planning figure of 160 hours per month for six months, and five hours per Whoami produced.) If the $2300 is spread over 192 Whoami units, the unit cost is about $12. That's less than the cost of overtime. But inventory costs for two months make it more expensive than the combination of overtime and inventory costs. And besides, to reduce inventory, you wouldn't really want to hire extra people for the entire six months. But that means that the hiring and termination costs (on a unit basis) go up again. Once more, Chris thought the tradeoff information was useful, but wasn't sure what to do with it.

Chris was about ready to formulate a plan when the plant manager, J. O. Elton, asked to discuss some issues with Chris. J.O. was about ready to place orders for the equipment to be used to make the Whoami. J.O. had selected a workstation design that cost about $350 per worker. J.O. asked, "How many of these workstations should I order? Should we plan on one shift or two? If we use a two-shift operation, we need one workstation for each two workers. Otherwise, this $350 is just like the training costs we incur when we gear up with a new employee. Each employee needs one."

Hanley Electronics had never operated a second shift. Chris and J.O. discussed the possibility at some length before they decided that the additional costs of supervision, security, utilities, shift differential, and other costs would just not be worth it for a six-month peak demand period. They concluded that any production plan should add the cost of the workstation to the cost of training, to obtain the complete cost of expanding the workforce.

Exercises for Hanley Electronics

1. This series of questions is designed to lead the modeler through the steps to construct an influence chart for Hanley Electronics.

   a. The objective for Hanley Electronics is to minimize the sum of the monthly costs, where each monthly cost consists of inventory cost, overtime cost, hiring cost, and firing cost. Show this in an influence chart.

   b. Inventory costs each month are assessed on the ending inventory for that month. The ending inventory is calculated as the beginning inventory, plus regular production, plus overtime production, less the units shipped. Regular production is influenced by the current workforce; overtime production is a decision variable. Include these variables in the influence chart, using appropriate shapes for decisions and constraints.

c. The overtime cost each month is the number of units made on overtime (a decision variable already included in the influence chart), multiplied by the additional unit cost for overtime production. Show this on the influence chart.

d. Hiring and firing costs are influenced by the number of workers hired, the number of workers fired, and the unit cost of each of these activities. Place this on the influence chart. Use rectangles to indicate the decision variables. Include all linkages between these variables and current workforce level, mentioned in step (b) above.

e. The feasibility of an overtime decision is based upon the "allowed but unused" overtime. This is influenced by the overtime limit and the overtime production. The overtime limit is influenced by the workforce level for that month. Show all of these variables on the influence chart. (*Remember:* include a variable only once on an influence chart. The current workforce level, for example, already appears on the influence chart.)

f. Include any additional variables necessary to complete the influence chart.

2. Construct a spreadsheet model from the influence chart constructed in the previous exercise.

3. Specify the optimization instructions to What's Best! for Hanley. Remember that inventory may not go negative. Include the requirement that the workforce for starting October must be sized to produce 2500 units of regular production.

4. Chris Hanley made several observations in the case about tradeoffs. "So overtime is cheaper than three months in storage, but more expensive than two months in storage." Another observation: "But inventory costs for two months are more expensive than the combination of overtime and inventory costs." Discuss the role of rules such as these in optimization modeling.

5. The workstation cost ($350) received a hasty treatment in the case scenario. The Hanley personnel observed that this cost is "just like the training cost we incur when we gar up with a new employee." Discuss the similarities and the differences between training costs and workstation costs.

6. Reconsider your answer to the previous question if you were dealing with a situation in which demand rises, falls, rises again, and so on. Is the approach recommended by the Hanley personnel appropriate for this different situation? Discuss.

7. Using the assumptions and values stated in the case, find the optimal plan for Hanley.

8. Chris Hanley was unsure about the firing cost, tentatively taken to be $1500 per employee terminated. Using optimization and your spreadsheet model, the production plans that are optimal for a $1000 cost (call this Plan A), a $1500 cost (already done—call this Plan B), and a $2000 cost (call this Plan C). Then find the cost of each of the three plans, A, B, and C, if the cost is actually $1000, $1500, and $2000. Array this information in the table shown below, and discuss its managerial use.

	Plan Used		
	A	B	C
Cost is $1000	_____	_____	_____
Cost is $1500	_____	_____	_____
Cost is $2000	_____	_____	_____

11

Optimization with Integer Variables

The optimization models discussed so far in this text have implicitly assumed that the decision variables (adjustable cells) could have fractional values. In many situations, this assumption isn't particularly important, because it is easy to round the decision variables to obtain a very usable set of integer values. From a managerial perspective, the data in the optimization spreadsheet are seldom of such precision that rounding makes any real difference! But if we are dealing with many decision variables which have small values (say, between 0 and 10) rounding may be difficult, and may lead to results which are not as close as we might like to the optimal integer solution. What's*Best!* provides a way of dealing with these situations. The main What's*Best!* menu has an **Integer** menu choice, which allows the modeler to specify which decision variables must have integer values. The first two menu selections from the **Integer** menu are **Binary** (values of either zero or one) and **General** (nonnegative whole numbers).

On the **Integer** menu, selecting **General** establishes ranges (or blocks) whose names start with WBINT. The optimizer accepts as integer variables all adjustable cells in ranges named WBINT or any other name starting with WBINT. After selecting **Integer**, then **General**, What's*Best!* will suggest the range name, WBINT, for these cells. (If there is more than one range of integer adjustable cells, range names such as WBINT1, WBINT2, WBINT3, . . . may be used to identify general integer adjustable cells.) After accepting the name WBINT or choosing another name such as WBINT1, the cells to be included in the named range are identified by the user in the usual spreadsheet manner. Binary decision variables are placed in ranges whose names begin with WBBIN.

Solving an integer optimization problem uses a procedure called *branch and bound* to search for the best integer solution. This search procedure finds a feasible integer solution, and then tries to improve it. By carefully evaluating the possibility of finding a better solution along a given search branch, it is seldom necessary to search a large portion of the possible integer solutions to the problem. However, these branch and bound searches can be quite time-consuming, particularly when used for a nonlinear optimization, also a time-consuming search. Textbook-size problems seldom require an onerous amount of computer time, but large problems may require hours or days of processing time, even with a fast computer. The message of this paragraph: Be prepared to wait a bit if you choose to invoke the menu option of integer variables!

Tip to Speed Up **What's***Best!* *Computations:* There are some important ways to speed the processing of optimization with integer variables. One of these is by specifying a value of the objective for a known feasible integer solution. If the **Known IP** menu choice is selected from the **Integer** What's*Best!* menu, the search omits all branches that would lead to a solution less attractive than the value of **Known IP**. A **Known IP** value sometimes can be found quickly by rounding the optimal continuous solution. The second way to speed processing is to specify the **Tolerance** the manager is willing to live with. If we specify a tolerance of 5% (0.05), the search process will only look for integer solutions which are 5% better (in terms of the value of the objective cell) than the current best feasible integer solution. The What's*Best!* help facility ([F1] key) and Appendix B explain both of these options in more detail.

From a managerial perspective, there is little else one needs to know about optimization with general integer variables. Solving integer problems is possible, but it often requires too much time. This suggests a need for managerial judgment as to whether the time is worthwhile! From a technical perspective, it may be useful to describe some of the vocabulary of optimization. Here are some key words in the technical vocabulary:

Discrete optimization typically refers to either linear or nonlinear optimization, in which some or all of the decision variables must have integer values.

Integer programming typically refers to linear optimization, in which all of the decision variables must have integer values.

Mixed is an adjective used to describe problems in which some, but not all, of the decision variables must have integer values. The most common usage is for *mixed integer programming* to describe a linear optimization problem with some of the decision variables requiring integer values.

General integer variables are decision variables which are restricted to the whole numbers 0, 1, 2, 3, ...

Binary variables are a special case of integer variables: the value must be either zero or one. Sometimes the term *zero-one* variables is used in

Figure 11.1

Influence Chart for Hiker's Knapsack

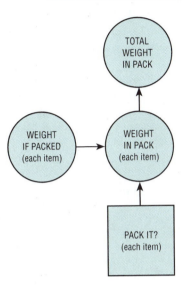

place of *binary variables*. These binary variables are often used much like an on/off switch. Managerial uses of binary variables comprise the remainder of this chapter.

A Knapsack Problem: Do I Pack It?

It is often useful to use optimization for answering "Do I or don't I?" questions. Should I build the plant? Should I purchase a new truck? Should I manufacture this product? Should I operate a second shift? Contrast these questions with most optimization problems, which deal with the question, "How much or how many?" How many decoys should be made? How many units should I ship from Tampa to Atlanta? How much cottage cheese should be used in cheesecake? The key ingredient that allows us to shift from the quantitative variable (how many?) to the choice variable (should I?) is the use of *binary* or *zero-one* variables. Just like a switch, a binary variable has two values or positions: zero for "no" and one for "yes." (Have you looked at the power switch on your computer recently?)

To understand a key building block for utilizing binary variables, consider a hiker deciding which of several items to include in a knapsack. We want to design a spreadsheet that will easily calculate the total weight of the selected items, using a value of zero to indicate an item is not selected, and a value of one to indicate the item is selected. An influence chart showing the situation is shown in Figure 11.1.

We want to know the total weight in the pack; if we know the weight of each item that is in the pack, we can easily find the total. We can find the weight that

----------- **Figure 11.2** -----------

Spreadsheet and Documentation for Hiker's Knapsack Problem

	A	B	C	D	E	F	G
1		Raincoat	Blanket	Lantern	Tent	Stove	Total
2	Pack It?	0	1	1	0	1	
3	Weight if Packed	2	3	1	4	5	
4	Weight in Pack	0	3	1	0	5	9

Pack It?[Raincoat]..Pack It?[Stove] are decision variables, to be adjusted

Weight if Packed[Raincoat]..Weight if Packed[Stove] are data values

Weight in Pack[Raincoat THRU Stove] = Pack It? * Weight if Packed
Weight in Pack[Total] = SUM (Weight in Pack[Raincoat] THRU Weight in Pack[Stove])

each item contributes to the pack by knowing whether it is packed, and its weight. The key steps are:

restricting the variable PACK IT? to values of either zero or one (no or yes), then

multiplying that value of zero or one by each item's WEIGHT IF PACKED.

This gives us the WEIGHT IN PACK for each item. Next:

Add up the individual values of WEIGHT IN PACK to find the TOTAL WEIGHT IN PACK.

This is illustrated in the spreadsheet of Figure 11.2.

It is important to distinguish these two concepts: the *potential* impact of doing it, and the *realized* impact of doing it. The Weight If Packed information is potential; it weighs nothing (in the knapsack) if it isn't packed, but we know its weight if it is packed. The model multiplies the Weight If Packed by Pack It? to set the realized value Weight in Pack to 0 if the item is not packed, and to its weight if it is packed. The link between potential weight and realized weight is the Pack It? variable, which is either zero (no) or one (yes). A simple multiplication performs the logic.

We now have the tools to complete the hiker's optimization problem. The hiker has subjectively determined a value associated with each item. There are knapsack limits of 10 pounds, and 1000 cubic inches. How should the knapsack be packed, so the hiker's value is as large as it can get, without violating either the weight or volume limit? The expanded influence chart is shown in Figure 11.3.

Figure 11.4 shows the data for each item's value and volume in the spreadsheet model and also the documentation. It shows the optimal solution to the hiker's knapsack problem. The optimization instructions are:

Binary Decisions: PACK IT?[*all items*]

Constraints: Volume in Pack[Total] <= Volume in Pack[Up Lim]
Weight in Pack[Total] <= Weight in Pack[Up Lim]

Objective: *Maximize* Value in Pack[Total]

Figure 11.3

Influence Chart for Hiker's Optimization Problem

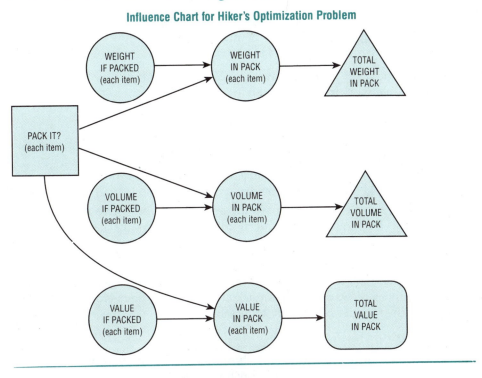

Figure 11.4

Spreadsheet and Documentation for Hiker's Knapsack Problem (Optimized)

	A	B	C	D	E	F	G	H	I
1		Rainct	Blankt	Lantern	Tent	Stove	Total	Cnstrnt	Up Lim
2	Pack It?	1	1	1	0	0			
3	Weight if Packed	2	3	1	4	5			
4	Weight in Pack	2	3	1	0	0	6	<=	10
5	Volume if Packed	105	525	350	775	225			
6	Volume in Pack	105	525	350	0	0	980	<=	1000
7	Value if Packed	6	12	9	14	5			
8	Value in Pack	6	12	9	0	0	27		

Pack It?[Raincoat]..Pack It?[Stove] are decision variables

Weight if Packed[Raincoat]..Weight if Packed[Stove] are data values

Weight in Pack[Raincoat THRU Stove] = Pack It? * Weight if Packed
Weight in Pack[Total] = SUM (Weight in Pack[Raincoat] THRU Weight in Pack[Stove])
Weight in Pack[Up Lim] = 10

Volume if Packed[Raincoat]..Volume if Packed[Stove] are data values

Volume in Pack[Raincoat THRU Stove] = Volume if Packed * Pack It?
Volume in Pack[Total] = SUM (Volume in Pack[Raincoat] THRU Volume in Pack[Stove])
Volume in Pack[Up Lim] = 1000

Value if Packed[Raincoat]..Value if Packed[Stove] are data values

Value in Pack[Raincoat THRU Stove] = Value if Packed * Pack It?
Value in Pack[Total] = SUM (Value in Pack[Raincoat] THRU Value in Pack[Stove])

Extending the Knapsack Problem

There are additional managerial considerations that can be modeled using binary variables. We'll introduce them into the hiker's scenario, and then describe how they can be handled in the spreadsheet model.

Warmth: The hiker believes that warmth is important; it can come from either a blanket or a tent (which provides shelter, and therefore warmth). One or the other must be included, but bringing both would not make sense.

Dry Stuff: Either the tent or the raincoat provides some protection against moisture. At least one item of dry stuff must be packed. It might make sense to bring both of them, because the tent provides protection while stationary, and the raincoat provides protection while hiking.

Lantern & Stove: The lantern uses the stove's fuel supply, so it doesn't make any sense to bring the lantern unless the stove is packed. On the other hand, it is OK to bring the stove without the lantern.

This scenario adds three requirements to the hiker's selection: warmth, dry stuff, and lantern and stove. To assure the hiker will bring either a blanket or a tent, the number of warmth items packed must equal one. From a modeling standpoint, the number of warmth items packed is:

```
Warmth Packed[Total] = Pack It?[Blanket] + Pack It?[Tent]
```

The model we will use will calculate this warmth requirement in a cell called Warmth Packed[Total], which will be constrained to be equal to 1.

To assure that there is some dry stuff, either a raincoat or a tent must be packed. Both may be brought. The number of dry items packed must be at least one. In modeling terms, the number of dry items packed is:

```
Dry Stuff[Total] = Pack It?[Raincoat] + Pack It?[Tent]
```

The model calculates a cell called Dry Stuff Packed[Total], which will be constrained by optimization to be greater than or equal to 1.

The "lantern & stove" requirement requires that you can't bring the lantern without the stove. Another way of saying the same thing is that the number of lanterns must be less than or equal to the number of stoves.

```
Pack it?[Lantern] <= Pack it?[Stove]
```

The model and the added documentation are shown in Figure 11.5, with the optimal solution using these optimization instructions:

Binary Decisions: Pack It?[Raincoat THRU Stove]

Constraints: Weight in Pack[Total] <= Weight in Pack[Up Lim]
                      Volume in Pack[Total] <= Volume in Pack[Up Lim]
                      Warmth Packed[Total] = 1
                      Dry Stuff Packed[Total] >= 1
                      Pack it?[Lantern] <= Pack it?[Stove]

Objective: *Maximize* Value in Pack[Total]

--------------------------------   **Figure 11.5**   --------------------------------

Spreadsheet and Additional Documentation for Hiker's Problem

	A	B	C	D	E	F	G	H	I
		Rainct	Blankt	Lantern	Tent	Stove	Total	Cnstrnt	Up Lim
1									
2	Pack It?	1	1	0	0	1			
3	Weight if Packed	2	3	1	4	5			
4	Weight in Pack	2	3	0	0	5	10	=<=	10
5	Volume if Packed	105	525	350	775	225			
6	Volume in Pack	105	525	0	0	225	855	<=	1000
7	Value if Packed	6	12	9	14	5			
8	Value in Pack	6	12	0	0	5	23		
9									
10	Warmth Packed						1	=	1
11	Dry Stuff Packed						1	=>=	1
12	Lantern & Stove							<=	

```
Warmth Packed[Total] = Pack It?[Blanket] + Pack It?[Tent]
Dry Stuff Packed[Total] = Pack It?[Raincoat] + Pack It?[Tent]
```

The Capital Budgeting Problem

The knapsack problem illustrates the modeling concepts of management's *capital budgeting* problem. Just as the hiker has many things that would be nice to pack, management faces a number of requests for capital funding. Just as the hiker can't fit everything into the knapsack, management can't fit everything into the plan given the resources that are available. The hiker had limitations from weight and volume; management faces limitations from available funds, staffing, buildings, and so on. The hiker had a mutually exclusive required choice between a tent and a raincoat; management has mutually exclusive required choice between competing plant sites. The hiker was required to choose at least one item for rain protection; management may be required to choose at least one building to renovate, but may choose more. The hiker had a contingent item: bringing the lantern was contingent upon bringing the stove. Management may face a decision to build a new warehouse, but the warehouse is contingent upon building a new plant where there will be enough space for the warehouse. For the hiker, the objective was to pack as much value as possible. In a capital budgeting problem, management's objective is to maximize the net present value* of the cash flows (in and out) from each project.

Location Problems: Where to Put Recycling Centers

The city of Placid Platz is developing plans for recycling centers at several locations throughout the city. The city's engineering staff has determined that are nine feasible locations, where the city has enough land and there won't be

----

*The present value of cash flows is also called the *discounted* cash flow. As discussed thoroughly in the finance literature, the operation called *discounting* adjusts future cash flows to reflect the preference of funds received now over funds received later.

Figure 11.6

Cost and Service Information for Recycling Centers in Placid Platz

Potential Location	Cost ($000)	Neighborhoods Served
A	6	1, 7, 8
B	15	2, 3, 9
C	11	3, 5, 6, 9, 10
D	14	1, 4, 7
E	9	3, 5, 6, 9
F	5	5, 7, 8, 10
G	8	1, 7, 8
H	13	2, 3, 9
I	17	5, 6, 9, 10

---

adverse reaction from the NIMBY* syndrome. Each of the proposed locations is evaluated on the basis of cost. The service of a proposed set of locations is evaluated by determining whether every neighborhood is within twelve minutes of a recycling center. If every neighborhood is within twelve minutes of a center, the service of the proposed set of locations is acceptable. There are ten neighborhoods in Placid Platz. Cost information for each location, and a table showing the neighborhoods each location can serve within twelve minutes, are shown in Figure 11.6.

The use of binary variables in this application is similar to the knapsack and capital budgeting problems. Each of the proposed locations will have a Build It? variable, with a value of one or zero indicating whether or not a center is built at a location. The new concept in this model is the potential service to each neighborhood provided by each location. This is represented as a matrix of zeros and ones, with one indicating a location provides service to a neighborhood. Using the information provided in Figure 11.6, the column for LocA shows service to neighborhoods 1, 7, and 8. This matrix of potential service is shown in the first part of the spreadsheet, Figure 11.7. It is a worthwhile exercise to verify the consistency between this potential service matrix and the third column of Figure 11.6.

The next section of the spreadsheet is the "Build it?" row showing values of zero for locations not selected, and values of one for locations that are selected. This row, multiplied in turn by each of the rows in the potential service matrix, shows what service is provided to each neighborhood. Logically, this means that:

> Actual service is provided to a neighborhood by a location if two conditions are met: the neighborhood is potentially served by the location, and a center is built at the location.

---

*The NIMBY syndrome is well-known in planning governmental facilities. Everyone wants them, but "Not In My Back Yard." A LULU (Locally Undesirable Land Use) may be OK but NIMBY. Sometimes planners invoke the principle of BANANA (Build Absolutely Nothing Anywhere Near Anything). In terms of optimization, these concepts may cause the set of feasible solutions to be null.

─── **Figure 11.7** ───

Spreadsheet for Placid Platz Recycling Centers

	A	B	C	D	E	F	G	H	I	J	K	L	M
1		LocA	LocB	LocC	LocD	LodE	LocF	LocG	LocH	LocI	Tot	Cnst	Lim
2	Pot'l Svc Nbh 1	1	0	0	1	0	0	1	0	0			
3	Pot'l Svc Nbh 2	0	1	0	0	0	0	0	1	0			
4	Pot'l Svc Nbh 3	0	1	1	0	1	0	0	1	0			
5	Pot'l Svc Nbh 4	0	0	0	1	0	0	0	0	0			
6	Pot'l Svc Nbh 5	0	0	1	0	1	1	0	0	1			
7	Pot'l Svc Nbh 6	0	0	1	0	1	0	0	0	1			
8	Pot'l Svc Nbh 7	1	0	0	1	0	1	1	0	0			
9	Pot'l Svc Nbh 8	1	0	0	0	0	1	1	0	0			
10	Pot'l Svc Nbh 9	0	1	1	0	1	0	0	1	1			
11	Pot'l Svc Nbh 10	0	0	1	0	0	1	0	0	1			
12													
13	Build it?	1	1	1	0	0	0	1	0	0			
14													
15	Actual Svc Nbh 1	1	0	0	0	0	0	1	0	0	2	>=	1
16	Actual Svc Nbh 2	0	1	0	0	0	0	0	0	0	1	=>=	1
17	Actual Svc Nbh 3	0	1	1	0	0	0	0	0	0	2	>	1
18	Actual Svc Nbh 4	0	0	0	0	0	0	0	0	0	0	Not >=	1
19	Actual Svc Nbh 5	0	0	1	0	0	0	0	0	0	1	=>=	1
20	Actual Svc Nbh 6	0	0	1	0	0	0	0	0	0	1	=>=	1
21	Actual Svc Nbh 7	1	0	0	0	0	0	1	0	0	2	>=	1
22	Actual Svc Nbh 8	1	0	0	0	0	0	1	0	0	2	>=	1
23	Actual Svc Nbh 9	0	1	1	0	0	0	0	0	0	2	>=	1
24	Actual Svc Nbh 10	0	0	1	0	0	0	0	0	0	1	=>=	1
25													
26	Cost if Built	6	15	11	14	9	5	8	13	17			
27	Incurred Cost	6	15	11	0	0	0	8	0	0	40		

This logic is implemented in the section showing the actual service to neighborhoods (Actual Svc Nbh). From a modeling standpoint, this logic is carried out by multiplying the values in the potential service row by the values in the Build it? row. Only if both values are 1 in a column will there be a value of 1 indicating service is provided to a neighborhood by a location. The final column shows the total number of number of locations which actually provide service to a neighborhood. If this total for all locations is at least one, the design requirements are met.

The final section of the spreadsheet shows cost computations, using logic similar to the value computations for the hiker's knapsack problem. The documentation for the logic of the model is shown in Figure 11.8.

The spreadsheet values for Build It? shown in Figure 11.7 are arbitrary. Note that neighborhood 4 has no service from the proposed (arbitrary) solution. The instructions for optimization are:

Binary Decisions: Build it?[LocA THRU LocI]

Constraints: Actual Svc Nbh 1[Total] >= 1

  . . . and so on for all neighborhoods 2..10

Objective: Minimize Incurred Cost[Total]

Figure 11.8

Documentation for Logic in Placid Platz Spreadsheet

```
Actual Svc Nbh 1[LocA THRU LocI] = Pot'l Svc Nbh 1 * Build it?
Actual Svc Nbh 1[Total] = SUM (Actual Svc Nbh 1[LocA] THRU Actual Svc Nbh 1[LocI])

Actual Svc Nbh 2[LocA THRU LocI] = Pot'l Svc Nbh 2 * Build it?
Actual Svc Nbh 2[Total] = SUM (Actual Svc Nbh 2[LocA] THRU Actual Svc Nbh 2[LocI])
```

. . . and so on for neighborhoods 3 through 10.

```
Incurred Cost[LocA THRU LocI] = Cost if Built * Build it?
Incurred Cost[Total] = SUM (Incurred Cost[LocA] THRU Incurred Cost[LocI])
```

The optimal solution is to build recycling centers at locations D, E, F, and H; the cost of this configuration is $41,000.

The Fixed Charge Problem: Using Binary Variables

The "Fixed Charge" problem arises whenever there is a fixed cost associated with "getting started" on an activity; this cost is avoided if the activity is not undertaken. We use the scenario of Chris's Printing Business (from Chapter 6) to illustrate the fixed charge. For convenience, the scenario is repeated here.

> Chris Hadley, a recent graduate of a leading business school, has developed several new paper products that are sold to souvenir stores throughout tourist areas. Each item requires cutting, printing, and folding on specialized equipment. Chris arranged with a large printing company to rent time during slack periods; unfortunately, there was not enough time available to meet all of the anticipated demand in Chris's plans. For the four items in the product line, Chris believed that there would be no difficulty in selling quantities within production capabilities at these prices:

> | | |
> |---|---|
> | Product A: | $5 |
> | Product B: | $7 |
> | Product C: | $3.25 |
> | Product D: | $3 |

Manufacturing each of the products required all three operations: cutting, printing, and folding. The printing company equipment had these operating rates, shown in units per hour for each product in each piece of equipment:

	Cutting	*Printing*	*Folding*
Product A	1000	4000	500
Product B	2000	1000	350
Product C	4000	1000	750
Product D	3000	3000	600

The agreement with the printer required Chris to pay for time used, and also set limits on the number of hours available:

Cutting	$100 per hour	12 hours available
Printing	$200 per hour	20 hours available
Folding	$300 per hour	30 hours available

The raw materials for each product are $0.30 per unit, for any of the four products.

To illustrate a fixed charge, we will make some modifications in the scenario. The original scenario contained the requirement that in order to present a balanced product line, it was necessary to make at least a thousand units of each of the four products. We replace that requirement with the following information:

Chris was not certain whether it made sense to try to make all of the products. There were costs incurred for setting up to make a product. For example, getting the plates to the printing press and installing them required some time. There are also machine adjustments to be made for cutting and folding, to assure they are performed correctly for each product. The cost to set up varied considerably with each product. For the four products, these set up costs are (in order) $2000, $5000, $500, and $200. These set up costs are incurred only if a particular product is produced. Furthermore, there are upper limits on the quantity of each product. These limits are 20,000 units for Products A, B, and D; 10,000 units for Product C.

The fixed charge is incurred if any of a product is made, but is not incurred if the product is not produced. We need to introduce these new rows into the spreadsheet:

Set up?: A binary decision variable for each product. If optimization adjusts this variable to 0, the product is not produced. If it is adjusted to a value of 1, the fixed charge is incurred so the product can be produced.

Potential Capacity: The upper limit on Units Made for each product, if the set up cost is incurred. These values are shown in the spreadsheet. In many problems, there is no direct limit; other resource limitations effectively place an upper bound on each activity. When there is no upper limit, the modeler simply inserts a number that is large enough not to interfere, such as 9999999.

Operating Capacity: The actual upper limit on a product. It is computed by multiplying the value of Set up? by the value of Potential Capacity. If Set up? has a value of 0, the Operating Capacity will have a value of 0. If the set up has been performed, operating capacity will be equal to potential capacity.

Cost to Set up: This is the value that must be subtracted from profit if any of a product is made.

Figure 11.9

Influence Chart for Fixed Charges

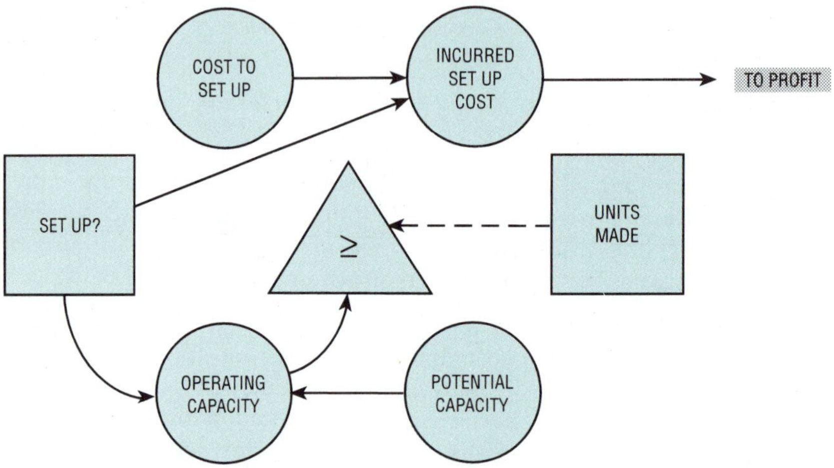

Incurred Set up Cost: This is computed by multiplying the value of Set up? by the value of Cost to Set up. If the set up is not performed, the value is 0. If the set up is performed, this value is equal to the cost to set up.

All of these variables are shown in the influence chart, Figure 11.9. The influence chart indicates that the INCURRED SET UP COST is to be linked to the PROFIT in the main part of the spreadsheet.

Figure 11.10 shows a complete spreadsheet model, with the fixed charge included. Values of the decision variables are arbitrary; they will be adjusted during optimization, according to the optimization instructions we are developing. The documentation for the model is shown in Figure 11.11. The first row of the fixed charge section is the Set up? row. The arbitrary values in the spreadsheet show all products are to be set up, except Prod C. There is a set up cost incurred for products A, B, and D; none is incurred for C. For each product, the Incurred Set up Cost is Set up? multiplied by Cost to Set up. Product D is interesting: the set up cost is incurred, and shows up in Profit as a loss of $200, even though no product is made. Economics and optimization concepts will assure that the optimized solution does not let this happen! For product A, the revenue is $5000, and Manufacturing Cost is $1050. Without the set up, the profit would be $3950. However, the profit shown in the model is $1950, reflecting the incurred set up cost of $2000.

Optimizing Chris's Spreadsheet with Fixed Charges

We have introduced a fixed charge for each product. The optimization instructions for the complete spreadsheet are listed here.

Figure 11.10

Spreadsheet Model Showing Fixed Charges

	A	B	C	D	E	F	G	H
1	Chris Hadley's Printing Business							
2								
3		Prod A	Prod B	Prod C	Prod D	Total	Cnstrnt	Limit
4	Units Made	1000	2000	3000	0			
5								
6	Selling Price	5	7	3.25	3			
7	Revenue	5000	14000	9750	0			
8								
9	Units Cut per Hr	1000	2000	4000	3000			
10	Cutting Hours	1	1	0.75	0	2.75	<=	12
11	Cutting Cost per Hr	100						
12	Cutting Cost	100	100	75	0			
13								
14	Units Printed per Hr	4000	1000	1000	3000			
15	Printing Hours	0.25	2	3	0	5.25	<=	20
16	Printing Cost per Hr	200						
17	Printing Cost	50	400	600	0			
18								
19	Units Folded per Hr	500	350	750	600			
20	Folding Hours	2	5.7142	4	0	11.714	<=	30
21	folding Cost per Hr	300						
22	Folding Cost	600	1714.2	1200	0			
23								
24	Unit Material Cost	0.3	0.3	0.3	0.3			
25	Material Cost	300	600	900	0			
26								
27	Manufacturing Cost	1050	2814.2	2775	0			
28								
29	Profit	1950	6185.7	6975	-200	14910.		
30								
31								
32	Set up?	1	1	0	1			
33	Potential Capacity	20000	20000	10000	20000			
34	Operating Capacity	20000	20000	0	20000			
35	Constraint	>=	>=	Not >=	>=			
36								
37	Cost to Set up	2000	5000	500	200			
38	Incurred Set up Cost	2000	5000	0	200			

Decisions (continuous):	Units Made [*all products*]
Decisions (binary):	Set up? [*all products*]
Constraints:	Operating Capacity[Prod A] >= Units Made[Prod A]
	Operating Capacity[Prod B] >= Units Made[Prod B]
	Operating Capacity[Prod C] >= Units Made[Prod C]
	Operating Capacity[Prod D] >= Units Made[Prod D]
	Cutting Hours[Total] <= Cutting Hours[Limit]
	Printing Hours[Total] <= Printing Hours[Limit]
	Folding Hours[Total] <= Folding Hours[Limit]
Objective:	*Maximize* Profit[Total]

Figure 11.11

Documentation for Chris Hadley with Fixed Charge

```
Units Made [Prod A THRU Prod D] are decision variables

Selling Price[Prod A]..Selling Price[Prod D] are data values
Revenue[Prod A THRU Prod D] = Units Made * Selling Price

Units Cut per Hr[Prod A THRU Prod D] are data values

Cutting Hours[Prod A THRU Prod D] = Units Made / Units Cut per Hr
Cutting Hours[Total] = SUM (Cutting Hours[Prod A] THRU Cutting Hours[Prod D])
Cutting Hours[Limit] = 12

Cutting Cost per Hr[Prod A] = 100
        Note:  Cutting Cost per Hr is constant for all products.  To simplify changes in the model,
               all columns refer to the data value for Product A.

Cutting Cost[Prod A THRU Prod D] = Cutting Hours * Cutting Cost per Hr[Prod A]

Units Printed per Hr[Prod A THRU Prod D.] are data values

Printing Hours[Prod A THRU Prod D] = Units Made / Units Printed per Hr
Printing Hours[Total] = SUM (Printing Hours[Prod A] THRU Printing Hours[Prod D])
Printing Hours[Limit] = 20

Printing Cost per Hr[Prod A] = 200
        Note:  Printing Cost per Hr is constant for all products.  To simplify changes in the model
               all columns refer to the data value for Product A.

Printing Cost[Prod A THRU Prod D] = Printing Hours * Printing Cost per Hr[Prod A]

Units Folded per Hr[Prod A THRU Prod D] are data values

Folding Hours[Prod A THRU Prod D] = Units Made / Units Folded per Hr
Folding Hours[Total] = SUM (Folding Hours[Prod A] THRU Folding Hours[Prod D])
Folding Hours[Limit] = 30

Folding Cost per Hr[Prod A] = 300
        Note:  Folding Cost per Hr is constant for all products.  To simplify changes in the model,
               all columns refer to the data value for Product A.

Folding Cost[Prod A THRU Prod D] = Folding Hours * Folding Cost per Hr[Prod A]

Unit Material Cost[Prod A THRU Prod D] are data values

Material Cost[Prod A THRU Prod D] = Units Made * Unit Material Cost

Manufacturing Cost[Prod A THRU Prod D] = Cutting Cost + Printing Cost + Folding Cost + Material Cos

Profit[Prod A THRU Prod D] = Revenue - Manufacturing Cost - Incurred Set up Cost
Profit[Total] = SUM (Profit[Prod A] THRU Profit[Prod D])

Set up?[Prod A THRU Prod D] are binary decision variables

Potential Capacity[Prod A THRU Prod D] are data values

Operating Capacity[Prod A THRU Prod D] = Set up? * Potential Capacity

Cost to Set up[Prod A THRU Prod D] are data values

Incurred Set up Cost[Prod A THRU Prod D] = Set up? * Cost to Set up
```

The reader is invited to construct the model and verify the optimal profit of $54,530.

Exercises

1. Using the knapsack problem shown in Figure 11.5, find the optimal solution. Then solve the problem again, with the weight limit at 8 pounds and the volume limit at 800 cubic inches.

2. Continuing with the knapsack problem in Figure 11.5 (with the original limits), an additional item has been suggested: waterproof thermal underwear. This item is both dry and warm. It has a weight of 2 pounds and a volume of 200 cubic inches. The value of thermal underwear is 11. Should it be packed?

3. The investment committee of a corporation is deciding projects to fund for the next year. Many departments have submitted proposals, which have passed some screening tests. All of the remaining projects (shown below) are attractive; the net present value and the investment capital required are shown in the following table:

Project	Capital Required	Net Present Value
1	$733,000	$883,000
2	464,000	558,000
3	588,000	704,000
4	235,000	281,000
5	614,000	719,000
6	946,000	1,231,000
7	615,000	699,000

Find the set of projects that maximizes the net present value of the selected projects, but does not require more than $2,500,000 of capital investment.

4. Continuing with the information from Exercise 3, we add these requirements:

   Exactly two projects must be selected from projects 1, 2, and 3.

   No more than two projects may be selected from projects 4, 5, 6, and 7.

   Project 4 is contingent upon project 3. If project 3 is not selected, project 4 cannot be selected.

Find the set of projects which maximizes the net present value of the selected projects, but does not require more than $2,500,000 of capital investment, and meets all of the requirements listed above.

5. Continuing with the information from Exercise 4, we add concerns about the second year cash requirements for each project. In the second year some projects require cash, while others generate cash. To the data and requirements of Exercises 3 and 4, and add the requirement that the projects selected cannot require more second-year cash than they generate, in the aggregate. The second year cash information is shown in this table:

Project	Second Year Cash Required	Second Year Cash Generated
1	39,000	0
2	52,000	0
3	0	35,000
4	57,000	0
5	0	27,000
6	0	38,000
7	0	10,000

Find the optimal set of projects.

6. This exercise builds on the Sunsoak Products case at the end of Chapter 1. In addition to the data and requirements presented in Chapter 1, we add this information:

   There is a fixed charge each day of $100 for setting up to make Screen, $1000 for Block, and $10,000 for Soak. This charge is avoided if a product is not made that day.

   Find the optimal production plan for tomorrow.

7. This exercise builds on the Citrimagination cheesecake problem, discussed in length in Chapter 6 and shown in the spreadsheet model in Figure 6.4. After some internal discussion, the standard cake cost of $1.5036 seemed too high. Management wanted to investigate trade-offs between cost and perceived consumer quality. Initially, rather strict nutritional requirements had been set: not too many calories, sufficient protein, not too much fat, and not too many carbohydrates. What would happen if they met only three out of these four nutritional requirements? Could a cheaper cake be made? What would its cost be?

   Hint: A binary decision variable can be used as a "switch" to turn off any one of the nutritional limits, by adding or subtracting a "big number" to the limit. But only one of the four can be turned off. There can be four binary variables, one for each nutritional requirement. Then a big number (such as 10,000), multiplied by this binary switch variable, is added to each of the "less than" limiting values, or subtracted from the "greater than" limiting value. Construct a model using this approach, and verify that a cake costing $1.091 can be produced meeting three of the four nutritional requirements.

8. Verify that the optimal location of recycling centers for Placid Platz (shown in Figure 11.7) results in a cost of $41,000.

9. Verify that the optimal solution for Chris Hadley with set-up costs, Figure 11.10, is $54,530.

CASE STUDY:
Long Plains Fire Services*

The City of Long Plains, Kansas, has a population of about 108,000 people, according to the 1990 census. Like many cities in the great plains, city services had not been modernized for some years. A shortage of tax revenues made it difficult for the city management to satisfy all of the demands for services.

A recent residential fire had focused attention on the fire services of Long Plains. A particularly tragic fire occurred when major road repairs had blocked a key thoroughfare; the situation was made more difficult by a voice that was

---

*This case is adapted from Donald R. Plane and Thomas E. Hendrick, "Mathematical Programming and the Location of Fire Companies for the Denver Fire Department," *Operations Research*, July–August, 1977.

Exhibit 11.1

Location of Fire Stations and Regional Demand Points—Long Plains, Kansas

*Fire Station Locations:

	Station 1	Station 2	Station 3	Station 4	Station 5	Station 6
X:	1	1.5	2.4	3.7	4.2	2.5
Y:	2	4.4	4.5	1.5	3.9	2.6

Regional Demand Point Locations:

	X	Y			X	Y
RDP 1	0.7	3.6		RDP 10	4.3	3.3
RDP 2	4	5		RDP 11	3.8	0.5
RDP 3	2.2	4.7		RDP 12	2.6	0.4
RDP 4	1.4	1.8		RDP 13	4.4	2.2
RDP 5	3.2	3.5		RDP 14	1.1	0.8
RDP 6	4.6	1		RDP 15	4.5	1.8
RDP 7	0.3	1.4		RDP 16	1.2	2.1
RDP 8	4.1	4.8		RDP 17	4.6	1.1
RDP 9	4.5	4.2				

Note: The City of Long Plains is square, five miles on each side. The point at the southwest corner of the city is the reference point for the fire station locations and the regional demand point locations. The X distance is the distance in miles between the western city boundary and the station; the Y distance is the distance in miles between the southern city boundary and the station.

---

particularly difficult to hear on the 911 line. Both of these factors, plus a rainy night, caused delays in fire equipment reaching the scene of the fire. The tragic death of four small children focused much attention on the fire department.

The Long Plains Fire Chief, Myrle Relisch, was a veteran of three decades of fire services. He had risen through the ranks of fire fighting, and knew the strengths and weaknesses of the Long Plains fire department. Ample water supply and an excellent road network were some of the favorable aspects of the department. Unlike cities in some parts of the country, Long Plains streets were typically North-South or East-West in orientation; there were no major lakes or industrial complexes to disrupt the regular grid of streets throughout the city.

A major difficulty in Long Plains was the lack of sufficient fire stations. There were currently six stations in the city; these provide the "supply" of fire services for Long Plains. Although there is potential demand for fire protection at any point in the city, the fire department had identified seventeen "regional demand points" throughout the city. If adequate fire protection is provided at each of these demand points, Chief Relisch believed that protection would be adequate throughout the city. The locations of the fire stations and the seventeen regional demand points are shown in Exhibit 11.1, along with a discussion of the way Long Plains coded locations.

--- **Exhibit 11.2** ---

Listing of Response Time Experiment

Sample Information: Response Time Experiment

Key:	Run Number	The serial number of the timed emergency response
	Station Number	The number of the station housing the vehicle
	Add-X	The distance of the address from the Western boundary
	Add-Y	The distance of the address from the Southern boundary
	Minutes	The time of the response in minutes

Run Number	Station Number	Add-X	Add-Y	Minutes	Run Number	Station Number	Add-X	Add-Y	Minutes
1	2	1.2	3.8	3.4	16	4	4.1	0.1	4.9
2	1	1.3	4.3	8.2	17	1	0.1	1.6	5.3
3	4	2.6	2.3	4.6	18	1	4	1.5	11.1
4	5	3.8	1.8	7.8	19	6	2.9	3.9	4.9
5	4	4	0.8	3.4	20	1	1.5	4.9	11.7
6	6	1.2	3.1	5.9	21	1	1.8	3.8	8.2
7	3	1.5	2.6	9.2	22	4	1.9	1.1	7.9
8	3	4	4.2	5.9	23	4	4.9	3	8.3
9	6	1.7	4.1	7.8	24	4	4.8	0.2	7.2
10	1	1.6	1.1	4.4	25	3	4	4.7	4.7
11	2	0.2	4.2	4.5	26	1	1.1	0.6	4.6
12	2	0.3	4	5.5	27	4	3.9	0.3	4.7
13	1	0.8	2.3	1.7	28	4	4.4	0.9	4.7
14	5	4.9	1.8	8.9	29	3	4.4	3.6	8.3
15	3	0.4	4.4	6.8	30	2	2.4	2.2	9.3

A recent study of response times to fires had been conducted in Long Plains. This information is shown in Exhibit 11.2. The locations of the address for which the responses were timed is shown using the same codes.

There is only one universally accepted standard for measuring the adequacy of fire department response times: quicker is better. Chief Relisch had included this comment in a memo written to the city manager explaining the standards of the Long Plains fire department:

> On the average, a fire vehicle should be able to get to any location in the city within a *maximum* time of five minutes. I believe that a full analysis of our performance will show that we are achieving that response time.

The city manager, Chris Charlesides, was not certain just how much fire protection Long Plains should try to provide. If more stations were added, what benefits would accrue? Where should they be located? Charlesides asked Chief Relisch to provide potential locations, if fire stations were to be added to the system. The chief provided these locations, using the codes of Exhibit 11.1 for locating the stations:

	Sta 7	Sta 8	Sta 9
X:	3.2	2.1	0.9
Y:	4.1	0.9	3.2

Before approving the chief's recommendation to build these three new stations, Charlesides wanted to learn more about the benefits (reduced response time) that would arise from building these stations. There are substantial economic costs associated with building new stations (capital outlay in excess of $500,000; annual operating costs in excess of $400,000). Furthermore, there are political costs of opening new stations (*Who wants the noise?*) and political costs of closing existing stations (*Don't close my fire station!*); on the whole, people are much more vocal about closing a station than about opening a new one.

Over the years, there has been some debate about an appropriate measure for fire protection. Although response time is almost always considered in measuring fire protection, it may be used in different ways. If the average response time is used, some parts of the city may have very poor response, while others may have excellent service. An alternative is to look at the maximum time to get to any Regional Demand Point from the nearest station. For a first cut at the analysis, Charlesides decided to evaluate a proposed change in fire stations by looking at the maximum time between any RDP and its closest station.

Discussion Questions

1. How far would a fire truck travel from a station with coordinates (1.5, 4.4) to a fire at location (3.5, 1.2)? How can you generalize the computation of the distance from a fire station to a fire?

   Hint: Assume vehicles always travel in a North-South or East-West direction, and there are no angled streets. Then the @ABS function can be used to determine the travel in the East-West (X) direction, and also in the North-South (Y) direction. Adding these two components will give the total distance traveled.

2. If you know the distance that a fire truck travels, how can you predict the time required to travel that distance? Develop a method to predict the time required for any distance that a fire truck might travel.

   Hint: The linear regression capability of the spreadsheet can be used to obtain this equation to predict time, knowing distance:

   TIME (MINUTES) $= 0.165 + 3.080 \times$ DISTANCE (MILES)

3. Which Regional Demand Points does Station 1 cover within 5 minutes? Which Regional Demand Points are not covered by any existing station within five minutes?

4. What is the minimum number of stations that can cover all Regional Demand Points within five minutes? Within six minutes? Within seven minutes? Within four minutes?

5. Develop information for Chris Charlesides to use in contemplating the tradeoffs between city budget expenditures and fire protection.

12

Inventory Analysis: An Example of Nonlinear Optimization

Many scenarios have a nonlinear relationship between the decision variables and the objective variable, or between the decision variables and any constraint. Although this change from linear to nonlinear may seem unimportant from a managerial standpoint, it makes a big difference to the solvers used in optimization. Large linear problems can be solved easily, with a great deal of mathematical precision, because linear optimizers follow a rigid set of steps that is guaranteed to reach an optimal solution. Nonlinear optimizers use a search procedure, taking many small steps. Many steps are required; there is no guarantee that an optimal solution will be reached. The starting point for the values of the decision variables is very important, because the solver searches with the initial spreadsheet decision values as the starting point for the search. Different starting points may cause different stopping points. These stopping points may be managerially similar (35.5 compared to 35.6) or drastically different (when there are several local optima, reached from different starting points).

Another important difference is that linear problems must have constraints, but nonlinear problems may not require constraints. Consider two different decisions faced in agriculture: the number of acres to plant, and the amount of fertilizer to use on a given field. There may be linearity between the number of acres and the profit, if the profit per acre remains constant over some relevant range of values for the number of acres. If there is no constraint (land available, water available, equipment available, planting time available, and so on), the linear optimization would conclude that an infinite number of acres should be planted, yielding an infinite profit. We know this doesn't make sense; linear optimization requires constraints! But if we have a model to use optimization to adjust the amount of fertilizer to use on a given field, we would expect the model to indicate that some fertilizer increases yield, but after a point (burn out?) more fertilizer decreases yield. So even without an explicit constraint, the nonlinear model would recommend a finite amount of fertilizer. Nonlinear models do not necessarily require constraints, although constraints are common in nonlinear optimization.

Inventory Management: An Example of Nonlinear Optimization

Inventories are present in almost any business. Many aspects of nonlinear optimization are illustrated by a study of inventory management. If inventory levels are very high, maintaining these inventories is expensive, but there may be benefits from obtaining larger lot sizes from suppliers. If inventory levels are low, the cost associated with keeping inventory on hand is small, but orders are placed frequently to replenish items "which are always running out of stock."

In this text we'll discuss only a small part of the very broad area of inventory management. We'll be addressing two questions for an end-product inventory item we purchase from another organization:

> How many should we order? (in this chapter), and
>
> When should be place an order? (in Chapter 15)

The methods in this text apply to inventory items whose pattern of demand is not controlled by the organization that manages the inventory. These methods might be used by a retailer, who carries inventory to sell to customers. The retailer does not control when a customer comes to the store to buy something. On the other hand, the methods here aren't appropriate for a manufacturer of household appliances who wants to develop an inventory policy for switches used in assembling washing machines, refrigerators, dryers, and dishwashers. The manufacturer controls the demand for switches by establishing a production schedule. Neither are these methods appropriate when one is asking the question "What should I make with the idle production facilities?" It is important not to let an inventory model drive production plans, because the production costs are not included in the inventory model.

The approach of this chapter is to present the scenario of Specialty Products Incorporated to bring out many of the conflicting forces at work in answering the question, "How many should I order?" The problem facing Specialty Products is addressed in familiar fashion: Build an influence chart, then a model that describes the outcome for a particular value for the decision variable(s). Then we apply optimization to find the "best" values to use.

Specialty Products Incorporated

Specialty Products Incorporated is a small industrial supplier with a contract to supply shower enclosures for a large student apartment complex that is under construction. These shower enclosures are relatively bulky; they are delivered from the factory in corrugated cardboard protective coverings, with some wood supports and steel banding so the units can be handled without excessive flexing.

Stev Oberlin, the owner of Specialty Products, was quite pleased to land the contract. The terms of the contract state that Specialty Products will provide about five enclosures each week for the job in nearby Bithlo. The contractor will pick up the enclosures as they are needed; this is convenient for Stev, because the only truck Specialty owns is a truck large enough to hold about eighty enclosures at one time. Stev could use this truck to deliver the enclosures to the job site three miles from Stev's office, but the contractor pickup made this unnecessary. In any event, the operating cost of $0.50 a mile for the truck would have been trivial, since the job site was only three miles away.

Specialty Products had already arranged to purchase the enclosures for $130 each, with the manufacturer loading the enclosures on Specialty's truck at the Atlanta factory. Since Stev's contract with the builder specified a price of $180 for each enclosure, Stev was looking forward to a weekly profit of $250 for very little effort. Stev's main concern was the cost of getting the enclosures from Atlanta to Bithlo, a distance of 400 miles. With a truck capacity of eighty enclosures, Stev figured a delivery cost of $5 per enclosure, which was acceptable. Stev made the trip to Atlanta for the first batch of eighty enclosures, and realized that other time commitments meant it would be necessary to hire a driver for subsequent trips, at a cost of about $250 for the trip.

But Stev uncovered the major problem in the analysis upon arrival at the office in Bithlo with eighty enclosures, and no place to put them. Although rainy weather would not hurt the enclosures themselves, it would damage the packaging, making the enclosures more vulnerable to damage. The eighty enclosures would need to be protected for up to sixteen weeks; Stev obviously couldn't keep the shower enclosures in the office, which was already as overextended as a professor's desk! A nearby self-serve garage-style warehouse provided an answer. Although there were various garage sizes available, they all seemed to work out to about $1.50 per enclosure per week. Stev rented enough garages to store the enclosures until they were to be delivered. Stev believed that the warehouse company provided fire and theft insurance as a part of the rental fee. Theft was not a major concern, anyway, because unoccupied shower enclosures are generally not considered to be attractive to those who might do evil. Unloading the enclosures costs $2 each, using casual labor which was usually available and sometimes reliable.

Specialty Products had a line of credit with a local bank. As a relatively new business, Specialty had to pay 1.2% per month for the funds used to purchase the enclosures.* The builder paid by check upon delivery, which allowed Stev to repay the bank on a weekly basis.

---

*For simplicity, the model that follows neglects the compounding of this monthly rate into an annual rate; we assume the annual rate is twelve times the monthly rate.

Discussion: Specialty Products Incorporated

In what way could Stev use a spreadsheet model to support the decision at hand? That question can hardly be answered without determining the decision variables. Although it might be tempting to suggest that the question Stev is answering is whether too much interest is being paid, that is more a symptom of a possibly bad decision rather than the decision itself. The underlying decision facing Stev is the number of enclosures that should be brought back on each trip to Atlanta. Even though the truck holds eighty enclosures, it may not be wise to bring back a whole truckload at one time.

What is the basis for determining whether some other number of enclosures is better than eighty? It would be myopic to look only at interest costs in determining how many to order at one time; one could make interest costs practically zero by going to Atlanta every week. Unfortunately, that would make delivery costs quite high. Stev's current decision (set the order quantity at eighty) is at the other extreme, with delivery costs as low as possible, which causes high interest and storage costs.

One of the factors that Stev contemplated during the analysis was the level of inventory to use in estimating the storage costs and interest costs. Right after a truck load had arrived from Atlanta, storage and interest costs were incurred on the quantity of enclosures in that truckload. But just before a truck arrived, Stev planned to have only a small garage warehouse (instead of several larger ones), so the rate of incurring storage and interest costs is about zero just before an order arrives. With relatively uniform withdrawal of enclosures from inventory, it was reasonable for Stev to decide to base the calculations of storage and interest charges on the average inventory level, which would be the average of the highest and lowest inventory level. The highest inventory level Stev planned was the order quantity; the lowest level Stev planned was zero. Hence, these costs are based on half of the order quantity, the average of the high and the low.

In terms of the components of an optimization problem, the objective is to make the yearly cost as small as possible. The decision to be made is the order quantity, which has an upper limit of eighty. Although there may be other constraints, none seems to be explicitly stated in the scenario. For example, there may be an upper limit on the line of credit available to Specialty Products. These unstated constraints tend to "come out of the woodwork" when a solution is presented which violates an unspecified constraint; management then becomes very explicit in stating why "that won't work" so the analyst can return to the worksheet and develop solutions that don't interfere with reality.

Figure 12.1 shows an influence chart for Specialty Products. The spreadsheet model constructed from the chart is shown in Figure 12.2. The verbal documentation for the model is shown in Figure 12.3. The numerical solution to the model uses Stev's first decision to get a full truck on each trip to Atlanta.

Figure 12.3 indicates that the annual costs of purchasing, shipping, storing, and unloading the shower enclosures, plus the cost of interest to buy the enclosures, is $40,301 when a full truckload is brought back from Atlanta on each trip.

Figure 12.1

Influence Chart for Specialty Products

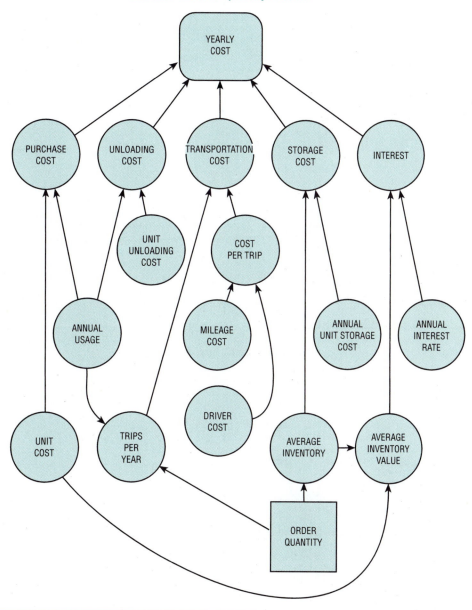

Formal optimization can be used to see if this can be improved. The characteristics of the optimization problem are:

Decision: Order Quantity (*technically, with an upper limit of 80*)

Objective: *Minimize* Yearly Cost

Figure 12.2

Spreadsheet Model for Specialty Products

	A	B
1	Specialty Products Incorporated	
2		
3	Yearly Cost	$40,301
4		
5	Purchase Cost	$33,800
6	Annual Usage	260
7	Unit Cost	$130
8	Transportation Cost	$2,113
9	Trips Per Year	3.25
10	Order Quantity	80
11	Cost per Trip	$650
12	Mileage Cost	$400
13	Driver Cost	$250
14	Storage Cost	$3,120
15	Average Inventor	40
16	Annual Unit Storage Cost	$78
17	Unloading Cost	$520
18	Unit Unloading Cost	$2.00
19	Interest	$749
20	Annual Interest Rate	14.40%
21	Average Inventory Value	$5,200

Figure 12.3

Documentation of Specialty Products

```
Yearly Cost = Purchase Cost + Transportation Cost + Storage Cost + Unloading Cost + Interest
Purchase Cost = Annual Usage * Unit Cost
Annual Usage = 5 * 52
Unit Cost = 130
Transportation Cost = Trips Per Year * Cost per Trip
Trips Per Year = Annual Usage / Order Quantity
Order Quantity = 80
Cost per Trip = Mileage Cost + Driver Cost
Mileage Cost = 0.5 * 400 * 2
Driver Cost = 250
Storage Cost = Average Inventory * Annual Unit Storage Cost
Average Inventory = Order Quantity / 2
Annual Unit Storage Cost = 1.5 * 52
Unloading Cost = Unit Unloading Cost * Annual Usage
Unit Unloading Cost = 2
Interest = Annual Interest Rate * Average Inventory Value
Annual Interest Rate = 0.012 * 12
Average Inventory Value = Average Inventory * Unit Cost
```

Optimization Tip: Occasionally, a nonlinear problem will have unusual behavior when unusual starting conditions are used. For example, if the initial spreadsheet value of the order quantity is 0, the value of the objective cannot be determined because a division by zero is taking place in the spreadsheet computations. This may cause problems for the optimizer! This reinforces the suggestion that nonlinear optimization start with "good" values of the decision variables, not merely convenient values. (In linear optimization, convenient values are fine, because the mathematical procedures are fast and effective.)

This formal optimization analysis shows that reducing the order quantity from 80 to about 60 reduces the annual costs to about $40,038, a saving of about $263. Stev's decision could be improved from the original full truckload, but the savings are relatively small in this situation.

In addition to the monetary factors considered in the model, other factors should be considered before a firm decision is reached. After all, models are used to support decisions, not to make them. These other factors include consideration of the advantages of larger inventory (ability to respond to surges in demand, if that is a factor), the advantages of smaller inventory (change in customer needs has less impact on a smaller inventory), the advantages and disadvantages of larger or smaller bank debt (bigger borrowers may be better bank customers; use of a line of credit means that those dollars can't be used for other needs), the managerial effort needed to arrange for more frequent deliveries, and so on.

Economic Order Quantity

Economic Order Quantity is included in many parts of the management literature. A formula to be used to determine the quantity of an item to be ordered at one time is often included in the literature of managerial accounting, production management, management science, financial management, managerial economics, marketing management, and perhaps a few more places. The ideas behind the simplest economic order quantity are these:

> The annual demand for an inventory item is known, and demand occurs at a constant rate throughout the year. We know the elapsed time between placing an order with the supplier, and the receipt of that order. Inventory is to be managed so that the entire replenishment order arrives from the supplier just as the last of the inventory is purchased by a customer. Every time we place a replenishment order, we incur a cost that we call the "cost of ordering." The cost of carrying inventory is based on the average level of inventory, which is half the order quantity; the annual cost of carrying one unit is called the "cost of holding." How many units should be ordered each time an order is placed?

Using the modeling approach, this classic problem can be addressed with an influence chart and a model. The modeler wants to calculate the total annual cost, which is the sum of the annual ordering cost and the annual carrying cost, as shown at the top of the influence chart in Figure 12.4. The lower portion of the influence chart shows the factors involved in calculating other cost elements.

To build a spreadsheet model to reflect this logic, we need to assume values for the three data elements shown in the influence chart. The three circles with

Figure 12.4

Influence Chart for Economic Order Quantity

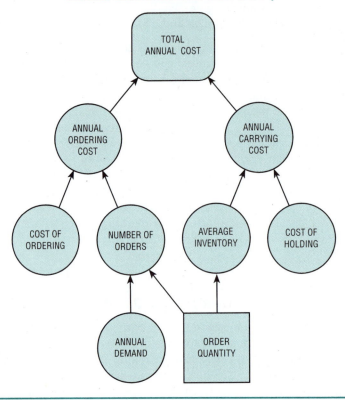

no arrows leading into them are the required data; the square, which has no arrows leading into it, is the decision variable. We use these data values:

ANNUAL DEMAND	10,000 units per year
COST OF ORDERING	$500 per order
COST OF HOLDING	$4 per unit per year

Arbitrarily, we construct the model with an order quantity of 1000. A few specifics about relationships in the model may be helpful. The number of orders placed is calculated by dividing 10,000 (the annual demand) by 1000 (the quantity ordered at one time). If the inventory is managed so that the last one goes out the door when the replenishment order arrives, the inventory goes to zero, then immediately jumps up to 1000 (the order quantity). Then it gradually and uniformly drops to zero again. Dropping from 1000 to 0 yields an average inventory of 500, which is half the order quantity. With these values, the model and its documentation are shown in Figure 12.5.

This model is ready for optimization with these instructions:

Decision:	Order Quantity
Objective:	*Minimize* Total Annual Cost

--- **Figure 12.5** ---

EOQ Model and Documentation

	A	B
1	Total Annual Cost	7000
2		
3	Annual Ordering Cost	5000
4	Annual Carrying Cost	2000
5		
6	Number of Orders	10
7	Order Quantity	1000
8	Average Inventory	500
9		
10	Annual Demand	10000
11	Cost of Ordering	500
12	Cost of Holding	4

```
Total Annual Cost = Annual Ordering Cost + Annual Carrying Cost
Annual Ordering Cost = Number of Orders * Cost of Ordering
Annual Carrying Cost = Average Inventory * Cost of Holding
Number of Orders = Annual Demand / Order Quantity
Order Quantity = 1000
Average Inventory = Order Quantity / 2
Annual Demand = 10000
Cost of Ordering = 500
Cost of Holding = 4
```

There are no constraints. Optimization yields an order quantity of 1581 units, or thereabouts, as the optimal or economic order quantity. With nonlinear optimization, the optimizer may identify decision values close to 1581 units as optimal, because of the nature of the search process. It makes no managerial difference in Total Annual Cost whether an order quantity of 1571, 1581, or 1591 units is used.

This economic order quantity is typically optimized by direct methods, using the differential calculus. The results of the calculus-based optimization are widely known as the EOQ or Economic Order Quantity, which occurs when

```
Order Quantity = @SQRT(2 * Annual Demand * Cost of Ordering / Cost of Holding)
```

Mathematics Tip: Those who are familiar with the calculus recognize the process: The derivative of Total Annual Cost, with respect to Order Quantity, is set to zero. The solution of the equation yields a relative minimum.

It is useful to view a graph showing Total Annual Cost, and its components Annual Ordering Cost and Annual Carrying Cost, plotted against various values for Order Quantity. From this graph (Figure 12.6) we see that there is a nonlinear relationship between Total Annual Cost and Order Quantity; this agrees with the diagnosis provided by What's*Best!*.

Analytical Tip: A characteristic of this optimization process is that the Annual Carrying Cost is equal to the Annual Ordering Cost at the optimal value of Order Quantity. On the graph, the two curves cross at the point which is the minimum value for Total Annual Cost. Although this is always true

─────────────────── **Figure 12.6** ───────────────────

Cost Elements for EOQ Model

EOQ Model: Total Annual Cost and Other Cost Elements

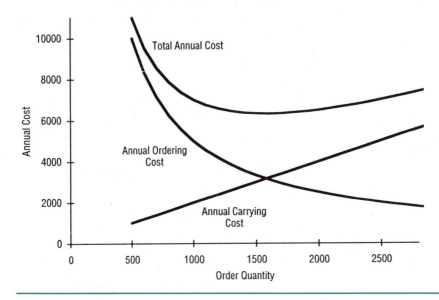

for models structured exactly like this one, it is a result that is not necessarily true for other optimization problems. This coincidence sometimes causes poor analysts to believe that balancing opposing costs by setting them equal to each other is the same thing as minimizing their total. Don't be misled by the marvelous intrigue of "balancing opposing costs"!

Economic Order Quantity for Specialty Products Corporation

Although we have used the optimization software to determine the optimal value of Order Quantity for Specialty Products, we could have come to the same results by finding these values for Specialty Products:

Annual Demand: 5 per week, for 52 weeks, for annual demand of 260 units.

Cost of Ordering: $250 for the driver, plus 400 miles each way or 800 miles round trip at $0.50 per mile, for a total of $250 + $400 or $650 per order.

Cost of Holding: Monthly interest is 1.2 percent of $130, $1.56 per month, or $18.72 per year. In addition, storage costs $1.50 per week, $78 annually, for a total of $96.72 to carry one unit in inventory for one year.

From these data values, we could calculate

EOQ = @SQRT(2 * 260 * 650 / 97.92) = 59, or about 60 units.

A Comparison: Modeling and Formulas

The results of "applying the formula" are the same as those we reached from modeling and optimization. If one is working on problems like this frequently, it obviously is simpler to know where to find the formula, and plug in the numbers. But its proper use requires a thorough understanding of the assumptions that were made in the EOQ formula. We make these observations:

> The scenario never used the term "Cost of Ordering" in describing Specialty Product's situation. For Specialty, the cost of ordering is really broken into two components, the cost of the driver and the mileage cost. But since these are costs that are incurred once for each order, they constitute the cost of ordering without using those words.

> The scenario never used the term "Cost of Holding" for Specialty. It shows up in the description as interest costs and storage costs. But since these are costs which apply to one unit held in inventory for one year, they constitute the cost of holding without using those words.

> The scenario painstakingly includes other numbers, which aren't used in the EOQ formula: a selling price of $180, a purported $250 weekly profit, and the unloading cost of $2 per enclosure. Is the user who "plugs numbers into formulas" going to be tempted to use these numbers, even though they are irrelevant?

Each of the points above can easily be handled by an analyst who understands the assumptions of the EOQ formula; any of them may lead to incorrect use of the EOQ formula by the "plug and chug" user. On the other hand, the modeling approach requires the modeler to understand the situation as it stands by itself, not as it stands in relation to a formula. It is not necessary to determine if the formula is appropriate, because modeling and optimization are general techniques, and generally applicable.

The modeling approach to Specialty's problem has a further striking advantage: What happens when something changes? To illustrate:

> The warehouse owner mentioned that the warehouse was about full now (contrary to its position a few months ago), so it would be necessary to enter into a year-long lease for storage space, in order to guarantee its availability. This changes the cost of storage from $1.50 per week per enclosure to $0.90 per week per enclosure, but it also means that the current practice of releasing space as soon as it is vacant may eventually result in space being unavailable.

If we assume that Stev is unwilling to consider a policy that may result in enclosures which have no place to be stored, enough garage space must be rented or leased on an annual basis. In terms of Specialty's influence chart (Figure 12.1) this is reflected by changing the chart so that STORAGE COST is influenced by ANNUAL UNIT STORAGE COST, and by ORDER QUANTITY (in place of AVERAGE INVENTORY). In the model, the value 1.5 is changed to 0.90 to reflect the new unit storage cost. Applying optimization gives the new value of the order quantity.

───────────────────── **Figure 12.7** ─────────────────────

Spreadsheet Model for an Inventory System with Six Items

	A	B	C	D	E	F	G	H
1				Inventory Item				
2		1	2	3	4	5	6	Total
3	Cost of Ordering	$400	$700	$100	$50	$400	$250	
4	Cost of Holding	$35	$10	$25	$20	$200	$50	
5	Annual Demand	5000	10000	30000	4000	5000	7000	
6	Classic "EOQ"	338	1183	490	141	141	265	
7	Unit Cost	500	250	800	3000	250	800	
8	Volume (Cubic Feet)	12	25	40	30	20	10	
9								
10	Total Annual Cost	$11,832	$11,832	$12,247	$2,828	$28,284	$13,229	$80,253
11								
12	Annual Ordering Cost	$5,917	$5,917	$6,122	$1,418	$14,184	$6,604	$40,163
13	Annual Carrying Cost	$5,915	$5,915	$6,125	$1,410	$14,100	$6,625	$40,090
14								
15	Number of Orders	14.8	8.5	61.2	28.4	35.5	26.4	
16	Order Quantity	338	1183	490	141	141	265	
17	Average Inventory	169	592	245	71	71	133	
18								
19	Avg Investment	$84,500	$147,875	$196,000	$211,500	$17,625	$106,000	$763,500
20	Avg Investment (1-3)							$428,375
21	Avg Investment (4-6)							$335,125
22	Average Cubic Feet	2,028	14,788	9,800	2,115	1,410	1,325	31,466
23								
24	Constraints Section							
25				Actual	Constr	Limit		
26	Avg Investment, All Items			$763,500	Not <=	400,000		
27	Avg Investment, 1 THRU 3			$428,375	Not <=	250,000		
28	Avg Investment, 4 THRU 6			$335,125	Not <=	250,000		
29	Avg Cubic Feet, All Items			31465.5	Not <=	28000		

An analyst who relies on formulas rather than modeling will have no easy way to handle this simple change, because textbook EOQ models are seldom developed for situations just like this. By focusing on the modeling process, the analyst develops skills that are useful in a wide variety of situations.

An Inventory System with Multiple Items

Nonlinear spreadsheet optimization allows the manager to address a wide variety of inventory management problems for a product line. As an illustration of this concept, we expand on the classic Economic Order Quantity. For an inventory system of six items, we use the classic assumptions of lump-sum receipt, known replenishment lead time, known and constant demand rate, and known cost of ordering and cost of holding, based on average inventory. There are additional considerations:

Investment in inventory is being scrutinized; the average dollar value of inventory may not exceed $400,000.

—————————————————— **Figure 12.8** ——————————————————

Documentation for Six-Item Inventory Model (Formulas Only)

```
Classic "EOQ"[1 THRU 6] = SQRT (2 * Annual Demand * Cost of Ordering / Cost of Holding)

Total Annual Cost[1 THRU 6] = Annual Ordering Cost + Annual Carrying Cost
Total Annual Cost[Total] = SUM (Total Annual Cost[1] THRU Total Annual Cost[6])

Annual Ordering Cost[1 THRU 6] = Number of Orders * Cost of Ordering
Annual Ordering Cost[Total] = SUM (Annual Ordering Cost[1] THRU Annual Ordering Cost[6])

Annual Carrying Cost[1 THRU 6] = Average Inventory * Cost of Holding
Annual Carrying Cost[Total] = SUM (Annual Carrying Cost[1] THRU Annual Carrying Cost[6])

Number of Orders[1 THRU 6] = Annual Demand / Order Quantity

Order Quantity[1 THRU 6] = 338, 1183, 490, 141, 141, 265

Average Inventory[1 THRU 6] = Order Quantity / 2

Avg Investment[1 THRU 6] = Order Quantity * Unit Cost / 2
Avg Investment[Total] = SUM (Avg Investment[1] THRU Avg Investment[6])

Avg Investment (1–3)[Total] = SUM (Avg Investment[1] THRU Avg Investment[3])

Avg Investment (4–6)[Total] = SUM (Avg Investment[4] THRU Avg Investment[6])

Average Cubic Feet[1 THRU 6] = (Order Quantity / 2) * Volume (Cubic Feet)
Average Cubic Feet[Total] = SUM (Average Cubic Feet[1] THRU Average Cubic Feet[6])
```

The inventory items are divided into two classes. Items 1, 2, and 3 are consumer items; items 4, 5, and 6 are sold to businesses. To diversify the inventory risk, neither category can have an average inventory value in excess of $250,000.

Warehouse space is limited. No more than 35,000 cubic feet of warehouse space will be available for these items. Managerially, the company has decided that the average inventory volume cannot exceed 80% of the 35,000 cubic feet warehouse capacity, or 28,000 cubic feet, to allow for fluctuations around the average volume.

The characteristics of the six inventory items are shown in cells A2..G8 of the spreadsheet model of Figure 12.7. Other information, which we'll be discussing shortly, is also presented in Figure 12.7.

Individually, each of these items meets the assumptions of the EOQ formula, before we consider the constraints placed on the system. The EOQ for each item is calculated in row 6 of the spreadsheet (Figure 12.7), using the information in rows 3, 4, and 5: Cost of Ordering, Cost of Holding, and Annual Demand. The spreadsheet also shows the aggregate impact on inventory investment and warehouse space, using the classic EOQ values as ordering quantities. The documentation of the model is shown in Figure 12.8.

What's **Best!** *Tip:* The values of Order Quantity, in row 16 of Figure 12.7, are keyed as constants; the constant values are determined from the calculated values in row 6. Adjustable (decision) cells must be constants, which requires entering the values in row 16 from the keyboard (or, for experienced spreadsheet users, with the 1-2-3 /**Range Value** command, or with the Quattro Pro command /**Edit Value**, followed by again specifying the adjustable cells).

In Figure 12.7 and the documentation in Figure 12.8 there are two rows in the spreadsheet that refer to order quantity: in the top section, the Classic "EOQ" is calculated using the familiar square root formula,

Classic "EOQ"[1 THRU 6] = SQRT (2 * Annual Demand * Cost of Ordering / Cost of Holding

By calculating the EOQ in the model and using it as the order quantity, we can determine whether the constraints are going to affect management's actions. In the lower section of the model, the order quantity is entered from the keyboard with the Classic "EOQ" values:

Order Quantity[1 THRU 6] = 338, 1183, 490, 141, 141, 265

When we use optimization, the Order Quantity row will contain the decision variables. We start out with the Order Quantity equal to the Classic "EOQ" to determine if we really need to use optimization. We compare the constraints described earlier with the reality of Figure 12.7, using the EOQ values:

Inventory investment limit:	$400,000
Inventory investment using EOQ values:	$763,500
Inventory investment limit, items 1–3:	$250,000
Inventory investment using EOQ values:	$428,375
Inventory investment limit, items 4–6:	$250,000
Inventory investment using EOQ values:	$335,125
Cubic feet limit:	28,000
Cubic feet used:	31,466

Optimizing the Multi-Item Inventory System

The model of Figure 12.7 is ready for optimization, with these instructions:

Decisions:	Order Quantity[1 THRU 6]
Constraints:	Avg Investment[Total] <= 400000
	Avg Investment (1–3)[Total] <= 250000
	Avg Investment (4–6)[Total] <= 250000
	Average Cubic Feet[Total] <= 28000
Objective:	*Minimize* Total Annual Cost[Total]

It is left as an exercise to demonstrate that the lowest feasible value of Total Annual Cost[Total] is $88,780.

What's **Best!** *Tip:* The computer processing time required for this nonlinear optimization may be longer than you expect, based on experience with linear models and with nonlinear models with only one or two variables. That is characteristic of nonlinear optimization. You may also encounter unusual behavior if you permit the optimizer to encounter unusual situations! Remember to start the search process with reasonable values for the decision variable, and limit the decision variables to reasonable values.

The role of the Classic "EOQ" calculated by the model is important. The nonlinear optimizer is a search process; searches may be quicker and more effective if they start at an intelligent starting point. The Classic "EOQ" value for each item serves as the intelligent starting point. There is no unique intelligent starting point; in this application, there is nothing particularly important about starting with precisely the value of the Classic "EOQ" calculated in the spreadsheet. This set of starting values is nothing more than one of many places the nonlinear optimizer search process can intelligently begin its work. The optimizer adjusts the values in the row labeled Order Quantity, which influences all of the constraints and the objective. The values in the row Classic "EOQ" are unchanged by optimization.

Managerial Information from Nonlinear Optimization

The manager of this multi-item inventory system is able to obtain the "optimal" order quantities for each of the items, considering all of the constraints. That is, of course, useful information in itself. But optimization can also be used to explore alternatives, and to help management know which constraints may be worth attacking.

One managerial issue is the difference between Total Annual Cost before optimization (based on EOQs and no constraints) and Total Annual Cost after optimization (which includes the cost of meeting the restrictions). Is the change in Total Annual Cost, from $80,253 (cell H10, Figure 12.7, before optimization) to $88,780 (optimal value) enough to make management reconsider whether the restrictions on inventory investment and warehouse space should be reconsidered?

The marginal values provided by the dual variables in What's Best! are useful to help determine which constraints to attack. The marginal value for the constraint on Avg Investment[Total] is about seven cents; this means that changing the limit on inventory by $1.00 reduces annual costs by about seven cents. This value already includes the carrying cost, valued at the appropriate holding cost for each item in the inventory. On the other hand, loosening the requirement for diversification in inventory (no more than $250,000 average investment for products 1–3 collectively) reduces total annual costs by only about four tenths of a cent per dollar change. Hence, it may be better to attack the total inventory limitation rather than the diversification requirement.

Quantity Discounts and Nonlinear Optimization

A common decision in inventory management is whether to buy enough to take advantage of a quantity discount. One aspect of quantity discounts is illustrated

─────────────── **Figure 12.9** ───────────────

Influence Chart for Economic Order Quantity with Price Breaks

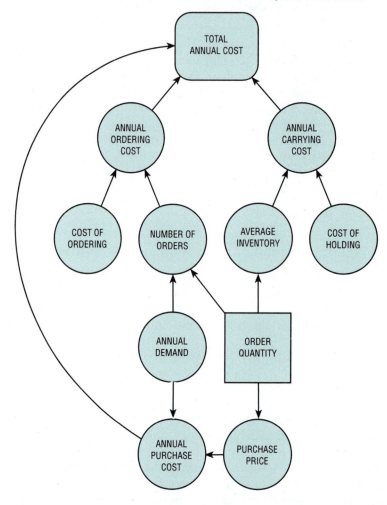

in this extension of the EOQ model presented in Figure 12.5. We use the information from the scenario for Figure 12.5:

Annual Demand	10,000 units per year
Cost of Ordering	$500 per order
Cost of Holding	$4 per unit per year

along with this price break schedule, which shows the smallest quantity eligible for each price. For example, a quantity of 200 receives the base price of $20.00. A quantity of 500 is just large enough to receive the first price break, $19.94. If the order quantity is, say, 2800, each unit would cost $19.90.

―――――――――――――――――― **Figure 12.10** ――――――――――――――――――

EOQ Spreadsheet Model with Price Breaks

	A	B	C
1	Total Annual Cost	206400	+B3+B4+B5
2			
3	Annual Ordering Cost	5000	+B7*B13
4	Annual Carrying Cost	2000	+B9*B14
5	Annual Purchase Cost	199400	+B12*B10
6			
7	Number of Orders	10	+B12/B8
8	Order Quantity	1000	Arbitrary Value
9	Average Inventory	500	+B8/2
10	Purchase Price	19.94	(see documentation)
11			
12	Annual Demand	10000	Data
13	Cost of Ordering	500	Data
14	Cost of Holding	4	Data
15			
16	Smallest Quantity to Obtain This Price		
17		Quantity	Price
18	Base	0	20
19	Break 1	500	19.94
20	Break 2	1200	19.92
21	Break 3	2500	19.9
22	Break 4	3000	19.88

	Quantity	*Price*
Base	0	20
Break 1	500	19.94
Break 2	1200	19.92
Break 3	2500	19.90
Break 4	3000	19.88

The last time we visited this scenario, we minimized the TOTAL ANNUAL COST, which was the sum of ANNUAL ORDERING COST and ANNUAL CARRYING COST, which were then the only costs that were affected by the decision variable, the order quantity. With the price schedule, we see that purchase cost also varies with the decision variable, so it cannot be ignored. We need to add to the influence chart the PURCHASE PRICE (influenced by the ORDER QUANTITY) and the ANNUAL PURCHASE COST (influenced by the PURCHASE PRICE, and having an influence on TOTAL ANNUAL COST). This is shown in Figure 12.9.

The spreadsheet model to implement these changes is shown in Figure 12.10. The new model requires these new definitions, in addition to the documentation in Figure 12.5:

Total Annual Cost = Annual Ordering Cost + Annual Carrying Cost + Annual Purchase Cost

Annual Purchase Cost = Annual Demand * Purchase Price

Purchase Price is determined with this long @IF function:

@IF(B8<B19,C18,@IF(B8<B20,C19,@IF(B8<B21,C20,@IF(B8<B22,C21,C22))))

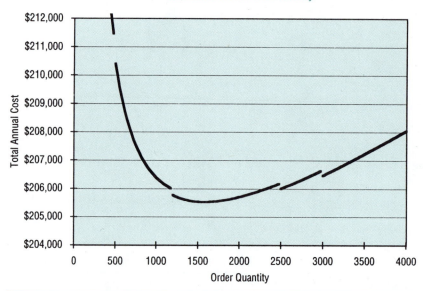

Figure 12.11

EOQ Model with Price Breaks

Inventory Model with Price Breaks
Total Annual Cost vs. Order Quantity

From a logical point of view, the model is ready for optimization. But recall the discussion in Chapter 10: This optimization problem involves a nonsmooth relationship between the decision variable (Order Quantity) and the objective (Total Annual Cost). To see the nature of this relationship, Figure 12.11 shows Total Annual Cost vs. Order Quantity; there are obvious gaps in the relationship. The reader is encouraged to apply the optimizer, using various starting points, and observe whether the same "solution" is obtained in each situation. Unfortunately, one cannot generalize from this experience!

Tip for Advanced Spreadsheet Users: One can use the **Data Table** (**Tool What-if** in Quattro Pro) capability of a spreadsheet to overcome some of the difficulties of optimization with nonsmooth nonlinearities. By establishing a spreadsheet column of order quantity values ranging from (say) 300 to 4000, construct a one-way data table showing values of cell B1, Total Annual Cost. In the data table command, identify cell B8 as the input cell. This produces the information graphed in Figure 12.11. One then scans the column showing the Total Annual Cost for various values of Order Quantity until the lowest cost is found. The use of the @MIN function also makes it easy to verify whether a particular value is really the lowest value in the column. This scheme works well for optimization with only one decision variable. A two-way data table works well for optimization with two decision variables; beyond that, this approach requires multiple data tables, which becomes cumbersome at best.

Exercises

1. An inventory item meets all of the assumptions for the classic EOQ model described in the chapter. Annual demand is 100,000 units; the cost of placing an order is $200; the cost of holding one unit for one year is 20% of the purchase price of $3.20. Find the Economic Order Quantity first using modeling and optimization, and then using the EOQ formula.

2. Three inventory items have these characteristics:

	Item 1	Item 2	Item 3
Cost of Ordering	$400	$700	$100
Cost of Holding	$45	$15	$20
Annual Demand	5000	10,000	30,000

   a. Find the Classic "EOQ" for each item.

   b. Recommend a policy if a total of no more than fifty orders can be placed in a year.

3. Verify that the lowest value of Total Annual Cost for Specialty Products (Figure 12.2) is $40,038. At what order quantity does this occur? Use optimization.

4. Verify that the multi-item inventory scenario modeled in Figure 12.7 has a lowest feasible value of Total Annual Cost[Total] of $88,780.

5. The text discusses this change in Specialty Products original scenario:

   The warehouse owner mentioned that the warehouse was about full now (contrary to its position a few months ago), so it would be necessary to enter into a year-long lease for storage space, in order to guarantee its availability. This changes the cost of storage from $1.50 per week per enclosure to $0.90 per week per enclosure, but it also means that the current practice of releasing space as soon as it is vacant may eventually result in space being unavailable. We assume that Stev is unwilling to consider a policy that may result in enclosures having no place to be stored, enough garage space must be rented or leased on an annual basis. In terms of Specialty's influence chart (Figure 12.1) this is reflected by changing the chart so that STORAGE COST is influenced by ANNUAL UNIT STORAGE COST, and by ORDER QUANTITY (in place of AVERAGE INVENTORY).

   Incorporate this change in the model, apply optimization, and recommend an order quantity.

6. Rangely Lakes* (Chapter 1) has still one more modification. The price of hangings is no longer fixed at $15. For every 10 hangings sold, the price must be reduced 2 cents to clear the market. Thus, if 100 hangings are sold, the price charged would be $14.80 ($15 less a two-cent reduction for 10 batches of 10). If 1000 hangings are to be sold, each of them would fetch a price of $13.00 ($15 less 100

---

*This problem has no direct relation to inventory models; it is included here because the optimization is nonlinear.

two-cent reductions). These reductions occur continuously, not in two-cent increments.) Before this modification, the optimal profit was $10,632.

a. What is the optimal profit with this new scenario? Modify the appropriate influence charts and models, and apply optimization to obtain the new optimum. Describe your results to J. L. Duckworth.

b. For those with a mathematical bent, develop an equation showing profit as a function of quantity for Decoys. Using this result, explain why an optimization problem of this form is called a *quadratic programming* problem.

c. Again for those with a mathematical bent and an understanding of microeconomic demand curves, straighten out the befuddled analyst who made this statement:

> This must be a linear programming problem! I constructed the demand curve for each product, and definitely find a straight line for the relationship between price and quantity. Someone is confused when they call this quadratic instead of linear.

Modeling Case: Economic Production Quantity

A situation commonly treated in the management science literature is a variation of the Economic Order Quantity. The assumptions are similar to the classic EOQ model, except lump-sum receipt is replaced by a flow of units arriving over a finite period of time. The complete set of assumptions is:

> The annual demand for an item in inventory is known, and occurs at a constant rate throughout the year. We know the time between placing an order with the supplier, and the receipt of that order. *When we start to receive the order, it arrives at a steady rate, or a constant number of units per day, until the entire order quantity has been received.* Inventory is to be managed so that a replenishment order begins to arrive from the supplier just as the last of the inventory is purchased by a customer. Every time we place a replenishment order, we incur a cost, which we call the *cost of ordering*. The cost of carrying inventory is based on the average level of inventory. *Average inventory is half the maximum inventory level, which occurs when the last unit in the order arrives into the inventory.* The annual cost of carrying one unit is called the *cost of holding*. How many units should be ordered each time an order is placed?

To see how this differs from the classic EOQ scenario, we introduce the same numbers of the example shown in Figure 12.5: 10,000 units per year, $500 per order cost of ordering, and $4 per unit per year cost of holding. We assume that there are 250 business days in a year; this means that demand is 40 units (10000/250) each business day. The shipment arrives in daily manufacturing batches of 100 units per day. This means that an order of 1000 units will arrive over a ten-day period; the maximum inventory level will be reached at the end of that ten-day

---------- **Exhibit 12.1** ----------

Time Path of Inventory Level—Lump Sum Receipts

Inventory Level vs. Time
Lump-Sum Receipt of Entire Shipment

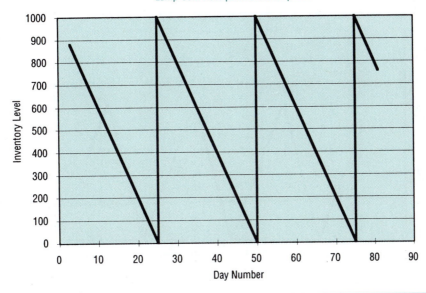

period. This maximum level will not be the order quantity, but the order quantity reduced by the demand during the ten days shipments have been occurring. During that period, demand will be 400 units, so the maximum inventory level will be 600 units.

It is worthwhile to visualize the difference between inventory levels with the classic EOQ and this situation. The graphs in Exhibits 12.1 and 12.2 show the time path of inventory levels over several order cycles:

a. Modify the influence chart of Figure 12.4 to include these new conditions. You may want to use these new variables:

PRODUCTION RATE (*data*)

DAYS OF SHIPMENT, *influenced by* PRODUCTION RATE *and* ORDER QUANTITY

DEMAND DURING SHIPMENT, *influenced by* DAYS OF SHIPMENT *and* DAILY DEMAND

DAILY DEMAND, *influenced by* DAYS PER YEAR *and* ANNUAL DEMAND

DAYS PER YEAR (*data*)

MAXIMUM INVENTORY, *influenced by* ORDER QUANTITY *and* DEMAND DURING SHIPMENT

With these new variables, AVERAGE INVENTORY is influenced by MAXIMUM INVENTORY, rather than by ORDER QUANTITY.

Exhibit 12.2

Time Path of Inventory Level—Daily Receipts

Inventory Level vs. Time
Receipt of 100 Units per Day

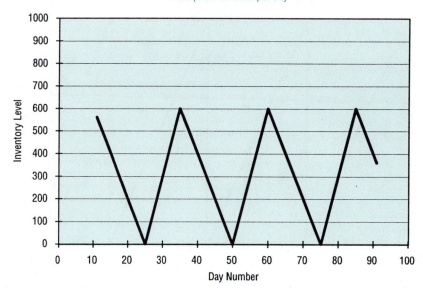

---

b. Incorporate these relationships into the spreadsheet model, Figure 12.5, using a production rate of 100 per day, and 250 days per year.

c. Using optimization, find the optimal order quantity.

d. Now include into this model the price breaks, introduced in Figure 12.10. Find the optimal order quantity using a graph similar to Figure 12.11. This question requires the use of the spreadsheet **Data Table** (or **Tools What-if**) command to generate the information for the graph.

CASE STUDY:
Golden Ear Audio Distributor (A)

G. E. Audo, manager of Golden Ear Audio Distributors, spent about an hour talking about managing the inventory of the Model 3581-X speaker.

How many Model 3581-X speakers should Golden Ear order at one time? These speakers are our premier product, and we want to do things just right. We've been carrying them for about a year now, and they do good business for us. The 3581-X speaker costs $400 each. We expect to sell 5000 speakers during the year, for an annual purchase cost of two million dollars. With this much money on the line, we insist on testing each speaker before we deliver it to our customers, who are high-end audio retailers. We like to order the speakers from the manufacturer in small batches, to keep our inventory investment as low as we can. But when we do that, it seems we are always in a state of turmoil. Although it doesn't take much time to process the paperwork for an order, speakers in this price range require individual testing when they arrive. We know that testing a speaker takes thirty minutes of technician time, which we cost out at $28 per hour. We also know that we're going to spend just as much time testing speakers if we order them in small lots or in large lots. But the kicker is that we need to set up the test facility for these speakers for each order as it arrives. This takes us several hours, with both technicians and helpers. All together, this costs us about $350. By the time we add in the cost of paperwork to process the orders, we come to an estimated $400 cost incurred for each order we place.

There are other costs as well: We're always amazed when we find out how much it costs us to keep inventory. The obvious part is the bank's interest cost: that's about 1.5% a month, which is $6 per month or $72 per year. We're committed to our warehouse space, and space is not currently a problem, so we don't need to consider the warehouse cost as a part of holding inventory. Obsolescence is another big problem. In this business, you never know how long a product will stay in favor. While there are sudden changes in some components, others are more gradual. For example, LP turntables are virtually dead now, and high-end tape players aren't doing too well either. But CD players are hot! Although this change started some years ago, it wasn't until the late 1980s that it was clear that we needed to keep our inventory levels quite low for turntables. Speakers, on the other hand, have been more stable. Current ideas such as the sub-woofer with extensive crossover networks are making inroads right now, but they aren't radical enough to cause a major restructuring (I think). Over the past three years, we've experienced losses due to obsolete speakers that have averaged an annual 4% of our average speaker inventory. We're content to apply that factor to the 3581-X. Since we built our new warehouse, we've been able to control shrinkage (theft) so well that we can ignore this factor.

An analyst looked at the assumptions of an EOQ approach, and the actual situation for Golden Ear Audio Distributions. This analysis is shown as Exhibit 12.3.

From the comparison of the assumptions and the case scenario, it appears that the EOQ formula can be used.

1. Construct an influence chart and model for Golden Ear. Use optimization to recommend an order quantity.

2. Use the EOQ formula shown in the text to recommend an order quantity for Golden Ear.

3. G. E. Audo looked at the results of the analyses performed in the previous two questions and exclaimed:

> "We'll be setting up our test facility so often that the cost of $350 for a test setup is outrageous! That cost is based on relearning the procedures each time; if you do it a couple of times a month you'll get better at it. While I haven't researched this, I think it would cost about $350 to set

─────────────────── **Exhibit 12.3** ───────────────────

Golden Ear Audio Distributors (A)

This analysis investigates whether the classic EOQ model fits Golden Ear's situation for the 3581-X speakers. Each assumption of the EOQ model is compared to the situation faced by Golden ear.

Assumption	*Golden Ear's Situation*
The annual demand for an item in inventory is known, and occurs at a constant rate throughout the year.	From the case, Golden Ear appears willing to plan based on an annual demand of 5000 speakers. No information is provided about whether it occurs at a constant rate. While it might be possible to make assumptions about factors such as seasonality) based on information about retail sales of other items, or upon intuition) we *assume* that demand occurs at a constant rate during the year. There is no real basis for this assumption other than simplicity.
We know the time between placing an order on the supplier and the receipt of that order. Inventory is to be managed so that a replenishment order arrives from the supplier just as the last of the inventory is purchased by a customer.	No information is given in the case about this aspect of managing the inventory. We are not focusing on inventory that is carried to allow for uncertainties (which will be discussed in Chapter 14). Again for simplicity and lack of information, we *assume* that we are able to manage the inventory so that a replenishment order is timed to arrive just as we are running out.
Every time we place a replenishment order, we incur a cost which we call the *cost of ordering*.	This point was addressed in the case. Golden Ear is willing to make plans based on a cost of $400 for placing an order (and performing all the other tasks that arise because an order is placed).
The cost of carrying inventory is based on the average level of inventory; the annual cost of carrying one unit is called the *cost of holding*.	Holding costs were addressed in the case. The holding costs that vary with inventory level are interest ($72 per year) and obsolescence (4% of $400, or $16 per year).

up for test if we order only once a year; twice a year, cost guess is $345; three times, $340; four times, $335. In general, I'd be willing to guess that the expression for unit setup cost for testing is about $355 less $5 for each setup we do in a year. However, I don't think this cost will ever get below $150, regardless of the number of setups we do in a year."

Alter your recommendation for order quantity with this new information.

───

CASE STUDY:

Golden Ear Audio Distributors (B)

After performing the careful analysis for Golden Ear Audio Distributors (A), G. E. Audo received an interesting letter from the manufacturer of the speakers. The important information from the letter is in this paragraph:

A careful review of our records shows that you typically order about 200 speakers at a time. With that purchase quantity, you have been one of our most valued customers. As we review our operations, we discover that we can occasionally offer better prices to customers who help us operate more efficiently. If you are able to adjust your practices and place an order of 250 speakers or more, we can offer you a price break of $2 per speaker. For orders of 500 speakers or more, we can offer an additional price break of $1 per speaker or a total reduction of $3. In summary, we are offering you this pricing schedule:

Order Quantity	Unit Price
0–249	$400
250–499	$398
500 or more	$397

Recommend an ordering policy, based on a $350 cost to set up the test procedures.

Case Illustration: An Efficient Portfolio*

One of the important areas of financial analysis of investments is *portfolio theory*. In a nutshell, portfolio theory selects the proportion or amount of a portfolio that should be devoted to each of several assets. A great deal of statistical analysis and theory is involved in the portfolio problem. There are two basic concepts at the heart of portfolio theory:

1. The expected profitability (or desirability, before accounting for risk) of a portfolio is measured by the expected return of the portfolio. If a portfolio is comprised of assets A and B, yielding 10% and 20% annually, the expected return of the portfolio is the weighted average of those yields, where the weights are the proportion of the portfolio invested in each. If the portfolio is divided equally between A and B, the expected return is 15%:

$$10\% \times 0.5 + 20\% \times 0.5 = 15\%$$

   If the portfolio is divided with 40% in A and 60% in B, the expected return is:

$$10\% \times 0.4 + 20\% \times 0.6 = 16\%$$

   This can be extended to any number of assets, by multiplying each annual return by the portfolio proportion, and adding these products.

2. The risk associated with a portfolio or an asset is measured by the standard deviation of the returns. From statistics, we know that standard deviation is a measure of variation. A portfolio that returns 10% in half of the years and 20% in the other half has an expected return of 15%; however, its risk is greater than the risk of a portfolio that returns 15% in each year. As this case analysis will describe, the measurement of the risk of a portfolio of several assets is not a trivial statistical exercise!

An investor seeking an *efficient portfolio*[†] will behave in one of these two ways: (1) select a portfolio that minimizes the risk for a given expected return, or (2) maximizes the expected return for a given level of risk. In terms of the vocabulary of optimization, the problem has either of these two forms:

---

*Although a portfolio may be viewed as an inventory, nonlinear optimization is the primary link between this case and the content of the chapter.

[†]For a text discussion of these concepts, see, for example, Edward A. Moses and John M. Cheney, *Investments: Analysis, Selection, & Management* (St. Paul: West Publishing Company, 1989), pp. 122–135. The basic model was developed by Harry M. Markowitz, "Portfolio Selection," *Journal of Finance* (March, 1952): pp. 77–91 and *Portfolio Selection* (New York: Wiley, 1959).

Problem 1:

Decision Variables:	The proportion of the portfolio to be invested in each of the assets which is under consideration for inclusion in the portfolio.
Constraints:	a. The expected return must be greater than or equal to a specified value.
	b. The sum of the proportions of the portfolio investment must be equal to 1.
	c. There may be other constraints. In the simplest situation, each asset's proportion is constrained so that it cannot be negative. (In financial terms, this prohibits borrowing or "short selling" of assets which are not owned.)
Objective:	Minimize the standard deviation (risk) of the portfolio.

Problem 2:

Decision Variables:	The proportion of the portfolio to be invested in each of the assets which is under consideration for inclusion in the portfolio.
Constraints:	a. The standard deviation of the portfolio, the measure of risk, must be less than or equal to a specified value.
	b. The sum of the proportions of the portfolio investment must be equal to 1.
	c. There may be other constraints. In the simplest situation, each asset's proportion is constrained so that it cannot be negative. (In financial terms, this prohibits borrowing or "short selling" of assets which are not owned.)
Objective:	Maximize the expected return of the portfolio.

The Expected Return for a Portfolio

The expected return for a portfolio can easily be calculated from the weights and the individual asset expected returns. If the three assets have expected returns of 9%, 12%, and 18%, and the weights are 0.1, 0.4, and 0.5, the portfolio return is:

$$9\% \times 0.1 + 12\% \times 0.4 + 18\% \times 0.5 = 14.7\%$$

The calculations for this illustration are shown in cells A4..C8 of the spreadsheet shown in Exhibit 12.4.

The Statistical Problem: Standard Deviation (Risk) for a Portfolio

If each asset behaved independently of all other assets, measuring the risk of a portfolio would be much easier than it is. But there is a great deal of dependence or correlation among the many assets considered for a portfolio. If two assets tend to have above normal returns in a given year, these two assets will be

---

Exhibit 12.4

Spreadsheet Model for Three-Asset Portfolio

	A	B	C	D	E	F	G
1	Three-Asset Portfolio						
2							
3	Asset Exp Ret	Asset Weights	ExpRt * Wt				
4	9	0.1	0.9				
5	12	0.4	4.8				
6	18	0.5	9				
7		=========	==========				
8		1	14.7	PORTFOLIO	EXPECTED	RETURN	
9							
10		Ingr 1c:	Asset STD		3	15	20
11		Ingr 1e:	Asset Weights		0.1	0.4	0.5
12							
13	Ingr 1b:	Ingr 1d:					
14	Asset STD	Asset Weights	Ingredient 1a:	Correlation	Coefficients		
15	3	0.1		1	0.2	0.7	
16	15	0.4		0.2	1	-0.3	
17	20	0.5		0.7	-0.3	1	
18							
19							
20							
21			Step 1:	Product of Ingrts (1a) thru (1f)			
22				0.09	0.36	2.1	
23				0.36	36	-18	
24				2.1	-18	100	
25							
26			Step 2:	Sum	105.01		
27			Step 3:	Square Root:	10.25	PORTFOLIO STD	
28							

---

positively correlated; two negatively correlated assets will tend to have dissimilar performance in a given year. In the finance literature, the correlation coefficient for the periodic returns for a pair of assets (i and j) is called rho$[i,j]$ or ρ_{ij}. The entire set of correlation coefficients for periodic returns is shown as a matrix, or as a square range (block) on a spreadsheet. The correlation coefficient matrix is one of three ingredients used in calculating the risk of a portfolio. The correlation coefficient matrix is calculated by many statistical software packages. On a spreadsheet, the correlation between a pair of assets can be calculated using the regression commands on a spreadsheet; the correlation coefficient is the square root of R squared, with the sign of the regression coefficient or slope. The data input required for this set of calculations is the periodic (i.e., annual) rate of return for each asset for the number of periods (years) in the relevant database.

The second ingredient in calculating portfolio standard deviation or risk is the standard deviation of the periodic (annual) returns for each asset in the portfolio. In the finance literature, the asset's standard deviation is called sigma$[i]$, or σ_i. This asset standard deviation is calculated with the STD function on spreadsheets, using the historical periodic (annual) returns as the arguments for the function.

The final ingredient in calculating the portfolio standard deviation is the weights or proportions for each asset in the portfolio. These are the decision variables in the optimization problem.

These three ingredients are combined to find the portfolio standard deviation, which measures the portfolio risk. The combination requires a pair-by-pair examination for all assets in the portfolio. If a portfolio could have two assets in it, there are four pairs of assets:

Asset A	*with*	Asset A
Asset A	*with*	Asset B
Asset B	*with*	Asset A
Asset B	*with*	Asset B

Note that this listing requires each asset be paired with itself, and also that both orders (or permutations) or a pair be included: A with B is included, and so is B with A. If there are three assets, there are nine pairs; four assets, sixteen pairs; five assets, twenty-five pairs, and so on.

The statistical theory for finding the portfolio standard deviation is outlined in these three steps, combining the correlation coefficient, the asset standard deviation, and the proportion for each asset. Cell references are given for the spreadsheet entitled "Three-Asset Portfolio" (Exhibit 12.4) shown with this case.

Step 1. For each pair of assets, find the product of these terms:

    a. The correlation coefficient for the pair of assets (E15..G18)

    b. The standard deviation of the first asset in the pair (A15..A18)

    c. The standard deviation of the second asset in the pair (E10..G10)

    d. The proportion (weight) for the first asset in the pair (B15..B18)

    e. The proportion (weight) for the second asset in the pair (E11..G11)

The products are calculated in cells E22..G22.

Step 2. Find the sum of all of the products from Step 1. (E26)

Step 3. Find the square root of the sum found in Step 2. (E27)

Spreadsheet Tip: There are number of subtleties involved in constructing the "Three-Asset Portfolio" spreadsheet. First of all, the asset weights are first shown in B4..B6. Any other occurrence of these weights refers back to these cells. These cell definitions are key:

    E11: +B4
    F11: +B5
    G11: +B6

    B14:+B4 *which copies to* B16..B17 *as* +B5 *and* +B6

Spreadsheet Tip: The /**Range Transpose** command (in Quattro, /**Edit Transpose**) is used to copy the keyed asset STD values from A15..A17 to E10..G10.

Spreadsheet Tip: The step for finding the product of ingredients 1a through 1e can be accomplished in one formula, which relies heavily on mixed absolute/relative addresses. This formula is copied to a rectangular range. The details are as follows:

This formula is keyed:

E22: +E15 * $A15 * E$10 * $B15 * E$11

It is then copied from E22 to E22..G24, which correctly gives the formula for each of the five-part products in Step 1 above.

Spreadsheet Tip: The sum in cell E26 is straightforward:

E26: @SUM(E22..G24)

The square root of this sum is the portfolio standard deviation.

From this point, finding an efficient portfolio is a straightforward optimization problem. Consider an investor who requires an expected return of 13%. To accomplish this with risk as small as possible, the optimization problem is to adjust the decision variables (the weights or proportions for each asset, cells B4..B6) in order to minimize the portfolio risk (cell E27). The constraints are that the sum of the weights must be equals to 1, and that the expected return must be at least 13.

Case Exercises

a. Demonstrate that the minimum portfolio standard deviation for a portfolio with an expected return of 13% is about 7.86%.

b. Solve ten optimization problems, with the expected return varying over the range of 9%, 10%, 11%, . . . , 18%. Find the minimum portfolio standard deviation for each expected return. Does the portfolio risk increase as the return increases, as you would expect?

c. Using spreadsheet graphics, plot the expected portfolio return (*x* axis) and expected portfolio standard deviation (*y* axis) from the ten portfolios you found above. This plot sketches out the *efficient frontier* for this set of assets.

Case Illustration: Stratified Sampling and Sample Allocation

Most students of statistics have studied the simplest sampling plan, which is called *simple random sampling*. In a simple random sample, each element of the population has the same chance as any other of being included in the sample. (This is a property of a simple random sample; it is not a definition of a simple random sample.) Although simple random sampling is widely discussed in textbooks, it is often inefficient for demographic research.

An alternative sampling plan is called *stratified sampling*, in which the population is divided into strata. Then a simple random sample is taken from each stratum. There are some easily understood concepts of stratified sampling. Suppose we could divide a population perfectly into two strata, with every member of a stratum just like all other members of that stratum. (The two strata may be quite different from each other.) In this extreme situation, a sample of one observation from each stratum would reveal everything possible about the population, because everyone in the stratum is just like the one sampled! Building on this concept, the goal of stratification is to develop strata that are internally similar, but different from the other strata. The managerial issue we will be addressing is the number of observations to take from each stratum, where there may be different sampling costs for the various strata and different variability within each stratum.

Statisticians have shown that the stratified sampling estimate of the population mean is the weighted average of the strata sample means, where the weights are the proportion of the population included in each stratum. Suppose we have a population of families, and have divided them into three strata which we call apartment dwellers, condominium dwellers, and freestanding-house dwellers. If the population has 20% apartment dwellers, 30% condominium dwellers, and 50% house dwellers, a stratified plan would weight the sample means from the strata accordingly. Suppose the average income in the sample from each stratum is:

Apartment:	$20,000
Condo:	$30,000
House:	$35,000

then the estimate of the population average income is:

$$0.20 \times 20000 + 0.30 \times 30000 + 0.50 \times 35000$$

which can easily be calculated on a spreadsheet.

Statisticians are very interested in calculating the margin of error for a sample estimate. As a useful approximation, the margin of error for a stratified sample estimate of a population mean can be calculated by first calculating the margin of error for estimating the mean for each stratum, treating each stratum as a population. This is a typical statistical procedure; the margin of error* for one stratum is:

```
2 * STD/@SQRT(sample size)
```

where STD refers to the standard deviation of the elements in the stratum, and sample size also refers just to the individual stratum. Usually, the sample standard deviation is estimated by the sample taken from the stratum. In this case, however, we are deciding how large a sample to take from each stratum, so we don't have a sample standard deviation. We must rely on information (or guesses) from past studies, or from a pilot sample.

The next step in estimating the margin of error for the overall stratified sampling estimate of the population mean is to find the weighted sum of the *squares* of the margin of error estimates for each stratum, where the weights are the *squares* of the proportion of population observations found in each stratum.

---

*For the technically inclined, this is approximately the half-width of a 95% confidence interval for the population mean. Purists are happier if we use 1.96 instead of 2; realistically, none of the data is precise enough to be particular about precise Z values from the table of the normal distribution. This discussion assumes that the sampling fraction from each stratum is negligible. If this is not the case, the values in cells G6..G8 need to be multiplied by the finite population correction factor, which is (STRATUM SIZE − SAMPLE SIZE THIS STRATUM)/(STRATUM SIZE − 1). This also ignores the managerially unimportant fact that @STD uses a divisor of n instead of $n − 1$.

Exhibit 12.5

Spreadsheet Model for Stratified Sampling from Three Strata

	A	B	C	D	E	F	G
1	Stratified Sampling from Three Strata						
2	Statistical Section of Spreadsheet						
3							
4	Stratum	Prop'n of	Estimated	Sample	Stratum	Prop'n *	Square of
5	Name	Population	Std Dev	Size	Mgn Err	Mgn Err	<==this
6	Apartment	0.2	6000	100	1200	240	57600
7	Condo	0.3	10500	225	1400	420	176400
8	House	0.5	12000	400	1200	600	360000
9							
10						Sum	594000
11						Sq Root	770.71
12	Cost Section of Spreadsheet						
13							
14		Cost per	Stratum				
15		Observation	Cost				
16	Apartment	3	300				
17	Condo	2.5	562.5				
18	House	6	2400				
19				Budget			
20	Total Cost		3262.5	4000			

Continuing with our example, suppose the estimates of the standard deviation of income for each of the three strata are:

Apartment:	$6,000
Condo:	$10,500
House:	$12,000

If we took a sample of 100 from the apartments, 225 from the condos, and 400 from the houses, the spreadsheet shown in Exhibit 12.5 shows the computations. This spreadsheet also shows the cost of the proposed sample, where each observation for an apartment costs $3, $2.50 for a condo, or $6 for a house. The sampling budget is $4000, so there is still some unused money that could be used to take a larger sample.

a. How should the budget be allocated to observations from the three strata? Verify that a plan can be developed that has a margin of error of about $688, while still meeting the budget.

b. Find the minimum-cost sample size necessary to have a margin of error of $500.

c. Suppose it had been decided to allocate observations to strata in proportion to the stratum size: condos 20%, apartments 30%, houses 50%. What would it cost to obtain a margin of error of $500?

13

Decision Analysis: Dealing with Uncertainty

Decision analysis brings the realism of uncertainty into an analysis; it recognizes that we don't always know what is going to happen. Uncertainty is typical in managerial decisions. This chapter describes some effective ways to use spreadsheet models to support decisions made in the face of uncertainty. A characteristic of these decision support techniques is that they deal with problems with only a limited number of choices. The decision analysis techniques we consider apply to decisions for which we can list the choices or courses of action; for the most part, we will evaluate "one by one" each of these choices in the list. Such a listing would be impossible (or at best, terribly unwieldy) for most optimization problems. Can you visualize how long the list would be for Rangely Lakes, if we consider each conceivable number of decoys along with each conceivable number of wall hangings?

Narrowing the Scope of the Analysis:
A First Step in Decision Analysis

We have already used optimization (Chapter 3, Figure 3.3) to recommend a plan for the souvenir business at the Rangely Lakes golf club. The plan J. L. Duckworth will implement, if the souvenir business is pursued in the winter, is to build about 2800 decoys (the value from optimization is 2794) and about 1850 hangings (the value from optimization is 1854). But this plan is based on certainty; J.L. realized that some of the planning factors may not materialize exactly as they were stated in the spreadsheet model that was optimized. J.L. addressed these uncertainties with these thoughts:

I'm really concerned about the prices we can get for our souvenirs; while I am comfortable with our guesses, when the sales force gets on

the road the prices may be as much as 30% lower than we have planned
(I hope not) or as much as 20% higher (I hope so). Should this uncertainty have much impact on whether I go ahead and get into the
souvenir business this winter?

There also is some concern about the estimates of lumber usage.
But this is a technological factor; it depends upon the care used in
cutting and the quality of the lumber. Both our workers and our
suppliers have demonstrated that they know what they are doing! At
the outside, the board feet per item may be 2% lower than planned
(sweet!) or 3% higher. Should this uncertainty have much impact on
whether I go ahead and get into the souvenir business this winter?

Labor usage is a different matter. We aren't sure just which people
will be staying around for the winter; the snow and wind also affect the
productivity of our workforce in making souvenirs. It could require 5%
less labor than we plan, if things work out well. But if this winter is
really bad, we may find that it really requires up to 20% more time per
souvenir than we think right now. But once we get going, we'll continue
until we have made the number of souvenirs planned, because that is
our production goal for the winter. Even if it takes a different number
of hours than we think, those production plans will stay firm to keep
the work incentive where I want it. Should this uncertainty have
much impact on whether I go ahead and get into the souvenir business
this winter?

We've done some pretty good checking about lumber prices. We're
pretty certain to be within 5% either way. Should this uncertainty have
much impact on whether I go ahead and get into the souvenir business
this winter?

How many uncertainties has J.L. identified? Although there are four items
discussed (price, board feet per item, hours per item, and price per board feet),
some of these items vary together and some vary independently. Here are J.L.'s
thoughts about this issue:

> The price of decoys will go along with the price of hangings. If the
> price turns out to be sour, it will affect both products. What I'm really
> concerned about is general market conditions, not the popularity of
> individual items. Conclusion: The same price factor (from down 30% to
> up 20%) applies to both prices.
>
> The lumber usage for decoys may be off one way, while the lumber
> usage for hangings will be off the other. Lumber quality affects the
> products in different ways, because the decoy requires blocks while the
> hanging requires boards. Conclusion: We need two separate lumber
> usage factors (from down 2% to up 3%), one for each product. These
> two factors are independent of each other.
>
> The labor usage depends upon the workforce, not on the product.
> Conclusion: The same labor usage factor (from down 5% to up 20%)
> applies to both products.

Figure 13.1

Rangely Lakes Worksheet After Optimization

	A	B	C	D
1		Decoy	Hanging	Total
2	Quantity	2793.733	1853.785	4647.519
3	Price	$12	$15	
4	Revenue	$33,525	$27,807	$61,332
5				
6	Board Feet Used	8101.827	8898.172	17000
7	Cost of Lumber	$10,532	$11,568	$22,100
8				
9	Hours Used	3073.107	926.8929	4000
10	Cost of Labor	$21,973	$6,627	$28,600
11				
12	Profit		$1,020	$9,612	$10,632
13				
14	Board Feet per Item	2.9	4.8	
15	Hours per Item	1.1	0.5	
16				
17		Data		
18	Price per Board Foot	$1.30		
19	Price per Hour	$7.15		

The price of lumber is the same for both products. Conclusion: The same lumber price factor applies to both products.

Putting all of this together, J.L. realized that there were five uncertain factors to be considered before making a firm commitment to the souvenir business for the winter. Before considering any of these items, J.L. anticipated a profit of about $10,600; in addition, the workforce would be kept busy, which would have other benefits not considered in the model. The optimized spreadsheet used for planning is shown again in Figure 13.1 (from Figure 3.3, Chapter 3). J.L. made temporary changes in the spreadsheet for each factor, and noted the Profit [Total] from each situation, as shown in Figure 13.2.*

After studying Figure 13.2, it was obvious to J.L. that some of the uncertainties made a big difference, and some were inconsequential. The worst case for selling price had a loss of about $7800; that would be enough to discourage Rangely from entering the souvenir business this winter. None of the other uncertainties produced a loss, even if their worst cases were realized. Furthermore, the profit swing from the selling price uncertainty was about $30,000 between the worst case and the best case. None of the other uncertainties had a range even close to that value. J.L. decided to focus on selling price as the important source of uncertainty for the decision to commit to the souvenir business for the winter. We use this situation to begin our study of decision analysis.

---

*There is a subtle issue that some readers are sure to raise if it is not addressed! When any of the factors change, the analyst should go back and optimize again with these new factors. This re-optimization is not shown in this chapter, because the purpose of the chapter is to illustrate concepts of decision analysis, and we have drawn upon a familiar case for illustration.

Figure 13.2

Profit Range for J. L. Duckworth's Uncertainties

Uncertainty: Price   *(applies jointly to two product prices)*

Worst Case: 30% below plan;   Profit: ($7,768)
Spreadsheet Changes: 12*0.7 *in cell* B3;   15*0.7 *in cell* C3

Best Case: 20% above plan;   Profit: $22,898
Spreadsheet Changes: 12*1.2 *in cell* B3;   15*1.2 *in cell* C3

Uncertainty: Board Feet per Item[Decoy]   *(applies only to this product)*

Worst Case: 3% above plan;   Profit: $10,316
Spreadsheet Change: 2.9*1.03 *in cell* B14

Best Case: 2% below plan;   Profit: $10,842
Spreadsheet Change: 2.9*0.98 *in cell* B14

Uncertainty: Board Feet per Item[Hanging]   *(applies only to this product)*

Worst Case: 3% above plan;   Profit: $10,285
Spreadsheet Change: 4.8*1.03 *in cell* C14

Best Case: 2% below plan;   Profit: $10,863
Spreadsheet Change: 4.8*0.98 *in cell* C14

Uncertainty: Hours per Item   *(applies jointly to both products)*

Worst Case: 20% above plan;   Profit: $4,912
Spreadsheet Changes: 1.1*1.2 *in cell* B15;   0.5*1.2 *in cell* C15

Best Case: 5% below plan;   Profit: $12,062
Spreadsheet Changes: 1.1*0.95 *in cell* B15;   0.5*0.95 *in cell* C15

Uncertainty: Price per Board Foot   *(applies to all lumber)*

Worst Case: 5% above plan;   Profit: $9,527
Spreadsheet Change: 1.30*1.05 *in cell* B18

Best Case: 5% below plan;   Profit: $11,737
Spreadsheet Change: 1.30*0.95 *in cell* B18

The spreadsheet changes shown in this analysis are temporary; after the change was made and profit determined for a particular case, the spreadsheet cells were restored to their original values for subsequent cases.

So far, J.L. has suggested that the selling price will be someplace between "down 30% and up 20%." That covers a lot of territory! But J.L. recognized that the worst and best cases were really quite extreme, and unlikely to happen. To simplify the analysis, J.L. was willing to consider just three values for the selling price factor. The three values J.L. selected were narrower than the best and worst cases:

1. The selling price for the souvenirs would be down 20%, or
2. The selling price for the souvenirs would be as planned, or
3. The selling price for the souvenirs would be up 15%.

Four Components of a Decision Analysis

The three selling price factors (down 20%, as planned, and up 15%) are the things that can happen as the souvenir business unfolds. These *events* in decision analysis are one of four major components. Events are sometimes called the "uncontrollables" in a decision:

> *Component 1.* The events in decision analysis are not controlled by the decision maker; rather, the events "happen." Events are sometimes called *states of nature*, which emphasizes the manager's inability to control which event will occur.

Next, J.L. contemplated the choices available: "Do I or Don't I? I'm either going to get into the souvenir business for the winter, or I'm not!" This illustrates the *acts*, another component of a decision analysis:

> *Component 2.* The set of acts are under the control of the decision maker. A decision is made when an act is chosen by the decision maker.

How well does J.L. like each end point for the souvenir business? How much profit will be made? This illustrates the *conditional payoff*, the third component of a decision analysis:

> *Component 3.* The conditional payoff, usually measured in dollars, shows the "bottom line" for each choice for the act, coupled with the occurrence of one event. The payoff is said to be conditional upon the choice of the act and the occurrence of the event.

Finally, J.L. recognized that some events are more likely than others to occur; this is described by the *probability* that is attached to each event. Thus, probability is the fourth component of a decision analysis.

> *Component 4.* Probabilities are associated with the events.

Probabilities may be familiar to some readers but not to others. Figure 13.3 presents some elementary ideas about the definition of probability, which might or might not be different from your use of the word in conversational English.

J.L. thought about the price uncertainty for the next season. Somewhat more than half of the time in the past, the price estimates used by Rangely had been "pretty close." J.L. wasn't optimistic about the next season; in fact, there were some forecasts that the retailers would be cutting back in anticipation of fewer summer tourists. So J.L. concluded that it was reasonable to assess a 50% probability that prices would be as planned. Rangely's history revealed that when the estimates were off, they were just as often too high as too low. Reflecting the pessimism about the coming season, J.L. assessed the probability for prices being down 20% at 0.30, and the probability for prices being up 15% at 0.20. J.L. was content to use these three probability numbers (0.3, 0.5, 0.2) as numbers that express the likelihood that each of the three events will occur.

The approach of decision analysis is to break a problem into various pieces, which are then put back together with *expected value*. To illustrate the calculations for expected value, we need to know the conditional payoff for each combination of an act and an event. If we choose "No" for the souvenir business, the condi-

---
Figure 13.3

A Brief Discussion of Probability

Uncertainty is usually described by *probability*, a concept which is familiar to each of us. Think about each of these statements:

The probability that a spare part (picked at random from a supply shelf) will work correctly is 0.94.

J.T. is the person on the repair shift this morning. From experience, I'd say there is an 80% probability we can start the repair by 9:30 A.M.

Although we've never submitted a bid for a contract like this before, our chances of winning with this bid are about 40%.

Each of these statements conveys something of meaning to most readers. We are considering three events:

1. The spare part will work correctly.
2. The repair can start by 9:30 A.M.
3. Our bid will be the winning bid.

From the probability values, we know that Event 1 is the most likely to occur, that the spare part will work correctly; this event has the highest probability of occuring. Although statisticians may spend hours and pages defining probability, a workable definition for our purposes is:

A probability is a number between 0 and 1 that expresses the likelihood that an event will occur. A probability of zero means that the event is viewed as impossible; a probability of 1 means that the event is viewed as certain to occur.

A probability of 0.75 can be interpreted as meaning that the event would happen "three times out of four" if it could be repeated, over and over again, under apparently identical situations. If the event is one that cannot be repeated (which is typical of most business decisions) the probability statement means that the event is as likely to occur as drawing (blindfolded) a red ball from an urn which contains 75 red balls and 25 green balls.

---

tional profit is $0, whether the price factor is off 20% or up 15%. If we say "Yes" for the souvenir business, the conditional profit can be calculated using the spreadsheet model shown in Figure 13.1. The reader is encouraged to verify these results:

"No" with any price	"Yes" with prices off 20%	"Yes" with prices up 15%
	Cell B3: 12*0.8	Cell B3: 12*1.15
	Cell C3: 15*0.8	Cell C3: 15*1.15
Profit: $0	Profit: ($1635)	Profit: $19,831

Payoff Table: Combining the Events, Acts, Payoffs, and Probabilities

A payoff table is a very useful way to portray the essential components of many decision problems. Note that J.L. has only one set of acts (Enter the business? "yes" or "no"), and only one set of events (What will happen to prices? Down 20%, as planned, or up 15%). When a decision problem has only one set of acts and only one set of events, a payoff table is useful and easy to construct. We construct the table by listing the set of acts across the top, listing the set of events

Figure 13.4

Payoff Table for Rangely's Decision

Event: Price Level	Acts		Probability
	Say Yes	Say No	
−20%	−$1,635	$0	0.3
As Planned	$10,632	$0	0.5
+15%	$19,831	$0	0.2

along the left margin, and showing the conditional payoff values at each act/event intersection. This is shown in Figure 13.4.

Expected Value: Combining Payoffs and Probabilities

Decision analysts use *expected value* to combine payoff values and probabilities into a number which is used to support a managerial decision. In general terms, the expected value for an act is calculated by multiplying (for each event) the payoff by the probability, and then adding these products for all events. Expected value for "Say Yes" is calculated in this way:

$$(-1635 \times 0.3) + (10,632 \times 0.5) + (19,831 \times 0.2) = \$8791.70$$

The expected value for "Say No" is calculated:

$$(0 \times 0.3) + (0 \times 0.5) + (0 \times 0.2) = 0 \quad \text{(which belabors the obvious!)}$$

Spreadsheet Tip: The use of the @SUMPRODUCT spreadsheet function (a native function in Quattro Pro, and an add-in function provided with What's-Best! for Lotus 1-2-3) fits this definition very nicely.

Decision analysts often recommend choosing the act with the highest expected profit. This is because the expected value for a choice of an act is the long-run average payoff that would result from making that choice when this decision is repeated many, many times. Expected value is the same concept as the statistician's concept of the arithmetic mean. If we unrealistically assumed that J.L.'s decision will be repeated 100 times, and result in 30 occurrences of "off 20%," 50 occurrences of "as planned" and 20 occurrences of "up 15%," then the total payoff would be:

$$(-1635 \times 30) + (10,632 \times 50) + (19,831 \times 20) = \$879,170$$

or an average payoff of $8791.70! This is why it is stated that the expected value is the same as the long-run payoff. Expected value is also the same as the weighted average of the payoffs, where the probabilities are the weights. Using Expected Monetary Value (EMV) as the criterion, J.L. would elect to "Say Yes" to the winter souvenir business, because $8791.70 is larger than $0.

Figure 13.5

Completed Payoff Table for Rangely's Decision

Event: Price Level	Acts		Probability
	Say Yes	Say No	
−20%	−$1,635	$0	0.3
As Planned	$10,632	$0	0.5
+15%	$19,831	$0	0.2
	$8791.70✳	$0	

If we assume that a decision will be repeated a large number of times regardless of the outcome of each replication of the scenario, decision analysts suggest choosing the act with the highest expected value. (This assumes we are dealing with profit; we would choose the lowest expect value when dealing with cost.) The basic assumption is that the long run is going to occur, so why not choose the act that will give us the most profit in the long run? Even if a particular decision will not be repeated a large number of times, there are many decisions in an organization. Expected value provides a way for a decision maker to make as much profit as possible in the long run, by averaging over a large number of decisions rather than over replications of one decision.

The difficulty with expected monetary value occurs when one outcome may affect the long-run viability of the organization. For example, assume J.L. needs at least $10,000 from this venture to be able to stay in the summer golf business. Then the payoff table shows that there is no way to stay in the summer golf business by saying no to the winter souvenir business! On the other hand, if the only way J.L. can have financial problems is by incurring a loss of more than a thousand dollars, it may be perfectly reasonable to look at the payoff table and decide to say no without calculating EMV. This guarantees that the business will survive into the golf season. In both of these situations, a particular outcome affects the long run viability of the organization, which makes expected value an inappropriate criterion. In most situations, expected value is a good decision criterion when the economic payoffs are "small" compared to the financial position of the firm. For larger problems, expected value may not be the major consideration in selecting an act.*

It is common practice to complete a payoff table by placing the expected values at the bottom of the table, and marking the best value with an asterisk. This is shown in Figure 13.5.

---

*The literature of decision analysis discusses alternatives to expected monetary value. The basic idea is to develop a measure that can be substituted for monetary conditional payoffs in a way that expected value usefully describes the decision maker's preferences. This form of analysis is often called risk preference analysis, and sometimes referred to as utility theory. Its consideration of uncertainty makes this form of utility theory substantially different from the utility theory discussed in microeconomics.

Comment: Payoff Tables and Their Uses

The discussion above clearly implies that payoff tables are very useful in supporting management decisions; payoff tables facilitate calculating the expected monetary value for various courses of action. But another important reason for using payoff tables is that the process of asking "What are the acts" and "What are the events" often provides structure to the problem, clarifying some aspect of the situation in the mind of the decision maker. During the construction of a payoff table, it may be advantageous for the decision maker to consider whether there are acts that have not been included in the payoff table. It has been said that choosing a "good" act from a rich set of alternatives is preferable to choosing the "best" act from a weak set of alternatives. Structuring a payoff table may stimulate the creativity that generates a richer set of alternatives.

An Illustration of Decision Analysis: Choosing a Production Process*

To reinforce the concepts of decision analysis, consider the scenario faced by J.D., owner of a specialty manufacturing and marketing organization. On June 1, J.D. signed a contract to deliver merchandise to be sold for $400,000. The administrative costs and factory overhead associated with the contract are estimated to be $140,000; the materials will cost $60,000. Labor cost is the major uncertainty remaining for J.D.

> *Comment:* J.D. and the case writer have already narrowed the scope of the analysis, by identifying labor cost as the remaining uncertainty. While this is easy to do in a textbook problem, the world seldom behaves so nicely! Hence, this example serves to illustrate the steps involved in breaking a decision into its four components and using expected value; it assumes away the task of deciding which uncertainties to consider in the decision analysis.

J.D. is in the midst of a labor dispute about the classification of workers who will be involved in making the merchandise. There has been no agreement between J.D. and the workers' union; an arbitrator will decide the cost of labor. The parties to the dispute have agreed to use the form of arbitration used by Major League Baseball: either the Union's position will prevail, with an award resulting in a labor cost of $12.00 per hour; or J.D.'s position will prevail, resulting in a labor cost of $8.00 per hour. The arbitrator will report a decision on August 15; the manufacturing must begin on September 1 to meet the terms of the contract.

> *Comment:* We can now identify one component of the decision problem, the *events*. Either the arbitrator will make an award of $8.00, or an award of $12.00. This represents an uncontrollable variable for J.D., who cannot choose the event. Rather, J.D. must wait for the event to occur.

---

*This illustration is modified from John Dinkel, Gary Kochenberger, and Donald Plane, *Management Science: Text and Applications* (Homewood, IL: Richard D. Irwin, Inc., 1978), pp. 18–51.

Figure 13.6

A Spinner Showing an Area of 70% for $8.00 and 30% for $12.00

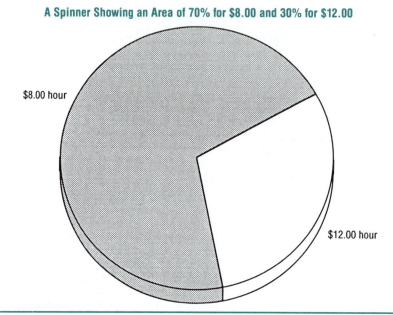

$8.00 hour

$12.00 hour

There are two production alternatives for J.D. The merchandise can be produced using either Process A or Process B. Process A, which is capital-intensive, will require 3600 labor hours. The cost of arranging the factory and obtaining the special-purpose equipment for this process will be $140,000. The alternative Process B requires an expenditure of $100,000 for a less costly factory arrangement and more general-purpose equipment. However, Process B requires 8000 hours of labor. In order to be ready to manufacture on September 1, J.D. must begin the process of setting up the factory and ordering equipment by July 1.

Comment: We can now identify another component of the decision problem, the *acts*. J.D. must make a choice of either Process A or Process B.

It was apparent to J.D. that the desirability of Process A and Process B is influenced by the arbitrator's award. Unfortunately, J.D. must make a decision before the occurrence of the uncertain event, the arbitrator's award.

Comment: The last paragraph emphasizes an important aspect of decisions made under uncertainty: a decision must be made before the decision maker knows what will happen. If we view events as states of nature, then the decision maker must decide what to do before nature reveals what is going to happen!

J.D. had a "good feeling" about the upcoming award, but wasn't completely confident of a victory. After some consideration, J.D. decided that the probability the arbitrator would make an award resulting in an $8.00 hourly labor cost was 0.7; this meant that the probability of a $12.00 hourly labor cost was 0.3, because

---

Figure 13.7

Computations of Conditional Payoff (Profit) for Each Act/Event Combination

Process Selected	A	Process Selected	B
Arbitrator's Award	$8	Arbitrator's Award	$8
Revenue	$400,000	Revenue	$400,000
Administration Costs	$140,000	Administration Costs	$140,000
Materials	$60,000	Materials	$60,000
Process Cost	$140,000	Process Cost	$100,000
Labor Cost	$28,800	Labor Cost	$64,000
Contract Profit	$31,200	Contract Profit	$36,000

Process Selected	A	Process Selected	B
Arbitrator's Award	$12	Arbitrator's Award	$12
Revenue	$400,000	Revenue	$400,000
Administration Costs	$140,000	Administration Costs	$140,000
Materials	$60,000	Materials	$60,000
Process Cost	$140,000	Process Cost	$100,000
Labor Cost	$43,200	Labor Cost	$96,000
Contract Profit	$16,800	Contract Profit	$4,000

---

one of those two events would occur. In order to contemplate the probability of an $8.00 hourly labor cost, J.D. had imagined a "spinner" similar to those found in board games, as shown in Figure 13.6. J.D. mentally adjusted the size of the solid and shaded areas, until J.D.'s personal belief was that the spinner was as likely to stop on the solid area as the arbitrator was to award an $8.00 hourly labor cost.

Comment: Another element of the decision problem, the *probabilities* for the events, has been identified. Although J.D.'s probabilities might be called *subjective* probabilities, other situations lend themselves to probabilities that rely upon substantial amounts of applicable data; such probabilities are said to be objectively determined.

J.D. next considered the economics of the situation with the four sets of computations shown in Figure 13.7. Each of the four sections deals with a combination of one act (Process A or Process B) and one event ($8.00 Award or $12.00 Award).

Comment: The final element of the decision problem, the *conditional payoff* or economic consequences arising from the various acts and events, has now been introduced into the problem. For this relatively small problem, these payoff values could have been calculated using a spreadsheet or paper and pencil. A case at the end of this chapter discusses a model used to construct the information shown in Figure 13.7.

Using a Spreadsheet for J.D.'s Problem

J.D. developed the payoff table (Figure 13.8) using the computations shown in Figure 13.7, and determined expected values with a few simple calculations.

--------- **Figure 13.8** ---------

Completed Payoff Table for J.D.'s Process Selection Decision

Events: Arbitrator's Award	Acts		Probability
	Process A	Process B	
$8	$31,200	$36,000	0.7
$12	$16,800	$4,000	0.3
Expected Value	$26,880*	$26,400	

Based on EMV, J.D. would choose to use Process A. However, the two values of EMV are so close to each other that J.D. might now choose to bring into the analysis factors that were discarded at the initial "narrowing" of the problem.

The reader is encouraged to verify the expected value computations shown in Figure 13.8. The time required on either a spreadsheet or a calculator would be about the same. But consider what would have happened if there had been five processes and six possible awards. This would have required thirty values for conditional profit; spreadsheet modeling would then win hands down. Two cases at the end of this chapter continue J.D.'s scenario, exploring spreadsheets to assist in this and a larger version of J.D.'s problem. Some readers may choose to pursue those cases at this point, while others may want to continue with additional topics in decision analysis before looking at spreadsheet modeling in the context of payoff tables.

Additional Information

Another important concept of decision analysis is *perfect information*. Conceptually, perfect information is the same thing as clairvoyance; we find out what is going to happen before we choose a course of action. While managerial decisions made with clairvoyance may seem to be irrelevant, there are many situations in which a decision maker may be able to obtain more information to reduce the amount of uncertainty. Sometimes a phone call will provide the information about a customer's intentions; a quick visit to a supplier may effectively provide clairvoyance about the supplier's position. One purpose of research is to generate information to use in a decision. Market research provides information about consumer behavior before a commitment is made to introduce a new product. But the observant reader has noticed that we started out discussing perfect information, yet the information we have described may be far from perfect. From a managerial perspective, the key factor is summarized:

> Never pay more for imperfect information than you would pay for perfect information.

While managers may not be able to find out exactly what will happen before committing resources, it may be possible to reduce the uncertainty with imper-

Figure 13.9

J.D.'s Process Selection Decision Evaluating Perfect Information

Events: Arbitrator's Award	Acts Process A	Process B	Best Payoff	Probability
$8	$31,200	$36,000	$36,000	0.7
$12	$16,800	$4,000	$16,800	0.3
Expected Value	$26,880*	$26,400	$30,240	

fect information. If perfect information is worth (say) $10,000, it is apparent that the manager would not pay $11,000 for information that is less than perfect.

Perfect Information for J.D.'s Problem

This section describes how to place a value on perfect information for a decision situation represented with a payoff table. This value is an upper limit on the value of any information that might be obtained before making a decision.

For illustration, we return to J.D.'s original decision shown in Figure 13.8, which is reproduced, with an additional column called "Best Payoff" as Figure 13.9. This shows the payoff the decision maker would obtain if clairvoyance (perfect information) always allowed the choice of a process to be made after it was known what event would occur.

The Best Payoff of $36,000 indicates that if the perfect information revealed that the Arbitrator's Award would be $8, then the decision would be to choose Process B, obtaining a profit of $36,000. On the other hand, if the perfect information revealed that the award would be $12, the decision would be to choose Process A, and the best payoff would be $16,800. Since the $8 award will occur with probability of 0.7, the best payoff will be $36,000 with probability 0.7; the $12 award will occur with probability 0.3, which is the probability of obtaining the best payoff of $16,800. Hence, with perfect information the expected monetary value of profit is calculated as:

$$(0.7 \times \$36,000) + (0.3 \times \$16,800) = \$30,240$$

To find the expected value of perfect information, the reasoning is straightforward. With perfect information, the expected profit is $30,240. Without additional information, the expected profit is $26,880. Perfect information increased the expected profit by:

$$\$30,240 - \$26,880 = \$3360$$

In general terms, the *expected value of perfect information* (EVPI) is the difference between expected profit with perfect information and the expected profit without perfect information. (If the decision is one in which we are minimizing expected cost, the expected value of perfect information is the difference between

Figure 13.10

J.D.'s Problem in Decision Tree Form

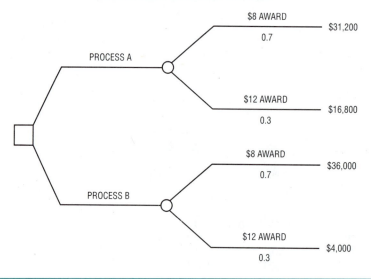

expected cost without perfect information and the expected cost with perfect information. The order of subtraction is reversed, because perfect information increases profit, but reduces cost.)

This value of perfect information, $3360, may be useful to J.D. in determining whether it is worthwhile trying to decide which process to use *after* the arbitrator's award, instead of before the award. Although the basic scenario presented much earlier made it clear that the decision must be made before the arbitrator made an award, knowing the economic benefit of finding ways around the original requirements may spur effective managerial action!

Decision Trees: Decision Problems with a Sequence of Decisions

Not all decisions under uncertainty are represented easily with a payoff table. In J.D.'s first problem there was an act, followed by the occurrence of an event. When the acts and events form a longer sequence, a decision tree may be a useful tool of decision analysis. Before we tackle a decision problem with a longer sequence of acts and events, let's look at J.D.'s original problem in tree form.

A decision tree shows a series of acts and events; on a tree, a square node represents an act, a circle node represents an event. Decision trees usually proceed in time order from left to right. Since the first node in J.D.'s problem is the act of deciding between Process A and Process B, the decision tree starts with a square node representing this act. Each branch growing from this node leads to an event, either the $8 award or the $12 award. This is shown in Figure 13.10. As J.D. views the decision problem, an act (select Process A or Process B) must first be chosen at the left-most node, which is a square. After J.D. has chosen an act (such as Process A), then an event occurs ($8 award or $12 award). Probability values are also shown on each event branch. At the right end of each final branch, the conditional profit values are shown. Since these are at the end of the sequence of acts and events, these conditional profit values are often called *terminal values*.

The tree has been constructed by working in time sequence, from left to right. It is analyzed in the opposite direction, working from right to left. Starting from any terminal value, proceed backwards to the next node. Then evaluate that node using these rules:

1. If the node is an event node, calculate expected value by multiplying each terminal value by its accompanying probability; then find the sum of these products.
2. If the node is an act node, choose the act with the best expected value (highest profit, lowest cost).
3. Proceed left to the next node, and start again with rule (1). When all nodes have been evaluated, the evaluation is complete.

It often happens that these rules cannot be applied, because one of the branches from the node being evaluated is itself not yet evaluated. When that occurs, move right from the unevaluated node to a terminal value, and start again with rule (1) above.

Eventually, rule (3) will signal us that the evaluation has been completed. When we apply these rules to the decision tree for J.D. in Figure 13.10, we might start with the uppermost terminal value. Moving to the left, we reach the event node. We compute the expected value:

$$(\$31,200 \times 0.7) + (\$16,800 \times 0.3) = \$26,880$$

This expected value is written at the event node, as shown in Figure 13.11. Continuing to the left, we reach an act node. We attempt to choose one of the branches, by comparing $26,880 with an unevaluated node. When we reach the unevaluated node, move to the right to a terminal value, and back up (left) one node. This event node is evaluated by finding the expected value:

$$(\$36,000 \times 0.7) + (\$4000 \times 0.3) = \$26,400$$

which is noted on the tree at the event node. Continuing to the left, we reach the act node, and compare $26,880 with $26,400. Preferring the higher EMV, we block off the choice of Process B. We cannot move left from this evaluated node, so the evaluation is complete.

To use these concepts of a decision tree in a situation with a sequence of acts and events, we expand J.D.'s scenario by introducing the possibility of appealing the arbitrator's award, if it is $12. The cost of this appeal is $4000, which is incurred whether J.D. wins or loses the appeal. Winning on appeal means that the actual labor cost will be $8 per hour; losing on appeal means that the actual labor cost will be $12 per hour. The probability of winning the appeal is 0.20. This

---

Figure 13.11

J.D.'s Decision Tree with Values Obtained in Evaluation

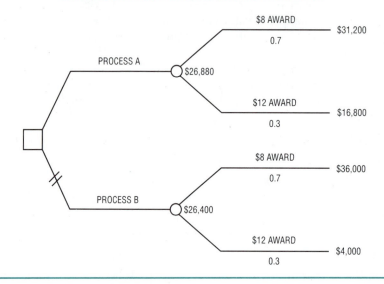

new situation is shown in Figure 13.12. This figure also shows the computations made in evaluating the tree using the rules described above.

When a sequential decision tree has been evaluated, it is necessary to interpret the tree into managerial language. The evaluation notations on the tree indicate that if Process A is selected and the $12 award occurs, J.D. should not appeal. However, if Process B is selected and the $12 award occurs, an appeal is appropriate. But the tree also indicates that J.D. should not choose Process A because the EMV is better for Process B. This can all be stated succinctly for J.D. with these instructions:

Choose Process B. If the arbitrator's award is for $12, appeal the award.

Note that these instructions tell J.D. the course of action to take for any decision node which might be encountered. There are no instructions about whether to appeal following a choice of Process A, because Process A is not recommended.

Computing Terminal Values for a Decision Tree

The terminal values in Figure 13.12 were easy to compute from Figure 13.11 (or from the payoff table, Figure 13.8). The appeal costs $4000; all terminal values following appeal nodes are exactly $4000 less than the corresponding values from the decision tree in Figure 13.10. Although this could have been incorporated into a spreadsheet model, this particular problem is small enough that it isn't worth the effort. In some situations, decision trees lack the regularity found in payoff tables, which makes it more difficult to present general concepts that can make spreadsheets useful in evaluating decision trees. On the other hand,

Figure 13.12

J.D.'s Decision Problem with Appeal

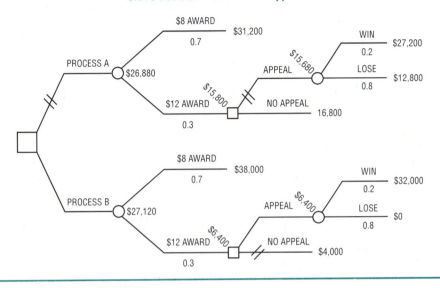

there are situations where spreadsheet models are extremely useful in calculating terminal values for decision trees. The case of the YumYum Corporation, included at the end of this chapter, would be much more difficult if one relied on a calculator rather than a spreadsheet!

Exercises

1. The Rangely Company analysis to determine the important uncertainties indicated that price was the most important variable, because it could be as much as 30% lower or 20% higher than planned. Suppose these values had been 5% lower to 10% higher than planned. Also consider a change in the uncertainty in the price of lumber changed, so that it could be as much as 40% below or 50% above plan. Parts of the analysis from Figure 13.2 will change; parts will not. Make the appropriate changes in the information in Figure 13.2 to reflect these new circumstances.

2. The Arno Corporation was contemplating entering the swimming pool surfacing business. The company's founder, D. L. Arno, had been in the swimming pool construction business for about thirty years; recent changes in the permitted chemical content of traditional swimming pool surfaces made newer fiberglass surfaces much more attractive. The rough planning figures Arno developed for the first two years of business served to encourage the company to enter the fiberglass surfacing market. Arno believed it would be at least two years before competitors would be able to enter the market; they would wait to observe Arno's success before making the substantial commitments required. Here is the

summary of Arno's projection for the first two years, showing the net gain from the plan. (For teaching purposes, factors such as taxes and interest are omitted; their inclusion is worthwhile from the standpoint of learning accounting and finance; to the beginning student of decision analysis, such important factors are better left for later!)

Revenue:	50 pools at $4000 each	$200,000
Expenses:		
Advertising and Promotion		40,000
Commissions		20,000
Employment and Training		40,000
Office Support		10,000
Materials		25,000
Installation labor		60,000
Net Gain		$5,000

All things considered, Arno was quite happy with this projection. If these plans work out, there would be a small gain for the two years, and Arno would be positioned to be a market leader in the local area.

There were numerous uncertainties. Arno thought about them, and made these notes about each of the items in the planning figures:

The number of pools could be off by 50% either way. The average selling price of $4000 is also a bit troublesome; it could be $3500, at worst, or $4500 at best. While there is a relationship between price and quantity, I'm willing to manage my decision as if those two things are independent of each other.

Advertising and promotion, employment and training, and office support are all pretty secure. In fact, those numbers will vary according to general price levels, which may vary by as much as 8% either way, if we go into the business. These expenses won't vary with the number of pools because we make those expenditures and commitments up front.

Commissions are a flat 10% of sales revenue. That fact won't change.

Materials and installation labor are figured at $500 and $1200 per pool. The materials won't vary on a per-pool basis, because that will be fixed by the franchise agreement. The installation labor per pool will vary the same amount as the other expenses which vary according to general price levels, that is, within 8% up or down.

a. Build an influence chart and a spreadsheet model to calculate the net gain for Arno. Verify the calculations for the base case, showing a net gain of $5000 for the "best guess" numbers.

b. Identify the three factors in Arno's scenario that are uncertain.

c. For each of the three independent uncertain factors, use the spreadsheet model to determine the dollar "swing" in net gain, for the range of uncertainty Arno describes in the scenario. The impact of the first factor is determined, then the value of that first factor is returned to its base case. Each source of uncertainty is analyzed, individually, with the remaining factors at the base case values.

d. Rank the independent uncertain factors according to their impact on net gain. Which factor should receive Arno's primary concern in a decision analysis?

e. Structure a payoff table, showing the acts available to Arno, and the events that may occur, based on your analysis of the impact of each of the uncertain factors. Use only the one uncertainty with the largest impact on net gain. Include the extreme values for this uncertaintainty, and the values halfway between the base case and the extreme. (We do not have probabilities for this payoff table.)

3. Find the expected profit for this payoff table, which shows conditional profit:

	Act A	Act B	Act C	Probabilities
Event No. 1	$25	$35	$55	0.4
Event No. 2	$40	$15	$25	0.6

4. Treat the payoff table in Exercise 3 as if the numbers show conditional cost. Recommend a course of action, based on minimizing expected cost.

5. A company must decide how many dozen sausage sandwiches to order for the concession stand at the baseball game. Each dozen costs $7.60 and sells for $18.00. Any sandwiches left over at the end of the day are of no value. Based on experience over the last several games with similar weather forecast, the probabilities for various number of dozens that will be demanded is estimated to be 0.4 for one dozen, 0.3 for two dozen, 0.2 for three dozen, and 0.1 for four dozen.

a. Construct a payoff table (assuming that sandwiches are bought and sold in batches of a dozen).

b. Using expected monetary profit, recommend a course of action.

c. Find the expected value of perfect information about demand.

6. [*Note:* The use of data table commands to construct a payoff table is described in the forthcoming case study, J.D.'s Decision (B). While this exercise can be assigned without using data tables, they are very helpful.] A news store must decide the order quantity for a "blockbuster" issue in January. The store pays $2.25 for the issue, which it sells for $3.50. Any left overs must be destroyed; it costs nothing to destroy a copy. The probability distribution for the number of copies demanded is shown here:

Number of Copies	Probability	Number of Copies	Probability
10	0.05	45	0.15
20	0.15	50	0.10
30	0.20	55	0.05
40	0.25	60	0.05

a. Assuming that copies are bought and sold in only the quantities shown in the table above, construct a payoff table for this problem.

b. Find the number of copies to purchase to maximize the expected profit.

7. Find the expected value of perfect information for the decision in Exercise 3.

8. Construct a decision tree for Exercise 3. Use the tree to find the best course of action. Explain the results.

9. Find the expected value of perfect information for the decision in Exercise 4.

10. Construct a decision tree for Exercise 4. Use the tree to find the best course of action. Explain the results.

11. Find the expected value of perfect information for the decision in Exercise 6.

12. Recommend a course of action to maximize EMV for the situation represented by the following tree. (Numbers without $ represent probabilities; numbers with $ represent profit.)

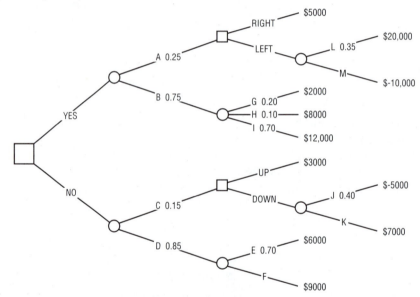

13. Mr. Weber, contracts manager, has just finished a cost and status review of the *Digger* project, a $500,000 cost-plus-fixed-fee government job. Three months remain to complete the final report required by the contract. He has requested an estimate of the cost to complete the final report, and, after several iterations during which the cost estimates are rethought and revised downward from $61,000, he receives what the engineering manager assures him is a "bare bones" estimate of $42,000. This estimate is accompanied by a plan to complete the report in the remaining three months. It makes a convincing package.

At the same time, Mr. Weber has been informed by the accounting department that only $28,000 remains in the contract to complete the effort.

In an effort to understand the problem better, Mr. Weber has called a meeting of Marketing, Engineering, and Estimating to investigate the possible alternatives. Engineering and Estimating have established three possible target costs for the final report: the $42,000 estimated earlier, an estimated $35,000 obtained by deleting those portions of the development that have been discussed in interim reports, and an estimated $28,000, which is unsatisfactory to Engineering and (in their words) based on, "If that's all you've got, that's all you get."

Engineering emphasizes that the $42,000 estimate represents a report the customer will like and accept, which is more than can be said for the other two estimates. Estimating points out that the historical median of the final report costs of this nature is between 10% and 12% of the total effort. Marketing asserts that the customer will insist on a satisfactory report, even if it requires additional funding, although no fee will be paid on any additional funds. Indeed, because some real costs of doing business are not allowed as costs on government contracts, work on overruns without fee not only hurts the firm's reputation but its pocketbook as well.

Engineering, with Marketing's concurrence, states that there is a 90% chance the $42,000 report will be accepted as is; but if it is not, there is an 80% chance that $700 of rework and travel will suffice. The maximum rework will be only $2000, and the customer will be happy in any case.

Engineering is pessimistic about the $35,000 report and feels there is a 70% chance the customer will question the report. If they do, Engineering is 90% sure it will cost $9000 to rework the final report; they believe there is only a 10% chance $2000 will satisfy. In addition, Engineering does not like doing a poor job in the first place. Marketing agrees with the likelihood and the possible rework required but does not feel the firm's reputation will be severely damaged.

All agree the firm's reputation will suffer if the customer does not accept the $28,000 final report. Engineering believes there is a 95% chance rework will be required and further, because the customer will feel insulted, that there is a 90% chance it will cost $25,000 more and only a 10% chance they can get by with as little as $18,000. There is no middle ground, because the estimates are based on excluding certain portions of the $42,000 report.

According to the contract, Mr. Weber must immediately notify the customer of any anticipated overrun. To further complicate matters, Marketing is planning to submit a proposal for additional work in a month. While they do not want to have an overrun against them, they want even less to face the charge of unsatisfactory technical performance on the current job. What should they do to minimize expected cost?*

CASES IN SPREADSHEET MODELING AND DECISION ANALYSIS
J.D.'s Decision (B)

The purpose of this case is to strengthen spreadsheet modeling skills, using the context of decision analysis. Using these skills, the analyst can easily construct and use large payoff tables. The organization of this case is nontraditional. At several points throughout the case, readers are asked to complete parts of the analysis before proceeding. Keystrokes are shown for Lotus 1-2-3 and for Quattro Pro.

After completing the analysis shown in the chapter, J.D. asked an analyst, Adrian Smythe, to pursue the use of spreadsheets to assist in this decision. J.D. wanted

*This exercise was contributed by Professor Donald Yale.

Exhibit 13.1

Incomplete Influence Chart for J.D.'s Decision

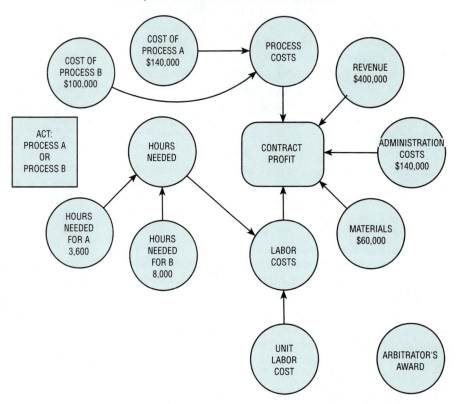

a robust model, to accommodate unknown changes which might come about in the next few weeks. Adrian started by constructing an influence chart showing the factors that influence the contract profit; the factors are revenue, labor cost, process cost, administrative costs, and materials. These are shown in the right side of Exhibit 13.1, connected by arrows.

The influence chart also shows an event, Arbitrator's Award, and an act, Process A or Process B. Several intervening variables are shown to relate these acts and events to contract profit. For convenience, all data values are shown next to the corresponding entries on the influence chart. Obviously, these cells with data values have no influences point to them.

Activity:

a. Draw arrows in the influence chart of Exhibit 13.1 to show the influences in the remaining part of the chart.

Adrian the analyst wanted to construct a model to generate the four situations shown in Figure 13.7 in the chapter. In particular, Adrian thought it would be useful to be able to enter the letter name for the selected process, A or B, into

---

Exhibit 13.2

Spreadsheet Model for J.D.'s Process Selection

	A	B	C
1	Process Selected	A	<== Note: User enters "A or "B here.
2	Arbitrator's Award	$8	<== Note: User enters 8 or 12 here.
3			
4	Revenue	$400,000	Note: Data Value
5	Admin Costs	$140,000	Note: Data Value
6	Materials	$60,000	Note: Data Value
7	Process Cost	$140,000	Note: IF logic, choosing B15 or B16
8	Labor Cost	$28,800	Note: Influenced by B11 and B14
9	Contract Profit	$31,200	Note: Influenced by B4..B8
10			
11	Hours Needed	3,600	Note: IF logic, choosing B12 or B13
12	Hours Needed for A	3,600	Note: Data Value
13	Hours Needed for B	8,000	Note: Data Value
14	Unit Labor Cost	$8	Note: Influenced by user's entry in B2
15	Cost of Process A	$140,000	Note: Data Value
16	Cost of Process B	$100,000	Note: Data Value

---

a spreadsheet cell, and base the calculation of Hours Needed and Process Cost on which letter is in the cell identifying the process selected. Adrian developed the spreadsheet shown in Exhibit 13.2.

In developing this spreadsheet, Adrian used the @IF function to test whether cell B1 contains A or B. The formula in B7 determines the process cost, by detecting which process is selected. Adrian first used this formula:

B7:   @IF(B1="A",B15,B16)

This formula correctly places in B7 the value $140,000 (from B15) if cell B1 contains the string of characters "A". If the test condition is false (cell B1 does not contain the string of characters "A") then B7 has the value of $100,000 (from B16). That formula works well if the user never puts any character other than "A" or "B" in cell B1. But if the user placed "AA" in cell B1, the logic of this model would assume that "*not* A" is the same as "B" and proceed!

Adrian then developed this more sophisticated formula:

B7:   @IF(B1="A",B15,@IF(B1="B",B16,@ERR))

This logic first tests if B1 contains "A"; if it does, it places in B7 the value in B15. Otherwise, it tests if B1 contains "B"; if it does, it places in B7 the value in B16. If both tests are failed, the user has made an error; the spreadsheet will place in B7 the function @ERR, which will indicate an error has been made. Adrian used a similar formula for cell B11.

To make the spreadsheet "look neat" Adrian instructed the user to enter in cell B1 the letter name for the process, preceded by a double quotation mark. Adrian did this to right-justify the letter position in cell B1. From a computational standpoint, it would not matter whether the entry was: "A, 'A, or ^A; these provide for right justification, left justification, or centering. In fact, if the user simply entered A (without a preceding character to indicate position) the

---

Exhibit 13.3

Outline for Data Table Generation of Payoff Table

	A	B	C	D	E	F
1	Process Selected	A				
2	Arbitrator's Award	$8				
3						
4	Revenue	$400,000			Process Selected	
5	Admin Costs	$140,000		31200	A	B
6	Materials	$60,000	Arbitrato	8		
7	Process Cost	$140,000	Award	12		
8	Labor Cost	$28,800				
9	Contract Profit	$31,200				
10						
11	Hours Needed	3,600				
12	Hours Needed for A	3,600				
13	Hours Needed for B	8,000				
14	Unit Labor Cost	$8				
15	Cost of Process A	$140,000				
16	Cost of Process B	$100,000				

---

spreadsheet inserts the left-justify character by default (unless the user has changed the global default values).

Activities:

   b. Construct a spreadsheet model to replicate Exhibit 13.2. Notes adjacent to cells B4..B16 are suggestions to the modeler; they need not be entered into the spreadsheet.

   c. Verify that all four situations in Figure 13.7 of the chapter provide results that agree with your model.

   d. Does it matter whether the user enters upper case or lower case letters?

   e. Does it matter whether the user enters a letter preceded by spaces, or followed by spaces?

   f. What would be the purpose of this formula in cell B14?

   B14:   @IF(B2=8,B2,@IF(B2=12,B2,@ERR))

Adrian realized that with this spreadsheet model of J.D.'s decision, the user enters values into the cells labeled Process Selected and Arbitrator's Award to find the conditional profit values. By entering four sets of values, (A,8; A,12; B,8; B,12) one at a time into the appropriate cells, the four values for conditional profit shown in the payoff table (Figure 13.8) can be obtained.

Adrian wanted to explore the spreadsheet's *data table* (or *what-if*) capability to find a quicker way to obtain the payoff table. Adrian added the structure of a two-way data table to the model; this is shown in Exhibit 13.3, with the data table emphasized in the range D5..F7. All of these elements must be provided before beginning the **Data Table** or **What-If** command:

   The upper left corner of the data table must show the value of conditional profit from the model; the formula in cell D5 is the simple formula

+B9. This means that whatever value is in B9, according to the award of $8 or $12 and the decision of A or B, will be in cell D5. The **Data Table (What-If)** will calculate this value for each act/event combination and place these values in the body of the table.

The next portion is a column, D6..D7, showing the values of the arbitrator's award (8 and 12). The **Data Table (What-If)** command will place these values, one at a time, into cell B2 for computing the contract profit.

The final portion is a row, E5..F5, containing the names of the process selections (A and B). The **Data Table (What-If)** command will place these values, one at a time, into cell B1 for computing the contract profit.

Adrian provided the text "Process Selected" (cell E5) and "Arbitrator's Award" (cells C6..C7) that are for the user; they do not enter into the computations.

Adrian next invoked the command to place the conditional profit values into the payoff table, using the selections **Data Table** for 1-2-3, or **Tools What-If** for Quattro. Adrian next provided this information, when prompted:

This is a "2-way" data table (or "2-variable What-If table"), meaning that we are using both a column of values (the event values) and a row of values (the act values) to form a table of conditional profit values (from the upper left corner of the data table).

The table is located in (D5..F7).

The cell on the spreadsheet into which the values from the left column of the data table are to be inserted is cell B2. Spreadsheets use the word *input*; these values are to be "inputted" or inserted into cell B2, next to the label Arbitrator's Award.

The cell on the spreadsheet into which the values from the top row of the data table are to be inserted is cell B1, next to the label Process Selected.

These instructions cause the spreadsheet to fill in the data table, giving the appearance of Exhibit 13.4. The **Data Table (What-If)** command is a "static" operation; the numbers for conditional profit are values, not formulas; changing any of the data for the model does not update the data table. (The most recent data table operation can be repeated by pressing [F8] with either Lotus 1-2-3 or Quattro Pro.)

Activities:

g. Add to your worksheet the structure shown in the exhibits, and use the commands to replicate Exhibit 13.4.

h. In cells G6..G7 enter the probabilities that are appropriate for the events. Place a label in G4 to indicate these are probability values.

i. In cell E9 enter the formula @SUMPRODUCT(E6..E7,$G$6..$G$7). Verify that this calculates the expected value for selecting Process A.

j. Copy cell E9 to F9. Verify that this calculates the expected value for selecting Process B.

––––––––––––––––––––––––––––– **Exhibit 13.4** –––––––––––––––––––––––––––––

Spreadsheet Model After Data Table

	A	B	C	D	E	F
1	Process Selected	A				
2	Arbitrator's Award	$8				
3						
4	Revenue	$400,000			Process Selected	
5	Admin Costs	$140,000		31200	A	B
6	Materials	$60,000	Arbitrato	8	31200	36000
7	Process Cost	$140,000	Award	12	16800	4000
8	Labor Cost	$28,800				
9	Contract Profit	$31,200				
10						
11	Hours Needed	3,600				
12	Hours Needed for A	3,600				
13	Hours Needed for B	8,000				
14	Unit Labor Cost	$8				
15	Cost of Process A	$140,000				
16	Cost of Process B	$100,000				

k. *Mind Expanding Exercise:* Invent processes C, D, E, F, G, and H, each with its own initial cost and its own hours needed. Put these into a table on the spreadsheet, and use @VLOOKUP functions for cells B11 and B7 to obtain the values for computation in the spreadsheet. This organization can be used to establish a very large payoff table with a very small model!

A Case Using a Decision Tree and a Spreadsheet: YumYum Corporation*

The YumYum Corporation makes nutritious candy bars. Next month (January) the company plans to sell nearly 200,000 pounds of candy (although they don't call it candy because they extol its nutritional value), which will be packaged as 600,000 bars; the price YumYum will receive is 18 cents ($0.18) for each bar. Production capacity for the plant is 640,000 bars per month. The cost estimates for next month are:

Fixed Costs (do not vary with number of bars made)

Fixed manufacturing costs (factory overhead)	$ 7,500
Fixed administrative costs (office overhead)	11,500
Advertising	4,500
Interest	4,100

Variable Costs (each of these is a "per bar" cost)

Labor	4 cents per bar
Materials	8 cents per bar

The planning horizon for YumYum is the next five months, January thru May. For January, the price will be $0.18 per bar; after that, the price will increase

*This example is adapted from Donald R. Plane, *Quantitative Tools for Decision Support Using IFPS* (Reading, MA: Addison-Wesley Publishing Company, 1986), pp. 32–36.

to $0.19 for two months, and then to $0.20 for two months. The number of bars made and sold is projected to begin at 600,000 bars, and then increase 2.5% each month until the capacity of 640,000 bars is reached. Because of the rapid growth, substantial increases in other costs are projected as follows:

Fixed manufacturing costs (factory overhead)	increase 5% per month
Fixed administrative costs (office overhead)	increase 7% per month
Advertising	increase 8% per month
Interest	will not change
Labor	increase 10% per month
Materials	increase 0.1 cents ($0.001) per bar each month

The GM is considering augmenting the advertising with a marketing campaign designed to increase volume. This additional advertising would cost $7500 in January and $1500 in each of the remaining four months of the planning horizon. These campaign costs are in addition to the advertising costs already discussed. Once started, the marketing campaign must continue. The thrust of the campaign is to enhance the quantity of bars sold at the prices projected above. The GM believes that the campaign will either be a flop (leaving the quantity sold as projected), be moderately successful (bringing about an 8% monthly increase in quantity sold, instead of 2.5%), or be very successful (bringing about a 15% monthly increase in quantity sold, instead of 2.5%). A decision to begin the campaign must be made within a day or two.

The campaign may not be a very good idea if the capacity limits (640,000 bars per month) are reached. Negotiations have taken place to obtain expanded facilities at the end of the first month, when it will be known if the advertising campaign is a flop, is moderately successful, or is very successful. The facilities expansion will cost $500 a month for the remaining four months, to increase capacity to 750,000 bars a month. Increasing the capacity to 1,000,000 bars a month would cost $1000 a month for the remaining four months. The capacity decision is made at the beginning of the second month; once made, it cannot be changed.

The probabilities of success for the campaign are flop, 0.1; moderate, 0.5; very successful, 0.4.

Where to Begin?

What is the GM's primary issue at this point? The first decision that must be made is whether to undertake the campaign. There is a secondary issue facing the GM: whether to expand the capacity of the factory. While it is known that there is enough capacity for January (planned production: 600,000 bars; capacity: 640,000 bars), it may be advantageous to obtain more capacity. If the campaign is started, the decision to obtain more capacity can be made after the first month's results are known. The GM believes that the growth rate in the first month will continue throughout the planning horizon. Oh, how wordy that has become! The purpose of the wordiness is to demonstrate vividly the ability of a decision

---
Exhibit 13.5

Decision Tree for YumYum's Campaign and Capacity Decisions

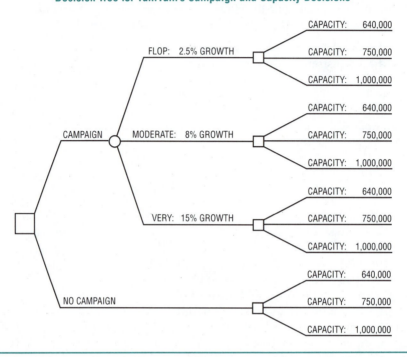

tree to communicate the sequence of acts and events. The structure of the decision tree for GM is shown in Exhibit 13.5.

The decision tree is not complete; it lacks probability values and terminal values for the Profit Before Taxes for YumYum Corporation. The scenario has provided the probability values, so they present no difficulty. The terminal values for profit will require substantial computation, however. A spreadsheet model is a useful way to calculate these terminal values. The model should calculate the profit before tax for any combination of campaign decision, campaign event (bar growth rate), and capacity decision. Rather than attempt to develop one model to simultaneously evaluate all end points, our approach will be to build one model that can be used to evaluate each end point by changing the values in a few cells.

A good place to start constructing the model is with an influence chart. The beginning of the influence chart is shown in Exhibit 13.6. This chart diagram begins with the "bottom line" or PROFIT BEFORE TAX, which is influenced by REVENUE, FIXED COSTS, and TOTAL VARIABLE COSTS. The decision nodes from the decision tree are shown at the bottom of the influence chart: CAPACITY and CAMPAIGN. The CAPACITY decision influences the NUMBER OF BARS, which in turn influences both REVENUE and TOTAL VARIABLE COST. The CAMPAIGN influences the CAMPAIGN COST. There is also a relationship (shown with a broken line on the influence chart) between the CAMPAIGN decision and the BAR GROWTH. This is shown as a broken line because the influence,

---

Exhibit 13.6

Influence Chart for YumYum (Incomplete)

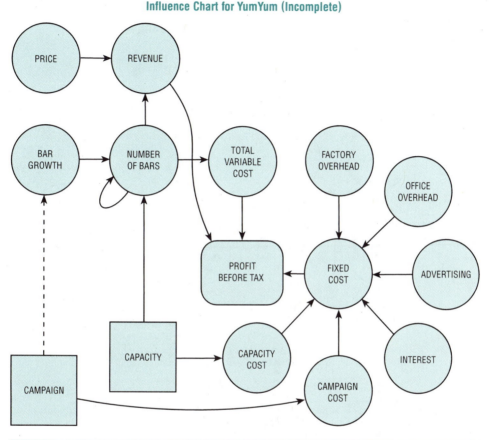

---

although real, does not exist formally in the model we will construct. Rather, the user of the model will vary the BAR GROWTH rate only in the part of the tree in which the CAMPAIGN has been undertaken.

Activities:

k. Additional items are included in the influence chart of Exhibit 13.7; these are not connected with arrows. Complete the influence chart to show how the "already connected" items are influenced by those we have just added. Note that several variables, such as UNIT LABOR COST and UNIT MATERIAL COST, have "loops" showing that a variable influences itself. This is artistic license indicating that the current value of that variable is affected by its previous value (as well as by other items).

l. Discuss other artistic license you may have taken in completing the influence chart. For example, we show that UNIT LABOR COST is influenced by its previous value. While this is true for February, is it also true for January?

Exhibit 13.7

Completed (but Unconnected) Influence Chart for YumYum

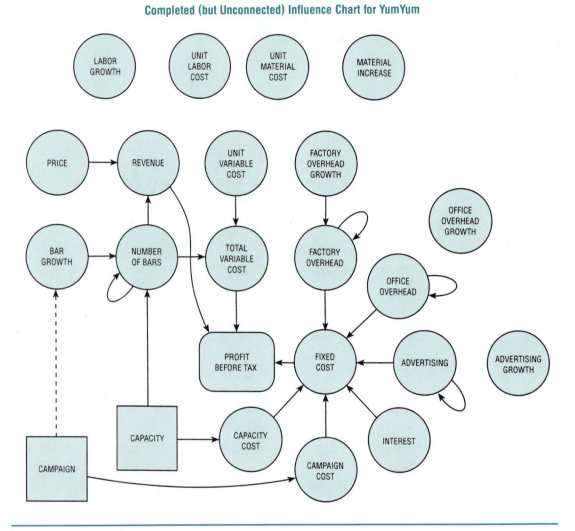

From the influence chart, the model of Exhibit 13.8 is constructed. This model is used to find the terminal values for the decision tree. To find the terminal value for the uppermost end point of the tree, the user of the model enters these values:

Campaign	Yes
Bar Growth	2.5%
Capacity	640000

--- **Exhibit 13.8** ---

Spreadsheet Model for YumYum's Decision Tree

	A	B	C	D	E	F	G
1		Jan	Feb	Mar	Apr	May	Total
2	Revenue	$108,000	$116,850	$119,771	$128,000	$128,000	
3	Price	$0.18	$0.19	$0.19	$0.20	$0.20	
4	Number of Bars	600,000	615,000	630,375	640,000	640,000	
5							
6	Profit B4 Tax	$900	$9,335	$5,286	$6,768	$846	$23,135
7							
8	Fixed Costs	$35,100	$30,640	$32,284	$34,039	$35,913	
9	Factory Ovhd	$7,500	$7,875	$8,269	$8,682	$9,116	
10	Office Ovhd	$11,500	$12,305	$13,166	$14,088	$15,074	
11	Advertising	$4,500	$4,860	$5,249	$5,669	$6,122	
12	Interest	$4,100	$4,100	$4,100	$4,100	$4,100	
13							
14	Campaign Cost	$7,500	$1,500	$1,500	$1,500	$1,500	
15	Capacity Cost	$0	$0	$0	$0	$0	
16							
17	Tot Vrbl Cost	$72,000	$76,875	$82,201	$87,194	$91,241	
18							
19	Unit Vrbl Cost	$0.1200	$0.1250	$0.1304	$0.1362	$0.1426	
20	Unit Lab Cost	$0.0400	$0.0440	$0.0484	$0.0532	$0.0586	
21	Unit Matl Cost	$0.0800	$0.0810	$0.0820	$0.0830	$0.0840	
22							
23	Bar Growth	2.50%	<==The user enters the appropriate growth here.				
24	Fact OH Growth	5.00%					
25	Ofc OH Growth	7.00%					
26	Advert Growth	8.00%					
27	Labor Growth	10.00%					
28	Matl Increase	$0.001					
29	Capacity	640,000	<==The user enters the appropriate capacity here.				
30	Campaign	Yes	<==The user enters 'Yes or No' here.				

Activities:

m. Construct the spreadsheet model shown in Exhibit 13.8.

n. Use the model to find all terminal values in the decision tree, Exhibit 13.5.

o. Complete the decision tree by placing probabilities on appropriate branches.

p. Use the tree to recommend a course of action.

14

The Monte Carlo Method: Incorporating Uncertainty into a Spreadsheet

The Monte Carlo method is a tool to help managers understand the uncertainty involved in a decision. Unlike decision analysis (which was *prescriptive*) the Monte Carlo method is *descriptive*. It helps a manager understand the uncertainty in a strategy when many sources of uncertainty are considered simultaneously.

The Monte Carlo method allows a spreadsheet modeler to define a spreadsheet cell as a random variable, or chance quantity. This random variable is based on the manager's assessment of the uncertainty in that value. Unlike the methods of decision analysis in Chapter 13, the Monte Carlo method allows the user to introduce uncertainty into a large number of variables.* Each uncertainty is introduced into a spreadsheet cell; each time the spreadsheet is recalculated, each of these chance quantities takes on a different value, according to the uncertainty specified by the modeler. With the Monte Carlo method, the spreadsheet is recalculated a large number of times, and records are kept of the "bottom line" values for each of these replications or recalculations. This permits the modeler to see how the specified uncertainty in the input variables extends into uncertainty in the output variables.

Generating Random Numbers on a Spreadsheet

Spreadsheets are able to generate *random numbers*. The value of a spreadsheet cell defined with the formula

@RAND

---

*Decision Analysis techniques more advanced that those introduced in this text can be used to extend the framework of decision analysis to problems with large numbers of uncertainties.

is equally likely to be any value between 0 and 1. Recalculating the spreadsheet (press the [F9] key) will change the value of the cell to some other randomly-selected value between 0 and 1. This capability provides the basis for the Monte Carlo method of introducing uncertainty into a spreadsheet.

As a very simple illustration of the use of @RAND on a spreadsheet, let's use the Monte Carlo method to simulate flipping a coin. Here's the logic we need:

> Draw a random number between 0 and 1 using @RAND; random numbers less than 0.5 are assigned to heads; other random numbers are assigned to tails.

This simulates a fair coin, because half of the random numbers are less than 0.5, and half of the random numbers aren't less than 0.5. The spreadsheet formula to display a label (showing either heads or tails) is:

$$@IF(@RAND<0.5,"Heads","Tails")$$

If you wanted to flip a coin one time and didn't have a coin handy, the statement above would take its place. If you wanted to do multiple flips (three out of five, for example), a simple way would be to recalculate the spreadsheet ([F9] key) once for each additional simulated flip of the coin. This process of generating random numbers on a spreadsheet to simulate some real-world system or phenomenon is called *Monte Carlo simulation*.

Using Data Tables (What-If) to Keep Track of Monte Carlo Replications

The process of recalculation for multiple flips is manageable for a small number of flips, but keeping track of a hundred flips would be tiresome. **Data Tables** (Lotus 1-2-3) or **What-If** (Quattro Pro)* provide a powerful way to perform multiple flips and keep track of the results at the same time. While flipping coins is more a teaching exercise than a meaningful managerial exercise, it does provide a simple way to understand a process that is useful in supporting managerial decisions. We'll illustrate the use of a data table to keep track of the results of ten flips of a fair coin. The following steps illustrate the process:

1. Starting in cell A2, enter a column of numbers from 1 to 10. This may be done by entering the numbers individually, or with a **Data Fill** (Lotus 1-2-3) or **Edit Fill** (Quattro Pro) in cells A2 through A11. The **Fill** starts with 1, steps 1, and stops at 10.

2. In cell B1, enter the formula @IF(@RAND<0.5,"Heads","Tails")

3. Create a data table, 1-way (/**DT1** for **Data Table 1**in Lotus 1-2-3, or /**TW1** for **Tools What-If 1-Variable** in Quattro Pro) and identify the range of the table as A1..B11. Completing this command will produce a table that shows the different values of the formula entered in cell B1. (If you have used

---

*The data tables in this chapter are "one-way" data tables. While they share some characteristics with the two-way tables used in Decision Analysis for constructing payoff tables, there are important differences in their construction. This chapter uses data tables in a non-traditional manner; it may require some rethinking by those familiar with traditional uses of data tables.

Figure 14.1

Spreadsheet Using Data Table for Monte Carlo Simulation

	A	B		A	B
1		@IF(@RAND<0.5,"Heads","Tails")	1		Tails
2	1		2	1	Heads
3	2		3	2	Tails
4	3		4	3	Heads
5	4		5	4	Heads
6	5		6	5	Tails
7	6		7	6	Heads
8	7		8	7	Tails
9	8		9	8	Tails
10	9		10	9	Heads
11	10		11	10	Heads

/DT1 or **/TW1** in other applications, you know that the numbers in the left column would be used in evaluating the formula in B1. However, our use of data (what-if) tables doesn't really make use of these numbers because the variation comes from the random number in the formula.)

4. When the spreadsheet asks you for the cell address of Input 1, give the address of any blank cell on the spreadsheet.

5. As soon as you have given the address of Input 1 (which really isn't used in this application), the spreadsheet will place the words Heads or Tails in cells B2 through B11. These ten cells simulate ten flips of a fair coin.

Figure 14.1 shows two steps in the preparation of this spreadsheet. At the left is the data table structure that must exist *before* issuing the **Table** command. Note that the **Text** format is used for cell B1, to show the formula that has been entered in that cell. At the right is the data table as it might appear after the table command. (The format for B1 is reset to its default general display). *The nature of Monte Carlo simulation is such that readers who are keying this into a spreadsheet will have different lists of Heads and Tails, because we have purposely interjected uncertainty using the @RAND function.*

If you wanted to simulate a thousand flips of the coin, you would extend the range of the data table so that there are a thousand rows in the body of the data table (plus row 1, which is the header row showing the formula to be repeatedly evaluated). Once these results have been obtained, you can count them, sort them, or use them with any appropriate spreadsheet operation.

Applying Monte Carlo Simulation to J.D.'s Problem

Now that the techniques have been described, let's use the information to address J.D.'s problem from the previous chapter, which is repeated here for convenience:

> J.D. is the owner of a specialty manufacturing and marketing organization. On June 1, J.D. signed a contract to deliver merchandise to be sold for $400,000. The administrative costs and factory overhead asso-

─────────────────── **Figure 14.2** ───────────────────

Spreadsheet and Documentation for J.D.'s Decision

```
           A              B
 1  Process Selected        A      <===Note:  User enters "A or "B here.
 2  Arbitrator's Award      $8      <===Note:  User enters 8 or 12 here.
 3
 4  Revenue           $400,000      Data
 5  Admin Costs       $140,000      Data
 6  Materials          $60,000      Data
 7  Process Cost      $140,000      @IF(B1="A",B15,@IF(B1="B",B16,@ERR))
 8  Labor Cost         $28,800      +B11*B14
 9  Contract Profit    $31,200      +B4-B5-B6-B7-B8
10
11  Hours Needed         3,600      @IF(B1="A",B12,@IF(B1="B",B13,@ERR))
12  Hours Needed for A   3,600      Data
13  Hours Needed for B   8,000      Data
14  Unit Labor Cost         $8      @IF(B2=8,B2,@IF(B2=12,B2,@ERR))
15  Cost of Process A $140,000      Data
16  Cost of Process B $100,000      Data
```

ciated with the contract are estimated to be $140,000; the materials will cost $60,000. Labor cost is the major uncertainty remaining for J.D.

J.D. is in the midst of a labor dispute about the classification of workers who will be involved in making the merchandise. There has been no agreement between J.D. and the workers' union; an arbitrator will decide the cost of labor. The form of arbitration used by Major League Baseball has been agreed to by the parties: either the Union's position will prevail, with an award resulting in a labor cost of $12.00 per hour; or J.D.'s position will prevail, resulting in a labor cost of $8.00 per hour. The arbitrator will report a decision on August 15; the manufacturing must begin on September 1 to meet the terms of the contract.

There are two production alternatives for J.D. The merchandise can be produced using Process A, which is capital-intensive, or process B, which is labor-intensive. Process A will require 3600 labor hours. The cost of arranging the factory and obtaining the special-purpose equipment for this process will be $140,000. The alternative Process B requires an expenditure of $100,000 for a less costly factory arrangement and more general-purpose equipment. However, Process B requires 8000 hours of labor. In order to be ready to manufacture on September 1, J.D. must begin the process of setting up the factory and ordering equipment by July 1.

It was apparent to J.D. that the desirability of Process A and Process B is influenced by the arbitrator's award. Unfortunately, J.D. must make a decision before the occurrence of the uncertain event, the arbitrator's award.

J.D. had a "good feeling" about the upcoming award, but wasn't completely confident of a victory. After some consideration, J.D. decided that the probability the arbitrator would make an award resulting in an

---
Figure 14.3

Continuation of Spreadsheet in Figure 14.2: Data Table for J.D.'s Model Using Process A

	A	B	
20			
21		+B9	Note: This data table used this
22	1	$31,200	formula for the award, cell B2:
23	2	$31,200	
24	3	$16,800	B2: @IF(@RAND<0.7,8,12)
25	4	$31,200	
	.		
	.		
	.		
71	50	$16,800	
72 Average		$27,456	@AVG(B22..B71)

$8.00 hourly labor cost was 0.7; this meant that the probability of a $12.00 hourly labor cost was 0.3.

Figure 14.2 shows the spreadsheet and the model that were developed as Exhibit 14.2 in the cases at the conclusion of the previous chapter. This model evaluates the economic consequences for any decision (which process?) and any event (what award from the arbitrator?). Note that notations have been added, showing the spreadsheet formulas adjacent to column B.

To simulate the arbitrator's award, with probability ($8) = 0.7, we can change cell B2, the value of the arbitrator's award, to this formula:

B2: @IF(@RAND<0.7,8,12)

This formula will give the cell the value 8 with probability 0.7, and the value 12 with probability 0.3. By using a data table (what-if), we can recalculate the spreadsheet and keep track of the results, as we did for the coin flip. The top row of the data table should have a cell (B21, Figure 14.3) whose value is equal to the Contract Profit from the spreadsheet. Each value in column B of the data table is either $31,200 or $16,800. If the average of all of the values for contract profit is found, it will be "close" to the expected value, $26,880. The average tends to get closer to the expected value as the number of replications (data table rows) gets larger. In this simple illustration, we have used Monte Carlo simulation to find an empirical estimate of the expected value of using Process A. In later simulations, we will use Monte Carlo simulation to estimate the expected value when it is impossible to calculate it using straightforward methods.

The process just above could be repeated after changing cell B1 so that the process selected is B. Repeating the data table would give a list of the simulated outcomes; the average of the values for contract profit should be close to the expected value, $26,880 for Process A and $26,400 for Process B.

Expanding J.D.'s Scenario

We have just introduced the Monte Carlo method for J.D.'s scenario, but we really accomplished nothing more than computing the expected value empirically, using the @AVG function for the list of simulated outcomes. The empirical computation is obviously not as good as the actual computation, because it is subject to experimental or sampling error. But for many situations it may be difficult for managers to calculate an expected value for a more complex situation. Suppose we change the scenario slightly, for Process A, in this way:

Change 1: The arbitrator is equally likely to select any wage rate value between $8 and $12. This means that $8.39 is as likely as $11.25, and so on.

Change 2: There is a new source of uncertainty: The hours required using Process A can be any value between 2600 hours and 4600 hours; any value is equally likely within this range.

Change 3: There is another new source of uncertainty: The cost of Process A can be any value between $100,000 and $180,000; any value is equally likely within this range.

A mathematician might be comfortable calculating the expected value for the contract profit under these conditions, but most managers are not equipped for this task. Instead, the manager is able to estimate the expected value empirically, using the Monte Carlo method.

How do we utilize @RAND to generate a value for the arbitrator's award, which is equally likely to be any value between $8 and $12? Consider this formula:

B2:   8+4*@RAND

If the value of @RAND is 0 (its lowest possible value), then the value of the formula is 8. If the value of @RAND is 1 (its highest possible value), then the value of the formula is 8 + 4 = 12. Because @RAND is equally likely to be any value between 0 and 1, the value of the formula is equally likely to be any value between 8 and 12. This is precisely the behavior we want for the cell containing the value of the arbitrator's award.

Using similar logic, the number of hours required for Process A can be described using the formula:

B12:   2600+2000*@RAND

The cost of Process A can be described using the formula:

B15:   100000+80000*@RAND

The Monte Carlo method can be used to determine empirically the expected value of profit under these new conditions. Each of these three formulas is inserted into the appropriate cell of the spreadsheet; a data table is used to develop a simulated list of profit values; the average of these profit values is an estimate of the expected value of profit. A spreadsheet showing this expanded model, a shortened version of the data results, and documentation for the model is shown in Figure 14.4.

The average Contract Profit, based on this simulation of 100 replications of the spreadsheet, is $24,304. This value is the empirical estimate of the expected

---

Figure 14.4

Model and Documentation for J.D. with Additional Uncertainty

	A	B	
1	Process Selected	A	Input
2	Arbitrator's Award	$11.21	8+4*@RAND
3			
4	Revenue	$400,000	Data
5	Admin Costs	$140,000	Data
6	Materials	$60,000	Data
7	Process Cost	$170,455	@IF(B1="A",B15,@IF(B1="B",B16,@ERR))
8	Labor Cost	$49,804	+B11*B14
9	Contract Profit	($20,259)	+B4ˇ2DB5ˇ2DB6ˇ2DB7ˇ2DB8
10			
11	Hours Needed	4,441	@IF(B1="A",B12,@IF(B1="B",B13,@ERR))
12	Hours Needed for A	4,441	2600+2000*@RAND
13	Hours Needed for B	8,000	Data
14	Unit Labor Cost	$11.21	+B2
15	Cost of Process A	$170,455	100000+80000*@RAND
16	Cost of Process B	$100,000	Data
17			
18	Average	$24,304	@AVG(B22..B121)
19	Std Dev	$23,698	@STD(B22..B121)
20			
21		+B9	This formula is displayed in Text format
22	1	($753)	
23	2	$55,430	
24	3	($7,095)	
25	4	$27,314	
26	5	$38,726	
27	6	$19,687	
28	7	($23,899)	
29	8	$43,141	
30	9	$32,594	
.	.	.	
118	97	$56,692	
119	98	$55,724	
120	99	$17,892	
121	100	$46,933	

---

value of contract profit. Like any estimate based on a sample, there is sampling error in this estimate; this sampling error could be made as small as we like by making the number of replications larger and larger. Procedures from statistical inference can be used to assess the magnitude of sampling error, either with confidence intervals or hypothesis testing.

Using the Results of J.D.'s Simulation: The Cumulative Frequency Distribution

Situations often arise in which the decision maker is interested in more than the expected value associated with a decision. In the previous chapter, we discussed the idea that expected value is primarily useful when the economic consequences of a decision are small, so the long-run viability of the organization is not affected by the results of one situation.

When the stakes are larger, the decision maker may be interested in questions such as these:

1. What's the most we could make by selecting Process A?

2. What's the most we could lose by selecting Process A?

3. What are the chances we'll make at least $10,000 by selecting Process A?

4. What are the chances we'll break even (zero profit or better) by selecting Process A?

5. What are the chances we won't lose more than $5000 by selecting Process A?

Questions 1 and 2 would be very easy to answer using the spreadsheets we have developed. The decision maker could simply enter the "best case" values ($8 arbitration award, 2600 hours, $100,000 cost) into the model, and the profit would be calculated for the best case. The "worst case" values ($12, 4600, $180,000) would provide an answer to question 2. But neither of these questions may be the questions the decision maker should be asking; it may be more appropriate to ask "What's the most I could reasonably expect to make?" or "What's the most I could reasonably expect to lose?" and then define *reasonably* with a probability value. The Monte Carlo method is required to answer any of these new questions.

The questions we posed above can be addressed by constructing a cumulative frequency distribution for the results in the data table of Figure 14.4. Sorting the column of results, cells B22..B121, into ascending order* shows the number of replications resulting in a particular profit value, or less, as shown in Figure 14.5, which is displayed in three columns to save space.

Based on these one hundred replications, we have learned this information about J.D.'s uncertainty:

1. What's the most we could make by selecting Process A? Only twice in one hundred replications would J.D. make more than $68,000. We could estimate that there is only about a 2% chance of making more than $68,000.

2. What's the most we could lose by selecting Process A? Only twice in one hundred replications would J.D. lose more than $19,000. We could estimate that there is only about a 2% chance of losing more than $19,000.

3. What are the chances we'll make at least $10,000 by selecting Process A? In the one hundred replications, there are 69 (100 − 31) occurrences of profit of $10,000 or more. We could estimate that there is a 69% chance of making more than $10,000.

4. What are the chances we'll break even (zero profit or better) by selecting Process A? Of the one hundred replications, 17 had profit less than

---

*The Lotus 1-2-3 sort commands are /**Data Sort**, then identifying the range as B22..B121, specifying the primary key any cell in column B within the sort range, selecting **Ascending**, and then **Go**. The Quattro Pro sort commands are /**Database Sort**, then identifying the block as B22..B121, specifying the first key any cell in column B within the sort range, selecting **A** for ascending, and then **Go**.

Figure 14.5

Sorted Monte Carlo Replications for J.D.'s Problem

1	($23,899)	21	$2,944	41	$16,820	61	$28,276	81	$47,148
2	($19,183)	22	$3,886	42	$17,523	62	$32,594	82	$53,130
3	($18,757)	23	$4,577	43	$17,892	63	$33,042	83	$53,893
4	($15,741)	24	$4,783	44	$18,226	64	$34,444	84	$54,039
5	($13,806)	25	$5,887	45	$19,102	65	$35,599	85	$55,302
6	($12,120)	26	$6,464	46	$19,458	66	$35,917	86	$55,430
7	($9,005)	27	$6,978	47	$19,687	67	$37,638	87	$55,640
8	($8,699)	28	$7,249	48	$20,002	68	$38,587	88	$55,724
9	($8,333)	29	$8,282	49	$20,952	69	$38,726	89	$56,541
10	($7,283)	30	$8,362	50	$21,037	70	$38,822	90	$56,692
11	($7,095)	31	$9,331	51	$21,164	71	$38,915	91	$56,890
12	($6,679)	32	$10,186	52	$21,715	72	$41,960	92	$57,230
13	($4,540)	33	$10,464	53	$23,108	73	$43,141	93	$58,941
14	($4,180)	34	$13,463	54	$24,203	74	$43,986	94	$59,102
15	($3,373)	35	$13,595	55	$24,236	75	$44,836	95	$60,565
16	($2,918)	36	$14,027	56	$25,383	76	$45,104	96	$63,626
17	($753)	37	$14,398	57	$25,536	77	$45,135	97	$64,359
18	$31	38	$15,504	58	$25,941	78	$45,394	98	$66,711
19	$1,867	39	$15,630	59	$27,314	79	$46,032	99	$68,356
20	$2,060	40	$16,609	60	$27,920	80	$46,933	100	$68,550

---

zero, while 83 had profit greater than zero. We could estimate that there is a probability of 83% of at least breaking even.

5. What are the chances we won't lose more than $5000 by selecting Process A? Based on the one hundred replications, we could estimate that there is a probability of 12% of losing more than $5000, or an 88% chance that we won't lose more than $5000.

We could sharpen these estimates as much as desirable by using more replications; statistical inference can be used to assess the magnitude of the sampling error for any number of replications.

Spreadsheet Tip: The data table operation is slowed substantially by @AVG and @STD formulas referring to the data table output in the worksheet. When you are performing a Monte Carlo data table, computation time is better, perhaps by a factor of five on some spreadsheets, by removing the @AVG and @STD formulas that calculate results from the data table. Entering these formulas at the completion of the data table takes very little time, and saves a considerable amount of waiting. Users of Quattro Pro may find that computation time is improved by using QP without What's *Best!* attached (DOS command **Q** instead of **WBQ**).

More Uncertainty for J.D.

Continuing with J.D.'s analysis of the process selection problem, consider these changes in the characteristics of Process B:

------------------------------ **Figure 14.6** ------------------------------

Cumulative Frequency Distributions for Processes A and B

J.D.'s Problem: Cumulative Probabilities for Process A and Process B

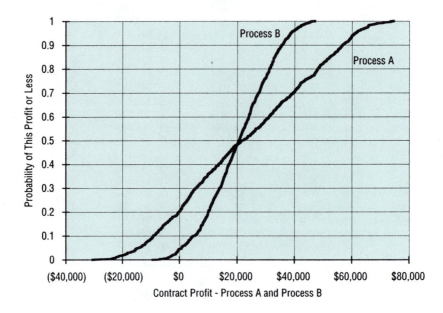

Change 4: There is a new source of uncertainty: The hours required using Process B can be any value between 7500 hours and 8500 hours; any value is equally likely within this range.

Change 5: There is another new source of uncertainty: The cost of Process B can be any value between $90,000 and $110,000; any value is equally likely within this range.

These changes can be incorporated into the model with these formulas:

B13:   7500+1000*@RAND   for the number of hours for Process B

B16:   90000+20000*@RAND   for the cost of Process B

After these changes, data tables have been constructed for the Contract Profit for Process A and for Process B, with one thousand replications for each. Rather than displaying the cumulative frequency distribution in tabular form (as in Figure 14.5), cumulative frequency distribution graphs have been prepared and combined into Figure 14.6, which is based on 1000 replications. Some spreadsheet details used to construct Figure 14.6 are explained in Figure 14.7 for Lotus 1-2-3, Figure 14.8 for Quattro Pro.

To verify your understanding of the cumulative probability distribution, consider these statements, and find the point on Figure 14.6 that verifies each of these statements:

Figure 14.7

Details for Graphing Cumulative Frequency Distributions (Lotus 1-2-3)

Starting with the spreadsheet shown in Figure 14.4, the first step is to make the necessary changes in cells B13 and B16, as described in the body of the text. Leave the label "A in cell B1. Then use the /**Data Fill** command to place the values of cumulative probability in cells A22..A1021, starting with 0.001, stepping by 0.001, and stopping at 1.000. Then perform the Monte Carlo simulation, using the data table methodology described in the chapter. The **Data Table** range is identified as A21..B1021.

Next, change B1 to "B, to simulate the randomness in Contract Profit when Process B is selected. To avoid disturbing the results of Process A, place the formula +B9 in cell B1023. Then use the fill command to place the values of cumulative probability in cells A1024..A2023. Then perform the Monte Carlo simulation, commanding the **Data Table** identifying A1023...B2023 as the range for the data table.

Next, sort B22..B1021 into ascending order; sort B1024..B2023 into ascending order. Erase the contents of cell B1023 (/**Range Erase**), because this cell will be part of a data range for the graph. The lower part of the spreadsheet now has this appearance:

	A	B
22	0.001	($30,602)
23	0.002	($29,440)
24	0.003	($25,570)
	.	.
	.	.
	.	.
1019	0.998	$73,501
1020	0.999	$73,637
1021	1.000	$74,582
1022		
1023		
1024	0.001	($9,476)
1025	0.002	($6,971)
1026	0.003	($6,912)
	.	.
	.	.
	.	.
2021	0.998	$45,528
2022	0.999	$45,923
2023	1.000	$47,046

Note: This section is for Process A

Note: It is important to have at least one blank row here.
Note: This section is for Process B

To construct the graph, the A range is the first column, A22..A2023; the X range is the second column, B22..B2023. The blank cells (between the largest profit for Process A and the smallest profit for Process B) cause the graph to be plotted as two unconnected lines. The labels "Process A" and "Process B" were inserted into the graph using the **Data Labels** option. The data labels for the first series might be placed in C22..C2023; the label, 'Process A, might appear in cell C660; the label, 'Process B, might appear in cell C1250.

---

a. With Process A, the probability that profit is negative (i.e., the probability that there is a loss) is approximately 0.20.

b. With Process B, the probability that profit is negative is approximately 0.04.

c. With Process A, there is a 90% chance that profit is less than (about) $56,000.

─────────────────────────── **Figure 14.8** ───────────────────────────

Details for Graphing Cumulative Frequency Distributions (Quattro Pro)

Starting with the spreadsheet shown in Figure 14.4, the first step is to make the necessary changes in cells B13 and B16, as described in the body of the text. Leave the label "A in cell B1. Then use the /**Edit Fill** command to place the values of cumulative probability in cells A22..A1021, starting with 0.001, stepping by 0.001, and stopping at 1.000. Then perform the Monte Carlo simulation, using the What-If table methodology described in the chapter. The What-If table block is identified as A21..B1021.

Next, change B1 to "B, to simulate the randomness in Contract Profit when Process B is selected. To avoid disturbing the results of Process A, place the formula +B9 in cell B1023. Then use the /**Edit Fill** to place the values of cumulative probability in cells A1024..A2023. Then perform the Monte Carlo simulation, commanding the **Tools What-If** identifying A1023..B2023 as the block for the table.

Next, sort B22..B1021 into ascending order; sort B1024..B2023 into ascending order. Erase the contents of cell B1023 ([Delete]) because this cell will be part of a data range for the graph. The lower part of the spreadsheet now has this appearance:

	A	B	
22	0.001	($30,602)	Note: This section is for Process A
23	0.002	($29,440)	
24	0.003	($25,570)	
	.	.	
	.	.	
	.	.	
1019	0.998	$73,501	
1020	0.999	$73,637	
1021	1.000	$74,582	
1022			Note: It is important to have at
1023			least one blank row here.
1024	0.001	($9,476)	Note: This section is for Process B
1025	0.002	($6,971)	
1026	0.003	($6,912)	
	.	.	
	.	.	
	.	.	
2021	0.998	$45,528	
2022	0.999	$45,923	
2023	1.000	$47,046	

To construct the graph, the first series is the first column, A22..A2023; the X-axis series is the second column, B22..B2023. The blank cells (between the largest profit for Process A and the smallest profit for Process B) cause the graph to be plotted as two unconnected lines. The labels "Process A" and "Process B" were inserted into the graph as interior labels, using the **Customize Interior** labels block option. The labels for the first series might be placed in C22..C2023; the label, 'Process A, might appear in cell C660; the label, 'Process B, might appear in cell C1250.

───

d. With Process B, there is a 30% chance that profit is greater than (about) $27,000.

From this graph, J.D. can observe that there is more variability in outcome for Process A than for Process B. J.D. might conclude that "there is more risk in Process A than in Process B." If this is viewed as a strategic decision, the amount of risk might be important to J.D. On the other hand, if J.D. wanted to base the decision on expected monetary value, the average profit (of the one thousand replications)

Figure 14.9

Shapes of Four Probability Distributions

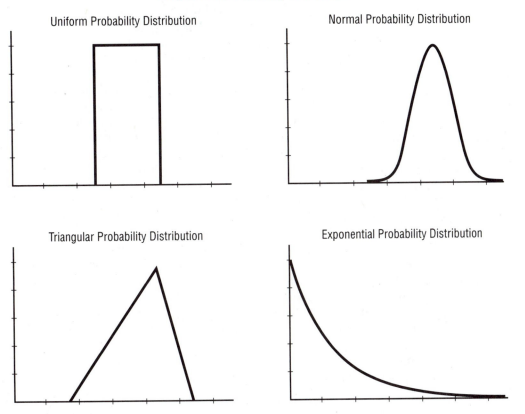

for each process would be used to estimate EMV. The average profit for Process A is $23,032; for Process B, the average profit is $20,517. Although J.D. would prefer Process A based on expected value, other considerations, which can be explored from information in Figure 14.6, may cause J.D. to choose Process B.

Generating Other Probability Distributions for Monte Carlo Analysis

All of the uncertainties used up to now have been based on the uniform probability distribution: The value of the random variable is equally likely to be any value within the specified range, such as between $8 and $12 for the arbitrator's award. Clearly, not all descriptions of uncertainty fit this uniform distribution. This section presents spreadsheet functions and formulas that can be used to generate the following distributions: normal distribution, triangular distribution, exponential distribution, and point (multinomial) distributions. Figure 14.9 shows the shapes of the uniform, normal, triangular, and exponential distributions.

The Normal Distribution

A normal distribution is a common tool of statistical analysis; it is often referred to as a "bell-shaped curve." The normal distribution has only one peak (the statistical term is unimodal); it is symmetrical (just as likely to be a given amount above the mode as that same amount below the mode). In order to use the normal distribution, its mean value (or its mode) must be specified. Increasing the mean shifts the distribution to the right (larger values of the random variable); reducing the mean shifts the distribution to the left. The standard deviation must also be specified to use a normal distribution. The standard deviation measures the dispersion or "scatter" of the values from the mean. A large standard deviation depicts a set of values that are "widely scattered" from the mean; a smaller standard deviation depicts values that are not as far away from the mean. A useful rule of thumb for the normal distribution is that about two-thirds of the values fall within one standard deviation on either side of the mean, while about 95% of the values fall within two standard deviations on either side of the mean. Virtually all of the values fall within three standard deviations on either side of the mean.

The supplement to this chapter describes special @ functions for Lotus 1-2-3 and for Quattro Pro for DOS Version 4 or 5. After these functions have been installed with the spreadsheet software, as described in the supplement to this chapter, they may be used to obtain random numbers for each of the distributions shown in Figure 14.9. It is assumed that these functions are installed for the remainder of this chapter. For more information about using thse functions, see the supplement.

A normally distributed random variable with mean 100 and standard deviation 20 may be obtained in 1-2-3 with this function:

$$\text{@NORMINV(@RAND,100,20)}$$

In Quattro Pro, this normally distributed random variable is obtained with this function:

$$\text{@WB.NORMINV(@RAND,100,20)}$$

Normally distributed random variables may also be obtained directly with spreadsheet formulas. For those readers who want to get "behind the scenes" or who need to obtain a normally distributed random number for another spreadsheet, here is the way to do it. A normally distributed random variable (whose mean is in the cell named AVG, and standard deviation is in the cell named STD) can be generated with this expression:

$$\text{@SQRT(}-2\text{*@LN(@RAND))*@COS(2*@PI*@RAND)*STD+AVG}$$

In this formula, each appearance of @RAND refers to a separate drawing from the spreadsheet's random number generator. Other functions may be unfamiliar to the user: @LN finds the "natural logarithm" of a number; @COS is a trigonometric function, cosine; @PI is the mathematical constant 3.14159 . . . , which is used to find properties of circles. The managerial user need not be concerned with the mathematics behind this formula; its use is not difficult, although it may look formidable!

The Triangular Distribution

The triangular distribution is quite useful because it handles nonsymmetric distributions, and because it is described in more "thinkable" terms than mean and standard deviation. A triangular distribution is described by three values:

> The lowest possible value of the random variable
> The most likely (or modal) value of the random variable
> The highest possible value of the random variable

Each of these three values is something that makes sense to managers (who may be less comfortable thinking about a standard deviation).

A triangular distribution, with a lowest value of 50, a modal (peak) value of 200, and a highest value of 700 may be obtained in 1-2-3 with this function:

> @TRIAINV(@RAND,50,200,700)

In Quattro Pro, this triangular random variable is obtained with this function:

> @WB.TRIAINV(@RAND,50,200,700)

For other spreadsheets, a triangular distribution, whose lowest value is in the cell named LO, modal value in the cell named MO, and highest value in the cell named HI, can be generated with this expression:

> @IF(RAND<(MO-LO)/(HI-LO),LO+@SQRT((MO-LO)*(HI-LO)*RAND),
> HI-@SQRT((HI-MO)*(HI-LO)*(1-RAND)))

In this formula, RAND refers to the same number, generated by use of the spreadsheet's @RAND random number generator. This expression is a bit cumbersome to use, because RAND must appear in a separate cell so that this same value is used each of the three times it's required in the formula.

Many probability distributions have a lowest, most likely, and highest value; not all such distributions are triangular. However, many situations are usefully described by this distribution.

The Exponential Distribution

The exponential distribution is used extensively in analysis of systems of waiting lines, a subject of a later chapter. For example, we may be interested in the time interval between successive fire alarms. Research has shown that phenomena such as this are often described by the exponential distribution. The exponential distribution is not symmetrical; it is said to be *skewed*, with a long right tail.

An exponential distribution with a mean of 36 may be obtained in 1-2-3 with this function:

> @EXPOINV(@RAND,36)

In Quattro Pro, this exponential random variable is obtained with this function:

@WB.EXPOINV(@RAND,36)

For other spreadsheets an exponential distribution, whose mean is contained in the cell named AVG, can be generated with:

−AVG*@LN(@RAND)

where @LN is the function which finds natural logarithms.

The Multinomial Distribution

In many situations, there are several discrete (point) values that may occur, each with its own probability. Returning to J.D.'s process selection problem from the beginning of this chapter, suppose the arbitrator's award for labor cost could end up being either $8, $9, $10, $11, or $12, with probabilities 0.1, 0.2, 0.3, 0.2, and 0.2. It is necessary to put the probabilities onto the spreadsheet in one block of contiguous cells, and the values into another block of contiguous cells. For example,

B3..B7 contains the values 0.1, 0.2, 0.3, 0.2, and 0.2

C3..C7 contains the values 8, 9, 10, 11, and 12

In 1-2-3, this distribution can be obtained with this function:

@MULTINV(@RAND,B3..B7,C3..C7)

The Quattro Pro function for this distribution is:

@WB.MULTINV(@RAND,B3..B7,C3..C7)

For other spreadsheets, the formula to replicate this distribution is:

@VLOOKUP(@RAND.TABLE.1)

where TABLE refers to this rectangular range on the spreadsheet:

0.00	8
0.10	9
0.30	10
0.60	11
0.80	12

The first column in the table starts with 0.00, and is incremented by each probability value. Random numbers which fall between 0.00 and 0.10 will correspond to a value of $8; this agrees with the 0.1 probability for an $8 award. Similarly, random numbers between 0.10 and 0.30 will correspond to a value of $9, in agreement with the 0.2 probability of a $9 award.

Converting Managerial Descriptions of Uncertainty into Spreadsheet Formulas

One purpose of this section is to examine several managerial statements, and convert them into appropriate spreadsheet formulas. In this way, we illustrate the connection between typical managerial thinking and spreadsheet descriptions. This section also shows a way that a spreadsheet can be created with all of the formulas described above. This spreadsheet can be combined into an empty portion of an existing spreadsheet, so that the formulas for any of the five probability distributions can be obtained without worrying about formulas.

Illustration 1

A manager used these comments to describe the uncertainty in the number of units of a new product that would be sold in its first year on the market:

> "Based on comparisons to similar products, my best guess is that we'll sell 5000 units next year. There's no way we could sell more than 20,000; a market that big would attract competitors faster than you would believe, which would limit us to maximum of 20,000 units. Frankly, it is highly unlikely in my mind that we'd sell anything close to that many. On the bad end, I'm sure we'll sell at least 2000 units; our customer interviews seem to say we'll be sure to sell 2000."

This description of the uncertainty in first year sales could describe a number of possible probability distributions. Of those we have presented, the triangular distribution best describes the situation. The lowest value in the distribution is 2000; the modal (most likely) value is 5000; the highest value is 20,000. In 1-2-3, this triangular distribution can be obtained with:

$$@TRIAINV(@RAND,2000,5000,20000)$$

In quattro Pro, this distribution can be obtained with:

$$@WB.TRIAINV(@RAND,2000,5000,20000)$$

Illustration 2

A manager used these comments to describe the uncertainty in the unit manufacturing cost of the new product that will be introduced soon:

> "I wish I knew what our cost will be for that product. The engineering department has a current best-guess of $830 unit manufacturing cost. I think a bell-shaped curved, centered on $830, represents a good distribution for the actual cost. Nineteen times out of twenty, I think we'll be within $100 of the $830 estimate."

The normal distribution is a likely candidate to describe this uncertainty. The mean of the distribution is $830. In a normal distribution, about 95% (nineteen out of twenty) of the values fall within two standard deviations of the mean; hence, two standard deviations is approximately $100. Each standard deviation has a value of $50. Combining these two parameters, we can describe the manufacturing cost by a normal distribution with a mean of $830 and a standard deviation of $50.

In 1-2-3, this normally distributed random variable can be obtained with:

$$@NORMINV(@RAND,830,50)$$

In Quattro Pro, this distribution can be obtained with:

@WB.NORINV(@RAND,830,50)

Illustration 3

A manager used these comments to describe the uncertainty in the price of the new product that will be introduced soon:

> "I know pricing is a difficult area for this new product. Our company policy for this product is to use cost-based pricing to avoid new competition caused by setting a price that is too high. I believe we'll end up pricing the product some place between 180% and 220% of cost. Frankly, it is as likely to be one value as any other within that range."

This description is easily recognized as the uniform distribution. To compute a cell containing a uniform random variable with these parameters, use this function with 1-2-3:

@UNIFINV(@RAND,1.8,2.2)

In Quattro Pro, this distribution can be obtained with:

@WB.UNIFINV(@RAND,1.8,2.2)

Illustration 4

A manager used these comments to describe the uncertainty in the number of development hours required to achieve the breakthrough that is necessary before production can begin:

> "The breakthrough to make this production process work could happen any time now. It could be today, it could be next week, it could be next month. I've been told that processes like this are like waiting for a collision of two blind fish in a fish tank: you know they'll run into each other sometime, but it isn't any more likely today than it was yesterday even though they swam all day! They call this a Poisson process, and the elapsed time between now and the fish collision, or the breakthrough, is described by the exponential distribution. My judgment tells me that the average time to the next breakthrough is five days. I hope it isn't too long, because each day costs us $250 in salaries."

The statement illustrates a random variable that is described by the exponential distribution with a mean of five days. The cell computing this exponential distribution would have this function in 1-2-3:

@EXPOINV(@RAND,5)

In Quattro Pro, this distribution can be obtained with:

@WB.EXPOINV(@RAND,5)

Illustration 5

A manager used these comments to describe the uncertainty in the number of salespeople needed to sell the new product:

"There's about a 25% chance we can get by with just one salesperson. However, I'd bet even money it will take two. There's a 15% chance we would need three, and a 10% chance we would need four. Each salesperson costs about $30,000 a year."

This comment describes a multinomial probability distribution. In tabular form, this probability distribution has this appearance:

Number of Salespeople	Probability
1	0.25
2	0.50
3	0.15
4	0.10

It is necessary to put the probabilities and values onto the spreadsheet. For example, suppose the number of salespeople is in A3..A6, and the probability values are in B3..B6. Then the function to obtain this distribution for 1-2-3 is:

@MULTINV(@RAND,B3..B6,A3..A6)

For Quatro Pro, the function is:

@WB.MULTINV(@RAND,B3..B6,A3..A6)

Exercises

1. A company sells in two markets. Analysis of past data, coupled with managerial judgment about the differences between the period of data collection and the outlook for the future, has suggested that the number of units sold in the first market will be described by a uniform distribution, with quantity equally likely to be any value between 1000 and 5000 units. For the second market, management believes the demand will be described by a uniform distribution, between 4000 and 6000.

   a. Use the Monte Carlo method to estimate a cumulative frequency distribution for the total units sold.

   b. Using your Monte Carlo analysis, make an empirical estimate for the expected value of the total units sold. If you are familiar with the statistical methods for interval estimates for a population mean, convert this point estimate into a confidence interval estimate.

2. The quantity sold is described by a normal distribution, with a mean of 1000 units and a standard deviation of 200 units. The price at which these are sold will be $100, less one cent for each unit sold. This means that if 900 are sold, the price will be $91; if 1142 are sold, the price will be $88.58. In addition, a discount must be applied to meet market conditions. It is estimated that the discount will be described by a normal distribution with a mean of 10% and a standard deviation

of 2%. Use the Monte Carlo method to estimate the expected value of revenue. Prepare a cumulative frequency distribution graph of revenue, and explain its meaning.

3. There are four cost elements; each is described by a triangular distribution with its own parameters. The four elements and their parameters (in order of lowest, mode, highest) are:

Labor cost	$10, $15, $25
Material cost	$17, $22, $24
Office cost	$1, $4, $5
Shipping cost	$1, $2, $3

Total cost is the sum of the four cost elements. Use Monte Carlo analysis to estimate the expected value of total cost. Prepare a cumulative frequency distribution graph of total cost, and explain its meaning.

4. The number of machines needed will be either 2, 3, or 4, with probabilities of 0.50, 0.40, and 0.10. The number of operators per machine will be either 5, 6, 7, or 8, with probabilities of 0.10, 0.20, 0.30, 0.40. Use Monte Carlo analysis to estimate the expected number of operators. Prepare a cumulative frequency distribution graph of the number of operators, and explain its meaning.

5. The company planning the new product introduction (Illustrations 1 through 5 in the chapter) wants to know the expected profit for the first year, based on the information given in the illustrations above. The profit realized next year will be the REVENUE (PRICE × QUANTITY) less all costs. The price will be the unit manufacturing cost, multiplied by the factor described as "equally likely to be anything between 180% and 220%." The costs include manufacturing cost (QUANTITY × UNIT MANUFACTURING COST), the development cost (250 × DAYS TO BREAKTHROUGH), and the salesperson cost (NUMBER OF SALESPEOPLE × 30,000). The company also wants a graphical description of the uncertainty in its profit for next year, based on the judgment that has been used to capture the uncertainty in the individual components that influence profit.

6. A production process calls for randomly selecting a shaft and a bearing from inventory. It is known from historical information that the shaft diameter is described by the normal distribution with a mean of 1.000 inches, and a standard deviation of 0.005 inches. It is also known that each bearing has a diameter described by the triangular distribution with a lowest value of 0.998 inches, a most likely value of 1.002 inches, and a highest value of 1.015 inches. A bearing fits the shaft if the bearing diameter is between 0.0005 and 0.008 inches larger than the shaft diameter.

   a. Using the Monte Carlo method, estimate the probability that the bearing fits the shaft.

   b. If the bearing specifications and the standard deviation of shaft diameter are outside the control of the company, but the average shaft diameter is controlled by the company, use Monte Carlo analysis to determine the average shaft diameter that maximizes the chances of a fit between

the shaft and the bearing. (It will be necessary to run repeated simulations, each with a different diameter, to find the best diameter.)

7. A "buy list" of common stocks has annual rates of return (for the past two years)
   that are adequately described by the uniform distribution with a lower limit of
   5% and an upper limit of 15%. If ten stocks are selected from this list by throwing
   darts, what is the probability that the portfolio will have an average rate of return
   between 9% and 11%?

CASE ANALYSIS

Using Monte Carlo to Support Novana's Decisions

The Novana Company was discussed extensively in Chapter 9. This case analysis
builds upon the information about Novana, presented in the discussion leading
to the spreadsheet model of Figure 9.10, and its documentation in Figure 9.11.
Following that model, optimization instructions were developed, resulting in an
optimal plan with an ending cash balance of $304,243. The results of applying
optimization are shown in the optimized spreadsheet, Exhibit 14.1.

Using Historical Data to Describe Uncertainty
in the Spreadsheet

S. T. Semoran realized that if Novana were to implement these schedules, they
really would not end up with results just like those shown in the spreadsheet.
The plan was based on a 50% split between credit card and COD sales, and upon
perfect ability to forecast sales for any number of ads scheduled. What would
happen if Novana experienced variation in sales type (credit card or COD) and in
the effectiveness of ads? To address this question, a report was prepared for S.T.,
as shown in Exhibit 14.2. This report shows the data that was behind Novana's
original modeling effort.

   This report provides the information necessary to include uncertainty in
Novana's planning. The data for the split between credit card and COD sales
could be used to estimate the month-to-month variability. The standard deviation
of these values is 3%, which could be used as the standard deviation for a
normally distributed random variable. It would be consistent with the information provided to describe the monthly split between credit card and COD sales
as normally distributed with a mean of 50% and a standard deviation of 3%.
(While there is no firm evidence that the normal distribution is appropriate,
there isn't much to the contrary, either. Another approach would be to develop
a histogram and observe the shape.) This normal distribution is inserted into
the spreadsheet for the Credit Card Percent. In Exhibit 14.1, only one cell was
required for the credit card percentage; as we modify the spreadsheet to introduce uncertainty, we'll need a row of values, one for each month, January
through May. Each cell is this row is defined with this formula:

$$@SQRT(-2*@LN(@RAND))*@COS(2*@PI*@RAND)*.03+.5$$

—————— **Exhibit 14.1** ——————

Optimized Spreadsheet for Novana

	A	B	C	D	E	F	G
		Jan	Feb	March	Apr	May	Total
1							
2	Beginning Cash Balanc	$10,000	$10,000	$10,000	$77,636	$252,600	
3	Cash Received	$75,000	$230,893	$279,214	$174,964	$51,643	
4	Credit Card Receipt	$75,000	$155,893	$123,321	$51,643		
5	COD Receipts	$0	$75,000	$155,893	$123,321	$51,643	
6	Cash Paid Out	$75,000	$230,893	$211,579	$0		
7	Paid to BenderMet	$15,000	$3,000	$0	$0		
8	Paid to Flexo	$0	$151,179	$198,293	$0		
9	Paid to TV	$60,000	$76,714	$13,286	$0		
10	Ending Cash Balance	$10,000	$10,000	$77,636	$252,600	$304,243	
11							
12	Beginning Inventory	1,000	(0)	0	689		
13	Units Sold	1,000	2,079	1,644	689		
14	Units Delivered to No	0	2,079	2,333	0		
15	BenderMet Deliverie	0	300	0	0		300
16	Flexo Deliveries	0	1,779	2,333	0		
17	Ending Inventory	(0)	0	689	0		
18							
19	Ads Run	40	51	9	0		100
20							
21			Data				
22	Selling Price		150				
23	BenderMet January Payment		50				
24	BenderMet Delivery Payment		10				
25	Flexo Delivery Payment		85				
26	Credit Card Percentage		0.5				
27	First Month Sales		25				
28	Second Month Sales		20				
29	Third Month Sales		10				
30	Ad Price		1500				

or the equivalent 1-2-3 function:

$$\text{@NORMINV(@RAND,0.5,0.03)}$$

or the equivalent Quattro Pro function:

$$\text{@WB.NORMINV(@RAND,0.5,0.03)}$$

where 0.03 (3%) is the standard deviation, and 0.5 (50%) is the mean.

The report also provides substantial information about the uncertainty in the number of units sold, given the ad schedule for this month and the previous two months. The regression report includes this line:

Std Err of Y Est   178.7600

which shows the standard deviation of the forecast error for each month, based on the regression analysis. Each month's value for Units Sold is subject to an "error term" whose standard deviation could be estimated to be 179. If the normal distribution seems to be a reasonable shape for these error terms (and it often is a reasonable shape for error terms), we add to the spreadsheet a row of

─────────────────────────── **Exhibit 14.2** ───────────────────────────

Data Estimates for Novana's Scheduling Model

Part A: Estimating the Breakdown between Credit Card and COD Sales

During the past year, we have kept track of the percentage of sales which are charged to credit cards, on a monthly basis. The results are shown here:

Month 1	50%	Month 5	48%	Month 9	51%
Month 2	45%	Month 6	51%	Month 10	50%
Month 3	46%	Month 7	45%	Month 11	56%
Month 4	52%	Month 8	47%	Month 12	51%

The average of these percentages is 49.3%; the use of a fifty-fifty split between Credit Card and COD sales is recommended, based on these data.

Part B: Estimating the Units Sold based on Ads Scheduled

For the past twenty-four months, we have run four cycles of ads for the SlimmerGymmer. The data for the number of ads and the number of units sold is shown below:

Number of Ads				Number of Ads			
This Month	One Month Ago	Two Months Ago	Units Sold This Month	This Month	One Month Ago	Two Months Ago	Units Sold This Month
30	0	0	750	50	40	25	2508
40	30	0	1737	35	50	40	2416
10	40	30	1459	0	35	50	1495
0	10	40	959	0	0	35	330
0	0	10	0	0	0	0	0
50	0	0	1302	30	0	0	590
40	50	0	2130	30	30	0	1326
50	40	50	2497	30	30	30	1408
50	50	40	2466	40	30	30	1994
0	50	50	1414	10	40	30	991
25	0	50	1160	0	10	40	748
40	25	0	1626	0	0	10	0

A regression analysis, using regression on a spreadsheet, has been performed with the Units Sold as the dependent variable, and the three columns for Number of Ads run as the independent variables. The results of this regression analysis are shown here:

```
            Regression Output:
Constant                    0.723148
Std Err of Y Est          178.7600
R Squared                   0.955638
No. of Observations               24
Degrees of Freedom                20

X Coefficient(s)   25.16572 19.85527 10.85157
Std Err of Coef.   2.194394 2.289746 2.194394
```

The numbers following "X Coefficient(s)" are estimates of the number of units sold per ad in the current month, in the following month, and in the second following month. These numbers (25.16572, 19.85527, and 10.85157) slightly modified by managerial input, were used to estimate that:

An ad sells 25 units in the current month
An ad sells 20 units in the following month
An ad sells 10 units in the second following month

Exhibit 14.3

Novana's Spreadsheet with Uncertainty

	A	B	C	D	E	F	G
		Jan	Feb	March	Apr	May	Total
1							
2	Beginning Cash Balanc	$10,000	($4,227)	($3,502)	$49,096	$215,967	
3	Cash Received	$60,773	$231,619	$264,176	$166,871	$57,589	
4	Credit Card Receipt	$60,773	$162,728	$117,519	$59,496		
5	COD Receipts	$0	$68,891	$146,658	$107,374	$57,589	
6	Cash Paid Out	$75,000	$230,893	$211,579	$0		
7	Paid to BenderMet	$15,000	$3,000	$0	$0		
8	Paid to Flexo	$0	$151,179	$198,293	$0		
9	Paid to TV	$60,000	$76,714	$13,286	$0		
10	Ending Cash Balance	($4,227)	($3,502)	$49,096	$215,967	$273,556	
11							
12	Beginning Inventory	1,000	136	152	985		
13	Units Sold	864	2,063	1,499	781		
14	Units Delivered to No	0	2,079	2,333	0		
15	BenderMet Deliverie	0	300	0	0		300
16	Flexo Deliveries	0	1,779	2,333	0		
17	Ending Inventory	136	152	985	205		
18							
19	Ads Run	40	51	9	0		100
20							
21	Credit Card Percent	46.9%	52.6%	52.3%	50.8%		
22	Forecast Error	-136	-16	-145	92		
23							
24			Data				
25							
26	Selling Price		150				
27	BenderMet January Payment		50				
28	BenderMet Delivery Payment		10				
29	Flexo Delivery Payment		85				
30							
31	First Month Sales		25				
32	Second Month Sales		20				
33	Third Month Sales		10				
34	Ad Price		1500				

---

forecast errors, for the months January through April, with each cell in the row defined with this formula:

$$@SQRT(-2*@LN(@RAND))*@COS(2*@PI*@RAND)*179+0$$

or the equivalent 1-2-3 function:

$$@NORMINV(@RAND,0,179)$$

or the equivalent Quattro Pro function:

$$@WB.NORMINV(@RAND,0,179)$$

where 179 is the standard deviation, and the mean forecast error is zero. For each month, the value of Units Sold would be as defined in the original model, plus the forecast error term just described.

The spreadsheet with these changes and its documentation are shown in Exhibits 14.3 and 14.4. (A reader who attempts to replicate the values shown in

―――――――――――――――――――――― **Exhibit 14.4** ――――――――――――――――――――――

Documentation for Novana's Spreadsheet with Uncertainty

```
Beginning Cash Balance[Jan] = 10000
Beginning Cash Balance[Feb THRU May] = PREVIOUS Ending Cash Balance

Cash Received[Jan THRU May] = Credit Card Receipts + COD Receipts

Credit Card Receipts[Jan THRU Apr] = Units Sold * Credit Card Percent * Selling Price[Data]

COD Receipts[Jan] = 0
COD Receipts[Feb THRU May] = (1 - PREVIOUS Credit Card Percent) *
    PREVIOUS Units Sold * Selling Price[Data]

Cash Paid Out[Jan THRU Apr] = Paid to BenderMet + Paid to Flexo + Paid to TV
Paid to BenderMet[Jan] = BenderMet Deliveries[Total] * BenderMet January Payment[Data] +
    BenderMet Deliveries[Jan] * BenderMet Delivery Payment[Data]
Paid to BenderMet[Feb THRU Apr] = BenderMet Deliveries * BenderMet Delivery Payment[Data]

Paid to Flexo[Jan THRU Apr] = Flexo Deliveries * Flexo Delivery Payment[Data]

Paid to TV[Jan THRU Apr] = Ads Run * Ad Price[Data]

Ending Cash Balance[Jan THRU May] = Beginning Cash Balance + Cash Received - Cash Paid Out

Beginning Inventory[Jan] = 1000
Beginning Inventory[Feb THRU Apr] = PREVIOUS Ending Inventory

Units Sold[Jan] = MAX (Ads Run[Jan] * First Month Sales[Data] + Forecast Error[Jan], 0)
Units Sold[Feb] = MAX (Ads Run[Feb] * First Month Sales[Data] +
    Ads Run[Jan] * Second Month Sales[Data] + Forecast Error[Feb], 0)
Units Sold[March THRU Apr] = MAX (Ads Run * First Month Sales[Data] + PREVIOUS Ads Run *
    Second Month Sales[Data] + PREVIOUS 2 Ads Run * Third Month Sales[Data] + Forecast Error, 0)

Units Delivered to Novana[Jan THRU Apr] = BenderMet Deliveries + Flexo Deliveries

BenderMet Deliveries[Jan]..BenderMet Deliveries[Apr] are documented in cells B15..E15
BenderMet Deliveries[Total] = SUM (BenderMet Deliveries[Jan] THRU BenderMet Deliveries[Apr])

Flexo Deliveries[Jan]..Flexo Deliveries[Apr] are documented in cells B16..E16

Ending Inventory[Jan THRU Apr] = Beginning Inventory - Units Sold + Units Delivered to Novana

Ads Run[Jan]..Ads Run[Apr] are documented in cells B19..E19
Ads Run[Total] = SUM (Ads Run[Jan] THRU Ads Run[Apr])

Credit Card Percent[Jan THRU Apr] = SQRT (-2 * LN (RAND)) * COS (2 * PI * RAND) * 0.03 + 0.5

Forecast Error[Jan THRU Apr] = SQRT (-2 * LN (RAND)) * COS (2 * PI * RAND) * 179 + 0

Selling Price[Data]..Ad Price[Data] are documented in cells C26..C34
```

Exhibit 14.3 will be unsuccessful, because different random numbers will be selected by the spreadsheet software.)

Using Novana's Spreadsheet with Uncertainty

The spreadsheet of Exhibit 14.3, incorporating the uncertainty in units sold and in the credit card percentage, was useful to S. T. Semoran in investigating the impact of uncertainty upon Novana's "optimal" plan developed earlier. Three important factors can be investigated with this model:

> How much uncertainty is there in the profit, as indicated by the May Ending Cash Balance?

> What are the chances that Novana will be able to keep inventory levels from become negative, which indicates a backorder position?

─────────────────── **Exhibit 14.5** ───────────────────

Cumulative Frequency Distribution for Ending Cash Balance

Novana Company Monte Carlo Simulation
Ending Cash Balance, 1000 Replications

What are the chances Novana will be able to keep a minimum ending cash balance of $10,000?

These questions are among those that can be answered by using the Monte Carlo method to perform a number of replications of the model's solution. For each of these replications, we need to keep track of:

The May ending cash balance

The lowest inventory during the four-month planning horizon

The lowest cash balance during the four-month planning horizon.

This can be accomplished by using a 1-way data table with three "result" columns, headed by these expressions (stated in documentation form):

```
Ending Cash Balance[May]
MIN (Ending Inventory[Jan] THRU Ending Inventory[Apr])
MIN (Ending Cash Balance[Jan] THRU Ending Cash Balance[Apr])
```

From each of these columns, we can create the cumulative frequency distributions shown as Exhibit 14.5, Exhibit 14.6, and Exhibit 14.7.

From Exhibit 14.5 it is apparent that there is a substantial variability in the results of applying the "optimal" plan for Novana. The optimized spreadsheet reports a May ending cash balance of $304,000. The graph in Exhibit 14.5 indicates that there is about a 10% chance that this balance will be less than $230,000, and a 10% chance it will be greater than $375,000. The average of the 1000 Monte

--- **Exhibit 14.6** ---

Cumulative Frequency Distribution for Lowest Inventory

Novana Company Monte Carlo Simulation
Lowest Ending Inventory, 1000 Replications

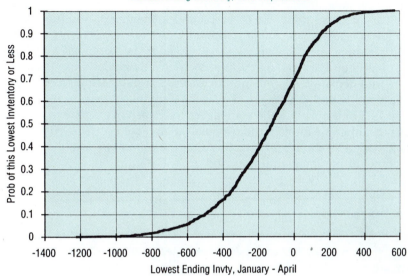

--- **Exhibit 14.7** ---

Cumulative Frequency Distribution for Lowest Cash Balance

Novana Company Monte Carlo Simulation
Lowest Cash Balance, 1000 Replications

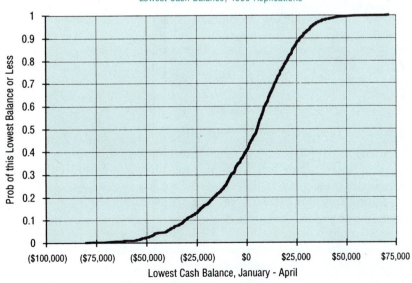

Carlo replications is $304,749. However, if Novana's management is making plans based on a May ending cash balance of $305,000, there is about a 50% chance they will not have a balance that large.

Exhibit 14.6 indicates there are serious inventory management issues not addressed by Novana. If the "optimal" plan for purchases is followed, there is about a 69% chance that there will be backorders sometime during the planning period. There is a 10% chance that a backorder as large as 500 units will occur during the planning period. This is not surprising; the "optimal" purchasing schedule is based on known demand; the Monte Carlo analysis has introduced uncertainty into demand. As demand fluctuates, the purchasing schedule does not change along with it.

Exhibit 14.7 indicates that there are also severe cash management problems for Novana to address. Although the "optimal" plan required a $10,000 minimum cash balance, there is about a 61% chance that the minimum will be below this level sometime during the planning period.

Exercises (Novana)

1. Develop a histogram to investigate the shape of the distribution of credit card percentage, from Exhibit 14.2 in the Novana case. What distribution appears to be appropriate?

2. Develop a histogram to investigate the shape of the distribution of forecast error, for the number of units sold each month, based on ad history. What distribution appears to be appropriate?

3. Use appropriate distributions to describe each of the uncertain quantities in this analysis. To decide on the values of the parameters of the distributions, study the histograms you developed in the two preceding exercises. Perform the simulations again, with these modifications. Is there a substantial difference in conclusions depending upon the shape and parameters of the distribution you use?

CASE STUDY:
Soft Ideas (B)

Sam Soft, owner of Soft Ideas (from Chapter 8), studied the information about the plans for the new office construction. The information Sam had received indicated that the project could be completed in 265 days at the "base" costs, without spending anything extra for crashing or expediting. Another option was to complete the project sooner, in 250 days, by crashing or expediting some activities. This would cost an additional $107,000, spent mostly for speeding up the interior construction. The description of Soft Idea's project network, showing the base times, is repeated here as Exhibit 14.8.

—————— **Exhibit 14.8** ——————

Planning Network for Soft Ideas

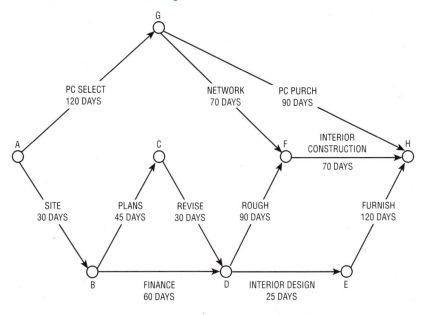

Anly, an analyst, had been working with Sam Soft in the planning process. In addition to the use of optimization for determining the minimum time in which a project can be completed, Anly had used a traditional method based on finding the earliest possible time of occurrence for each event. This *critical path method* is straightforward, and works easily on a spreadsheet for relatively small networks. Anly began with the convention that the first event (A) would start at a time called 0. For each remaining event, the earliest it could occur is the latest time that each of the predecessor activities can be finished. On an event-by-event basis, this is summarized using B to note the time that event B can occur, and so on.

> Event A will occur at time 0
>
> Event B can occur 30 days after A, or at time A + 30.
>
> Event C can occur 45 days after B, or at time B + 45.
>
> Event D can occur at whichever of these is later:
> > 30 days after C, or at time C + 30
> > 60 days after B, or at time B + 60
>
> Event E can occur 25 days after D, or at time D + 25.
>
> Event F can occur at whichever of these is later:
> > 30 days after G, or at time G + 30
> > 90 days after D, or at time D + 90

Event G can occur 120 days after A, or at time A + 120.

Event H can occur at whichever of these times is later:
90 days after G, or at time G + 90
70 days after F, or at time F + 70
120 days after E, or at time E + 120

In preparation for developing a spreadsheet model to determine the earliest occurrence of each event, the relationships above were generalized by replacing the time for an activity with its name:

Event A will occur at time 0

Event B can occur SITE days after A, or at time A + SITE

Event C can occur PLANS days after B, or at time B + PLANS

Event D can occur at whichever of these is later:
REVISE days after C, or at time C + REVISE
FINANCE days after B, or at time B + FINANCE

Event E can occur INT DES days after D, or at time D + INT DES

Event F can occur at whichever of these is later:
NETWORK days after G, or at time G + NETWORK
ROUGH days after D, or at time D + ROUGH

Event G can occur PC SELECT days after A, or at time A + PC SELECT

Event H can occur at whichever of these times is later:
PC PURCH days after G, or at time G + PC PURCH
INT CONST days after F, or at time F + INT CONST
FURNISH days after E, or at time E + FURNISH

The spreadsheet model for this network is easy to construct. It involves two lists, one for events and one for activities:

a list of all events, showing the earliest time of occurrence for each event, using the logic shown above, and

a list of the activities, showing the time required for each activity.

The spreadsheet model and an added column showing formulas, are shown in Exhibit 14.9. Note that the documentation is shown using range names, established using the

Range Name Labels Right command sequence (Lotus 1-2-3) or

Edit Name Labels Right command sequence (Quattro Pro).

The time of completion of the project is the earliest time of occurrence for event H, the last event on the project network. If any activity duration is changed, the worksheet is automatically recalculated, reflecting the new duration.

Sam was particularly concerned about the ability of the contractors to meet a schedule that showed completing the project in 265 days. Although the assumption of certainty was made throughout the analysis, it is an unrealistic

---

Exhibit 14.9

Spreadsheet (with Added Documentation) for Soft Ideas Network

	A	B
1		Earliest
2		Time of
3	Event	Occurrence
4	A	0
5	B	30
6	C	75
7	D	105
8	E	130
9	F	195
10	G	120
11	H	265
12		
13	Activity	Duration
14	SITE	30
15	PLANS	45
16	REVISE	30
17	FINANCE	60
18	ROUGH	90
19	INT DES	25
20	FURNISH	120
21	INT CONST	70
22	PC SELECT	120
23	PC PURCH	90
24	NETWORK	70

```
Cell Formulas for Column B (using Range Names)

+A+SITE     (The value of SITE is 30, from B14)
+B+PLANS    (The value of PLANS is 45, from B15)
@MAX(C+REVISE,B+FINANCE)
+D+INT DES
@MAX(G+NETWORK,D+ROUGH)
+A+PC SELECT
@MAX(G+PC PURCH,F+INT CONST,E+FURNISH)
```

assumption. For example, selecting a site was planned to take exactly 30 days —no more, no less. Sam's thoughts:

> How unrealistic! In some ways, selecting and purchasing a site is one of those things that you just keep working on until you find what you need. Oh, yes, there is some time spent evaluating, but if an evaluation shows that none of those in the list will work, you just keep looking. I know we can't finish this step in less than 15 days. I think the 30-day estimate is a good value for the most-likely time. But the scary part is that this process could go on for perhaps 75 days. We've planned as if the "best guess" will actually happen. Frightening!

Anly, the analyst listening in on Sam's thoughts, wrote that SITE is described with a triangular distribution, with time values of 15 (best), 30 (most likely), and 75 (worst).

Sam thought about each of the other activities, and the analyst wrote down notes summarizing the thoughts. At the end of this session, the analyst's notes were reproduced as Exhibit 14.10. Each of the probabilistic descriptions of an activity time was consistent with the earlier information, because each distribution has either the average time or the most likely time as the (certain) time from the previous analysis, without crashing or expediting.

Exhibit 14.10

Adding Uncertainty to Soft Idea's Project: Notes About Uncertainty

Activity	Description of Uncertainty
SITE	Triangular (15, 30, 75)
PLANS	Normal (45, 5)
REVISE	Triangular (20, 30, 60)
FINANCE	Uniform (45, 75)
ROUGH	Triangular (80, 90, 120)
INT DES	Normal (25, 3)
FURNISH	Uniform (100, 140)
INT CONST	Triangular (60, 70, 100)
PC SELECT	Triangular (45, 120, 140)
PC PURCH	Triangular (60, 90, 100)
NETWORK	Normal (30, 5)

Notes: For a triangular distribution, the three values are the shortest possible time, the "best guess" or modal time, and the longest possible time.

For a normal distribution, the two values are the mean or average time, and the standard deviation of time.

For a uniform distribution, the two values are the shortest possible time and the longest possible time.

Exercises (Soft Ideas (B))

1. Based on the probabilistic descriptions of time, what is the average or expected time required to complete all of the activities leading to Soft Idea's move?

2. What is the probability the project will be completed in 265 days?

3. Assuming a scheduled completion date based on the original 265 day project completion time, what is the probability the project will be completed:

    a. 30 days early?   d. 30 days late?
    b. 15 days early?   e. 45 days late?
    c. 15 days late?

4. Prepare a graph showing probability of projection completion time. Explain the graph in language suitable for nontechnical managers.

5. Use the "crash" schedule developed in Chapter 8, by crashing SITE 5 days, PLANS 2 days, INT CONST 8 days, and PC SELECT 2 days. Change the probability distribution for these crashed activities by reducing all values of a uniform or triangular distribution by the days crashed, and by reducing the mean time of a normal distribution by the days crashed.

Random Number Generation with What's *Best!* Functions

What's *Best!*, software provided with this textbook, generates random numbers described by various probability distributions for Lotus 1-2-3 Release 2.x and for Quattro Pro for DOS Versions 4 and 5. These new functions have the ability to generate random numbers distributed as any of these distributions:

> Normal distribution
>
> Triangular distribution
>
> Exponential distribution
>
> Uniform distribution
>
> Point or Multinomial Point distribution

Examples of the use of each of these distributions, and the requirements for the arguments of the distribution, are shown in the examples below. A typical requirement is that arguments must be specified individually rather than as ranges. If three parameters for the triangular distribution, Lo, Mode, and Hi, are in A1, A2, and A3, the function arguments must be specified as individual cell addresses, A1, A2, A3, or as numbers, such as 2, 5, 6. Use of the equivalent range A1..A3 is not allowed, and would result in an error. (There is one exception, noted below, for the multinomial distribution.)

These new functions were installed during the What's *Best!* installation. You may use Lotus 1-2-3 by commanding **123**; you need not use the **WB** command. You may use Quattro Pro by commanding **Q**; you need not enter through What's *Best!* (**WBQ**).

Normal Distribution

A random variable described by the normal distribution with a mean of 100 and a standard deviation of 10 is obtained with the function:

> Lotus 1-2-3:   @NORMINV(@RAND,100,10)
>
> Quattro Pro: @WB.NORMINV(@RAND,100,10)

Limitations: The standard deviation (second argument) must be non-negative.

Triangular Distribution

A random variable described by the triangular distribution with a lower limit of 100, a mode (peak value) of 200, and an upper limit of 500 is obtained with the function:

Lotus 1-2-3: `@TRIAINV(@RAND,100,200,500)`

Quattro Pro `@WB.TRIAINV(@RAND,100,200,500)`

Limitations: The numbers must be logically consistent; i.e., the lower limit may not be larger than the mode, and the upper limit may not be smaller than the mode.

Exponential Distribution

A random variable described by the exponential distribution with a mean of 100 is obtained with the function:

Lotus 1-2-3 `@EXPOINV(@RAND,100)`

Quattro Pro `@WB.EXPOINV(@RAND,100)`

Limitations: The mean must be a positive value.

Uniform Distribution

A random variable described by the uniform distribution with a lower limit of −300 and an upper limit of −150 is obtained with the function:

Lotus 1-2-3: `@UNIFINV(@RAND,−300,−150)`

Quattro Pro: `@WB.UNIFINV(@RAND,−300,−150)`

Limitations: The numbers must be logically consistent; i.e., the lower limit may not be larger than the upper limit.

Point (Multinomial) Distribution

A random variable described by the point (multinomial) distribution is shown in this table:

	A	B
1	Value of the	Probability of
2	Random Variable	This Value
3		
4	100	.40
5	50	.30
6	250	.25
7	−30	.05

In 1-2-3, this random variable is obtained with the function:

`@MULTINV(@RAND,B4..B7,A4..A7)`

Note that each value is followed by its probability.

In Quattro Pro, this random variable is obtained with the function:

`@WB.MULTINV(@RAND,B4..B7,A4..A7)`

Limitations: This function must have two ranges or blocks as the final two arguments. The blocks must be columns or rows of identical length. You may not specify individual cells or values with this function. The probability values must not be negative; and their sum must be equal to 1.

15

Uncertainty in Inventory Management: Analysis & Simulation

Uncertainty is a part of nearly every inventory management decision. We don't know exactly how many units will be demanded during any time period, and we don't know when replenishment orders will arrive from our suppliers. In spite of these uncertainties, inventory decisions are made routinely by nearly every business organization. One way of dealing with uncertainty is to assume it away! That is what this text did earlier, when nonlinear optimization was used to determine how many units should be ordered each time an order was placed with a supplier. This illustrates common practice: in determining order quantity, use single-valued estimates for uncertain quantities, such as annual demand. Experience has shown that this is often a good way to manage inventories. *In summary, uncertainty is often ignored in determining the order quantity.* The first part of this chapter will introduce Monte Carlo simulation for inventory management, and illustrate the reasonableness of determining order quantity by ignoring uncertainty. This serves to illustrate the technique of Monte Carlo simulation for inventory management.

The other major part of inventory management is deciding when to place an order. A common inventory management system uses a *reorder point*: when the inventory level reaches the reorder point, a replenishment order is placed with the supplier. Experience has shown that it is usually unacceptable to assume away the uncertainties in determining the reorder point. To illustrate, suppose it takes two weeks from the time we place an order until we receive it from our supplier; average demand during a two-week period is 100 units. Suppose we wait until we have exactly 100 units, and then place an order; on the average, we'll run out just as the replenishment order is arriving from the supplier. But in reality we stand a chance of running out before our stocks are replenished. Indeed, if the shape of the probability distribution of demand is symmetrical, this reorder policy would cause us to run out half of the time, before the replenishment order has arrived. *In summary, uncertainty is seldom ignored in determining the reorder point.* The second part of this chapter will show inventory analysis techniques to determine the reorder point for inventory management under uncertainty. The validity of that analysis will be investigated with a Monte Carlo inventory simulation illustration.

Monte Carlo Simulation in Inventory Management

Monte Carlo simulation is widely used to improve the rules (or policies) for managing inventories. In these simulations, we may use random numbers or we may use historical data; we will repeat a scenario over and over, just as we did in Chapter 14. But there is a new feature in inventory simulation: the repetitions occur over an extended sequence of time periods, one time period (day, week, month) after another. The end of one time period is the beginning of the next time period; the ending inventory one time period is the beginning inventory for the next time period. (In Chapter 14, we looked at the same scenario over and over again, starting each replication with the same conditions.)

A major use of Monte Carlo simulation is to describe how well something works; it doesn't tell us how to improve the way something works. But if we know how a system operates under one set of rules or policies, we can compare this behavior with the system under another set of rules or policies. If we can compare two proposed policies, we can choose the better; repeating this process with a number of policies may help the analyst find a good policy, but not necessarily the best policy.

Throughout this chapter, we continue to limit our discussion to the management of those inventory items (supplied by outside vendors) whose demand is not controlled by the organization carrying the inventory.

Inventory Simulation: Golden Ear Audio (C)

A dictionary might define simulation with words such as "assuming the appearance of without the reality." We use the spreadsheet to estimate the appearance over time of an inventory system, without disturbing the real system. A version of the Golden Ear Audio Distributors case provides the illustrations for inventory analysis and simulation.

> G. E. Audo, manager of Golden Ear Audio Distributors, spent about an hour talking about managing the inventory of the Model 3581-X speaker.
>
> How many Model 3581-X speakers should Golden Ear order at one time? How low should we let our inventory get before we place a replenishment order? These speakers are our premier product, and we want to do things just right. We've been carrying them for about a year now, and they do good business for us. The 3581-X speakers cost $400 each. We expect to sell 5000 speakers during the year, for an annual

purchase cost of two million dollars. With this much money on the line, we insist on testing each speaker before we deliver it to our customers, who are high-end audio retailers. Every speaker we order must be tested; every batch we receive requires us to set up the test facility. This setup costs us about $350. By the time we add in the cost of paperwork to process the orders, we come to an estimated $400 cost incurred for each order we place.

There are other costs as well: We're always amazed when we find out how much it costs us to keep inventory. The obvious part is the bank's interest cost: that's about 1.5% a month, which is $6 per month or $72 per year. We're committed to our warehouse space, and space is not currently a problem, so we don't need to consider the warehouse cost as a part of holding inventory. Obsolescence is another big problem. In this business, you never know how long a product will stay in favor. While there are sudden changes in some components, others are more gradual. Over the past three years, we've experienced losses due to obsolete speakers that have averaged an annual 4% of our average speaker inventory. We're content to apply that factor to the 3581-X. Since we built our new warehouse, we've been able to control shrinkage (theft) so well that we can ignore this factor.

Because of the importance of this speaker to our business, we are concerned about the level of service we provide our customers. Our customers (retail outlets) hardly ever carry much inventory of these speakers, because they are so expensive. So they rely on us to use overnight express to get them there the next day, in many cases. If a retailer calls to order, and we are out of stock, we haven't provided very good service to that customer. We look at what we call the *service level* for these speakers: if we place 100 replenishment orders, and 95 of them arrive before we run out, we have a service level of 95%. I'm not sure that is high enough for this product. We can raise it by having a higher reorder point, but that will raise our inventory holding costs.

Data were available for the number of speakers demanded on the last 250 business days, as shown in Figure 15.1.

The graph shows a distinct pattern of increasing demand for the first portion of the year, with a relatively stable demand level for the end of the year. It is reasonable to consider the portion of the data "after the demand has leveled off" rather than for the entire period. We choose the last hundred days as the relevant days for the demand history for speaker 3581-X. This is assuming that these last hundred days are management's projections of demand for the planning horizon.

Simulating a Hundred Days:
Historical Demand, Next-Day Replenishment

For our first inventory simulation we use the historical demand (days 151–250) for Golden Ear item 3581-X speaker system, with next-day replenishment of

———————————————— **Figure 15.1** ————————————————

Demand History for Golden Audio Distributors

Golden Ear Audio: Item 3581-X

Daily Demand for First Year

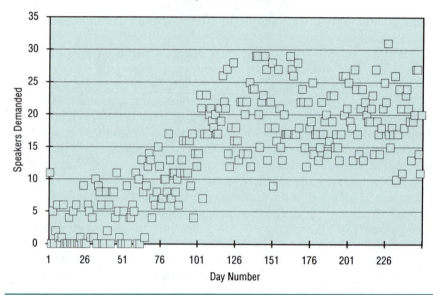

speakers. Our purpose is to demonstrate inventory simulation; we choose a rather arbitrary inventory management policy and see how it behaves. The inventory management policy we will simulate is:

> At the end of each business day, Golden Ear examines its inventory level; if there are 15 or fewer speakers available, an order will be placed for 100 speakers. (These numbers are not "recommended" numbers for controlling the inventory; they are used for demonstrating simulation.) Speakers ordered at the end of one day will be available for selling to customers the next day.

Our task is to construct a spreadsheet showing each day's speaker activities. To evaluate a policy, we need to know:

> The costs incurred each day
>
> How many replenishment orders are received during the simulation
>
> How many replenishment orders were received in time to avoid a stockout

The influence chart for the simulation model is shown in Figure 15.2. This influence chart contains three major components: a cost component, an ordering decision component, and an inventory component.

To understand the logic of the model, it is useful to look at the spreadsheet to see the first several days of the simulation, shown in Figure 15.3 and docu-

Figure 15.2

Influence Chart for Golden Ear's First Simulation

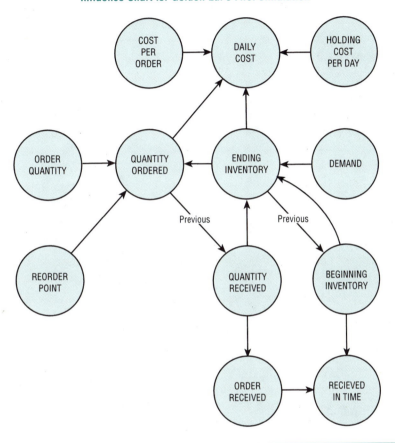

mented in Figure 15.4. The top part of the spreadsheet shows information that applies to each period: the cost per order ($400); the daily holding cost (annual interest, $72, and annual obsolescence, $16, divided by 250 business days per year; this is $0.352 per unit per day); the reorder point and the order quantity (the policy variables for this simulation). Column C, Demand, was shown graphically in Figure 15.1.

The inventory simulation begins with an *initial condition* of 6 speakers on hand. From the historical demand, the day 151 demand is 9 speakers, leaving an inventory of −3. We assume that this is backordered, and will be filled as soon as inventory is available. At the end of day 1 the ending inventory (−3) is compared to the reorder point (15), and an order of 100 (the order quantity) is placed. On day 152, the beginning inventory is the same as the previous ending inventory; 18 speakers are demanded, and 100 speakers are received (from yesterday's order). Day 152 ends with an ending inventory of 79 speakers, which exceeds the reorder point so no order is placed. An order was received that day,

---
Figure 15.3

Golden Audio's First Simulation

	A	B	C	D	E	F	G	H	I
1	Cost per Order			400					
2	Holding Cost per Day			0.352					
3	Reorder Point			15					
4	Order Quantity			100					
5									
6	Average						96.67		85.0%
7									
8	Day Beginning	Demand	Quantity		Ending	Quantity	Daily	Order	Rec'd
9	Inventory		Received	Inventory	Ordered		Cost	Rec'd	in Tim
10									
11	151	6	9	0	-3	100	400	0	0
12	152	-3	18	100	79	0	27.808	1	0
13	153	79	16	0	63	0	22.176	0	0
14	154	63	27	0	36	0	12.672	0	0
15	155	36	21	0	15	100	405.28	0	0
16	156	15	15	100	100	0	35.2	1	1
17	157	100	13	0	87	0	30.624	0	0
18	158	87	20	0	67	0	23.584	0	0
19	159	67	17	0	50	0	17.6	0	0
20	160	50	17	0	33	0	11.616	0	0
21	161	33	17	0	16	0	5.632	0	0
22	162	16	29	0	-13	100	400	0	0
23	163	-13	27	100	60	0	21.12	1	0
	.	.	.	.	.	.	.	.	.
	.	.	.	.	.	.	.	.	.
	.	.	.	.	.	.	.	.	.
100	240	92	24	0	68	0	23.936	0	0
101	241	68	21	0	47	0	16.544	0	0
102	242	47	19	0	28	0	9.856	0	0
103	243	28	13	0	15	100	405.28	0	0
104	244	15	19	100	96	0	33.792	1	1
105	245	96	20	0	76	0	26.752	0	0
106	246	76	27	0	49	0	17.248	0	0
107	247	49	27	0	22	0	7.744	0	0
108	248	22	14	0	8	100	402.816	0	0
109	249	8	11	100	97	0	34.144	1	1
110	250	97	20	0	77	0	27.104	0	0

---

but the negative beginning inventory for day 152 indicates it was not received in time to prevent a stockout.

During the period of the simulation, the average cost and the service level were computed. As shown in the spreadsheet, the average daily cost was $96.67, with a service level of 85.0%. To illustrate some additional methods of inventory simulation, we proceed next with a longer simulation before we attempt to improve the policy.

A Longer Simulation: Generating Random Demand Data

During the hundred days of the first simulation, only twenty orders were placed. If we want a better estimate of long-term behavior of the system with these

---------------------------------- **Figure 15.4** ----------------------------------

Documentation for Golden Audio's First Simulation

```
Cost per Order = 400
Holding Cost per Day = (72 + 16) / 250
Reorder Point = 15
Order Quantity = 100

Average[Daily Cost] = AVG (Daily Cost[Day 151] THRU Daily Cost[Day 250])

Average[Rec'd in Time] = SUM (Rec'd in Time[Day 151] THRU Rec'd in  Time[Day 250]) /
    SUM (Order Rec'd[Day 151] THRU Order Rec'd[Day 250])

Beginning Inventory[Day 151] = 6
Beginning Inventory[Day 152 THRU Day 250] = PREVIOUS Ending Inventory

Demand[Day 151]..Demand[Day 250] is documented in cells C11..C110

Quantity Received[Day 151] = 0
Quantity Received[Day 152 THRU Day 250] = PREVIOUS Quantity Ordered

Ending Inventory[Day 151 THRU Day 250] = Beginning Inventory +  Quantity Received − Demand

Quantity Ordered[Day 151 THRU Day 250] = IF (Ending Inventory <=
    Reorder Point THEN Order Quantity ELSE 0)

Daily Cost[Day 151 THRU Day 250] = IF (Quantity Ordered > 0  THEN Cost per Order ELSE 0) +
    IF (Ending Inventory > 0 THEN  Ending Inventory * Holding Cost per Day ELSE 0)

Order Rec'd[Day 151 THRU Day 250] = Quantity Received > 0

Rec'd in Time[Day 151 THRU Day 250] = (Order Rec'd = 1) #AND#  (Beginning Inventory >= 0)
```

> Note: The spreadsheet logical formula for Rec'd in Time uses the logical operator AND,
> which must be enclosed between the # symbols. Examples of logical formulas
> are shown in Figure 15.15 at the end of this chapter.

---

decision rules (reorder point, 15; order quantity, 100) we need to simulate more days. However, we only have about a hundred historical days of stable demand. If we assume that demand is random from day to day (a topic investigated in a supplement to this chapter), we can generate more demand data by using the Monte Carlo method to randomly select demand values in the same proportions they appear during the period of data collection. The spreadsheet **Data Distribution** (Lotus 1-2-3) or **Tools Frequency** (Quattro Pro) command helps us gather information about demand. We'll use this information with the @VLOOKUP spreadsheet function to generate more random demand data which has the "look and feel" of the original demand.

Figure 15.5 shows the spreadsheet used to develop the random demand generator for Golden Audio's 3581-X Speaker. We start with the daily demand, in columns A and B. The **Data Distribution** (**Tools Frequency**) command counts the occurrence of each demand value (from cells B6..B105) and puts these counts in the bins the user establishes. Here are the steps:

First, establish the bins for the various levels of demand. These are the integers 9..31 placed in cells D6..D28 in Figure 15.5. This can be done by keystrokes, or by **Data Fill** (Lotus 1-2-3) or **Edit Fill** (Quattro Pro).

Next, respond to the **Data Distribution** (or **Tools Frequency**) command prompts by identifying the values range (block) B6..B105 to be distributed (or counted to obtain the frequency).

—————————————— **Figure 15.5** ——————————————

Spreadsheet for Random Demand Generation, Golden Ear Audio

	A	B	C	D	E	F	G	H
							Proportion	
						Number	Less	
	Day	Demand		Bins	Counts	Less Than	Than	Demand
1	Golden Ear Audio: Hundred-Day Demand History, Item 3581-X							
2							Proportion	
3						Number	Less	
4	Day	Demand		Bins	Counts	Less Than	Than	Demand
5	===	======		====	======	=========	========	======
6	151	9		9	1	0	0.00	9
7	152	18		10	1	1	0.01	10
8	153	16		11	2	2	0.02	11
9	154	27		12	1	4	0.04	12
10	155	21		13	6	5	0.05	13
11	156	15		14	6	11	0.11	14
12	157	13		15	6	17	0.17	15
13	158	20		16	2	23	0.23	16
14	159	17		17	15	25	0.25	17
15	160	17		18	7	40	0.40	18
16	161	17		19	9	47	0.47	19
17	162	29		20	6	56	0.56	20
18	163	27		21	7	62	0.62	21
19	164	26		22	6	69	0.69	22
20	165	17		23	4	75	0.75	23
21	166	17		24	5	79	0.79	24
22	167	28		25	3	84	0.84	25
23	168	18		26	4	87	0.87	26
24	169	22		27	6	91	0.91	27
25	170	24		28	1	97	0.97	28
26	171	22		29	1	98	0.98	29
27	172	15		30	0	99	0.99	30
28	173	12		31	1	99	0.99	31
29	174	22			0	100	1.00	
30	175	18						
31	176	19						
	.	.						
	.	.						
	.	.						
102	247	27						
103	248	14						
104	249	11						
105	250	20						

Finally, respond to the prompts by identifying the bins as the range (block) D6..D28. The counts will immediately be placed in the cells adjacent to the bin values, column E in Figure 15.5.

The next step is to develop a running total of the counts, the Number Less Than, shown in F6..F29. This range starts in F6 with 0, because there are no demand values less than 9. Next, this expression is placed in F7:

$$\text{F7:} \qquad +\text{F6}+\text{E6}$$

which is then copied to F8..F29. This produces the running total. These values are converted to proportions in column G, by dividing by the total number of values (100, shown in F29):

G6:   +F6/$F$29

which is then copied to G7..G29. The final step is to construct a table for the @VLOOKUP function; the values from column D are copied into the same rows in column H. The following formula will generate a random demand, with the probabilities coming from days 151 to 250:

@VLOOKUP(@RAND,$G$6..$H$29,1)

A formula such as this can be used to generate each day's demand, replacing the third column of Figure 15.3. This table (columns G and H) could be keyed into a new spreadsheet.*

Spreadsheet Tip: The @VLOOKUP function looks up values in a table. The function has three arguments, separated by commas. In this illustration, the first argument (called the *search argument*) is @RAND, a random number between 0 and 1. This argument is used to search the table to find the correct row of the table. The table being searched is shown in the second argument, $G$6..$H$29. The spreadsheet goes down the first column of this table (which are cumulative probabilities in our example) and finds the first row of the table that *exceeds* the value of the search argument. It backs up one row, and moves to the right the number of columns indicated in the third argument (1 column in this illustration). The number in that cell is the value of the @VLOOKUP function.

Simulation Tip: It's not at all obvious that the @VLOOKUP function really generates demand the way we want. Here's the explanation. Let's focus on the fifth row of the table, a demand of 13 speakers. Six out of 100 days (0.06 or 6%) had this demand; the random numbers greater than 0.05 (cell G10) up to and including 0.11 (cell G11) correspond exactly to this 6%. Suppose the random number 0.07515 (which is in the 0.05 to 0.11 range) is drawn by the spreadsheet. The @VLOOKUP function searches from G6 down, until a number greater than 0.07515 is found; that number is 0.11, but then the spreadsheet backs up one row, to the row where demand is 13. The @VLOOKUP function will have a value of 13 when the random number 0.07515 is found. This will be the case for any random number greater than 0.05, and less than or equal to 0.11; this is exactly 6% of the random numbers, corresponding to 6% of the days with demand of 13.

A simulation worksheet identical to Figure 15.3, but with random demand and 1000 days, has been used to generate the table in Figure 15.6 and the graph of Figure 15.7. A series of simulations investigated the system behavior, using the same reorder point of 15 speakers. Various order quantities, from 150 speakers to 270 speakers, were investigated. As the order quantity increases, the average daily cost first decreases, then increases, as we would expect from our discussion

---

*There are other ways to get the information into a simulation spreadsheet. One method is to name the range G6..H29, save the file, retrieve the simulation spreadsheet, then combine this named range into the simulation spreadsheet. Another method is to extract the range G6..H29 into a new file, then combine that new file into the simulation worksheet.

Figure 15.6

Results of Multiple Simulation Runs, Reorder Point: 15 Speakers

Order Quantity	Average Daily Cost	Service Level
150	$76.72	76.6%
160	$75.31	86.7%
170	$73.89	82.3%
180	$73.85	84.3%
190	$72.77	73.5%
200	$72.39	81.3%
210	$72.37	74.7%
220	$72.44	77.5%
230	$72.76	81.0%
240	$72.67	66.3%
250	$74.35	83.3%
260	$74.80	81.3%
270	$75.03	81.7%

---

of cost behavior we observed in discussing economic order quantity. The service level wanders from 66% to 86%, with no apparent trend. As we would expect, the average daily cost appears to reach a low point in the vicinity of the Economic Order Quantity, which is 213 speakers. This illustrates the assertion, made at the beginning of the chapter, that it is often reasonable to disregard uncertainty when determining the order quantity. Note that the randomness inherent in a Monte Carlo simulation shows up as a "wiggle" in the graph. These wiggles could be smoothed by increasing the simulation beyond 1000 days.

Early in this chapter we explained that simulation doesn't tell us how to improve the way something works; it allows us to make comparisons. The information in Figure 15.6 compares many inventory policies, so that a good policy can be selected. But we can only find the best of those policies we have tried. We only tried policies with a reorder point of 15 speakers, so we have no way of knowing (yet) whether there are better policies. We next explore ways of setting the reorder point.

Inventory Analysis: When Should I Reorder?

If there were no uncertainty, deciding when to reorder would be straightforward: Place an order so it will arrive just when the last unit goes out the door. But as soon as demand becomes uncertain, or delivery lead times become uncertain, the problem becomes more difficult. The Golden Ear Audio Distributors case has illustrated inventory simulation with one arbitrary value for the reorder point. Our next task is to look at analysis of inventory systems to determine good values for the reorder point.

One piece of information we need is the *replenishment lead time*, the length of time between placing an order and receiving the speakers. We also need to know the *demand during a lead time*, or how many speakers are demanded during the replenishment lead time. Suppose there is no uncertainty: It always takes three

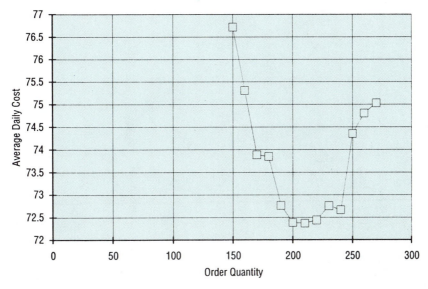

Figure 15.7

Average Daily Cost for Various Values of Order Quantity

Golden Ear Audio, Item 3581-X
Inventory Simulation, 1000 Days

days to get speakers from the manufacturer and have them available for shipment, and that we have demand for twenty speakers each business day. Then we should place an order when our stock gets down to sixty speakers. For the remainder of this chapter, we consider the Golden Ear Audio case with new information, that the replenishment lead time is three days. This allows us to continue with the same scenario, but learn more about inventory simulation. Our first analysis is to use a a historical approach, based on the history of demand for the last one hundred days.

Demand During a Lead Time: A Historical Approach

The historical data shows one hundred values of daily demand, days 151 through 250. Three days are required from the time an order is placed until it arrives; an order placed on day 155, for example, would be available for shipping to Golden's customers on day 158. We need information about demand during three-day intervals. This is done with a moving total, as shown in Figure 15.8. Column B of this worksheet shows the demand for the last hundred days; column C shows the total demand for successive three-day intervals. The first number is the total demand for the three days beginning at day 1; next is the demand for the three days beginning at day 2, and so on. In cell C7, this formula was entered:

C7:   @SUM(B7..B9)

which was copied from C7 to cells C8..C104.

-- **Figure 15.8** --

Golden Ear Audio: Worksheet for Determining Service Level

	A	B	C	D	E	F	G
	Golden Ear Audio: Hundred-Day Demand History, Item 3581-X						
1							
2				Sorted			
3			3-Day	3-Day	Service		
4	Day	Demand	Demand	Demand	Level		
5							
6	===	======	======	======	=======		
7	151	9	43	82	100.00%		
8	152	18	61	78	98.98%		
9	153	16	64	74	97.96%		
10	154	27	63	73	96.94%		
11	155	21	49	72	95.92%		
12	156	15	48	72	94.90%		
13	157	13	50	70	93.88%		
14	158	20	54	70	92.86%		
15	159	17	51	68	91.84%		
16	160	17	63	68	90.82%		
17	161	17	73	68	89.80%		
18	162	29	82	68	88.78%		
19	163	27	70	68	87.76%		
	.	.	.	.	.		
	.	.	.	.	.		
	.	.	.	.	.		
95	239	23	68	49	10.20%		
96	240	24	64	48	9.18%		
97	241	21	53	48	8.16%		
98	242	19	51	47	7.14%		
99	243	13	52	47	6.12%		
100	244	19	66	45	5.10%		
101	245	20	74	45	4.08%		
102	246	27	68	45	3.06%		
103	247	27	52	45	2.04%		
104	248	14	45	43	1.02%		
105	249	11					
106	250	20					

One way to make use of this information about demand during three-day intervals is to specify the level of service Golden Audio wants to provide for this speaker. Suppose management wants to provide service "so that 95% of the replenishment orders arrive before we have run out of speakers." If we sort the demand during three-day intervals, the sorted values shown in column D are obtained. In column E, we see percentages. The top number indicates that if we had reordered when the inventory level reached 82 units, we would have have provided service for 100% of the replenishment cycles, based on the hundred-day demand history. If we had placed an order whenever we reached an inventory level of 78 speakers, we would have provided service for 98.98% (97 out of 98) of the replenishment cycles. To provide 95% service, a reorder point of 72 speakers would have been appropriate.

Spreadsheet Tip: The 3–Day Demand shown in column C is computed with formulas in column C. These formulas need to be converted into values so they can be sorted. The formulas from column C are converted into the values in the adjacent cells in column D. (In Lotus 1-2-3, the commands are /**Range Value**; in Quattro, the commands are /**Edit Value**.) These value commands are nearly identical to the copy commands, except the formulas are converted to values when they are inserted into the destination range. After the values have been copied to column D, the **Data Sort** (or **Database Sort**) command is used to sort the range (block) D7..D104, using cell D7 as the primary (first) key, descending order.

Demand During a Lead Time: A Statistical Approach

The demand during a lead time can also be obtained using a statistical approach, if we are willing to assume that demand is *random* from day to day. Roughly speaking, demand is random from day to day if knowing one day's demand is no help in predicting the next day's demand. (A statistical investigation of randomness is presented in the supplement to this chapter.) The statistical approach also assumes that the shape of the frequency distribution of demand is somewhat close to "bell shaped" in appearance. The mean and standard deviation of the hundred days in the demand history are computed, using the spreadsheet functions @AVG and @STD. The values are:

$$\text{AVG} \quad 19.29 \text{ speakers}$$
$$\text{STD} \quad 4.68 \text{ speakers}$$

Statistical theory tells us that when we have random demand, the average demand and the standard deviation of demand over a three-day interval are found in this way:

THREE-DAY AVERAGE: $3 \times$ AVERAGE FOR ONE DAY

THREE-DAY STANDARD DEVIATION: STANDARD DEVIATION FOR ONE DAY $\times \sqrt{3}$

To apply this information to select the reorder point, we evaluate the mean and standard deviation for three days:

THREE-DAY AVERAGE: $3 \times 19.29 = 57.9$ SPEAKERS

THREE-DAY STANDARD DEVIATION: $4.68 \times \sqrt{3} = 8.1$ SPEAKERS

This can be generalized for a lead time of any length, say k days:

k-DAY AVERAGE: $k \times$ AVERAGE FOR ONE DAY

k-DAY STANDARD DEVIATION: STANDARD DEVIATION FOR ONE DAY $\times \sqrt{k}$

To find the reorder point, we first select a multiplier which depends upon the service level we desire. Various values of the multiplier are:

Service Level	Multiplier*
80%	0.84
90%	1.28
95%	1.64
98%	2.05
99%	2.33

The multiplier, times the three-day standard deviation, gives the "safety stock" that is needed to provide protection against uncertainties in demand during a three-day replenishment lead time:

SAFETY STOCK = MULTIPLIER × STANDARD DEVIATION OF DEMAND DURING LEAD TIME

Adding the average demand during a lead time to the safety stock gives the reorder point:

REORDER POINT = AVERAGE DEMAND DURING A LEAD TIME + SAFETY STOCK

REORDER POINT = 57.9 + (1.64 × 8.1) = 71.2

which compares closely with the value obtained from the historical analysis of demand.

The use of the statistical approach is based upon two factors: the applicability of the Central Limit Theorem, and whether demand is random. These two considerations are addressed in the supplement to this chapter.

Simulation of Golden Ear Audio with Three-Day Replenishment Lead Time

Our next inventory simulation uses the policies determined from analysis for the three-day replenishment lead time. We will use simulation to see how the Golden Ear Item 3581-X would have behaved for days 151 through 250, if we had placed an order for 213 speakers when we reached the reorder point of 72 speakers. From EOQ analysis and the simulation earlier in this chapter, we know that an order quantity of 213 speakers comes close to minimizing the sum of ordering and holding costs. From the reorder point analysis, a reorder point of 72 speakers should provide a 95% service level, meaning that 95% of the replenishment orders should arrive before the inventory has been exhausted. Will the system really behave this way?

When the replenishment lead time is more than one day, we can't base the reorder decision on the ending inventory level. Suppose we place an order on day 1; the order will be ready for customers on day 4. Unless a previous order arrives on day 2 or 3, we know the inventory level will be below the reorder point until day 4, when the order arrives. The reorder decision must be based on the total number of speakers *on hand and on order*. This means we need to keep track of the replenishment orders that have been placed, but are not yet on hand. The

---

*These values are from a table of the normal distribution. Readers who are familiar with the normal distribution are encouraged to verify these numbers from the complete table. Other readers are encouraged to accept their validity.

Figure 15.9

Influence Chart for Golden Ear Audio, Three-Day Lead Time

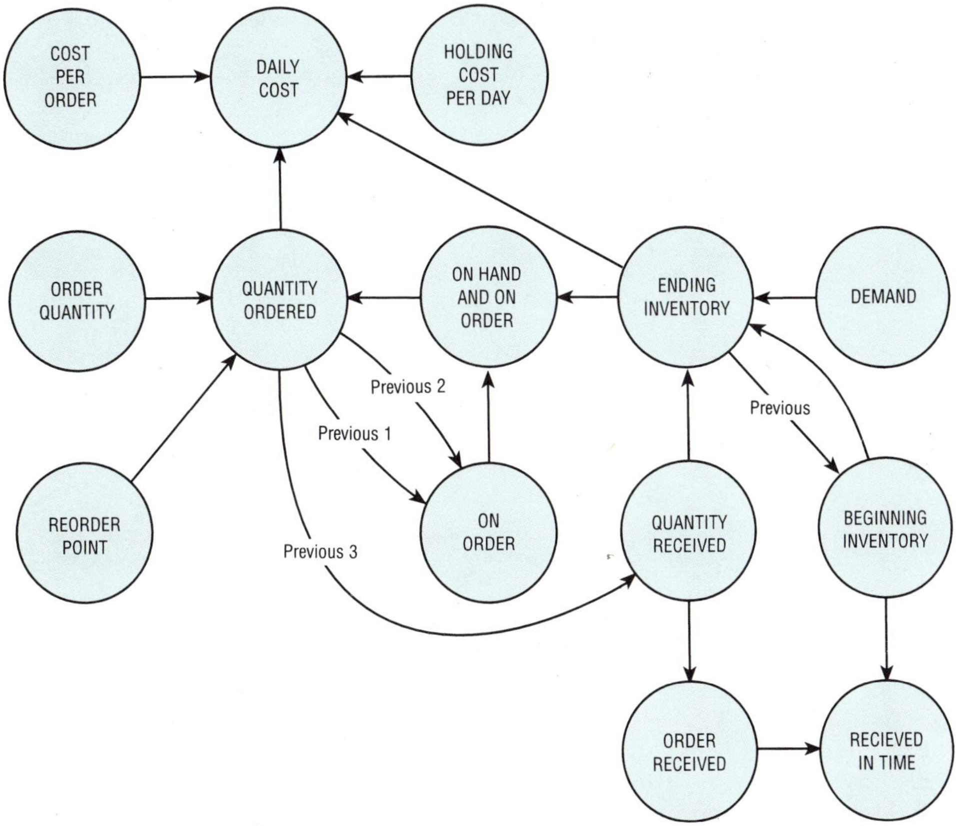

expanded influence chart is shown in Figure 15.9. The spreadsheet with the simulation is shown in Figure 15.10; the documentation of the model is shown in Figure 15.11.

The simulation begins in day 151 with 6 speakers on hand; demand is 9 speakers. Immediately, there is a stockout. The order is placed at the end of day 151, but the shortage continues into days 152 and 153. No orders are placed on these days, however, because the quantity on hand and on order exceeded the reorder point. The simulation results in an average daily cost of $80.69, and a 90% service level. Closer scrutiny of the results indicates that the only stockout was days 151 through 153; a total of ten orders were received during the simulation, and nine were on time. Clearly, the initial stockout was not typical of the system's behavior: it started with a handicap! With only 6 speakers on hand, and none on order, there was no way to avoid the stockout.

The initial conditions chosen for the simulation in Figure 15.10 were conditions that were virtually impossible for the system to experience; with a reorder point of 72 speakers, an order would have been placed in a period prior to the

────────────────────── **Figure 15.10** ──────────────────────

Spreadsheet Simulation for Golden Ear Audio, Three-Day Lead Time

	A	B	C	D	E	F	G	H	I
1	Cost per Order		400						
2	Hold Cost / Day		0.352						
3	Reorder Point		72						
4	Order Quantity		213						
5									
6	Average						80.691		90.0%
7									
8	Day	Begin	Demand	Qty	End	On	On Hd	Qty	Daily	Order	Rec'd
9		Invty		Recvd	Invty	Order	& On Or	Ordrd	Cost	Rec'd	in Time
10	===	=====	======	=====	=====	=====	=======	=====	=====	=====	=======
11	151	6	9	0	-3	0	-3	213	400	0	0
12	152	-3	18	0	-21	213	192	0	0	0	0
13	153	-21	16	0	-37	213	176	0	0	0	0
14	154	-37	27	213	149	0	149	0	52.448	1	0
15	155	149	21	0	128	0	128	0	45.056	0	0
16	156	128	15	0	113	0	113	0	39.776	0	0
17	157	113	13	0	100	0	100	0	35.2	0	0
18	158	100	20	0	80	0	80	0	28.16	0	0
19	159	80	17	0	63	0	63	213	422.17	0	0
20	160	63	17	0	46	213	259	0	16.192	0	0
21	161	46	17	0	29	213	242	0	10.208	0	0
22	162	29	29	213	213	0	213	0	74.976	1	1
23	163	213	27	0	186	0	186	0	65.472	0	0
	.	.	.	.	.	.	.	.	.	.	.
	.	.	.	.	.	.	.	.	.	.	.
	.	.	.	.	.	.	.	.	.	.	.
100	240	209	24	0	185	0	185	0	65.12	0	0
101	241	185	21	0	164	0	164	0	57.728	0	0
102	242	164	19	0	145	0	145	0	51.04	0	0
103	243	145	13	0	132	0	132	0	46.464	0	0
104	244	132	19	0	113	0	113	0	39.776	0	0
105	245	113	20	0	93	0	93	0	32.736	0	0
106	246	93	27	0	66	0	66	213	423.23	0	0
107	247	66	27	0	39	213	252	0	13.728	0	0
108	248	39	14	0	25	213	238	0	8.8	0	0
109	249	25	11	213	227	0	227	0	79.904	1	1
110	250	227	20	0	207	0	207	0	72.864	0	0

beginning of the simulation. Hence, the simulation result is not realistic system performance because of the poor starting conditions. We address this problem in two ways: try to start the system with realistic conditions, and throw away the first part of the simulation run. With this simple system, we could have easily determined realistic initial conditions (such as a starting inventory of 100, and none on order), but this is more difficult in some complex situations.

Another problem is that only 100 periods of simulation is hardly enough to confirm the service level, which we attempted to set at 95%. Using the random demand generation and 1010 periods of simulation (10 periods to discard from the beginning to allow for initial conditions, and 1000 periods of simulation), four simulations using different reorder points were run. The resulting values of service level are shown in Figure 15.12. These results are substantially different

---
Figure 15.11

Documentation for Golden Ear Audio, 3-Day Lead Time

```
Cost per Order = 400
Hold Cost / Day = (72 + 16) / 250
Reorder Point = 72
Order Quantity = 213

Average[Daily Cost] = AVG (Daily Cost[Day 151] THRU Daily Cost[Day 250])

Average[Rec'd in Time] = SUM (Rec'd in Time[Day 151] THRU Rec'd in Time[Day 250]) /
    SUM (Order Rec'd[Day 151] THRU Order Rec'd[Day 250])

Begin Invty[Day 151] = 6
Begin Invty[Day 152 THRU Day 250] = PREVIOUS End Invty

Demand[Day 151] = 9
Demand[Day 152] = 18
Demand[Day 153] = 16
    .    .    .    .
    .    .    .    .
    .    .    .    .
Demand[Day 248] = 14
Demand[Day 249] = 11
Demand[Day 250] = 20

Qty Recvd[Day 151 THRU Day 153] = 0
Qty Recvd[Day 154 THRU Day 250] = PREVIOUS 3 Qty Ordrd

End Invty[Day 151 THRU Day 250] = Begin Invty + Qty Recvd - Demand

On Order[Day 151] = 0
On Order[Day 152] = Qty Ordrd[Day 151]
On Order[Day 153 THRU Day 250] = PREVIOUS Qty Ordrd + PREVIOUS 2 Qty Ordrd

On Hd & On Ord[Day 151 THRU Day 250] = End Invty + On Order

Qty Ordrd[Day 151 THRU Day 250] = IF (On Hd & On Ord <=
    Reorder Point THEN Order Quantity ELSE 0)

Daily Cost[Day 151 THRU Day 250] = IF (Qty Ordrd > 0 THEN Cost per Order ELSE 0) +
    IF (End Invty > 0 THEN End Invty * Hold Cost / Day ELSE 0)

Order Rec'd[Day 151 THRU Day 250] = Qty Recvd > 0

Rec'd in Time[Day 151 THRU Day 250] = Order Rec'd > 0 #AND# Begin Invty >= 0
```

Figure 15.12

Service Level for Various Reorder Points, Based on Simulation

Reorder Point	Service Level
60	89%
65	93%
70	100%
75	100%

Note: Replications of the experiment to generate service level information will have different results, because new experiments will be based on new values of randomly determined demand.

---

from the results suggested by our analysis. Some possible explanations for these differences include:

The reported results have experimental error, because they come from a Monte Carlo simulation run or experiment. Repeating the experiment would give different results.

The historical approach to setting the reorder point suggested that a reorder point of 72 should achieve a 95% service level. The simulation used random demand, which was justified by the statistical analysis using the runs test (shown in the supplement to this chapter). While the statistical analysis did not reject the notion or hypothesis that demand is random, it may be that the test simply was not powerful enough to detect any nonrandom behavior of demand. Hence, the historical analysis (which did not assume random demand) gives service levels different from the simulation which assumed random demand.

The statistical approach to establishing demand during a lead time is based upon the Central Limit Theorem. It may be that the shape of the frequency distribution of demand during a three-day lead time is not close enough to a normal distribution (which is a bell-shaped curve).

The analysis assumes continuous review of inventory levels, so that an order can be placed at the instant the inventory level goes below the reorder point. The simulator, on the other hand, makes ordering decisions and performs bookkeeping chores only once each day. This may cause a difference between the simulated results and the analysis. In this particular simulation, we have assumed that orders are placed after knowing the daily demand, and that replenishment orders arrive in time to meet the current daily demand. An order placed on day 1 is received on day 4; however, there are really only two days of demand (days 2 and 3) in between. The analysis assumed that there were three days of demand in a replenishment cycle.

The difference between analysis and simulation illustrates both the usefulness and the frustration of Monte Carlo simulation. We use analysis to recommend decisions; these analyses are based on assumptions. We then use simulation to "try out" the recommendations; the simulation may require different assumptions. We get different results from analysis and simulation because each uses its own assumptions. While neither is "right" each has its own usefulness.

Exercises

1. The demand for laser printers is 5 printers for the first 10 days, then 3 printers for the next 10 days. Every evening you check your inventory level. If you have 4 or more printers, you do not place an order. If you have 3 or fewer printers, you place an order for 7 printers. These printers will be delivered first thing tomorrow morning. All printers demanded with none in stock are backordered and filled from the next delivery. The first day begins with 11 printers on hand.

a. Build a spreadsheet simulator to keep track of ending inventory with the inventory policy described in the scenario.

b. Add to the simulator the logic to keep track of the service level. To do this, you will need to keep track of the number of orders received during the simulation, and whether there are any backorders at the time each order is received.

c. Add to the simulator the logic to keep track of costs, which are $100 for each order placed and $1 for each printer in stock at the end of each day.

2. Using the scenario and simulator from Exercise 1, try various reorder points in addition to the base scenario which calls for a reorder point of 3 printers. Prepare a table that shows the cost and the service level for reorder points of 1, 2, 3, 4, and 5 printers.

3. Build a simulator for Exercise 1 with this change: printers that are demanded when there are no printers in stock are lost demand; customers will not accept backorders, but will order elsewhere. The costs are $100 for each order placed, $1 for each printer in stock at the end of each day, and $500 for each printer whose demand is lost. Prepare a table showing the total for reorder points of 1, 2, 3, 4, and 5 printers, with an order quantity of 7 printers.

4. The demand for boxes of notebook paper is 100 boxes per day for 5 days, then 120 boxes per day for 5 days, then 80 boxes per day for 5 days, then 90 boxes per day for 5 days. This entire cycle repeats itself for the next 20 days, and then again for another 20 days. The reorder point is 95 boxes; the reorder quantity is 250 boxes. The inventory level is checked at the end of each day; orders are placed (according to the rules) in the evening, for delivery first thing the next morning. The system starts with 75 boxes on hand.

a. Build a spreadsheet simulator to keep track of ending inventory with the inventory policy described in the scenario.

b. Add to the simulator the logic to keep track of the service level. To do this, you will need to keep track of the number of orders received during the simulation, and whether there are any backorders at the time each order is received.

c. Add to the simulator the logic to keep track of costs, which are $10 for each order placed and $0.04 for each box of paper in stock at the end of each day.

5. Using the scenario and simulator from Exercise 4, try various reorder points in addition to the base scenario. Prepare a table showing the cost and the service level for reorder points of 80, 90, 100, 110, and 120 boxes.

6. Using the scenario from Exercise 4, calculate the Economic Order Quantity and average demand over the entire sixty days. Using the simulator from Exercise 4 and a reorder point of 120 boxes, estimate the average daily cost of operating the inventory system, with the order quantity at the EOQ as you have calculated it, and at values both 50% above and 50% below that EOQ value.

7. Modify the scenario from Exercise 1 so that printers ordered at the close of one day are available at the beginning of the second day following the order placement. Printers ordered Monday evening are available Wednesday morning. The reorder point, based on printers on hand and on order, is 5 printers; the order quantity is still 7 printers. All printers demanded with none in stock are backordered and filled from the next delivery. The first day begins with 11 printers on hand.

   a. Build a spreadsheet simulator to keep track of ending inventory with the inventory policy described in the scenario.

   b. Add to the simulator the logic to keep track of the service level. To do this, you will need to keep track of the number of orders placed during the simulation, and whether there are any backorders at the time each order is placed.

   c. Add to the simulator the logic to keep track of costs, which are $100 for each order placed and $1 for each printer in stock at the end of each day.

8. Using the scenario and simulator from Exercise 7, try various reorder points in addition to the base scenario which calls for a reorder point of 5 printers. Prepare a table that shows the cost and the service level for reorder points of 3, 4, 5, 6, 7, 8, 9, and 10 printers.

9. Modify the scenario from Exercise 4 so that there is a three-day replenishment lead time. Orders placed Monday evening are available Thursday morning, and so on. The reorder point, based on boxes on hand and on order, is 300 boxes. The reorder quantity is still 250 boxes. The system starts with 75 boxes on hand, and none on order (which is unreasonable; why?).

   a. Build a spreadsheet simulator to keep track of ending inventory with the inventory policy described in the scenario.

   b. Add to the simulator the logic to keep track of the service level. To do this, you will need to keep track of the number of orders received during the simulation, and whether there are any backorders at the time each order is received.

   c. Add to the simulator the logic to keep track of costs, which are $10 for each order placed and $0.04 for each box of paper in stock at the end of each day.

10. Repeat Exercise 9, but start with an initial inventory of 400 boxes. Discuss the importance of the starting conditions for generalizing from your experiments.

11. Demand for printer ribbons for a popular computer printer averages 15 ribbons per week, with a standard deviation of 4 ribbons. Using the statistical approach, what is the distribution of demand during a four-week replenishment lead time? What reorder point would you recommend to achieve a 95% service level? Describe any assumptions you have made in answering this questions.

12. Daily demand for 100 watt light bulbs is described by this history of 128 days:

Daily Demand	Number of Days
0	50
1	35
2	21
3	14
4	6
5	2

a. Find the average and standard deviation for daily demand. *Spreadsheet Note:* To find values for these statistics, enter a value of 0 in a cell, then copy it to the next 49 cells below it. Then enter a 1 into the next cell, and copy it into the 34 cells below it. Continue this for all observations in the sample. Using this column of 128 observations in the sample, use @AVG and @STD to find the statistics for the sample.

b. Using the statistical method, determine the reorder point to provide 80% service level for a two-day replenishment lead time.

c. Using the statistical method, determine the reorder point to provide 80% service level for a ten-day replenishment lead time.

d. Next to each of the 128 observations in the sample, enter a formula to find a random number, @RAND. Shuffle the list of demands by sorting these two columns, using the column of random numbers as the sort key. Using this randomly generated demand as historical data, find the reorder point to provide 80% service level for two-day replenishment lead time, and again for ten-day replenishment lead time.

e. Why might your results from (d) differ from the results for (b) and (c)?

13. Generate 100 days of daily demand from a triangular distribution with lowest value of 100, modal value of 120, and highest value of 160. After these demand values have been generated using a spreadsheet formula, convert them from formulas to values (/**Range Value** in Lotus, or /**Edit Value** in Quattro).

a. Using the statistical method, determine the reorder point to provide 90% service level for a two-day replenishment lead time.

b. Using the statistical method, determine the reorder point to provide 90% service level for a ten-day replenishment lead time.

c. Using the historical method, find the reorder point to provide 90% service level for a two-day replenishment lead time, and again for a ten-day replenishment lead time.

d. Why might your results from (c) differ from the results for (a) and (b)?

14. An inventory item has daily demand described by a normal distribution with an average value (mean) of 25 units and a standard deviation of 10 units. Replenishment orders are received the day after they are placed. The current inventory policy is to order 150 units any evening when the closing inventory falls to 35 or fewer. These units will be delivered first thing the next day. The inventory carrying cost is $1 per unit per day, based on ending inventory. The cost or ordering

is $100. Construct a simulator to track inventory levels and daily cost using this policy. What service level is provided? What is the average daily cost? Assume that items demanded when there is a stockout are filled when the next replenishment order arrives. The simulator developed for Exercise 1 can easily be modified for this exercise. Change the demand for each period to the function or formula that will generate the normal distribution:

$$\texttt{@SQRT(-2*@LN(@RAND))*@COS(2*@PI*@RAND)*10+25}$$

Start with a reasonable starting inventory (such as 75), and extend the simulator for more periods (such as 500).

15. Modify your simulator (Exercise 14) so that the order quantity is the economic order quantity. Run the simulation a number of times, with the reorder point at 20, 25, 30, 35, 40, 45, and 50 units. Develop information for management that shows the service level provided, along with the cost of the inventory system that provides that level of service.

SUPPLEMENT

The Central Limit Theorem
& The Runs Test

To use the statistical approach to determine the demand during a lead time, we need to consider two things: the applicability of the Central Limit Theorem, and whether demand is random. The Central Limit Theorem states that the sum of independent daily demands is approximately described by the normal distribution, and that this approximation gets better as the number of days in the lead time increases, and as the shape of daily demands is closer to unimodal (single peak) and symmetrical. Generally, the shape is unimportant if the number of daily demand values in the summation is large—say, larger than about 20 or 30. But if the number of daily demand values in the summation is small—say, three as for Golden Ear—then the daily demand values should have a shape which is unimodal and reasonably symmetrical to justify using the statistical method.

The histogram of Figure 15.13 shows the shape of daily demand; it is peaked, but not quite symmetrical. Judgmentally, it is reasonable to use the statistical approach, providing the test of randomness (below) is passed.

The statistical approach to determining the reorder point assumes that the demand is random. This can be investigated by a statistical test called a "runs test." A runs test can be conducted by first identifying whether each day's demand is above or below the average demand. (Some other value, such as the median, could just as well be used. However, the average is easier to calculate on a spreadsheet, so we use the average demand in this discussion.) A "run" is a

Figure 15.13

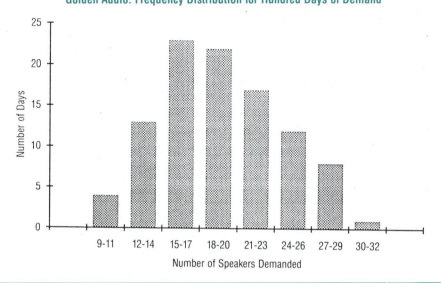

Golden Audio: Frequency Distribution for Hundred Days of Demand

sequence of days all above the average demand, or a sequence of days all below the average demand. First we discuss counting runs on a spreadsheet, then we explore the statistical theory used to tell us about how many runs there should be, if daily demand is random.

To see how to count runs, look at the spreadsheet shown (abbreviated) in Figure 15.14. The average daily demand is 19.29. Each day's demand is marked with a 1 or 0 to indicate whether it is above or below the average demand. Each day is also marked (in the last column) with a 1 if that day begins a run, and with a 0 if it does not begin the run. From this figure we see (from Sum) that there are 44 daily demand values above the mean (and therefore 56 values below the mean), and there are 46 runs.

The spreadsheet logic to generate the ones and zeros may need some explanation. Although the spreadsheet could be developed using the @IF function to assign the values of 0 and 1, we use this opportunity to describe the use of logical formulas on a spreadsheet. A logical formula compares two values, using the logical operators shown here:

=	is equal to
<	is less than
>	is greater than
<=	is less than or equal to
>=	is greater than or equal to
<>	is not equal to

A logical formula has a value of one (1) if the formula is true; it has a value of zero (0) if it is false. Figure 15.15 shows some examples of logical formulas.

——————————— **Figure 15.14** ———————————

Worksheet for Daily Demand: Counting Runs

	A	B	C	D
1	Golden Ear Audio:		Daily Demand for First Year, Item 3581- X	
2		Average:	Sum:	Sum:
3		19.29	44	46
4			Above (1)	Beginning
5	Day	Demand	Below (0)	of a Run?
6	===	======	=========	========
7	151	9	0	1
8	152	18	0	0
9	153	16	0	0
10	154	27	1	1
11	155	21	1	0
12	156	15	0	1
13	157	13	0	0
14	158	20	1	1
15	159	17	0	1
16	160	17	0	0
17	161	17	0	0
18	162	29	1	1
19	163	27	1	0
	.	.	.	.
	.	.	.	.
	.	.	.	.
95	239	23	1	1
96	240	24	1	0
97	241	21	1	0
98	242	19	0	1
99	243	13	0	0
100	244	19	0	0
101	245	20	1	1
102	246	27	1	0
103	247	27	1	0
104	248	14	0	1
105	249	11	0	0
106	250	20	1	1

The logical formula to determine whether a value is above the average compares each value to the average. The logical formula in cell C7, Figure 15.10, is:

C7:   +B7>$B$3

which can be copied throughout the C column.

The logical formula to determine whether a run begins in a row compares the Above or Below indicator with the same indicator a row above. The logical formula in cell D8 is:

D8:   +C8<>C7

If it is true that C8 is not equal to C7, a run has been started; otherwise, no run has been started. We use the logical formula with a value of 1 to indicate the start of a run in a given row; the value 1 appears in D7, D10, D12, . . . to mark the beginning of runs.

Figure 15.15

Some Examples of Logical Formulas

Suppose a spreadsheet has these values in row 1:

	A	B	C	D	E
1	4	12	JOE	160	3
2					

Then the logical formula

$$+A1+B1=11$$

would have a value of 0 (false), while the logical formula +D1/A1>5 would have a value of 1 (true). The reader is encouraged to verify the value of each of these expressions:

Expression	Value
+A1<>4	0
+A1>4	0
+A1>=4	1
+C1="JOE"	1
+C1<>"Mage"	1
+C1="Joseph"	0

What do we do with the number of runs? Statistical theory* tells us how to compute the expected number of runs, by knowing the number of values above the average and below the average (44 and 56, in this example). Using the symbol A to denote the number of values above the average, and B to denote the number of values below the average, the expected number of runs is:

Formula for Expected Number of Runs:

$$1 + \frac{2AB}{A+B}$$

or in spreadsheet form

$$1+2*A*B/(A+B)$$

Values for Expected Number of Runs for Daily Demand:

$$1+2*44*56/(44+56)=50.28$$

We observed only 46 runs. Are there too few runs? If the series of daily demand values is not random, perhaps there are clusters of runs below the average, and clusters above the average. This would show up as too few runs. But is 46 too far away from 50.28 to be of concern?

Statistical theory helps us determine if the observed number of runs is "too far" from the expected number of runs. This is done by calculating a value called the *standard error* of the number of runs. This value is calculated in this way:

---

*The discussion that follows is a *"Wall Street Journal* discussion" of hypothesis testing. Those who are thoroughly grounded in hypothesis testing may find it is sufficient to skim this material. The material is intended for those whose background in testing statistical hypotheses may be somewhat distant, weak, or null.

Formula for Standard Error for Number of Runs:

$$\sqrt{\frac{2AB(2AB - A - B)}{(A + B)^2[(A + B) - 1]}} = 4.90 \text{ runs}$$

or in spreadsheet form

@SQRT(2*A*B*(2*A*B–A–B)/((A+B)^2*(A+B–1)))=4.90

Values for Standard Error for Number of Runs for Daily Demand:

@SQRT(2*44*56*(2*44*56–44–56)/((44+56)^2*(44+56–1)))=4.90

Again from statistical theory, we know that "most of the time" (roughly, about 19 times out of 20) the number of runs we observe will be within two standard errors of the expected number of runs, if it is true that the time series is random. Statisticians use the term *Z-value* as jargon for the number of standard errors between the *observed* number of runs and the *expected* number of runs. The Z-value is calculated in this way:

$$Z\text{-}value = \frac{\text{OBSERVED NUMBER OF RUNS} - \text{EXPECTED NUMBER OF RUNS}}{\text{STANDARD ERROR}}$$

Numerically,

Z=(46–50.28)/4.90=–0.87

This calculation means that the observed number of runs is 0.87 standard errors below the expected number of runs. "Most of the time" (when demand is random) the observed number of runs will be within two standard errors of the expected number of runs, so we have no statistical reason to doubt the premise of randomness of demand.

A Warning: This method of testing demand for randomness requires that we have at least (about) thirty observations, and at least ten observations above the average, and at least ten observations below the average. If you have at least thirty observations, but fewer than ten above (or below) the mean, choose the median rather than the average for determining whether a demand value is above or below. (Another problem sometimes arises: What do you do with values exactly on the median. Pragmatically, avoid this problem by choosing a point of demarcation just slightly above or slightly below the median, so ties are completely avoided.)

CASE STUDY:

Golden Ear Audio (D)

In addition to speaker 3581-X, Golden Ear Audio has taken on an additional product, item 4811-X. This new item is supplied by the same supplier as Item 3581-X; if both speakers are ordered jointly, the ordering cost (including the test procedure setup) is $500. Ordering just this additional item incurs an ordering cost of $300. The annual holding cost for 4811-X is $50 per speaker per year. Only fifty days of stable demand data are available for this speaker; demand information, including a test for randomness, is shown in Exhibit 15.1.

─────────────── **Exhibit 15.1** ───────────────

Demand Information for Item 4811-X

	A	B	C	D	E	F	G
1	Demand for Item 4811-X					Avg Dmd:	15.04
2						Std Dmd:	2.591987
3			Sum:	Sum:			
4			19	22		Above and Below Avg:	
5			Above	Start		Above:	19
6		Day	Demand	Avg?	Run	Below:	31
7		===	======	=====	=====		
8	1	14	0	1		Number of Runs:	
9	2	14	0	0		Expected:	24.56
10	3	19	1	1		SE:	3.293511
11	4	13	0	1			
12	5	16	1	1		The observed number of	
13	6	20	1	0		runs, 22, is within two	
14	7	14	0	1		standard errors (2*3.2935)	
15	8	15	0	0		of the expected number	
16	9	13	0	0		of runs (24.56). Hence,	
17	10	13	0	0		we do not reject the	
18	11	16	1	1		hypothesis that demand	
19	12	13	0	1		is random.	
20	13	16	1	1			
21	14	18	1	0			
22	15	17	1	0			
	.	.	.	.			
	.	.	.	.			
	.	.	.	.			
53	46	10	0	0			
54	47	17	1	1			
55	48	12	0	1			
56	49	16	1	1			
57	50	19	1	0			
58							
59	Data Distribution for Random Demand						
60							
61	Demand	Number	Days	Prop'n	Demand		
62		of Days	LessThan	LessThan			
63	10	1	0	0	10		
64	11	3	1	0.02	11		
65	12	4	4	0.08	12		
66	13	6	8	0.16	13		
67	14	10	14	0.28	14		
68	15	7	24	0.48	15		
69	16	5	31	0.62	16		
70	17	5	36	0.72	17		
71	18	2	41	0.82	18		
72	19	4	43	0.86	19		
73	20	2	47	0.94	20		
74	21	1	49	0.98	21		
75		0	50	1	0		

What are reasonable order quantities for the two speakers? Using an annual demand of 15 speakers per day, for 250 business days a year, the EOQ if the new item is ordered by itself is:

$$\sqrt{\frac{2 \times \text{ANNUAL DEMAND} \times \text{ORDER COST}}{\text{HOLDING COST}}}$$

or

$$\text{SQRT}(2*250*15*300/50)=212$$

If we consider only the incremental order cost of $100, the EOQ value is:

$$\text{SQRT}(2*250*15*100/50)=125$$

For the original item 3581-X, the EOQ value assuming the item is ordered by itself has already been discussed; its value is 213 speakers. If only the incremental ordering cost of $100 is considered, the EOQ value is:

$$\text{SQRT}(2*250*20*100/88)=107 \text{ speakers}$$

From this analysis, it is reasonable that the average order quantity for 3581-X should be someplace between 107 speakers and 213 speakers; for item 4811-X it should be someplace between 125 and 212 speakers.

We need to determine reorder points for each speaker, to guarantee that at least a desired service level will be attained. Based on the information in Figure 15.14, we estimate that a reorder point of about 67 speakers will provide a service level of approximately 95% for item 3581-X. A reasonable reorder point for item 4811-X, using data from Exhibit 15.1, is:

$$\text{REORDER POINT} = \text{AVERAGE DEMAND DURING LEAD TIME} + \text{SAFETY STOCK}$$

$$\begin{aligned}\text{AVERAGE DEMAND DURING LEAD TIME} &= 3 \times \text{DAILY DEMAND} \\ &= 3 \times 15 \\ &= 45 \text{ speakers}\end{aligned}$$

$$\begin{aligned}\text{SAFETY STOCK} &= 1.65 \times \text{STANDARD DEVIATION OF DEMAND DURING LEAD TIME} \\ &= 1.65 \times 2.59\sqrt{3} = 7.4, \quad \text{or about } 7\end{aligned}$$

From these computations, we will use a reorder point of 52 speakers for Item 4811-X. With these reorder points fixed, we can use simulation to evaluate a variety of reorder policies for these two items. We list here two of many different "reasonable" policies to consider:

Policy A: Make independent ordering decisions for each items. When item 3581-X reaches its reorder point of 67 speakers, order 213. When item 4811-X reaches reaches its reorder point or 52 speakers, order 212 speakers.

Policy B: Whenever either item reaches its reorder point, order its quantity (213 or 212). At the same time, order the "incremental EOQ" of the other product: 125 speakers 3581-X, or 107 speakers 4511-X.

--- **Exhibit 15.2** ---

Hundred Day Two-Item Simulation for Golden Ear Audio, Policy A

	A	B	C	D	E	F	G	H	I	J	K	L	M	N	O	P	Q	R
1	Cost per Order		400							Cost per Order			300	or	100			
2	Hold Cost / Day		0.352							Hold Cost / Day			0.2					
3	Reorder Point		72							Reorder Point			52					
4	Order Quantity		213							Order Quantity			212					
5													Primary		Secondary			
6	Average							80.582										44.282
7	Item 3581-X....................................									Item 4811- X....................................								
8	Day	Begin	Demand	Qty	End	On	On Hd	Qty	Daily	Begin	Demand	Qty	End	On	On Hd	Qty	Order	Daily
9		Invty		Recvd	Invty	Order &	On Or	Ordrd	Cost	Invty		Recvd	Invty	Order &	On Or	Ordrd	Cost	Cost
10	===	=====	======	=====	=====	=====	=======	=====	=====	=====	======	=====	=====	=====	=======	=====	=====	=====
11	1	6	21	0	-15	0	-15	213	400	25	20	0	5	0	5	212	100	101
12	2	-15	10	0	-25	213	188	0	0	5	13	0	-8	212	204	0	300	0
13	3	-25	13	0	-38	213	175	0	0	-8	18	0	-26	212	186	0	300	0
14	4	-38	20	213	155	0	155	0	54.56	-26	11	212	175	0	175	0	300	35
15	5	155	24	0	131	0	131	0	46.112	175	15	0	160	0	160	0	300	32
16	6	131	18	0	113	0	113	0	39.776	160	17	0	143	0	143	0	300	28.6
17	7	113	15	0	98	0	98	0	34.496	143	12	0	131	0	131	0	300	26.2
18	8	98	13	0	85	0	85	0	29.92	131	16	0	115	0	115	0	300	23
19	9	85	21	0	64	0	64	213	422.52	115	17	0	98	0	98	0	100	19.6
20	10	64	17	0	47	213	260	0	16.544	98	16	0	82	0	82	0	300	16.4
21	11	47	17	0	30	213	243	0	10.56	82	14	0	68	0	68	0	300	13.6
22	12	30	17	213	226	0	226	0	79.552	68	11	0	57	0	57	0	300	11.4
23	13	226	17	0	209	0	209	0	73.568	57	11	0	46	0	46	212	300	309.2
24	14	209	20	0	189	0	189	0	66.528	46	14	0	32	212	244	0	300	6.4
25	15	189	18	0	171	0	171	0	60.192	32	18	0	14	212	226	0	300	2.8
26	16	171	17	0	154	0	154	0	54.208	14	12	212	214	0	214	0	300	42.8
27	17	154	15	0	139	0	139	0	48.928	214	14	0	200	0	200	0	300	40
28	18	139	17	0	122	0	122	0	42.944	200	17	0	183	0	183	0	300	36.6
29	19	122	23	0	99	0	99	0	34.848	183	15	0	168	0	168	0	300	33.6
30	20	99	21	0	78	0	78	0	27.456	168	16	0	152	0	152	0	300	30.4
31	21	78	20	0	58	0	58	213	420.41	152	14	0	138	0	138	0	100	27.6
32	22	58	20	0	38	213	251	0	13.376	138	12	0	126	0	126	0	300	25.2
33	23	38	14	0	24	213	237	0	8.448	126	16	0	110	0	110	0	300	22
34	24	24	13	213	224	0	224	0	78.848	110	15	0	95	0	95	0	300	19
35	25	224	20	0	204	0	204	0	71.808	95	14	0	81	0	81	0	300	16.2
36	26	204	19	0	185	0	185	0	65:12	81	13	0	68	0	68	0	300	13.6
37	27	185	22	0	163	0	163	0	57.376	68	18	0	50	0	50	212	300	310
38	28	163	23	0	140	0	140	0	49.28	50	11	0	39	212	251	0	300	7.8
39	29	140	19	0	121	0	121	0	42.592	39	20	0	19	212	231	0	300	3.8
40	30	121	15	0	106	0	106	0	37.312	19	15	212	216	0	216	0	300	43.2
41	31	106	9	0	97	0	97	0	34.144	216	16	0	200	0	200	0	300	40
42	32	97	20	0	77	0	77	0	27.104	200	14	0	186	0	186	0	300	37.2
43	33	77	25	0	52	0	52	213	418.30	186	10	0	176	0	176	0	100	35.2
44	34	52	17	0	35	213	248	0	12.32	176	14	0	162	0	162	0	300	32.4
45	35	35	17	0	18	213	231	0	6.336	162	14	0	148	0	148	0	300	29.6
46	36	18	21	213	210	0	210	0	73.92	148	14	0	134	0	134	0	300	26.8
47	37	210	21	0	189	0	189	0	66.528	134	14	0	120	0	120	0	300	24
48	38	189	17	0	172	0	172	0	60.544	120	11	0	109	0	109	0	300	21.8
49	39	172	13	0	159	0	159	0	55.968	109	13	0	96	0	96	0	300	19.2
50	40	159	20	0	139	0	139	0	48.928	96	19	0	77	0	77	0	300	15.4
51	41	139	27	0	112	0	112	0	39.424	77	12	0	65	0	65	0	300	13
52	42	112	22	0	90	0	90	0	31.68	·65	17	0	48	0	48	212	300	309.6
	.	.	.	.	.	.	.	.	.	.	.	.	.	.	.	.	.	.
105	95	174	18	0	156	0	156	0	54.912	136	14	0	122	0	122	0	300	24.4
106	96	156	26	0	130	0	130	0	45.76	122	15	0	107	0	107	0	300	21.4
107	97	130	19	0	111	0	111	0	39.072	107	13	0	94	0	94	0	300	18.8
108	98	111	24	0	87	0	87	0	30.624	94	15	0	79	0	79	0	300	15.8
109	99	87	23	0	64	0	64	213	422.52	79	10	0	69	0	69	0	100	13.8
110	100	64	17	0	47	213	260	0	16.544	69	18	0	51	0	51	212	300	310.2

Analysis of Policy A

Exhibit 15.2 shows a hundred day simulation worksheet for both items, using the decision rules which are documented in Exhibit 15.3. These decision rules implement Policy A. All of the logic for keeping track of each item is exactly the same as shown in Figure 15.13. Demand is randomly generated, using the frequencies shown in Figure 15.8 and Exhibit 15.1. The average cost values are for the entire

─────────────────────────────── **Exhibit 15.3** ───────────────────────────────

Logic of Decision Rules for Golden Ear Audio's Two-Item Simulation shown in Exhibit 2, Policy A

```
Qty Ordrd Item 3581[Day 1 THRU Day 100] = IF (On Hd & On Ord Item 3581 <=
    Reorder Point Item 3581 THEN Order Quantity Item 3581 ELSE 0)

Daily Cost Item 3581[Day 1 THRU Day 100] = IF (Qty Ordrd Item 3581 > 0 THEN Cost per Order
    Item 3581 ELSE 0) + IF (End Invty Item 3581 > 0 THEN End Invty Item 3581 * Hold Cost /
    Day Item 3581 ELSE 0)

Qty Ordrd Item 4811[Day 1 THRU Day 100] = IF (On Hd & On Ord Item 4811 <=
    Reorder Point Item 4811 THEN Order Quantity Item 4811 ELSE 0)

Order Cost Item 4811[Day 1 THRU Day 100] = IF (Qty Ordrd Item 3581 > 0 THEN Cost per Order
    Item 4811[Secondary] ELSE Cost per Order Item 4811[Primary])

Daily Cost Item 4811[Day 1 THRU Day 100] = IF (Qty Ordrd Item 4811 > 0 THEN Order Cost
    Item 4811 ELSE 0) + IF (End Invty Item 4811 > 0 THEN End Invty Item 4811 * Hold Cost /
    Day Item 4811 ELSE 0)
```

hundred-day period. The cost of ordering item 3581-X has always been set at $400; the `Cost per Order` for item 4811-X is set at $300 if the other item is not ordered that day, but at $100 if the other item is ordered that day. The average daily cost for this system is estimated by this simulation to be

$$\$80.58 + \$44.28 = \$124.86$$

This value has experimental error. Different demand values, different initial conditions, and simulations of different number of days would lead to different results.

Analysis of Policy B

Exhibit 15.4 shows a hundred-day simulation worksheet for both items, using the decision rules which are documented in Exhibit 15.5. These decision rules implement Policy B. All logic for keeping track of each item, and the method of demand generation, is exactly the same as shown in Exhibit 15.2. The attribution of ordering cost is arbitrarily set for $400 for item 3581-X, if both are ordered. The average daily cost, subject to experimental variation as explained in the analysis of Policy A, is estimated by the simulation to be

$$\$84.96 + \$34.75 = \$119.71$$

Based on these two simulation experiments, there is reason to suggest that Policy B is more attractive than Policy A.

Case Exercises

1. For Policy A, extend the simulation to (say) 500 days, and discard (say) the initial ten periods. Then compare policies A and B, allowing randomness to determine the demand sequence for evaluating policy A and different random demand sequences for evaluating policy B.

─────────────────── **Exhibit 15.4** ───────────────────

Hundred Day Simulation for Policy B

	A	B	C	D	E	F	G	H	I	J	K	L	M	N	O	P	Q	R
1	Cost per Order		400							Cost per Order			300	or	100			
2	Hold Cost / Day		0.352							Hold Cost / Day			0.2					
3	Reorder Point		72							Reorder Point			52					
4	Order Quantity		213	or	125					Order Quantity			212	or	107			
5				Primary		Secondary							Primary		Secondary			
6	Average								84.958									34.756
7		Item 3581- X...								Item 4811- X...								
8	Day	Begin	Demand	Qty	End	On	On Hd	Qty	Daily	Begin	Demand	Qty	End	On	On Hd	Qty	Order	Daily
9		Invty		Recvd	Invty	Order	& On Or	Ordrd	Cost	Invty		Recvd	Invty	Order	& On Or	Ordrd	Cost	Cost
10	===	=====	======	=====	=====	=====	=======	=====	=====	=====	======	=====	=====	=====	=======	=====	=====	=====
11	1	6	21	0	-15	0	-15	213	400	25	13	0	12	0	12	212	100	102.4
12	2	-15	25	0	-40	213	173	0	0	12	12	0	0	212	212	0	300	0
13	3	-40	20	0	-60	213	153	0	0	0	12	0	-12	212	200	0	300	0
14	4	-60	18	213	135	0	135	0	47.52	-12	14	212	186	0	186	0	300	37.2
15	5	135	19	0	116	0	116	0	40.832	186	11	0	175	0	175	0	300	35
16	6	116	13	0	103	0	103	0	36.256	175	20	0	155	0	155	0	300	31
17	7	103	19	0	84	0	84	0	29.568	155	13	0	142	0	142	0	300	28.4
18	8	84	19	0	65	0	65	213	422.88	142	17	0	125	0	125	107	100	125
19	9	65	21	0	44	213	257	0	15.488	125	11	0	114	107	221	0	300	22.8
20	10	44	21	0	23	213	236	0	8.096	114	14	0	100	107	207	0	300	20
21	11	23	18	213	218	0	218	0	76.736	100	19	107	188	0	188	0	300	37.6
22	12	218	19	0	199	0	199	0	70.048	188	19	0	169	0	169	0	300	33.8
23	13	199	13	0	186	0	186	0	65.472	169	12	0	157	0	157	0	300	31.4
24	14	186	20	0	166	0	166	0	58.432	157	19	0	138	0	138	0	300	27.6
25	15	166	21	0	145	0	145	0	51.04	138	12	0	126	0	126	0	300	25.2
26	16	145	15	0	130	0	130	0	45.76	126	11	0	115	0	115	0	300	23
27	17	130	21	0	109	0	109	0	38.368	115	14	0	101	0	101	0	300	20.2
28	18	109	26	0	83	0	83	0	29.216	101	11	0	90	0	90	0	300	18
29	19	83	25	0	58	0	58	213	420.41	90	16	0	74	0	74	107	100	114.8
30	20	58	17	0	41	213	254	0	14.432	74	13	0	61	107	168	0	300	12.2
31	21	41	16	0	25	213	238	0	8.8	61	18	0	43	107	150	0	300	8.6
32	22	25	28	213	210	0	210	0	73.92	43	19	107	131	0	131	0	300	26.2
33	23	210	17	0	193	0	193	0	67.936	131	14	0	117	0	117	0	300	23.4
34	24	193	21	0	172	0	172	0	60.544	117	17	0	100	0	100	0	300	20
35	25	172	19	0	153	0	153	0	53.856	100	14	0	86	0	86	0	300	17.2
36	26	153	17	0	136	0	136	0	47.872	86	17	0	69	0	69	0	300	13.8
37	27	136	14	0	122	0	122	0	42.944	69	14	0	55	0	55	0	300	11
38	28	122	17	0	105	0	105	125	436.96	55	12	0	43	0	43	212	100	108.6
39	29	105	24	0	81	125	206	0	28.512	43	12	0	31	212	243	0	300	6.2
40	30	81	26	0	55	125	180	0	19.36	31	13	0	18	212	230	0	300	3.6
41	31	55	15	125	165	0	165	0	58.08	18	17	212	213	0	213	0	300	42.6
42	32	165	26	0	139	0	139	0	48.928	213	15	0	198	0	198	0	300	39.6
43	33	139	11	0	128	0	128	0	45.056	198	17	0	181	0	181	0	300	36.2
44	34	128	17	0	111	0	111	0	39.072	181	16	0	165	0	165	0	300	33
45	35	111	17	0	94	0	94	0	33.088	165	19	0	146	0	146	0	300	29.2
46	36	94	25	0	69	0	69	213	424.28	146	17	0	129	0	129	107	100	125.8
47	37	69	26	0	43	213	256	0	15.136	129	16	0	113	107	220	0	300	22.6
48	38	43	13	0	30	213	243	0	10.56	113	11	0	102	107	209	0	300	20.4
49	39	30	20	213	223	0	223	0	78.496	102	21	107	188	0	188	0	300	37.6
50	40	223	20	0	203	0	203	0	71.456	188	13	0	175	0	175	0	300	35
51	41	203	22	0	181	0	181	0	63.712	175	15	0	160	0	160	0	300	32
52	42	181	22	0	159	0	159	0	55.968	160	15	0	145	0	145	0	300	29
	.	.	.	.	.	.	.	.	.	.	.	.	.	.	.	.	.	.
	.	.	.	.	.	.	.	.	.	.	.	.	.	.	.	.	.	.
105	95	45	17	0	28	213	241	0	9.856	128	17	0	111	107	218	0	300	22.2
106	96	28	27	213	214	0	214	0	75.328	111	13	107	205	0	205	0	300	41
107	97	214	11	0	203	0	203	0	71.456	205	19	0	186	0	186	0	300	37.2
108	98	203	14	0	189	0	189	0	66.528	186	12	0	174	0	174	0	300	34.8
109	99	189	20	0	169	0	169	0	59.488	174	17	0	157	0	157	0	300	31.4
110	100	169	15	0	154	0	154	0	54.208	157	15	0	142	0	142	0	300	28.4

2. Repeat Exercise 1, using the same two demand series you used for policy A with the decision rules for policy B. Does this simulation strategy (holding random elements constant across policies) impact on experimental error?

3. Develop other decision rules that seem reasonable, and evaluate them using simulation.

Exhibit 15.5

Documentation for Decision Rules, Policy B

Qty Ordrd Item 3581[Day 1 THRU Day 100] = IF (On Hd & On Ord Item 3581 <= Reorder Point
Item 3581 THEN Order Quantity Item 3581[Primary] ELSE IF (On Hd & On Ord Item 4811 <=
Reorder Point Item 4811 THEN Order Quantity Item 3581[Secondary] ELSE 0))

Daily Cost Item 3581[Day 1 THRU Day 100] = IF (Qty Ordrd Item 3581 > 0 THEN Cost per Order
Item 3581 ELSE 0) + IF (End Invty Item 3581 > 0 THEN End Invty Item 3581 * Hold Cost /
Day Item 3581 ELSE 0)

Qty Ordrd Item 4811[Day 1 THRU Day 100] = IF (On Hd & On Ord Item 4811 <= Reorder Point
Item 4811 THEN Order Quantity Item 4811[Primary] ELSE IF (On Hd & On Ord Item 3581 <=
Reorder Point Item 3581 THEN Order Quantity Item 4811[Secondary] ELSE 0))

Order Cost Item 4811[Day 1 THRU Day 100] = IF (Qty Ordrd Item 3581 > 0 THEN Cost per Order
Item 4811[Secondary] ELSE Cost per Order Item 4811[Primary])

Daily Cost Item 4811[Day 1 THRU Day 100] = IF (Qty Ordrd Item 4811 > 0 THEN Order Cost
Item 4811 ELSE 0) + IF (End Invty Item 4811 > 0 THEN End Invty Item 4811 * Hold Cost /
Day Item 4811 ELSE 0)

16

Simulation & Analysis of Waiting Lines

The body of mathematical knowledge called *queuing theory*, or *waiting line theory* describes characteristics of waiting lines, which occur in many situations. A waiting line arises when clerks wait in line to make copies in an office copy center. In another situation, customers wanting to place telephone orders wait "on hold" for an order clerk. Airplanes arriving to land form a waiting line or stack near a busy airport. Papers pile up in an in-basket waiting to be processed. Bank customers wait in a corral for a teller. Grocery customers wait in a line for checkout. All of these waiting lines involve economic costs, both for waiting time and for the resources used to provide the services. A study of a waiting line system may lead to lower cost, better service, or both.

There are two major branches of managerial analysis of waiting lines: mathematical analysis, and simulation. Both have advantages; both have disadvantages. While both analysis and simulation can be used by a nontechnical manager for some situations, many queuing studies will require the efforts of a professional management scientist. The purpose of this chapter is to describe the use of both analysis and simulation for simple waiting lines, to equip the manager with tools that can be used quickly for relatively simple situations. We'll start with a very simple scenario, and show how analysis and simulation can be used. As more data are needed, we'll provide that data to demonstrate its use. A major case study, North-South Insurance Company, will illustrate many of the techniques that bridge the gaps between simple problems and more realistic applications.

Case Example: Quick-Serve Software Help

The Quick-Serve Software Help Corporation is planning a telephone service to provide assistance to local users of several software packages. The main customers

371

—————— **Figure 16.1** ——————

Exponential Probability Distribution

The literature of queuing analysis is filled with the terms *Poisson* and *exponential*. They sound more forbidding than they are; these explanations are intended to give a manager enough understanding of the terms to know how to use them for queuing analysis. Throughout this discussion, more attention is paid to managerial understanding than to technical perfection.

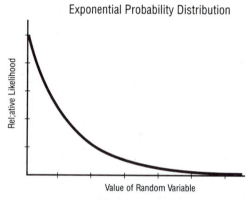

Exponential Probability Distribution

The term *exponential distribution* is often applied to service time. This distribution was introduced in Chapter 14; it is a skewed distribution (with a long right tail), which has its highest value at zero. Graphically, the exponential distribution has the shape shown in the accompanying graph. There are many interesting properties associated with the exponential distribution. From the graph, several characteristics are apparent. First, the most likely time is zero! (Note that the graph of the exponential distribution reaches its highest point at the Y axis, where time has a value of zero.) In the case of the Software Help line, this would suggest that there are many very short calls, perhaps analogous to "turn the switch on before you try to read the screen." On the other hand, there is no theoretical upper limit for call length. Perhaps the most fascinating theoretical property of times described by an exponential distribution is that the length of time required from "now" to the completion of service is not influenced in any way by the elapsed time from the start of service to "now." The amount of time the software help analyst has already been talking provides absolutely no information about how long the call will go on from here.

of the service will be small businesses that have only two or three people using personal computers for word processing, spreadsheets, and databases. The company will provide telephone service to these people, who have no "local guru" to provide assistance. The planning parameters for the service are:

The system will be open nine hours each day, from 8:00 A.M. to 5:00 P.M. It is anticipated that there will be an average of thirty-six calls a day, or four calls an hour, or one call every fifteen minutes. Experience in a related business indicates that an average time of nine minutes is required to handle each call. Multiple telephone lines will be provided, so that a customer will wait "on hold" until the single software analyst is available to provide help. How well will this system provide customer service? Incidentally, the manager of the company has heard of the

---
Figure 16.2

The Poisson Distribution

The Poisson distribution is often used to describe the number of arrivals in a given time interval. During the evening hours, one might say that the number of fire alarms received in a city's fire alarm center is described by the Poisson distribution, with an average of five alarms per hour. In a rough sense, this arises when alarms are "randomly" thrown at a time line; a fire that is "waiting to happen" is just as likely to occur between 5:04 and 5:05 as it is between 5:15 and 5:16, or between any other two points in time one minute apart.

There is an important relationship between the Poisson distribution and the exponential distribution: if the *number of arrivals* is described by the Poisson distribution, the *time between arrivals* is described by the exponential distribution. If arrivals are described by a Poisson distribution, with an average of four (4) arrivals per hour, they are also described by the exponential distribution, with an average of 0.25 (or 1/4) hours between arrivals. This time between arrivals is called the *interarrival time*. In this chapter, we will deal with arrivals according to their interarrival times; they are still referred to as Poisson arrivals, but we utilize the fact that the time between arrivals is described by the exponential distribution.

---

terms "exponential distribution of service times" and "Poisson arrivals" and believes they would apply to this situation. Figure 16.1 provides a managerial description of the exponential distribution; Figure 16.2 provides a description of the Poisson distribution. Depending upon your background, this may be a good time to learn about these distributions, which are widely used in waiting line analysis.

Analysis of Waiting Lines with Poisson Arrivals and Exponential Service Times

The Quick-Serve Software Help Company describes a very simple waiting line situation. Here is the way a queuing analyst would describe the situation:

Single server (there is only one software analyst to provide service).

First-come first-served rules for managing the waiting line, with no one leaving.

Exponential service times with an average of nine minutes.

Poisson arrivals with an average of four arrivals per hour, or an average time between arrivals of 0.25 hours or 15 minutes.

Mathematicians have been successful at providing formulas to describe the ongoing system behavior for a single-server waiting line just like the one for Quick-Serve Software Help. With Poisson arrivals, exponential service times, first-come first-served waiting line rules with no one leaving the system until they have been served, formulas are available to calculate these items, with the values for Quick-Serve shown in parentheses:

The average number of customers waiting in the line (0.9)

The average number of customers in the entire system (line and service combined) (1.5)

Figure 16.3

Worksheet for Exponential Interarrival Times, Exponential Service Times, Multiple Parallel Channels

```
        A        B          C
1   Waiting Lines:  Exponential Time Between Arrivals
2                   Exponential Service Times
3                   Multiple Parallel Channels
4
5   Enter Data Between the Arrows:
6   ========>       15 <==== Average Time between arrivals
7   ========>        9 <==== Average Service Time
8   ========>        2 <==== Number of Servers (in parallel)  LIMIT:  15
9
10
11          30.00% Percent Utilization (or Percent saturation)
12
13        0.059341 Average Number of Customers in the Line
14        0.659341 Average Number of Customers in Entire System
15         0.89011 Average Waiting Time in Line
16         9.89011 Average Time Spent in the System
17
18          53.85% Probability that the facility is completely idle
19           4.15% Probability that there is a waiting line
20          86.15% Probability that a customer is served immediately
```

The average time a customer spends waiting in the line (13.5 minutes)

The average time a customer spends in the entire system (22.5 minutes)

The probability that the facility is completely idle (40.0%)

The probability that there is a waiting line (36.0%)

The probability that a customer is served immediately, without waiting (40.0%)

Rather than showing formulas that would be used by very few people reading this book (who obviously have spreadsheet software), we present a worksheet with the formulas entered. The user needs to provide the average time between arrivals and the average service time, and the software does the rest. The worksheet named EXP–EXP.WK1 was used to calculate the values shown above.

This worksheet also allows for *parallel servers* with a single waiting line, which would arise if another software analyst is hired who is also able to serve customers in an average of nine minutes. Customers would wait "on hold" and be served on a first-come first-served basis by whichever analyst is available when their turn comes. The results of this analysis are shown in Figure 16.3, where the user has provided this information:

15 minutes between arrivals

9 minutes average service time

2 servers in parallel

From a managerial standpoint, changing from one to two software analysts has doubled the cost of analysts; but the benefits, according to the waiting line analysis, decrease the average waiting time from 13.5 minutes to 0.89 minutes. With one analyst, 40% of the customers are served immediately; with two analysts, 86% of the customers are served immediately. This provides information to help the manager decide whether to use one or two analysts.

Poisson Arrivals?

There are three assumptions that merit consideration at this point. The first is Poisson arrivals (exponential interarrival times), the second is exponential service times, and the third is the "steady state behavior" that is described by the mathematical analysis. The first assumption, Poisson arrivals, often holds true in practice. For example, the Quick-Serve Software Help Company may find that within each hour (for example) the assumption of Poisson arrivals is reasonable. But if there are more calls for help between (say) 10 A.M. and 11 A.M. than between 8 A.M. and 9 A.M. it may be desirable to analyze each hour separately. All of the analytical results for waiting lines that we use in this text require the assumption of Poisson arrivals (or exponential interarrival times).

Exponential or Arbitrary Service Times?

Statistical methods are available for investigating whether a set of data fits a specified distribution. The North-South Insurance Company case (later in this chapter) illustrates a simple graphical approach to help decide whether the exponential distribution is a reasonable fit for a set of service times or interarrival times. In a nutshell, this method constructs a histogram (or bar graph) showing the frequency distribution for service times. The shape of this histogram is judgmentally compared to the shape of the exponential distribution shown in Figure 16.1.

If the assumption of exponential service times is not met, other tools of mathematical analysis may be useful. Mathematicians have been successful in analyzing a waiting line with one server (and first-come first-served queue discipline), Poisson arrivals, and any arbitrary distribution for service times. This requires the analyst to know only the average and standard deviation for service times. Worksheet EXP–ARB.WK1 shows this situation. Suppose we are still dealing with the single server, Poisson arrivals (15 minute interarrival time), service times with an average time of nine minutes and a standard deviation of 20 minutes. This situation is shown in the worksheet of Figure 16.4. This situation has an average waiting time of 40.08 minutes, compared to a waiting time of 13.5 minutes with the exponential distribution describing service times. As the standard deviation of service times increases, the average waiting time also increases.

Steady State or Transient Behavior?

Perhaps the most important assumption about the use of the waiting line formulas in the worksheets is that they describe *steady state behavior* of the waiting line. The assumption is made that the system has been operating long enough that any behavior caused by startup has been worked out of the system. As an example, on the average the number of people in the system may be (say) 4.5;

――――――――――――――― **Figure 16.4** ―――――――――――――――

**Worksheet for Exponential Interarrival Times,
Arbitrary Service Times (with known average and standard deviation), Single Channel**

	A	B	C
1	Waiting Lines:		Exponential Time Between Arrivals
2			Arbitrary Service Times (AVG and STD known)
3			Single Channel
4			
5	Enter Data Between the Arrows:		
6	========>	15	<==== Average Time between arrivals
7	========>	9	<==== Average Service Time
8	========>	20	<==== Standard Deviation of Service Times
9			
10		60.00%	Percent Utilization (or Percent saturation)
11			
12		2.672222	Average Number of Customers in the Line
13		3.272222	Average Number of Customers in Entire System
14		40.08333	Average Waiting Time in Line
15		49.08333	Average Time Spent in the System
16			
17		40.00%	Probability that the facility is completely idle

when the system gets started every morning it starts empty, with the server idle. When these initial conditions are influencing system behavior, the system is said to be in a *transient state*; after these conditions have disappeared, the *steady state* prevails. It is usually judgmental whether a system is in a transient state or in the steady state. Unfortunately, most managerial situations (involving people) are always in transient behavior, because people change their habits over the course of a day. Every day, people come to work, take coffee breaks, have lunch, and go home. The next morning, the system may start over again. The arrival rate may be constant for an hour, but there are hours that are busier than other hours, day in and day out. For these reasons, managers may be more interested in transient behavior than in steady state behavior. Unfortunately, the mathematics required for transient behavior analysis are not managerial in nature. The transient behavior of simple waiting line systems can be simulated on a spreadsheet, with tools no more difficult than those we have been using. Simulation is also useful when the Poisson and exponential assumptions do not apply.

Spreadsheet Simulation of a Single-Server Waiting Line

To illustrate spreadsheet simulation, we'll consider a simple situation where customers arrive *exactly* fifteen minutes apart. Service times are described by the exponential distribution, with an average service time of nine minutes. Chapter 14 demonstrated the way to generate exponentially-distributed random variables; the service time can be generated with this formula:

$$-9*@LN(@RAND) \quad \text{where 9 is the average service time}$$

Because there is no uncertainty in arrivals—they arrive every fifteen minutes, on

--- **Figure 16.5** ---

Influence Chart for Copy System Simulation

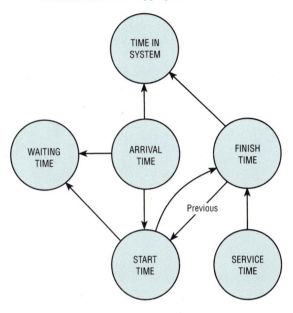

schedule—lines won't build as rapidly as with Poisson arrivals, because there will be no "bunching" of arrivals.

Basically, the spreadsheet simulator will keep track of all events for each arrival. We want to know (for each arrival) the time it spends in the system and the waiting time. In constructing the influence chart of Figure 16.5, the analyst might contemplate steps like these:

TIME IN SYSTEM *is influenced by* ARRIVAL TIME *and* FINISH TIME

WAITING TIME *is influenced by* START TIME *and* ARRIVAL TIME

ARRIVAL TIME *is scheduled every fifteen minutes*

FINISH TIME *is influenced by* START TIME *and* SERVICE TIME

SERVICE TIME *is described by the exponential distribution*

START TIME *is influenced by* ARRIVAL TIME *and by the previous* FINISH TIME *(whichever is later)*

Figure 16.6 shows the spreadsheet implementing the logic of the influence chart; in verbal form, the logic for this spreadsheet is:

```
Time in System = Finish Time - Arrival Time
Waiting Time = Start Time - Arrival Time
Finish Time = Start Time + Service Time
Start Time = @MAX(Arrival Time, Previous Finish Time)
Service Time = -9*@LN(@RAND)
Arrival Time is scheduled for fifteen minute intervals
```

--------- **Figure 16.6** ---------

Spreadsheet for Waiting Line Simulation with Arrivals Every 15 Minutes

	A	B	C	D	E	F	G
1	Customer	Arrival	Service	Start	Finish	Time in	Waiting
2	Number	Time	Time	Time	Time	System	Time
3							
4	1	0	7.9	0.0	7.9	7.9	0.0
5	2	15	2.1	15.0	17.1	2.1	0.0
6	3	30	22.5	30.0	52.5	22.5	0.0
7	4	45	16.9	52.5	69.4	24.4	7.5
8	5	60	14.4	69.4	83.8	23.8	9.4
9	6	75	2.1	83.8	85.9	10.9	8.8
10	7	90	22.3	90.0	112.3	22.3	0.0
11	8	105	3.1	112.3	115.5	10.5	7.3
12	9	120	1.4	120.0	121.4	1.4	0.0
13	10	135	14.4	135.0	149.4	14.4	0.0
14	11	150	2.2	150.0	152.2	2.2	0.0
15	12	165	4.4	165.0	169.4	4.4	0.0
16	13	180	19.4	180.0	199.4	19.4	0.0
17	14	195	9.8	199.4	209.2	14.2	4.4
18	15	210	36.4	210.0	246.4	36.4	0.0
19	16	225	4.7	246.4	251.2	26.2	21.4
20	17	240	17.2	251.2	268.3	28.3	11.2
21	18	255	2.1	268.3	270.4	15.4	13.3
22	19	270	6.6	270.4	277.0	7.0	0.4
23	20	285	2.1	285.0	287.1	2.1	0.0
24	21	300	4.6	300.0	304.6	4.6	0.0
25	22	315	5.2	315.0	320.2	5.2	0.0
26	23	330	6.1	330.0	336.1	6.1	0.0
27	24	345	8.5	345.0	353.5	8.5	0.0
28	25	360	4.1	360.0	364.1	4.1	0.0
29	26	375	16.8	375.0	391.8	16.8	0.0
30	27	390	2.9	391.8	394.6	4.6	1.8
31	28	405	0.6	405.0	405.6	0.6	0.0
32	29	420	23.8	420.0	443.8	23.8	0.0
33	30	435	13.8	443.8	457.6	22.6	8.8
34	31	450	37.3	457.6	494.9	44.9	7.6
35	32	465	15.7	494.9	510.6	45.6	29.9
36	33	480	2.5	510.6	513.2	33.2	30.6
37	34	495	13.4	513.2	526.6	31.6	18.2
38	35	510	2.5	526.6	529.1	19.1	16.6
39	36	525	0.3	529.1	529.4	4.4	4.1
40							
41	Average		10.3			15.9	5.6

Because the arrivals occur every fifteen minutes, and the company is open nine hours each day, thirty-six customers will be served. The spreadsheet model shows the simulated behavior for the system. You are encouraged to follow several lines of the spreadsheet, to verify that you fully understand the logic used in the simulator.

From the spreadsheet, various characteristics can be calculated. The average service time is 10.3 minutes; the "luck of the draw" has resulted in an average slightly longer than the expected value of nine minutes. The average waiting

---------- **Figure 16.7** ----------

Single Server Simulator, Poisson Arrivals, Exponential Service Times, Empty Start

	A	B	C	D	E	F	G
	Customer	Arrival	Service	Start	Finish	Time in	Waiting
1	Number	Time	Time	Time	Time	System	Time
2							
3							
4	1	55.3	4.6	55.3	59.9	4.6	0.0
5	2	73.0	4.8	73.0	77.8	4.8	0.0
6	3	73.4	8.6	77.8	86.4	13.1	4.5
7	4	86.4	14.8	86.4	101.2	14.8	0.1
8	5	126.7	4.9	126.7	131.7	4.9	0.0
9	6	140.4	16.2	140.4	156.5	16.2	0.0
10	7	169.2	7.5	169.2	176.7	7.5	0.0
11	8	179.1	0.9	179.1	180.0	0.9	0.0
12	9	181.3	7.4	181.3	188.6	7.4	0.0
13	10	208.8	3.3	208.8	212.1	3.3	0.0
14	11	215.9	13.4	215.9	229.3	13.4	0.0
15	12	221.9	7.4	229.3	236.7	14.8	7.4
16	13	237.0	2.2	237.0	239.2	2.2	0.0
17	14	247.3	27.9	247.3	275.2	27.9	0.0
18	15	254.0	6.8	275.2	282.0	28.0	21.1
19	16	260.2	16.0	282.0	298.0	37.8	21.8
20	17	266.7	1.9	298.0	299.8	33.1	31.2
21	18	287.1	8.5	299.8	308.4	21.3	12.7
22	19	306.0	13.3	308.4	321.7	15.7	2.4
23	20	334.8	20.0	334.8	354.8	20.0	0.0
24	21	344.7	32.4	354.8	387.2	42.5	10.1
25	22	392.4	7.2	392.4	399.5	7.2	0.0
26	23	425.1	0.6	425.1	425.7	0.6	0.0
27	24	436.7	0.3	436.7	437.1	0.3	0.0
28	25	446.2	3.7	446.2	449.9	3.7	0.0
29	26	447.3	2.4	449.9	452.3	4.9	2.5
30	27	447.8	1.1	452.3	453.4	5.6	4.5
31	28	476.5	0.9	476.5	477.4	0.9	0.0
32	29	477.3	4.3	477.4	481.8	4.5	0.1
33	30	482.6	6.0	482.6	488.6	6.0	0.0
34	31	483.9	34.4	488.6	523.0	39.1	4.7
35	32	491.9	8.3	523.0	531.3	39.4	31.1
36	33	498.5	1.8	531.3	533.1	34.6	32.8
37	34	500.1	1.4	533.1	534.5	34.4	33.0
38	35	522.3	19.4	534.5	553.9	31.6	12.2
39	36	532.2	11.4	553.9	565.3	33.1	21.7
40	37	539.9	3.9	565.3	569.3	29.3	25.4
41							
42	Average		8.9			16.5	7.6

time is 5.6 minutes; the average time in the system is 15.9 minutes (which will always be the sum of the service time and the waiting time). Note that the theoretical model (with Poisson arrivals) has an average waiting time of 13.5 minutes, considerably longer than our simulation shows. Although some of this difference may be due to randomness in the simulation, much of it is caused by the regularity of arrivals.

It is useful to modify this simulator for Poisson arrivals, which we have already studied with the mathematical results. The only change in the logic is that the arrival times are now calculated from the interarrival times and the arrival time for the previous customer. The interarrival times are from the exponential distribution with an average of fifteen minutes:

Arrival Time = Previous Arrival Time + (−15)*@LN(@RAND)

This simulation is shown in Figure 16.7, this time with thirty-seven customers, enough to fill the nine hours or 540 minutes. The average waiting time for these customers is 7.6 minutes, although the theoretical average is 13.5 minutes in steady state. While this simulation in Figure 16.7 is only one sample result, it often requires a surprisingly large number of customers for a system to reach steady state, after an "empty and idle" start. Experience has shown that as the time required to provide service (here an average of nine minutes) becomes closer to the time between arrivals (here fifteen minutes), it takes more customers to reach steady state. If the time required to provide service is longer than the time between arrivals, the waiting line will theoretically grow without bound; in reality, the assumptions that everyone who arrives will wait for service becomes impossible to maintain if the service capacity is insufficient to serve the arrivals.

Now that we have seen the fundamental tools for dealing with waiting lines, we are ready to describe a more realistic example. This case study will show many of the decisions that a managerial analyst may need to make in applying the concepts of waiting lines in an organization.

CASE STUDY:

Lines at the Copier, North-South Insurance Company

Rob Shirley, manager of office systems for the Atlanta office of North-South Insurance Company, was perplexed about the problems that always seem to arise over access to a copy machine. The Atlanta office has several hundred clerical workers who support the sales representatives through the southeast. Although a lot of information is stored on computers, there is a need to have paper copies to use in clients' offices and homes.

Last Tuesday, May 29, had been a miserable day at the copy machine. There were really two problems: The Memorial Day holiday had caused a backlog of paperwork and copy requests, and the copy machine was out of service from 3:15 P.M. until 5:00, the end of the work day. The service technician was able to repair the machine by Wednesday morning. When the machine is "up" there is theoretically enough capacity to handle the copy needs. The machine has a rated speed of ten copies per minute; previous studies had shown a "typical" daily copy activity of 500 copies, or just over one per minute for the eight-hour day. By this crude (and misleading) comparison, the copy machine was operating at only 10% of capacity. But this average rate of utilization didn't keep lines from building up during peak hours of peak days, even when the machine was "up" all day.

Rob decided that both the reliability problem and the peak load problem could be solved by a new machine. Several vendors had been asked to submit proposals for a new machine. After studying the costs and reliability information, and talking with purchasers of copiers from several vendors, two copiers (from the same vendor) were being considered. Both were faster than the present copier (to address the peak load problem); the reliability issue would be addressed by replacing the current machine which had grown increasingly unreliable in the last year, as it reached its fifth year of service. Both of the proposed machines, model X-20 and X-35, utilized sophisticated automatic document feeders that kept the machines running close to their rated capacity, after the copying had begun. The operating characteristics of the two machines were summarized in these paragraphs:

Model X-20 has a rated speed of twenty copies per minute. This means that *ideally* twenty copies of a single document can be made in one minute, after the document is loaded in the machine and the proper control buttons are pushed. Because some operations (such as stapling and collating) slow down the machine, an actual rate of sixteen copies per minute will be used. After users were trained, it required approximately 42 seconds from the time one user had completed a copy job until the next user had pushed the appropriate controls so that copies could be delivered at the rate of sixteen per minute.

Model X-35 has a rated speed of thirty-five copies per minute. However, its document feeder is limited to thirty copies per minute. Recognizing the realities of collating and stapling, Rob decided to use twenty-four copies per minute as the actual speed of the machine. The controls of this machine were slightly simpler, giving a 36 second estimate of the elapsed time from the completion of one job to the start of the next.

While Rob realized that it was "nice" to look at the characteristics of the two machines, what really mattered was the impact each machine would have on time spent waiting in line for the copier and making the copies. The current machine was perfectly adequate for slow days, but would either of the proposed machines really help out during the peak times of the peak days? Rob decided that a useful test for comparing the two machines would be the copy system's behavior on Tuesday, May 29, which is still remembered as the bad day at the copier. The daily copy log for May 29 had collected data that made it possible to go back and simulate (on a spreadsheet) what would have happened on May 29 if either of the proposed machines had been present, up to the time of breakdown (3:15 P.M.) The daily log was kept at the entrance to the copy room; each employee entered the time of arrival (copied from a digital clock prominently displayed at the pedestal holding the log), the account to be charged, and the number of copies. When the machine was down on Tuesday, the log was not filled out because no copies were run.

Rob decided to break the analysis into two components: the behavior from 8:00 to 3:15, based on historical demand for copies, and the behavior from 3:15 to 5:00, based on estimated demand for copies. Rob made another critical decision: simulation would be used, to incorporate the actual arrival information and actual service time data for May 29. It would be much more convincing to show

--- **Figure 16.8** ---

Arrival Times and Copy Times, May 29, 8:00 A.M. to 3:15 P.M.

	A	B	C	D	E	F	G
1	Customer	Arrival	Times	Calculated	Number	Time to	make
2	Number	(from log)		Arrival	of	Copies	....
3	======	Clock	Time.....	Time	Copies	Model	Model
4		Hours	Minutes	Minutes	======	X20	X35
5		=====	=======	Since		===	===
6				8:00 AM			
7				=======			
8	1	8	3.3	3.3	16	1.700	1.267
9	2	8	12.0	12.0	4	0.950	0.767
10	3	8	24.3	24.3	4	0.950	0.767
11	4	8	39.5	39.5	17	1.763	1.308
12	5	8	40.6	40.6	7	1.138	0.892
13	6	8	45.2	45.2	17	1.763	1.308
14	7	8	49.5	49.5	20	1.950	1.433
15	8	8	50.4	50.4	14	1.575	1.183
16	9	8	52.1	52.1	15	1.638	1.225
17	10	9	2.5	62.5	3	0.888	0.725
18	11	9	4.0	64.0	11	1.388	1.058
19	12	9	4.2	64.2	11	1.388	1.058
	.						
	.						
	.						
138	131	15	3.6	423.6	3	0.888	0.725
139	132	15	3.7	423.7	9	1.263	0.975
140	133	15	3.9	423.9	7	1.138	0.892
141	134	15	4.6	424.6	4	0.950	0.767
142	135	15	5.5	425.5	16	1.700	1.267
143	136	15	8.3	428.3	4	0.950	0.767
144	137	15	11.0	431.0	11	1.388	1.058
145	138	15	11.2	431.2	15	1.638	1.225
146	139	15	13.7	433.7	5	1.013	0.808

what would have happened on May 29 with each of the new copiers, than to show analysis based on data somewhat further from reality, which is the way some people might view it if Rob used the terms "Poisson arrivals and exponential service times." Anyway, Rob was convinced that the service times couldn't be exponential, because each proposed copier had a "get ready" time of 42 or 36 seconds, so the real data do not mimic the exponential distribution's property for a service time of zero to be the most likely. Another part of Rob's reasoning was that the steady state (which is the output from mathematical analysis of waiting lines) really never arises at the company. There may be changes in arrival rate throughout the day, which are reflected in the real data but not in the theoretical models.

Rob's Analysis: 8:00 to 3:15, Tuesday, May 29

Rob's first step was to take the log for May 29 and enter the information onto a spreadsheet. All times were entered as minutes since 8:00 A.M., to make arithmetic simple. The time required for Model X-20 was calculated as 0.7 minutes (42 seconds) plus one minute (or fraction) for each 16 copies required. For Model

---

Figure 16.9

Spreadsheet Model for Simulating Copy Room with Model X-20

	A	B	C	D	E	F
1	North-South Insurance Company Simulation:				May 29	
2			Average			Average
3			1.466			2.392
4	Customer	Arrival	Service	Start	Finish	Time in
5	Number	Time	Time-X20	Time	Time	System
6	======	====	========	====	====	======
7	1	3.3	1.700	3.300	5.000	1.700
8	2	12.0	0.950	12.000	12.950	0.950
9	3	24.3	0.950	24.300	25.250	0.950
10	4	39.5	1.763	39.500	41.263	1.763
11	5	40.6	1.138	41.263	42.400	1.800
12	6	45.2	1.763	45.200	46.963	1.763
13	7	49.5	1.950	49.500	51.450	1.950
14	8	50.4	1.575	51.450	53.025	2.625
15	9	52.1	1.638	53.025	54.663	2.563
16	10	62.5	0.888	62.500	63.388	0.888
17	11	64.0	1.388	64.000	65.388	1.388
18	12	64.2	1.388	65.388	66.775	2.575
		.				
		.				
		.				
137	131	423.6	0.888	426.312	427.200	3.600
138	132	423.7	1.263	427.200	428.462	4.762
139	133	423.9	1.138	428.462	429.600	5.700
140	134	424.6	0.950	429.600	430.550	5.950
141	135	425.5	1.700	430.550	432.250	6.750
142	136	428.3	0.950	432.250	433.200	4.900
143	137	431.0	1.388	433.200	434.587	3.587
144	138	431.2	1.638	434.587	436.225	5.025
145	139	433.7	1.013	436.225	437.237	3.537

X-35, the time required was calculated as 0.6 minutes (36 seconds) plus one minute (or fraction) for each 24 copies required. This information is shown in the spreadsheet of Figure 16.8.

The next step was to simulate the behavior of the copy system with each copier model. Although clerks complain about the amount of time they spend waiting (without regard for how long it takes to make the copies), the time in the copy system (room) is really the important information from the company's standpoint. To construct a simulator, logic identical to the logic of Figures 16.5 and 16.6 was used. Both the arrival time and the service time come from Figure 16.8, column D (arrival times), column F (service times, X-20), and G (service times, X-35). The simulator is shown in Figure 16.9 for the X-20, and Figure 16.10 for the X-35.

By averaging the values in the column Time in System, Rob is able to determine that from 8:00 A.M to 3:15 P.M. Wednesday, the average copy job required 2.39 minutes of time in the copy room for X-20, and 1.46 minutes for X-35. For the period from 8:00 to 3:15, 139 clerks came to the copy room. With Model X-20, the time for copying and waiting would total 139 × 2.39, or 332 minutes. With

—————————————— **Figure 16.10** ——————————————

Spreadsheet Model for Simulating Copy Room with Model X-35

	A	B	C	D	E	F
1	North-South Insurance Company Simulation:					May 29
2			Average			Average
3			1.111			1.456
4	Customer	Arrival	Service	Start	Finish	Time in
5	Number	Time	Time-X35	Time	Time	System
6	======	====	========	====	====	======
7	1	3.3	1.267	3.300	4.567	1.267
8	2	12.0	0.767	12.000	12.767	0.767
9	3	24.3	0.767	24.300	25.067	0.767
10	4	39.5	1.308	39.500	40.808	1.308
11	5	40.6	0.892	40.808	41.700	1.100
12	6	45.2	1.308	45.200	46.508	1.308
13	7	49.5	1.433	49.500	50.933	1.433
14	8	50.4	1.183	50.933	52.117	1.717
15	9	52.1	1.225	52.117	53.342	1.242
16	10	62.5	0.725	62.500	63.225	0.725
17	11	64.0	1.058	64.000	65.058	1.058
18	12	64.2	1.058	65.058	66.117	1.917
	.					
	.					
	.					
137	131	423.6	0.725	423.842	424.567	0.967
138	132	423.7	0.975	424.567	425.542	1.842
139	133	423.9	0.892	425.542	426.433	2.533
140	134	424.6	0.767	426.433	427.200	2.600
141	135	425.5	1.267	427.200	428.467	2.967
142	136	428.3	0.767	428.467	429.233	0.933
143	137	431.0	1.058	431.000	432.058	1.058
144	138	431.2	1.225	432.058	433.283	2.083
145	139	433.7	0.808	433.700	434.508	0.808

Model X-35, the total time would be 203 minutes. This additional 129 minutes (332 − 203) is a way of measuring the benefits of the faster machine, which can be compared to the costs of the faster machine.

Rob's Analysis: 3:15 P.M. to 5:00 P.M. Tuesday, May 29

Rob's next concern was how to handle the period of time from 3:15 P.M. until 5:00 P.M., when no data had been gathered on May 29. His research strategy was first to determine if the arrival rate is constant throughout the day. Then he would decide whether to use the exponential distribution for interarrival times.

Arrival Rate: Before 3:15 P.M. and After 3:15 P.M.

Rob looked at the last week of data, to see what had been happening to the number of clerks (customers) coming to the copy machine during the two parts of the day (before 3:15, and after 3:15). For the week before May 29, Rob learned that a substantial portion of the day's customers arrived after 3:15. On Monday, there were 65% as many customers after 3:15 as before, even though there are only 24% as many minutes after 3:15 as before. For the next four days, the comparable value was 57%, 63%, 59%, and 62%. Over the course of the entire week, 61% as many customers arrived after 3:15 P.M. compared to the time period before 3:15 P.M. This means that the 139 customers Rob had logged on May 29 could be used to predict about 61% × 139 or about 85 customers would arrive during the last 105 minutes (from 3:15 P.M. to 5:00 P.M.). This is an average of 1.24 minutes between customers. By comparison, the average time between arrivals was 3.12 minutes between 8:00 A.M. and 3:15 P.M.

Analysis of Arrivals: 8:00 A.M. to 3:15 P.M.

Rob wanted to know if the exponential distribution was a good fit for the time between arrivals for the clerks arriving between 8:00 and 3:15. But before Rob could look at that question, it was necessary to see if the entire time period from 8:00 to 3:15 could be considered at once, or if it was necessary to divide it into smaller time intervals, each with its own arrival rate. If there are busy times and slow times, the interval needs to be split into several intervals. During a busy time period, the time between arrivals would be short; during a slow time, the time between arrivals would be long. Thus, fluctuations in the arrival rate during the course of a day should show up as groups of "short" and "long" times between arrivals. If there is no fluctuation in the arrival rate during the day, the "short" and "long" times should be randomly spread throughout the day. Rob applied the runs test for randomness, described in Chapter 15, and concluded that the sequence of inter-arrival times was reasonably considered to be random. Thus, Rob could use the entire set of arrivals from 8:00 to 3:15 to investigate whether arrivals were Poisson, by studying whether the interarrival times were exponential.

Analysis Tip: A Review of the Runs Test. To find the sequence of interarrival times, subtract each time of arrival from the time of arrival of the previous customer. A runs test for randomness can be applied by marking each interarrival time with a "1" if it is above the average interarrival time, and with a "0" if it is below the average interarrival time. For the 138 values of the interarrival time, 45 were above the average, and 93 below the average. The number of runs of successive 1s or 0s is counted; for the data for May 29, there were 62 runs above and below the mean. Using the formulas shown in Chapter 15, the expected number of runs (61.1) and the standard error of the number of runs (5.1) were calculated. Obviously, the observed number of runs is quite close to what is expected, giving no reason to doubt that the sequence of runs is random. Interestingly, however, thge data conclude with a single run of 14 observations below the mean, suggesting that things may be "heating up" just as the machine is about to break!

One way to investigate whether the exponential distribution is reasonable is to construct a histogram (or bar graph) showing the shape of the observed frequency distribution of interarrival times. One convenient way to do this is the **Data Distribution** command (Lotus 1-2-3) or **Tools Frequency** command (Quattro Pro). This finds the frequency distribution for a set of values (the interarrival times), by counting the number of observations in various categories or "bins."

─────────────────────── **Figure 16.11** ───────────────────────

Proportion of Interarrival Times Falling Into Various Bins for the Exponential Distribution

Bin	Proportion	Upper Bin Limit
1	39.3%	0.5 * AVG
2	23.9%	1.0 * AVG
3	14.5%	1.5 * AVG
4	8.8%	2.0 * AVG
5	5.3%	2.5 * AVG
6	3.2%	3.0 * AVG
7	2.0%	3.5 * AVG
8	1.2%	4.0 * AVG
9	0.7%	4.5 * AVG
10	0.4%	5.0 * AVG

Although there is no "correct" way to determine the bin limits, a useful rule is to establish these bins, using AVG to stand for the average value of the time between arrivals for the data being studied:

Bin 1:   from 0 up to and including 0.5 × AVG
Bin 2:   greater than 0.5 × AVG, up to and including 1.0 × AVG
Bin 3:   greater than 1.0 × AVG, up to and including 1.5 × AVG
Bin 4:   greater than 1.5 × AVG, up to and including 2.0 × AVG

· · ·

Bin 10: greater than 4.5 × AVG, up to and including 5.0 × AVG

Data that follow the exponential distribution will distribute itself in approximately the proportions tabulated in Figure 16.11. The shape of this "theoretical" distribution is shown in Figure 16.12; the North-South Copy Machine interarrival times (8:00 to 3:15) have been placed into bins, giving the histogram or bar chart shown in Figure 16.13. Either judgment or statistical tests* can be used to decide whether the exponential distribution is an appropriate assumption for the mechanism generating interarrival times. Based on the similarity in the shapes shown in Figure 16.12 and in Figure 16.13, Rob decided to use the exponential distribution. While this analysis investigates only the time period before 3:15 P.M., Rob had no data after 3:15 to use. So it was decided to use the exponential distribution for interarrival times after 3:15, based on a study of times before 3:15. (As an alternative approach, Rob could have studied interarrival times after 3:15 for another time period, such as the previous week. The techniques used here would apply to such an analysis.)

─────────────

*The chi-square test for goodness of fit can be used with the "binned" data, after combining the right-tail classes so that the expected number of observations is greater than about five for each category. Another test that can be used is the Kolmogorov-Smirnov test for goodness of fit, using the cumulative frequency distribution. These tests are described in many beginning statistical texts. See, for example, Donald R. Plane and Edward B. Oppermann, *Business and Economic Statistics* (Plano, Texas: Business Publications, Inc., 1986), 3rd edition, Chapters 13 and 14.

–––––––––––––––––––––– **Figure 16.12** ––––––––––––––––––––––

Theoretical Shape, Exponential Distribution

Exponential Frequency Distribution

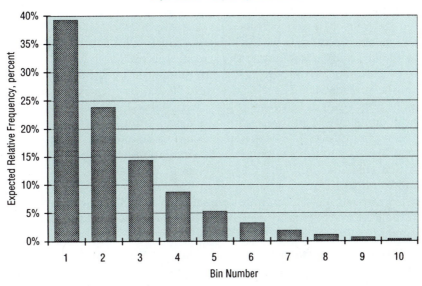

–––––––––––––––––––––– **Figure 16.13** ––––––––––––––––––––––

Empirical Shape, Time Between Arrivals to Copy Machine

Histogram of Time Between Arrivals
May 29, 8:00 A.M. to 3:15 P.M.

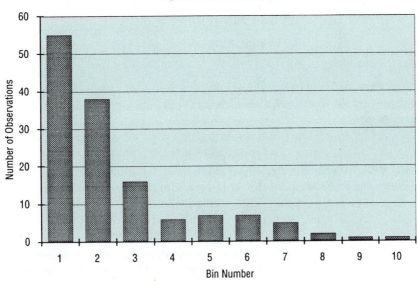

To generate these random interarrival times, exponentially distributed with an average of 1.24 minutes between arrivals, Rob used this spreadsheet formula:

$$-1.24*@LN(@RAND)$$

By copying this expression to (say) 150 cells in a column on a worksheet, Rob generated 150 times between arrivals. The next step was to get an unbiased set of random values; holding down the [F9] (CALCulate) key for several seconds and releasing the key without looking at the screen, Rob was getting a set of values for the time between arrivals which was not influenced by Rob's looking at the values on the spreadsheet. These values were "fixed" by using the **Range Value** command (Lotus 1-2-3) or **Edit Value** command (Quattro Pro), which work much like a copy command except that values rather than formulas are placed into the cells receiving the values. The next step is to use these interarrival times to find the time of arrival for each customer in the simulation, starting with customer 140, the first customer after the customers from the previous simulations of Figures 16.9 and 16.10. The last customer in the previous simulation, customer number 139, arrived at 433.7 minutes after 8:00 A.M (cell B145, Figure 16.9 or 16.10). If the interarrival time for customer 140 is 3 minutes, the arrival time for this customer is 436.7 minutes after 8:00 A.M. In general,

TIME OF ARRIVAL = PREVIOUS TIME OF ARRIVAL + INTERARRIVAL TIME

With this formula, a column of arrival times, starting with customer 140, can be developed on a spreadsheet. Later, this information will be combined into a spreadsheet for the completed simulator.

Service Times: 3:15 P.M. to 5:00 P.M.

The next step to prepare a simulator for the period from 3:15 to 5:00 is a decision about service (copy) times during the last part of the day. From experience and analysis of logs of the past week, there seemed to be no difference in the number of copies per customer during various parts of the day. Rob's decision was to take the column of service times for each proposed copier, and "shuffle" the list using random numbers. Then these times would be used in their shuffled order for the simulation. Rob followed these steps to accomplish this:

Retrieve the worksheet shown in Figure 16.8.

In column H of this worksheet, fill each row with a random number using @RAND.

Sort all rows of the worksheet, using as the primary sort the column of random numbers. Unless recalculation has been set to manual (for Lotus 1-2-3, **Worksheet Global Recalculation Manual**; for Quattro Pro, **Options Recalculation Mode Manual**), the sorted random numbers won't appear to be sorted. Each time a sort is performed, the random number is recalculated automatically. The customer numbers are no longer in sequence, however, indicating that sorting has been accomplished.

This column of service times is now ready for inclusion in a simulator covering the entire day of May 29; Figure 16.14 shows these service times in columns F and G.

Figure 16.14

Randomly Sorted Service Times (Columns B..D Are Hidden)

	A	E	F	G	H
1	Customer	Number	Time to make		Random
2	Number	of	Copies........		Number
3	======	Copies	Model	Model	======
4		======	X20	X35	
5			===	===	
6					
7					
8	26	10	1.325	1.017	0.00825
9	44	7	1.138	0.892	0.01284
10	62	6	1.075	0.850	0.01306
11	10	3	0.888	0.725	0.02195
12	95	1	0.763	0.642	0.02414
13	12	11	1.388	1.058	0.03458
14	17	30	2.575	1.850	0.04543
15	132	9	1.263	0.975	0.04781
16	125	10	1.325	1.017	0.04801
17	41	11	1.388	1.058	0.05672
18	2	4	0.950	0.767	0.07064
19	135	16	1.700	1.267	0.07406
20	76	18	1.825	1.350	0.07497
21	80	11	1.388	1.058	0.08818
22	59	6	1.075	0.850	0.09895
23	93	17	1.763	1.308	0.10304
24	.				
25	.				

Constructing the Simulator: 3:15 P.M. to 5:00 P.M.

All of the parts are now described so that the simulators shown in Figures 16.9 and 16.10 can be extended with enough arrivals to occupy the time of missing data, from 3:15 P.M. to 5:00 P.M. We need to augment Figures 16.9 and 16.10 with the arrival times and the service times for customers starting with customer number 140. One way to do this is to retrieve the simulator worksheet (Figure 16.9 for X-20; Figure 16.10 for X-35). Then combine into a blank section of this worksheet (starting, say, at column G) the worksheet with the arrival times. Then in another blank section (say, column K) combine the worksheet with the service times (Figure 16.14). Then copy the new information into the proper position, the arrival times starting in cell B146, and the service times starting in cell C146. In Lotus 1-2-3, the file combine commands are:

     File   **Combine**   **Copy**   **Entire file**

   . . . *and respond to the prompt with the appropriate filename.*

In Quattro Pro the file combine commands are:

     Tools   **Combine**   **Copy**   **File**

   . . . *and respond to the prompt with the appropriate filename.*

The logic of the simulator carries into the remainder of the arrivals, through customer number 210, who arrives just before 5 P.M. (540 minutes after 8 A.M.) The simulators are shown in Figures 16.15 and 16.16.

Figure 16.15

Simulator for Copy Machine X-20, 8 A.M.–5 P.M., May 29

	A	B	C	D	E	F
1	North-South	Insurance	Company	Simulation:		May 29
2			Average			Average
3			1.477			2.392
4	Customer	Arrival	Service	Start	Finish	Time in
5	Number	Time	Time-X20	Time	Time	System
6	======	====	========	====	====	======
7	1	3.3	1.700	3.300	5.000	1.700
8	2	12.0	0.950	12.000	12.950	0.950
9	3	24.3	0.950	24.300	25.250	0.950
10	4	39.5	1.763	39.500	41.263	1.763
	.					
	.					
	.					
142	136	428.3	0.950	432.250	433.200	4.900
143	137	431.0	1.388	433.200	434.587	3.587
144	138	431.2	1.638	434.587	436.225	5.025
145	139	433.7	1.013	436.225	437.237	3.537
146	140	434.496	1.325	437.237	438.562	4.066
147	141	434.795	1.138	438.562	439.700	4.904
148	142	436.089	1.075	439.700	440.775	4.686
149	143	438.294	0.888	440.775	441.662	3.368
150	144	439.571	0.763	441.662	442.425	2.853
151	145	439.589	1.388	442.425	443.812	4.223
152	146	441.327	2.575	443.812	446.387	5.060
	.					
	.					
	.					
201	195	508.780	1.450	518.162	519.612	10.832
202	196	508.804	1.763	519.612	521.375	12.570
203	197	509.245	1.700	521.375	523.075	13.829
204	198	514.665	1.638	523.075	524.712	10.047
205	199	517.260	1.825	524.712	526.537	9.277
206	200	517.783	1.200	526.537	527.737	9.954
207	201	522.242	1.700	527.737	529.437	7.195
208	202	524.514	2.138	529.437	531.575	7.060
209	203	524.873	1.950	531.575	533.525	8.652
210	204	525.532	1.013	533.525	534.537	9.005
211	205	527.967	1.388	534.537	535.925	7.958
212	206	528.094	1.763	535.925	537.687	9.593
213	207	529.136	1.763	537.687	539.450	10.313
214	208	529.776	2.138	539.450	541.587	11.811
215	209	535.323	2.325	541.587	543.912	8.589
216	210	539.292	2.200	543.912	546.112	6.820

Using the Simulators for Decision Support

The first step in comparing the two machines is the average time a customer spends in the system (copy room) for each model. From the spreadsheets:

X-20:   Average Time in System: 2.392 *minutes*

X-35:   Average Time in System: 1.865 *minutes*

Figure 16.16

Simulator for Copy Machine X-35, 8 A.M.–5 P.M., May 29

	A	B	C	D	E	F
1	North-South Insurance Company Simulation:				May 29	
2		Average				Average
3		1.118				1.865
4	Customer	Arrival	Service	Start	Finish	Time in
5	Number	Time	Time-X35	Time	Time	System
6	======	====	========	====	====	======
7	1	3.3	1.267	3.300	4.567	1.267
8	2	12.0	0.767	12.000	12.767	0.767
9	3	24.3	0.767	24.300	25.067	0.767
10	4	39.5	1.308	39.500	40.808	1.308
		.				
		.				
		.				
142	136	428.3	0.767	428.467	429.233	0.933
143	137	431.0	1.058	431.000	432.058	1.058
144	138	431.2	1.225	432.058	433.283	2.083
145	139	433.7	0.808	433.700	434.508	0.808
146	140	434.496	1.017	434.508	435.525	1.029
147	141	434.795	0.892	435.525	436.417	1.621
148	142	436.089	0.850	436.417	437.267	1.177
149	143	438.294	0.725	438.295	439.020	0.725
150	144	439.571	0.642	439.572	440.213	0.642
151	145	439.589	1.058	440.213	441.272	1.682
152	146	441.327	1.850	441.328	443.178	1.850
		.				
		.				
		.				
201	195	508.780	1.100	509.001	510.101	1.320
202	196	508.804	1.308	510.101	511.409	2.604
203	197	509.245	1.267	511.409	512.676	3.430
204	198	514.665	1.225	514.665	515.890	1.225
205	199	517.260	1.350	517.261	518.611	1.350
206	200	517.783	0.933	518.611	519.544	1.761
207	201	522.242	1.267	522.243	523.510	1.267
208	202	524.514	1.558	524.515	526.073	1.558
209	203	524.873	1.433	526.073	527.506	2.633
210	204	525.532	0.808	527.506	528.315	2.782
211	205	527.967	1.058	528.315	529.373	1.406
212	206	528.094	1.308	529.373	530.681	2.587
213	207	529.136	1.308	530.681	531.990	2.853
214	208	529.776	1.558	531.990	533.548	3.771
215	209	535.323	1.683	535.323	537.006	1.683
216	210	539.292	1.600	539.292	540.892	1.600

But do these numbers tell the whole story? Rob constructed a graph showing the time each customer spent in the system, for each copier model. These are shown in Figures 16.17 and 16.18. Rob studied these graphs, and decided that there is more to evaluating the copiers than looking at the average time in the system.

With the slower copier, the pickup in business at 3:15 seemed to cause major problems in the copy room. There is a distinct tendency for copy room time to

---
Figure 16.17

Time in System for Each Customer Model X-20

Time Spent in System for Each Customer

Machine X-20, 8 A.M.–5 P.M., May 29

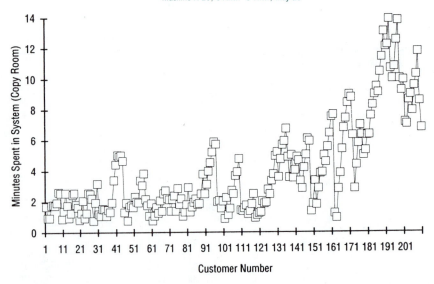

Figure 16.18

Time in System for Each Customer Model X-35

Time Spent in System for Each Customer

Machine X-35, 8 A.M.–5 P.M., May 29

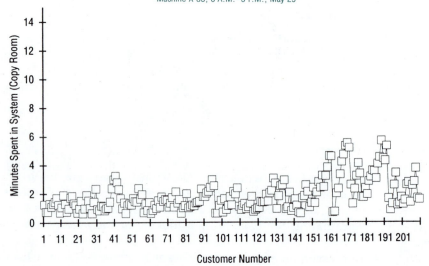

---

get longer as it gets closer to 5 P.M.; this indicates that a line is building. Rob did a quick calculation: From the spreadsheet, the average time required to service the first 139 customers was 1.466 minutes. Unfortunately, from 3:15 P.M. onward the average time between customers was 1.24 minutes. If you can't service customers as they arrive, you have a *saturated* system. Something must give:

> Lines may build up without limit
> Customers may leave
> Customers may not make as many copies as they intended

The copy room might never experience an ever-increasing waiting line, because customers will leave or make fewer copies. But the ever-increasing line will occur over the long run if customers arrive quicker than they are served, and nothing happens that changes the service rate or the workload. But if Rob decided to use the X-20 copier, plan to receive complaints at the end of busy days!

With the faster copier, there is an obvious increase in the time in the system starting around 3:15 (customer number 140). However, the average service time is 1.111 minutes, which is less than the average time of 1.24 minutes between arrivals, so the system is not quite saturated with the faster copier, even at the end of a busy day.

Simulation of Waiting Lines

Rob Shirley has used simulation to study the copy room behavior on May 29, with conditions different from those that actually prevailed on May 29. Using the worksheet as a laboratory, Rob was able to design an experiment to investigate changes in the copy room without actually disturbing the copy room. In the process of performing these experiments, Rob made several tactical decisions about the use of simulation.

Decision 1:

Rob decided to use historical data where possible. Rob was fortunate; there was a fairly large body of historical data. If it had been possible to obtain data for only a small number of customers, it would be necessary to make some assumptions about interarrival times and service times. To the extent possible, these assumptions should be validated with statistical analysis, such as developing the histogram for the shape of the distribution of arrival times. An advantage of using assumed theoretical distributions is that the tails of the distributions (unusually long service times, unusually short and bunched interarrival times) may not be present in short historical data, leading to potential distortions in the results. On the other hand, is one justified in assuming that these extreme values belong in the data, when they are not observed in historical data?

Decision 2:

Start the simulator at 8:00 A.M. with no one in the copy room. In waiting line simulation, this is referred to as an "empty and idle" start. While this makes sense for the copy room, it might not make sense at all for a manufacturing facility. If an expensive machine services products as a part of a manufacturing process, it may be desirable to have a long line of "customers" in the form of work in process inventory. If the normal system behavior is to have a queue of a hundred items waiting for service, starting the system "empty and idle" would give very misleading information until the simulator had sufficient time (number of customers) to build up a long waiting line of items. This illustrates the difference between *steady-state behavior* and *transient behavior* of a queuing system. In the steady state, there will be fluctuations but no trends. Although waiting times will go up and down, and lines will come and disappear, there is no long-term tendency for behavior "next week" to be different from behavior "today." The copy room simulation was apparently in a steady state until 3:15, but the change in interarrival times caused transient behavior. For the slower copier, this transient behavior would continue indefinitely, with ever-increasing lines, because the system is saturated. For the faster copier, transient behavior would be present until the shock of the changed interarrival times worked its way out of the system.

Decision 3:

The two copy systems were compared with identical streams of input data. For each simulator, there were two inputs: the arrival times (calculated from the interarrival times) and the number of copies (from which the service times were calculated). The streams of input data may be viewed as the experimental media, which were held constant to focus on the differences that arise because of copy speeds rather than differences that arise because of the input data.

Decision 4:

There was no investigation to determine whether the observed differences were sensitive to other streams of input data. Rob Shirley should consider studying the system with "shuffled" input data for the number of copies and for interarrival times. (Be careful! With the two distinct periods and different interarrival times, shuffle each period separately.) An alternative to shuffling would be to use random generation, as described in Chapter 14.

Decision 5:

Rob used the entire stream of values of "time in system" for evaluating the results between 8:00 A.M. and 3:15 P.M. This makes sense, because the "empty and idle" starting conditions were indeed typical for the copy room. Each morning the copy room starts empty and idle, and all clerks leave the copy room at 5:00 P.M. In other simulations, the end of the work day leaves everything in place, to start up the next morning with those pre-existing conditions. If the steady-state is the focus of the study, the results from the initial customers may be transient, and should be discarded from the analysis so that the steady-state conditions are the ones being analyzed.

Exercises

1. If an average of two customers arrive per hour, what is the average time between arrivals? If the average service time is twenty minutes, how many services can the server complete in an hour, on the average, if there is always someone waiting for service? *Note:* This question emphasizes a language that commonly

occurs in waiting line discussions. The arrival rate counts the average number of arrivals in a period of time; the service time is measured as the elapsed time between start and finish.

2. For a single-server waiting line system with Poisson arrivals (two per hour) and exponential service times (twenty minutes, average), what are the steady-state system characteristics?

3. For the system of Exercise 2, customer time is valued at $20 per hour, for all time spent in the system (in line or in service). What is the expected cost of customer time for each customer? What is the expected cost of customer time for each hour (when an average of two customers arrive)?

4. For a waiting line system with three parallel servers, Poisson arrivals and exponential service times, the following information is available:

> Arrival rate: 50 customers per hour, or an average interarrival time of 0.02 hours.
>
> Cost incurred per hour that a customer is in the system: $150
>
> Average service time: 0.04 hours
>
> Hourly cost per server: $100

   a. How many customers arrive in an hour, on the average?

   b. How long does each of these customers spend in the system, on the average?

   c. On the average, what is the total hourly cost for customers in the system?

   d. What is the cost per hour for providing service?

   e. On the average, what is the total cost per hour (cost for customers in the system plus service cost)?

5. Arrivals occur according to a Poisson process, with an average of two hours between arrivals. Service time distribution is unknown (arbitrary), but it is known to average 1.5 hours, with a standard deviation of 5 hours. Describe the characteristics of the system.

6. Modify Exercise 5, so that the standard deviation of service times is only 0.5 hours. Judgmentally predict whether average waiting time will increase or decrease. Then use the appropriate analytical worksheet to determine the system characteristics. Compare them with your results to Exercise 5.

7. It is known that the exponential probability distribution has a standard deviation which is equal to the average. Compare these two queuing systems, each with a single server:

   System 1:   200 minute average interarrival time, exponentially distributed
   125 minute average service time, exponentially distributed

   System 2:   200 minute average interarrival time, exponentially distributed
   125 minute average service time, 125 minute standard deviation of service time, unknown distribution

8. Add a column to the simulators of Figure 16.9 and Figure 16.10 to calculate the time each customer spends waiting. *Note:* WAITING TIME = START TIME − ARRIVAL TIME.

9. Add a column to each of the simulators of Figure 16.9 and Figure 16.10 to calculate the time the copy machine is idle. *Note:* IDLE TIME = START TIME − PREVIOUS FINISH TIME.

10. For each simulator (Figures 16.9 and 16.10), show that the average waiting time, plus the average time spent actually making copies is equal to the time in the system.

11. For each simulator, show that the total time from 8:00 A.M. until the last customer is finished is equal to the time spent making copies plus the time the machine is idle.

12. Suppose waiting time costs $10 per hour, while time making copies costs $6 per hour. Calculate the difference in the total of these two costs for the two machines, for the 210 customers, as shown in Figures 16.15 and 16.16. Why might management believe that it costs more for a clerk to be standing in line than for the same clerk to be making copies?

13. Discuss whether cost calculations such as those from Exercise 12 are sufficient to make a decision about the selection of a copier.

14. Discuss the potential for erroneous information in the log used to determine activity in the copy room.

15. Verify that 139 customers between 8:00 and 3:15 is equivalent to 3.12 minutes between customers. Verify that 85 customers between 3:15 and 5:00 is equivalent to 1.24 minutes between customers.

16. Distribute the service times from column F, Figure 16.8, into bins, as described in the chapter. Judgmentally, would the assumption of exponential service times be appropriate for the copy room?

17. Rob Shirley's analysis of the North-South Insurance Copy Room indicated that the distribution of interarrival times is reasonably described by the exponential distribution, and that service times are not exponentially distributed. Further, Rob concluded that the rate of arrivals was reasonably constant between 8:00 A.M. and 3:15 P.M. For this time period, compare the results of the simulator (Figure 16.9) with the appropriate results from analytical models.

18. One hundred pieces must be processed serially through two machines. The first machine, a shaping operation, requires time described by a uniform distribution with a lower limit of eight minutes and an upper limit of twelve minutes. The second operation, a drilling operation, requires time described by a uniform distribution with a lower limit of five minutes and an upper limit of fourteen minutes. For the first piece to be processed, the first operation will be started at once; the second operation will be started as soon as the shaping is completed for the first piece. For all subsequent pieces, the first operation will be started as

soon as the previous piece has completed the first process. The second operation will be started when the first operation is completed, but not sooner than the previous piece has been completed by the second operation. The desire is to complete all hundred pieces as quickly as possible.

a. Construct a simulator to determine these characteristics for each piece:

> START TIME OPERATION 1
> TIME REQUIRED FOR OPERATION 1
> FINISH TIME OPERATION 1
> START TIME OPERATION 2
> TIME REQUIRED FOR OPERATION 2
> FINISH TIME OPERATION 2

b. The job is complete when piece number 100 has finished operation 2. Using the data table method for implementing the Monte Carlo method, find the average time for completing the hundred pieces.

c. Management has tentatively planned to make room for no more than two pieces that have been shaped but not drilled. To determine whether this is sufficient, the following logic is useful (using piece 10 as an example):

> If piece 10 finishes operation 1 before piece 10 starts operation 2, there is need for at least one piece to be stored between operations.

> If piece 10 finishes operation 1 before piece 9 starts operation 2, there is need for at least two pieces (pieces 9 and 10) to be stored between operations.

> If piece 10 finishes operation 1 before piece 8 starts operation 2, there is need for at least three pieces (pieces 8, 9, and 10) to be stored between operations.

Determine the probability that there will be a need for the third storage location sometime during the production of 100 pieces.

19. Construct a simulator for a single server, with exponential interarrival times averaging ten minutes between arrivals, and exponential service times averaging four minutes. For the first hundred arrivals, calculate the average waiting time in the line and the average time spent in the system.

a. Compare these results with the theoretical results.

b. Develop a graph showing the time spent in the system for each of the first hundred arrivals.

c. Does it appear the system has reached steady state within the first hundred arrivals?

Installing What's*Best!*

(Some of this material is taken from the What's*Best* user's manual,
Copyright © 1993 LINDO Systems, Inc. Used with permission.)

System Requirements

The student version of What's*Best!* will run on 286, 386, and 486 PCs operating under DOS. A hard disk with at least 1.5Mb free space is required for installation. At least 2Mb installed RAM (conventional, extended, or expanded) is recommended for solving larger problems; a minimum of 1.5Mb installed RAM is required for program execution.

The student version of What's*Best!* solves optimization problems in conjunction with Lotus 1-2-3 Release 2.x, and with Quattro Pro Release 2, 3, or 4. Execution speed is substantially enhanced by using a hard disk (instead of a floppy disk) for worksheet files. Although the execution time required for optimization is independent of the spreadsheet software in use, Lotus 1-2-3 permits quicker problem setup before optimization and provides quicker return to the spreadsheet. Operation with Quattro Pro may be enhanced by the use of additional expanded memory.

Spreadsheet size is limited to 800 numeric cells. This limit should be sufficient for all problems in this text. Large problems may require substantial processing time for optimization on older (slower) computers. To avoid surprises, instructors are encouraged to solve problems using a typical student computer before making student assignments. Various larger versions of What's*Best!* are available commercially, with support for coprocessor hardware. Commercial versions also may be used in conjunction with other releases of Lotus 1-2-3, and in conjunction with Excel. For information about commercial versions of the solver, contact LINDO Systems, Inc., 1415 North Dayton Street, Chicago, IL 60622, (312) 871-2524.

Quick Installation

The Install Program

The What's*Best!* Install program places the appropriate What's*Best!* files into the proper directories on your hard disk and integrates the What's*Best!* commands into your spreadsheet program. To get you up and running quickly, the following briefly covers the information needed to install What's *Best!*. Material at the end of this appendix covers installation in more detail and should be referred to if:

- You're running spreadsheet software from a network server
- You don't understand an error message during installation

Installing with Lotus 1-2-3 Release 2.X

Before you run the What's *Best!* Install program, please note which drive and directory on your hard disk contains your 1-2-3 system files. You'll need this information at hand as you proceed.

1. Insert the What's *Best!* disk into your floppy disk drive.
2. At a DOS prompt with your floppy as the default drive, type WBINST and press [←Enter] to load the installation program. If you have a monochrome display, type WBINST MONO.
3. Specify 1-2-3 and whether you wish to install just the What's *Best!* system files or the example worksheets as well. The example worksheets contain some example optimization models and files that are useful in Chapters 14, 15, and 16.
4. Enter the appropriate drive and directory information, and follow the instructions on the screen.

Now you're ready to use What's *Best!*. To load the program, type WB from your 1-2-3 directory and press [←Enter]. This will automatically load 1-2-3, attach the What's *Best!* add-in(s), and leave you at a blank worksheet.

The What's *Best!* menu can be invoked by pressing the [Alt] key combination that you assigned to What's *Best!* during the installation, or by typing:

[Alt]-[F10], Invoke, **WBMENU** [←Enter]

The use of a startup worksheet such as AUTO123.WK1 may interfere with What's *Best!*.

Installing with Quattro Pro 4.0

Before running the What's *Best!* installation program please note the drive and directory of your hard disk that contains the Quattro Pro system files.

1. Insert the What's *Best!* disk into your floppy disk drive.
2. At a DOS prompt with your floppy as the default drive, type WBINST and press [←Enter] to load the installation program. If you have a monochrome display, type WBINST MONO.
3. Specify Quattro Pro as your spreadsheet and whether you wish to install both the What's *Best!* system files and example worksheets or just the system files. The example worksheets contain some example optimization models and files that are useful in Chapters 14, 15, and 16.
4. Enter the appropriate drive and directory information, and follow the instructions on the screen.

Now you're ready to use What's *Best!*. To load the program, type WBQ from your Quattro Pro directory and press [←Enter]. This will automatically load Quattro Pro, and the What's *Best!* menu will appear as **WB!** at the far right of the Quattro Pro menu bar.

The use of a startup worksheet such as QUATTRO.WQ1 may interfere with What's *Best!*.

Installation Details

This section covers the following Installation Details that are outside the scope of the preceding discussion of *Quick Installation*:

- Comments about the What's *Best!* Add-ins with 1-2-3
- Running What's *Best!* on a network

If you encounter a problem running the WBINST installation program or running the program for the first time, refer to the section *Quick Installation* and to the sections below for instructions on correcting the problem. If, after reading these sections, you continue to have problems running What's *Best!*, please contact a technical support representative by phone at (312) 248-0465 or by fax at (312) 871-1777.

Attaching and Detaching the What's *Best!* Add-ins with Lotus 1-2-3 Release 2.2, 2.3, 2.4

When running with 1-2-3 Release 2.2 or 2.3, What's *Best!* uses two add-ins— WBMENU.ADN and WB.ADN. The WBINST installation program should have copied these two files to your spreadsheet directory. They can be manually attached, or installed for automatically attaching with the following commands from within 1-2-3:

/**W**orksheet	
Global	
Default	
Other	
Add-in	
Set	*[select an unused setting between 1 and 10]*
WBMENU[←Enter]	*[select unassigned key* [Alt]-[F7] *through* [Alt]-[F10]*]*
No	*[do not invoke the add-in when spreadsheet is started]*
Set	*[select another unused setting between 1 and 10]*
WB[←Enter]	
Quit	
Update	
Quit	

After you attach the What's *Best!* add-ins you are ready to use What's *Best!*. Exit the spreadsheet, and invoke What's *Best!* with the **WB** command from the Lotus 1-2-3 directory.

If you decide you no longer want the What's*Best!* add-ins to automatically attach when you enter 1-2-3, they must be detached. Detach the What's*Best!* add-ins with the following commands from within 1-2-3:

/**W**orksheet
Global
Default
Other
Add-in
Cancel [*select the setting between 1 and 10 to which* WBMENU *was assigned*]
Cancel [*select the setting between 1 and 10 to which* WB *was assigned*]
Update
Quit
Quit

When the WB add-in is canceled the computer will beep and display the message "Cannot detach @function add-in." This add-in will no longer appear on the list on the default settings screen, but will remain loaded in memory until 1-2-3 is exited.

Running What's *Best!* on a Network

There are two important issues concerning running What's*Best!* on a network: proper licensing and proper installation. Before installing What's*Best!* on a network, you should be sure you've purchased a network license for What's*Best!*, or that you have the ability to limit the number of concurrent What's*Best!* student edition users to the number of What's*Best!* copies licensed to your institution. If you have questions regarding your version of What's*Best!*, or the number of copies licensed to you, please call the Technical Support Line at (312) 248-0465.

Installing What's*Best!* on a network involves setting up separate directories for each user. A separate directory should be assigned to each user from which What's*Best!* is started. The user must have write privileges in this directory and, while it need not contain all the spreadsheet system files, it must contain at least the minimum files to run the spreadsheet. For complete information on installing What's*Best!* on a network, see the README file supplied with the What's*Best!* software files.

Nor should two users employ the same directory for their spreadsheet data files. During optimization, What's*Best!* uses the spreadsheet data directory to save and analyze your model (WBTO) and write the optimized file (WBFR). If What's-*Best!* uses the same data directory for optimization runs for more than one user, data files for one could mistakenly be overwritten with another's files. The use of the **R**eport **S**olutions **E**nable option requires naming a file and pathname where the user has write privileges.

Installation Related Problems

Most errors during installation result in clear on-screen messages and instructions for remedying the errors. If, for instance, you specify installation to a nonexistent directory, the Install program asks you if you want to create such a directory now or quit installation. Missing spreadsheet software, unfound configuration files, and incorrect spreadsheet release, are all handled similarly.

After following all on-screen instructions, if you still have trouble installing What's*Best!*, call the Technical Support Line: (312) 248-0465.

What's*Best!* Commands & Error Messages

(Some of this material is taken from the What's*Best!* user's manual, Copyright © 1993 LINDO Systems, Inc. Used with permission.)

The material in this appendix complements the description of What's*Best!* in Chapter 3 by serving as reference material.

The What's*Best!* Commands

The first four commands in What's*Best!* are used to specify and solve the optimization problem. These commands are *Adjustable*, *Best*, *Constraints*, and *Solve*.

Adjustable

Adjustable lets you tell What's*Best!* if the values in cells can be changed during solution, and if they can be negative. These cells are the decision variables for the optimization problem.

Adjust

The **A**djust command specifies the *adjustable cells* in the model. Before What's*Best!* can solve a problem, it must know which cells it can change in its search for the optimum answer. These are the adjustable cells. They will return nonnegative values unless you specify otherwise.

What's*Best!* will not alter the contents of cells specified as adjustable that contain equations or text or are blank. These cells are usually inappropriate as adjustable cells.

Free

Use the **F**ree command to specify that certain adjustable cells may take negative values. (Until you use the **F**ree command, all adjustable cells are restricted to being greater than or equal to zero.) Adjustable cells that are not restricted to a positive value are sometimes referred to as *free variables*.

When you choose **A**djustable **F**ree, What's *Best!* asks you to identify the WBFREE range name with up to ten characters beginning with the letters WBFREE, then specify the cell or range you want to be free variables. To remove a free variable designation, simply use the commands in your particular spreadsheet to delete the range name (beginning with WBFREE) that identifies the cell or cells in question.

A negative adjustable cell representing the number of widgets to produce may not be extremely meaningful. But there are situations in which it's useful to allow an adjustable cell to be negative. For example, if you have the ability either to buy or sell a stock, you could have a single adjustable cell representing buy/sell transactions. A positive value represents the amount to buy—and a negative value represents the amount to sell.

Reset

The **R**eset command returns an adjustable cell to its fixed (nonadjustable) state. By default, a cell is fixed until it has been specified as adjustable.

After solving a model, you may wish to fix some of the adjustable cells at new values (turning them into constants) and solve again for the remaining adjustable cells.

Best

Under **B**est, you can choose whether your objective is to maximize or minimize —or neither one.

Cost/Minimize and Profit/Maximize

The **C**ost/Minimize and **P**rofit/Maximize commands are used to specify the *best cell*.

For optimization models you must define a best cell. The best cell, sometimes called the *objective of the optimization*, is the cell whose value is to be minimized or maximized during the optimization process. You can't specify more than one cell to be maximized or minimized. Specifying a cell to be maximized or minimized overrides any previously specified best cell.

In a situation that has multiple goals, you should consider maximizing or minimizing one goal and constraining the others, or combining goals into a single equation to be maximized or minimized. For example, if the goals for your factory are to maximize production output and minimize costs, there are clearly trade-offs between the two goals. You can choose to maximize output while constraining costs to be less than some value, or minimize costs while constraining output to be greater than some level. Or you can combine your goals into a single equation and maximize total value of the output minus the cost.

None

If no best cell is specified, What's *Best!* will try to find a solution that satisfies all constraints and relationships in the model. This is referred to as *goal-seeking* or *backsolving*. **N**one can be used to void any previously specified best cell.

If you solve a model in which no best cell has been specified, a warning may appear in the status report after an attempt to solve has completed. The "No

`Best Cell specified"` warning is intended to notify the user that the specification of a best cell may have been inadvertently omitted. You have the option of turning this warning on or off, as discussed later in this Appendix.

Constrain

In the real world, decisions are always constrained in some way. In the steel business, for example, you can't acquire infinite amounts of ore, coke, alloy metals and power for free: you have a budget. And if you don't deliver your customers' orders on time and up to specifications, you won't be in business very long.

There are always such limits, which are imposed by *constraints*. In What's-*Best!* you can use **G**reater than, **L**ess than, or **E**qual to constraints.

Creating Constraints

Let's consider the following constraints: a *resource limitation* constraint, "Advertising expenditures must be no more than ($\leq$) \$10,000," and a *performance requirement* constraint, "Advertising exposures must be at least ($\geq$) 100."

	A	B	C	D	E
1	Advertising Projection				
2		Expenditure		Budget	
3		\$0.00	<=	\$10,000	
4					
5		Exposures		Requirement	
6		0	Not >=	100	
7					

In this What's *Best!* model, if an adjustable cell representing the advertising expenditure were in cell B3, and D3 were a fixed cell with a value of 10,000, you could enter the @WB constraint formula B3 <= D3 anywhere in the spreadsheet to enforce the first constraint. It makes good sense to enter this constraint in cell C3 where it makes visual sense. Likewise, in cell C6, the @WB constraint formula B6 >= D6 enforces the second constraint. (See the table of formulas on page 408 for the exact constraint syntax used in your particular spreadsheet.)

What's *Best!* would then optimize so as to satisfy these constraints. With B3 selected as the minimize objective, the program will select at least 100 exposures that add up to the lowest possible expenditure. With B6 selected as the maximize objective, the program will select the highest number of exposures over 100 whose summed cost is less than \$10,000.

The constraint formula returns the *indicator* (<=) if the constraint is satisfied. If the constraint is not satisfied, the indicator is preceded by the word *Not* (Not <=). If the constraint is tightly satisfied, the indicator is preceded by the equal sign (=<=). A tightly satisfied constraint is one in which the value of the constrained cell is equal to the constraining cell, value, or expression; in this case, if B3 were equal to D3, =<= would be returned in the constraint cell.

If you wish, you may select **O**ptions **C**onstraint **WB** and choose to display the *slack* returned by the constraint function, instead of the indicator. The slack is the amount by which a constraint is violated or exceeded; thus, if the indicator displayed were =<=, the slack displayed would be zero. If the indicator displayed were <=, the slack displayed would be some positive number. And if the indicator displayed were Not <=, the slack displayed would be some negative number. Here's a table with some examples for the constraint B3 <= D3.

If B3 is . . .	and D3 is . . .	then Indicator is . . .	and Slack is . . .
1	2	<=	1
2	2	=<=	0
4	2	Not <=	−2

You could do away with cell D3 and use the formula B3 <= 10000. In Lotus 1-2-3, the **C**onstrain command lets you enter single-cell references or a range on the left-hand side, and single-cell references, a range, or a single value on the right-hand side of your formula. When a range is entered on the left-hand side, a range on the right-hand side must be of the same dimension. When a range is entered on the left-hand side and a single cell or a value on the right-hand side, the same right-hand side applies to each cell in the range. In Quattro Pro 4, the **C**onstraint command lets you enter single-cell references on the left-hand side, and a single-cell reference or a value on the right-hand side of your formula. When entering a constraint formula manually, you have the additional option of entering an expression on either side of the indicator, such as B3–B11 <= D3+D11.

> *Note:* This release of What's *Best!* also supports a form of constraint formula that employs the spreadsheet @IF function. This form lets you exchange models between spreadsheets, and it's required by Quattro Pro 2 and 3. Details of the @IF function are in the next paragraph.

Constraint Formulas

Depending on the spreadsheet you're using, What's *Best!* will write constraint formulas according to various syntaxes. If you want to write the formulas yourself, rather than allowing the program to do it, here is a table of the formulas by spreadsheet for the constraint G8 >= H8.

Lotus 1-2-3:	@WB(G8,">=",H8)
Quattro Pro 4	@WB.CON(G8,">=",H8)
"IF" style	@IF(0>=0,G8–H8,0)

Solve

Once the optimization problem has been specified, you can **S**olve your model. Choosing the **S**olve command sends your model directly to the What's *Best!* solver under the filename WBTO (with the extension native to the spreadsheet), retrieves the file WBFR, and writes the error file WBERR.PRN. (These filenames are defaults; to change them, see **O**ptions **F**iles command description.)

Error Messages from Solve

There are some situations that arise from improper specification of an optimization problem, or from failing to understand the scenario completely. These are displayed by What's *Best!* in the WBERR.PRN file after a solution has been attempted. Here is a description of some of these common errors.

Too Few Constraints—Unbounded Solutions. If you forget to include some of the constraints in your model and try to optimize, you may not represent reality. For example, if you forget to specify limits on the resources you used, What's *Best!* may give an error message indicating `Solution Status: Unbounded`. This is because without the constraints, there's no limit on the profit you could make, because there are no resource limits. You could increase profit without limit by producing an infinite supply! What's *Best!* knows you've left out one or more constraints, and rather than giving an infinite profit as a result, indicates that the problem is unbounded. Or What's *Best!* might give you an unbounded error message if you maximize the wrong cell, or maximize the objective cell when in fact you really wanted to minimize it.

Anytime What's *Best!* finds the objective heading toward infinity, you'll see the *unbounded* error message.

No Feasible Solution Found—Linear. What if you add a constraint that contradicts one or more of the existing constraints? In the Rangely Lakes problem, if you add a requirement that the amount of lumber used must be greater than or equal to 25,000 board feet, What's *Best!* will return the `Solution Status: No Feasible Solution Found` message. The original constraint requires that *no more* than 17,000 board feet be used, but this new constraint requires the usage of at least 25,000 board feet, exceeding the limitation of the first constraint.

Anytime What's *Best!* can't find a solution to a linear problem that satisfies all constraints, you'll see the `No Feasible Solution Found` error message. By looking at the state of the constraints in the returned infeasible solution, you may find how to reformulate and eliminate the infeasibility.

No Feasible Solution Found—Nonlinear. In a nonlinear problem, the `Solution Status: No Feasible Solution Found` message may not mean that there is no solution that satisfies all constraints—only that none can be found from the starting values you've entered in the adjustable cells. If you know or suspect there *is* a feasible answer to the problem, enter adjustable cell values that yield the feasible or near-feasible objective, and try solving from that starting point.

One other possible course to follow is to view the constraints in *slack* form rather than *indicator* form. This will let you determine which constraints are furthest from being satisfied. Then enter "educated guesses" in the adjustable cells—values that cause the constraints to come closer to being satisfied, and try solving again from these starting values.

Advanced Commands

The remainder of the What's *Best!* menu and commands are more advanced features. They are discussed in the order in which they appear in the menu.

Dual

What's *Best!* provides three **D**ual value commands. The first one, **V**alue, lets you find the dual value of a cell or range of cells. The second two, **U**pper and **L**ower, let you find the upper and lower ranges for dual values. These are discussed in more detail in Chapter 5.

Value

Use the **V**alue command to calculate the dual value of a cell. To use it, put the cursor in the cell for which you want to find the dual value and choose **D**ual, then **V**alue, from the What's *Best!* menu, then specify where you want the dual value displayed.

In Lotus 1-2-3, you can specify ranges in both parts of the command, as long as the ranges are identical in dimension. In Quattro Pro, you must enter single cells.

Upper and Lower

Use the **U**pper and **L**ower commands to calculate the upper and lower valid ranges for a dual value. To use them, put the cursor in the cell for which you want to find the dual value and invoke What's *Best!*. Choose **D**ual, then **U**pper or **L**ower, and then specify where you want the dual value displayed.

In Lotus 1-2-3, you can specify ranges in both parts of the command, as long as the ranges are identical in dimension. In Quattro Pro, you must enter single cells.

About Dual Value

Dual Values and Multiple Optima. Dual values are generally nonzero for adjustable cells that have a zero value in the optimal solution. An exception to this occurs when there are multiple optima—more than one combination of adjustable cell values that yield the same optimal solution—because no penalty is incurred in moving from one optimal solution to an alternative one. If your model yields zero dual values for adjustable cells that are zero after optimization, it's likely that there are multiple optima for your model.

Dual Values in Nonlinear and Integer Problems. Dual values in a nonlinear problem can be interpreted usefully only for small changes in the right-hand side. It may not be possible to make assumptions about the effect of large changes in a nonlinear model. You may want to investigate the effect of such changes manually by inserting proposed changes and resolving. The dual values in integer problems may be meaningless.

Valid Ranges for Dual Values. The range commands can find the upper and lower ranges of any specified dual value. Changing the right-hand side of a constraint, or using more or less of a resource, eventually will cause a change in the dual value. The valid range for a dual value is the amount of change in the right-hand side of a constraint, or in resource use in an adjustable cell, which is possible before such a change in the dual value will occur. This is discussed more fully in Chapter 5.

In some problems, the range of a dual value may be very small or zero. When this occurs you may find that different starting solutions result in different dual values. This may also indicate that more than one combination of the adjustable cells will result in the optimal value of the objective cell; in this case your model is said to have *multiple optima*. In any event, before making use of dual values in decisions of economic importance, you should investigate the range over which they're valid.

Valid Ranges in Nonlinear Problems. Because solvers cannot assign meaningful values to upper and lower ranges in nonlinear problems, What's*Best!* will always return a zero if you use the **U**pper or **L**ower command in such a case. There is no useful interpretation of ranges in a nonlinear problem.

Dual Value Formulas. Depending on the spreadsheet you're using, What's*Best!* writes dual and range formulas under various syntaxes. If you want to write the formulas yourself, here is a table of the formulas, by spreadsheet, for a dual value of cell H8.

Lotus 1-2-3	@WBDUAL(H8,0)
Quattro Pro 4	@WB.DUAL(H8,0)
"IF" Style	@IF(0=H8,0,0)

To write an upper or lower range formula, simply substitute the word "UPPER" or "LOWER" for the word "DUAL" in the appropriate formula. In the "IF" style, replace "=" with the greater than sign (>=) for an upper range, and the less than sign (<=) for a lower range.

To see dual values for every possible cell without entering dual value formulas in the worksheet, use **R**eport **S**olution **E**nable.

Integer

What's*Best!* provides four **I**nteger commands. The first two, **B**inary and **G**eneral, let you specify that cells must return zero or one (binary) or any whole number (general) values. The second two, **T**olerance and **K**nown IP, change the way the program solves problems involving integer variables.

Binary

Binary integer variables are useful in making yes/no, open/close, or buy/sell decisions, and in formulating piecewise linear functions.

If a cell is specified as Binary, What's*Best!* will find the best solution that returns a zero or a one in that cell. When you use the **I**nteger **B**inary command, you'll be asked to identify the range you want to be Binary with up to ten characters, then to select the range. This range name must begin with WBBIN. Typical range names might be WBBIN, WBBIN3, WBBINAPPLE, or WBBINFATSO.

To remove a binary integer designation, simply use the commands within your particular spreadsheet to delete the range name that identifies the cell or cells in question.

General

General integer variables (0, 1, 2 . . .) can be useful when answers with fractions are of limited or no value. If a cell is specified as General, What's*Best!* will find the best solution that returns a whole number in that cell. When you use the **I**nteger **G**eneral command, you'll be asked to identify the range you want to return whole numbers with up to ten characters, then to select the range. What's-*Best!* designates general integers with range names starting with "WBINT."

To remove a general integer designation, you simply use the commands within your particular spreadsheet to delete the range name that identifies the cell or cells in question.

Runtime Concerns in Integer Problems

The use of integer variables can considerably increase the time required to find the best answer; another thing to remember is that in most nonlinear models that include integer variables, your chances of reaching an optimum in a reasonable amount of time are not very good, unless the problem is extremely rudimentary or constrained in very specific ways.

Having said all this, using **T**olerance and **K**nown IP can significantly decrease the optimization time on some integer problems. The first step to understanding how **T**olerance and **K**nown IP work is to understand how integer problems are solved without these options. If neither **T**olerance nor **K**nown IP is used, What's*Best!* solves integer problems using the following steps:

1. First, What's*Best!* solves what is known as the continuous problem. This involves finding the optimal answer if the integer variables are constrained to be *any nonnegative value* rather than constraining them to be *whole numbers*. This sets a theoretical limit: The integer answer can't be better than the answer to the continuous problem.

2. Next, it uses optimization to find a feasible integer solution.

3. After finding a feasible integer answer, What's*Best!* uses a solution method called branch-and-bound to find the best integer answer. The number of potential "branches" in the search tree goes up exponentially with the number of integer variables. During branch-and-bound, What's*Best!* will investigate every branch with a possibility of yielding a better answer than the current best integer answer. When a better integer answer is found, the value of the best cell and the value of each integer variable is stored, and the search for an even better answer continues. Branch-and-bound is not complete until there are no branches remaining that could yield a better answer than the best integer answer stored.

Both **T**olerance and **K**nown IP can be used to reduce runtime by reducing the number of branches in the search tree that What's*Best!* will investigate. Some experimentation may be required to find the best values for these options to achieve the results you need.

Tolerance

After a feasible integer solution has been found, the **T**olerance command can sometimes significantly reduce remaining runtime by accepting a tolerance of variation from the true integer optimum. Rather than searching every branch that might yield a better answer than the current best integer, What's*Best!* can be set to search only those branches that may improve the current best integer by the percentage specified with **T**olerance. When you set a **T**olerance, you may not find the mathematically optimal answer, but the answer is at least within the specified percentage of the best integer answer—and may in fact be much closer than that. As a rule, the greater the **T**olerance value, the shorter the solution time.

For example, to set a tolerance of 5%, select the **T**olerance command under **I**nteger and enter 0.05 as the value. (You'll also select a cell address in which to store the value.) If What's*Best!* is maximizing and finds a feasible integer answer of 100, then a branch will not be investigated if it cannot lead to a solution of 105 or better.

In evaluating the final answer of a model using **T**olerance, you should compare the integer solution with the theoretical limit. If in the above example the final integer answer is 100 and the theoretical limit is 101, then the final answer is within 1% of the true integer optimal answer even though the **T**olerance was set at 5%.

Known IP

The **K**nown IP command can significantly reduce the time required to find an acceptable integer answer. With **K**nown IP specified, What's*Best!* will not spend time searching for any feasible integer solution unless it is at least as good as the bound value specified by **K**nown IP. After such a feasible integer solution is found, What's*Best!* will continue the branch-and-bound, searching all branches that may improve that integer answer (unless the **T**olerance command is used in conjunction with **K**nown IP).

If you set a **K**nown IP value *better* than the optimal integer answer, What's-*Best!* will return an infeasible error message, since no feasible answer can satisfy the bound you've set. **K**nown IP is different from **T**olerance: If you use it by itself and an integer answer is found, it will yield the true optimal integer answer.

For example, if you're confident the best integer answer is at least 95 for a maximization problem, choose **K**nown IP under **I**nteger and input the value 95. (You'll also enter a cell address in which to store the value.) What's*Best!* won't consider any branch that doesn't yield an answer of at least 95. If in fact the best integer answer is only 93, you will eventually get the infeasible error message.

Options

Options contains commands that let you change the ways in which What's*Best!* displays, processes, and saves information and data.

Constraint

This command permits automatic building of constraint formulas in either the WB form, using the custom constraint function built into the What's*Best!* add-in, or the IF form, which uses a syntax understood by all spreadsheets.

If you're writing and running a model solely in Lotus 1-2-3, for instance, you'll probably want to use the WB form. If you have a model that you expect to export to other spreadsheets, you'll probably want to use the IF form. In Quattro Pro 2 and 3, only the IF form is allowed.

The **C**onstraint **WB** command also allows the constraint cells in your model to return either their **S**lack value or **I**ndicator. The *slack* is a value that lets you know how close you are to satisfying the constraint; it's the result of a simple calculation that depends on the kind of constraint involved. For instance, the constraint A1>=B1 yields the slack calculated by A1–B1; A1<=B1 yields that calculated by B1–A1. A positive slack means the constraint is satisfied. As the slack reaches zero, the constraint is tightly satisfied. A negative slack means the constraint is not satisfied.

Warnings

Warnings lets you activate and deactivate six warnings:

Nonlinear—nonlinear functions or formulas in the model

Blank Cell—blank cells referenced

Function—an unsupported function in the model

Objective—no best cell is specified

Conditions—optimality conditions uncertain in nonlinear problems

Error Screen—when toggled on, the error screen is displayed whenever there's an error. When off, the error screen is not displayed; What's *Best!* prompts you for a cell address to which an error code can be written in this event.

Translate

Translate allows two kinds of translation. **T**ranslate **M**odel translates all constraint and dual value formulas in models built in What's *Best!* Release 1.X to the newer format required by this release. **T**ranslate/**C**onstraints allows translation between the WB and IF formats of constraint and dual value formulas.

Constraints: The **T**ranslate/**C**onstraints command allows translation between the WB and IF formats of constraint and dual value formulas. This facilitates moving models between spreadsheet packages.

For spreadsheets with the appropriate capabilities, What's *Best!* allows the expression of constraint and dual value information in two formats—special WB functions or native IF formulas. The WB functions are easier to read and interpret, but they can't be directly read by other than the native spreadsheet program. For example, a model created in 1-2-3 Release 2.3 using the WB functions could be read by other 1-2-3 Release 2.X spreadsheets (with the appropriate add-in attached), but, if the model were read by Quattro Pro, the WB functions would be lost.

To use a model with WB functions in a different spreadsheet package, follow these steps:

1. Use the **O**ptions **T**ranslate **M**odel **I**F command to convert all WB functions to IF function form.

2. Save the model.

3. Import the file into the other spreadsheet.

4. Use the **O**ptions **T**ranslate **M**odel **WB** command to convert all IF functions back to WB function form.

Model: The **T**ranslate **M**odel command can be used to prepare models built with What's*Best!* Release 1.X to run in this release of What's*Best!*. This is typically not used in the Student Edition of What's*Best!*.

Omit

Areas of the worksheet specified with **O**mit are completely ignored during optimization. These areas do not contribute toward the numeric cell limit of What's*Best!*.

When you use the **O**mit command, What's*Best!* asks you to identify the WBOMIT range name with up to ten characters beginning with the letters WBOMIT, then specify the cell or range you want to be omitted during optimization. To remove an omit designation, you simply use the commands in your particular spreadsheet to delete the range name that identifies the cell or cells in question.

Where To Use Omit

Reporting Equations—Some cells in the spreadsheet may be used for evaluation and reporting and aren't pertinent to the solution process. If these cells contain unsupported spreadsheet functions, using **O**mit will eliminate the error message caused by the equations. If they contain equations that depend upon adjustable cells, using **O**mit can shorten the time required for solving.

Extraneous Equations or Numeric Cells—Cells that are not necessary to perform the optimization still count toward the problem size limits of What's*Best!* and, if they depend upon the adjustable cells, may significantly slow optimization. These cells can be included in omit ranges.

Where Not To Use Omit

Since What's*Best!* ignores the values and equations of every cell within an omit range, it is very important not to include in such a range any optimizable cell that is pertinent to optimization. Thus, **O**mit should *not* be used in the following situations:

Adjustable Cells—Any adjustable cell within an omit range will be ignored during the solution process.

Constraint Cells—Any constraint cell within an omit range will be ignored during solution. Do not include in an omit range any cell that you intend to function as a constraint.

Cells Precedent to Equations Outside Omit Range—Referencing cells in an omit range in an equation outside the omit range will cause solution to halt and the original worksheet will be returned.

Limit

A limit on the number of tries (LP iterations) can be placed on the What's*Best!* optimizer. To use this command, choose **L**imit and type in the maximum number of tries that you want attempted, then specify the cell to which you want the number written. (There is no default limit to the number of tries.) This cell is given the range name WBLIM.

To undo the **L**imit command, simply use the commands within your spreadsheet to delete the WBLIM range name.

Display

During optimization the status is set up to be updated on the bottom of the screen every few tries (LP iterations). You can vary the frequency of update by choosing the **D**isplay command and typing in the new number of tries between status updates, then specifying the cell to which you want the number written. This cell is given the range name WBTRACE.

To undo the **D**isplay command, simply use the commands within you particular spreadsheet to delete the WBTRACE range name.

Files

Files offers three commands: **T**o lets you assign a name to the file What's *Best!* looks for to optimize; **F**rom specifies the filename to which What's *Best!* will write the optimized spreadsheet; **E**rror names the file to which cell classification statistics for your model, and any errors or warnings, will be written. Changes made with the **F**iles command are specific only to the active file.

The default filenames are: WBTO.W?? for the file to be optimized, WBFR.W?? for the optimized file, and WBERR.PRN for the statistics and errors file. When you change the filenames, you're also responsible for the extensions.

Macro

When optimizing from a macro, you may want to perform a macro immediately on returning from optimization; the **M**acro command lets you specify a macro to be executed when the optimized file is retrieved.

In 1-2-3 2.x, we prompt you for the cell location of a macro to run after optimization, then for a blank cell in which to store the What's *Best!* auto macro. In Quattro Pro, we prompt you only for the cell location of the macro to run after optimization.

Report

Under **R**eport you'll find commands relating to three different reports, and one informational command to help you organize your model.

Locate

Locate has three commands to let you search for three special kinds of cells.

Adjustable (Lotus 1-2-3 Only): **A**djustable allows you to find the next adjustable cell relative to your present position in the spreadsheet. The search is by row: If you are in A1 and if B1 and A2 are adjustable, the next cell found will be B1.

Best: **B**est takes you to the objective cell if one has been designated. If no best cell exists, What's *Best!* lets you know.

Constraint: **C**onstraint allows you to find the next or previous constraint cell relative to your present position in the spreadsheet. The search is by row: If you're in A1 and if B1 and A2 are constraints, the next cell found will be B1.

Error

Error opens a text file with the error report for the last **S**olve attempt.

Algebraic

Algebraic gives you three choices of action with regard to a text file containing the *algebraic formulation* of your model.

> *Enable:* **E**nable lets you specify that, during optimization, the algebraic formulation will be written to a text file. You'll be prompted for a file name to which you want the formulation written, then for the cell in which to store the filename. The default filename is WBFORM.PRN. The resultant output file may be used as an input file with the LINDO linear programming package.

> *Disable:* **D**isable turns off the above option.

> *Retrieve:* **R**trieve opens the created text file.

Solution

Solution gives you three choices of action with regard to a text file containing a detailed *solution report* on your model.

> *Enable:* **E**nable lets you specify that a solution report will be written to a text file. The report contains a listing of constraint locations, types, and formulas; the formula, type, and location of your objective; and complete range reports. You'll be asked to type in the file name to which you want the solution report written, then to specify the cell in which to store the filename. The default filename is WBSOLN.PRN. Unless a path is specified as a part of the filename, the WBSOLN.PRN file will be saved in the subdirectory containing your spreadsheet programs.

> *Disable:* **D**isable turns off the above option.

> *Retrieve:* **R**etrieve opens the text file created.

Macro Capabilities of What's*Best!*

Any What's*Best!* command can be executed from a spreadsheet macro. They behave as normal keyboard macros. There are separate commands for 1-2-3 Release 2.X and Quattro Pro.

Macro Commands for 1-2-3 Release 2.2 and 2.3

For Release 2.2 and 2.3, the **Add-in** menu macro commands to invoke What's-*Best!* are:

/AIWBMENU   (**A**dd-In **I**nvoke **WBMENU**[←Enter]

If you want a macro to run after optimization, use the What's*Best!* command **O**ptions **M**acro.

What's *Best! Macro Commands for Quattro Pro*

What's *Best!* commands may be used in your Quattro Pro macros exactly as if they were native Quattro Pro commands.

Messages for Errors and Troubleshooting

This section lists problems and messages that may occur, and messages that may be returned when solving a worksheet. If you generate an error message that is not discussed here, please call LINDO Systems Technical Support at (312) 248-0465.

Operational Errors

These messages generally occur due to an error in operation.

Operating Problems

Symptom: After typing WB or WBQ at the DOS prompt, the message "Bad command or file name" was displayed by DOS.

Problem: Either you are not in a directory from which you can run your spreadsheet, or What's *Best!* hasn't been correctly installed to this directory.

Symptom: After typing WB or WBQ at the DOS prompt, the spreadsheet was not loaded and you were left at a DOS prompt.

Problem: What's *Best!* was unable to load your spreadsheet because it was not in the directory from which you typed WB or WBQ.

Symptom: (Applies only to Quattro Pro) After optimizing, user is left at the DOS prompt.

Problem: You have failed to start Quattro Pro by typing WBQ at the DOS prompt. You have opened WB.WQ1 from within the application. To ensure proper operation, always start What's *Best!* by typing WBQ at the DOS prompt; never open WB.WQ1 from within Quattro Pro.

Unable to Load Solver Messages

The following messages appear if the What's *Best!* solver is unable to load.

Unable to load WBOPT.EXE, File not found.

Problem: WBOPT.EXE is not in your spreadsheet directory or on the DOS path. Reinstall the What's *Best!* system files to the correct directory.

Unable to load WBOPT.EXE, Insufficient memory.

Problem: There is not enough free conventional RAM memory to load WBOPT.EXE. Check the README file on your What's *Best!* disk for the minimum RAM requirements.

Insufficient memory to load WBOPT.EXE, or exceeded limit while solving.

Problem: Either there isn't enough memory to load `WBOPT.EXE`, or a limit was exceeded while solving your worksheet. If a smaller model solves successfully, the original problem is beyond the limits of this version of What's *Best!*. If a small model won't solve, check the `README` file on your What's *Best!* disk for the minimum RAM.

`Unable to solve, 123 not loaded through WB.EXE`

Problem: In order to successfully optimize your worksheet, 1-2-3 must be loaded by the `WB.EXE` controlling program. First, save your worksheet and quit Lotus. Then, type WB at the DOS prompt to load both the controlling program and 1-2-3.

`Unable to solve, The WBMENU add-in must be set to attach automatically.`
`Unable to solve, The WB add-in must be set to attach automatically.`

Problem: Solution can only occur if the `WB` and `WBMENU` add-ins have been specified to be loaded automatically whenever 1-2-3 is started. For more information on setting up add-ins to be loaded automatically, turn to the Installation Instructions in Appendix A.

`Unknown key or block name:` [MOUSE] (*Applies only to Quattro Pro*)

Problem: A What's *Best!* command has been entered while `WB.WQ1`, the What's *Best!* macro sheet, was not open. You may have started Quattro without typing WBQ at the DOS prompt or `WB.WQ1` was inadvertently closed. Save worksheet changes, quit, and restart by typing WBQ.

Solution Status Messages (Errors)

Messages described here will be written to the "error" file and displayed on the screen.

Blank Cell

If a formula within a worksheet refers to cells that have neither numbers nor formulas within them, then What's *Best!* presumes that these blank cells have a value of zero. It displays a warning to this effect and lists all such cells. The error message displayed is titled:

`BLANK CELL REFERENCE WARNING`

The cell addresses listed on the screen have been referenced in formulas but are either blank or contain text. During the solution search their values have been taken as zero. This message can be turned off from the **Options Warnings** menu. The typical default settting for the student version is for this message to be turned off. It can be enabled through the What's *Best!* menu.

There are three possible reasons for this error. (1) An omission in entering the numbers or formulas. If so, check the addresses of blank cells listed in the error message and enter the proper values. (2) The formulas that refer to these blank cells are incorrect. Find the formulas that refer to these cells, and check to see if they should in fact be referring to some other cells. Correct the formulas if they are incorrect. (3) You have intentionally referred to blank cells, perhaps in a shortcut such as summing an entire range, and you don't mind these cells being taken as zero. If so, you don't have to make any changes.

Equation Length Limit

What's *Best!* generates its own algebraic formulation of your model. When one of your equations results in a statement of inordinate length, the error message displayed is titled:

    EQUATION LENGTH LIMIT

The solver has been halted because the addressed cell contains an equation that is too long to store in algebraic form. Try breaking up the calculation into multiple cells. Please report this error to a LINDO Systems Technical Support Representative.

Interrupt

If the [End] key is pressed before completion of the solution process, the error message displayed is titled:

    INTERRUPT

The solver was interrupted before the solution could be found. What's *Best!* returns the adjustable cell values for the best solution found up to the point when the [End] key was pressed. However, the returned answer may not be feasible, and is likely to be suboptimal for optimization models. If a feasible integer solution is found for an integer optimization model, restoring the best integer solution may take a significant amount of time.

Irreconcilable Constraint Formulas

If a constraint does not depend upon any adjustable cells, What's *Best!* will not be able to affect whether or not that constraint is violated or satisfied. If What's *Best!* encounters violated constraints that do not depend upon adjustable cells, then these constraints will be ignored. The error message displayed is titled:

    IRRECONCILABLE CONSTRAINT FORMULAS

The cells listed on the screen contain violated constraints that do not depend upon adjustable cells, and, therefore, cannot be reconciled. These constraints were ignored during the solution process. An example of an irreconcilable constraint would be (1,"<=",0). Please check to see that these constraints have been entered correctly and that all adjustable cells have been specified.

This error could occur if a constraint or equation that it depends upon is improperly formulated. Also, make sure all cells that you intend to be adjustable have been properly specified.

Iteration Limit

What's *Best!* itself does not put a limit on the number of tries. By using the **O**ptions **L**imit command, you may limit the number of tries. When the program has executed the specified number of tries without finding a solution, the error message displayed is titled:

ITERATION LIMIT

The limit for the maximum number of tries, N, was reached before the solution to the problem could be found.

Multiple Max or Min Cells

If an error message with the following title appears, you've manually created a spreadsheet range called WBMAX when a range called WBMIN already exists (or vice versa), or you have created a WBMIN or WBMAX range with multiple cells.

MULTIPLE MAX/MIN

There are multiple cells specified for maximize, minimize, or both. What's-*Best!* only allows one cell to be maximized or minimized. If you have several objectives, they can be combined into one formula by weighting their importance.

No Adjustable Cells Specified

Adjustable cells represent activities that are under direct managerial control. These are the cells that are allowed to be changed during the optimization process. If there are no adjustable cells in the model, the error message displayed is titled:

NO ADJUSTABLE CELLS SPECIFIED

No cells have been specified as adjustable. You must use the **A**djustable command to specify the cells you want What's *Best!* to adjust to find the solution. These cells must contain numbers. Cells specified as adjustable that are blank or contain formulas or text will be ignored by the solver.

If there are no adjustable cells in the worksheet, reformulate the model to create some. Check to be sure that cells in the worksheet that should be adjustable are specified as such.

No Best Cell Specified

Every *optimization* problem must have an objective. It could be profit maximization, cost minimization, or some other criterion that can be represented as a formula referring directly or indirectly to some adjustable cells. If your model is *not* an optimization problem, you will probably want to turn this warning off with **O**ptions **W**arnings **O**bjective **D**isable. With the warning turned on, a model with no max or min cell will display an error message titled:

NO BEST CELL SPECIFIED

Either no cell has been specified to be maximized or minimized, or the cell that is marked is not a function of any adjustable cells. If this is an optimization model, use the options under the **Best** menu to specify an appropriate cell as the objective of the optimization. This message can be turned off from the **Options Warnings Objective** menu.

If you failed to indicate a best cell before solving, specify a cell to be maximized or minimized and resolve. If the problem doesn't need a best cell, consider turning off this warning. Keep in mind that disabling this warning will cause it to be suppressed for all models until you re-enable it. Problems without an objective are often called goal-seek or back-solve problems.

No Feasible Solution Found

A *linear optimization* model containing constraints that can't be met simultaneously by What's *Best!* is said to be infeasible—there's no solution that simultaneously satisfies all the constraints. In *nonlinear* models, it's possible that a feasible solution exists, but What's *Best!* was unable to reach it from the starting adjustable cell values you specified. In either case, What's *Best!* tries to find a solution to the problem that satisfies as many constraints as possible, and returns an error message titled:

```
SOLUTION STATUS: NO FEASIBLE SOLUTION FOUND
```

No solution was found that satisfies all of the constraints. If the model is linear, there is no solution that satisfies all constraints. If the model is nonlinear, a feasible solution may exist that What's *Best!* was unable to detect. If you suspect this to be the case, try changing the initial values of the adjustable cells and resolving. Keep in mind that there are many situations that have no feasible solution. Imagine the dilemma of an employee who is told by one supervisor to "make at least a dozen" and told by the parts department that "we only have parts for ten." The scenario, if faithfully modeled on the spreadsheet, should indeed show no feasible solution.

If a *linear* or *nonlinear* problem is reported to be infeasible, determining whether the error indicates a logically infeasible situation, or whether a situation has been incorrectly modeled, can be a very complicated task. The first step is to find which constraints contribute to the infeasibility. *Unsatisfied* constraints will display "Not =," "Not <=," or "Not >=." Investigating their relationships to *satisfied* constraints may help you find the conflicts. Next, find all the constraints that are contradictory to the constraints identified in the first step. Finally, eliminate all the contradictory constraints except the ones that most accurately model your business situation.

If a *nonlinear* problem returns this error message and you suspect there is a feasible solution, change the starting adjustable cell values to a feasible or near-feasible solution and solve again. Note that a very discontinuous problem may have a feasible solution that can only be "found" by starting at the solution point itself.

Nonimplemented Function

During solving, What's *Best!* treats the cells that contain nonimplemented functions as fixed, and doesn't recalculate their values during solution. It uses their pre-solution values for the required calculations. The error message displayed after solving is titled:

```
FUNCTION ERROR
```

The addressed cells contain spreadsheet functions that are not implemented in What's *Best!*. The numeric values for these cells are taken from the spreadsheet directly without recalculation.

If these formulas are used for reporting only, then they can be included in a `WBOMIT` range. If they are necessary to the solution, they must be expressed or approximated in terms of equivalent operations that are implemented in What's*Best!*.

List of Supported Functions and Operators

The following spreadsheet functions are supported by What's*Best!*. Those functions shown in *slanted* type are discontinuous; their use may result in long solution times or nonoptimal answers.

ABS	COS	LOG	SIN
ACOS	EXP	*MAX*	SQRT
ASIN	FALSE	*MIN*	SUM
ATAN	*IF*	*MOD*	SUMPRODUCT
ATAN2	*INT*	NPV	TAN
AVG	LN	PI	TRUE

The following spreadsheet operators are supported by What's*Best!*.

$$^\wedge \qquad * \qquad + \qquad -$$

The following spreadsheet logical operators are discontinuous. They are supported by What's*Best!* for numeric arguments but not for string (alphanumeric) arguments. Their use may result in long solution times or nonoptimal answers.

$$< \qquad <= \qquad <> \qquad = \qquad > \qquad >= \qquad AND \qquad NOT \qquad OR$$

Nonlinear Expressions

If the Nonlinear Expressions warning is enabled, the warning screen will be displayed if the optimization model is nonlinear. The warning is suppressed if the optimization is linear, even if there are nonlinear *reporting* cells. What's*Best!* will list all cells that contain nonlinear relationships after a solution try. What's-*Best!* can solve problems made up of linear and nonlinear relationships, but problems expressed entirely of linear relationships tend to solve faster with a higher degree of confidence. For further discussion of identifying linear and nonlinear expressions see Chapter 4. The message displayed is titled:

NONLINEAR EXPRESSIONS

The cells listed on the screen contain nonlinear expressions. This message can be turned off from the **Options Warnings** menu.

When possible, formulate your problem using linear expressions. Evaluate the equations in the cells identified above to determine if they can be reformulated into linear expressions, as discussed in Chapter 10. In many cases linear reformulation may not be possible. If your model contains inherently nonlinear expressions, you may choose to turn off this nonlinear warning with **O**ptions **W**arnings **N**onlinear **D**isable. Keep in mind that disabling this warning message will cause it to be suppressed for all models until you enable it again.

Numeric Cell Limit Exceeded

All cells that have a number or formula within them are referred to as *numeric cells*. Also, blank cells referred to in formulas (such as using the SUM function across a range that includes some blank cells) are classified as numeric cells with a value of zero. If the number of numeric cells in a worksheet is greater than the limit of the What'sBest! version being used, the error message displayed on the screen is titled:

NUMERIC CELL LIMIT EXCEEDED

The number of numeric cells exceeds the limit of N. (N is the limit of the What'sBest! version being used.) A numeric cell is any cell containing a number or equation. In addition, blank cells that are referenced in equations are stored as numeric cells with values of zero. Any numeric cell that is not used in the What'sBest! model can be put in a WBOMIT range. Numeric cells in WBOMIT ranges do not count toward the numeric cell limit.

The only ways to lower the number of cells that count toward the numeric cell limit are to erase them or include them in a WBOMIT range. Candidates for elimination could include any cell that is not an adjustable cell, constraint cell, or the best cell, and is not referenced directly or indirectly by a constraint or by the best cell.

Since What'sBest! counts the number of cells *referenced* in your model, not the number used, erasing a cell referenced in an equation won't reduce the number of numeric cells counted by What'sBest! (unless the equation is in a WBOMIT range). Including a cell in a WBOMIT range that is referenced in an equation outside a WBOMIT range will cause an error—see the WBOMIT cell error message later in this section.

Optimal

When optimization has been successfully completed, the following message will be written to the error file:

Solution Status: OPTIMAL
Optimality Conditions: SATISFIED

The mathematical requirements for optimality are met. In linear problems, this means that a global optimum has been found; in nonlinear problems, it means that a local optimum has been found.

Optimal To Tolerances

When optimization has been successfully completed, the following message will be written to the error file:

Solution Status: OPTIMAL TO TOLERANCES
Optimality Conditions: UNCERTAIN

Given the tolerances programmed into What'sBest!, the optimizer was unable to find a better point. The current solution may not be optimal.

Although it is uncertain whether the mathematical requirements for optimality have been met, What'sBest! was unable to find a nearby point that improves the value of the cell to be maximized or minimized. However, it is likely that the returned solution is a local optimum. When the optimality conditions are uncertain, the dual value information may not be completely accurate.

Problem Capacity Exceeded

What's*Best!* assigns memory dynamically to its tasks so that all available memory is used efficiently, but sometimes a model is too large, resulting in a message titled:

```
PROBLEM CAPACITY EXCEEDED
```

This model is too large to be solved by this version of What's*Best!*. If possible, reduce the size of the model. Please report this error to a LINDO Systems Technical Support Representative.

Unbounded

If, without violating any constraints, the value of the cell specified to be maximized can be increased to infinity, or the value of the cell specified to be minimized can be decreased to negative infinity, then the problem is said to be unbounded. The message displayed is titled:

```
SOLUTION STATUS: UNBOUNDED
```

The value of the cell to be maximized/minimized can be increased/decreased without limit, and without violating a constraint. The problem may be incorrectly formulated. Be sure that the best cell has been correctly specified and all equations and constraints have been correctly formulated. Because very few real problems have the opportunity for infinite profit, it is unlikely that a correctly-modeled situation will be unbounded. It may often be possible to drive costs to infinity levels, so one cause for this error is maximizing cost or minimizing profit.

Check the formulation of the problem to ensure that adjustable cells, best cell, and constraint information have been properly specified and no constraints have been left out. The returned worksheet will display a large positive or negative number in the best cell, and may have large numbers in one or more adjustable cells. This information can give you an indication of where formulation errors lie. An incorrectly specified best cell or constraint (i.e., maximizing a cell that should be minimized or incorrectly specifying a greater than constraint as a less than constraint) may be causing the problem.

Undefined Arithmetic Value

If a formula contains an operation that evaluates to an undefined value, What's*Best!* gives an error message along with the cell address of the offending formula. Examples are: division by zero, multiplying by a text string, and evaluating to a number larger than 10^{99}. In such cases, the message displayed is titled:

```
UNDEFINED ARITHMETIC VALUE
```

The solver has been halted because the cell listed on the screen contains an equation that has an undefined value (e.g., attempting division by zero). If possible, change the initial values of the adjustable cells to move away from this undefined region and attempt to solve again.

If the cells are unrelated to solving the model, include them in a WBOMIT range or delete them. Otherwise, change the initial values of the adjustable cells to move away from the undefined region. In some situations, starting a nonlinear model with adjustable cells at values of zero makes logical sense, but causes errors from dividing by zero. Using positive values for the adjustable cells will often eliminate this problem. In other situations, it may be necessary to incorporate constraints to keep adjustable cells from getting close to troublesome values, such as zero.

Undetermined

When an error occurs that is not recognized by What's *Best!*, the following message will be displayed:

SOLUTION STATUS: UNDETERMINED

The optimizer encountered a serious error and was unable to continue the optimization. If this message appears, please call technical support at (312) 248-0465.

Unexpected Operation

If a formula contains an unexpected, inappropriate, or unrecognized operation (e.g. SUMPRODUCT(A1..C1*A1..C2) where a comma is expected instead of the multiplication operator, What's *Best!* may not know how to proceed. The message displayed is titled:

UNEXPECTED OPERATION

The solver has been halted because the cell listed on the screen contains an equation that has an unrecognized or unexpected operator. Please check the formula in this cell for abnormalities or contact LINDO Systems Technical Support. Check to be sure the formula has been constructed properly. If the formula still results in this message, and the cell is used only for reporting purposes, you may consider putting it in a WBOMIT range.

WBOMIT Cell Error

Cells within WBOMIT ranges cannot be referenced in cell formulas outside of any WBOMIT range. If this occurs, the message displayed is titled:

WBOMIT CELL ERROR

The solver has been halted because the cells listed on the screen are in WBOMIT ranges and have been referenced by formulas. Eliminate references to cells in WBOMIT ranges or include all referencing formulas in a WBOMIT range.

C

Using the Solvers in Excel 4.0 & Quattro Pro for Windows 1.0

Some spreadsheets have solvers (optimizers) as a part of the software package. There are some differences between the capabilities of these solvers and the capabilities of What's *Best!* that the user should understand. This section is not intended to be exhaustive, but it is sufficient to assist the reader in making productive use of these solvers. While all of the examples in the chapters have been solved with What's *Best!* there may be situations in which nonoptimal results are obtained from solvers not tested with these models.

Using the Solver in Excel Release 4.0

The solver provided with Excel 4.0 can address all of the optimization problems in this text. There are some differences which the user should understand.

The most important difference is that the decision variables (which Excel identifies as *changing cells*) are allowed to take on negative values. In What's *Best!* the adjustable (decision) variables cannot take on negative values, unless they are specifically identified as **F**ree variables from the **Adjustable** menu choice. When it is logically impossible for a decision variable to be negative, which is usually the case in managerial optimization problems, the Excel solver requires the user to add a constraint for each decision variable, so that it will be >= 0.

Another important difference is that the Excel solver contains no expertise to determine whether a linear solver may be used. The user may specify the use of a linear solver, and an imperfect "after the fact" test determines whether the linear assumption was correct. However, this test for linearity may yield incorrect results under certain conditions.

The Excel solver has the capability to produce integer solutions. If binary solutions are desired, an integer value is specified, with a lower limit of 0 and an upper limit of 1. An unsuspecting reader may not be able to find the integer specification; it is included as a choice for the type of constraint, along with <=, =, and >=.

The Excel solver has the capability to use spreadsheet functions that What's*Best!* cannot understand. In certain modeling situation, functions such as VLOOKUP and DSUM can simplify models which are otherwise complex. For example, the VLOOKUP function can be used to find the purchase price in an inventory model with price breaks. The DSUM function can be used to greatly simplify network flow problems.

Using the Optimizer in Quattro Pro for Windows Version 1.0

The solver provided with Quattro Pro for Windows 1.0 can be used to address many of the optimization problems in this text. There are some differences which the user should understand.

The most important difference is that the decision variables (which QPW identifies as *variable cells*) are allowed to take on negative values. In What's*Best!* the adjustable (decision) variables cannot take on negative values, unless they are specifically identified as **Free** variables from the **Adjustable** menu choice. When it is logically impossible for a decision variable to be negative, which is usually the case in managerial optimization problems, the QPW solver requires the user to add a constraint for each decision variable, so that it will be >= 0.

Another important difference is that the QPW solver contains no expertise to determine whether a linear solver may be used. The user may specify the use of a linear solver, and an imperfect "after the fact" test determines whether the linear assumption was correct. However, this test for linearity may yield incorrect results under certain conditions.

The QPW solver has no capability to produce integer or binary solutions.

The QPW solver requires a constant on the right hand side of each constraint, according to the documentation. According to empirical results, the right hand side of a constraint may also be a formula, as long as that formula does not depend upon any decision variable. In contrast, What's*Best!* allows general formulas on both the right and left sides of a constraint. That capability has been used in the text. However, there is an easy "workaround" to use the QPW solver. As an example, suppose the logic of a What's*Best!* constraint is:

$$\text{Quantity[Decoy]} >= \text{Quantity[Hanging]}$$

where both variables are decision variables. To include this constraint in QPW, these changes might be used:

Define a new variable as

$$\text{Excess Decoys} = \text{Quantity[Decoy]} - \text{Quantity[Hanging]}$$

And then include this constraint:

$$\text{Excess Decoys} >= 0$$

The QPW solver has the capability to use spreadsheet functions that What's*Best!* cannot understand. In certain modeling situation, functions such as @VLOOKUP and @DSUM can simplify models which are otherwise complex. For example, the @VLOOKUP function can be used to find the purchase price in an inventory model with price breaks. The @DSUM function can be used to greatly simplify network flow problems.

Using the Quattro Pro Version 4.0 Optimizer

The Optimizer in Quattro Pro Release 4.0 is very similar to Quattro Pro for Windows 1.0. The major difference is that the QP 4.0 optimizer will accept only one rectangular block of decision variables. Many of the models in this text have noncontiguous blocks of decision variables. Although it may be possible to rearrange a spreadsheet to accommodate this requirement, the spreadsheet tends to be come more difficult to understand.

Optimizers in Quattro Pro 2.0 and 3.0

The optimizers in Quattro Pro releases prior to 4.0 are generally incapable of solving optimization problems as they have been set up in this text. These optimizers are designed for linear problems whose formulation is based on the traditional "coefficient" approach as described in the chapter on Linear Programming.

INDEX

A

Absolute cell addresses, 37–38, 155
Absolute key, 38
Activity in project scheduling, 142
Acts, 275
Ad hoc modeling, 1
Add-ins with 1-2-3, 336–338, 401–402
Additional information in decision
    analysis, 282–283
Adjustable cell (cells), 46, 50–53, 405–406
Adjustable cell locate, 416
Adjustable cells not specified, 421
Agribusiness case, 116–117
Algebraic report, 417
Alphanumeric strings and What's Best!, 423
Amusement devices example, 109–112
Anchored range (block), 36–37
Andrews, V. L., 186
Arbitrary distribution by fractiles, 338
Arcs, 139
Artistic license in influence charts, 48,
    104, 180
Assignment problem, 129–134, 139
Assignment solution methods, 134

B

Bad command or file name message, 418
BANANA, 226
Best cell, 47, 406–407
Best cell locate, 416
Best cell not specified, 421–422
Binary (integer menu), 410

Binary variables, 220–221
Binary variables for fixed charge, 228–232
Binary variables in What's Best!, 219
Black Bird Function, 337
Blank cell warning, 414, 419–420
Blending example, 193–198
Bodily, Samuel E., 2
Borrowing in time-based models, 180–184
Branch and bound, 219–220

C

CPM, 140
Capital budgeting problem, 225
Cash planning example, 169–172
Cell limit, 424
Central limit theorem, 352, 356, 360–361
Cheesecake example, 99–104
Cheney, John M., 263
Chi-square test, 386
Chris Hadley example, 105–109, 282–232
Citrimagination example, 99–104
Coefficient matrix for linear
    programming, 74
Components of optimization problems,
    46–47
Computer system requirements, 399
Conditional payoff, 275
Conditions warning, 414
Constrain(t) command, 407–408
Constraint (option menu), 413–414
Constraint cell locate, 416–417

Constraint formulas or functions, 54, 408
Constraint translate, 414–415
Constraint variables (cells), 46, 51–53
Copier waiting lines case, 380–394
Corner point solutions for linear programming, 80
Correlation coefficient, 255–256
Cost in network flow model, 157–158
Cost of admission, 94–96
Cost/Minimize, 406
Crashing an activity in project scheduling, 147–150
Critical Path Method, 140
Critical activity, 146
Critical path, 146
Cumulative frequency from Monte Carlo, 309–315
Customize interior of graph, 314

D

Data labels on graph, 313
Data tables for Monte Carlo, 304–305
Data values in influence charts, 48
Decision analysis, 271–287
Decision analysis components, 275
Decision tree rules for analysis, 285
Decision trees, 284–287
Decision variables (adjustable cells), 46, 50–53, 405–406
Delta Company case, 137–138
Demand during a lead time, 348, 366
Demand during a lead time, historical, 349–351
Demand during a lead time, statistical, 351–352
Demand generation with historical data, 344–347
Developing a new product example, 99–104
Dinkel, John, 279
Disable reports, 417
Discounted cash flow, 221
Discrete optimization, 220
Disk space required, 399
Display (options menu), 416
Documentation of models, 7–8, 16–17
Dual command, 409–411
Dual value for decision variables, 95
Dual value formulas, 411
Dual values and multiple optima, 410

Dual values for constraints, 89–92
Dual values in integer problems, 410
Dual values in nonlinear problems, 410
Duality, 87
Dumb answers suggest new constraints, 193

E

Economic Order Quantity, 245–248
Economic Order Quantity vs. modeling, 249–250
Economic Production Quantity, 258–26
Efficient portfolio case, 263–267
EMV, 277–278
Enable algebraic report, 417,
Enable solution report, 417
End key to interrupt, 420
End-user modeling, 1–2
EOQ, 245–248, 348, 366
EOQ vs. modeling, 249–250
Equation length limit, 420
Error (report menu), 417
Error messages, 418–427
Error messages from solve, 408–409
Event in project scheduling, 142
Events (decision analysis), 275
EVPI, 283–284
Excel 4.0 solver, 427–428
Expected monetary value, 275, 277–278
Expected value, 275, 277–278
Expected value estimated by Monte Carlo, 308–309
Expected value of perfect information, 283–284
Exponential distribution, 317, 321, 337, 372–373
Exponential distribution test, 385–387
Extrapolation revealed by optimization, 193

F

Fast Pack Delivery Company example, 151–158
Feasible region in linear programming, 75
File save, 42
Files (options menu), 416
Fire station location case, 234–237
Fish, 321
Fixed charge problem, 228–232

Flow chart, 2
Flows and cost in networks, 157–158
Flows in networks, 151–158
Flows in time-based models, 170
Fluctuating market purchases, 165–169
Folding back a decision tree, 285
Fractiles, 338
Free (adjustable cells), 405–406
Function warning, 414, 422–423

G

Gap, 191–192, 255–256
General integer variables, 219–22, 410–411
Global optimum, 190–191, 424
Golden Ear Audio Distributors case,
    260–263, 340–356, 366–370
Graphical solution for linear
    programming, 74–81
Graphing cumulative frequency, 313–314

H

Hanley Electronics case, 212–217
Heavy Haulers example, 112–114
Hendrick, Thomas E., 234
Hesse Corporation example, 165–169
Highint Company example, 169–172
Historical demand for simulation, 344–347
Hunt, Pearson, 186
Hypothesis testing, 363–364

I

IF logic and piecewise linearity, 203–206
Influence chart, 2
Influence chart advantages, 12–14
Influence chart construction, 2–6, 8–11,
    25–28
Influence chart for model construction,
    6–8, 11, 28–42
Influence chart guidelines, 5–6
Influence chart shapes, 47
Influence charts and artistic license, 48,
    104, 180
Influence charts and data values, 48
Influence diagram, 2
Initial condition in simulation, 343,
    393–394
Installing What'sBest!, 399–403

Integer

Integer command, 411–412
Integer programming, 220
Integer solution to assignment problem,
    132, 134
Integer solutions and runtime, 412–413
Integer solutions and solution time, 220
Integer variables and optimization,
    219–232
Integer variables in What'sBest!, 219
Interrupt, 420
Inventory model with multiple items,
    250–253
Inventory models, 241–263
Inventory on hand and on order, 352
Inventory simulation, 339–356
Irreconcilable constraint formulas, 420
Iteration limit, 415–416, 420–421

J

J.D.'s problem, 279–287
J.D.'s problem and Monte Carlo, 305–315
Jan Chalk's blending example, 193–198

K

Kink, 191–192
Knapsack example, 221–224
Known IP (integer), 220, 412–413
Kochenberger, Gary, 279
Kolmogorov-Smirnov test, 386

L

Levels in time-based models, 170
Limit (options menu), 415–416
Limiting values for constraints, 49
LINDO, 74, 417
Linear programming, 65–81
Linear programming graphical solutions,
    74–81
Linear programming, mathematical
    definition, 71–72
Linearity, 66–69
Loans in time-based models, 180–184
Local optimum, 190–191, 424
Locate (report menu), 56, 416–417
Location example, 225–228
Logical formulas, 361–362, 423
Long Plains Fire Services case, 234–237

Lower limit for dual value, 93, 410
LULU, 226

M

Macro (options menu), 416
Macros for WB commands, 417–418
Management science, 1
Marginal values, 89–92
Marginal values for advertisement
limit, 180
Marginal values for project scheduling,
145–147
Marginal values from What's*Best!*, 91–92
Marginal values in inventory model, 253
Markowitz, Harry M., 263
Maximize, 406
Maximum flow in network, 151–157
McNamee, Peter, 2
Memory requirements, 399
Minimize, 406
Minimum cost of network flow, 157–158
Mixed absolute-relative cell addresses, 155
Mixed integer programming, 220
Model construction from influence chart,
6–8, 11, 25–42
Model documentation, 7–8, 16–17
Models in management science, 1
Models with many columns, 14–17
Monte Carlo method, 303–323
Moses, Edward A., 263
Moving between Quattro and 1-2-3, 414
Multi-item inventory model, 250–253
Multi-item inventory simulation, 366–370
Multinomial distribution, 317, 321–322,
337–338
Multiple Max or Min Cells, 421
Multiple optima, 410

N

Network flows, 151–158
Network installation (README) file, 402
Networks, 139–160
New product development example,
99–104
NIMBY, 226
No Adjustable cells specified, 421
No Best cell specified, 421–422
No Feasible Solution, 409, 422

Nodes, 139
None (no best cell), 406
Nonimplemented function, 422–423
Nonimplemented function warning, 414,
422–423
Nonlinear optimization, 189–193, 239
Nonlinear programming, 190–192
Nonlinear warning, 414, 423
Nonlinearities for reporting, 69–71
Nonsmooth nonlinearities, 190, 255–256
Normal distribution, 316, 320, 336
North-South Insurance Company case,
380–394
Novana Company case, 172–184, 324–332
Numeric cell limit, 424

O

Objective, 47, 406
Objective coefficients, 74
Objective warning, 414
Omit (options menu), 415
Omit range in What's*Best!*, 70–71, 423–424
On hand and on order, 352
Operators supported by What's*Best!*, 423
Oppermann, Edward B., 386
Optimal termination messages, 424–425
Optimal to tolerances, 425
Optimization defined, 46
Optimization modeling characteristics,
57–58
Optimization models involving time,
165–184
Optimization problem characteristics,
56–57
Optimization problem components, 46–47
Options command, 413–416

P

Parallel servers, 374
Payoff, 275
Payoff table, 276–278
Perfect information in decision analysis,
282–284
PERT, 140
Piecewise linearity and IF logic, 203–206
Piecewise linearity in Production Planning,
205–206

Piecewise linearity in Rangely Lakes, 201–205
Placid Platz case, 225–228
Point distribution, 337–338
Point mode in spreadsheets, 32
Poisson distribution, 373
Poisson process, 321
Portfolio optimization, 263–267
Portfolio risk, 266
Postoptimality analysis, 87
Present value of cash flows, 221
Previous period on influence chart, 167
Price breaks in inventory models, 253–256
Probabilities, 275–276
Problem capacity exceeded, 425
Process selection example, 109–112
Processor required, 399
Production Planning case, 206–209
Production Planning example, 205–206
Production quantities example, 105–109
Profit lines in graphical linear programming, 77–78
Profit/Maximize, 406
Program Evaluation and Review Technique, 140
Project scheduling, 139–150
Project scheduling with uncertainty, 332–336
Project scheduling, optimization view, 143–147
Purchases in a fluctuating market, 165–169

Q

Quantity discounts in inventory models, 253–256
Quattro Pro 2.0 and 3.0 optimizers, 429
Quattro Pro 4.0 optimizers, 429
Quattro Pro for Windows optimizer, 428–429
Queuing theory, 371–376
Queuing theory spreadsheets, 374–376
Quick installation, 399–401
Quick-Serve Software case, 371–380

R

RAM required, 399
Random demand, 351–352
Random number functions, 335–337

Random number generation, 315–317
Random numbers, 303
Randomness test, 360–365, 385
Rangely Lakes Case with kinks, 201–205
Rangely Lakes Case with piecewise linearity, 201–205
Rangely Lakes LP in mathematical format, 73–74
Rangely Lakes case and dual information, 88–97
Rangely Lakes case optimization, 43–56
Rangely Lakes case, model construction, 21–22, 25–42
Rangely Lakes nonlinear example, 257–258
Rangely lakes and decision analysis, 271–278
Ranging, 87
Ranging in decision analysis, 271–274
Real estate development case, 118–124
Rectangles (rounded) in influence charts, 47
Rectangular distribution, 320–321, 337
Recycling Center Location case, 225–228
Reduced cost, 95
Regression analysis, 237, 326
Relative cell addresses, 37–38, 155
Reorder point, 339–340, 366
Replenishment lead time, 348
Report command, 56, 416–417
Reset adjustable cells, 406
Retrieve reports, 417
Right-hand side, 72, 74
Rounded rectangles in influence charts, 47
Runs test for randomness, 360–365, 385
Runtime concerns for integer solutions, 412–413

S

Safety stock, 352, 366
Sample allocation, 267–269
Saturated waiting line system, 393
Saving a file, 42
Sawgrass Canning Company case, 186–188
Schrage, Linus, 74
Screen update, 416
Sensitivity analysis, 87
Sequential decision problems, 284–287
Service level, 341, 350–352, 354–356
Set-up cost as fixed charge, 229

Shadow price, 90
Shapes for influence charts, 47
Shortest path through a network, 158–160
Simplex method, 80
Simulation defined, 340
Simulation input data, 394
Simulation of inventory systems, 339–356
Slack on project activity, 144
Soft Ideas case example, 140–150, 332–336
Solution report, 56, 96–97, 417
Solution time for integer solutions, 220, 412–413
Solve command, 54, 408
Solve error messages, 408–409
Solvers in other spreadsheets, 429–431
Sparkling Clean case, 199–201
Specialty Products Incorporated case, 240–245
Squares in influence charts, 47
States of nature, 275
Steady-state behavior, 375–376, 394
Stimulation tactics, 394–395
Stocks in time-based models, 170
Stratified sampling case, 267–269
String variables, 423
SUMPRODUCT function, 128–129
Sunsoak Products case, 22–24
Supported functions, 423
Supported operators, 423
System requirements, 399

T

Tactical decisions for simulation, 394–395
Terminal values on decision tree, 285
Time-based optimization models, 165–184
Timing in time-based models, 170, 193
Tolerance for integer solutions, 220, 412–413
Too few constraints, 409
Top down modeling, 2
Transient behavior, 375–376, 394
Translate (options menu), 414
Translate constraints, Quattro and 1-2-3, 414–415
Transportation problem, 125–129, 139
Transportation solution methods, 134
Triangles in influence charts, 47
Triangular distribution, 316–318, 337

Tries limit, 415–416
Troubleshooting messages, 418–427
Tucker Development Corporation case, 118–124

U

Unable to . . . messages, 418–419
Unbalanced assignment problem, 132–134
Unbounded solution, 409, 425
Uncertainty, 271–287, 303–323
Uncertainty in inventory analysis, 339–356
Undefined arithmetic value, 425–426
Undetermined solution status, 426
Unexpected operation, 426
Uniform distribution, 320–321, 337
Unknown key or block name, 419
Unsupported function, 422–423
Unsupported function warning, 414, 422–423
Upper limit for dual value, 93–94, 410
User's manual, 399–427

V

VLOOKUP function, 347
Vacation budget example, 3–8
Valid ranges (dual), 410–411
Validity range for marginal values, 92–94, 410–411
Value (dual), 410
Von Lanzenauer, Christoph Haehling, 118

W

Waiting line simulation, 376–394
Waiting lines, 373–394
Warnings (option menu), 414
WBERR file, 416
WBERR.PRN file, 408
WBFORM.PRN, 417
WBFR file, 52, 54, 416
WBFREE, 406
WBLIM, 415–416
WBOMIT, 423
WBOMIT cell error, 426
WBOMIT range, 415
WBOMIT range, 424
WBSOLN.PRN, 417

WBTO file, 52, 54, 416
WBTRACE, 416
What's*Best!* commands, 405–418
What's*Best!* solver, 49–50
What's*Best!* and Lotus 1-2-3, 50–52
What's*Best!* and Quattro Pro, 52–54
What's*Best!* files, 52, 54, 416
What-if cells, 46
What-if tables (data tables) for
    Monte Carlo, 304–305
Worksheets with many columns, 14–17

X

Xaja Construction Company example,
    129–134

Y

Yale, Donald, 291
Young, C. W., 186
YumYum Corporation case, 298–301

Z

Z-value for runs test, 364
Zero-one variables, 220–221
Zero-one variables for fixed charge,
    228–232